The People

The publication of this book was made

possible by generous support from the

S. J. and Jessie E. Quinney Foundation

Words and Photographs by Stephen Trimble

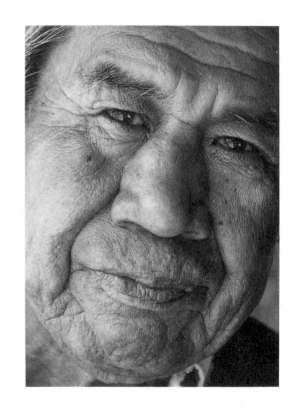

SAR PRESS SANTA FE

SCHOOL OF AMERICAN RESEARCH

The People

Indians of
the American
Southwest

School of American Research Press
Post Office Box 2188
Santa Fe, New Mexico 87504

Director of Publications: Jane Kepp
Editor: Joan Kathryn O'Donnell
Art Director: Deborah Flynn Post
Maps: Deborah Reade
Typographer: Tseng Information Systems, Inc.
Printer: Edwards Brothers, Inc.
Color: Mercantile Printing Company, Inc.
Designed by Richard Hendel

Distributed by the University of
    Washington Press

Library of Congress
Cataloging-in-Publication Data
Trimble, Stephen, 1950–
    The People : Indians of the American
Southwest / words and photographs by
Stephen Trimble. — 1st ed.
        p.   cm.
    Includes bibliographical references (p.   ) and
index.
    ISBN 0-933452-36-5 (cloth : acid-free paper) :
$50.00.
    — ISBN 0-933452-37-3 (paper : acid-free paper) :
$29.95
    1. Indians of North America—Southwest, New.
I. Title.
E78.S7T75   1993
979'.00497—dc20   93-12510
                CIP

Printed in the United States of America

FOR ALL MY RELATIONS

especially for my daughter, Dory Trimble,

her mother, Joanne Slotnik,

and her grandmothers,

Isabelle Trimble and Beatrice Slotnik,

in whose strength and love live our family's

past, present, and future

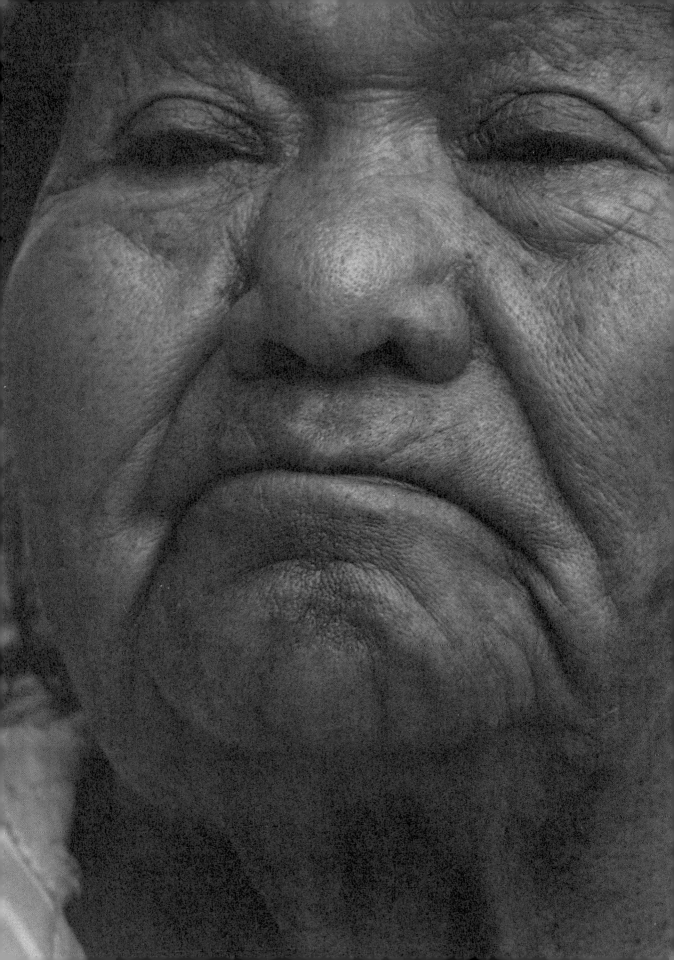

Being Indian, from Acoma to Pine Ridge, Tahlequah to Tacoma, Wounded Knee to the Hopi mesas, upstate New York to down-home Ohio, would seem, finally, to be doing something about seeing or being or defining oneself Indian. It can be working with Headstart children from farming communities to urban poverty areas. It can include bringing goods and concern to the old ones, staying to listen to their memories and wisdoms. Being Indian is as much behavior and attitude, life style and mind-set, as a consequence of history or bloodline . . . Being a "now day Indi'n" would seem, as with most positive human values, more active than passive, although the past obviously informs tribalism through cultural continuity and a sense of common heritage.

Dawson No Horse told his people, gathered in a Lakota *yuwipi* ceremony the summer of 1981 at Wakpamni Lake, Pine Ridge Reservation: "We're gonna make it as we go along, generation to generation, addin' on an' addin' on."

Kenneth Lincoln, Native American Renaissance, 1983

Contents

Preface

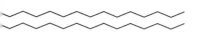

This book, despite its heft, is an introduction. I am an outsider and a student, not an anthropologist. I came to Indian Country to listen and have tried to learn from both the words and the silences. I write for other beginners, for nonspecialists.

While reading about and listening to Indian people over the last ten years, I have been astonished at my own ignorance. Though I have lived in the Four Corners states all of my life, remarkably little about the Indian peoples of my home ever reached me. The dominant culture has other stories to tell. It has been an honor to have this opportunity to construct for readers a story about the People from what I have found in libraries and from what Indian people have wanted me to hear.

Native words for tribal groups usually mean "The People" or "The Human Beings." Hence my title for this book. Today, the People call themselves "Indians" more often than they use the term "Native Americans," and so I use this misnomer without apology.

The vitality of the People is exhilarating. They remain fiercely dedicated to preserving their lands, their families, and their ethnicity. Even with all of the challenges they must deal with — economic, cultural, social — I have no doubt that in one hundred years, the Indians of the Southwest will remain unique and distinct. I believe that is a good thing.

The Southwest. We all have unique images triggered by these words: secret places, memory-laden smells, piquant tastes, unforgettable people. Where does this place begin, where does it end? Anthropologists have one definition, historians another, and naturalists still another. Every defining factor changes with time. Look at Southwestern peoples in A.D. 1200, and one boundary seems to make sense. Look at tribal territories interacting with Spanish colonialism in the 1700s, and another definition results. History unreels, people move, and cultural geography evolves.

To define the Southwestern landscape, begin with its rivers. They flow from the mountains to the sea — and in doing so, make sense out of a major sweep of the continent. Two great river systems, the Colorado and the Rio Grande, flow through the arid lands. Rivers, mountains, climate, and vegetational history define the limits of agriculture, forming yet another boundary for the region — one with powerful meaning for native peoples.

The River of the West, the Colorado, tumbles down from the Rocky Mountains in a red torrent and plunges southwestward toward the ocean. The River of the East, the Rio Grande, arcs away from the Colorado Rockies and then runs due south, bisecting New Mexico. Trace the basins drained by these rivers and their tributaries, and much of the Southwestern landscape is clear. Desert lands away from the rivers include the harshest terrain on the continent. The Southwest also contains peaks rising to fourteen thousand feet, crowned with near-permanent snow and alpine tundra — watersheds to the great rivers.

On the eastern boundary of the Southwest runs the Pecos River, leading south from the Rockies between the Basin and Range deserts and the beginnings of the flat inland sea of grass at the heart of the continent. On the western boundary, beyond the Colorado River, lies California, a different place.

The Southwest extends deep into Mexico. (Mexican historians would rephrase this: "The Mexican Northwest once extended north to the Grand Canyon.") The international border slices through desert basin and mountain range, bisecting the homelands of the Cocopah, O'odham, and Apache peoples. In this book, I focus on that part of the Southwest within the United States. This "American" Southwest omits the "other" Southwest's Tarahumara, Mountain Pima, Paipai, and many other Mexican native peoples with strong linguistic and trading ties north of the border. (Another Southwest definition, however, is "the area of close and continuous contact between Hispano-American, Anglo-American, and Amerindian" — a definition that excludes these Mexican tribes beyond continuous Anglo contact.)

On the north, some historians limit the Southwest by the northward limit of Spanish influence, though Spanish missions and place names, of course, reach to San Francisco. In The People, my boundary for the Southwest penetrates Colorado from New Mexico to include the San Luis Valley and the drainages south of the San Juan Mountain crest. In Utah, the Southwest includes the drainage of the San Juan River to its confluence with the Colorado River and southwestern Utah along the base of the High Plateaus. Southernmost Nevada hovers on the edge of the Southwest, with Las Vegas sitting smack on the boundary. Northward beyond this line, not only do Indian communities disappear for a long distance, but, historically, Hispanic influence is minimal.

Two cultural groups commonly left out of the anthropological Southwest live in this Southwest of The People. The Southern and Ute Mountain Utes skirt the southern foot of the Colorado Rockies. And Southern Paiute territory connects the north rim of the Grand Canyon and the High Plateaus of Utah with oases in the Nevada desert. Archetypal Southwestern places lie within Ute and Paiute homelands, both historically and today — Las Vegas, Zion Canyon, Navajo Mountain, Glen Canyon, Mesa Verde, the Sangre de Cristo Range. I include these peoples here.

Change runs through the history of both Southwestern peoples and landscape. Southwestern deserts have existed for less time than humans have lived here. Once, Southwestern people hunted mastodon and mammoth and lived by wetlands where today there are only dry *playas*. Only later did they find it necessary to adapt gradually to the desert.

Today, the People adapt to the booming Sunbelt economy, to ever-challenging swings in federal policy, and to continuing ignorance (with the potential for paternalism and racism) on the part of many non-Indians. I hope this book can dispel a little of that ignorance blocking the path of Southwest native peoples by increasing awareness of their lives and hopes and dreams — and by recounting enough history to make sense out of the present. As I finished the book, I realized how many stereotypes and naive notions of my own I lost in the course of research; every issue was more complicated than it initially seemed.

My emphasis is contemporary; I do not include complete ethnographies of each tribe's pre-contact lifeways or extensive recounting of tribal myths. As readers will discover in the text, I have talked with several hundred Indian people in the fifty reservation communities across the Southwest, as well as in the region's major cities. I deeply appreciate the generosity extended to me when I showed up on doorsteps unannounced. I apologize to all of the members of these tribes I did not seek out or missed. I have tried to emphasize the positive statements made to me and avoid either romanticizing the People or ignoring the huge problems they face. As Stan Steiner said of his 1968 classic, *The New Indians*: "What I have written is not a study, but a book of people full of the truths and lies people tell." Those "truths and lies" are simply the stories every person tells in his or her own way. Other members of their communities would tell different stories. I try to provide a chorus of stories that, together, communicate the distinct personality of each people.

Though *The People* includes events through 1992, this book will inevitably be out of date even before it reaches your hands. The interviews span eight years, concentrated in the late 1980s. Economic plans change quickly; events like the 1990 flash flood at Supai in Havasu Canyon alter the course of tribal history in one afternoon. People leave jobs and move from state to state; *The People* provides a snapshot of their lives and homes at the moment I happened to intersect them. For further developments in Indian Country, read periodicals such as *High Country News*, *The Navajo Times*, and *The Indian Trader*.

I have tried to photograph with care, to refrain from taking advantage of people. Except for my photographs of participants in public events, I have received permission from my subjects. At the end of the four-day White Mountain Apache girl's puberty ceremony that resulted in the pictures in this book, I asked my companion, the late San Carlos Apache medicine man Philip Cassadore, whether it was really acceptable to publish these images. With a wry spark in his eye, he reassured me: I had a wordless model release from the entire community. "You took the picture there at the ceremonial ground in front of two hundred Apaches, and no one stopped you. If somebody is going to stop you, they'll stop you right there. Nobody stopped you; that means okay."

There will be Indian individuals and entire communities who will read this book and feel that I have divulged too much, that a white man should not be treading this territory; I regret offending them. And there will be Indian people who resent other members of their communities speaking about their shared culture, though virtually all the people I interviewed made clear that they spoke only for themselves. In interviews, I did not pursue such sensitive subjects as ritual and ceremony. If one of the People chose to share sacred aspects of culture, he or she did so, and I took notes. Hopi and Zuni people talk openly about katsinas; Acoma, Santo Domingo, or San Felipe Pueblo people would never talk about such matters with anyone outside the pueblo. In my text, I have tried to strike a middle ground. I know I have taken some risks. Everett Burch, language and education coordinator for the Southern Utes at the time I visited him, said to me: "We've given you a piece of our lives. You then have the responsibility to give something in return."

This book is my gift. I have done my best to honor my responsibility, to speak fairly. I cannot truly repay Southwest Indian people, but each year I share royalties from *The People* and from the annual calendar based on it with the Native American Rights Fund, the Indian Law Resource Center, and other organizations working to preserve and protect Native American rights through education, policy, and the law.

Several people, both Indian and non-Indian, deserve individual recognition. First comes my friend Robert Breunig. In 1984, Bob invited me to work on the audio-visual program that introduces the "Native Peoples of the Southwest" wing at The Heard Museum — a program that became the show and the book *Our Voices, Our Land*. That fieldwork — and Bob's guidance — introduced me to contemporary Indians in my home landscape, and *The People* grew from that initial experience.

I often found a pivotal teacher whose thoughtful words guided me in my search for the distinct spirit of each tribal group. Some of these teachers and scholars I have only read, others I have interviewed once, and still others have become friends. Some, alas, are no longer with us. At times, local contacts, both Indian and non-Indian, took charge of my schedule to make sure I spoke to the "right" people. On the road, many friends gave me shelter and moral support.

For such help, the following individuals deserve special thanks: Barney Burns, Philip Cassadore, Steven Darden, Vine Deloria, Jr., Rick Dillingham, Jan Downey, Joseph Enos, Amelia Flores, Bunny Fontana, Bob Helmer, Richard Howard, Elbys Hugar, Peter Iverson, Joe Keck, Kathleen and Reed Kelley, Pat Mariella, Nancy Cottrell Maryboy, Kalley and Jan Musial, Gary Nabhan, the Nahohai family, Nora Naranjo-Morse (and the rest of her remarkable family, especially Rina Swentzell), Floyd O'Neill, Alfonso Ortiz, Malinda Powskey, Holly Roberts, Bertha Russell, Joe Sando, Susan Shaffer, Stan Steiner, Abby Stevens, Gregory Thompson, Gary Tom, Octaviana Valenzuela Trujillo, Tom Vigil, Dave Warren, Cindy and Philbert Watahomigie, and Verna Williamson.

I thank The Heard Museum and the School of American Research for permission to quote from interviews conducted under their auspices while working on previous projects. Bea Slotnik made it possible for me to work without interruption when she joined our household to await the birth of her grandson, Jacob.

For their time and care spent in critiquing early drafts of all or part of the text, I thank Keith Basso, Janice Colorow, Raymond J. Concho, Jr., Jennifer Dewey, Tony Dorame, Amelia Flores, Peter Iverson, David Lavender, Nancy Maryboy, Gary Nabhan, James Officer, Sally Pablo, Tim Priehs, Joanne Slotnik, Bill Sutherland, Gregory Thompson, Gary Tom, Don Trimble, Octaviana Valenzuela Trujillo, Harry Walters, Dave Warren, and Cindy Watahomigie. L. Edward Purcell edited the completed text with consummate professionalism; all writers dream of such intelligent and critical attention applied to their manuscripts. Joan O'Donnell applied her attentive eye to the last copy-edit, further improving the manuscript. Remaining misinterpretations, naivetes, and omissions, of course, remain my own.

I am delighted to once again work with Rich Hendel, the finest book designer I know. Ben Altman, in Salt Lake City, made the black-and-white prints of my photographs with care; I thank him for maintaining his cheerfulness and enthusiasm for this project through five years of running back and forth to my house. Deborah Reade loves maps as much as I do, and I thank her for caring about getting the details of our maps exactly right. T. J. Priehs, executive director of Southwest Parks and Monuments Association, originally commissioned this project; I thank him for his vision and trust.

From the moment he first heard about this project in The King's English bookstore in Salt Lake City, James Freed, board member of the Quinney Foundation, has voiced his morale-building enthusiasm. I deeply appreciate his conviction that the book merited the foundation's financial support.

And lastly, to Jane Kepp, Joan O'Donnell, Deborah Flynn Post, and Peter Palmieri at the School of American Research Press: it was a thrill to have such care and expertise applied to my book during production. Thanks for understanding so clearly what I was trying to communicate after this long, enlightening, and satisfying journey.

Stephen Trimble
Salt Lake City

Introduction

WE ARE THE PEOPLE

From the doorways of hogans and cinder-block ramblers, elders still pray at dawn to the spirits of sacred mountains — here, Four Peaks in the Mazatzal Mountains, seen from the Fort McDowell Yavapai Reservation, Arizona, 1988.

We have lived upon this land from days beyond history's records, far past any living memory, deep into the time of legend. The story of my people and the story of this place are one single story. No man can think of us without thinking of this place. We are always joined together.

Taos Pueblo man, in an appeal for the return of Blue Lake, 1968

"We are the People. We were here." George Rocha, a middle-aged Hualapai man, smiled at me. "I'm real proud. I love this land. I've been back East. It's beautiful, it's green. But after three or four days I feel everything closing in. And when I arrive back in Arizona, especially back to the reservation, I feel real loose and comfortable.

"This is my land."

A modern map of the United States includes both large and small "Indian reservations" clearly distinguished from surrounding areas. Fifty of these Indian nations lie within the Southwest. Drive from Las Vegas, Nevada, to Santa Fe, New Mexico, from El Paso, Texas, to Cedar City, Utah, or from Yuma, Arizona, to Durango, Colorado, and you still can experience this land as an Indian land.

Imagine this Indian Southwest. Conjure the continent before these reservation boundaries. Imagine the grasslands unbroken and regularly burned. Imagine the forests huge, their plants and animals managed to increase the diversity and yield of wild foods. Imagine the rivers restored. Chant the litany of tribal names covering the land. The land regains, once again, its mythic and native proportions.

Native cultures multiplied and migrated, ebbed and flowed — covering the Southwest with a skein of stories that marked sacred places in forty languages. People wandered far beyond their homes, trading, visiting, and exploring. Choose most any nook or cranny of this land, and some hunter, fisherman, or seed gatherer knew its plants and animals. Native residents learned how to manage those wild beings to create an abundance of food, construction and craft materials, and habitat for other desirable creatures.

Today, Southwestern Indians remain vital, their lives rich. They make saguaro cactus fruit into ceremonial wine. They mourn their dead in the old ways. Sacred mountains stand in black silhouette above Indian homes; elders stand at dawn in the doorways of both hogans and cinder-block ramblers to pray to the spirits of those mountains. Rain clouds follow, in response to faith, respect, ritual, and receptivity — and the beat of the drum.

The People value their history, but they must forge a workable present to survive into the future. They are physicists, Episcopalians, and suburbia dwellers as well as shamans and farmers. Sometimes, one person may be all of these. Native peoples are constantly challenged by the dilemmas of finding a livable path between two opposing worlds.

Landscape sustains them: plateau, mountain, and desert. Their ancient connection with *place* abides—an intimacy that helps define them as unique peoples. As Indian communities maintain and modify old lifeways while adopting new ones, the land continues to run through their days and their lives, helping to make them Indians of the Southwest.

Plateau, Mountain, Desert

At the heart of the Southwest lie the canyons and mesas of the Colorado Plateau surrounding the Four Corners. Here the village-dwelling Pueblo people span the continuum from prehistory to history to modern times in ancient villages: Hopi, Zuni, Acoma, and the Rio Grande communities in New Mexico. Despite their sharing of culture, modern Pueblo people speak half a dozen different languages and live in more than thirty villages in twenty modern reservations scattered from Taos to Hopi (with one remnant southern village, Tigua Pueblo at El Paso). To their west, along the southern rims of the Grand Canyon, live the Pai, today's Hualapai and Havasupai, who speak a Yuman language. The Navajo, Athapaskan speakers who came late to the Southwest, perhaps about A.D. 1400, have made their home in the vast plateau lands between the Rio Grande pueblos in New Mexico and the Grand Canyon, filling in the wild spaces between the old villages.

Mountains rise on most every Southwestern horizon: islandlike from the northern plateaus, in a band of highlands across central Arizona and New Mexico, and from the low deserts of southern Arizona. These dry mountains gave life to tribes who cycled with the seasons of hunting and gathering. Bands of Yavapai (speakers of nearly the same dialect of Yuman as their traditional enemies, the Pai) held central Arizona's rugged interior. The Southern Paiutes and Utes lived on the High Plateaus and on the flanks of the Southern Rockies at the northern edge of the Southwest, along the borders of today's Utah and Colorado; their cultural and linguistic connections lie to the north, in the Great Basin and Rocky Mountains. After the 1500s, the Athapaskan-speaking Apaches filtered into mostly unclaimed country through most of the rest of the upland Southwest.

Below, in the deserts, two primary language groups covered southern Arizona. The O'odham, speakers of Piman, lived along the Gila River (the Pima) and in the Sonoran Desert to its south (Tohono O'odham—proper name for the Papago—and Sand Papago, or Hia-Ced O'odham). Along the Colorado River, an oasis of moisture

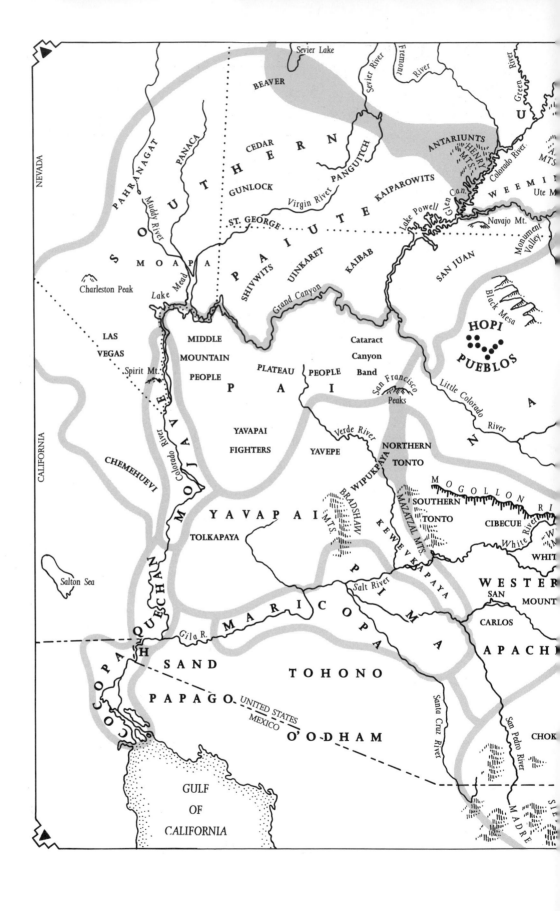

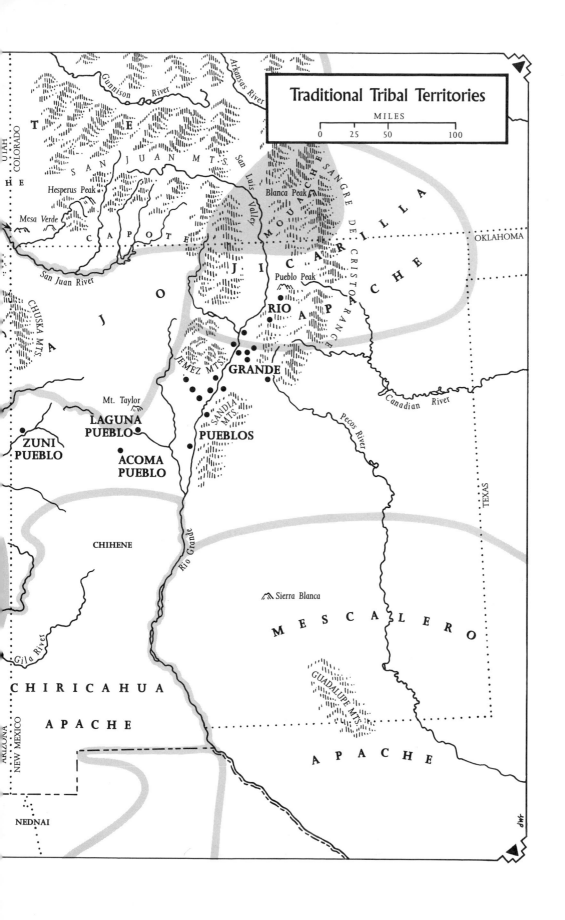

Traditional Tribal Territories

MILES

0   25   50   100

UTAH
COLORADO

T   E   E

Gunnison   River

Arkansas River

SAN   JUAN   MTS.

Hesperus Peak

San Luis Valley

Blanca Peak

M O U A C H E

SANGRE

Mesa Verde

C A P O T E

San Juan River

J O

J I C A R I L L A

Pueblo Peak

DE   CRISTO   RANGE

A P A C H E

OKLAHOMA

CHUSKA MTS.

RIO   AP

A

JEMEZ MTS.

GRANDE

Canadian   River

Mt. Taylor

SANDIA MTS.

Pecos River

**LAGUNA
PUEBLO**

PUEBLOS

**ZUNI
PUEBLO**

**ACOMA
PUEBLO**

TEXAS

CHIHENE

Rio Grande

Sierra Blanca

M   E   S   C   A   L   E   R   O

Gila River

GUADALUPE MTS.

ARIZONA
NEW MEXICO

C H I R I C A H U A

A P A C H E

A   P   A   C   H   E

NEDNAI

In canyons and mesas at the heart of the Southwest, the Pueblo people span the continuum from prehistory to modern times in ancient villages like Walpi on the Hopi Mesas in Arizona. Photo by John K. Hillers, 1873. (Smithsonian Institution photo no. 1851)

threading the continent's harshest deserts, River Yuman–speaking tribes divided the bottomlands: the Mojave in the north, the Quechan (Yuma) in the south, and the Cocopah near the delta. One River Yuman group, the Maricopa, migrated up the Gila to live with the modern Pima on the Gila and Salt rivers. A Paiute-speaking group, the Chemehuevi, came to the Colorado River to live with the Mojave. Finally, Cahitanspeaking Yaqui refugees escaping north from Sonora's Rio Yaqui country at the end of the nineteenth century established small colonies near Phoenix and Tucson, eventually to become the Pascua Yaqui tribe.

Anthropologists remain vague on a definition for "tribe." The word describes a social group with a distinctive language or dialect, a group that practices a distinctive culture — more than a band but less than a chiefdom (the latter requiring a redistributive economy). In the real world, tribes create these distinctions, incorporate them in their identities, and change them as necessary through time. For Indians, communities are defined by family relationships, not by place of residence or "culture."

Analysts of United States census data similarly gesture with frustration when they attempt to define the "Indian" population. Race, ethnicity, blood quantum, biological definitions based on physical characteristics such as earwax type or blood peculiarities all have their limits; in the end, an American Indian is anyone who identifies his or her race as Indian and who is recognized as such by Indian communities.

As Native American anthropologist Jack D. Forbes writes: "The behavioral pattern systems of human groups are like currents in the ocean. It is possible to point out generally where a particular current exists, especially at its center or strongest point, but it is not ordinarily possible to neatly separate that current from the surrounding sea."

Villagers before History

Ancestors to these Native Americans once were Native Asians. They crossed the land bridge between Siberia and Alaska during the Ice Ages of the Pleistocene and peopled the American continents from the Bering Strait to Tierra del Fuego. The Bering land bridge was exposed intermittently between 23,000 and 8000 B.C. Groups of people may have migrated to the new lands in several waves.

Indian peoples had certainly reached the Southwest by about twelve thousand years ago. Their fluted and chipped stone spearpoints remain lodged in the buried skeletons of the game animals they hunted on the New Mexico plains. In the rich interior of the continent these Paleo-Indian hunting peoples stalked mammoth, giant bison, horses, camels, antelope, sloth, and tapir. Nearly all of these prey animals were extinct by 8500 B.C., and the effective skills of the recently arrived hunters may have hastened such extinctions.

Through the millennia that followed, Southwestern peoples gradually shifted their activities from hunting to plant gathering. Archaeologists call this period, from about 5500 B.C. to A.D. 100 the Archaic. Archaic times began with the final drying cycle of the wet glacial climate and the establishment of today's deserts; the cold steppes with their herds of mammoths were gone. During these centuries, Southwesterners

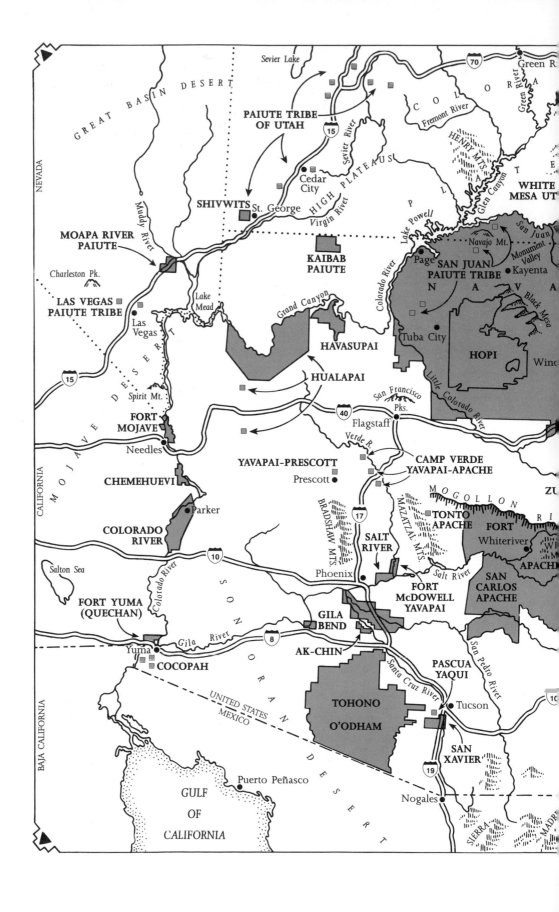

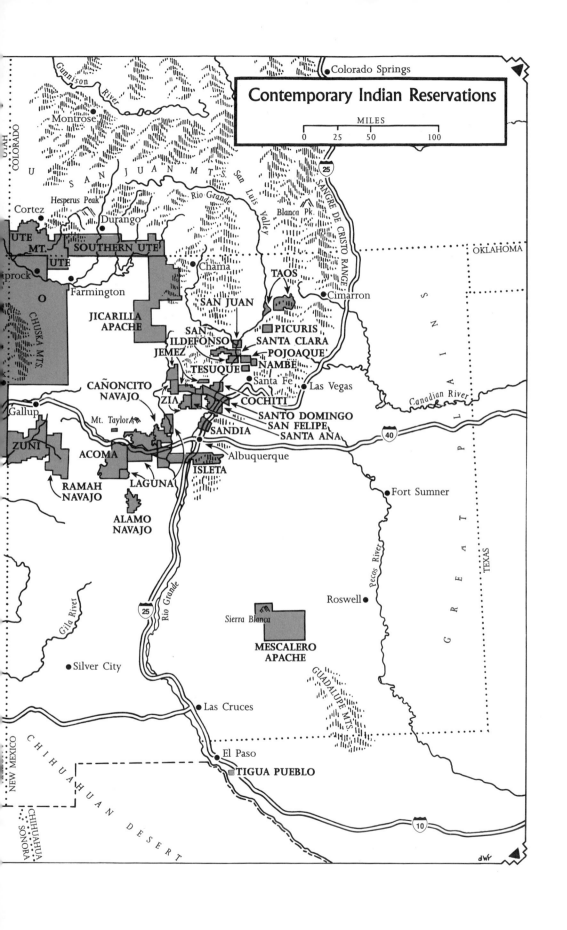

Contemporary Indian Reservations

MILES

0   25   50   100

Colorado Springs

Gunnison River

Montrose

UTAH
COLORADO

SAN JUAN MTS.

San Luis Valley

Hesperus Peak

Rio Grande

Blanca Pk.

Cortez

Durango

SANGRE DE CRISTO RANGE

UTE MT. UTE

SOUTHERN UTE

OKLAHOMA

prock

Farmington

Chama

TAOS

Cimarron

O

CHUSKA MTS

JICARILLA APACHE

SAN JUAN

PICURIS

SANTA CLARA

SAN ILDEFONSO

POJOAQUE

P L A I N S

JEMEZ

TESUQUE

NAMBE

CAÑONCITO NAVAJO

Santa Fe

Las Vegas

Canadian River

Gallup

Mt. Taylor

ZIA

COCHITI

SANTO DOMINGO

SAN FELIPE

SANTA ANA

ZUNI

SANDIA

40

ACOMA

Albuquerque

ISLETA

RAMAH NAVAJO

LAGUNA

Fort Sumner

ALAMO NAVAJO

Gila River

25

Rio Grande

Roswell

Pecos River

Sierra Blanca

G R E A T

TEXAS

MESCALERO APACHE

Silver City

GUADALUPE MTS.

Las Cruces

NEW MEXICO

CHIHUAHUAN

El Paso

TIGUA PUEBLO

CHIHUAHUA
SONORA

D E S E R T

10

dWr

In southernmost Nevada stands Spirit Mountain, pierced by canyons whose petroglyphs tell how all peoples spilled into this world — created by Mastamho, according to the Yumans. The Yuman tribes stayed closest to Spirit Mountain, where they live today. 1984.

began to develop their modern lifeways, gathering many wild food plants and hunting modern animals: bison, deer, jackrabbits, and pronghorn.

Humans have been hunters and gatherers for most of their history. They have lived by the folk wisdom accumulated over centuries, such as the teachings passed on to Hualapai elder Bertha Russell by her grandparents: "There are some animals you don't eat, there are some animals you eat. Eat what the birds eat. The birds, they know."

By 1000 B.C., the hunters and gatherers of the Southwest began to cultivate corn and squash, the first crops to be traded up from Mexico. At first, the People planted patches of corn in the spring and went about their rounds of gathering and hunting, returning in the fall to harvest their fields. Later, some groups gradually increased their dependence on farming and began creating irrigation systems and settling down in villages. With settlement came further change, and by A.D. 1, the great regional cultures of the prehistoric Southwest were beginning to take shape.

Between about A.D. 200 and 900, Southwesterners built a scatter of communities across a vast frontier. People lived in these hamlets year-round or moved out seasonally to field or hunting camps. Most of these settlements were no more isolated from each other than nineteenth-century Anglo-American homesteads.

After about A.D. 750, and more so after A.D. 1000, hamlets began to grow into villages and villages into towns and even cities. Native architects adapted the design of half-buried pithouses to the ceremonial chambers called kivas; aboveground, they joined masonry and adobe houses in structures that we now call pueblos (after the Spanish word perhaps best translated as "community"). Villagers in the deserts of southern Arizona built massive irrigation works to bring water to the dry fields beyond the river bottoms; northern farmers refined dry-farming techniques. Highland, desert, and plateau people each developed distinctive pottery.

Closest to what became Mexico, the Hohokam lived in the Arizona deserts, and the Mogollon held the uplands that would eventually become Apacheria. Mesoamerican civilizations strongly influenced these cultures (as seen in everything from the Mogollon's early adoption of pottery to the Hohokam's ball courts and religious platform mounds). Along the Colorado River dwelled the Patayan peoples, the least-known culture of the prehistoric Southwest. Farther north, on the Colorado Plateau, the ancestral Pueblo people, the Anasazi, built their villages on mesas and in canyons. Within these major cultures existed an array of more local groups, such as Sinagua, Salado, and Mimbres.

The prehistoric Southwest culminated most spectacularly at Chaco Canyon, in present-day New Mexico, where during the 1100s the Anasazi built five-story pueblos with hundreds of rooms (now preserved in Chaco Culture National Historic Park). After only two centuries as a focus of Southwestern culture, however, the Chaco people ceased new building and resumed a simpler life.

Southern peoples tried out urban lifeways as well — the Hohokam at places like Snaketown, between Tucson and Phoenix; the Mogollon (sparked by an influx of Mesoamerican traders) at the city of Paquimé (Casas Grandes) in Chihuahua, Mexico. Smaller, dispersed communities lasted longer than the aggressive, expansionist risk takers. Patayan peoples lived simply throughout the times of the great cities.

Momentous events came during the boom years, when the dynamic Anasazi absorbed the more conservative Mogollon. The Anasazi continued to build pueblos, inventing cliff dwellings at the very end of their history in the Four Corners country, moving into the sandstone alcoves of Mesa Verde, Canyon de Chelly, the Tsegi canyons (now within Navajo National Monument), and elsewhere. Some archaeologists believe the People chose these difficult-to-reach sites because they needed to defend themselves against marauders. Rina Swentzell, an architectural historian from Santa Clara Pueblo, suggests another reason: "Maybe they just wanted to live closer to the sky!"

Change jolted the quiet unfolding of this long history even before the invasion of the continent by bearded white-skinned men in clanking armor. By 1300 (a little later for Hohokam), the urbanized bastions of Anasazi and Hohokam cultures disintegrated. The Hohokam retreated to their core territory along the Gila and Salt rivers (though within this reduced area, the new villages grew quite large), with a dispersed population in Papaguería — the harsher deserts of southwestern Arizona. A century-long gap in the archaeological record separates the last of the Hohokam from the written Spanish chronicles.

Though the Anasazi people had long been mobile, commonly shifting village sites to take advantage of changing climatic conditions, they now withdrew from vast areas of the Colorado Plateau. The People colonized new country, created new styles of pottery, and found themselves dealing with new neighbors.

The New Wave

Hohokam, Mogollon, Anasazi, and Patayan had been Southwesterners all along. Into their world came new peoples — the ancestral Ute, Paiute, and Chemehuevi from the Great Basin and, later, the Athapaskan Apache and Navajo from Canada. Dates for the arrival of these incoming peoples are impossible to pin down. Each tribe's mythology states they have been here forever, living where the Creator meant for them to live.

Listen to Steve Darden, a young Navajo orator: "Mother Earth told me, 'The Holy People placed your Navajo people in this place. We have the four sacred mountains placed at the four sacred directions, and you are to live within that place. And you are to respect that place. We have created this place for you where you will have plenty, you will not want.' These things I learned."

Paiutes may have moved south into Anasazi country sometime after A.D. 1100; Utes may have been Archaic residents of the northern periphery of the Southwest for 6,000 years. Either way, these hunters and gatherers lived a simpler life that probably did not threaten the more settled Anasazi.

The Athapaskans reached the Southwest about 1400. Apaches filtered into the mountains between the Pueblo-held valleys. One Apachean group, who came to be called Navajo, lived for a time with Pueblo people, adopting many of their skills and religious beliefs and creating a unique lifeway that has proven immensely successful. Anthropologist Gary Witherspoon describes this creative synthesis: "Navajo culture is not just a food-gathering strategy; it is an artistic way of life." The Navajo, relative newcomers to the region, today dominate the Indian Southwest.

A critical meeting between Indian and non-Indian came in 1540, with Coronado's venture northward in search of legendary riches. The conquistador and his retinue marched north from Mexico through Apacheria — the central uplands of Arizona and New Mexico — describing the land as uninhabited. The expedition sought the fabled golden cities of Cíbola and Quivira and just may have been lured north by tales sparked by golden Hopi bowls — to the Spaniards' chagrin made from golden-hued clay rather than beaten metal.

Cíbola turned out to be Zuni Pueblo, its adobe walls burnished gold only by the sunset. Quivira proved to be Kansas, Coronado's deepest penetration of the continent. Despite these disappointments, the expedition and its supporting mariners in the Gulf of California saw the Rio Grande and the Colorado River, visited Yuman peoples at the mouth of the Gila, peered into the Grand Canyon, and made enemies of every Pueblo community from Hopi to Taos and Pecos.

Coronado understood the diversity of Southwestern Indians by the time he left the region. He found farmers living in sixty compact adobe towns in what we call New Mexico and at Hopi in northern Arizona; these he called the Pueblo Indians, a generic term with no counterpart among the unrelated languages spoken by the village dwellers. His men glimpsed the more loosely knit *rancheria* communities of the Yumans. Of raids by the Apaches, he heard only stories.

When Spain invaded North America, some two to five million Indians lived on the continent. The Spaniards sketched out what they saw of the tribes, and — with the help of the traditions of the Southwest Indian peoples themselves — archaeologists and historians have tried ever since to understand the link between prehistory and history.

Anasazi became Pueblos. The urban Hohokam people may have lived on in the Piman-speaking O'odham or in some Hopi clans. Patayan people evidently fractured into the Yuman-speaking Pai, Yavapai, and Colorado River tribes. Athapaskans were shadowy in colonial records until the Apaches acquired horses lost or stolen from Spanish expeditions and began to appear on ridgetops mounted on the new animals with an equestrian skill that belied its newness.

Today's Indian people recognize these connections with their distinctive pasts. Pueblo potters find inspiration in Anasazi designs on potsherds and historic pots

Dowa Yallane, sacred Corn Mountain, rises behind Zuni Pueblo and its cornfields, 1985. A critical encounter took place here in 1540, when Coronado's legendary golden city of Cíbola turned out to be Zuni, its adobe walls burnished gold only by the sunset light.

preserved in museums. Carol Antone, a Tohono O'odham, hears her parents' words ringing in her ears: "Ever since we were children, they say 'Respect your Huhugam [O'odham for Hohokam]. They were here when times were hard and they survived.' We are a continuance of that."

Waves of epidemic disease washed northward everywhere ahead of settlement, reducing some tribes by 80 percent long before they had to fight for their home ground. During the sixteenth century, the native population of the Southwest fell from hundreds of thousands to tens of thousands. As Navajo Jennie Joe says: "I often wonder how history would have been different if the Native American population had not been so decimated by communicable diseases."

The Spanish came back to New Mexico in force in 1598 — still intrigued by rumors of gold — to found the first non-Indian settlement in the Southwest, adjacent to San Juan Pueblo. Over the next ninety years, they converted and persecuted and enslaved the native peoples, until in 1680 the Pueblos rebelled — exiling the Spanish for twelve years from the king's northernmost colony. Refugees from the pueblos dislocated by the revolt and reconquest moved to northwestern New Mexico, where they intertwined their lives with the resident Navajos (barely differentiated from their Athapaskan Apache kin at this early date).

The Spanish frontier crept north into Sonora and Arizona more slowly than it had in New Mexico. Friars based at the Rio Grande pueblo missions had been at work "civilizing the savages" for twenty years before the first Yaqui baptisms took place, and nearly a century before Padre Kino began his work among the O'odham and the Colorado River tribes in 1687. By then, Spain had to contend with Apache raiders on every frontier.

Apaches themselves began to retreat from the plains in the 1700s in the face of even fiercer nomads, the Comanches. By the early 1800s, Anglo-Americans from the new country far to the east began to appear in the Southwest, and their presence would eventually bring the Indian people an entirely new world.

First, however, came the Mexican Revolution in 1821. New Spain became Mexico. Most Southwestern Indian peoples paid this change little heed. Only on the southern frontier, where the Yaqui and O'odham had to defend their land from Mexican settlers and where Apaches terrorized the frontier presidios, did the change in empire matter much.

When the United States won the Mexican War, however, a single turbulent generation transformed Southwestern Indian life. The Gadsden Purchase of 1853 completed the American takeover of the Southwest. Mining rushes came next, and then, after the Civil War, settlers arrived in a flood. During these years a complicated relationship with the United States government grew from treaties, wars, and the bewildering oscillations of federal Indian policy. The complications persist. Today, this "special relationship" has as much to do with defining Indian people as do their creation stories, languages, and lands.

Turning American Indians into Indian Americans

The vigorous young United States pushed westward. At first, the Americans swept native peoples ahead of them to "Indian Territory," where banished and conquered tribes (at least those who avoided extermination) attempted to live in isolation. The federal government signed treaties with tribes (as had European colonial powers), recognizing tribal entities as separate nations — a precedent that would do much to protect native rights over the years.

The United States Constitution specifically identified Indian tribes as governments with executive, legislative, and judicial powers. Tribes signed treaties that ceded most of their territory in exchange for the promise that their remaining lands would be held permanently in trust for them. Unrecognized as United States citizens until 1924, Indians had to rely on their unique relationship with the federal government for any help with the non-Indian political and economic world.

When the Mexican War brought the Southwest into the sphere of the United States, the Americans initially left the "civilized" tribes, farmer-villagers like the Pueblo and Pima, to their own devices. The first task of the conquerors was to subdue the "wild" Navajo, Yavapai, Hualapai, Ute, and Apache.

These more nomadic peoples lived in enormous territories. The Yavapai, for instance, used some nine million acres in central Arizona (an area twice the size of New Jersey). Their strongholds lay in rugged mountains where they moved through the seasons from wild plant harvests to agriculture to the hunt. When settlement and mining operations disrupted their rounds, they began to starve and they began to fight back.

Army campaigns defeated tribe after tribe. Crushed by starvation and battle, the hunter-gatherers were too often marched off to some inhospitable spot far from their homes. Worn down by disease and heartbreak, the survivors eventually trickled back to small reservations — tiny remnants of their former territory, usually devoid of resources capable of supporting even the remaining few dozen families.

Traditional use areas surrounding the reservations were cut back. Battles for resources, for farmland and water, were won and lost. More sedentary peoples, however, tend to remain in their ancient homelands today — lands either too dry to have attracted much permanent Anglo-American settlement (Tohono O'odham, Hopi, and the pastoralist Navajo) or village sites permanent enough to withstand the onslaught of Westernization (Mojave, Quechan, Pima, and Rio Grande pueblos). Most of these desert and plateau peoples can still look to the horizon and find there the silhouettes of their sacred mountains. Mojave elder Joe Sharp understated the importance of this fact when he said to me: "You don't have roots. We have roots. It's very hard for an Indian to leave his own country."

Gradually, federal dealings with Indians shifted from the military to the bureaucracy. In 1849, the Bureau of Indian Affairs (BIA) was moved from the Department of War to the Department of Interior. The BIA reservation agents continued to act without much guidance from the "Great Father" in Washington, and corruption was rampant. In 1871, Congress ceased making treaties with Indian nations and unilaterally began legislating Indian policy, excluding Indians from the process.

After the Civil War, a wave of reform hit the Indian Bureau. The newly established Bureau of American Ethnology, directed by John Wesley Powell, helped provide scientific data for use in policymaking. When President Grant instituted his "peace policy" and assigned reservation agencies to various religious groups, he hoped for ethical behavior from his appointees. Historian Francis Paul Prucha calls the peace policy mostly a state of mind, "a new emphasis on kindness and justice." At the same time, Indian wars still raged and the Army was much in evidence, making the way clear for the incoming rush of settlers.

By the 1880s, virtually all the Southwestern tribes lived on reservations (with the Rio Grande pueblo lands guaranteed by Spanish land grants). The frontier had swept into more and more remote country, and the most isolated of reservation communities had Anglo neighbors. In the Great Plains, whites had destroyed the buffalo; in the Southwest, they proceeded to destroy the rivers.

With the end of the Apache Wars in 1886, the People ceased making war to protect their homelands from trespass. Wide-ranging tribes confined to reservations avoided starvation only through government-issued rations. For the non-Indians who administered Indian policy, isolationism gave way to a new notion: assimilation.

The Dawes Act of 1887 formalized efforts to legislate a national solution to the "Indian Problem" after the takeover of their lands. The Dawes reformers hoped to "raise up" their "children," the inferior Indians, from savagery to civilization — to replace Indianness with Americanness. That Americans were Christians who observed the Protestant ethic went without saying. Unspoken fear and hope underlay the reformers' fervor: fear of the diversifying American population and hope that civilized society could demonstrate its ability to incorporate just about anybody by incorporating Indians. The crux of the issue was society's definition of a civilized person: a property-owning farmer.

Under the Dawes Act scenario, tribally owned reservations would break up into

Tom Toslino, Navajo, arrived at the Carlisle Institute in Pennsylvania in 1882. Three years later, the school had done its best to "civilize" him. Photos by John N. Choate. (Courtesy Denver Public Library, Western History Department)

individually owned (allotted) lands, Indian children would attend distant boarding schools far from the barbaric influence of their irredeemably primitive parents, and native religions would wither. The tribes had little to say about the program; reservation communities remained without political representation in the Anglo power system.

The Dawes Act, however, failed to generate quick assimilation — much to the surprise of its true believers. The program, like all efforts at assimilating Indian people, had not taken into account the persistent and unyielding determination of the tribes to remain distinct. Earl Ray, a young Salt River Pima interested in reviving his traditions, explained that resistance to me in this way: "Native Americans won't assimilate totally. They are like Pima baskets: the strongest part is the middle, the first part to be made."

The disruption of families as their children were herded onto wagons and railcars to be shipped off to Carlisle, Pennsylvania, to Riverside, California — or even to relatively nearby Albuquerque, New Mexico — had devastating effects. One-fourth or more of the Southwestern Indians coming of age between the 1890s and the 1930s experienced boarding school.

The late Bertha Russell, a Hualapai elder, spoke to me of her introduction to boarding school in a voice filled with sorrow and outrage: "When I went to school, the interpreter told us, 'You are not in your world anymore. So from here on, you talk the English language.' When we would talk our own language, the matron would pick us up. She says that she gives us a good spanking; today when I look at it from here, that was a beating. We were tortured. Words cannot describe how we were punished in school.

"They tell us, 'Forget your Hualapai language. Forget your Indian food. Forget your culture. Forget your stories. Forget the names of the mountains and the rivers and the mud tanks. And above all, forget your language. Just speak English.'"

Southwestern Indians were old hands at dealing with religious persecution. The Spaniards had initiated such campaigns three hundred years before, and many important ceremonies had been secreted away from Hispanic and Anglo eyes ever since. Rather than the hoped-for Christianization, the Indian Bureau instead watched the spread of peyote religion and its formalization in the early twentieth century as the Native American Church. In the 1890s, the Ghost Dance caught fire — sparked by the Northern Paiute prophet Wovoka, who promised the disappearance of the whites and the return of native ways.

Alfonso Ortiz, from San Juan Pueblo, describes what his elders told him of religious conflicts in his home in the early twentieth century: "The resident priest regularly told the people that, if they did not stop dancing and praying to the sun, moon, and stars, they would all go to hell. A half a century later, the people there are still singing, dancing, and praying to the sun, moon, and stars, and so far as we know, no one has gone to hell. Everyone knows there are no Indians in hell. It is not a place designed for us."

Though many Native Americans have become Christians, conversion requires a revolution in their thinking. Historian Mary Young sums up the trade-offs in beliefs:

> For many spirits — friends, enemies, grandmothers, grandfathers, mothers, sisters, and brothers — substitute a single, exclusive, distant, perpetually invisible, patriarchal God; for animal friends, enemies, and relatives, substitute animals as distinct and subordinate species; for a common afterlife to which most relatives' spirits might make the final journey, substitute a final segregation between converted kin who go to heaven, and the unconverted who go to hell. For visible violations of correct standards of conduct, remediable by ceremonies that restore the individual's proper relations with his community and its guardian spirits — here and now — substitute innate sinfulness and perhaps irremediable depravity.

Even those Indian people who convert usually interpret Christian doctrine uniquely, in light of their persisting traditional beliefs. Tony Ringlero, an Apache/ Pima who works at the Phoenix Indian Center as a counselor for school dropouts, is a member of the Church of Jesus Christ of the Latter-Day Saints, but he says: "Being Indian comes before being Mormon. The Indian way is basically a spiritual way of living. It's nothing like Christianity, with a church and a single holy day. Being Indian is what you feel in your heart."

Through the early decades of reservation life, the educational aims of the evangelical peace commissioners were scaled back to simple vocational training for the "incompetent" Indians, creating a labor pool for low-paying migrant jobs. Many newly "competent" Indians were granted title to their allotted land. Most quickly lost their allotments to Anglo sharpies and disappeared into rural poverty. With the exception of the Utes, however, allotment did not devastate the reservations in the Southwest as terribly as those in many other parts of the country.

The reservation agents (now called BIA superintendents) became more and more powerful. Agency towns grew up around their offices. Their control of federal budgets split tribes into those who sought jobs with the agency and those who lived apart — often labeled the "progressives" and "conservatives," respectively, by the superintendent.

With an average tenure of just three years, superintendents could learn little about the cultures of their charges. Budgets were low, disease and poverty rampant. The reform dreamed of by the Dawes Act supporters died within a rusting bureaucracy, defeat hastened by surrounding Anglo residents quick to swoop down on allottees to whom land ownership was a foreign concept. Instead of solving the Indian problem, assimilation policies devastated tribal self-sufficiency and self-rule while offering no practical replacements.

The first two decades of the twentieth century were dismal times for Indian Country. The nation dismissed Indians with the maudlin and inaccurate notion of "the vanishing race." Tribes indeed had lost lands and traditional lifeways, but they continued to exist — without much help from anyone. Especially hard times came during the influenza epidemic following World War I. During the worst of one flu outbreak, people died in such numbers at San Juan Pueblo that the church bell tolled day and night, without a lull.

These were the years, too, when the last western territories became states with full representation in Congress (Utah entered the Union in 1896, Arizona and New Mexico in 1912). Western Anglos, in those days virtually all "boomers," wanted to open up the reservations; opposing them were Eastern reformers (who lived a long way from Indian reservations). The Westerners often won.

Non-Indians took over "surplus" reservation land, used allotment as a camouflage to steal Indian land, and created leases to put to use "underdeveloped" tribal resources. Between 1887 and 1933, the nation's tribes lost 87 million acres — 60 percent of all the land guaranteed by treaty to native peoples in 1880. Anthropologists predicted that Indians would disappear and studied the old cultures with vigor, freezing the popular image of Indian people with their documentation of "traditional" tribal life in about 1880.

The United States Supreme Court and the Congress occasionally verified old treaty rights with surprising forcefulness. In 1913, the Court upheld the Pueblos' rights to the same relationship with the federal government as all other tribes. Five years later, a bill prohibiting peyote religion was defeated.

In 1921, however, the BIA commissioner appealed to Indian people: "I do not want to deprive you of decent amusement or occasional feast days, but you should not do evil or foolish things or take so much time for these occasions. No good comes from your 'giveaway' custom and dances and it should be stopped. It is not right to torture your bodies or handle poisonous snakes in your ceremonies. All such extreme things are wrong and should be put aside and forgotten."

The commissioner did not reckon with the stubborn resistance of Indian identity. Deprived of their traditional lands and means, native peoples did not instantly metamorphose into Jeffersonian farmers. They became disheartened and impoverished — and dependent on the very government trying to make them independent citizens. Given what they saw of the ethical nature of "civilization," however, it made little sense to trade away their Indianness. They remained Indians. And they slowly began to increase in numbers from the nadir of 210,000 counted in the 1910 census.

John Collier's New Deal

The 1920s began with the fight against the Bursum Bill, a thinly disguised attempt to steal title to the best Pueblo lands. In the battle to defeat this bill, new organizations for reform grew powerful; John Collier — opinionated, intense, and effective — led the fight. With his help, the Bursum Bill was greatly modified.

Collier began his career as a social worker in New York City and believed passionately in using social science to restore America to an idealized democracy. He visited Taos Pueblo at Christmas in 1920, and there discovered the model for his dream: a "Red Atlantis," filled with secrets of successful communal life. Collier's new, appreciative, and activist romanticism replaced the older version based on passive lamentation for the vanishing race.

Throughout the twenties, the reform movement — in which Collier grew ever more conspicuous — began to look at conditions on reservations and try to improve them. The 1924 extension of citizenship (while still recognizing special tribal rights) came after 10,000 Indians served in World War I and the country wished to reward

John Collier speaks to a crowd on the Tohono O'odham Reservation, Sells, Arizona, 1940.
The controversial New Dealer, an impassioned orator and wily bureaucrat, created the Indian
Reorganization Act in 1934. (Courtesy of the Arizona Historical Society/Tucson)

their patriotism. Unfortunately, the bill did little to spark fair treatment for native peoples. New Mexico and Arizona managed to prevent Indians living on reservations from voting until 1948; Utah stood steadfast by legal technicalities that blocked the reservation Indian vote until 1957.

In 1928, the Meriam Report brought the focus of the national press to bear on problems resulting from the failure of assimilation policies. Other reports revealed deficient justice systems and problems with irrigation projects and range conservation. Indian education had stalled. At the end of the twenties, there was no Indian school operating exclusively as a high school, and just six high school programs existed nationwide, all tacked on to elementary and junior high schools.

The stage was set for effective reform when John Collier became Indian commissioner under newly elected President Franklin Delano Roosevelt in 1932.

Federal reform is almost never revolutionary, but Collier's program was an exception to this axiom. The Indian Reorganization Act (IRA) was introduced, debated, amended, and passed in Congress in an intense four months during 1934. Indian peoples have been dealing with its complicated, flawed, and unavoidable effects ever since.

Collier took the bold step of asking Indian tribes for their reactions to the proposed bill in regional congresses; tribal reactions were mixed. Collier's policy of reducing herds of sheep, goats, and horses to combat overgrazing made the Navajo suspicious of the bill. The Tohono O'odham were concerned about applying centralized self-government to their scattered villages. Pueblos, however, supported the legislation because it reinforced their already firmly implanted system of governing officers. The persuasive Anglo and his staff won over most, but not all, of the doubting tribes.

The bill as eventually passed (taking effect *unless* a tribe voted to reject it) spelled out procedures for establishing tribal constitutions, electing councils, and chartering tribal corporations (with access to revolving credit funds, unfortunately funded at meager levels). The IRA ended allotment for tribes who did not reject it and authorized the Interior Department to establish new reservations for landless Indians. The bill budgeted scholarship funds, mandated conservation programs, and gave preference to Indian applicants for BIA jobs. The act developed mechanisms for restoring tribal status for allotted lands and consolidating reservations "checkerboarded" with private or public domain land. On the other hand, special-interest amendments severed Tohono O'odham mining rights to certain disputed — and profitable — lands.

In an effort to make the new programs safe from most legislative whims, Collier's legal advisor, Felix Cohen, wrote an opinion defining tribal rights. His interpretation harked back to John Marshall's 1830 phrase describing tribes as "domestic dependent nations" whose permanent and inherent powers predated the formation of the United States. Cohen clearly stated the facts of tribal autonomy: tribes retain full internal sovereignty, even after turning over their external sovereignty to the conqueror, the United States; all other powers of government remain with the tribe, unless specifically qualified by treaties or legislation. In the words of Sioux writer/attorney Vine Deloria, Jr. (and his associate Clifford Lytle): "Modern tribal sovereignty . . . begins with this opinion."

Collier believed he had helped tribes to create updated versions of the old tribal consensus he revered. He set up roadless areas — Indian wilderness — within eleven reservations and encouraged native religious freedom (the latter probably the most enduring effect of the IRA in the Southwest). For BIA teachers, he set up cultural training sessions taught by anthropologists, an unheard-of attempt to match the curriculum to the culture. He pushed through an Indian Arts and Crafts Board to help tribes market traditional art.

As the tribes used IRA-style government to help climb out of their economic depression, they discovered the problems inherent in the bill. The powers of the Secretary of the Interior over their lives had actually increased. The new procedures favored Indian bureaucrats over traditionalists, who felt that an arbitrary form of white-style government had been forced on them. An administrative conception of tribe firmly replaced the old definitions of band and people, creating new entities from disparate reservation communities. At its most complex, the process has created new cultures like the CRIT Indians — the Colorado River Indian Tribes formed from intermarrying Mojave, Chemehuevi, Hopi, and Navajo of the Colorado River Reservation — and the Yavapai-Apaches of Camp Verde. With new guarantees to their rights and new challenges to their identities, Indians began to define themselves in new ways.

World War II and the Barren Years

During World War II, tribal governments and enterprises (and BIA programs, as well) virtually ground to a halt. More than 65,000 (some estimates say 113,000) mostly young people left the reservations to fight or to work in war-related industries — the first great off-reservation migration. Pueblos competed with each other in buying war bonds, using money from pottery sales, photo fees charged to tourists, and benefit dance performances. Collier had hoped for all-Indian units to preserve Indian culture; the 25,000 Indians who served in the military were integrated, however — with enormously powerful effects on their world view, and sharp boosts in their family economies while they served.

After the war, many Indians never returned to live full-time on the reservations. Those who did sent reservation unemployment statistics soaring. Federally subsidized agribusiness was continuing its inexorable displacement of small farmers and cattlemen: in 1945, Indian farm families still had a net annual income of just $501. Indian employment statistics, however, can mislead. A man at Santa Ana Pueblo or in an isolated Tohono O'odham village may take care of the community ceremonial building, organize graveyard cleanup crews, plant two fields, cut wood, gather food and medicinal plants, care for and teach grandchildren, spend time on weaving or leatherwork, help with ceremonial tasks, serve on the village council — and receive in trade from the rest of the community a variety of food, goods, and free transportation. Is this man "unemployed?"

Veterans came home to grandfathers who performed purification rituals to exorcise their ghosts. Even after the ceremonies, the returned GIs grappled with the

Private Jimmy D. Benallie, a Navajo marine from Gallup, New Mexico, on Okinawa in 1945.
During World War II, more than 65,000 (some estimates say 113,000) mostly young people left
the reservations to fight or to work in war-related industries — the first great off-reservation migration.
U.S. Department of Defense photo by McElroy. (Courtesy Special Collections Department, University of
Utah Libraries)

tragedies they had seen and with two opposing ways of life. Some men drank to forget. Others used their GI Bill benefits to attend college. Elders wondered how many more changes would be needed before "we won't be Navajo (or Pueblo or O'odham) anymore."

Collier's resignation as commissioner inaugurated what Deloria and Lytle call "the barren years," the decades from 1945 to 1965. As controversial, abrasive, and stubborn as Collier was, the New Dealer was an impassioned orator and a wily bureaucrat. He fought with Congress wholeheartedly, and with his absence, assimilation and integration once again became the doctrines of federal policy.

The post-Roosevelt Congress sought to dismantle the New Deal. Opponents of the IRA and of BIA protection of Indians saw their chance to preserve the assimilationist momentum generated by the war. If Indians now could govern themselves, as

Collier had said, earn their own livings, and assimilate successfully as the soldiers had done, then by God let them take care of themselves!

The creation of the Indian Claims Commission in 1946 gave tribes a crucial forum for resolving land claims. The commission also was seen as a means to prepare the way for termination, unilaterally invalidating treaties and severing the trust relationship — the federal responsibility for both Indian lands and social services, for which Indians had exchanged most of the continent. Alfreda Mitre, chair of the Las Vegas Paiute band, noticed that lawyers often pushed tribes to settle claims cases in the fall, just when Indian children returned to school and they need money the most: "Desperate people do desperate things."

As scholar Michael Dorris has pointed out, "Congress often seems to regard reservations and treaty rights as transitional stages" rather than as permanent government-to-government relationships. The legal guarantees of dual rights to Indians as both tribal members and American citizens are unique; no wonder few non-Indians understand them.

Termination became official federal policy in 1953, when the resolution designed to "free Indians" passed Congress unanimously. Unfortunately, the strategy instead set Indian communities adrift — without training, without support, without capital. None had experience with entrepreneurship or in finding social services outside of familiar channels. The more than one hundred tribes devastated by termination included both small bands and large, resource-rich tribes. In the Southwest, only the Southern Paiute bands in Utah suffered termination. Like many terminated tribes, they found their trust obligations assumed by local banks and subsequently lost most of their land.

Along with termination, the Bureau convinced some sixty thousand Indians to move to cities in a program aimed at relocation of Indian people from reservations to urban areas; the program continued until the mid-1970s. In 1967 alone, relocation's climactic year, 5,800 Indians moved to the cities. Once there, the Bureau offered little support. Throughout these years, many Indians found urban life alienating, and about half the relocatees moved back home after weeks or months. Anthropologist Joseph Jorgensen summed up the program: "Indians are pushed from rural poverty to urban poverty with the promise of crumbs of wealth in the city."

Today more than half of all American Indians live in cities. Most maintain their ties to reservation and tribe; they maintain a sense of community in the city through churches or powwows. Los Angeles has the largest urban Indian concentration in the country, numbering almost ninety thousand in 1990, a more than tenfold increase since 1955. Phoenix, Tucson, Denver, Albuquerque, and Salt Lake City all have (or have had) Indian Centers, born of the 1960s — crucial places for these otherwise near-

Today more than half of all American Indians live in cities. Most maintain their ties to reservation and tribe, preserving a sense of community through churches or powwows. Gathering of Nations Powwow, Albuquerque, 1991.

invisible minorities to celebrate their ethnicity. According to census records, nearly fifty thousand Indian people lived in those five cities in 1990.

With bloodlines mixed by intermarriage, these more acculturated Indians can feel displaced both in the city and on the reservation. Pima/Apache Tony Ringlero went to California on a Latter Day Saints high school placement program. He says: "You take on roles, you adapt; no one wants to be a nerd. I hung out with Spanish, surfers, Blacks, and Polynesians; I acted, dressed, and spoke like each group. Then I went to Brigham Young University and met a Sioux/Winnebago guy and started learning singing and dancing from him. I learned what tradition was all about from other northern Plains mentors. Then I came home to Arizona.

"When I go to San Carlos, I am a San Carlos Apache. When I go to Salt River, I am a Salt River Pima. On a daily basis, I'm both. Identity is a matter of moments in time."

The New Buffalo

As the termination movement gained in strength after the war, Indians were developing their first effective national lobbying groups, thinking of themselves as more than isolated tribal peoples. The National Congress of American Indians formed in 1944 and soon began to push for self-determination. Though these Indian rights advocates could not stop the initial termination legislation, by 1958 they had achieved sufficient clout to halt the policy of terminating a tribe against its will.

One rather cynical, though realistic, effort to blunt termination came when sympathetic members of Congress pushed reservation leases from ten years to fifty years. They knew that non-Indian lessees would join with tribes to fight termination if only to protect long-term investments. With the Kennedy administration, the lease term grew to ninety-nine years — effectively a transfer of tribal land to corporate America.

The 1960s once again brought federal money to the reservations, funneled from the Office of Economic Opportunity. During the War on Poverty, tribal governments became just as eligible as city or county governments to sponsor a multitude of federal programs. Civil rights advances encouraged minority participation, though Indians pressing for voting rights in local elections continue to provoke opposition from non-Indians fearful of losing their all-white representation.

The chance to run their own programs revolutionized tribal governments. As Washington increased funds and programs, the tribal hierarchy grew in order to manage them. Federal money became, in the words of one tribal administrator, the Indian's "new buffalo." Instead of a new hunting technology, tribal leaders learned a new language of federal acronyms. Allen Turner, a sociologist working with the Kaibab Paiutes in the 1970s, offers the following daunting example of the impact of this new federal language, overheard from a tribal bureaucrat: "The CHR should meet with the NCOA's at Title Four to talk about 437 IHS and 641 HSA planning." The effective meaning of this sentence is simply, "John and the elders should meet at the community center to talk about health planning."

In reaction to this sudden flowering of self-government, younger Indians began searching for ways to assert Indian pride. The National Indian Youth Council was founded in 1961, and the American Indian Movement (AIM) developed in Minneapolis in 1968. The moderate National Congress of American Indians became more radical. Energy resource-rich tribes banded together in 1975 in a Council of Energy Resource Tribes (CERT), in hopes of having some of the clout of an OPEC.

New housing, industrial parks, community centers, and tribal headquarter complexes sprouted all over the Southwest. The Institute of American Indian Art (a two-year college program for young Indian artists) began operating in Santa Fe in 1962; the first Indian-operated college, Navajo Community College, opened in 1968. Zuni and Salt River each signed contracts in 1970 in which the tribe took over administration of all BIA programs. The unlikeliest of men, Richard Nixon, became the most sensible administrator of Indian policy in decades, stating that his goal was "to strengthen the Indian's sense of autonomy without threatening his sense of community."

In 1968, the Indian Civil Rights Act passed, greatly complicating Indian self-government. Aiming to strengthen both the civil rights of individual Indians and tribal self-government, the bill called for tribal courts considerably more independent from tribal councils than they formerly had been. This bill and other legislation raised fine points of law and jurisdiction (tribal versus state versus federal, in criminal, civil, and taxation issues) that still constitute the primary legal problems for Indian Country.

The Indian Education Act of 1972 gave new funding to Indian school programs but did not answer the demands from many Indian educators for a curriculum different from one designed for middle-class whites. As Vine Deloria, Jr., puts it, "Indians were placed within the process of education but not allowed to determine its content." He goes on to plead for placing education in the context of tribal culture and history, asking Indian students always to ask, "How does what we receive in our educational experience impact the preservation and sensible use of our lands and how does it affect the continuing existence of our tribes?" Deloria believes this can lead to a remarkable future where Indian communities walk into and right through the Western world view, emerging "on the other side" with innovative, integrating, and influential ideas.

With the passage of the 1975 Indian Self-Determination and Educational Assistance Act, Indian people could take from the Bureau some power over their schools. Funding, however, became more complicated than ever. The movement to design schools for Indian needs continued to face counterpressures to make Indian schools fit into the demands of the wider society — obtaining regional accreditation, for example. Many middle-aged Indians, boarding-school educated, bemoaned the passing of the BIA boarding schools, convinced that the rigid discipline had been good for them. Nonetheless, by the 1980s only 15 percent of Indian students attended BIA-run schools. Nearly all of the rest were in public schools.

The Indian Child Welfare Act of 1978 limited state control in an effort to halt forced adoption, which had claimed up to a third of all Indian children in the early 1970s. As still more bills followed, refining the notion of tribal sovereignty and legislatively repudiating termination, tribal communities have become increasingly involved with federal politics and law and with agencies outside the BIA. Mona Fernandez, a Hopi/Havasupai member of the Colorado River Indian Tribes, has seen her elders' teachings grow broader and more political: "Our relationship with the government is not based on race, it is based on the political relationship that Indian nations have with the government. Young Indian people don't understand that. The media makes us out to be dependent, but to me we're not. There has to be an *exchange* for land and water taken.

"These may not be traditional teachings, but they are our history, and important to us maintaining ourselves as Indian tribes, Indian governments."

"The United Indians of All Tribes"

National Indian movements grew from the cities. In 1940, less than 5 percent of the Indian population lived in cities; by 1950, almost 20 percent did. Some Indians who stayed on after the urban relocation efforts of the fifties acquired street smarts that they applied to activist confrontations in the years that followed. "The United Indians of All Tribes" was a new idea — invented along with the concept of Red Power in the 1970s.

The seventies began with the demands for Indian rights that climaxed in the Trail of Broken Treaties and the takeover of the BIA headquarters in Washington, D.C., the confrontation at Wounded Knee, and the occupation of Alcatraz Island in San Francisco Bay. Gail Russell, Chemehuevi/Camp Verde Apache, was married to a Sioux and living in Salt Lake City when the Trail of Broken Treaties caravan came through town. Her husband said: "This is history in the making." The couple went on to Washington, D.C., where Russell saw what she describes as "the beginning of Indian people coming together for a common cause and trying to make some changes. Our world became smaller after that; we had friends all over the country."

Russell and her husband also were at Wounded Knee, and she was tear-gassed in Custer, South Dakota. She says: "AIM was the catalyst. It took the warriors coming in like that to effect change. Then came the spiritual people." Russell's experiences in the 1970s "made me want to help and do more. Some of us just went home after that; others will just go change their lives." Today, she directs the Indian Walk-In Center in Salt Lake City.

The AIM warriors, though somewhat subdued by legal prosecution following their initial militancy, changed the perception of Indians in America. Elementary textbooks could no longer speak blithely of "squaws" and "bucks." Indian Studies departments blossomed on university campuses. The report of the 1977 American Indian Policy Review Commission stated clearly that the "right to exist as separate tribal

In 1972, the Trail of Broken Treaties cross-country caravan ended with the takeover of the Bureau of Indian Affairs headquarters in Washington, D.C. The Indian activists proclaimed the BIA building the Native American Embassy — a symbol of the emerging Red Power movement and the drive for self-determination. (Courtesy UPI/Bettmann)

groups with inherent authority to rule themselves and their territory" is "the cornerstone of federal Indian policy . . . Self-government (i.e., sovereignty) in conjunction with the trust relationship, is truly the inheritance of Indian people." Thoughtful non-Indians sincerely tried to understand the desire of Indian people to remain separate and distinct rather than disappear into the melting pot of a sentimentalized America.

Urban-dwelling Indians seek to forge an identity, to create a new tribalism. They find their inspiration in the traditional elders of reservation communities, who speak to moral and ethical concerns, who understand Indian identity in a whole sense, inseparable from land and ceremony and work and animals and ancestors. Ironically, for the traditionalists themselves, the problems remain tribal — fulfillment of specific treaty rights, for instance.

To keep reservation communities afloat, tribal officials look to the short-term processes of politics, economics, and legislation. As their prime means of access to federal power and money, tribal governments need the BIA — just as the BIA needs tribal dependency as the justification for its bureaucratic existence. These tribal bureaucrats have years of managerial experience earned through administering government grants. They can become the Indian entrepreneurs that reservation economies need. Meanwhile, as Janice Colorow, librarian at Ute Mountain, says: "Our history is created on a daily basis. A council decision last Thursday affects everybody now and for the next generation."

Matching funds for grants and money to meet budget shortfalls has to come from somewhere. As Geneal Anderson, chair of the Paiute Tribe of Utah, says: "People think trucks pull up here every day and unload money." They do not. Anthropologist Joseph Jorgensen describes the plight of reservation Indians: "They do not have access to capital to use their own resources, the skills to use their own resources, adequate counsel to use their own resources, nor ultimate control over their own resources."

Governments of small tribes remain poor and subject to charges that they are doing nothing for their people. Tribes with energy resources (Navajo, Hopi, Laguna) have leased land to corporations for rapid development but do not have the clout necessary to make fair deals with the corporations; such tribal governments face charges of selling out their people for short-term gain and few jobs, leaving land ravaged by strip mining and creating chronic radiation hazards from uranium waste.

Like so many aspects of the modern native dilemma, however, the two sides are not easily reconciled. Balanced, yes, but not welded together. Tribal economies need to be developed but in ways that maintain some relation to Indian values. Tensions will continue; politics will paralyze reservations; and young Indian people will be challenged to search for a path between conflicting values. They have no choice but to acknowledge both sides. In the words of Sioux attorney Sam Deloria, director of the American Indian Law Center at the University of New Mexico: "To refuse, in the name of cultural purity, to learn the skills of survival in the world as it exists is to perpetuate paternalism."

The federal government has not helped. The 1980s and early 1990s have brought conservative Republican administrations, whose cuts in financial and social aid reflect a philosophy similar to that of supporters of termination in the 1950s. Reservations have drifted into desperate economic straits. In 1981, for example, the Reagan administration called for an 82 percent slashing of federal funds for tribal economic development. Alfonso Ortiz calls this "de-facto termination . . . by de-funding."

Indian communities can ill afford cuts in social services. Half of the American Indian population suffers from alcoholism to some degree, which means that *all* Indian people have alcoholics in their closest circles. Alcohol-related deaths and diseases for Indians are three to six times the national averages. At Fort Apache, for instance, as many as 20 to 30 percent of Apache children suffer from the effects of maternal drinking during pregnancy. The historic social pressures that, in some tribes, encourage drinking as a reinforcer of solidarity and identity make battling its horrendous consequences even more difficult.

Carl Valley, the young Acoma Pueblo postmaster trained as a historian, takes a pessimistic view of the future. "Tribal governments really are not recognized. Any chance to say 'national emergency!' and the federal government could annex what-

Young Indian students dressed as Pilgrims at a boarding school far from home — both geographically and culturally. (Courtesy Special Collections Department, University of Utah Libraries)

ever reservation they wanted. Things will come around to the way they were. Bust, boom, bust, boom. It happened with uranium, it happens with nations, too."

Once more, policies encouraging cultural pluralism have given way to some of the old assumptions of forced assimilation. These assumptions never go away: a syndicated column by Andy Rooney published in 1992 voiced the ignorance that too many people still share: "American Indians . . . hang onto remnants of their religion and superstitions that may have been useful to savages 500 years ago, but which are meaningless in 1992 . . . Someone should tell the Indians living on reservations that the United States isn't a bad country to be part of."

In such a climate, the restoration of the Paiute Tribe of Utah (1980) and the recognition of the Pascua Yaqui (1978) and San Juan Paiute (1989) tribes are near-miracles. Indians form a tiny minority in American society, but as an array of dozens of tribal governments, each with its own legal relationship to the federal government, they actually exert considerable political influence given their numbers. Increasingly sophisticated Indian activists have ensured that no statute has passed Congress over Indian opposition since 1968. Many tribes are undergoing a cultural renaissance as young people assert their identity.

The late Hopi artist and teacher Terrance Honvantewa spoke with me in his little office at the Hopi Cultural Center Museum, where he worked as curator and director:

"Anthropologists are forever telling us that our culture is dying out. They don't realize the commitment that we do have into the ceremonial life that is our identity. I still have a field. I still plant my corn. Because why should I participate and pray for rain if I don't have any plants for the rains to come and nourish?

"You are born with that spirit, but it's up to you to be responsible to it, to develop it in a way that you would be proud to say, 'I'm a Hopi,' or 'I'm a Navajo.' It's a tradition. It's a language. It's an identity.

"The teachings of the Hopi stay with you no matter how far and how long you venture away from the center of the universe, which is here. And when you come back, the teachings are still here. This is what makes the Hopi people strong."

The People will need all the strength they can muster from land, family, community, ceremony, language, and government. Arrayed against them are the challenges rampant at the end of the twentieth century: poverty, unemployment, substance abuse, homogenization of culture through television, and fragmentation and urbanization of families.

Honvantewa believed the teachings of the People remain strong enough for them to survive as Indian people. Acoma Pueblo poet Simon Ortiz agrees: "Only when the people of this nation, not just Indian people, fight for what is just and good for all life, will we know life and its continuance. And when we fight, and fight back those who are bent on destruction of land and people, we will win. We will win."

ONE

In the Canyons and Mesas

PLATEAU PEOPLES

Yei Bi Chei Rocks and hogan, Monument Valley Tribal Park,
Navajo Reservation, Arizona, 1988.

From the mouth of the Colorado River at the Sea of Cortez, the Southwest rises northward in steps — concentric semicircles from desert basin to desert mountain to the Colorado Plateau and, finally, to the Rockies themselves. Keystone to this circular Southwest, ringed by dry mountains, standing like a huge island above the deserts, the

Colorado Plateau seems timeless. Its landscapes are icons of wilderness and natural beauty. Its rocks are old, its canyons still new, its geology laid bare to even the least observant eye. Its aridity and isolation have preserved Indian ways as much as anywhere in the West.

Dawn in Monument Valley. Orange sand ripples the foreground, Navajo sheep graze through the background, their bells clanking in the still air. One hundred and fifty miles to the west, Havasupai children swim near Supai Village in the blue-green waters of Havasu Creek. Below Third Mesa, dry cornhusks rustle underfoot as a Hopi farmer harvests his field. At Zuni Pueblo, families gather for a feast day in cool adobe rooms, eating their fill of sweet blue corn *atole* and pungent red chile. These images come from the lives of the native peoples of the Colorado Plateau.

The Colorado River slices in deep canyons through a vast plateau-land between the Rocky Mountains and the deserts, a grand stairway of mesa and cliff named for the river that carves it. Born in the Colorado Rockies, then joined deep in the canyon country of Utah by the Green River bearing snowmelt from Wyoming, the Colorado meets the San Juan River. The combined forces of all three streams pour through the greatest gorge of any Southwestern river, the Grand Canyon. When the Colorado leaves the Grand Canyon, the river flows into the lowland deserts, leaving plateau country behind.

While the surrounding crust of the Earth folded into mountains, faulted into basins and ranges, and stretched open in rifts, the plateau lay still in a vast block — an island with a nearly continuous stratigraphic record of geologic history exposed in mesas and buttes and canyons at the heart of the Southwest. Today, the entire plateau has been uplifted, and its average five-thousand-foot elevation generates sufficient rainfall and snowfall to carry it out of the ecological category of "desert" — barely.

In southwestern Utah and along the rims of Grand Canyon, smaller plateaus within the greater plateau have been uplifted higher still, to ten thousand and twelve thousand feet — still flat-topped but high enough to become mountains. Here, the rivers carve deep to find their way through. Volcanic island mountains eroded in contrasting curves and angles rise from the plateau surface: San Francisco Peaks, Mount Taylor, the Chuskas, Shiprock, Ute Mountain, Navajo Mountain, all sacred to the Indian people who live near them.

In prehistoric times, the plateau was the heartland of the Anasazi. Today, their descendants, the Pueblo people, live in villages spanning a 350-mile crescent from the Hopi Mesas of northeast Arizona to the Rio Grande pueblos near Albuquerque and Santa Fe and, finally, north to Taos, in the Rockies themselves. Along the fertile strip of the Rio Grande, modern Pueblo farmers have moved from canyons into irrigable bottomlands — they are people with their heritage in the mesas but their feet in the good earth and brimfull ditches of northern New Mexico.

Deep in the Grand Canyon live the Havasupai; on the rims above them are their kin, the Hualapai. And in a huge reservation — the largest of any Southwestern tribe — the Navajo have taken over land once held by Pueblo, Ute, and Southern Paiute. Arriving with their Apache relations long after other Southwestern tribes, the Navajo have flourished here — sheepherding, farming, and adapting. Today, the Diné, the Navajo people, live in what they call the Navajo Nation, the most populous Indian reservation in the United States.

Great spaces and high elevations make for stark clarity of vision, both literally and spiritually. The rock, time, space, and color of the Colorado Plateau forge a bond between people and land that gives rise to archetypal images: Acoma Pueblo perched on its mesa, halfway to the sky. Supai cradled deep within Grand Canyon. Navajo hogans facing east toward the rising sun below chiseled sandstone buttes and spires.

If the Southwest is Indian Country, the Colorado Plateau is its heart.

The Pueblos

Survival, I know how this way.

This way, I know.

It rains.

Mountains and canyons and plants

grow.

We travelled this way,

gauged our distance by stories

and loved our children.

We taught them

to love their births.

We told ourselves over and over

again,

"We shall survive this way."

. . . And so you tell stories.

You tell stories about your People's birth

and their growing.

You tell stories about your children's birth

and their growing.

You tell the stories of their struggles.

You tell that kind of history,

and you pray and be humble.

With strength, it will continue that way.

That is the only way.

That is the only way.

Simon J. Ortiz, *A Good Journey*, 1977

Son'ahchi.

Pueblo tales begin with a formal opening: *Son'ahchi* in Zuni, *Aliksa'i* in Hopi. Translations vary from "Attention!" to "Let us take up the story where we left it." The stories continue with identification of place, not time. Pueblos, and Indian people in general, care more for where a story happened than when.

When elders from Zia, Jemez, and Santa Ana pueblos submitted a land claim in 1950, they made clear the relationship of land and stories: "This has always been our land. We know these matters not merely because our grandparents told us vague stories when we were children, but because our parents and grandparents, and their parents and grandparents before them, made sure to tell us so exactly and so often that we could not forget."

Every year around the first of December, ten-foot-high courier katsinas — the Shalakos — come to visit special houses in Zuni. They dance all night, celebrating the connections between modern Zuni people and the spirits of their ancestors. Photo by Matilda Coxe Stevenson, 1897–98. (Smithsonian Institution photo no. 2374)

Son'ahchi. The Zuni people live at Halona. Of the legendary cities of Cibola that drew the Spaniards north, forever altering the lives of Southwestern Indians, only Halona remains. Every year near the first of December, ten-foot-high courier katsinas, the Shalakos, return from Katsina Village, *Ko/lhu/wa/a la:wa,* to visit special houses in Zuni. Other katsinas — the Council of the Gods — accompany them.

These spirit messengers from the gods dance all night, celebrating the connection between modern Zuni people and the spirits of their ancestors. The Shalakos ensure that the blessings of life will continue to come to the families sponsoring Shalako houses, to the Zunis, and to all people. Vinton Zunie, a Zuni man in his thirties who works as tribal youth coordinator, says: "Even little kids commit to the year-long Shalako involvement. And the schools let out for Shalako now that Zunis have control of the school district."

On Shalako night, I walk around the village in frosty darkness. I stop to warm by a fire built in a generous Zuni's front yard. The stars are brilliant, the air brittle with cold. In the darkness beyond, two *Sa'Li'Mo:Be'ya'* katsinas rustle by, their ruffs of raven feathers stiff beneath domed and beaked heads. These two War Brothers of the nadir and zenith brandish swords of green yucca leaves; they menace anyone who dares to fall asleep during the dance of the Shalako. A swish of embroidered kilts and the soft clatter of rattles mark their passage.

The warrior katsinas enter the nearby Shalako house, and as the door opens, a shaft of white light leaps out across the packed earthen yard. I glimpse close-packed Pueblo, Navajo, and Anglo bodies — all dwarfed by the Shalako dancing behind them, an immensely powerful and appealing being with wide eyes, buffalo horns, and an eagle feather headdress. The open door lets out a gust of warm, stuffy air laden with the smell of roast mutton, a phrase or two of drum-beat and chant, and the clacking of the great Shalako's beak. Then the door closes and the bonfire leaps up to the stars.

Energetic Lea Pinto, director of the Wellness Center at Zuni, says: "The Shalako prayer talks about everything in the universe — all the animals, all the seeds known in the Zuni language. Even the seeds men and women have in them are honored."

Thousands of other guests have visited Zuni for Shalako. Lea Pinto believes that "we've kept a lot of our culture because we have been so open." Her grandmother said of the white people coming to dances: "Let them come: they don't understand anyway!" Beginning in 1990, however, the Zuni tribal council closed Shalako and summer rain ceremonies to tour groups of non-Indian visitors. Individuals are still welcome, but too many tourists had defied the rules prohibiting photography, sketching, and tape recording, and the religious leaders of the pueblo felt it necessary to limit attendance in order to "safeguard our religious well-being and privacy."

It is an old and depressing story. Spanish soldiers and missionaries, federal functionaries, anthropologists, commercial exploiters, and well-meaning but ignorant travelers all have tested the patience and resilience of Pueblo people over nearly five centuries. In 1936, anthropologist Elsie Clews Parsons dedicated her monograph on Taos Pueblo to "My best friend in Taos, the most scrupulous Pueblo Indian of my acquaintance, who told me nothing about the Pueblo and who never will tell any white person anything his people would not have him tell, which is nothing." Today, the Taos people remain hostile toward Parsons' work and just as uninterested in talking about their ceremonial life with outsiders.

Parsons ended her monograph with this statement: "The kiva groups will tend to become mere clubs, vaudeville groups perhaps. Pueblo ceremonialism will break down . . . How soon? Shall we say fifty years, *más o menos*?"

Her arrogant prediction was wrong. The Pueblos have survived and flourished, retaining more of their old ways on their journey than any outsider can know. Diane Reyna, from Taos, who works as a video producer and camerawoman in Santa Fe, told me that Parsons' informants are still ostracized. Reyna also said: "A lot of outsiders want to get into the crux of Indian religion. They need to accept the simpleness of it all. All you have to do is be thankful that the sun is coming up. Acknowledging what you have and being thankful — that's the essence of Pueblo life."

The Living Anasazi

Pueblo people have no doubts about where they come from. Rina Swentzell, from Santa Clara, talks about the "sense of connectedness" that comes from continuity: "The relationship that has been established here over thousands of years with the land, clouds, and mountains is unique because it is so strong."

Edmund Ladd, from Zuni, archaeologist and curator of ethnology for the Museum of New Mexico, says: "The Anasazi are well and happy in the Rio Grande valley." When pressed for a Hopi word for those whom Anglos call "traditional," Moenkopi people gave anthropologist Shuichi Nagata the word they use for Anasazi, *hisatsinom* ("ancient people").

Lillian Salvador, Acoma potter, spent a day camped on a Mimbres ruin in southern New Mexico. "It made me feel we were at home and they were there, too. I felt that we were all just talking. When I got home, I started painting, and my animals just came out. It made me feel so good." She brought home Mimbres potsherds, as well, grinding them into her clay as temper, building the Pueblo past into her pots.

Pueblo people lived in the Four Corners and Rio Grande country from the

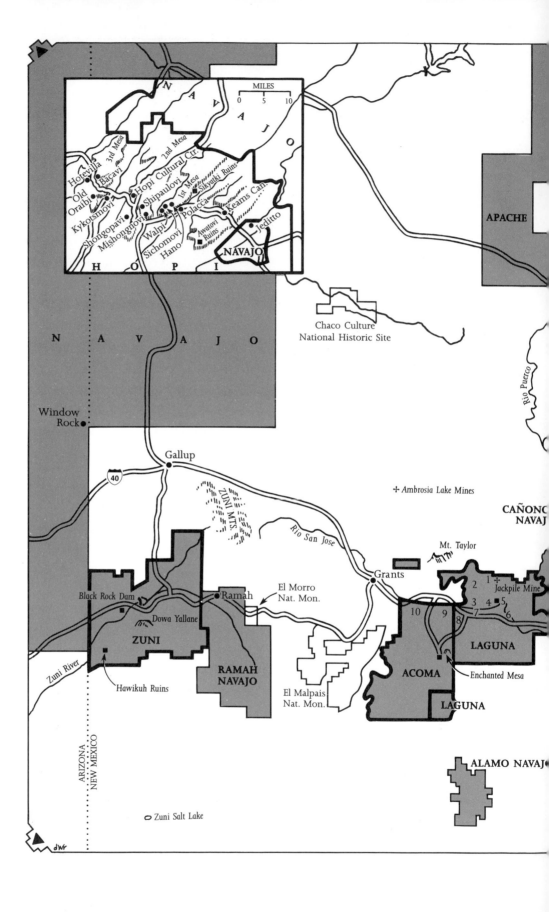

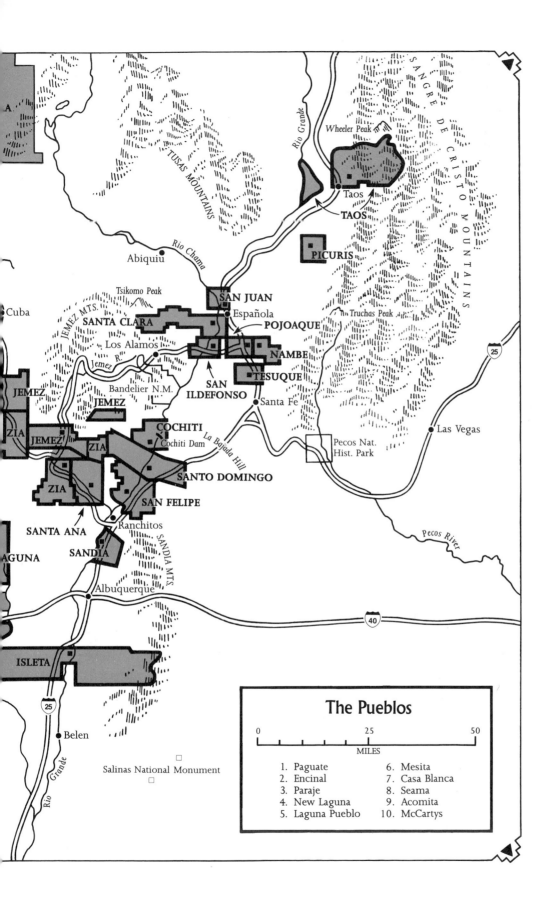

A

Rio Grande

Wheeler Peak

SANGRE DE CRISTO MOUNTAINS

TUSAS MOUNTAINS

Taos

TAOS

Rio Chama

Abiquiu

PICURIS

Tsikomo Peak

SAN JUAN

Cuba

JEMEZ MTS.

SANTA CLARA

Española

POJOAQUE

Truchas Peak

Los Alamos

NAMBE

Jemez R.

I-25

JEMEZ

Bandelier N.M.

SAN ILDEFONSO

TESUQUE

ZIA

JEMEZ

Santa Fe

COCHITI

Cochiti Dam

La Bajada Hill

Las Vegas

ZIA

JEMEZ

Pecos Nat. Hist. Park

ZIA

SANTO DOMINGO

SAN FELIPE

SANTA ANA

Ranchitos

Pecos River

SANDIA MTS.

SANDIA

LAGUNA

Albuquerque

I-40

ISLETA

I-25

Rio Grande

Belen

Salinas National Monument

The Pueblos

0   25   50

MILES

1. Paguate
2. Encinal
3. Paraje
4. New Laguna
5. Laguna Pueblo
6. Mesita
7. Casa Blanca
8. Seama
9. Acomita
10. McCartys

Rina Swentzell, Santa Clara Pueblo writer and architectural historian, Santa Fe, 1989.

beginning, growing from the ancient Archaic traditions. In adobe and masonry villages (called *pueblos* by the Spanish), they created a society based on communal farming and worship.

As Santa Clara writer Rina Swentzell puts it: "The adobe structures flowed out of the earth, and it was often difficult to see where the ground stopped and where the structures began . . . As we are synonymous with and born of the earth, so are we made of the same stuff as our houses . . . The structures were interactive. We built them, tasted them, talked with them, climbed on them, lived with them, and watched them die . . . The entire community was the house."

Writer Peter Nabokov speaks of Acoma Pueblo as a "veritable food factory," with storage rooms, corn-grinding rooms, and *piki* (paper-thin blue corn bread) preparation rooms scattered through the house blocks. In the streets below stand the *hornos*, the beehive-shaped bread ovens as essential to village character as roof beams, kiva ladders, and piñon woodsmoke.

Modern Hopis, as one older Bacavi man told anthropologist Peter Whiteley, live their lives "as a destiny we are fulfilling," a life prophesied by "those priests and chiefs who planned this all out for us." The great "disappearance" of the Anasazi may well have been just another set of destinies prophesied by the wise men of the People.

In the 1200s, the Anasazi encountered a whole set of climatic and social stresses. Drought, arroyo cutting (perhaps aggravated by tree felling in watersheds), political upheavals (maybe even war), disease, religious pronouncements — some unknown combination of factors led these prehistoric Pueblo people to abandon much of the canyon country that had been their heartland. These migrations make sense to Rina Swentzell: "There is that easy flow through life. Build up this community, something happens, time to go, move on to the next place, leaving the pot sitting there, walking away from it, without any need to pack it and take all your possessions with you. The thing that you took with you was creative capability, and that was all you needed."

In those years of upheaval in the thirteenth and fourteenth centuries, the Anasazi frontier — the upper Rio Grande valley, Acoma and Zuni, Hopi country — increased in population. Archaeologists detect no great cultural shift: these were Anasazi joining communities of their kin. They spoke diverse languages and embraced many heritages, but their core — religion, world view, and economy — stayed remarkably similar through time and across many miles. As Cochiti artist Joe Herrera points out: "Regardless of how they dress, or how they put on the paraphernalia, it is still the same, the same belief."

Time passed, migrations gathered new combinations of people, and Anasazi life changed. Anasazi religion incorporated katsinas (the more accurate spelling of the Anglicized "kachinas") — yet another cultural contribution, according to the anthropologists, to come to the Southwest from Mexico. The Pueblo people do not think of spirit beings "migrating" from anywhere; for them, katsinas have been here from the beginning.

Today, more than three hundred different kinds of katsinas come to Hopi for six months each year, arriving in February at Bean Dance (Powamuy) time and departing for the San Francisco Peaks and other holy places after the Home Dance (Niman) in July. Uninitiated children hold the katsinas dancing in the plazas "in awe," in the words of the late Hopi teacher Terrance Honvantewa. Hopi artist Michael Kabotie says: "The katsinas are an ideological handle for children, to help them understand and relate to the spirits of nature, which are more complex and intangible." Kabotie always includes in his paintings the home of the katsinas — the silhouette of the San Francisco Peaks — as "homage to those here before us, a signature of the spirits around this sacred place."

"Hopis don't worship katsinas," says Ramson Lomatewama, a Hopi educator and poet who attended Goddard College in Vermont and dances at Hotevilla as a sacred clown. "Katsinas are intermediaries between the Creator and humankind. They deliver the blessings of life — health and happiness and hope. Katsinas provide living examples of how life is conducted. I can't think of many words to describe the

Katsinas like these come to Hopi for six months each year, arriving in the February Bean Dance (Powamuy). Hopi artist Michael Kabotie says: "The katsinas are an ideological handle for children, to help them understand and relate to the spirits of nature." Photo by James Mooney, 1893. (Smithsonian Institution photo no. 1821-A-2)

feelings that I get when I watch these dances. I can say that I'm inspired, that I'm moved, but it goes beyond that. They're there showing us; they're there giving us — something."

The Pueblo people have continued to thrive, building new villages as they abandoned old ones. To write their history is to write of a loosely knit network, with each pueblo (even those with barely two hundred people) comparable to a city-state — complete, self-sufficient, and independent. Specifics vie for attention with regional and "national" trends, and the story is not simple.

The People remind me, however, that much of what they believe is indeed comprehensible and far from esoteric. Nora Naranjo-Morse, Santa Clara potter, says: "The spiritual connection is the most important thing. The older people spent time talking to the sun and wishing it well. They had a strong grasp that it was just *okay*." She adds, sadly, that now, too often, people spend their time asking, "Am I okay?"

Lea Pinto told me: "During winter solstice we bring in all our seeds and pray that those seeds will be reborn. It teaches you about growth — the seed that you are, the seed that you are becoming. Your prayer, even if only one, will help the environment, giving respect to what makes us survive as a people."

As Anasazi grew corn, Pueblo people grow corn. In Zuni, *dowa* means both "corn" and "ancient." Ramson Lomatewama has learned about Hopi corn from his elders: "When a person planted corn, they would be raising these corn plants up as their children. We were taught to sing to our corn, sing to our children, talk to our children, to love our children, to care for them. Corn provides us with food. It is the center of life and the essence of life. Our ceremonies are prayers for rain in order that our corn will grow. When we plant corn or when we plant melons or squash or beans, we are showing our faith in life."

Learning about one thing extends outward to all things. Says Lomatewama: "You can't learn anything without giving something up. And you have to learn by trial and error. I learned about the Hopi Way just by being involved in the culture, listening to older people speak, and living. The more you live, the more you learn."

Unity and Diversity

Since Europeans came to the Southwest in the sixteenth century, Pueblo people have abandoned at least sixty-one former villages. Today, anthropologists divide the more than thirty modern Pueblo villages into "western" and "eastern" traditions, the two groups differing in social organization. Pueblo administrators speak of "northern" and "southern" Pueblos. Tourist guides tend to focus only on those pueblos with spectacular architecture or flourishing crafts (Taos, San Ildefonso, and Hopi, for example), to the exclusion of pueblos like Sandia or Pojoaque. Santa Clara Pueblo potter Jody Folwell, however, can feel the shared core within all of these pueblos: "Spiritual power exists there in those villages a hundred times more so than in any other community."

At the far west lie the thirteen Hopi villages, isolated along the southern rim of Black Mesa in northeastern Arizona, the driest place chosen by any Pueblo people as a home. The three main clusters of villages blend into the sandstone of three peninsulas dropping away to the desert, named in their order of approach from the east: First, Second, and Third mesas. The Hopis joke that they chose their mesas in part because no one else would want to live there, and so the world would leave them in peace. They have earned a reputation as the most skilled dry-farmers in the world; ecologists have called them "environmental wizards." Hopi elder Fred Kabotie spoke interchangeably of learning to be "a good Hopi" and learning to be "a good farmer."

Zuni Pueblo, too, lies deep within the Colorado Plateau, at the foot of the Zuni Mountains near the Arizona–New Mexico state line, in almost as dry a place as Hopi. Edmund Ladd points out that Zuni "is a kind of crossroads, a composite of many cultures. It grew out of a long trading and cultural movement — Anasazi mostly, but Hohokam, Mogollon, Mimbres, Sinagua, and Hopi, too."

Farther east, Acoma and Laguna stand on mesas near the Rio San Jose on an age-old travel route now followed by both the Santa Fe Railroad and Interstate 40, "improvements" critical to the history of these peoples. The rest of the pueblos spill over from plateau country into the Rocky Mountains and the deserts of the Basin and Range. These eastern or Rio Grande pueblos all have been built near or on the great river. The only modern pueblos south of Albuquerque are Isleta, and, far to the south, Tigua Pueblo at El Paso.

Travel north, beginning in the urban sprawl of Albuquerque. Along the Rio Grande and its tributary, the Jemez River, lie the seven pueblos of Sandoval County: Sandia, Santa Ana, Zia, Jemez, San Felipe, Santo Domingo, and Cochiti. The next major geographic break comes as Interstate 25 climbs La Bajada Hill, a long grade cutting through basalt cliffs just north of Cochiti. This line of cliffs separates the lower river, the Rio Abajo, from the upper river, the Rio Arriba. It separates the desert from the Rockies and divides southern from northern pueblos.

Above La Bajada Hill lies northern New Mexico.

Indian lands begin again in a ruddy bowl of badlands north of Santa Fe, nestled between the Jemez and Sangre de Cristo mountains — southernmost ranges of the Rockies. Within this bowl lie six closely related pueblos: Tesuque, Nambe, Pojoaque,

Hopi farmer with melon, early 1900s. The Hopis measure up to their reputation as the most skilled dry farmers in the world, joking that they chose their dry mesas because no one else would want to live there and so the world would leave them in peace. Photo by Herbert Gregory. (Courtesy Special Collections Department, University of Utah Libraries)

San Ildefonso, Santa Clara, and San Juan. Finally, northernmost (and the only pueblos truly within the mountains), come Picuris and Taos.

In 1942, anthropologist Leslie White wrote: "Unemployment and destitution are blights which cannot affect the Pueblo Indians while they retain their lands." Though sadly this has not remained an absolute, land for growing the old and sacred corn and bean plants still forms an axis for Pueblo culture.

Language adds another layer to Pueblo relationships. The Hopi speak a distinct language related to Ute and Paiute. Zuni stands alone, with only a remote possible connection to Penutian, a central Californian Indian language family. Acoma, Laguna, and the Rio Grande pueblos of Santa Ana, Zia, San Felipe, Santo Domingo, and Cochiti speak Keresan, a language that also stands by itself. Anthropologist Leslie White wrote in 1935: "Santo Domingo is the largest, most typical and most important of Keresan Pueblos." (The Domingo people remain almost as conservative as in White's day. Interracial marriages are few; Keresan is spoken in most homes. The People divulge little to outsiders.)

All other Rio Grande Pueblo peoples speak dialects of Tanoan (a language group that includes Kiowa). Tanoan includes four Pueblo languages: Southern (Isleta and Sandia) and Northern (Taos and Picuris) Tiwa; Tewa (Tesuque, Nambe, Pojoaque, San Ildefonso, Santa Clara, and San Juan); and Towa (Jemez). Edmund Ladd believes Tanoans are the closest kin to Anasazi (though all Pueblo groups may carry Anasazi blood).

Pueblos that today go by the names of their Spanish missions (Santa Ana and San Juan, for example) identify themselves by entirely different names in their own languages. San Juan calls itself by the untranslatable name of Okhe, but also has a sacred ritual name meaning "village of the dew-bedecked corn structure." As San Juan scholar Alfonso Ortiz points out, this phrase ties the San Juan to their past, where always they have lived with corn and moisture, recalling "endless times and places, ever on the edge of an equally endless dawn." Still, the generic "Pueblo" for "village Indians" may not be so far off: Taos is an adaptation of the Tiwa *Teotho*, meaning "houses of the people" or "in the village."

Confusing? Yes. Tony Martinez, from Taos, says: "I don't know the difference between Tewa and Tiwa, but when someone tells me they are from San Juan, I have a reference point." Hartman Lomawaima, from the Hopi village of Shipaulovi, says that for centuries, "in droughts it was not unusual for kids to be sent to other pueblos and other Pueblo kids to Hopi. This developed into a sort of 'student exchange program,' just to give you some perspective on yourself."

A Jemez person is at once Jemez Indian, Pueblo Indian, speaker of Towa, speaker of Tanoan, citizen of a pueblo transitional culturally between western and eastern pueblos, and member of a southern pueblo. That same person may live in Santa Fe and speak English and Spanish, as well. This Jemez person may move on to work in New York or Paris, learn to speak French or Swahili — but all the other defining statements remain true, and each Jemez person may return home for important feast days almost every year, dancing in the plaza after ceremonial purification in the kiva.

As Ada Melton, a Jemez woman in her thirties who lives in the city, says: "Albuquerque has a pretty good urban Indian community, but *all* of us have very long umbilical cords!"

San Felipe Pueblo, circa 1935. The Pueblo world begins at the plaza — the "heart-place" of each village, where all the balanced forces of the universe come together. Conservative Santo Domingo and San Felipe, especially, quietly radiate this spiritual heartbeat. Photo by T. Harmon Parkhurst. (Courtesy Museum of New Mexico, neg. no. 3436)

The Pueblo Way

The Pueblo world begins at the center, at the "heart-place," the plaza of each village. All the balanced forces of the Pueblo world come together here — the sacred mountains of the four cardinal directions, the Sun above and Earth below, winter and summer, male buildings and female space. Here the People dance to bring good things to all people, to create unity, to celebrate the whole. They dance, says Taos artist Pop Chalee, "because it is part of their life. The dances are prayers."

Joe Herrera, Cochiti artist, spoke to writer Tryntje Seymour of plaza dances: "We do it for the whole universe. We don't just do it for our own people. We want peace. We want love. We want care. We want to be blessed. We want people to be blessed. We want them to live as long as they can. We want more animals — to be bountiful."

Herrera's wishes extend to all the dances, from the buffalo and deer dances usually performed in winter to the corn and harvest rituals danced in summer and

Feast day, Santa Clara Pueblo, 1987. Joe Herrera, Cochiti artist, says of plaza dances: *"We do it for the whole universe. We don't just do it for our own people."*

San Ildefonso circa 1920, when a new south plaza isolated the northside with its landmark old cottonwood tree from the southside with its round kiva. Even in these difficult times, the plaza, Black Mesa rising behind, remained the place to feel "the heartbeat of the earth," in Rina Swentzell's words. Photo by Kate Chapman. (Courtesy School of American Research)

fall; from the Hopi Snake Dance to the secular Comanche dances of the Tewa Pueblos, danced largely for pleasure. They embrace a Nambe Pueblo Butterfly Dance of seven shy teenagers and the overwhelming spectacle of hundreds of Santo Domingo corn dancers.

Here in the plaza the sacred clowns — the striped koshares and the knob-featured mudheads — perform the acts prohibited to normal Pueblo people — beyond all rules, scary, funny, sexy, and outrageous. "They make the sacred relevant to the everyday," in Alfonso Ortiz's words. Hopi artist Michael Kabotie calls clowns the "priests of Life." He recites the clown's prayer: "With one smile may there be enlightenment."

In the plaza, often, stands the kiva, its ladder reaching upward toward a lapis sky filled with life-giving clouds, its inner chamber sunk in the secure and sacred earth. Inconspicuous in the dust of the plaza, a half-buried rock with a scatter of prayer feathers and cornmeal indicates the center of the center, the "navel of navels," the symbol of the emergence place. Here, in Rina Swentzell's words, "is where cosmic regions intersect; where the heartbeat of the earth is felt; where the water of the sky is welcomed; where laughter is easy; where the people meet the outside world."

On the horizons stand the sacred mountains in all their strength. They bound the Pueblo world. They are snowy and therefore holy; the katsinas live on them. Within their shelter, the Pueblo people live enmeshed in a network of reciprocal relationships with each other, with every being of the Earth, animate and inanimate, and with the cloud-spirits of the sky. Pueblo time whirls in cycles and circles, not the linear plod of Anglo-American history. Clan, religious society, planting and harvest, ceremonies, hunting, preparations for war, and curing: these order the year; leaders of religious societies are the leaders of the pueblo. The rhythm repeats annually, from solstice to solstice, equinox to equinox.

Within this Pueblo world view reside as many variations as villages (or as many, some would say, as individual Pueblo people!). Katsinas dance for all to see at Hopi. On the Rio Grande, after centuries of secrecy, none but initiated Pueblo people see the katsinas, though such dances performed in secret still are done for the benefit of all humankind. When anthropologists say that "the katsina cult is weak" at Taos and Picuris, they may simply be expressing their own lack of knowledge — and documenting the success of Pueblo guards and the ability of the People to compartmentalize their lives.

Clans, whose membership depends on one's mother's lineage, dominate at Hopi, growing less important to the east. On the Rio Grande, the religious associations dominate (called moieties by the anthropologists because they divide the pueblo in two: Winter and Summer People, Turquoise and Squash People, Made People and Dry Food People, north and south kiva groups).

"In the west, all activities are subordinated to religion," Edward Dozier, Santa Clara anthropologist, said. The reason? In the dry plateau country, rain must come or the People die. And the only way to ensure rain is through prayer and dance and ritual. Only in this way can the Hopi keep the contract they entered into with Maasau-u, keeper of this Fourth World, when they emerged from below, agreeing to act as caretakers for his land in return for his permission to live here.

Prayers grow ever more difficult to complete. Tourists steal prayer feathers, and gravel-mining operations desecrate shrines. Prayers are more than simple blessings. Anthropologist Jane Young quoted the young son of a noted Zuni religious leader:

> "I once asked my father
> to teach me the shortest prayer he knew.
> It took him twenty minutes
> just to say it once."

On the Rio Grande, irrigation is possible, and Dozier believed that this fact explains the intertwining in the east of government with religion, to regulate major irrigation projects effectively. Rio Grande people direct their magic at curing illness. Dozier calls the Tanoans "pragmatic." The Keresans are intermediate — a bridge between east and west.

Alfonso Ortiz says: "One is not born a Tewa but rather one is made a Tewa . . . once made, one has to work hard continuously throughout one's life to remain a Tewa." Young Pueblo people listen to endless theological discussion, watch the rounds of dances, and as they near puberty, undergo initiation in the kivas under the tutelage of a ceremonial father. The crux is not personal transformation but initiation into the community; knowledge leads to responsibility and to proper living.

Tony Dorame, Tesuque leader and entrepreneur, says: "I try to pattern myself after the old people. They could do *everything* — make their breakfast, plant their fields, sing, pray, make beautiful things."

At Hopi, fewer men undergo the year-long initiation into the Wuwtsim religious society, but katsina societies include most people over about ten years of age; in Tewa pueblos, only a select group belong even to katsina societies. Pueblo women do not dance as katsinas, and in some villages they remain uninitiated (as children are everywhere) — and thus still believers in the katsina dancers as real katsinas, not as prayerful masked human dancers.

Hopi men who dance as katsinas call the mask their "katsina friend." A dancer acquires the power of the katsina. Though the experience is transfiguring, historian Joanne Kealiinohomoku points out that "the work is tiring, the sun is hot, the headpieces are often heavy or strangely balanced to uphold (especially in a wind) and one sweats and itches inside the faces; the evergreen ruffs scratch the chest; the arm bands pinch; and the turtle shell rattles beat on the calf muscles." However, Hopi men have told her, "the more uncomfortable they are, the more they must be spiritually in tune." Hopi Emory Sekaquaptewa told me, with a twinkle in his eye, that he "was pleased to be approaching the age where he could stay in the kiva as a katsina father and not have to go out and dance in the winter cold!"

Plaza dances remain a normal part of people's lives, for all of their sacredness and seriousness. Village members — usually younger men — compose new songs for the summer dances each year. Hopi people bring cassette players to the dance to record the songs and chants, playing them over and over until the next year, when they record new ones.

I interviewed Hopi potter Susanna Denet on a dance day. We sat in her living room, with a door open to the Sichomovi plaza filled with dancing katsinas. The Hopi elder gazed serenely out the window at these spirit beings while she spoke with me about the more mundane details of clay and paint. The juxtaposition was exhilarating — but it made it hard to concentrate on taking notes.

Susanna Denet, Hopi potter, watches from her living-room couch as katsinas dance in the Sichomovi plaza, 1986. Gazing serenely at these spirit beings, she spoke with me about the more mundane details of clay and paint.

Nathan Begay, Hopi/Navajo potter, went home to "look through the windows and see the dancing going on, but the children were ignoring this, sprawled on the floor glued to the TV." This saddened him, but one can imagine a still sadder scenario, when dances become so rare that children do *not* take them for granted.

Leadership comes from different sources of strength within each community. Bear Clan members become village kikmongwis at the Hopi villages, Antelope Clan members govern at Acoma; the Bow priests were the executives of Zuni; the Tewas have dual village leaders, the heads of the Winter and Summer moieties each ruling the pueblo for a half-year.

A cacique (kikmongwi, at Hopi), appointed for life, rules a pueblo in all matters of traditional religion. As Leslie White put it for the Santo Domingo cacique: "He is regarded as the father and mother of the people." Historian Richard Clemmer calls the Hopi kikmongwi "more an interpreter of Hopi tradition than a legislator." His assistants, the war chief and war captains, administer everything from ceremonies to hunts to planting. These prominent religious and social leaders inevitably acquired political power, as well.

The Spanish overlaid a governor and tribal council on this theocracy, but, as Joe Sando points out, the Pueblos coopted this system so confidently designed for Spanish domination: "The governor . . . protected the spiritual leaders."

Today, six pueblos (Isleta, Laguna, Pojoaque, San Ildefonso, Santa Clara, and Zuni) elect their governors and councils. The Hopi elect a council, but in the 1990s fewer and fewer villages recognize its authority. At the other pueblos, the caciques appoint the governor each year and the council generally is made up of former governors. But the caciques and kikmongwis remain powerful everywhere and can disband even elected councils, as they did in the mid-1980s at Zuni, when they believed the elected officials to be corrupt. Hopi lacks the traditional array of Spanish-inspired officials, presumably because Hopi ceremonial life could flourish even without this protective bureaucracy.

Precise rituals prescribe proper living. There are no words in Pueblo languages for "religion." When speaking to outsiders, the People call sacred rituals "Indian doings." They learn more and more about their meaning the longer they live, until, as Hopi katsina doll carver Wilfrid Duwenyie puts it, "things finally open up to you" and you grow old enough to "talk in riddles."

The most profound Pueblo elder I have listened to was the late Percy Lomaquahu of Hotevilla. His history challenged my assumptions about Pueblo people who live away from home: he lived in Winslow for forty years, but returned to Third Mesa every weekend to plant and participate in kiva life. His words, in turn, challenged my assumptions about the Hopi tribe. "Hopi" is not a unifying *political* concept any more than is "Tewa" for the Tewa. Being Hopi is more a philosophy, an ideal. The Hopi owe primary allegiance to their village kikmongwi, not the tribal council. When Anglo writer Oliver La Farge wrote the Hopi constitution in 1936, he effectively invented the Hopi "tribe."

In Lomaquahu's own Third Mesa dialect, Hopi means "good in every respect." He told me this "riddle" about the nature of Hopi people, the nature of Pueblo people: "Humbleness means peace, honesty — all mean Hopi. True, honest, perfect words — that's what we call Hopi words. In all the languages, not just in Hopi. We strive to be Hopi. We call ourselves Hopi because maybe one or two of us will become Hopi. Each person must look into their heart and make changes so that you may become Hopi when you reach your destination."

The First American Revolution

Most of these villagers lived close to where they live today when the first Spaniards came wandering out of Mexico in 1539. First came the Moor, Estevan, scout for Fray Marcos de Niza. When Estevan swaggered into Zuni demanding honor and women, the Zunis executed him. Fray Marcos peered at Zuni from a distance before returning south.

De Niza boasted of riches he had found, and Coronado followed his trail northward the next year with a military expedition. Once more, the Pueblos resisted — first at Zuni, later, at Pecos and elsewhere. Ed Ladd points out one little-noted fact: "I sincerely believe that if Coronado had arrived at Zuni four days later or earlier, he would have been welcomed. He arrived during the summer solstice, and the night before he arrived he was attacked. These had to be Bow Priests protecting pilgrims headed for the sacred lake."

Wherever they waged war, the captain-general's three hundred soldiers beat the Indian warriors; they executed hundreds of Pueblo people. Spain's reputation with the People had not begun well.

By the time don Juan de Oñate received the royal contract to settle New Mexico in 1598, another four Spanish expeditions had reached Pueblo country. Only one Spanish leader (Espejo) had come in peace — and he found the People friendly. The others had demonstrated to the Pueblos their superior arms. The People would need wilier methods of dealing with the invaders.

Oñate came with a full-blown state loaded on his carts and horses: farmers, soldiers, missionaries, servants. He met with a group of Pueblo leaders (the first time the Pueblos deemed necessary an All Indian Pueblo Council, an organization that Jemez historian Joe Sando calls "a kind of Pueblo United Nations" and which has existed sporadically ever since) and extracted what the Spaniard understood to be a pledge to submit to his authority. He established his first capital across the river from San Juan Pueblo (newly named by the Spanish), at a site he called San Gabriel.

By the end of 1598, all the pueblos were conquered, but Acoma did not submit for long. That same year, the Acomas killed an aide of Oñate's, along with a dozen of his men. The next year the Spanish retaliated, virtually destroying the pueblo, killing hundreds of people, and subsequently sentencing five hundred Acoma prisoners to have one foot chopped off (adult males only) and to serve twenty years "of personal servitude." Children were taken away to monasteries and convents. Oñate, relieved of his governorship, eventually was permanently banished from New Mexico for this unwarranted slaughter.

Governor followed governor, friar replaced friar. Santa Fe replaced San Gabriel as capital of New Mexico in 1610. Churches were built at all the pueblos — though not until after 1629 at Zuni and Hopi. Both these pueblos lay on the frontier, and after 1621 they received exemptions from paying tribute.

In 1620, a royal decree created civil offices for each pueblo, including a governor, *fiscales* to oversee the church, and *mayordomos* to supervise the ditches; silver-headed canes symbolized each governor's authority. By 1630, the missionaries claimed sixty thousand converts. But conflicts between the Spanish military, governors, land-grant owners, and religious authorities grew more and more bitter. Competition for profits and power centered on the produce and forced labor of the Pueblos, who were caught in the middle, taxed by all comers in a feudal economy and growing ever more resentful.

The Roman Catholic Church believed it had converted all the Pueblos. The friars enforced their conversions with such tactics as whipping any men caught worshiping in the old ways until they were "bathed in blood," then tarring their wounds with hot turpentine. Even so, the priests realized by mid-century that native religion continued as strong as ever within the secrecy of the kivas.

In the 1660s, the friars raided kivas and destroyed hundreds of katsina masks, as well as many native altarpieces. The governor hung three and publicly whipped forty-three Pueblo leaders accused of sorcery in 1675. Apache and Comanche raiders, the slave trade, overgrazing by Spanish cattle leading to erosion, drought, and famine — all complicated the crisis. For the Pueblo people, the message became ever clearer: Spanish rule was intolerable — and not inevitable.

Pueblo caciques (religious leaders) and their war captains began conferring about the possibility of revolt against the Spanish sometime in the 1670s. Tradition names a single leader, Popé of San Juan, who was among those whipped in 1675. (Popé's

Cochiti artist Tonita Peña and her husband, Epitacio Arquero, 1940. As governor of Cochiti, Arquero cared for the two canes given to each Pueblo governor, the first by the king of Spain in the 1600s and the second by President Abraham Lincoln when he reaffirmed Pueblo land grants. Photo by Sekaer. (Courtesy National Archives, photo no. 75-N-PU-532)

reputation among the Pueblos today as a sorcerer may come from his thirst for power after the rebellion, or simply from the distaste and jealousy Pueblo people feel when one of their number makes himself too conspicuous.) Jemez historian Joe Sando takes the more reasonable view that each pueblo offered leaders, and he names a dozen in addition to Popé, conspicuous among whom were Luis Tupatu of Picuris, Alonzo Catiti from Santo Domingo, and Antonio Malacate of the Cochiti village of Cieneguilla. These men were the heroes of the most successful uprising of Southwestern Indians in their history of conflict with Europeans. Their names and their deeds should not be forgotten.

On 10 August 1680, the Pueblos acted. Beginning at Tesuque, and from Taos to Hopi, the People gave the priests a choice (according to Sando): leave or die. Twenty-one of 33 missionaries were killed, and 375 of the 2,350 colonists died in battle. The Pueblos laid siege to Santa Fe, took the Palace of the Governors, and allowed the rest of the Spaniards and loyal mixed-bloods to retreat south to El Paso — an act of mercy unmatched in centuries of retaliation by the Spanish.

Only one modern pueblo — Isleta — did not join the revolt. Some twenty-nine other pueblos south of Albuquerque (speaking still other Pueblo languages, Piro and Tompiro), remained obedient to the Spanish Crown. The Piro and the Tiwa-speaking Isletans retreated south with the governor; some eventually returned to Isleta, while descendants of others remain today in El Paso in what is now called Tigua Pueblo.

Such unity of action was unique to this time in Pueblo history. Only when necessary would the fiercely independent villages join forces. Once the Spanish were evicted, each community returned to its own concerns.

When the Spaniards gathered their forces under Diego de Vargas for the reconquest in 1692, they met no united defense of New Mexico. After initially accepting the return of the oppressors, some pueblos rose up once again; others fought alongside the Spaniards.

Enormous changes took place in the next decades. Groups of refugees joined forces to live in new villages, dispersed, migrated to Hopi, returned, were caught up in disputes between pro- and anti-Spanish leaders, and created new communities. The Zunis all lived atop Corn Mountain (Dowa Yallane) for years. Rebel Tewas fought from the top of Black Mesa between Santa Clara and San Ildefonso during 1694; the Keresans made Enchanted Mesa, near Acoma, into a fortress from that same year until 1698. Whole areas were abandoned and entire language groups absorbed. The Tewa-speaking village of Hano, on First Mesa at Hopi, and the village of Laguna both date from this time.

Historians tend to write of Pueblos as rocks, geographically and metaphorically: steadfast amidst the swirl of nomads and invaders, stubborn and unchanging in every way. This, of course, is true only in part. Even the migrations of the clans spiraling in to each home village only hint at how dynamic the People could be. Besides Hopi and Zuni (whose villages were by no means changeless), by the 1700s only Taos, Picuris, Isleta, and Acoma had not moved their locations since the Spaniards arrived.

Pueblo people were great travelers, and they remain so to this day. To spend so much time so far from home, they needed to be multilingual: the kiva conversations where initiated religious leaders planned the Pueblo Revolt took place in at least six languages. Early on, Pueblo people became fluent in Castilian. All along, they have combined tenacity and elasticity in astounding ways.

Throughout the 1700s, the pueblos declined in population and prosperity and suffered smallpox epidemics and accelerating raids from the mounted Apache, Ute, and Comanche. The People maintained their religion underground, away from the disapproving eyes of the Spaniards. They worked out an alliance with the settlers, as well, to fight with the Spaniards against the nomadic tribes. Joseph Naranjo, of Santa Clara, became the best-known leader of the pueblo auxiliaries, his loyalty to the Spaniards extending so far that he fought against his brother Lucas when the latter led rebel forces against the returned Spaniards in 1696.

These were the years during which Pueblo and Hispanic created a unique New Mexican blend through intermarriage and interchange. Pueblo people incorporated new crops in their diet: wheat, melons, apples, peaches, pears, tomatoes, and chile (the latter two imports from Mexico). A complicated array of terms indicated one's genetic heritage and social position: *casta, genízaro, mestizo, coyote, mulatto, zambo, indio.* Culturally, almost any of these mixed-bloods could choose to live as Indians. In turn, hispanicized Pueblo people moved into the settlers' villages.

The Hopi, and to a lesser extent, the Zuni, retained the luxury to pick and choose among these influences. Zuni's mission church was abandoned for a century after 1821. The Hopi, in anthropologist Edward Spicer's words, "are probably the most famous 'apostates' in the history of Spanish Christianity." They lived too far from Santa Fe for the Crown to dictate its will.

After the 1680 rebellion, the Hopi moved all their villages to the tops of the mesas, making them virtually impregnable. Especially after Apache raids closed the frontier, the Hopi were free to live as Hopi. The Spaniards focused their attention mostly on trying to persuade Rio Grande refugees at Hopi to return to New Mexico. Their success was mixed, and Tewa Village (Hano) stands today on First Mesa.

The authority of the Hopi traditionalists peaked in 1700. Antimissionary feelings centered in the Third Mesa village of Oraibi, the largest Hopi village, whose powerful kikmongwi at the time was a man called Espeleta by the Spaniards. Only one Hopi village, Awatovi, retained an active mission church.

In a surprise night attack, forces from Oraibi and Shongopavi combined with the antimissionary faction from Awatovi. Awatovi men who resisted were killed, women and children were dispersed into the other Hopi villages, and Awatovi was destroyed. In one act, the pro-Christian "wicked" forces were erased from Hopi (though some modern Hopi believe that the destroyers were "a new people" living at the edge of Hopi, later rejected because of their action against Awatovi). No missions came again to Hopiland until the 1890s.

The Hopi Way, the Tewa Way — the Pueblo Way — has remained strong right up to today. The Pueblo Revolt remains vivid to Pueblo people. In 1980, they celebrated its tricentennial with pride. Runners made the trip from Taos to Hopi. Hopi schoolchildren drew the story — complete with gods, katsinas, and warriors coming to the Hopi mesas to kill "black-robed Spanish monster priests" and throw their bodies over the cliffs.

Citizens without Rights

Though "reconquered" in 1692, in some ways the Pueblos succeeded in their revolt. Though the People continued to decrease in population and suffer Hispanic encroachment and missionary efforts, the Spanish, followed by the Mexicans, pushed the Pueblos no further toward abandoning their Indian identity. Tribute ceased permanently. Hopi and Zuni had virtually no contact with the Mexican government and saw comparatively little interaction with Hispanics or Anglos until the 1880s.

In 1821, Pueblos became citizens of Mexico. In Joe Sando's words, during its administration of the People's lands Mexico succeeded only in "confusing Indian land title, ignoring the illegal taking of Pueblo land, and responding passively when Indian boundaries were violated."

New Mexico citizens, both Indian and Hispanic, rebelled in 1837 when Mexico installed a non-New Mexican governor who was rumored to be considering heavy taxation. After a successful revolt, Jose Gonzales from Taos Pueblo ruled as governor of New Mexico for a remarkable few months before the Republic recaptured Santa Fe and executed this first Indian governor of all the peoples of the state.

The endless battle against Apache and Navajo raiders brought the most cooperation between sedentary Pueblos and Hispanics. Nonetheless, the raiders forced abandonment of a number of pueblos, most notably Pecos, the largest Rio Grande pueblo in Oñate's day. Smallpox, factions intensified by the Spaniards so near at hand, decreases in farming, and pressures on Pecos land from Hispanic settlers all combined with the effects of the raiders; Pecos lost nearly 75 percent of its population in three generations. The last twenty-one Pecos Indians moved to Jemez Pueblo in 1838.

Jemez and Pecos pueblos formally consolidated in 1936, and most modern Jemez people trace their bloodlines to both villages. They maintain a spiritual connection to the land surrounding Pecos, returning to pray in shrines near the abandoned village, now Pecos National Historic Park.

When the United States annexed the Southwest in the Mexican War, it found an attenuated array of stubborn Pueblo villages scattered in the same crescent from Taos to Hopi that Coronado himself had found; in 1832, only five of the villages had resident priests.

The American administration spent its first forty years fighting to defeat the "wild" Navajo and Apache and generally ignoring the Pueblos. An exception occurred early on, when a group of Taos people, both Indian and Hispanic, killed the American governor, Charles Bent, in 1847, in a supposed gesture of support for the Mexicans. Only a few Pueblo people were involved, but in retaliation the Americans slaughtered more than 150 Taos Indians and burned their church. Mid-century saw the lowest Pueblo population ever — about nine thousand total.

Pueblo warriors had few calls to battle after this. Anglo colonists began to flood the Southwest as peace reigned. By the 1880s, railroads passed near virtually all the pueblos — even within seventy-five miles of isolated Hopi. One current within the Anglo flood that had particular importance to the Pueblos was the tide of anthropologists flowing west to study the villages. Zuni saw four generations of these scientists, inspired by the 1879–83 residency at Zuni of Frank Hamilton Cushing.

Cushing became a Bow Priest, learned the language, and essentially lived as a Zuni, while instituting innovations like the first ground-level door in the pueblo. He wished the best for the Zuni people, but as an Anglo scholar he wrote voluminously about his experiences, openly discussing the most sacred of Zuni ceremonies. He took a delegation of Zunis to the East Coast in 1882, including Lai-iu-ah-tsai-lu (who also used the name Pedro Pino) and his son, Ba:lawahdiwa (Patricio Pino) — between them governors of Zuni from 1830 to 1885. These two leaders, who emphasized "progressive" and peaceful relations with whites, influenced Zuni life well into this century.

The Zunis brought home bottles of water from the Atlantic Ocean to use in rain ceremonies, to keep their land fertile. They would need all its power.

As their numbers increased, Anglos took Hispanic land, and the Hispanic farmers, in turn, took Pueblo land. Anglo cattle and sheep herds devastated the western range not already devoured by Hispanic herds. Pueblo watersheds were no exception.

The United States ratified no treaties with the Pueblos. In 1858, they instead recognized the Spanish land grants which "gave" the Pueblos their lands. This put the

Anthropologist Frank Hamilton Cushing (seated on floor) took a delegation of Zunis to the East Coast in 1882. Photographed in Boston, the group included Lai-iu-ah-tsai-lu (Pedro Pino, seated at left) and his son, Ba:lawahdiwa (Patricio Pino, center) — governors of Zuni Pueblo from 1830 to 1885. Photo by James W. Black. (Courtesy Museum of New Mexico, neg. no. 9146)

Pueblos in a unique and difficult situation — outside the array of rights decreed for Indian people by ratified treaties and acts of Congress. A long struggle for land rights had begun.

Anglos saw the Pueblos as so different from the "wild, wandering savages" that made up the nomadic tribes that they legally defined the villagers as "citizens" rather than "Indians." This well-meaning oversimplification deprived the Pueblo people of their trust relationship with the government; though the BIA gave them agencies and agents, Pueblo lands came under heavy pressure from squatters and entrepreneurs.

After a parade of lawsuits in the late 1800s, which the Pueblos lost, in 1913 the federal government for the first time acknowledged its jurisdiction over the Pueblo Indians. To achieve their rights, the Pueblos ironically had to convince the courts that they were just as "primitive . . . crude . . . uninformed, and inferior" as other Indians!

New Mexicans who "owned" land within Pueblo grants were upset. Their worries led to the infamous bill promulgated by Senator Holm Bursum of New Mexico, a thinly veiled attempt to make legal the theft of the most choice Pueblo land — and the water to irrigate it. The All Indian Pueblo Council began to meet once again.

Strong leaders reorganized the council in 1922: Sotero Ortiz, from San Juan. Pablo

Abeita from Isleta. Alcario Montoya from Cochiti. Martin Vigil from Tesuque. Their statements in print and in person to audiences from New York City to San Francisco helped to defeat the Bursum Bill. They were ready for the boldest of moves. When Stanley Paytiamo, former governor of Acoma, told me the story of these men, he clutched a handful of pens in his fist and thrust them at me: "In 1922, the governors took their canes back to Washington and threatened to break them, as the treaties were threatened to be broken."

The appeal against the Bursum Bill, signed by all nineteen New Mexico pueblos, ended with these words: "This bill will destroy our common life and will rob us of everything which we hold dear, our lands, our customs, our traditions. Are the American people willing to see this happen?"

Senator Bursum was too late. The tide had turned in the twenties, and the era of John Collier was dawning. Instead of the Bursum Bill, Congress passed the Pueblo Lands Act, which created a board that over the next fifteen years confirmed title to all Pueblo grants. With Congressional funding, all but four pueblos increased their land holdings and grazing permit areas, by 1944 adding 50 percent to their 1933 holdings. In a series of court decisions and congressional acts, the United States acknowledged its trust responsibilities and the Pueblos once again became "Indians."

Throughout these years, multilingual Pablo Abeita, astute and articulate, interpreted each side to the other. St. Michael's College in Santa Fe awarded Abeita two honorary degrees, including a doctorate. The Isleta leader claimed to have met every president from Grover Cleveland to FDR. He spoke at length with Teddy Roosevelt in Washington, D.C., and Roosevelt promised the Pueblo man a visit when he came to Albuquerque. The two had to conspire to steal away to Isleta for lunch. Abeita disguised Roosevelt in a blanket and walked him through a protective shield of secret service agents at the Alvarado Hotel. When Abeita returned Roosevelt to the hotel in his wagon, the secret service men were in a frenzy at the loss of their president — and Abeita and Roosevelt were pleased with their getaway.

The Dynamic Village

Pueblo people live closely together. Community life has its pleasures — dances, jokes, and shared social interactions with many different groups. Strong and endlessly interwoven ties bind together families and neighbors in a pueblo like Zuni, with fifteen clans, six kiva groups, various priesthoods and medicine societies, political officers, school boards, and cattle, farm, and irrigation associations. The control necessary to keep such a community healthy often makes individuals resentful.

As in all small communities, Pueblo people gossip about their neighbors and complain about their leaders — sometimes even accusing them of witchcraft. Disputes occasionally reach the point where every member of a village must choose sides. Such "factionalism" is just as central to the Pueblo character as is the stereotypical dutiful and stoic behavior of each cog-in-the-wheel member of the communal society.

The pueblos are far from static. Only some of the smallest pueblos and rigorously conservative larger villages such as Santo Domingo have avoided major dislocations and rifts. As one Cochiti elder summed things up for anthropologist Charles Lange in the 1950s: "Anyone who thinks that everything in an Indian Pueblo is all calm and cooperation just simply doesn't know anything about Pueblo politics."

Lagunas, for example, live now in Old Laguna, New Laguna, Mesita, Encinal, Paraje, Paguate, Seama, and Casa Blanca — and a group of Laguna people migrated to Isleta in 1880, revolutionizing that pueblo's religion and pottery. These people left after a major break precipitated by several white Protestants marrying into Laguna — the two Marmon brothers even served as governors, after writing the first constitution to be adopted by a pueblo.

Leslie Marmon Silko, the eloquent Laguna writer, says of these men in *Storyteller*:

> A good deal of controversy surrounded
> and still surrounds my great-grandfather and his brother
> who both married Laguna women.
> Ethnologists blame the Marmon brothers
> for all kinds of factions and trouble at Laguna
> and I am sure much of it is true —
> their arrival was bound to complicate
> the already complex politics at Laguna.

Silko knew her great-grandfather only from family stories and photos. Her own understanding of his role in her people's history comes from what she believes she can see in his eyes, something that explains much of Pueblo politics:

> For him at Laguna
> that was the one thing he had to remember:
> > No matter what is said to you by anyone
> > you must take care of those most dear to you.

Santa Ana virtually abandoned Tamaya, its old pueblo, beginning in the 1700s. The Santa Anans spent more and more time living near their more productive fields at Ranchitos, which they purchased from Spanish colonists on the east side of the Rio Grande just north of Bernalillo. Today, Tamaya is open to non-Pueblo visitors only on major feast days. The Santa Anans live in their farming community, away from any historical markers announcing their presence, maintaining their kivas and ceremonies in Tamaya, keeping alive the old ways with less outside interference than many other pueblos.

In 1942, anthropologist Leslie White said of Santa Ana: "The old Pueblo is by way of becoming a sort of shrine, a place for sacred ceremonies, of sentiment, of good times and feasting, isolated and shut off from the world, while Ranchitos is a very prosaic, workaday place very much in the modern world."

San Ildefonso went through a catharsis in the twenties, its people building an entirely new south plaza, isolating the northside with its landmark old cottonwood from the southside with its round kiva. North- and south-side village factions took over from the traditional Summer and Winter moieties because the Winter People had almost died out in the influenza epidemics of the previous decade. The dominant north plaza held the governor's office for many years. Though civil authority was eventually reconciled and the houses dividing the two plazas removed, even today the schism remains as an undercurrent in tribal politics.

Modern Hopis see the split between "Friendlies" and "Hostiles" as such a pivotal event in tribal history that they refer to it as "the Revolution." Early in this century, the major village of Oraibi fragmented into Old Oraibi, Hotevilla, Bacavi, Kykotsmovi (New Oraibi), and Moenkopi (which divided again in the thirties). Today, Old Oraibi — inhabited at least since 1150 and for centuries the "capital" of Hopiland — is a village of little more than one hundred people, with minimal vitality and ceremonial activity. (Anthropologist Peter Whiteley has recently investigated the split from the perspective of the village of Bacavi, and his work influences my story here.)

The Hopi split began as Hopi isolation ended. Jacob Hamblin and his Mormon missionaries made annual trips from Utah between 1858 and 1873 and founded Tuba City, near the westernmost Oraibi farming colony of Moenkopi, in 1875–76. The Anglo residents gave Moenkopi its first insurance against Navajo raiding, and the Hopi colony became a permanent village. The Mormons named their own "city" after Teuvi, one of their four or five Hopi converts, but in 1903 the federal government bought out the white farmers. Though Anglo visitors came and went, until the late 1800s Hopis lived secure in the belief that their katsinas and their commitment to the Hopi Way were successfully protecting them from outsiders.

A school opened at Keams Canyon, thirty miles east of Oraibi, in 1887 — the same year that the Dawes allotment act passed. As did so many tribes, Hopis saw their children captured and forced into wagons and carried off to boarding school, a practice continued at Hopi as late as 1911. In 1890, troops came into Oraibi to demand stu-

dents. The next spring, surveyors plotted the Hopi farms into allotments, intending
to move the villagers into houses on individual farms.

The Oraibi "Hostile" leaders pulled up the survey stakes and confronted the
troops in an armed phalanx complete with major katsinas, including the Warrior
Twins and Maasau-u, the powerful deity associated, in part, with fire and death. Fighting
was avoided, but soon afterward nine Hostile leaders were imprisoned.

In the 1880s, with a mandate from Washington, Anglo missionaries and BIA officials
divvied up the reservations among religious dominations. Even the Catholic
Rio Grande pueblos saw Protestant evangelists, whose work was often a difficult-to-
reconcile combination of good deeds toward individuals, narrow-minded persecution of groups, and denigration of traditional wisdom. Hopi happened to go to the
Mennonites, and the Reverend H. R. Voth came to Oraibi in 1893.

Voth became a major nuisance. He set out to learn as much as possible about Hopi
religion — but only in order to destroy it, to show the Hopi that their beliefs were
little more than "stacks of straw and chaff." Voth documented Hopi kiva rituals more
completely than anyone. Notwithstanding his opposition to other kinds of Anglo
interference, modern Hopis hate him. Not long after Voth's time, the Hopi prohibited all photography of ceremonies. Even today, Victor Masayesva, Jr., says of himself
and other Hopi photographers: "Refraining from photographing certain subjects has
become a kind of worship."

For ten critical years, the Oraibi situation deteriorated. Allotment — a ridiculous notion for Hopi farmers — was opposed by everyone from the Friendlies to Reverend
Voth to explorer/ethnologist John Wesley Powell. The program was abandoned in
1894 (though revived briefly some fifteen years later, when Moenkopi was allotted).
The U.S. Army imprisoned nineteen Hostile leaders on Alcatraz in 1894–95. (At the
same time, ironically, the Santa Fe Railroad was publishing elaborate booklets pro-
moting Hopi as a tourist attraction.) Ceremonial societies became exclusively Friendly
or Hostile, sometimes performing two rival versions of the same ceremony and following two kikmongwis. In 1899, a particularly zealous agent–school superintendent
came to Keams Canyon; in the next several years he went to extreme lengths to round
up Hopi children for school, forcibly cut the hair of all Hopi men (whose long hair
marks initiation into manhood and symbolizes rain), and encouraged brutal physical
discipline in the schools. Hopi children who had never seen a clock were punished
for missing the opening bell of school.

The experience Don Talayesva described in *Sun Chief* was typical: "When my sister started, the teacher cut her hair, burned all her clothes, and gave her a new outfit

and a new name, Nellie. She did not like school, stopped going after a few weeks, and tried to keep out of sight of the Whites who might force her to return. About a year later she . . . was captured by the school principal who . . . compelled her to return . . . The teachers had then forgotten her old name, Nellie, and called her Gladys."

Drought came to Hopi in 1902, and the springs failed in 1906, suggesting to the Hopis that all was not in harmony between them and the Cloud People. Navajos lay in wait to take advantage of Hopi weakness and commandeer crops and stock. Oraibi's growth was putting pressure on available farmland.

Hostiles and Friendlies agreed on a scenario: they would draw a line, face off, and whoever pushed their rivals over the line would remain in Oraibi. On 7 September 1906, the Friendlies, led by Tewaquaptewa, forced the Hostiles from Oraibi; the latter left to found Hotevilla that very day.

Over the years, older Hopis have gradually opened up to talking about the secret deliberations behind these events. It appears that a plot underlay the historic story: the leaders of Oraibi, both Friendly and Hostile, acted together to carry out a prophesied destruction of the village. In Albert Yava's words, recorded in Big Falling Snow, "Tewaquaptewa proclaimed the end of Oraibi's ceremonial life," and then set about ensuring that his prophecy would come true.

Federal intervention continued to complicate relations between the two groups. The Hostiles in on the plot (one Hotevilla man calls them the "intellectuals") founded Bacavi in 1909 and have phased out many ceremonies in the decades since the split. The people at Hotevilla, mostly ignorant of the plot, believed in their stand as Hostiles and tried to revive a full traditional ceremonial calendar. But over the years they too have seen ceremonies die as older leaders refused to pass on ritual knowledge. The last Snake Dance at Hotevilla, for instance, took place in 1980. Oraibis who wished to adopt more "American" or Christian ways moved to Moenkopi or Kykotsmovi. Since the thirties, Oraibi itself has stabilized at about 120 people.

The legacy of these antagonisms remains today throughout Hopiland. The leadership and politics of these villages are complex, and serve as a metaphor, to some extent, for other pueblos.

At First Mesa, the Tewa of Hano have dramatically influenced community values. Initially welcomed as warriors, the refugees from the Rio Grande long felt ostracized by the Hopi. Hopi and Tewa did not often intermarry until the nineteenth century. The Tewa have maintained their language and separate culture all along, while learning to speak Hopi and to practice many Hopi ways.

Already bicultural, Hopi-Tewa took to the new economic opportunities promoted by whites (livestock, wage work, pottery, schools) with more ease than the majority of Hopi. Three pivotal "Hopis" who began to open up Hopiland to Anglos in the late 1800s were actually Tewas from Hano: Nampeyo, who began making art pottery for sale; Tom Polacca, who acted as interpreter for all Hopi; and Tom Pavatea, who opened the first Indian-owned and operated trading post in the nation. Today, First Mesa has become more and more integrated, with the Tewa taking the lead.

Moenkopi has the most complicated politics at Hopi, and Upper Moenkopi, according to one anthropologist, may be the "most Americanized village of all." Hopis truly live as a minority in this area: though thoroughly Hopi culturally, even their farming and grazing lands are administered by the Navajo Tribe. Wil Numkena, raised at Upper Moenkopi, says: "Other than tribal distinctions, Tuba City as a community has engulfed Moenkopi. Lower Moenkopi claims they are clinging to traditional Hopi life. But there's really no distinction between Upper and Lower. We're all related; both go to school, drive automobiles, buy their clothing at the stores in Flagstaff."

Shongopavi, Hotevilla, Old Oraibi, and Lower Moenkopi generally reject the authority of the tribal council. Bacavi, Kykotsmovi, and Upper Moenkopi, on the other hand (along with consistently "progressive" First Mesa villages and some elements from Second Mesa), usually support the council. Hotevilla has resisted powerlines and water and sewer lines. But many "Traditionalists" drive pickups and use mechanized farm equipment, and many Hotevilla people use propane for lights and cooking and run television sets off car batteries. The Hopis say they don't oppose the conveniences, they just don't want to hire a white-run corporation to administer their utilities. Self-contained solar energy systems for individual households may be a workable alternative.

Only Shongopavi — the Second Mesa community that was the first Hopi village founded by the Bear Clan, the first clan to arrive in Hopi country — has a full and flourishing ceremonial life, far more active than that of the Traditionalist stronghold of Hotevilla. Yet Shongopavi has allowed powerlines into much of the village.

One group of Traditionalists receives extensive press coverage and opposes the council with enough vehemence to make it a true opposition party. The group owes its authority to a 1948 meeting at which Hopi spiritual leaders (led by Dan Katchongva of Hotevilla) divulged prophecies long held secret. The leaders appointed official spokesmen to the outside world to communicate these prophecies (most notably, Thomas Banyacya) and pledged to revitalize Hopi culture through increased initiations, thus assuring perpetuation of ceremonies. The Traditionalists laid out their beliefs in an eloquent letter to President Harry Truman in 1949. In this oration, they stated their opposition to the land claims process with an argument that epitomized the everyday Hopi talent for interpreting myth, creating prophecy, and translating both into political ideology.

From these activities of the "Hopi Traditional Chiefs," in part, grew the spiritual

Hopi tribal headquarters, Kykotsmovi, Arizona, 1984. Though just two of thirteen villages were represented on the tribal council in 1992, the council remains, in theory, the main arena for problem solving among the Hopi villages.

renewal of young Indian people that flowered in the sixties. Hopis achieved recognition as conscientious objectors during the Vietnam War. More than seventy young Hopi men served their alternate service as C.O.s after 1966, with deferments granted upon documentation of their initiation into katsina or Powamuy societies. Many young Hopis take the pronouncements of the traditional leaders seriously. Wilfrid Duwenyie says, flatly: "Prophecies are keeping the young people here."

These orators do not receive the same adulation inside Hopi as they do in the non-Indian world — largely because of suspicion at such outside attention and the well-meaning but misguided New Age converts who make pilgrimages to Hopiland with unrealistic expectations. As Hopi anthropologist Hartman Lomawaima says: "In summer, we get inundated by people coming to seek the real religion."

Everyone — supporters, antagonists, and the majority of nonpolitical Hopis — criticizes the tribal council, voted into existence by a minority of Americanized Hopi in 1935 but with no seated members until 1955 (when it was hastily made workable just in time to submit a land claim). Only two of the thirteen villages were represented on the council in the spring of 1992. In several other villages, organizations have sprung up to oppose the council, and Shongopavi has gone so far as to sue the council in tribal court over development projects. (Shongopavi, along with First Mesa villages, also closed katsina dances to non-Indians in 1992, to protest the film version of Tony Hillerman's story *The Dark Wind*, which they felt demeaned Hopi religion.) Nonetheless, the council remains, in theory, the main arena for problem solving among the Hopi villages — and government now provides the Hopis with three-fourths of their jobs. In 1991, tribal chairman Vernon Masayesva began a dialogue with traditional village leaders to work out a statement clarifying the roles and responsibilities of village and tribe.

The Hopi Way allows for conspicuous heterogeneity. Anthropologist Edward Spicer offers a fascinating explanation: "It was possible with much greater ease for a Hopi to remove himself from the restraint of a given village atmosphere merely by moving a few hundred yards to an off-mesa village, and yet still feel strongly Hopi, since he still lived on the Hopi land and in the Hopi milieu. The dissident Eastern Pueblo, on the other hand, had to move into an Anglo-American community and thus move more definitely in the direction of renouncing his Indian heritage." Michael Kabotie suggests another way of dealing with being "a loner": "Flexible strength is better than inflexible. Let the storm flow over you, and then pop back up."

Percy Lomaquahu spoke to me about the confusing nature of even the most classic Hopi personality, the "true traditionists": "Who's really the traditionist? No one. Nobody knows it anymore, because our customs and culture have changed. I might say, 'I'm the true traditionist.' But I wouldn't be telling everything right because you can see how I'm dressed now." Like many rural Pueblo men, Lomaquahu wore Sears-style work clothing. "Those that were before us — three, four generations ago — they carry the true culture, the true religious principles.

"Nevertheless, we keep the principles of our tradition in our hearts."

Outsiders never quite seem to grasp the intensity of commitment to their lifeway that Pueblo people feel. Perhaps the most astonishing result of that feeling lives on at Tigua Pueblo, among the nearly forgotten people of Ysleta del Sur in Texas.

Tigua: The Forgotten Pueblo

"Just because we live in the city doesn't mean we aren't Indians." Miguel Pedraza, governor of Tigua Pueblo in 1970, was talking to writer Stan Steiner. "Just because we talk English, or the Spanish, and talk not much of our own language, Tiwa, doesn't mean we don't have Indian blood in our veins.

"We have Indian hearts. We will always be Tigua."

And who are the Tigua? A sherd of Pueblo history, surviving in a tiny corner of west Texas.

Sweeping changes blew through New Mexico in the late 1600s. Drought and famine hit the pueblos of the "Saline province"—the Tompiro-speaking villages near important salt deposits—pueblos whose ruins now stand preserved in Salinas National Monument. Already under pressure from Apache raids, the People abandoned their homes, moving to the Rio Grande south of Isleta to live with their kin in villages that spoke Piro.

When the Southwestern world turned upside down in the Pueblo Revolt, Spanish colonists of the Rio Abajo took refuge at Isleta before retreating south to El Paso. They took with them in 1680 more than three hundred Indians from Isleta and the Piro villages, either as loyalists, captives, or refugees who feared reprisal from the victorious pueblos they had not joined. (The Piro claimed that no one had informed them of the coming revolt!)

A year later, Spain sent a force northward to reconquer Santa Fe. Defeated, the Europeans returned to El Paso, this time with 385 Tiwa-speaking Isletans as prisoners. All of these displaced Pueblo people settled in new villages in El Paso, the Isleta people at Ysleta del Sur, the Piros at two other villages nearby (their inhabitants eventually absorbed by either Ysleta or the surrounding Mexican communities). The People brought with them from Isleta their patron Saint Anthony and built a mission church in his honor in 1682—today the oldest church in Texas.

After the reconquest of New Mexico, the People remained. After Spain gave way to Mexico and then to Texas and the United States, they remained. They had the bad luck, however, to live in Texas at crucial times for Indian policy making. First, during the Civil War, when President Lincoln acknowledged New Mexico pueblo land grants with a second set of silver-headed canes to augment the original canes given by the king of Spain, Ysleta Pueblo, Texas, stood within the Confederacy—and was ignored. During the 1870s, while President Grant's Peace Policy helped to set aside federal reservations elsewhere, the Texas legislature did its best to transfer Indian land "legally" to the non-Indian town of Ysleta, and largely succeeded.

The Tiguas disappeared from the historical record, going about their lives, known only to their neighbors in El Paso. Their men served as scouts for the Texas Rangers and the U.S. Army in campaigns against the Comanche and Apache. Their farms prospered. Their children attended Albuquerque Indian School in the early 1900s.

Piros and Tiguas left Ysleta to work in the fields of the newly formed Doña Ana colony at modern Las Cruces, New Mexico, in 1843. By 1854 some one hundred so-called

*Old Ysleta Mission, Tigua Pueblo, El Paso, 1988. On feast days, the Tigua beat the tribal drum —
brought from New Mexico 300 years ago — and march, singing, from the tribal meeting house, the
tusla, to the church.*

Tortugas lived outside Las Cruces, and they live there still — unrecognized by the federal government and considerably diluted in Indian blood.

The Tortugas community within the Las Cruces neighborhoods of San Juan and Guadalupe incorporated as La Corporación de Indígenas de Nuestra Señora de Guadalupe in 1914, deeding part of their forty acres for a church that year and more for an elementary school in 1916. The school closed in the 1970s, and the land was returned to the corporation in 1986. The Tortugas hope to remodel the structure into a community museum. Meanwhile, about half the members live on the corporation's forty acres.

Any Catholic can be a member of the corporation, so few full-blooded Indians remain. A cacique is chosen from the male lineage with the greatest Indian blood quantum, though rifts in the corporation have developed between non-Indian and Indian members. Vestiges of the Tiwa language surface when the People sing. Though they no longer know the literal meanings of the lyrics, they continue to mark their Indian heritage each year with a community rabbit hunt and a major celebration each December in honor of the Virgin of Guadalupe.

The Virgin's feast climaxes with the four-mile pilgrimage to the top of the nearby Tortugas Mountains. On the night of 11 December, the pilgrims light bonfires on their descent, outlining the mountain with trails of orange flame that seem to float in the sky above Las Cruces.

The Tigua at Ysleta, too, lost their everyday use of the native language, but they mix many Tiwa words and phrases into their Spanish and English. And they remember the songs. On the Feast of Saint Anthony (13 June) the People bring out the tribal drum, brought down from New Mexico three hundred years ago. They march from the tribal meeting house, the *tusla*, through the Old Pueblo — across highways and past bars and cafés and dance halls — to the church, and then to the newer housing area. The dancers stop and perform before the house of anyone bearing the saint's name.

George Candelaria, a young tribal council member, told me: "The mission is ours, but we only use it for feasts and going to church."

In the 1960s, the Tigua caught the attention of the public, and, in particular, of El Paso attorney Tom Diamond. At the time, the average Tigua had finished just three years of school. The average Tigua family made $400 a year. Virtually every Tigua home faced tax foreclosure. Diamond began to set up meetings between government officials and tribal leaders — the cacique, war captain, and governor. Before each discussion, the Tigua "talked" with the tribal drum, which told them "which way to go and what to say."

In 1967, the state of Texas recognized the Tiguas, and federal recognition came the following year. The BIA transferred administration of the Tiguas to the Texas Indian Commission. In 1988, the state commissioner was Tigua.

The creation of a tribal roll brought forth many people who had long been embarrassed by their Indian blood. Newly proud of their heritage, the more acculturated Tigua added their names to the core of perhaps two hundred traditionalists. With a one-eighth Tigua blood requirement, the rolls closed in 1984 with 1,124 certified tribal members.

George Candelaria says: "Little by little, the blood quantum is slipping away. It's hard on kids. Even if they aren't enrolled, we treat them as Tiguas. We make sure they don't forget their history, their culture, because they are the ones that will have to carry it on."

The tribe owns some sixty-seven acres, with more than eight hundred resident

members, many of them in a new 113-house HUD development. The tribally owned
Arts and Crafts Center in a historic hacienda grossed more than a million dollars in
1987. The center includes a gift shop, a restaurant (serving steaming Tigua chile and
award-winning fajitas), and a living history museum, where Tiguas perform social
dances in season. Tigua women paint wheel-thrown pottery with designs inspired by
prehistoric Hueco Tanks pottery from the mountains to the north. The tribe hopes to
have these Hueco lands — traditional hunting and herb-gathering grounds — returned
when their land claims case is resolved.

Meanwhile, the Tigua have renewed contacts with Isleta Pueblo. At feast times
they trade visits with the Tortugas (some half of whom are on the Tigua rolls). The
tribe hopes to become the newest member of the All Indian Pueblo Council, and in
the 1990s Tigua women have moved toward demanding their right to vote in tribal
elections.

The Tigua have the advantage of jobs close at hand and a thriving tribal business,
even if they lack a substantial land base. Water and land are their dreams, but even
those pueblos with such resources must fight long battles to preserve them. The Taos
people found this out with a vengeance.

Taos and the Return of Blue Lake

As you drive north from Santa Fe and Española, you round a last corner
and climb up onto the Taos plateau. Here, the Rio Grande gorge makes its astonishing cut through the level sagebrush plain. Beyond, the curves of Pueblo Peak carry
your eye up to the summit of the Sangre de Cristos. As Diane Reyna says, it's a shot of
"double-aweness."

High on the flanks of the range, in what the Taos people call "the Bowl," a small
lake lies cupped in spruce-fir forest. From here at Blue Lake flows El Rio de Pueblo de
Taos, the lifeline of the Taos people.

"The mountain symbolizes Taos," says Diane Reyna. "The way it looks, the way it
feels bigger than life. Life comes from there." Tony Martinez, also from Taos, told me
that "Blue Lake is the most sacred place in our world, the Taos world."

The Taos people have always known this, of course. Not everyone else has. When
the pueblo heard a rumor in 1904 that their mountain was to be set aside in a national
forest, they assumed that the act would protect their land. They petitioned the government for exclusive use of the lake.

Instead, in 1906, Theodore Roosevelt proclaimed 130,000 acres of these most
sacred Taos lands a public forest reserve. Despite repeated petitions for the return of
their land during the next decade, the Taos people saw their holy mountain opened

to grazing by non-Indian permittees during World War I. Anglo campers came to Blue Lake. The People were horrified.

Over the next fifty years, the conflict between the government and the pueblo ground on. Federal officials saw Blue Lake as a land rights issue. Taos Pueblo fought its crusade for religious rights, to protect the source of all life. Severino Martinez, long-time governor and a leader of the Blue Lake fight, said: "Religion is the most important thing in our life. That is the reason why this Blue Lake is so important to us."

Tolerance of tribal religion hit a low point in 1924, with the BIA Commissioner ranting about the "hideous and revolting" ceremonies conducted by Taos elders he dismissed as "half animal." Not until 1927 did the Forest Service recognize the pueblo's annual August pilgrimage to the lake with a three-day exclusive use permit.

In 1951, the Taos elders solemnly submitted their case to the Claims Commission. The commission did not rule until 1965, when it established tribal title to the lost 130,000 acres. The standard procedure at that point was of course to calculate a cash payment for the lost lands. Taos only wanted Blue Lake.

Throughout these many decades, the cacique, Juan de Jesus Romero, gave quiet, strong support to the council for their fight. He died in 1978 at 103, a hero to his people. In addition to Romero and Martinez, many other Taos men spoke strongly over the years, including John Reyna, Querino Romero, Frank Marcus, and Paul Bernal. They enlisted the aid of Anglo writer Oliver La Farge in the fifties and sixties; later, after La Farge's death, his secretary, Corrine Locker, took the Taos case to the nation.

Blue Lake became a national symbol of Indian rights, and when President Richard Nixon took office, he chose to support the pueblo in its fight against the Forest Service and entrenched New Mexico Senator Clinton Anderson. True, this did wonders for Nixon's image with minority groups — but for complex reasons, Nixon consistently pursued a humane Indian policy.

In 1970, Congress passed and Nixon signed a bill returning 48,000 acres of land surrounding Blue Lake to Taos Pueblo — the first tribal land ever restored for traditional religious reasons. Against huge odds, the Taos people had prevailed.

The harmony of the Blue Lake celebration could not last in a community continually on the brink of change. Like other conservative pueblos, Taos Pueblo has no constitution or elections. The cacique appoints a new governor each year, and opposing forces on the all-male council effectively prevent movement off dead center. The conservative status quo prevails.

The old pueblo now houses fewer than one hundred people. Most families have moved outside the village walls, some to old adobe farmhouses, others to HUD

Replastering homes with adobe, Taos Pueblo, 1985. The old pueblo now houses fewer than 100 people, who endure a daily onslaught of tourists. Most Taos families have moved outside the old village, some to adobe farmhouses, others to HUD crackerboxes.

crackerboxes. The people in the old village live with a daily onslaught of tourists drawn by this terraced icon of the Pueblo world, recognized formally by the United Nations as a World Heritage Site. (Most other modern Pueblos have removed their second and third stories — defensive architecture no longer necessary.)

Sharon Reyna told writer Nancy Wood: "There was never a day when some tourist wasn't there when I went in or out the door. One day I was taking a bath in the living room and this man walked in the door. He thought it was a curio shop . . . After that I thought, Who needs it? I moved away from the village."

Reyna went on, talking about how everyone will move on in time, sick of tourists, tired of hauling water. And then when the pueblo tumbles down, looking "like Mesa Verde," the People will return to visit. And "the tourists will still be there taking pictures of my great-grandkids looking at the house where I used to live."

Reyna may sound cynical, but Taos Pueblo, like all Indian communities, is a mixture of ingredients set for a long simmer. The old ways mellow, changing in texture but never disappearing. New ingredients spice the pot. Every individual yields a unique result.

One object serves as a metaphor for that unique, evolving amalgam of old and new. A 1960s-vintage Taos Buffalo Dance headdress noted by art historian Ralph T. Coe was made from a buffalo head in the traditional way — with an inverted Sears infant seat as the interior support, forming a perfect headrest.

Rina Swentzell, whose family moved from Santa Clara to Taos when she was in high school, felt that Taos in the fifties "was an older-feeling place, darker, too, with that feeling that the world has many more levels of existence than we generally recognize. At Taos they were recognized."

Tony Martinez (son of strong old Severino Martinez), with an M.B.A. from Baylor, years of experience running his own business in Dallas, and strong opinions about everything, works as operations manager for the Eight Northern Pueblos regional organization. He told Nancy Wood: "There's no center now, no core, nobody to set an example or be a role model." And yet, "there's only one way to preserve the Indian and that's tourism. Tourists want to see 'the noble savage' in his native habitat, so why not take their money and let their fantasies run wild?"

In my own talk with Martinez, he said: "I think there's an optimism in the People's day-to-day thinking. You have to be optimistic. There's a balance, a harmony that's very subjective. You can't see it. It's a state of mind. It's simple when you toil day in and day out and you know the value of things."

Can you feel that harmony when you live in a HUD tract house rather than an adobe room in the ancient pueblo? Certainly, but it must be harder. Drum-maker Red Shirt Reyna moved enthusiastically into a new frame house, but he told Wood, "it didn't breathe like the one I was used to." He returned to his adobe — one of those homes described by another Taos man as not "just a shelter" but "what the earth stands for, the center of our being."

As the People stream away from the pueblo, they do less to maintain it. Those who remain number too few to care for the high-maintenance adobe walls, and many fear the pueblo has passed beyond the point of affordable restoration. Conservatives protecting sacred ground and those who say they simply desire "modern" amenities battle over electric lines, which have yet to enter the main village.

Santana "Sam" Romero spoke to Nancy Wood about his duties as a kiva leader. His words sum up this mix of change and optimism: "We're even starting to speak English in the kivas now, so some of the boys will understand. I was against it. I said, 'Let them learn the language,' but some of the older ones said, 'It's the only way they'll learn.' It hurt me to see this happen, but what could I do? . . . These boys are like my own. Someday when I'm gone, one of them will take over. That's how we pass it on. I don't think our religion will ever die out."

Foot races, San Geronimo feast day, Taos Pueblo, 1893. Diane Reyna, Taos film-maker, says: "For Pueblo people, there's more to come home to — a good, strong, spiritual connection. And so I never miss San Geronimo Feast Day at home; it's my New Year's." Photo by George E. Stewart. (Courtesy Colorado Historical Society)

Diane Reyna agrees: "Being raised on the reservation, it seemed like the whole world was your playground. It really, really attaches to your heart. For Pueblo people, there's more to come home to — a good, strong, spiritual connection. And so I never miss Christmas Eve or San Geronimo at home; San Geronimo Feast Day [30 September] is my New Year's. I can see myself going back to Taos when I'm sixty; I'll be an elder then, and I'll have more tolerance. But I value my privacy too much to live there now."

People may leave the Pueblo during their middle years to "see what the world is like," in Tony Martinez's words. But, he adds: "They *always* come back. Taos is a sanctuary."

Keeping the Sanctuary Alive: Development versus Subsistence

"I work here in this office so that other San Juan people can choose to live in the Pueblo." Sam Cata spoke bluntly to me. A San Juan man in his forties, in 1988 he was Assistant Director of Indian Affairs for New Mexico. "There are a lot of advantages to a slower-paced life. It's important to understand the computer age, too. You need to have some of your people understand the latter so the rest of your people can live that slower life."

Cata went on: "The main issues for future success are land and water. Our main job is to educate Indian people about their rights. To be advocates, we need to understand tribal government, state government, and federal government. We have to understand where the pots of money come from. And yet, we need to encourage the young to understand and preserve the life that no one has proven anything better than!"

Peter Pino, tribal administrator for the small pueblo of Zia, tries to "go down the middle" between the exclusively traditional people and exclusively business-oriented people. He guesses that an individual from either group wears about fifteen hats. Pino, who makes a dual commitment, wears thirty hats. That burden can be exhausting. The Hopi teacher Polingaysi Qoyawayma described her own efforts to carry that burden as a "struggle to span the great and terrifying chasm between my Hopi world and the world of the white man."

Dave Warren, from Santa Clara, spoke to me of the location of the Rio Grande pueblos along a "strategic corridor" of development in the booming Sunbelt economy of New Mexico. The planning team for the Eight Northern Pueblos Council, Walter Dasheno and Leon Tafoya, both from Santa Clara, want to take advantage of that opportunity. Their efforts include offering technical assistance to farmers to make even a small operation viable; generating a computer data base to include all craftspeople, to help them with sales and invitations to shows such as the huge annual Eight Northern Pueblos Arts and Crafts Show; and developing water quality standards for each pueblo. Says Dasheno: "I'm very optimistic. We are trying to retain and create jobs, reestablish our self-sufficiency. The bottom line is education. The next generation will be more apt to accept that and still never sacrifice their traditional culture."

Pueblos must reassert old claims to land as Anglos begin to use it more heavily. Jemez Pueblo successfully fought a geothermal development in the Jemez Mountains in 1982. Sandia Pueblo began fighting for rights to the east flank of the Sandia Mountains above Albuquerque in 1983. Joseph Lujan, governor in 1988, repeated the so-often-dismissed tenets of Pueblo faith: "The mountain is our mother. We believe in that mountain. We pray to that mountain." To the Anglos, Lujan adds, the mountain "is just a plaything."

Long surrounded by Albuquerque, Sandia has had the advantage of wage work close at hand, but has been forced to be particularly secretive about religion. This small pueblo has maintained considerable pueblo-wide cooperation and a strong ceremonial life.

The Sandia people have used the mountain for their ceremonies all along, but now must perform those ceremonies at night to keep them private. Says Lujan: "There are so many hikers sometimes that we have to hide." Sandia people have promised to recognize all rights of private landowners within their claim; they ask only for title, to give them some measure of control over sacred territory, with the U.S. Forest Service continuing to manage the tract as wilderness. The Forest Service, however, has fought the pueblo to a standstill, and the case remains in the courts.

Crucial water lies at the root of other conflicts. Acoma and Laguna, for instance, have been arguing over the Rio San Jose's trickle ever since Laguna's founding. Some threats come on a grander scale. Frank Tenorio, longtime San Felipe spokesman, put it this way: "Water is the blood of the Pueblo people . . . If the blood of the people stops its life-giving flow, or becomes polluted, all else will die and many thousands of years of our communal existence will come to an end."

Tenorio continued: "With the ever-expanding and wasteful urbanization of Indian country, we Indian people of the Southwest find ourselves with the last good land and the last good water left. As the white man wastes his resources, he casts a covetous eye on what we have preserved for our own needs."

Litigation follows. Indeed, Indian law expert Charles Wilkinson believes that no more complex litigation exists in the federal or state courts than Indian water rights cases — with the possible exception of antitrust suits.

Frank Tenorio described the battle: "We have survived the Spanish, the Anglos, and the technological revolution. But now we face our greatest enemies. They do not go by the name of Coronado, or Cortez, or Custer, but by the name of the Army Corps of Engineers, San Juan–Chama Diversion Project, Salt River Project, and so forth."

In some ways, the Cochiti Dam project serves as a microcosm of this whole legal nightmare. A dam constructed in the thirties increased irrigation farming at the pueblo. In the 1960s, work began on a huge earthen dam to replace the old one; the new dam would create a major flood-control and recreational reservoir. In the process, archaeological sites were drowned, Cochiti potters lost their best source of clay, and seepage under the dam has made much of the "reclaimed" land useless to the few Cochiti farmers still active.

In 1975, the dam closed its head gates. Cochiti signed a controversial ninety-nine-year lease to turn the seventy-five hundred acres of Cochiti land surrounding the reservoir into a retirement and bedroom community with a potential population of forty-five thousand and a guarantee of ninety thousand acre feet of Cochiti's water rights. The population of Cochiti Pueblo itself hovers around a thousand people.

Since then, only 165 houses have been built in the lakeshore subdivision, the development has gone bankrupt, and the local water system has become over-committed. More than a million people each year use the lake's recreational facilities. As

Fred Bowannie, Cochiti governor in 1988, politely put it, this "desecration of our land has not led to economic prosperity." In 1986, Cochiti Pueblo bought out the original developer, so at least the People now possess some control over the future of the lakeshore.

The latest controversy has been over hydroelectric development and efforts to reclaim land lost to seepage. Regis Pecos, an intense young Cochiti man and Director of Indian Affairs for New Mexico, says: "Many people can't understand how we could forego all the money from this plant to preserve the sacred site that is the only feasible place for that plant. That place is the very heart of our spiritual being. I've gone to Congress to introduce legislation. When it finally passed, my uncle, when I told him, before he uttered a word he took off his glasses and tears were in his eyes. When you see grown men cry because they feel so much for something that is the essence of our lives, that is the ultimate statement. That is the ultimate explanation."

In working through these conflicts, successfully applying their age-old, religion-based, constitutionless government to decision making, the Cochitis also have created a comparatively good economy for themselves. Unemployment is low for a reservation—about 20 percent. Two-thirds of the tribe have graduated from high school—almost twice the numbers for San Carlos Apache, for example.

Western states continue to ceaselessly challenge the basic principles of Indian water rights. The crux of those rights lies in the *Winters* case of 1908, which stated that Indians retain reserved water rights to all practically irrigable land on reservations. Winters rights supersede the otherwise universal doctrine of prior appropriation (whoever diverts the water first owns its rights).

Subsequent court cases have both supported and whittled away at the Winters doctrine. The Department of Interior houses both the BIA and the Bureau of Reclamation, and the water rights interests of the two are frequently at odds—a major conflict of interest. In 1966, a court battle began in which all of these issues play a part.

New Mexico brought the suit (known as *New Mexico v. Aamodt*), claiming jurisdiction over the water rights of the Nambe-Pojoaque watershed, which includes four of the Tewa pueblos. Twenty-five years later, the case is still lost in the appeals process. But along the way, courts have decreed that the pueblos may not be entitled to Winters rights, limiting their rights to historical uses only, and that the state should control watershed rights—both devastating possibilities for pueblo economic futures.

The tribes have appealed; the All Indian Pueblo Council rallied to the cause in the mid-1970s, under the strong leadership of Delfin Lovato, a San Juan/Santo Domingo; the voices of eloquent pueblo leaders again echoed in the press.

Robert Lewis of Zuni: "The Indian finds himself in a life and death competition for a water supply rapidly becoming inadequate to meet all demands." Frank Tenorio of San Felipe: "We did not derive our rights from any sovereign, but these rights are our immemorial rights which our forefathers knew and handed down through the generations to us, to cherish and protect." Joe Sando of Jemez: "If . . . the most critical task facing the Pueblo people is the development of a sustained economy, it is dead certain that such economic development cannot be separated from Indian rights to the use of water . . . Without their water rights, the Pueblos are virtually uninhabitable."

Water, land, development, religion, survival. For the Pueblo people, these are inseparable. Tesuque Pueblo found this out in the 1970s. After much debate, the tribal council signed a ninety-nine-year lease with a land development corporation in 1970. The plan: to build "Las Colonias de Santa Fe" on more than five thousand acres of Tesuque land, including a golf course, resort hotels, and houses for fifteen thousand non-Indian residents. Tesuque signed over a portion of its water rights, as well.

A legal storm erupted that involved battles over jurisdiction with the state, county, and city of Santa Fe (just nine miles away), environmental impacts, and accusations of misconduct on all sides. Some said the developers had Mafia connections. Others saw the whole plan not as a well-intentioned effort of the council on behalf of their people but as yet another fleecing of "gullible" Indians.

In one public hearing, Tesuque women spoke against the development. Their words were passionate. One elderly woman said afterward to Stan Steiner: "It has come to this. Will our men follow the white's government? And ruin our land? Or will our men follow their women? And save our land?"

Tesuque canceled the lease and the development plan in 1976. In 1990, when I spoke with Tony Dorame, then Tesuque lieutenant governor, it was clear the pueblo had moved on. He described the Tesuques as "progressive traditionalists" and explained what he meant: "The best tribal governments operate well when they are based in their values and traditions — whether they use so-called modern management techniques or not. We do maintain our values and traditions, and yet, we were one of the first pueblos to have electricity, one of the first to have HUD housing. We're using management techniques that are progressive.

"For instance, we have a biological farming project. It sounds like traditional farming — chemical-free, using alfalfa as 'green manure' — but it is a mixture of the old and new, with a consulting specialist in agriculture."

Tesuque has long had a reputation for conservatism. Just over the hill from Santa Fe, the Tesuques needed to be fierce to maintain their independence. Dorame maintains that the pueblo and city have nothing to do with each other: "I don't even think about the place." But as he admits: "The key to Pueblo survival has been adaptation. We haven't been static."

Jose Lorenzo Pino, war captain, Tesuque Pueblo feast day, 1985. Pino and the other administrator-guards of the dance stand watch as the sounds of the ceremony wash over them: the beat of the drum, the cries of the hunter-dancers, the clatter and shush of deer-hoof anklets and gourd and tortoise-shell rattles, and the stamping of dozens of leather-padded feet on the earth of the plaza.

Dorame speaks with frustration of how slow the changes come. "We don't live in a local economy anymore. We need to get out of this narrow mind-set and think a little more globally. I keep thinking back to the way it used to be hundreds of years ago. Tesuque traded through all of North and South America. Now we only think of development within our reservation boundaries.

"Now tribal government is the entrepreneur. That's not the complete answer. Development here brings jurisdictional headaches, environmental problems, people within the tribe fighting over money.

"Individuals need a shot at entrepreneurship, too. Self-reliance paradoxically makes us stronger communities. There are so many hidden talents, dormant skills in the pueblo. Maybe what we're after is a Renaissance of sorts. I can see a blossoming everywhere. Not just in the arts. The fields are turning green here again, with corn and beans and chile."

We had our conversation the weekend before Tesuque Feast Day on 12 November. On dance day, Tony Dorame wore his moccasins and best turquoise. His hands

whitened with clay, he acted as a guard to the dancers, directing traffic, watching
for violators of rules prohibiting photography, standing alert beside seventy animal
dancers. The sounds of the drum, the cries of the hunter/dancers, the rattle of gourds
and deerhoof ankle rattles, and the stamping in unison of the dozens of leather-
padded feet on the earth of the plaza filled the space between the adobe walls of the
old village.

Later that week, Dorame was back at his management consulting firm, with
photos from his travels in the Air Force and of his year in Thailand on his office walls,
back teaching at the University of New Mexico in the graduate school of public administration. He says: "An Indian well grounded in his or her Indian world of values
has the necessary tools to do well in any situation. I am not an amalgam of values,
rather I am Indian because of Indian values. That is what I mean when I say, 'I carry
my values everywhere.'"

Mother Earth, Money, Mines — and Mined-Out

"Companies complain about double taxing on energy extraction [taxed by
the state, taxed by the tribe], but when they take that resource out, we're left with
nothing." Carl Valley, the young postmaster of Acoma Pueblo, takes a measured view
of his people's lives; he has a degree in history from Colorado College. He goes on:
"Uranium was good money while it lasted, but I don't know what the long-term effects
will be."

Randy Chavez, Acoma tribal secretary in 1990, does know: "My father worked
at the mill for Anaconda. He died of leukemia." Chavez says that "when we had the
uranium mines, everybody had the idea that when we got out of high school, we
would go to work at the mines and make all the money there was to be made." That
expectation ended as the 1980s began and the last big mines closed. Closure of the Am-
brosia Lake mines put three hundred people out of work; unemployment at Acoma
remained near 60 percent in 1990. When the Jackpile Mine at Laguna closed, tribal
unemployment went from 20 percent to 80 percent.

The Jackpile was the largest uranium mine in the world. When the mine opened
in 1953, Laguna had no tribal offices and the contract paperwork was stored in a trunk.
The pit eventually displaced 24 million tons of ore on 8,000 acres leased from Laguna
by Anaconda (now a division of Atlantic Richfield). The mine closed in 1982. During
the intervening thirty years, eight hundred people (70 percent of them from Laguna)
had well-paying jobs. The tribe invested millions of royalty dollars, and it remains the
wealthiest of the New Mexico pueblos. But the mine took its toll, too.

The Jackpile Mine blasted its way to within eight hundred feet of Paguate village. According to Laguna writer Leslie Marmon Silko, before the fall in uranium prices Anaconda wanted to relocate the entire village to reach the richest ore — directly under old Paguate. The People refused, says Silko: "They were bound to refuse, because there is a small mossy spring that bubbles out of the base of a black lava formation on the west side of Paguate village. This spring is the Emergence Place." So the mining company simply sank their shafts at an angle to reach the ore they wanted.

Yellow clouds of radioactive dust drifted over the village for thirty years — over its lines of laundry, drying fruit, and running children — while no one monitored exposure to radioactivity. Lagunans stayed inside during the noon blasting to avoid the potato-sized rocks that fell from the sky. They built houses from the ore and used crushed Jackpile rock in their road construction. Today, radon wafts from the closed mine, and tailings leach radioactive silt into the river and groundwater. The yellow uranium dust has a virulent vitality, "bright and alive as pollen," as Silko puts it in her novel, *Ceremony*.

The old mine is a disaster waiting to be reclaimed. Anaconda had made strong commitments to reclamation in its contracts, and in 1987 the company agreed to pay almost $47 million for the pueblo to take over reclamation. Nonetheless, Lagunans fear their people will inevitably be hit by an epidemic of radiation-related diseases: lung cancer, leukemia, birth defects, cataracts, chromosomal damage, and pulmonary fibrosis. Research cannot tell the miners and their families exactly how high their risks are, but the risks are clearly there.

Laura Graham, who has managed a variety of social services for the tribe over the years, lives in a house at Paguate that looks toward the mine. She says: "A lot of people who have died recently died of cancer. No one ever heard of it before. But nobody wants to say it. I look out there over this mine and I feel sad. I was alive in the time of my grandfather, and the mine would have made my grandfather cry.

"But it's bought a little something for us. I went to school. My kids all went to school. I wish we could have gotten that money some other way, but it's done."

Confronted with such dilemmas, the Pueblo people worry about their economic future. Lee Sarracino of Laguna works as a traffic controller during road construction; he invited me into his kitchen on a day too snowy for the crew to work. He said of his tribal leaders: "They're always trying to bring in new jobs, but they're afraid of it all going down the drain."

Each pueblo stands alone in the marketplace. San Juan has a lucrative gas station on the outskirts of Española. Nambe operates a trailer park. Picuris opened a major hotel in Santa Fe in 1991, with a loan guaranteed by the BIA and with non-Indian financial partners. Tiny Pojoaque Pueblo (uninhabited for a decade before being resettled in 1934 by a group of dispersed Pojoaques led by Antonio Jose Tapia) has developed a shopping mall on nearby U.S. Highway 285. Santa Clara encourages tourism at Puye Ruins and in Santa Clara Canyon. Pueblo profits remain low, however. As Joe Sando says: "It sometimes seems as though everyone in New Mexico earns money from tourism except the Indians." Several pueblos run lucrative bingo operations, including Sandia, where abundant bingo jobs pushed unemployment down to 2 percent in 1992.

As anywhere, innovations require creative leaders. Ronald Solimon of Laguna is one such leader. Trained as an attorney, Solimon acted as legal advisor to the tribe in the 1970s and early 1980s, grappling with the federal bureaucracy and the tribe's corporate opponent, Anaconda. "Nothing comes easy here," he says.

In 1985, the tribe provided Solimon with a line of credit based on the lucrative years of uranium royalties and a building from which to launch Laguna Industries. Since then, as president and general manager, he has created a model reservation business, manufacturing communications and electrical components, primarily for sale to the U.S. Army and defense industry — sales that already had reached $18 million annually in 1988.

In 1989, Solimon became New Mexico's "Small Business Person of the Year." Laguna Industries now is the largest employer on the reservation (90 percent of the firm's 240 workers are Laguna), contributing about $10 million annually to the local economy. Solimon says proudly: "The Pueblo of Laguna tribal leadership was able to set aside politics in order to meet the employment needs of its people." He credits his grandparents with teaching him "the spirit of entrepreneurship."

Without the capital from uranium leases, Acoma has had a harder time coming back from the uranium bust. Some eighty thousand people a year visit the old pueblo atop Acoma Mesa (they have paid fees to do so since 1928 and entered only with an Acoma guide since the 1980s), but they do not stay long. Much of the tribal investment has been in land; regaining aboriginal holdings yields great satisfaction but no quick returns.

The tribal fishing lake at Acomita had to be drained in 1984 when contaminated wastewater from the town of Grants, upstream, made it unsafe. Stanley Paytiamo, former Acoma governor and, in 1990, tribal planner, spoke to me optimistically of reclaiming the lake. He sat in his office, the walls behind him plastered with computer printouts and projections:

"We have to dredge and make the lake again. We're losing $100,000 a year and fourteen to twenty jobs a year there. We bought the land at Exit 102 on Interstate 40, and tribally owned businesses there [laundromat, conference/bingo center, motel/restaurant, truckstop plaza] could create 227 jobs. We plan a tourist center/foundation on the edge of El Malpais National Monument."

Paytiamo sounds philosophic when he talks about El Malpais. He spent much of his governorship in the mid-1980s fighting to preserve Acoma shrines within the proposed monument. Acoma lost — perhaps, thinks Paytiamo, because "we always had to leave some things secret. We couldn't explain ourselves fully."

Gilbert Ortiz, Acoma land development coordinator, helped fight the National Park Service, as well. He says: "The New Mexico congressional delegation refused to understand; to them, that was just more public domain. To us, those were our aboriginal lands — our lands. And the media never explains why Indians feel so intense about the land." Paytiamo cheers himself with the belief that "the younger generation can say that the leaders in the eighties fought with all they had."

Ortiz jokes that he and Stanley "are always being accused of too much planning and not enough results." Many of Paytiamo's statements lack any trace of planning jargon, however: "Pueblos — we live together. We do things together as a community. Maybe that's why we're poor capitalists. If you give an Indian a million dollars, he'll share that with everybody. A non-Indian will put it in the bank."

While the Acomas plan and discuss, "Albuquerque is moving up this way," as Randy Chavez puts it. "We're trying to get some company to look at us." Carl Valley says: "There will never be enough jobs on the reservation without a resource to sell." Gil Ortiz agrees, and says "the thing that holds us back is money. Indian tribes are always faced with the challenge of not enough venture capital."

Ortiz points out that "law and politics determine the fate of native people until they begin to control their own destiny. Culture and tradition has such a stronghold, change happens very slowly. We lose some of our Acoma-ness by becoming more capitalistic. But in developing a new kind of Acoma person, it takes much more than hoping and praying that the old ways won't disappear; it takes active decision-making along the way."

The Acomas have as their ace Sky City — Old Acoma — one of the grand architectural treasures of the Southwest, which will always draw tourists. From the overlook on the approach road, sandstone buttes rise from a bowl of grass yellow-gold in the spring sunset light. Acoma cows drift through the dry stems. Enchanted Mesa stands alone to the left — just far enough away to be mysterious, but close enough to be a constant presence — a perfect crucible for stories.

It takes a minute to spot the pueblo in the distance. The foreground buttes catch my eye first. The whole cluster of rock outcroppings assembles and rises, however,

Aurelia Pasquale, Acoma potter, 1988. The vitality of Pueblo art belies any claims that traditions are disappearing. Techniques may change, content may evolve, but the essential Pueblo-ness of what the People make remains, built into every coil, stroke, and stitch.

climaxing at Acoma Mesa itself. The old church dominates the skyline, giving away the village. Without the mission, the pueblo would be even harder to spot.

Even the old mesa-top town has its pitfalls as a money-maker. Stanley Paytiamo told me that the "elderlies give us a lot of static; they are afraid that the state might want to take over Sky City." They fear the Acoma Restoration Project, which "wants us to restore those buildings to their original state." Paytiamo says, mostly serious, that if given full control over the ancient pueblo: "We would tear down some of the buildings and start over — to make the buildings livable and safe for our people."

Most Acomas live year-round below the mesa, in Acomita or McCartys. Now, says Randy Chavez, other than potters, "the only people up there year-round for sure are the field-chief's family. Some of those like the peace and quiet so much, they stay." Carl Valley sums it all up: "If people had to go back to subsistence living, they might go back up. The old Pueblo will always be a place for Acomas."

Upstream and Downwind: Connections with the Outside Earth

"I've put environmental quality and health as our number one priority," says Verna Williamson, former Isleta governor. "What's the use of economic development if we're all sick? If you have people who are dying, it doesn't matter how much you make from Indian bingo. We better be healthy before we start talking about being rich!"

Isleta lies fifteen miles south of Albuquerque, the first community downstream along the Rio Grande from an egg-producing chicken farm, a meat packing plant, and a city landfill that stores one-half million tons of garbage each year. Isleta's managed recreational lakes (which generate important tribal revenue) suffer pollution from all of these. Perhaps most alarming, the meat waste causes "accelerated growth of plant life in the lakes" — eutrophication — according to lake manager Murray Vatsattie.

Williamson told one scholar this story: "By tradition, men doing Winter ceremonies have to cleanse off their body paint in river water. One recent winter, we got a call from the Albuquerque waste treatment facility upstream two days before that ceremony. They said they'd had a major sewer line break, and there would be raw sewage diverted into the river for several days."

Land is a resource for Isleta to cherish and protect — and to save for the future, believes Williamson: "We have prime land, virgin land — more than 200,000 acres to be developed if we want. It doesn't have to be factories or bingo palaces." That "we're sandwiched between Albuquerque and all these bedroom communities to the south" is both an opportunity and an administrative challenge: "This is going to go on for a long time. We're dealing with huge numbers of people passing through our reservation, and we don't have clear jurisdiction."

And yet, living right outside of Albuquerque, "We can get jobs. We *have* opportunities. There are no excuses."

Isolation at pueblos like Zuni and Hopi limits job opportunities but cannot shield the pueblos from the effects of surrounding settlement. The Zuni Reservation, for example, has been badly eroded, its watersheds stripped, and 90 percent of its arable land washed away. Zuni governor Robert Lewis blames loggers, ranchers, and a century of federal mismanagement.

By 1900, Zunis had lost 80 percent of their land base to Anglo settlers. Their reservation, fenced in 1939, includes less than 3 percent of their original holdings. To consolidate Zuni farming, the BIA engineered an irrigation development in 1904, just east of the village: Black Rock Dam, built on sand, collapsed immediately after completion in 1909.

The Black Rock project — and the smaller dams built to try to fix its failure — permanently changed traditional communal agriculture at Zuni. Available land decreased, springs were eliminated, and streams sliced down into eroded channels where the Zuni farmers cannot use the water. Overall acreage farmed at Zuni decreased at least 83 percent between 1911 and 1988. Zunis could no longer support themselves as farmers and stockmen even if they wanted to.

As the twentieth century passed, silverwork became more and more important in the Zuni economy. The Zuni learned to work silver when the Navajo smith Atsidi Chon taught Lanyade, a Zuni, in 1872 (Lanyade, in turn, taught the craft to the Hopi craftsman, Sikyatala, in 1898). Beginning in about 1920, Zuni silversmiths began making pieces for sale through traders to non-Indians. Initially, their products reflected "the Indian's idea of the trader's idea of what the white man thought was Indian design," in the words of anthropologist John Adair. By 1932, they had begun to focus on the inlay work they are known for today. By 1945, wage labor and arts and crafts brought in 65 percent of tribal cash income. By the 1960s, 90 percent of all Zunis were working at least part-time on silver jewelry; in 1978, they brought in some $5 million — tens of times more than Zuni stockmen. This growth constituted what Adair calls "an economic revolution."

Joe Dishta, job coordinator for the Zuni tribe, says that "95 percent of Zunis are artistically inclined!" Other jobs are hard to come by. "A lot of people with skills and certification are not willing to go to Albuquerque or Phoenix for jobs. There's a tie that holds people here. We had seventy-five applicants for one secretarial position."

In 1951, Zuni elders voted against pursuing a land claims case, thinking they were voting against allotment. But gradually political power at Zuni shifted from the priests to the politicians. In the 1970s, Zunis went to court with an array of issues.

The People won the return of Zuni Salt Lake, home of Old Salt Woman and an important pilgrimage site, in 1978. In 1984, the most sacred pilgrimage site of all, Katsina Village, *Ko/lhu/wa/a la:wa*, sometimes called "Zuni Heaven," was added to the reservation. The tribe won a land claim compensating them for almost 15 million acres in 1987. And they now are suing for damages done to their lands and resources, hoping for a negotiated settlement with Congress that will provide money to rehabilitate and restore their reservation.

The Hopi, too, have seen their lands shrink and the resource management techniques they had used successfully for centuries scrapped in favor of grand technology. The grandest of all are the Black Mesa mines operated by Peabody Coal Company.

The Black Mesa controversy now stretches over more than twenty-five years. Peabody signed its first leases with the Navajo and Hopi tribal councils in 1966, obtaining permission to mine 400 million tons of coal on 65,000 acres of land managed jointly by the tribes. At Hopi, there were no open hearings or community meetings regarding the decision, which was made unilaterally by the council. Every Hopi village except those entrenched on the council opposes strip mining. One Oraibi man told Richard Clemmer in 1970: "It's not a Hopi council, it's a government council."

The Kayenta Mine ships 7 million tons of coal annually to the Navajo Generating Station at Page, Arizona, by electric railroad. The Black Mesa Mine sends 5 million tons of coal to the Mohave Generating Station, westward on the Colorado River, through a pipeline almost 300 miles long. To do so means mixing the coal in a slurry with water — 3.9 million gallons of water per day, pumped up from aquifers thousands of feet below the surface of the earth.

This is a provocative scenario, needless to say. Both tribes are underpaid for their minerals and water. One early estimate projected life-of-mine revenues over thirty-five years: $14 million to the Hopi tribal council; $58 million to the Navajo tribal council; $750 million to Peabody Coal; and at least $75 million to Arizona in taxes. Renegotiating the leases in 1987 was expected to send those numbers higher.

The enormous drain on water supplies has led to the most recent battles. Hopi farmers believe that the Peabody deep wells are drying their springs and eliminating runoff from their washes; the water table has dropped by seventy feet already.

Vernon Masayesva, Hopi chairman in 1991, acknowledges that 70 percent of the tribe's operating budget comes from the $9 million annual receipts in coal royalties. Four hundred Hopis work for the mining operation. But, he adds, "it just seems foolish to be using water as a transportation method from a desert climate where you have an average rainfall of six to seven inches."

The mining leases are just one aspect of the greater battle between the development-oriented tribal council and the staunch traditionalists of Hopi society. The traditionalists, most vocally led by people like Thomas Banyacya and the late Mina Lanza, longtime spokesperson for Old Oraibi, spoke strongly against the mining leases for years. Implicit in their thinking was the position that neither the tribal council nor any other people had the right to sign leases to mine sacred earth. They brought a lawsuit against the council on this basis in 1971.

Though the suit came to naught and the mining continues, Black Mesa served as a warning to other tribes seeking to avoid exploitation, and no such controversial development has happened since in Indian Country.

The ethical position of the traditional Hopi brought them many Anglo followers but has made little dent in the courts of the tribal council's business dealings. Intent on investment, the council spent its first lease money, made from mineral exploration in the 1960s, on an underwear factory in Winslow (which closed in 1975) and the Hopi Cultural Center motel/museum complex at Second Mesa, which opened in 1970 and continues to be an important community center for both tourists and Hopis.

Abbott Sekaquaptewa, leader of the council in the 1970s, felt passionately about both pushing for additional mineral leases and regaining rights to Hopi land usurped by Navajos. His brother published the primary Hopi newspaper, so the chairman had an effective soapbox. His lawyers were effective, too, and Hopi interests in the courts did well.

The Hopi council's lawyer, John Boyden of Salt Lake City, worked diligently for years on their behalf. He was, in anthropologist Richard Clemmer's words, "the mainstay of the Hopi Tribal Council's economic and political position" after 1955. Much of the council was Mormon, as was Boyden. His son, Stephen Boyden, followed him as counsel to the Hopi council.

John Boyden made a great deal of money — and enemies. He represented the Peabody Coal Company at the same time he represented the Hopi. He also won cases. First came *Healing v. Jones*, in 1962.

The roots of the Hopi-Navajo land controversy reach back more than a century. The Hopi Reservation drawn in 1882 embraced a 2.5-million-acre rectangle carved from traditional Hopi lands. It also embraced at least three hundred Navajos living within its boundaries, who continued to live there and to increase in numbers.

The light use the Hopis made of their land seemed like no use at all to the Navajo, who pushed the BIA to transfer lands to them. The BIA asked the two tribes to sit down at a conference in 1930 and settle their differences. The Hopi leaders came, but they refused to consider any proposal to reduce their lands. They pointed out that their concentration on the mesas was a recent phenomenon (typical only of the last three hundred years or so), required only because of Athapaskan raids through the 1700s and 1800s. Before, they had made more use of their far-flung territory.

As journalist Catherine Feher-Elston puts it: "The Navajo view of land acquisition and settlement is more comparable to the American view; if land appears empty, settle on it and wait to see what happens. Hopis view this as aggressive exploitation; Navajos and Americans view it as homesteading."

In *Healing v. Jones*, federal courts decreed in 1962 that the two tribes had a joint interest in the 1882 reservation (outside the grazing district immediately surrounding the Hopi villages, within which Hopi had exclusive use — an area that had been the de facto Hopi Reservation since the stock reduction days of 1942). Neither tribe liked this arrangement (and it certainly complicated lease negotiations for the Black Mesa Mine), and their pursuit in Congress of a more definitive settlement led to the 1974 Navajo and Hopi Land Settlement Act (essentially written by John Boyden).

In the 1974 law, each tribe received exclusive use of half of the 1.8 million acres of jointly held land. Any Navajo or Hopi living on the "wrong" side of the partition line was required to move by 6 July 1986. About 100 Hopi had to move — and did so. More than eight thousand Navajo had to move, but many refused and still live on their old lands.

Today, the Hopi remain adamant about their rights to the land, and they refuse to take money in exchange for it. They note that partition actually gave formal recognition to *reducing* the area of the 1882 Hopi Reservation. As Oraibi elder John Lanza put it in 1971: "Young generations are the ones that go for money. But we depend on the *Earth* to make our living. It's our social security."

Opposing the Hopi are Navajo families at Big Mountain, north of the Hopi villages and within the now-designated Hopi partition area, who have vowed never to move. Peabody Coal, accused of conspiring to help the Hopi (perceived as more compliant in granting leases), claims to have no interest in mining the Big Mountain area.

Another court battle involves millions of acres still farther west in the Navajo Reservation — territory that includes the Hopi villages at Moenkopi and the de facto western Navajo capital, Tuba City. The Hopi Tribal Council and its attorneys claim this huge area as traditional Hopi land, but the Navajo Reservation has administered it since 1934. This dispute also involves the newly recognized San Juan Paiute, who want land of their own. From 1966 to 1992, the BIA restricted improvements on tribal homes in the area. A 1992 ruling lifted the development freeze and gave the Navajo

"We Are the People. We Are the Land."

Jeannette Larzelere, painted with clay, sits transfigured by the power of the earth on the fourth and last day of her puberty ceremony. Whiteriver, Fort Apache Reservation, Arizona, 1984.

Eugene Sekaquaptewa works in the Eagle Clan cornfield below the old village of Oraibi on Third Mesa.
Hopi Reservation, Arizona, 1984.

Shipaulovi village rises from the rocky prow of Second Mesa. Hopi Reservation, Arizona, 1984.

A Navajo stone hogan below Shiprock — Tsébit'a', the great Rock with Wings — on top of which the Navajo culture hero Monster Slayer killed the evil Monster Bird. Navajo Reservation, New Mexico, 1989.

Orian Box,
Southern Ute council
member and artist,
in his studio. Ignacio,
Colorado, 1989.

Sierra Estrella,
sacred to the Pima,
seen from the Ak-Chin
O'odham Reservation.
Arizona, 1987.

At the annual Gathering of Nations Powwow, dancers assemble from all over the West to proclaim and nourish their Indianness. Albuquerque, New Mexico, 1991.

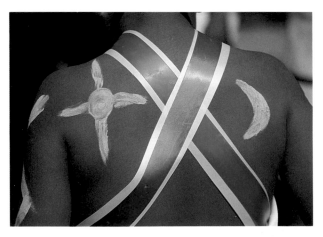

The painted back of a young Tohono O'odham dancer at the O'odham Tash celebration. Casa Grande, Arizona, 1992.

Opposite: Native traditions live and evolve: Amber Ljunggren, Head Start student, dressed for a Buffalo Dance performance. Laguna Pueblo, New Mexico, 1990.

The Hualapai honor their
dead at the annual Memorial
Powwow, singing, dancing,
and mourning under a ritual
ramada for a day and a
night, then burning the
ramada at dawn. Peach
Springs, Arizona, 1984.

exclusive rights to 6.9 million acres, the Hopi 40,000 acres around Moenkopi, and
created a new joint-use area of 70,000 acres; the court ruled that only Congress can
create a San Juan Paiute Reservation. This saga is certain to continue.

The Hopi have refused to renegotiate the 1974 partition along with this new disputed territory; their chairman for much of the 1980s, Ivan Sidney, says simply: "This land is not for sale." Peterson Zah, Navajo tribal president, says: "I support a comprehensive solution and a negotiated settlement because it is better if we work it out ourselves without allowing these lawyers to make money off the Navajo and off the Hopi . . . I think that the two tribes just simply have to resolve this issue." Resolution may have been reached in late 1992, when federal mediation led to a proposal granting Navajos in the disputed area a seventy-five-year lease and Hopis some 480,000 acres of forest land on the Coconino Plateau, south of the Grand Canyon.

As one elder told Feher-Elston: "This land fight is tearing us all to pieces. Moving back and forth, fighting with each other, how can our cultures continue with so much outside interference?"

The Living Traditions of Pueblo Art

Outside interference can help, too. Interactions with outsiders have been crucial in transforming art into a viable Pueblo profession.

Pueblo people have always approached their lives as an artistic undertaking, whether cooking chile verde, hollowing a cottonwood log to make a drum, weaving a sash, tending corn, building a shed, telling a joke, making a pot, or painting a kiva mural. Art is not separate from life.

As Rina Swentzell says: "I value tremendously the unselfconsciousness, and absence of aesthetic pretension, which led to doing everything straightforwardly yet which still considered the context and the connections . . . That thing which connects us is the breath. That's why everything takes on life . . . We all breathe of the same breath the plants do, the rocks do." Nothing could be more inclusive.

For many modern Pueblo artists, that fundamental connection remains. Jose Rey Toledo, Jemez elder and painter, says: "I am striving to express my life through the medium of art." (Toledo's strivings range from health education to murals to serving as master of ceremonies at the Indian Pueblo Cultural Center and announcer for the New Mexico State Fair's Indian Village.)

Many traditional arts began to disappear toward the end of the nineteenth century. The old ways, after all, are hard work. Though the railroads completed in the 1880s displaced handcrafted products with manufactured products, they also brought tourists looking for ethnic and exotic curios. Many older women tell stories of selling

Waiting for customers, Santa Fe Railway, Laguna Pueblo, late 1800s. Many older Laguna and Acoma women remember carrying pots to sell at the nearby railroad, waving down trains with small white flags while holding high their family's work. Photo by C. B. Waite. (Courtesy of The Southwest Museum, Los Angeles. Photo no. 20267)

their Hopi pots for a dime or a quarter to Anglos camped out for the Snake Dance, of carrying Acoma pots by horse to the nearby Santa Fe Railroad and holding up their pots for sale while they flagged down trains with little white flags, or of taking Isleta pots to sell to travelers at the Albuquerque train station.

When Anglos began to take an interest in native knowledge and crafts, a handful of pivotal Pueblo people took the lead in creating a new profession: Indian artist. These pathmakers owed their success to a happy combination of creativity, openness to white people, and entrepreneurial skills.

In the 1880s, Nampeyo watched the spectacular pottery being excavated from the old Hopi village of Sikyatki, and with her husband, Lesou, began working to reproduce the designs on her own pottery. More than a century later, her fourth-, fifth-, and sixth-generation descendants are still among the preeminent Hopi and Hopi-Tewa potters.

At San Ildefonso, Maria and Julian Martinez developed their matte-black on high-polish-black pottery style in about 1919, singlehandedly creating a flourishing market for San Ildefonso art pottery. By 1920, one-third of San Ildefonso families made their living from hand-coiled, stone-polished pottery, and Santa Clara was joining the revival.

Over succeeding decades, innovators and teachers and entrepreneurs have stood out in every Pueblo art form. Potters at many pueblos kept working through the lean periods of the thirties and World War II, keeping tradition alive: Virginia Duran at Picuris, the late Lucy Lewis at Acoma, Eudora Montoya at Santa Ana.

The late Fred Kabotie, dean of Hopi painters, created the Hopi overlay style of silverwork with Paul Saufkie after World War II. Their immediate goal was to employ Hopi veterans and incorporate their sense of design in an art form essentially new to Hopi. The late Charles Loloma took Hopi silver in new directions; even his most abstract inlay work, however, hid within its designs and colors katsina faces and dance chants.

When Loloma's niece and protege, Verma Nequatewa, began working with him and looking for ideas, she found "there were sculptures everywhere — sticks, rocks, all made into little sculptures by Spider Woman. And going to the dances and seeing all the colors — it comes back in the jewelry."

The Santo Domingos, masters of pump-drilled *heishi* beads for centuries, today make finer and more even necklaces, using previously unheard of materials like malachite. In keeping with their more conservative values, more of their work is unsigned than any other Pueblo art I know. Their flair for business and trade, however, makes them the dominant group at such places as the portal of the Palace of the Governors on the Santa Fe plaza.

Dan Namingha and Michael Kabotie incorporate the visions of abstract expressionism and impressionism in their paintings of Hopi landscapes, katsinas, and dreams. Kabotie, with four other Hopi painters, joined in the creative group Artist Hopid in 1973. "We are trying to smooth the sharp edges of the clash between the two cultures, to have a dialogue through the arts," he told Tryntje Seymour. "We still maintain the Hopi point of view — just using a Western tool."

As Michael's father Fred put it: "'These Hopi painters have been influenced by Picasso,' visitors tell me. 'No, Picasso was infuenced by the Hopis,' I explain."

In 1964, Cochiti potter Helen Cordero made her first storyteller figure, with five children hanging from a seated grandfather: "His eyes are closed because he's thinking; his mouth is open because he's singing." As many as thirty children swarm over her later pieces. Inspired by her success, more than two hundred Pueblo potters today make figurative pottery; one-fourth are Cochiti. Droll Ivan Lewis even makes mermaids: "Cochiti mermaids? Sure, they live up in Cochiti Lake!"

Michael Naranjo, blinded in Vietnam, came home to Santa Clara to sculpt emotion-filled figures cast in bronze. Manfred Susunkewa revived the old vegetal paints for his Hopi katsina dolls, and the market veered off to accommodate his vision. He says: "I started out as a protest against detailed, contemporary, acrylic-painted dolls. My dolls look primitive. My dolls blow up on you — they're frightening." Ramona Sakiestewa has taken the classic designs of Hopi weaving and added to them ideas inspired by Japanese yarn, Chinese philosophy, and Andean and African weavings.

The list goes on and on. Pottery seems to be the art form that most happily blends Pueblo culture and Anglo taste. Potters who make $5,000 pots for galleries may also shape cooking bowls for their feast days and ceremonial jars for their kivas. As Rina Swentzell says: "The women have held . . . it's almost like holding onto the clay, onto the earth itself, through the pottery." Though less widely practiced, katsina doll carving (at Hopi), weaving, drum making, and basket weaving also fit into the Pueblo craft continuum. Silverwork and easel painting may seem foreign, but both have ties to prehistory, when ancestral Pueblo jewelers worked with turquoise and shell and religious leaders painted murals on kiva walls.

Katsina dolls once were carved only for the dancers to give, with a blessing, to young girls at Powamuy, the Bean Dance. Such dolls are "a present from unseen spiritual people," in Percy Lomaquahu's words. Manfred Susunkewa says: "Everything that is on this earth is represented by a katsina. Dolls were to educate the female youngsters. When they possess these things, they will learn how to care for them and then in turn, when they grow older, they will learn how to take care of their people."

The carvers work with cottonwood root — yet another petition for water, according to Hartman Lomawaima, since cottonwood roots search out water. The dolls are still given to young Hopi girls by katsina dancers. Lomawaima says: "The rows of dolls on the walls of Hopi homes are like bar graphs: they tell you how many daughters and how old they are!"

With mentors available in the old crafts, a need to find work, and a market augmented by the enormous national passion for "Santa Fe Style," Pueblo people can choose to live in the old villages, create art, and make a living. They still find their work inseparable from their lives. Zuni High School even offers an academic course in traditional pottery making.

Alex Seowtowa has spent the years since 1970 painting life-size katsina figures on the walls of the freshly renovated Our Lady of Guadalupe Mission Church at his pueblo of Zuni. Three of his sons have helped him in this enormous project. When visitors come to the pueblo for Shalako, Seowtowa gathers them in the church, introducing the katsinas they will see by interpreting his fifty-foot-long panels of painted dancers. In 1992, he planned to finish his lifework in four years.

Nora Naranjo-Morse, Santa Clara potter, finds ideas everywhere for her clay people, figures that tell stories rich with humor and wisdom. Going to the post office, "the angle of the body of a big woman bending over to open her mailbox" inspires her:

Our Lady of Guadalupe Mission Church, Zuni Pueblo, 1988. With the help of three of his sons, Alex Seowtowa has spent the years since 1970 painting 50-foot-long panels of life-size katsina figures on the interior walls of the church. He plans to finish in 1996.

"I dash home and do something with that." She knows that the continuity of her life confounds many Anglos. For instance, she and her husband recently built their own adobe house. "I met a woman at the hardware store where I was buying two-by-fours. She was shocked and said, 'You should be home making pottery!'" Naranjo-Morse's dream: "To help open doors for others who are interested in preserving their culture in their own way."

Indian and non-Indian worlds interact in unpredictable ways. Stella Loretto, a Jemez potter, has traveled and studied art in Belgium, Oaxaca, India, Nepal, Japan, Iran, and the South Pacific; all these experiences influence her figurines. Crucita Melchor from Santo Domingo grew so tired of explaining to tourists what the birds on her pots were doing that she painted musical notes next to their faces, to make it clear that "they sing." Stella Teller, from Isleta, sometimes has to refire her unsold pots after exhibits to burn off the greasy, sticky fingerprints left by people who have been eating fry bread and honey. Emma Lewis Mitchell, Acoma potter, jokes that she and her family keep Argentine corned beef companies in business because the women so much like the lids from the tinned meat to use as scrapers to smooth their pots.

Al Qoyawayma, a Hopi man who worked for many years as an engineer and administrator for the Salt River Project in Phoenix, has applied his knowledge of structure and form to pottery, pushing the limits of his bowls and jars. He measured the old Sikyatki pots and found that the older potters had been unable to make the same shapes he had been unable to make; they, too, had pushed their pottery to its artistic and structural limits.

The individualization of Pueblo art challenges the anthropological maxims. In the old way, for instance, Hopi men wove, Hopi women on First Mesa made pottery, Hopi women on Second Mesa made coiled baskets, and Third Mesa Hopi women made wicker baskets. Today, exceptions to all these generalizations exist, though as trends, they still stand.

Young artists learn by trial and error, watching their aunts and uncles and grandmothers and grandfathers and mothers and fathers. They learn by living. "The uncles, the grandparents are always dispensing that information," says Hopi educator Wil Numkena. "You ask questions, for clarification." Michael Kabotie, Hopi painter, says: "My father was an artist. The ceremonies are a form of art, and I began to participate when I was a kid. Between the two, I became an artist automatically."

Others have learned art in schools. In the early twentieth century, people like Fred Kabotie and Awa Tsireh from San Ildefonso had to struggle to find any art instruction. In the 1930s, Dorothy Dunn, first at the Santa Fe Indian School, then at The Studio in Santa Fe, created a training center for a whole generation of Indian painters. San Juan painter Geronima Montoya took over as director of The Studio in 1937 and remained for twenty-five years. The pan-Indian style that grew from these schools created a strong sense of community, but by the fifties had become stagnant.

In part to inject new life in Indian art, Santa Fe's Institute of American Indian Art opened in 1962. Since then, Pueblo artists have been able to start with a foundation of teaching and scholarship, moving on to their own lives in their own communities — both on the reservations and in Santa Fe, San Francisco, or New York. Many of today's most innovative young Pueblo artists started at IAIA.

Laura Fragua, from Jemez, graduated from IAIA in 1984 — the year I interviewed her at Santa Fe Indian Market, when she won a major award for her sculpture. She said, with an ironic smile: "Pueblo women have the more passive role: stay home, have the kids, raise them. Pueblo women should be quiet. It's the same way with sculpting. Females should be painting or drawing, not working with big chisels and hammers."

Fragua speaks of the spiritual bedrock underlying her work. "First, we're artists because we want to create. And then, being an Indian, my art will reflect some of my Indianness. This is how I'm going to express myself, thanking the creator for what he's done." She also says, "You might have a Calvin Klein pair of pants on, but that doesn't change the way you feel in your heart."

Nora Naranjo-Morse sums up what comes through in her art: "All the things that affect me — an American Indian woman making pottery now, in this year — all, good and bad, come out in my work. All of my childhood gets stored in this vessel." (She holds her hand to her heart.) "Now I'm bringing that all out." Naranjo-Morse writes poetry, too. Sometimes the writing feeds her ideas for pottery, sometimes she makes something and then writes about it. And, sometimes, "I get ideas for both when I'm rolling out tortillas. That's really living for me!"

Many young artists have told me that their elders approve of their innovations, as long as their piece bears their respect for the culture. As Ralph T. Coe points out in *Lost and Found Traditions*, the elders know their job: to complain and lament the passing of the old ways, and at the same time to teach those ways to the young. Innovative Hopi/Navajo potter Nathan Begay says: "Tradition is a state of mind." (He adds, "It's the Hopi side of my ancestry that does the pottery!") Gabrieleta Nave, longtime director of the San Juan Pueblo crafts cooperative Oke Oweenge, told Coe: "We don't have a word for tradition, but we do have words for 'old-timey' and 'done in the right way,' because these are important to us."

The vitality of Pueblo art belies any notions about disappearing traditions. Mary Esther Archuleta, married into San Juan and the daughter of Santa Clara pottery matriarch Margaret Tafoya, says: "I think it's really hereditary. It just comes down the line like anything else — people in medicine, lawyers. Pottery is the same thing. You find the patience, you make the time." Her cousin, Mary Cain, puts it this way: "My grandmother has been doing it, and her mother, and their mothers have been doing it — the black pottery, all in a line, all through their lives."

Hartman Lomawaima talks about the process of "Hopifying" new concepts to make them one's own. When Zunis willingly incorporate new bits of technology, they then consider them thoroughly Zuni. Techniques may change, content may evolve, but the Pueblo-ness of what the People make with their hearts and hands remains, built in with every coil, stroke, and stitch.

Pueblo Identity at the Multicultural Crossroads

Holding on to Pueblo identity is the challenge of the twenty-first century — maintaining ethnicity in the face of overwhelming Anglo dominance. Pueblo people know where their roots lie; they return home for dances. Some remain permanently among those roots. Others move outward from there.

Pueblo people speak warmly of quiet childhoods. Ada Melton teases her father, who worked in Albuquerque all his life, about "abusing child-labor laws, working us in his fields at home in Jemez! Those are fun memories for me." Produce from such fields fuels an underground economy that makes the horrendous unemployment figures for the pueblos a little less devastating.

Melton, who works as the student resource specialist for the Native American Studies program at the University of New Mexico, has thought hard about these issues. She defines "multicultural" as "accepting and embracing something and making it a part of your belief system. It's a skill — to view the world through the lens of the people you are participating with. You go back and forth on a regular basis. It's a continuum, but it's not linear. The paths meet every now and then, and those are our strongest points. My mother would clench her hands together when she talked about those crossroads."

Verna Williamson, former Isleta governor, puts it even more bluntly: "Being an Indian is schizoid. You completely change your role in a matter of seconds. You better be able to adapt that quick! Talk about coping — no wonder people get drunk!"

Melton believes: "I can complement my peers who choose not to be multicultural, who choose to be purely Jemez. I can look out for them by using my education to protect Jemez rights, Jemez land, to refuse economic opportunities that are going to exploit us. In turn, they preserve the culture for us."

The in-between culture — the Spanish-speaking descendants of the conquistadores — suffer from all the challenges of being in that middle position. The more successful the Pueblos have been at achieving federal recognition of their rights, the more disenfranchised New Mexico Hispanics have become. Indians compare themselves with the Anglos now dominant in New Mexico rather than with Hispanics; no one wants to be the bottom rung of society. Hispanics bitterly resent the attention given by the top-rung Anglos to the Pueblos and their "Indian doings," especially after five centuries of Hispanic certainty of superiority over their pagan Pueblo neighbors — whom they always viewed as primitives.

The "primitives" remain stubbornly unreconstructed, however. Though nominally Catholic, most neither take communion nor go to confession. As Leslie White described the Santa Anas, they "do not belong to the Roman Catholic church; rather, they have accepted and adopted bits of Catholic ideology, ritual, and paraphernalia, and these bits belong to them." In 1965, when the Isletas became convinced that their priest of ten years was impossibly insensitive to the traditional ceremonial life, they set him down outside the village and told him never to come back.

Nevertheless, not every potter listens solely to Clay Old Woman: Gladys Paquin of Laguna told me that "the Lord Jesus put a desire in me to make pottery." At Santa Clara, Teresita Naranjo has a homily from Christian theology for every step in her potterymaking. She says: "My pottery is the handiwork of God."

Quiet intensity emanates from conservative pueblos like Santo Domingo and San Felipe — unlike anything that comes from more open pueblos. I drive into San Felipe one November. Chile ristras — waxy red and brilliant in the sun — hang from roof beams. Here and there a tumble of drying blue corn cascades from someone's porch. Blazing gold cottonwoods beginning to frost to burnt-orange line the river and ditch banks. Dogs, kids, older women circle around the hornos, the beehive-shaped bread ovens. Soft-cornered adobe stands in every stage from ruins to gray stucco ready for painting to classic mud-and-straw-plastered walls, every nuance of texture revealed by the crystalline clarity of late afternoon.

This is a living community, steeped in Pueblo-ness.

Old and new, tradition and change, conservative and progressive. These dichotomies lead to conflict and to adaptation. Regis Pecos, from Cochiti, says: "We believe duality to be a means of balance; others see it as something where conflict evolves." At Acoma, Stanley Paytiamo quotes the refrain of the elders: "Grandpa says: 'You have to carry on our culture as long as it will last.' Grandpa and Grandma have all the basic skills to get you anywhere." Both Grandpa and Paytiamo know, however, that "we can't totally live the Indian way. We have to live in the present and future, too." His fellow Acoma, Gilbert Ortiz, admits that "as you opt for becoming progressive, there are true losses for Acoma society. It's a sacrifice."

Says Stanley Paytiamo: "In the end, I tell my children, there's no way I can tell you how to be an Acoma, how to be an Indian. You have to experience it."

Experiencing Acoma-ness, Pueblo-ness, begins at home. It is the experience of

Stanley Paytiamo, Acoma Pueblo planner and former governor, 1990. "Pueblos," he says, "we live together as a community. Maybe that's why we're poor capitalists. If you give an Indian a million dollars, he'll share that with everybody. A non-Indian will put it in the bank."

dance practice in kivas, weeding cornfields with your grandfather, serving endless bowls of steaming chile on feast days, waiting for school buses on crisp autumn mornings in front of an old adobe mission, and living within a few hundred feet of a dozen family members.

Sharing has a great deal to do with living a Pueblo life. In the old days, a Hopi bride's family would grind eight hundred to a thousand pounds of corn in just a few days for wedding feasts. They needed the help of every aunt and clan sister to do so. Even today, cooking for feast days is a huge responsibility. When visitors sit down to such a meal, they eat in shifts. I took my turn at Petra Gutierrez's house at Santa Clara on the 12 August saint's day one year; she periodically walked to the table from the busy kitchen, repeating, "Just help yourself; eat all you want," as a blessing, a benediction.

Pueblo people who grow up in reservation communities have the chance to begin their lives steeped in Pueblo values. Hopi/Navajo Rosanda Suetopka-Thayer was raised in California. Before I met her, she was described to me as a "Hopi who talks like Bette Midler." That isn't far off. When her daughter was born in the early 1980s,

Suetopka-Thayer and her spouse moved their family home to Hotevilla, where she had always spent summers with her father's people ("How can you really know your grandparents if you don't see them?"). She says: "I had no idea I was Indian for a real long time — till fifth or sixth grade. I knew I was different but not so different that I couldn't get over it. Only in the last couple of years do I see how deep it is. I feel so blessed."

Parents and grandparents and uncles and aunts tend not to discipline Pueblo children physically, but through endless teasing and lecturing young people learn to follow the Pueblo way. Even the tribal justice systems maintain old ways. When Ada Melton worked for the Laguna tribal courts, she realized that "we didn't see all the deviants and criminals and J.D.'s. The villages were taking care of them in their own way — through family gatherings as the first forums, and then village gatherings with officials as mediators/arbitrators. You participate in the resolution, and you will be responsible for your actions."

Education in Context: Pueblo Culture 101

The chance for transforming Pueblo values into Anglo assets is always there. One success story has been running. Zuni High School's track team practices along the base of Dowa Yallane (Corn Mountain), carrying on the excellence of the old Zuni stick racers. At Jemez, the license plates on the pickups read "Track Town, USA — Jemez Pueblo, New Mexico." The Pueblo has long regarded the winners of ceremonial long-distance races as local heroes. Legends tell of one runner of the thirties, Jose Tosa, who supposedly could run down and capture wild horses.

Today, those same ceremonial race winners have carried the Jemez Valley High School cross-country team to more than a dozen state championships and to the national championship, as well. Runners like Steve Gachupin and Al Waquie have long lists of record times. Gachupin himself has been a track coach at the school since 1965.

Controlling their schools has become crucial to Pueblo communities as they build a foundation of Pueblo-ness — beginning with Head Start and day-school programs. Most Pueblo kids go to public schools, many to schools with overwhelmingly Indian student bodies. Pueblos taking over their school boards must overcome what Hayes Lewis, Superintendent of Zuni Schools, describes as "physical facilities that should have been condemned" and old "poisons" left over from misguided administrators. They must struggle with young people whom Edmund Ladd characterizes as "undermotivated, undereducated, and underemployed."

They must overcome facts like these: from 1976 to 1979, the (non-Indian) Cibola County school board spent $38 per student attending Laguna-Acoma High School and

$802 per student at Grants High School (with mostly non-Indian enrollment). Anglos who justify this by pointing out that Indians do not pay property taxes on tribal lands must explain the $40 million paid by Laguna in severance taxes on Jackpile Mine revenues.

Zuni took over its school system in 1980 (becoming the first public school district in New Mexico whose boundaries match the reservation's), and Harvard-educated Hayes Lewis, son of longtime Zuni governor Robert Lewis, is proud of what they have accomplished since. He told me: "We believe in the empowerment of people to direct their own destiny. It takes a little longer but it's consensus building; it's a liberating experience. Parents are involved in every decision at the new middle school; it allows people to buy in and be responsible for their choices."

Lewis goes on: "Language and culture history are the top priority now. Zuni people want Zuni literacy taught in K through 12. Once, they said families could do it. Now, they want Zuni placed in equal value to German and Spanish. So we have to implement training, dictionaries, orthographies." Edmund Ladd says: "Language is a vehicle for carrying spirit, life, family. Language, religion, and land base are the three things that characterize culture. Without the language, you have little religious life. But when I go back and speak Zuni to youngsters, they look at me like I'm from Mars."

Lewis dreams of an immersion approach: "Maybe on some days — Monday, Wednesday, Friday — everything will be taught in English. On Tuesdays and Thursdays, everything will be in Zuni." He leaned back from his desk and stared at a calligraphed "Goals for Schools" plaque on the wall: "I had intended to go to law school but got pulled into this. There's always another thing left to do. It's a humbling, energizing, challenging, complicated experience to be in this job."

Joe Abeyta, superintendent of Santa Fe Indian School, would agree. With 560 students, more than 80 percent of them from Rio Grande pueblos (and many of the rest Hopi and Navajo), his staff is about 85 percent Indian, his board members are Indian, and the school is owned by Indian people, contracting with the BIA.

The contracting began when the All Indian Pueblo Council took over administration of the Albuquerque Indian School in 1977 — a historic event engineered by the council's chair, Delfin Lovato of San Juan. In 1981, the school moved from the decaying Albuquerque campus back to the old Santa Fe Indian School campus, which had closed in 1962. Says Abeyta, now: "It's our school, we're responsible for it. It's us."

Abeyta bubbles with energy and enthusiasm. He emphasizes that his charges go home on weekends, that the school teaches an Indian perspective. Abeyta himself commutes from his home in Santa Clara, where, he says, "I love my mud home; we don't recognize our strengths." He told me: "The responsibilities that my kids are growing up to are greater than nine-tenths of the general population. They will be governors, council members. They've got to be ready. Every kid I have here from a small pueblo like Tesuque will have leadership roles there eventually."

Abeyta's board chairman, Regis Pecos, explained the school's goals: "The Pueblo concept of an extended family drives this school. That's what makes it unique. This whole environment is culturally relevant — recreates that extended family, administration through staff. The easier road would have been to create a school for the elite, a 'Pueblo Academy.'" Instead, the school accepts all Indian students on a first-come, first-served basis. Says Pecos: "Where we are now is where we should have started."

Language is crucial to Pueblo-ness. Joe Sando describes Jemez people who cannot speak Towa as "lost in the cold air of fragmentary existence." Stanley Paytiamo says of his Acoma language: "I prefer to talk in Keresan. English is too short, it doesn't fully explain things. You say something in Keresan, it explains itself." Verma Nequatewa agrees: "One Hopi word can explain a lot. English can't do it."

Emory Sekaquaptewa, a Hopi scholar who teaches anthropology at the University of Arizona, is helping to edit the first dictionary of written Hopi. At Hopi, you must speak the language to be initiated; Sekaquaptewa notes that "the language has certain ritual forms that are used in secrecy, by an exclusive group. Those who don't have access work harder to gain it."

Sekaquaptewa says: "The most creative medium in the Hopi language are the songs of the katsinas. In the songs, we find words that dwell on natural forces at work for the benefit of mankind, language filled with the energy of Hopi thought. One katsina song has cloud maidens grinding rain just as a Hopi maiden grinds corn, to prepare it, to bring this life force to the People. How does one proceed to capture these images and organize them into more contemporary literary applications?"

There has never been a written Hopi language, for all its ancientness and eloquence. The Hopi oral tradition has force and power and a distinct style, but it is more like theater or poetry than prose. Can such performances be translated to print? Can the exclusivity of access to true meaning be maintained? Is that appropriate?

Sekaquaptewa wonders, with awe, as he works on the dictionary project with a team of non-Hopi linguists to create a standardized orthography and with Hopi elders who double-check accuracy of syntax and grammar and subtlety of meaning: "What happens to a person and his world view and his view of himself when you switch him from oral to written words? Words, spoken words, carry the meaning and power of the Hopi Way not out of context, but in context. In the context of ritual forms, ceremonial formation, architecture (relation of houses to ceremonial places), place names."

Sekaquaptewa hopes that the dictionary will "inspire younger Hopis to begin to produce written Hopi text — Hopi literature" for the first time in the long history of the language. He dreams of seeing this literature move beyond the oral tradition of stories and legends to "bring the reader the historical, moral realities of life today at Hopi."

Perhaps the most likely place for Hopi literature to blossom will be Hopi High School, opened in 1986 between Second and Third mesas after years of campaigning by Hopi parents to bring their young people home from boarding schools. The school is a federally funded BIA school, but its board is entirely local and Hopi. According to the tribe's secondary education specialist, Radford Quamahongnewa, the focus is "to provide students a chance to be more involved in cultural activities, a chance for parents to give their children daily guidance," to be there to answer their children's questions — the crucial method for Pueblo culture to be passed from generation to generation. Quamahongnewa certainly understands this issue; he is a Snake Society priest at Shongopavi.

Fridays are preparation days for dances, and the high school (grades seven to twelve), lets students out for those days. Dances rotate from First Mesa on to Second and Third mesas, and so not all students are out at one time. Quamahongnewa hopes to eventually establish a four-day school week for all students.

In 1991, there was no Hopi language instruction at the school, the former instructor having died a year earlier without replacement. Conflicts over which dialect to teach (First, Second, or Third mesa) have also prevented full acceptance of the new dictionary based on Third Mesa's dialect.

As the Hopi create the best possible environment for learning and creativity — keeping their students in Hopiland, giving them the incredible new tool of a written Hopi language, and providing them the gamut of experiences from computer labs to kivas — unpredictable and innovative ways of articulating Hopi-ness surely will result.

Joe Sando lists the first Pueblo college graduates, starting with two Laguna teachers: Suzy Rayos Marmon (Bloomsburg State Normal School, Pennsylvania, 1906) and Miguel Trujillo, Sr. (who also initiated the lawsuit in 1948 that led to Indians obtaining the right to vote in New Mexico). Beginning in the 1940s, others followed, including the Tewa Ph.D.s in anthropology, Edward Dozier and Alfonso Ortiz, and the first Pueblo physician, Beryl Blue Spruce, Laguna/San Juan, who obtained his M.D. in 1964. Dozier, in fact, in 1952 was the first Indian from any tribe to receive a Ph.D. in the humanities. In 1969, when the All Indian Pueblo Council took over scholarship programs from the BIA, college enrollment "skyrocketed," in Sando's words.

Though Pueblo people have since entered many professional and academic fields, they still struggle with an educational system at odds with many of their values. While

Raymond Concho, Jr., was attending college, he took home Leslie White's monograph on Acoma Pueblo to show to his grandfather. His grandfather glanced at the illustrations, listened to Concho read the text, and returned the book to the young Acoma man, saying, "This isn't true." Says Concho: "Who would I believe more, an anthropologist or my grandfather?"

Ted Jojola, another Ph.D. Pueblo anthropologist, from Isleta, directs Native American Studies at the University of New Mexico. He believes that Indian college students stand little chance of finishing their degrees until they have attended for three continuous semesters. Jojola's gut feeling for the reasons behind Pueblo students leaving college: "They aren't competitive in the classroom. That highly paternalistic Indian education system is the root cause, not their culture." The solution: "Early intervention. Teach them that just because they have to be competitive here, they don't have to do it in their communities." Joe Sando makes community values even more central and suggests that each pueblo work with students, matching them to the community's needs and creating "a planned society, with the greatest possible improvement in the lives of the people."

Jojola's staff member Ada Melton notes a common thread among Indian students with problems: "They cannot articulate their needs." She resents the litany Pueblo kids hear from their parents: " 'You need an education to survive.' It's a loaded statement. I want to replace that with 'You need an education to be successful.' "

The Modern Circle: Commuters and Community

One Pueblo person successful at the dance between Pueblo-ness and Anglo-ness is Isleta's forty-two-year-old Verna Williamson, governor from 1986 to 1990. Her family "pushed her," she told me, but gave her self-confidence, too. Her father's family was full of entrepreneurial energy, especially her grandfather, who "kept bees, grew corn, did silver, helped run a gas station. He exposed me to the work world and taught me to be independent." Her mother "came from a very poor, very traditional family. She gave us a balance; we had it made."

The middle of seven kids, "I learned from both ends." After sixth grade, she went to public school, "with all kinds of people." One older brother went to law school, another has a Ph.D. in political science. When Williamson tagged along with her father to council meetings where there were no women, no one thought much about it, since she was only a kid. When her father died, she was thirteen; she continued tagging along to tribal meetings with her brother.

"When my brother began to go out from the pueblo, I was in high school. I continued to go to meetings, and the council threw me out. One older woman who had

Verna Williamson, councilwoman and former governor, Isleta Pueblo, 1990. Even today, most Pueblo women wield their power from the home, not the tribal office. Williamson speaks proudly of being an exception, by her election giving "women more ownership of the community."

taught in Oklahoma and retired home to Isleta became my mentor. She taught me to go for whatever I wanted. One time after I had been thrown out of council, she went back with me. They let us stay.

"After leaving Isleta in the sixties, I came back home and decided to live here for the rest of my life. This was *home*. I'm very strongly connected to my clan. I wanted to have children and bring my children up here.

"I started working for the tribe on the youth program, focusing on children from dysfunctional families. I became real disgusted with the way the council members made their decisions. I had these values drummed into my head as the Indian ways, but I didn't see them in council. I headed up a petition drive to protest a council decision to let Shell Oil drill for oil all over the reservation. We felt there were other means to bring about economic development. We won by ten votes.

"Women got the vote here in 1971 — as a necessary political move to get rid of a particular governor that the men couldn't get rid of by themselves. Opponents said, 'A baby is being born with this change; it will grow up, and someday it will bite you in the butt.'

"I am that baby."

Four months after she reached thirty-six, the lower age limit for governor decreed in the tribal constitution, Williamson went to the elders to ask their opinion of her running for the office. "I was real comfortable with the elders. Growing up in the village, most of my neighbors were old people. I asked them: will this be okay, for me to run? They knew there was going to be trouble, but they said, 'The government came to us from the Spanish. It didn't come out of Blue Lake with all those holy and sacred things. This is recent history — only three or four hundred years ago.'" They saw no barriers in "the Indian Way." And so she ran and was elected in 1986, to the horror of the old-guard male Isleta politicians.

Female leaders in Pueblo culture are not completely unknown. At the time of the founding of the Hopi village of Moenkopi in the mid-1800s, far from the Oraibi kikmongwi, the settlers chose Nashileowi, a woman of the Pi:kyas Clan, to be their political spokesperson. This was a secular position, with Moenkopi dependent on Oraibi ceremonially, but anthropologist Shuichi Nagata notes that Nashileowi had a firmer economic base than any other village chief in Hopiland. Other Hopi kikmongwis have recently designated their sisters as successors. Even today, however, most Pueblo women wield their power from the home, not the tribal office. Frances Tenorio, at Santo Domingo, says: "We will never have a woman governor here — not in my lifetime, anyway. Woman have plenty of power, nonetheless."

Williamson rallied through a constitutional amendment in the fall of 1990 to create a more representative council that could establish codes for water quality, natural resource management, and children's law and order without being "sabotaged" by the old guard. She left the governor's office in 1990 but remains on the council.

When Williamson became governor, she was very nervous about going into the kiva for the first time with all the men, to perform the governor's duties in a place where never before had there been a woman governor. The elders were her quiet supporters, so she knew in the end all would be well. They neglected to tell her, however, that one did not inhale sacred tobacco. When it came time to smoke, "one of the old guys laughed at my coughing and said, 'Check the governor out: she swallowed the smoke!'"

Verna Williamson speaks proudly of what she has accomplished: "It certainly has brought about opportunities for our young women. Now they know they can do things. This gave women more ownership of the community. It just makes us a better people. I see so many good, intelligent young people who have so much potential; I can hardly wait for them to be involved in tribal government!"

Opinionated, brash, feisty, and idealistic, she is also positive, sharing, and kind. Says Williamson of her optimism: "As long as you keep a good heart, you always win. Because good overcomes evil."

Pueblo leaders grapple with many issues. Health problems remain one of the most intractable. Reservation communities continue to breed more than their fair share of disease, just as they did in the days of smallpox, trachoma, and tuberculosis. Urban Indian people struggle to obtain decent health care. Alcohol and substance abuse are deadly; AIDS is on the increase among urban Indians and cannot help but eventually reach the pueblos.

Frances Tenorio, from Santo Domingo, has worked as a Community Health Educator for twenty years. She takes health education directly to a dozen Indian communities in northern New Mexico. "I enjoy working with grades K–3 on health issues. I like working with young adults, teaching them to not abuse alcohol so they can have healthy babies. But diabetes is rampant; there are more and more cases of cancer. A lot of our people don't have physicals; they go in too late."

Today, Indian Health Service hospitals cooperate with native healers. Theodora Sockyma, Hopi medicine woman and healer, says: "Before, the doctors at Keams Canyon had nothing to do with medicine men and sorcerers; they say it's just nothing but mumbo-jumbo. Now we're working together. It's not a question of competition — we work for this one person that's ailing, we need him to stand up again.

"If the doctors can't find anything wrong, it usually has something to do with our culture. If there's sickness of the mind, worriness, the People would rather go to their own medicine people than a psychiatrist. They need someone to sit down to talk to them. You don't just give them medication, you have to find out what it's all about.

"I'm glad I don't live in Salem: I would have been burnt long ago!"

Health, for Tewa people, means balance, harmony, connectedness, having a "heart that connects with the earth," in the words of Rina Swentzell and Tito Naranjo. This ideal is fast becoming rare. Frances Tenorio lists how "our life styles have changed. People used to have their own crops; now we buy more things, do more sedentary work, and people are not working off their fuel."

Tenorio emphasizes prevention. She fights the feeling of the elders that "we're immune to things like AIDS. We're not."

Those proud elders really count. Not only do they carry with them the core of the culture, but almost one-fourth of all rural American Indians are over sixty-one years old. The reason? Though one-third of Indian people leave reservations when they reach adulthood, well over half of those people come home when they grow old. They don't always return to an easy retirement.

Though almost 20 percent of reservation families still contain three or four generations, such extended families have been disrupted by housing developments, health problems, and the increasing insularity of the aged. Some sociologists believe that Indian elderly are the "most deprived group in the United States."

The key to well-being in old age is to live as an elder, not an elderly. To live as Millie Touchin's mother, at Laguna, lives: "My mother is seventy-three and sometimes she won't let my boys chop wood for her. She says it keeps her in shape." Or as her grandfather lived: "My grandfather used to pray every night for people out there with their cattle, for single parents — he prayed for everybody before he prayed for us in the household. Every morning he was out there again with his cornmeal."

As long as the community recognizes elders and gives them opportunities to fulfill their roles in tribal and ceremonial life, elders remain vital and purposeful. Santa Clara Pueblo is one pueblo actively creating a place where this can happen, breaking ground for a new Santa Clara Senior Citizens Community Center in May 1990.

One of the prime movers in creating this center is Tessie Naranjo. She says: "I imagine the community center as a collecting place of resources. The elders are the hosts, the storehouse of cultural information.

"We put the center across the street from the day school. We want to create a space to bring together elders and kids. Through designed interaction, cultural sensitivities get passed on. Just being together could create respect."

In the old days, of course, such "being together" happened without planning it. Tessie Naranjo's great-grandmother, for instance, raised more than thirty people, relations and nonrelations.

One of Naranjo's older sisters, Rina Swentzell, emphasizes women as the "stronghold of the community." She says, swirling her hands in the air: "My mother always has this thing going on around her. There's always someone coming to her for help or support. We become part of that swirl. One of the best things that ever happened to me was my great-grandmother taking me home. I'm raising two of my own grandchildren now. Those connections just go out . . ." She started swirling her hands again.

Tessie Naranjo smiled. "I don't know if I am a sociologist by personality, but I want to know the soul of the community. That's why I need to be here. I've had a long regard for generational things: pottery, cultural things, participation in dancing, extended family. Only in that way does culture survive; only in that way is culture active.

"It's the most precious thing I can think of to know absolutely where you belong. There's a whole emotional wrapping-around-of-you here. You see the same rock, tree, road, clouds, sun — you develop a nice kind of intimacy with the world around you. To be intimate is to grow, to learn. To be intimate with emotional space, physical space, that is what is absolutely fulfilling. Intimacy, that's my magic word for why I live here."

For most village residents, such intimacy fills only half of one's life; wage work turned Pueblo people into commuters. Only the growth of federal programs and tribal government has eased this burden. Winslow early on became the key urban area for the Hopi, their closest source of wage work. When Los Alamos was built during World War II, the Tewa pueblos had a new and dependable source of jobs. Frances Tenorio had eight brothers and sisters: "Here at Santo Domingo, the extended family is still strong. We all lived together. We all commuted. I have never lived in Santa Fe or Albuquerque." But, as Tessie Naranjo says: "You have to reach out to Santa Fe and Albuquerque to make your world wider, for education, organizations, friendships."

Wil Numkena commutes farther than most Pueblo people. One of only four Hopis living in Salt Lake City (as he told me in 1991), his home village of Upper Moenkopi lies nine hours of fast driving away. He says: "There is a void for me here in the city, both in physical surroundings and in your spirit or soul. I have to go back to my Hopi-ness to bring balance and harmony into my heart. I come back rejuvenated."

Today, the intimacy of living in the pueblo includes new experiences, new ways of living within the circle of Pueblo sacred mountains. As Lea Pinto says of her job directing the Zuni Wellness Center: "I never thought I would be able to combine my education in community health, recreation, and physical education with my responsibilities to my clan. The Wellness Center does that."

Dora Tse-Pe Peña of San Ildefonso is one of the great Pueblo potters. She comes from a traditional Zia family; she dances for feast days and goes to the kiva when she is called. All the basics of her pottery-making techniques resemble the age-old ways

Buffalo dancer, Head Start class, Laguna Pueblo, 1990. Controlling their schools has become crucial to Pueblo communities as they build a cultural foundation — beginning with Head Start and day-school programs.

of her People. But she also speaks frankly of the innovations she uses to create two-tone, high-polish pots by using a blowtorch to oxidize the light areas. "There's an art to that, too."

I stopped at Laguna to photograph the old mission on a stormy winter day, and found Joni Mooney, Antonette Silva, and Claressa Lucas rolling in the snow down the hill alongside the outer wall of the church. The bright colors of their coats and sweat pants and the laughter from the three delighted Laguna girls contrasted sharply with the still image of the church sitting with dignity atop the pueblo's hill. Down the road, the Laguna Head Start three-year-olds were dancing for a tour group in the tribal auditorium, wearing Eagle and Buffalo Dancer headdresses over their Teenage Mutant Ninja Turtle t-shirts decorated with dinosaur stickers.

I visited Zuni potters Randy Nahohai and Rowena Him and watched their toddler son, J.C., playing with his collection of stuffed animals, circling them around one of Randy's pottery katsina figures, making "hoo-hoo" katsina noises. He had just been to his first night dance. His parents said: "He behaved well, just sat and listened." The katsinas gave him arrows and a bow, which J.C. was playing with.

As I left San Ildefonso after a Buffalo Dance, a trio of youngsters in jeans and sweatshirts were mimicking the dance steps of the initiates, stomping in a tight circle in the bed of a pickup at the edge of the plaza. At Hopi, families gather in the kivas for February night dances with respect, but also with the enthusiasm of small town people waiting in line for the Saturday night double-feature at the only movie theater in town.

The sacred clowns embody the combination of old and new in both easy and powerful ways. Marcellus Medina, at Zia, tells the story of his grandfather being asked to dance at the Gallup Inter-Tribal Ceremonial in the fifties. He had no costume, so he gathered together odds and ends from the Gallup galleries and invented a crow or raven dancer, "a scavenger, a sort of clown." According to Medina, this figure is now danced regularly.

At Zuni, people speak of a summer rain dance when the clowns climbed atop the kivas and mimicked the stiff-legged gait of astronauts walking on the moon. As anthropologist Jane Young points out, the Zuni were shocked by the moon landers, "who heedlessly walked on the body of the moon mother and pierced her with metal instruments in order to bring back samples." One Zuni insisted to Young that the clowns could foretell this event, and danced their moonwalk the year *before* the first moon landing!

Tessie Naranjo says: "All the Pueblos are egotistic about their own community, but the similarities are more important than the differences. One good example is the

matriarchal beginning—feminine, nurturing. I asked a Taos nurse who worked at
Santa Clara Clinic, 'What makes a person healthy?' Without hesitation, she said, 'If my
parents are healthy and my children are healthy, I'm healthy.'" Edmund Ladd quotes
an old saying of his people: "The Zunis say, 'Nobody on his own strength has ever
succeeded.' You need the spiritual assistance, the guidance of those who have gone
before." As Hopi Terrance Honvantewa told me: "We are here on this Earth to be
teachers."

Even at those pueblos often dismissed as Hispanicized and secularized—like
Picuris, Nambe, or Pojoaque—it does not take long to find thoroughly Pueblo people.
When Cora Durand at Picuris or Virginia Gutierrez at Nambe/Pojoaque talk about
their pottery, you hear the statements of age-old connection between artist and clay
and spirit.

San Ildefonso potter Blue Corn believes that "if my children and grandchildren
carry on the pottery making that they have a lot of hope. If they are doing the pottery
making in the traditional way, with their hands without using a machine at all, it's
really a miracle—to them and to me, too."

As always, the Pueblo definitions of "health" and "hope" take in more than most
of us can imagine. Tony Dorame says: "It's hard to say where original Indian culture
ends and begins anymore." Everything is connected. It's much as Hopi-Tewa potter
Dextra Quotskuyva says of her sophisticated pieces: "Most of my designs are from
the dreams that I had, and from looking at the earth. Everything in the universe—the
plants, the rocks—everything in the earth inspires you. Everything seems to have life."

Nora Naranjo-Morse speaks of the circle that connects her with her clay people—
a circle that takes in thousands of years of history and connections to clouds and
mountains, spirits and underworlds. The Pueblo people live and pray and dance and
shape pots to maintain these connections.

I climbed one of the sacred mountains of the Tewa one autumn, the peak that loomed
over my own home in New Mexico. To protect the shrine, I won't say just which
mountain. A San Juan says: "It is the chief of all the mountains, the most sacred thing
we see each day." For this reason, some Tewa believe no human blood can be shed
on its slopes.

At the summit, ravens circled, swallows whizzed by. Trails came up from two
directions, from Tewa and Cochiti country, ending abruptly at the shrine in a quick
surprise, a slap of grace. A gray jay flew to the top of a conifer and called com-
panionably.

The shrine is a three-quarter circle of rocks, banked into the hillside, three feet
across, open to the east, to the rising sun. The mountain drops off to a far ridge with a

splotch of golden aspen, then to the Rio Grande valley below, then across to another distant sacred mountain — all in a knife-edge line with the shrine, with the summit. Offerings lay tenderly across the earth and cobbles of the shrine: spruce boughs, pot-sherds, prayer feathers made from turkey plumes, corn cobs, corn husks, cornmeal, deer molars.

The shrine rests at the top of the world, very close to the Cloud People. The mountain indeed feels like a sheltering presence. To the west, forested ridges roll on through wild country. To the east, the Rio Grande valley lies protected. It looks like a good place for the People to live.

The Navajo

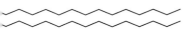

Navajo hitchhiker, Shiprock, New Mexico, 1989.

What we do to the land can destroy what gives us life. Even now there are springs that no longer run. I am talking not only for myself, but for those who may be born tonight. We have to think of them. How will they drink? How will they live? What kind of life are we giving them?

My father always told us that from the time of the Long Walk our ancestors' strongest advice was never to leave this land again, trade it, or sell it, because they suffered grief, tears, and death for their land.

I say to you, my children: Study! Prepare for a job! Plan for the future! But don't forget the land and the people who went before you. They will be your blessing and will make you strong.

Charles Yazzie Morgan, Towering House Clan, *Between Sacred Mountains*, 1982

"My clan is Bitter Water. I am Bitter Water. That's my identity." Navajo poet Luci Tapahonso goes on: "My connection to the land, to creation, to religion, is directly connected with the beginning: Bitter Water Clan created by the Holy People through Changing Woman."

Over and over again, Navajos speak of their powerful sense of identity. Place "ensures identity," as Tapahonso puts it — the place where you are born, where your placenta is buried, the tree next to the family sheep corral under which your umbilical cord lies. All mark your home, your place — where the Navajo, who call themselves Diné, the People, have woven their creation story from the fabric of the land. Tapahonso also says: "Your mother is your home. Having a mother is everything."

"The Navajo religion is *being* Navajo," says Jennie Joe, a Navajo educator and medical anthropologist: "Religion is something that you live every day. We get blinded by the word 'culture.' We would be far better off if Kluckhohn [the Anglo anthropologist who co-wrote *The Navaho*] had called us 'a religious sect.' We are much like the Amish, whose religion dictates their way of life. But we are not worried. We know who we are."

For Harry Walters, curator of the museum at Navajo Community College, "religion is culture." Period. He told me: "You often hear: 'All the old ways are gone.' In some ways, this is true. Yet we are still Navajos. The language may be a little different, ceremonies a little different. We may use a pickup instead of a horse to carry the ceremonial wand on the first day of Enemyway. Nevertheless, we are still a unique people."

Walters goes on: "Being a medicine man says you have to possess wisdom, leadership quality, knowledge in theology, art; you need to know colors associated with

Potter Kate Davis, Deeschii'nii Clan, 123
in front of her hogan. Cow Springs,
Arizona, 1986.

The Navajo

the cardinal directions, how to carve fetishes — it's all rolled into one. Every Navajo person, whether six or eighty-nine, possesses to some degree this knowledge."

At the same time, every publication about Navajos emphasizes their adaptability. The Diné came late to the Southwest and created their traditional culture from a diversity of sources: from their Athapaskan roots, from neighboring Pueblo and Paiute and Pai, from the borrowed technology and livestock of the Spaniards, and now from what they deem useful in the Anglo world. New peoples became Diné, and new clans were created to describe their kinship: Naakaii Dine'é (Mexican Clan), Naasht'ezhi Dine'é (Zuni Clan). After centuries of such incorporations, sixty Navajo clans exist. (Diné are "born to" their mother's clan and "born for" their father's.)

Diné integrated these beliefs within only a couple of generations of thoughtful living. New landscapes grew rich with myth, new ways became gifts of the Holy People, new beliefs passed into the Creation story.

Scholar Peter Iverson distinguishes between tradition, which connotes conservative, unchanging approaches to life, and style, which reflects change and choice, "ethnicity with room to maneuver." The Diné people retain a powerfully distinct

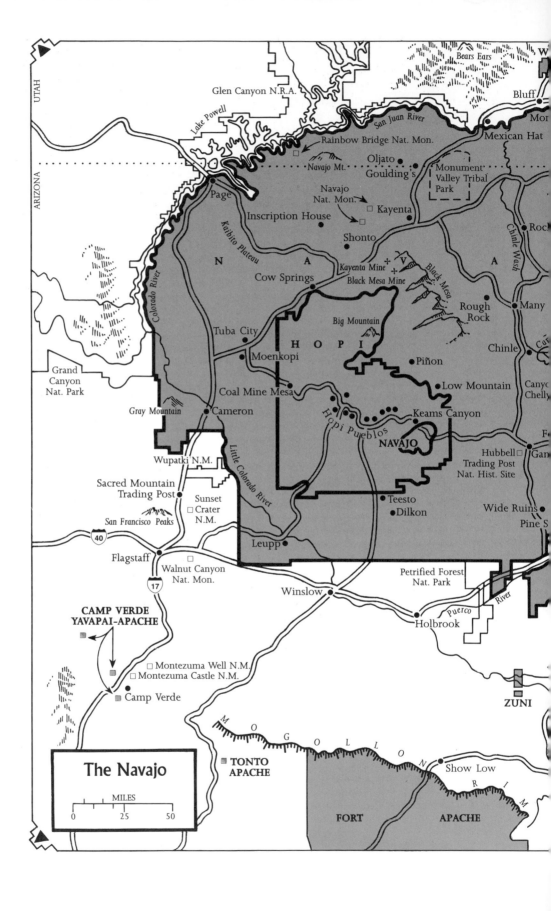

The Navajo

MILES

0   25   50

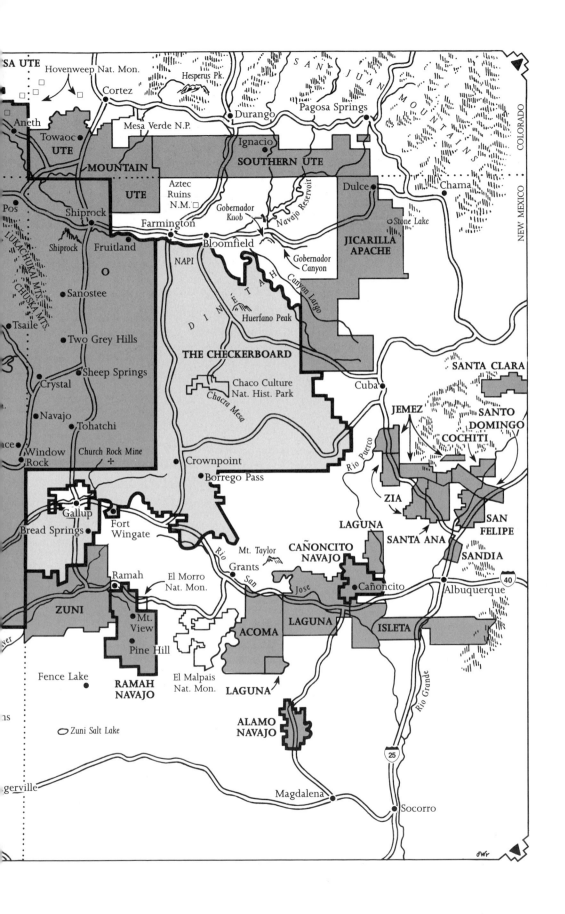

style; they live as Diné with great success. As the young Navajo teacher Rex Lee Jim says: "My students hear 'tradition' and they think of old things. Our *adaptability* is a tradition."

The resulting sturdy sense of Diné identity has carried the Navajo from their past to their present. Today, they number more than 200,000 — the nation's largest reservation-based Indian tribe, by far. They dwell in the Navajo Nation, 24,000 square miles of plateau lands, the nation's largest reservation, by far. Although the percentage of fluent Navajos decreases each year, 125,000 Diné on the reservation still spoke Navajo fluently in 1987. As Jennie Joe says, with awe as well as pride: "I see a Navajo Nation, not a tribe. I see Navajo students getting into Harvard Medical School. We have a full-time lobbyist for the Navajo Nation in Washington, D.C. I meet Navajos at Heathrow Airport in London and walking down the streets of Paris."

Peterson Zah, tribal president in 1992, has a prescription for dealing with the astonishing present and challenging future of his people: "My mother taught me, 'The most important thing in your life is that you will never lose sight of who you are and where you came from. Use your culture as a canoe. The white culture can put you in the mainstream. But your Navajo culture will keep you afloat.' Without that understanding of family and traditional values — intact, deep down inside of their hearts — Navajo people can't figure out the conflicts, and they tend to sink."

With that understanding, the People maintain a way of life that anthropologists have been studying for more than a century, without any slowdown at all in ethnographic publishing. (Indeed, an old joke lists the members of a Navajo family as a grandmother, her married daughters, their spouses and children, and one anthropologist! An updated version adds a filmmaker, an FBI undercover agent, and a white psychologist in search of "a separate reality.")

Navajos share much with outsiders, but much lies beyond the ken of any non-Diné. The languages simply diverge. Harry Walters says, with a wry grin: "I think in Navajo; but when I write in English what I'm thinking doesn't always appear on the page!" As one specialist in Navajo language said to me of my conversations in English with Walters: "It's like talking to him through a keyhole."

Even many Navajos have no deep understanding of what their key concept, *hózhǫ́*, really means. This makes sense; most Christians and Jews spend little time pondering their core beliefs. A Thomas Aquinas or Immanuel Kant or Martin Buber comes along once in a century. Great Navajo singers who dedicate their lives to study and ritual are rare.

What they study is the Navajo core. They study what it means to be alive, how to live responsibly, how to be Diné.

Living in Hózhǫ́

Sǫ'ah naaghéí bik'eh hózhǫ́.

These four nearly untranslatable words sum up Navajo philosophy. The last, hózhǫ́, often is used as an abbreviation for the whole, but Navajo teachers stress that both the phrase and the abbreviation possess power in ceremonial context, not in isolation. Ritual acts carry its meaning. A prayer need not end with this phrase as a benediction, for the essence of hózhǫ́ suffuses the whole prayer — and the Navajo language itself. Navajo people strive to maintain hózhǫ́, to live with hózhǫ́.

The earliest translators summed up the meaning of hózhǫ́ as "long life and happiness," which sounds suspiciously like the facile answer given by people worldwide when an outsider asks of a prayer, design, or amulet, "What does it mean?" Later, ethnologists strung together lists of all the things embraced by the concept of hózhǫ́: beauty, perfection, harmony, goodness, normalcy, success, well-being, blessedness, order, and ideal. All that we know is involved in hózhǫ́, thus everything is sacred.

Efforts at understanding how hózhǫ́ permeates Diné life fill scholarly bookshelves. More casual use of the concept extends to the names of small businesses across the Southwest and to the sermons and ceremonies conducted by non-Indian ecumenicists.

In one recent Anglo effort to explicate Navajo philosophy, John Farella concludes in his book, *The Main Stalk*, that *Sǫ'ah naaghéí bik'eh hózhǫ́* embraces wholeness, life force, rootedness in the Earth, completeness, "continuous generational animation."

The most important ceremonial symbol of hózhǫ́ is the Mountain Earth bundle. A singer presides over this powerful object, which contains pinches of soil from the tops of the four sacred mountains that bound Navajo Country. The earth nestles in a wrapping made from buckskin tanned from a deer run to exhaustion and killed by suffocation with a bag of corn pollen. The mountains give life to the land; the soil is the Earth's very flesh; the deerskin retains its life-force.

The bundle has the power of life. It can return an individual to hózhǫ́ during the restorative chants of a Blessingway ceremony, "reanimating" and bringing harmony as that Diné person moves back into everyday life and takes the risks associated with growth and adaptation. As singer George Blueeyes puts it:

> Because of this bundle we gain sheep, horses,
>   and cattle.
> We gain possessions and things of value,
>   turquoise, necklaces, and bracelets.
> With this we speak, with this we pray.
> This is where the prayers begin.

The prayers end with the certainty that hózhǫ has been restored; that statement of certainty is repeated four times. As Steve Darden, who has taught Navajo culture at Tuba City High School, says: "When we pray, we say 'It is finished in beauty.' We don't say, 'I hope it will be finished in beauty.' We say, 'It is.'"

The young Navajo artist Shonto Begay remembers "winter nights, gathered around our father, listening to stories passed down through generations."

We sat in expectation as we journeyed up from the womb of the Mother in creation stories. We sat mesmerized by coyote stories. Laughing at his antics and frightened by his cruelties. We sat in awe as First Man and First Woman brought forth life upon the Fourth World. We journey back from the west, the home of Changing Woman, into the midst of the Four Sacred Mountains after the creation of our clans. "Slayer of Enemies" and "Born for Water," the hero and savior of the fourth world, came alive for us these nights. I felt the pain of their fathers' testing in the roaring fire of the hearth. Their war with the Monster Gods raged as the snow storm dusted outside our door, snow sifting through the cracks of the door. Shadows leaping on cribbed wall of the *hooghan* brought to life the animal beings as the shoe game was created. As the nights wore on, the youngest ones of us fell asleep where we sat. My mother's spindle scratching the floor set the tempo of these late night journeys . . . back."

Stories structured into prayers become the "medicine" of singers, who chant to bring the attention of the Diyin Diné, the Holy People, to exorcise evil, to restore hózhǫ to the patient. Steve Darden describes ceremonies as "blueprints to recreate beauty." Diné prescribe ceremonies whenever anyone seems to be ill or in trouble, thrown out of balance by contact with corpses, whites (*bilagaana*), ghosts, or witches ("skinwalkers" or "human wolves"). Witchcraft constantly threatens, but with proper ceremonial protection, the witch's evil backfires and the witch dies soon after. In the past, Navajos took great precautions in burying a dead person (along with the belongings of the deceased) and purified themselves afterward. Today, more and more Diné avoid such contact by using funeral homes and cemeteries, and several Navajos have become morticians. Nonetheless, several thousand dollars of silver and turquoise still may be buried in the Anglo-style casket alongside the deceased loved one.

Harry Walters says of the twenty-four chantway systems: "The two main branches are Holyway (for healing and blessing) and Protectionway (or Warriorway)." *Sǫ'ah naaghéí bik'eh hózhǫ* permeates the Holyway but is not used in Protectionway. Each chant is its own mini-religion; only about eight still are sung frequently. The Enemy-way (called the Squaw Dance by Anglos) is performed only in summer; Nightway is a

Navajo dancers from the Nightway, a winter ceremony, 1930s or 1940s. The ceremony climaxes on its ninth night with the Ye'ii Bicheii dance (named for Talking God, the "grandfather of the Ye'ii"). Photo by Burton Frasher. (Courtesy Museum of New Mexico, neg. no. 74870)

winter ceremony, climaxing on its ninth night with the Ye'ii Bicheii dance (named for Talking God — the "Grandfather of the Ye'ii," the group of Holy People impersonated by the dancers). Diné sing the Blessingway anytime, to "repair those torn threads in this tapestry of the universe," as Jennie Joe says. They sing Blessingway as a prayer and a precaution, to keep the winds of life blowing strong and harmoniously, to stay in tune with the Holy People. Blessingway is the backbone of the Navajo ceremonial system. Harry Walters notes that ceremonies have incorporated new technology, but: "You never hear of Monster Slayer or Born For Water herding sheep or riding horses!"

From the Blessingway singers came the peace chief for each community, chosen for his oratorical power and knowledge of the chant. War chiefs not only showed skill in battle but knew the Warway Chants, as well.

Birth brings life, and so sexuality and birth are sacred. A young woman's coming of age is good and powerful, and her "womanhood ceremony," her kinaaldá, is a time for celebration, reanimation, a time for Blessingway. Kinship stands at the center of Navajo morality because it connects a Diné person with the movement of generations. Navajo elders admonish the People to "act as if everybody were related to you."

In its turn, death reanimates the Earth. Diné educator Rose Hulligan says: "The Earth has a song; the Earth has a prayer." Movement, change, adaptation — all intertwine with the core of the Navajo outlook on the world. Danny Blackgoat, Navajo teacher, says: "We are one with the universe, not 'we are part of . . .'"

No wonder historians and anthropologists conclude their books with exclamations about the Navajos' ability to incorporate, integrate, and adapt — all the while remaining Diné. Jennie Joe isn't so surprised: "We wouldn't be called 'Children of Changing Woman' if we were not!"

Dinétah: The Journey In, the Journey Out

Unique among Southwestern Indians, the Apacheans (Apaches and Navajos) speak Athapaskan languages. Their linguistic kin live far to the north, in Canada and Alaska and on the Pacific Coast. In a never-ending debate, anthropologists have tried to track the Apachean migration southward. They may have come through the mountains; they may have moved south on the plains along the base of the mountains. Different groups may have used different routes. Dating their travels has proved well-nigh impossible.

Hunters and gatherers leave meager evidence: tipi rings, brush wickiups, mescal roasting pits, and buffalo kill sites — even the more substantial ruins of Navajo hogans are hard to find three hundred years later. Languages, however, carry history within them. Linguists can analyze the differences between dialects and estimate how long any two have been separated. By such wisps of evidence, the Apacheans seem to have started moving south about A.D. 1000. Before 1400, the Athapaskan speakers who would become Navajo moved into the Southwest.

Only then did the people who call themselves Diné begin their life within the four sacred mountains: to the east, Sisnaajiní, Blanca Peak in the Sangre de Cristo Range in Colorado; to the south, Tsoodził, Mount Taylor, standing high above north-central New Mexico; to the west, Dook'o'oosłííd, the San Francisco Peaks at Flagstaff, Arizona; and to the north, Dibé nitsaa, Hesperus Peak in the La Plata Mountains at Durango, Colorado.

All mountains are sacred, full of stories and power, and many other landmark peaks in Navajo Country rise past the Earth Horizon. The great dividing highlands of the region stand in balance: the male Chuska Mountains and the female Black Mesa, with her head northward at the pivotal blue dome of Navajo Mountain. Rain and snow drawn to these summits nourish medicinal herbs. The sacred mountains rise with grace above tan and rust-colored mesas and the intricate, interfingering sandstone canyons, into the shining sky. Prayers, songs, and myths repeat the names of these sacred places — a powerful grounding.

Navajo tradition tells of the first home of the People in northwesternmost New Mexico: a place called Dinétah ("among the Navajo"). Here the Spaniards found the Diné in 1600, when they called them the "Apaches de Nabajo." The Diné flourished in this land beyond the Pueblo frontier: the Spaniards spoke of them as a numerous and important tribe.

Unlike their northern Athapaskan kin, these people had learned to farm (indeed, "Nabajo" is probably derived from a Tewa word for "planted fields"). They had learned pottery making and, perhaps, weaving, on their journey southward. In this new land, northern ways became southwestern ways. Even the language shows traces of the journey: the Diné word for the flight of an owl is the northern Athapaskan word for the motion of paddling a canoe; Diné "gourd dipper" comes from Athapaskan "horn spoon."

Here, near the mesa today called Huerfano Mountain, lived First Man and First Woman, emerging into Dinétah from the Third World. Here, Talking God showed how to build a hogan, the round Navajo home. Here, Coyote flipped a blanketful of stars into the heavens, creating the Milky Way. Here, in Red Rock Canyon on the east flank of the Lukachukai Mountains, One Walking Giant taught the People how to play the shoe game. Here, First Man and First Woman found the infant Changing Woman on top of Gobernador Knob.

Changing Woman grew up in Dinétah. The first puberty ceremony was performed here for her by the Holy People. Here she gave birth to the Twins who would rid this Fourth World of its monsters.

Here lie the roots of Diné.

When the Spaniards arrived in the Southwest, the Navajo and Apache had surrounded the Pueblos. Sometimes Navajo and Pueblo warred; between skirmishes they traded together, the Navajo frequenting Jemez and Santa Clara pueblos, in particular. Navajos helped the Pueblo people in their revolt against Spain in 1680. Pueblo refugees fled west in the years of the Spanish reconquest, and this became a pivotal time for the Diné.

Tewa, Jemez, Keresan, and Zuni people lived with the Diné in the southern tributaries of the San Juan River (between today's Jicarilla Apache Reservation and Farmington), in Dinétah. The Pueblo people came to the canyons in numbers; they brought with them the full wealth of their culture, including clans passed on through female lineages, decorated pottery, innovative weaving techniques, katsina dances, and masonry homes. The resulting Pueblo-Diné "pueblitos" — built in such canyons as Largo and Gobernador — were complexes of defensive towers, hogans, and small pueblos, whose people left behind distinctive rock art and "Gobernador polychrome" pottery.

When the Utes began to pressure these *pueblitos*, the stability of Pueblo and Athapaskan living side-by-side fractured. But the incubation period of the Gobernador years made permanent the incorporation of Pueblo traits into Navajo culture. When the Diné expanded outward from Dinétah in the mid-1700s, they were essentially the Navajo as we know them today. Pueblo refugees who went west with them became Diné, with clan designations to identify their roots.

They carried west a new way of life forged from what Pueblo ways the People favored combined with their Athapaskan bedrock — all sanctioned by Blessingway. Some Anglo scholars think of these transformed Diné as "biological and cultural hybrids, neither Athapaskan nor Puebloan, but a product of both," as ethnohistorians Garrick and Roberta Bailey put it.

The People took with them, too, their goats, sheep, and horses, originally stolen from the Spanish and Pueblos but long since raised by Navajo. Sheep gave the Navajo an economy unique for Southwestern Indians (and the new lands the Diné now pioneered made better sheep country than Dinétah, whose tortuous canyons were more suited to goats).

They hunted, they gathered, they farmed; they raided and traded with Hispanic and Pueblo settlements; they raised livestock. With sheep as a dependable source of protein, the Navajo eliminated much of the risk in exclusive dependence on the vagaries of wild crops or weather-dependent agriculture. As long as sheep could forage, the Navajo ate well.

And with sheep to shear, the weaving of wool became a staple of the Navajo economy. (One old tradition speaks of raiding Hopi primarily to capture weavers —

Navajo orator Steve Darden explains that sheep are "gifts from the Holy People. While we are herding sheep, we are their mother, the sheep are the children. When we butcher that sheep, then that sheep is taking care of us. It is giving us life." Photo by William M. Pennington, 1940. (Courtesy Denver Public Library, Western History Department)

Pueblo men to teach Navajo women.) Women, who owned the sheep and wove blankets from their wool, became the most dependable contributors to a Diné family's economy.

That fact remains true. When Isabell Deschinny and her husband, Daniel, were living in Washington, D.C., while he attended law school, they ran out of money. Isabell sent word home to Arizona, and her mother, the legendary weaver Mabel Burnside Myers, sent yarn and tools. Isabell then "wove us out of that predicament," in Daniel's words.

Herders, Warriors, Slaves

Diné people in the eighteenth century shared a language, ceremonial system, clan-based kinship, and economy, but they did not share a tribal consciousness. Each extended family (often a woman and her spouse plus her daughters and their families) roamed a valley or mesa with their sheep, moving between summer and winter hogans up to forty miles apart. Once they became sheepherders, the People were no more nomadic than an Anglo rancher with a home place and a summer sheep camp in the mountains.

Several related families in an area ("outfits") cooperated in larger farming, herding, and ceremonial tasks. Even today, says Rose Hulligan: "The man doesn't just marry his wife, he marries the whole family!" For the English word "family," with its more limited "nuclear" meaning, the Diné use a Navajo term that means "one-hogan group."

The best summer homes had bottomlands and sufficient water for farming; winter homes needed to be low enough in elevation to have sheep forage not often covered by snow but high enough to have a sufficient wood supply for heating hogans. Winter homes nestled against sheltering landforms to absorb warmth from the southern sky. Anthropologists Klara Kelley and Peter Whiteley sum up the requirements for Navajo families depending on farming and stock raising for their lives: "water, wood, forage, and land subject to at least 130 frost-free days, and either twelve inches of annual precipitation or irrigation water."

The movement of Navajo people in numbers into country they had only lightly used—beyond the Chuska Mountains to Canyon de Chelly, south to Chacra Mesa (near Chaco Canyon), and still farther south into the land around Mt. Taylor—proceeded in relative peace for decades. The Diné and the Spaniards needed each other as allies to fight the Utes. After 1773, however, New Spain allied itself with the Ute and Comanche enemy, and war became unavoidable for the Navajo.

The next decades were an endless round of raid, retaliation, peace treaty, and renewed raiding. The People did well for themselves in defending their lands and held their own against encroaching settlement from the east. The crucible of battle began to forge them into a nation, though primary loyalty remained with local headmen and with clans.

In January 1805, Antonio Narbona led Spanish troops and Indian (Pueblo and Mexican Opata) auxiliaries right into de Chelly, defeating a group of Navajo in their stronghold. The People took refuge in a high alcove now known as Massacre Cave in Cañon del Muerto, "the Canyon of Death" — the canyon named later for burials found in its Anasazi ruins, but named appropriately nonetheless.

When Mexico achieved its independence, slave raids against the Navajo accelerated — conducted by slavers both from Mexico and from other Indian tribes. In retaliation, Navajo men raided the settlements and pueblos, returning with metal tools, firearms, and women. These captives and their children became Diné, increasing their numbers. While Navajo men hunted and raided, the women gathered herbs, herded the flocks, kept the mutton stew pot full, and raised children. The Navajo flourished, completely beyond Hispanic control, even though the wars continued.

Not every Navajo band approached these conflicts in the same way. Navajo families who had lost their women and children to captivity on the Rio Grande were the most passionate speakers when outfits and their headmen met to discuss the future. Those who favored peace with the whites (and who later scouted for U.S. troops in campaigns against their own people) came to be called "Enemy Diné." As early as 1818, or earlier, one such group began to isolate itself from the main group of Diné, living a more settled and agricultural existence close to Spanish settlements, even agreeing to listen to Christian missionaries for a couple of years; today, this group lives alone on the Cañoncito Reservation, below Mt. Taylor near Laguna Pueblo.

When the United States won the Southwest in 1846, Pueblos and New Mexicans demanded protection from Navajo raiders. The United States Army found Navajo headmen to sign peace treaties but never realized that each Diné leader spoke for at most a few hundred people amongst the more than ten thousand Navajo. The Navajo term for headman, *naat'aani*, did not translate as "chief;" it derived from the verb, "to orate."

Then, as now, Navajo Country lay out in the mesas and canyons of the Colorado Plateau — land wanted by few others. The tribes already there — Hopi, Zuni, Southern Paiute, and Pai — used much of northeastern Arizona and southeastern Utah lightly. Diné herders gradually took advantage of the considerable room left them, transforming the land, in the words of Navajo journalist Marshall Tome, into "this place that is all of us and we are all of it."

Today, Navajo homesteads make the land inhabited, but they scatter across the open country inconspicuously. The homesteads have the same horizontal lines as the land. I drive through this "empty" land and when I look beyond the highway, homes stand in every reasonable site — below cliffs, between mesas, on hilltops, in swales — denser than you think. When I search for a dirt road campsite off the highway, I must look long and hard to avoid camping in someone's front yard. My best bets prove to be stock tanks and windmills, the closest thing to public lands I can find.

Each family has its own separate relationship to the sun — a more intimate relation with nature than with each other. Even when HUD houses or trailers stand alongside a hogan, the new houses generally face east. It's as if a giant magnet swept through and aligned every structure with a force greater than human choice.

I stood on a ridge at the base of Red Mesa in Utah, talking with a young Navajo man who had lived "away" for seven years before his recent return home. He talked about the houses three or four miles away, telling me the stories of the people who lived there. They were clearly the neighbors, the way suburban families facing each other across a street are neighbors. But these Diné neighbors were so far away, I had to look closely even to see them. My acquaintance had "Navajo eyes."

Between 1846 and 1850, northwestern New Mexico reported nearly 800,000 sheep and cattle and 20,000 horses and mules lost to the Diné, perhaps no more than a twofold exaggeration. The army marched through Navajo Country to discipline the People, but the Diné would not fight unless attacked.

In 1849, however, the American cavalry escalated its campaign. On 31 August, troops discussed peace with the Diné headman, Narbona, at Two Grey Hills. A dispute over a stolen horse left Narbona and six other Navajos shot in the back. Narbona was father-in-law to the great warrior Manuelito, who was not prone to make peace after this event.

Diné leaders who signed peace treaties often were the ricos, "rich men" with great herds; they could not control the poorer Navajo who had no choice but to raid for food, wealth, and status. The fifteen years following Narbona's murder played out the usual misunderstandings and injustices. Navajo history was revolutionized in the process.

The Long Walk

During the 1850s, New Mexicans moved their herds into Navajo grazing lands. Slave raids continued unabated. And rumors of mineral wealth influenced the decisions of army generals. In 1851, the army set up Fort Defiance (near today's Win-

Navajo farmstead near Chaco Canyon, New Mexico, 1982. Each family has its own relationship to the sun — a more intimate relation with nature than with other families. Even when HUD houses or trailers stand alongside a hogan, the new houses generally face east. Photo by Paul Logsdon. (Courtesy Marcia L. Logsdon)

dow Rock); it was built on a sacred site. The Navajo saw the post as a formal invasion of their country, and conflict was virtually inevitable.

An honest and sympathetic Indian agent, Henry Linn Dodge, kept relative peace in the first half of the 1850s; he also brought an Anglo blacksmith and his Mexican silversmith assistant to Fort Defiance, and Navajo silverwork flourished from this time on. In 1858, a new anti-Navajo commanding officer at Fort Defiance appropriated Navajo grazing land surrounding the post for his horses. Any Navajo horses found in the pastures were shot. Not long after, a Navajo shot the servant of Captain William Brooks, the commandant.

Brooks insisted, over the protests of more reasonable officers, that if the local Navajo did not produce the killer, he would go to war with the whole nation. The hotheads prevailed, and within a month, an army colonel had issued a unilateral declaration of war on the Navajo. Succeeding campaigns killed scattered groups of peaceful Navajos and alienated many who had signed peace agreements. Each new treaty whittled away at the eastern Navajo grazing lands, making it more and more unlikely that the Diné would cease raiding.

On 30 April 1860, more than one thousand Navajos under Manuelito of the Tohatchi area, Barboncito of the Canyon de Chelly area, and Herrero attacked and came close to taking Fort Defiance. In succeeding forays, both regular troops and New Mexican volunteers disrupted the People, killing those Diné they could catch, including the important leader Zarcillas Largo.

As the Civil War drew the attention of the military, slave raiders from New Mexico operated against the Navajo with almost a free hand. Fort Defiance was abandoned; the army left only a small force at Fort Fauntleroy (near modern Gallup), later called Fort Wingate. One estimate tallied up to six thousand Navajo slaves in New Mexico. In turn, Navajos began raiding as far as Santa Fe and Zuni.

General James Carleton put an end to this power struggle in 1863. He had arrived from California too late to fight Confederate troops in New Mexico, so he turned his attention first to the Mescalero Apache, whom he defeated in five months. Carleton then revived the already-formulated army plan to remove Navajos from their homeland, ending once and for all their "murders . . . robberies . . . [and] atrocities." For the new Navajo home he chose the Mescalero concentration camp of Fort Sumner, at Bosque Redondo on the Pecos River. In Carleton's mind, this "tribal reformatory, away from the haunts and hills and hiding places of their country," would surely be a place where the "wild Indians" could be civilized.

The general assigned Colonel Kit Carson to the Navajo campaign. The old mountain man believed war with the Navajo unnecessary, but he nonetheless carried out his orders with frightful thoroughness.

Carson's volunteers began their campaign in August 1863. They systematically burned fields and hogans, took livestock, chopped down orchards, and killed the few Diné they could find (an official total of 301 for 1863). The surrounding tribes, old enemies of the Navajo, took this chance to raid with unchecked force. As the Navajo storytellers put it: "The Utes did so, the Mexicans did so, the Pueblo Indians did so, the Hopi did so."

After Carson's foray into Canyon de Chelly in January 1864, many starving Navajo came in under a flag of truce to determine the consequences of surrender. They learned of the plan for a reservation at Bosque Redondo, where they would be clothed and fed and allowed to retain their stock. Two hundred Navajo surrendered within the next few days, and Carson made good on his promises. Word spread through the land of the People, and by the end of February, twenty-five hundred starving Navajo had come in to Fort Canby (the rebuilt Fort Defiance), another twelve hundred to Fort Wingate. The first fourteen hundred Navajo reached faraway Fort Sumner in late January.

More followed throughout the year, many fighting through winter blizzards.

Hundreds died on the way, sick and weakened by the scorched-earth campaign, or old
and unable to keep up. Beyond the comparatively benevolent command of Carson,
soldiers shot stragglers. Other Diné lost their children to slavers hovering along the
route eastward. The way led across New Mexico for 370 miles (an alternate route
added 100 miles).

This was the Long Walk.

The Long Walk remains vivid in the minds and hearts of the Diné, though little
more than half the Diné made the trip. During their four-year imprisonment, hundreds of Navajos escaped from Fort Sumner and made miraculous journeys home.
The thousands of Diné in hiding were self-sufficient — herding, farming, gathering
plants, and hunting — already rebuilding the life of the Diné before the rest of the
People came home from the Long Walk.

Edward Spicer equates the magnitude of the experience for the Navajo to that
of the Civil War for the South. Today's elders heard the stories told to them by their
grandparents who lived through the ordeal. Those of us who do not have Navajo
grandparents can listen to *Navajo Stories of the Long Walk Period*, reminiscences of forty
Diné published by Navajo Community College Press in 1973:

Howard Gorman, Ganado, Arizona, Bitter Water Clan: "These Navajos had done
nothing wrong. For no reason they had been taken captive and driven to Hweeldi
(Fort Sumner). While that was going on, they were told nothing — not even what it
was all about and for what reasons. The Army just rounded them up and herded them
to the prison camp."

Curly Tso, Page, Arizona, Many Goats Clan: "Personally, I often wondered, after I
became aware of White Men's laws, why our ancestors were treated so unjustly. White
Men make and preach about all kinds of laws, laws that protect individual rights; and
where were these laws then?"

Bosque Redondo made a poor home for nine thousand Diné. Alkaline water made
the People sick. Firewood was scarce, and became scarcer during four years of Navajo
imprisonment. The same lack of timber made proper hogans impossible. The People
attempted to honor the army demand that they farm, and labored to plant six thousand acres; each year caterpillars, drought, hail, or floods destroyed their crops. Smallpox killed more than two thousand Diné in 1865. Ration deliveries were contracted to
crooks, and few of the already meager appropriations reached the People. Comanches
stole their horses.

Manuelito had hidden in the northern frontier of Navajo Country, but in the
autumn of 1866, Ute raids finally wore him down. He, too, surrendered and joined
the Bosque Redondo captives.

Manuelito in 1866, the year the great war chief surrendered and joined the Bosque Redondo captives. He remained a major leader of the People for another 20 years, serving as head chief after the return of the Diné from the Long Walk. Photo by Charles Bell. (Courtesy Museum of New Mexico, neg. no. 23130)

The federal government spent over $2 million in 1865 to manage the Navajo in this new "home." Carleton's critics ranted about his misguided ethics (and they weren't thrilled with so many Indians in the midst of eastern New Mexico ranchland, either). By anyone's reckoning, the Bosque Redondo scheme was a disaster. General Carleton was relieved of his command in the fall of 1866.

The whites designated a dozen leaders, including Herrero, Ganado Mucho, and, of course, Manuelito, the war leader. Barboncito, a peace chief, acquired far more power than he would have in normal Navajo times. The army contemplated sending the People to Texas or Oklahoma. But the Diné orators spoke passionately, declaring their resistance to further displacement. Barboncito said: "I hope to God that you will not ask me to go to any other country except my own."

Navajo singers used Visionway to ask questions of the Holy People about the future of the captive Diné. The medicine men knew cures for their people's troubles but would not perform some chants so far beyond the four sacred mountains. Near the end, the People conducted the Put A Bead in Coyote's Mouth ceremony. They encircled a female coyote in a ring of Diné. Barboncito placed in her mouth a piece of specially carved white shell. She left the circle, headed west. Barboncito said, "There it is, we will be set free." The People negotiated with the soldiers with new confidence, blessed with the power of Coyote.

On 1 June 1868, the headmen made their marks on the Treaty of Bosque Redondo. The Navajo Wars ended. The Diné went home to what anthropologist Ruth Underhill called their "third beginning," equal in historic moment to their arrival in the Southwest and the exodus from Dinétah. Medicine men performed hundreds of Enemyway ceremonies to purge the Diné of the white man's evil and to bring them back into balance with their world.

The Invention of the Navajo Tribe

The People returned to rejoin their kin. Every clan has stories of families who hid from Kit Carson in the rugged country around Navajo Mountain, with the Apache along the Mogollon Rim, in Paiute Country north of the San Juan River, or in Monument Valley (under the headman Haashkeneinii, or "Hoskinnini"). Some small groups allied themselves with Paiutes in the rough country of the Kaibito Plateau, much as refugee Pueblos had allied themselves with Diné two centuries before. No wonder the Diné were not destroyed by the experience. No wonder they did not confine themselves to their new treaty reservation.

The satellite communities of Navajos in New Mexico got their starts after the return from Bosque Redondo. The Ramah community grew from the family of Many

Beads, who escaped from Fort Sumner, took refuge with the Chiricahua Apache, and returned to the Ramah area, joining another family centered around a man named Cojo. Bidaga, the son of Many Beads, was the longtime patriarch of the Ramah community, living until 1956.

The Enemy Navajo, led by Delgadito Chiquito, returned to their homes at Cañoncito. And the Alamo (also called Puertocito) Navajos west of Socorro became permanently distinct when the Bosque returnees joined their kin already living at Alamo — previously escaped refugees both from Carson and Carleton and from Spanish slave masters in Socorro. Each of these three Diné groups eventually grew into a permanent reservation.

When, at Fort Sumner, the federal government elevated Barboncito to "Head Chief of the Navajo," with Manuelito and Ganado Mucho as "sub-chiefs," half the population of Diné watched. The years at Bosque Redondo impoverished the People, and when they returned home, they had to depend on rations for several years before they could support themselves again from fields and herds. These two experiences new to the People dominated the next two decades: tribal "chiefs" and the federal government as a supervising force in their lives.

In 1869, the government lived up to its promise to give fourteen thousand sheep and a thousand goats to the Diné. Intensive hunting in these years when stock numbers stayed low led to most game being hunted out. Goats became the Navajo mainstay, for they yielded milk and cheese in addition to meat. Navajo herds began to grow; Navajo families began to look for new grazing land.

The 1868 treaty designated a rectangle of reservation land that embraced about 10 percent of what had been Navajoland. Non-Indian stockmen believed more in the reservation boundaries than did the Diné herders. A decade later, Navajos lived across nine million acres — twice the area of the treaty reservation.

Ganado Mucho, the wealthy owner of "many cattle," and Manuelito both took their turns as head chief after the death of Barboncito in 1870. In that same year, Manuelito was the first chief to use force to stop raiding by other Diné. In 1872, he became head of the "Navajo Cavalry" invented by the agency to police his people. Manuelito grew dispirited in his last years and took to whiskey. In 1884, the agent appointed Henry Chee Dodge to replace the aged warrior.

Chee Dodge, then only twenty-four, had grown up around Fort Defiance and learned more fluent English than any other Navajo. Half Mexican by blood but thoroughly Navajo by culture, he became primary interpreter between Anglo and Diné. With these skills, he rose quickly from chief herder to special courier to chief of scouts, and then, to head chief. He would continue to hold a pivotal leadership role for more than sixty years.

When the Diné herders demanded new land, their heartland of canyons and plateaus had yet to prove attractive to Anglo and Hispanic homesteaders. Between 1878 and 1886, the original 3.5 million acres defined by the treaty grew by 8 million acres, in five executive-order additions (including the 1882 Hopi-Navajo Joint Use Reservation that came to be so controversial in the late twentieth century). The Navajo already living in these areas acquired legal protection. Dinétah grew into Diné Bikeyah, Navajo Country.

As the People increased in numbers, they began to jostle against the margins of the non-Indian world, encountering Mormons expanding southward from Utah, other Anglos moving north from the new Santa Fe Railway line, and Hispanics moving west from New Mexico. The Diné hotly contested grazing lands, for without raiding, stock raising grew preeminent. Throughout the 1880s, with the chance to ship cattle east on the railroad, cattle numbers grew and sheep numbers fell. In turn, by 1883 Indian agents reported overgrazing.

Though homesteading was technically open to Navajos, efforts to homestead beyond the reservation boundaries never worked. Whites refused to acknowledge hogans and *ramadas* as the investments required to "prove up." Many times Navajos came home to a summer or winter camp to find their hogans destroyed and their homestead land usurped.

When today's Navajos speak of the old, traditional life, they think of the quiet decades from the 1870s to the 1920s. Hogans began to evolve from a forked-stick, mud-covered dwelling to the cribbed-log octagon made feasible by wagons to haul wood and surplus railroad ties, and sawmills and steel axes to cut them.

The tribe grew in population — to twenty thousand in 1900 and to forty thousand by 1930. Their herds grew with them, in the 1890s for the first time reaching numbers that could support Navajo families with no supplemental farming, hunting, or gathering. Indeed, at about this time, the wealthier Navajos chose to trade for their corn and other crops rather than farm themselves. This certainly did not testify to lack of Navajo skill in farming: in 1879, the Navajo agent stated that "a Navajo with a sharp stick and hoe can get one-half to one-third more returns than a white man with the best machinery."

Merino and Rambouillet rams brought into the reservation by government breeding programs added their genes to the hardy little churro sheep descended from the Spanish herds. These new breeds may have made better meat producers, but they diminished the quality of Navajo wool, for nothing could beat the smooth, long-staple, non-oily wool of the churro. (In the 1980s, range scientists began restoring churros to the Navajo.) A shift to Angora goats emphasized commercial mohair production over milking potential.

Navajo family, 1930. When today's Navajos speak of the old traditional life, they think of the quiet decades from the 1870s to the 1920s. As the tribe grew in population — from 20,000 in 1900 to 40,000 by 1930 — their herds grew with them, setting the stage for the trauma of stock reduction. Photo by T. Harmon Parkhurst. (Courtesy School of American Research)

Herds grew to enormous numbers — a million and a half sheep and goats by 1892. The prosperous Navajos ranged far beyond the reservation borders with their stock; their economic success made them independent of most government and missionary attempts to Americanize them. They were the only American Indian tribe rapidly increasing in numbers in these years.

Disaster lurked, however. Disputes between Anglo cowboys and Diné sheepmen led to sporadic violence. The Panic of 1893 ruined the wool market. A severe drought in the summer of that year followed by a terribly harsh winter began ten years of

unpredictable weather that dropped Diné livestock numbers by 75 percent. When
the tribe began to rebuild its economy in the early twentieth century, the People
switched from subsistence herding to raising stock for market. Wage labor became
more common. Navajo children began attending school in larger numbers.

Though BIA-appointed chiefs served as an interface between the People and the
government, local headmen retained their influence. The years between 1868 and
1924, as Edward Spicer notes, resulted in steady decentralization of power — in some
ways a return to the old days of independence.

In 1915, the BIA divided the reservation into five districts, with agencies at Tuba
City, Leupp, Shiprock, Crownpoint, and Fort Defiance (plus the Hopi Agency at Keams
Canyon, which administered to many Navajo, as well). These agencies divided the
tribe, to some extent, and within each area a loose council of local headmen took
precedence over any tribal authorities. In 1955, a reorganization created sub-agencies
at Tuba City (which absorbed the Leupp area), Shiprock, Crownpoint, Fort Defiance,
and Chinle. These communities retain their character as government towns today.

Leupp formed the earliest local business council in about 1904; the Leupp BIA
superintendent created local chapters in 1927, a new level of organization of about five
hundred related people surrounding a trading post. Within ten years, nearly all Diné
both on and off the reservation belonged to chapters. In 1991, the tribal council approved its 110th chapter, Nahat'a'Dzil, south of Sanders, Arizona, in new lands granted
the Diné in the Navajo-Hopi land partition. Chapters now average about twelve hundred people each and form the primary community-level political unit.

Education, too, played a larger and larger role. Families initially kept the stronger children at home to herd and learn the old ways. A decade after the return from Bosque
Redondo, the Fort Defiance school served only eleven Navajo students. Efforts to en-
force attendance began in 1887, and the Navajos, like all Southwestern Indians, tell
stories of children rounded up and hauled away to die of tuberculosis far from home.
In 1892, of eighteen thousand Diné, less than a hundred Navajos attended school.

The exposure of nineteen headmen and younger leaders to the non-Indian world
of Chicago when they went to the 1893 Columbian Exposition changed the course
of Navajo education. The first day school opened at Tohatchi in 1895. Many families
began sending their strongest children to school. They began to heed old Manuelito's
words: "It is as though the whites were in a grassy valley, with wagons, plows, and
plenty of food, we Navajos up on a dry mesa. We can hear them talking, but we cannot
get to them. My grandchild, school is the ladder. Tell our people this."

Some Diné still protested compulsory education, most notably the Utah Navajo
headman Ba'ililii in 1907, who was imprisoned without trial for a year and a half for

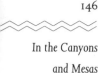
taking his stand against forced removal of all local Navajo children to the Shiprock boarding school. By 1913, however, the eight BIA boarding schools on the reservation — in addition to more distant off-reservation schools and several mission schools — began educating hundreds of Navajos in Anglo ways.

In those days, families traveled at least as much as they do today. As Amos Coggeshall, an elder from Rock Point, says in *Between Sacred Mountains*: "We traveled so much in those days. We did not worry about our hogans and blankets and valuable things. When we came back they would all be there." Diné traveled with their flocks, to find grass, to the piñon harvest. They traveled between winter and summer hogans, between fields and firewood. They traveled far for ceremonies. They traveled to hear stories.

And they traveled to the trading posts.

Traders to the People

The People returned home from the Long Walk with a new taste for coffee sweet with sugar and for fry bread made from milled wheat flour (the modern standard is Bluebird flour, milled in Cortez, Colorado). These ingredients did not come from any "plant people" within their four sacred mountains. They had to come from traders. And what would the Navajo trade? Meat. Weavings. Silver. Anasazi artifacts (for those who overcame their fear of contamination by the dead in the interest of profit). And, especially, wool.

Traders came to Diné Bikeyah, Navajo Country, to take advantage of this business opportunity, beginning in 1868. They lasted only if they enjoyed the life, only if they became friends with their Navajo customers. In turn, they became the primary link to the outside world for the People — right up to the 1960s. The traders acted as interpreters, funeral directors and grave diggers, scouts for new ideas and bits of technology, bankers (by pawning jewelry and other valuables like rifles), doctors, gossip columnists, postmasters, and business managers. Traders held surprising power for outsiders; Ruth Underhill called them "Navajo shoguns."

The Navajo had long traded their blankets to Indians and non-Indians; in the mid-1800s, some Diné made yearly trading trips as far as Fort Bridger in Wyoming. Stripes and terraces and diamonds on Navajo ponchos and shoulder-blankets did not fit the styles in Philadelphia and Toledo, however. Anglo traders encouraged Diné women to weave specifically for Anglo markets. The businessmen supplied weavers with commercial wool, dyes, and rug patterns, and circulated catalogs in the East. Anglos placed their orders for "Navajo rugs," and the rough and simple Navajo saddle blanket and woman's blanket dress began to evolve away from their roots.

Goulding's Trading Post, Monument Valley, 1947. Through the 1960s, traders served the People as interpreters, funeral directors and gravediggers, scouts for new ideas and technology, bankers (pawning jewelry and other valuables), doctors, gossip columnists, postmasters, and business managers. (Courtesy Special Collections Department, University of Utah Libraries)

Enter the Pendleton blanket and calico skirt for the People. Exit from hogans to Anglo markets the eye-dazzler woven from commercial Germantown yarns, the Ganado red floor rug favored by don Lorenzo Hubbell at his trading post in Ganado Mucho's old domain, and, later, the Two Grey Hills tapestry, the oriental-flavored Teec Nos Pos designs, and the storm pattern — the latter three probably inspired by trader J. B. Moore. By 1908, weaving had become the major income source for Navajos along the San Juan. As anthropologist James Downs notes, the Navajo rug became "a symbol of the relationship between the People and the trader."

Still later, in the 1920s, came the Chinle weaving revival. Encouraged by trader Cozy McSparron and Anglo patron Mary Cabot Wheelwright, Navajo women developed the soft-hued multicolored Wide Ruins, Crystal, and Pine Springs vegetal-dyed wall hangings. Also in the twenties, medicine man Hosteen Klah wove his sandpainting rugs, to ensure preservation of chantway ritual designs — and to make part of his living, as well.

Design trends followed the news. Navajo weavers made American flag blankets during the Spanish-American War to capitalize on the patriotic fever that always accompanies a war. When I visited weaver Beverly Allen in April 1991 — a few weeks after the Persian Gulf War — she had just finished a small rug with an American eagle design.

After World War II, weavers made about five cents an hour for their time spent in washing wool, carding, dyeing, spinning, and weaving. A 1973 estimate pegged their wages at thirty cents an hour. Today, smaller rugs that sell for several hundred dollars still pay poorly per hour. But they do pay, dependably.

Weaver Kalley Musial says of her childhood at Gray Mountain: "I started to weave when I was six. My grandma was going blind. One day she couldn't see and she said, 'It's your turn. There is no other way we can get food.' She didn't teach me, she just said, 'You've seen me weave all these years; you should know if you've got it in you.'"

Musial began weaving again in the seventies when her kids began school. She says: "I rarely tell anyone what feelings I put into my rugs. My pieces are as traditional as they can be because they are from me, not from a trader." Musial teaches weaving to Anglos, and she has discovered that: "The patience has to come from you. The rug cannot teach you to be patient. Whatever is happening in your life, that's where you get your peace from, and peace will give you patience."

Tsaile weaver Beverly Allen notes some of the changes in sharing over the years: "A long time ago, everyone would help one another. If someone comes to visit, they would help you with whatever you are doing — even weaving. Now, if someone comes, they just say 'That's pretty,' and watch." She laughed: "But on the day you sell a rug, people who are related to you come to ask for a loan!"

Eventually, analyzers of regional styles gave up trying to keep pace with the creativity of Navajo weavers. Today, individual weavers still follow the teachings of Spider Woman, who taught them how to weave; they may choose to weave a Crystal or a storm pattern; but they also create their own fine art that fits no scheme of classification other than one of personal "creative transformation," to use the term favored by ethnologist Gary Witherspoon.

Barbara Ornelas (left) and her sister Rosann Teller Lee, Santa Fe Indian Market, 1987. Their Two Grey Hills weaving — at 5 × 8½ feet the largest recorded contemporary Navajo tapestry, a category defined by its exceptionally fine weaving — won Best of Show and sold for $60,000. It took four years to complete.

Silverwork went through similar transformations. Before the Long Walk, one Navajo man was known for working iron — the headman, Herrero, whose name in Navajo was 'Atsidí Sání, "Old Smith." He learned to work iron and silver from the Mexican smith brought to Fort Defiance in 1853. By 1867, several Navajo men (at first, all relatives or students of 'Atsidí Sání) were making buttons and bracelets, stamping designs with homemade punches. Not until 1880 did the Diné silversmiths begin to set turquoise, probably learning from the Santo Domingos. About the turn of the century, the Fred Harvey Company tapped into the Navajo silver market for tourist souvenirs — lighter in weight than pieces the People made for themselves — giving the jewelers a guaranteed sales outlet.

Silverwork has continued to evolve. Ambrose Roanhorse and Kenneth Begay were influential teachers and bold artists of the forties and fifties. Navajo educator Ruth Roessel points out that, in contrast to weavings, "among contemporary Navajo silver, the best is to be found on the reservation being worn by Navajos." Dozens of fine silversmiths make pieces that they may give to their family or clan relations. Non-

Navajo silversmith, 1892–93. By 1867, a number of Navajo men were making silver buttons and bracelets; not until 1880 did Diné silversmiths set turquoise stones. In the early 1900s, the Fred Harvey Company commissioned tourist souvenirs from Navajo jewelers, providing a guaranteed market. Photo by Buckwalter. (Courtesy Colorado Historical Society)

Indians and non-Navajo tribal people buy considerable Navajo silverwork, as well, enough to provide full-time skilled silversmiths with a decent living. Their uniquely personal work fills galleries across the country, carrying with it a bit of hózhǫ́ to grace whoever wears it.

When traders established the pawn system after the 1880s, Navajo families invested their savings in silver and turquoise that could be pawned when the sheep market crashed, and in good years retrieved from the trader's vault. Eventually, unsecured credit became even more important. James Downs equates the importance of the trader with that of the shepherd and medicine man.

Navajos themselves are also the best customers for "Navajo wedding baskets," the distinctive shallow plates required for so many ceremonies, decorated with an unclosed ring of black mountains with a band of russet-red within the terraced black. San Juan Paiutes make most of these baskets — sold and used and traded and resold, acquiring a permanent blessing of cornmeal dust within their stitches from years of sings and chantways. Recently, more Navajo basket weavers have been active; Sally Black may well be the best known, the creator of huge pieces decorated with yei figures — clearly conceived as art pieces from the first coil.

Pitched pottery, too, died down to a whisper for decades, with only a small output of pipes and ceremonial drums for Enemyway. With the encouragement of key traders and museum curators, especially Bill Beaver at Sacred Mountain Trading Post north of Flagstaff, Navajo pottery has become yet another Southwest native art in renaissance. Many of the best-known potters are related, learning from two pivotal teachers, Faye

Louise Goodman, Navajo potter, Cow Springs, Arizona, 1986. Following a decline that began in the late 1800s, Navajo potters made only a small number of pipes and ceremonial drums for Enemyway. A renaissance reversing this trend began in the Shonto–Cow Springs area in the 1960s.

Tso at Tuba City and Rose Williams of Shonto–Cow Springs. The latter area remains the center of activity for Navajo pottery, both for potters working in older styles and for innovators like Alice Cling (daughter of Rose Williams), who creates pots with the same elegance and smoothness as fine Pueblo pottery.

One Navajo commercial art, sandpainting, was never made in permanent form before the development of today's market. Singers have made sandpaintings as integral parts of curing ceremonies for centuries, especially during Holyway chants. Anglo anthropologist Gladys Reichard, a lifelong student of Navajo religion, called sandpaintings as used in ritual, "ceremonial membranes" that absorb the power of the Holy People depicted in them and transfer that power to the patient who sits on them. The singer (or several singers, for large paintings) works with colored pigments: ground stone, oak charcoal, cornmeal, flower petals, and pollens. At the end of the ceremony, the singer erases the sandpainting and carries the sand outside the hogan.

With the Anglo discovery of Navajo ceremonialism, sandpainting designs began to turn up in Navajo easel paintings, on rugs, and in jewelry. Some singers, overcoming their feelings of blasphemy for transforming the sacred into the secular, demonstrated sandpainting in museums. Anthropologists cultivated friendships with particular singers, who allowed them to sketch ceremonial sandpaintings. Finally, in the early 1950s, as scholar Nancy Parezo notes in her history of the craft, the Diné began to make commercial sandpaintings.

An Anglo couple developed the techniques of gluing sand to boards, and the late Navajo singer and sandpainting demonstrator Fred Stevens, Jr., from Sheep Springs, New Mexico, saw their work and began making permanent sandpaintings. His motivations included, in Parezo's words, "economics, ethnic pride, historical obligation, and aesthetic preferences." In the sixties, Stevens taught his family and clan members. In the decades that followed, virtually all Navajo sandpainters learned from this one pioneering Diné artist or his students. Today, artists like Joe Ben, Jr., strike out on their own, taking sandpainting to new frontiers of elegant precision.

By substituting, transposing, eliminating, simplifying, adding, or in some other way changing the sacred prescription of a design, commercial sandpainters avoid offending the Holy People, though some controversy still exists regarding their activities. The artists favor safe subjects that stress the attraction of good: Mother Earth and Father Sky, Sun, Corn, and Rainbow People rather than monsters, White Thunder, snakes, and bears. The power of the Holy People carried in these works buys food and vehicles and houses for their makers.

Other Diné have chosen other art forms, both as a playful way to create and as

A Navajo medicine man adds a bear to a sandpainting, circa 1930s to 1940s. For centuries an integral part of curing ceremonies, especially the Holyway chants, sandpaintings absorb the power of the Holy People depicted and transfer that power to the patient who sits on them. Photo by Joseph H. McGibbeny. (Courtesy Special Collections Department, University of Utah Libraries)

a way to make a living. Wood carvings, cardboard cutouts, and sandstone carvings of pickups can all be found today in trading posts.

Easel painters have established a rich tradition, beginning with the "deer-and-horses" genre and flat-perspective ceremonial scenes that grew out of the Santa Fe Studio, exemplified by Harrison Begay, Andy Tsihnahjinnie, and the self-taught Jimmy Toddy (Beatien Yazz), who also paints dreamlike images from his experiences in the Native American Church. Their successors include the prolific and wealthy R. C. Gorman, Clifford Beck, and younger, experimental painters like Robert Draper, Bahe Whitethorne, and W. B. (Bill) Franklin.

Bill Franklin's experience includes boarding schools, the occupation of Alcatraz, a college education in Flagstaff, silversmithing, and awards for his paintings during the 1980s at Santa Fe Indian Market. He learned to paint, he says, "through prayer and through study. I'm careful in how I paint, and stay along the lines of Beautyway. My paintings are Navajo paintings because I am a Navajo."

Some traders, like Navajo Chee Dodge, accumulated wealth in herds. Most traders were Anglo, passing on their businesses through several generations; most did not get rich. Ed Smith traded for forty years at Oljato, just around the corner from Monument Valley. He told me in 1986: "You didn't make any money. If you didn't like living there you were wasting your time." Smith told stories of trading groceries for coyote skins and sending the hide on to his suppliers to let them figure out how to value it. Like most of his compatriots, he had to close up shop in the 1980s, as Bashas and FedMart and video stores and pizza parlors came to Window Rock and Kayenta and Chinle and Tuba City. His customers did the rest of their shopping in Gallup and Farmington and Page, lured by advertising broadcast in Navajo.

Indeed, the structure of the Diné language tends to make an advertisement sound like a command; Diné-preferred brands of condensed milk were known to change overnight after the initiation of advertising campaigns on the Navajo radio stations. The disappearance of trading posts also opened the way for Navajo entrepreneurs — not all of them one-person businesses: Don Davis owns the Chevrolet agency in Tuba City, for instance.

Today's Diné artists and artisans sometimes still sell to the local trader or take their work to the big wholesalers in Cortez or Albuquerque or Flagstaff. But much of the best work is sold right off the loom or workbench, to gallery owners who come out to the back roads of the "rez" every spring to buy up all that the People can produce, to sell to their customers in Chicago, San Diego, or Miami.

Out there, Navajo women still keep a loom in the hogan next to their houses. Navajo men keep their silversmithing tools on a workbench in the corner of the living

room. Betty Manygoats, near Shonto, walks through the rabbitbrush and saltbush to
her pottery-making studio, an old hogan. Manygoats, known for her hand-coiled wedding vases with appliqued horned toads perched on them, works hard on her craft.

I watched as she fired one April day. Winter-cool air warming to summer; hot sun
on the gray wood of the hogan. From out of the juniper ashes left from the firing the
pot emerged, dull tan and blackened on one side. Manygoats carried the vase outside
to a table where she brushed hot pine pitch — pitch the consistency of refrigerated
maple syrup — into the baked clay. The smell cut the clear air: steam and smoke, sharp,
pungent, fresh, elemental.

The People weave and hammer and coil their spirit into such pieces. Hózhǫ́
travels outward from the sacred mountains, unspoken but eloquent. As Navajo weaver
Kalley Musial said of her rugs to writer Tryntje Seymour: "It is a piece of art — it is a
piece of you.

"I don't think we ever realized or thought of any form of craft or hobby as art. It
was done for ceremonial purposes, and it was done for trade.

"In many ways that is the way it still is. And it is still a way to express something
that you can't say out loud."

How Many Sheep Is Too Many Sheep?

By the 1920s, the Navajo Reservation had grown by millions of acres over its
size at the turn of the century. Decent superintendents and missionaries sparked the
political action that led to these additions. However, checkerboarded alternate sections granted to the railroad as it pierced the West and wheeling and dealing by white
homesteaders and mineral corporations for allotted Navajo lands made the borders
of this new territory a jurisdictional morass. These same pressure groups periodically succeeded in having Navajo lands returned to the public domain or won mineral
leases on the reservation.

Who spoke for the Navajo about such issues? The BIA needed a mechanism to
give voice to the Diné as a whole. Though initially the Bureau acted for its own con-
venience, it nonetheless gave birth to the Navajo Nation.

First came a business council appointed by the Secretary of Interior in 1922,
chosen to arrange oil leases for the tribe. On 7 July 1923, a newly appointed tribal
council of twelve men chose Chee Dodge as the first tribal chairman. Though heavily
constrained by the BIA, these men nonetheless took stands and argued issues.

The issues included education. In 1925, the tribal council moved to prohibit
primary-grade students from being sent to off-reservation boarding schools. The BIA
ignored their position. Times were changing, however. Once John Collier took office

as Indian Commissioner in 1933, the day school program expanded rapidly and encouraged the study of Navajo language and culture.

The 1928 council discussed for the first time the idea of stock reduction to eliminate overgrazing. This would become the dominant issue of the 1930s. Two groups
within the council began to face off: one led by Chee Dodge (a Catholic), who believed
in Anglo education programs while remaining primarily oriented toward traditional
Navajo values. Dodge was a mediator; he cooperated with the BIA in order to form a
true tribal consciousness. He also was a man wealthy from sheep and trading interests. Fundamentalist missionary Jacob Morgan, from Shiprock, led the other faction,
whose gospel included total assimilation. Morgan wanted oil royalties spent in his
own district and wasn't much concerned about poor herders elsewhere. His following lay with the boarding school–educated Navajos looking for wage work, who had
no land or herds with which to make their way.

Jacob Morgan decided that Collier represented a return to tribalism rather than
full-speed assimilation; many Navajos would not agree. Morgan fought Collier at every
step. As scholar Peter Iverson points out, "John Collier made Jacob Morgan's political
career."

This Morgan-Collier-Dodge feud became entwined with the need to limit overgrazing — either by land acquisition or stock reduction. Executive-order additions to
the reservation had ended in 1918. But Navajos continued to multiply, and so did
their herds; with government encouragement, the Navajo economy depended almost
solely on stock raising. Even the influenza epidemic of 1918, when eastern Navajo
Country lost almost 20 percent of its population, did little to slow Navajo population
growth. To meet the needs of Diné herders, the federal government allotted new public domain lands. After 1928, the government funded the outright purchase of new
land. Additions to the reservation, however, were no longer feasible.

Navajos' feelings for their flocks reached deep. Livestock meant more than
money. A Diné speaker at a 1935 meeting in Shiprock said: "What good is just money?
You earn it, have it, spend it, or save it, but it doesn't grow or hatch or increase."

Navajo historian Clyde Benally points out: "Before 1868, the man's role was protector; that was honor, dignity. Then, we were told we cannot be protector any more.
We were told to go home and be farmers and stock raisers. To the Navajo male, that
was the woman's role, that was her sheep, her farming plot, her hogan.

"But by the turn of the century, Navajos were running huge herds; there was
honor and dignity in having huge herds. Then came the 1930s. The federal government again said, 'You shall not have honor, you shall not have dignity, by having so
many sheep and cattle.' We were told we have to go out and do wage work."

Steve Darden articulates the Navajo belief that sheep are "gifts from the Holy

Beginning in 1884, Henry Chee Dodge served as the primary interpreter between Anglos and Diné. He led his people for more than 60 years, in roles ranging from chief herder to tribal chairman. His death in 1947 symbolically marked the dividing point between the post-treaty period and the modern Navajo Nation. (Courtesy Museum of New Mexico, neg. no. 9866)

People. While we are herding sheep, we are their mother, the sheep are the children. Where we were once the mother, then we become the child. When we butcher that sheep, then that sheep is taking care of us. It is giving us life. Corrals represent the womb; the opening is to the east, much like our hogan is. When we take our sheep out in the morning, we take it first to the east, where life comes from. You took your sheep grazing in the four directions.

"The concept of overgrazing we don't understand. How can you eat up your mother? The holy mother, our Earth, takes care of us, our sheep . . ."

In 1933, the BIA judged two-thirds of the Navajo range to have been destroyed by overgrazing. Reluctantly, the Navajo Council submitted to stock reduction, believing it unavoidable and hoping for land guarantees in trade. With Morgan equating Collier's Indian Reorganization Act with stock reduction, the tribe — "those stubborn Navajos," in Peterson Zah's words — voted to reject the IRA in 1935. Zah believes their message was: "We ought to remain as we are and exercise our true sovereignty." The BIA proceeded with stock reduction anyway. By dividing the reservation into grazing districts, each stock owner could graze only in his or her district, compounding difficulties for the strapped herders.

Political maneuvering filled the next several years. Collier chose Window Rock, near old Fort Defiance, as tribal headquarters, and saw to it that WPA money made possible the construction of the council building — a grand rock hogan still in use today. In 1936, with Collier's urging, the council voted to reorganize and create its own constitution. No constitution passed, but a set of rules was adopted that, with many modifications, forms the basis for Navajo self-government today. (The Diné still have no constitution. As Peterson Zah told journalist Catherine Feher-Elston: "The only way for it to happen is to have the concept [of a constitution] . . . come from the schools, it has to come from the families. It has to come from the younger generations. It has to then work its way into the chapter houses, it has to go to the agencies and then it has to work itself into the council.")

Morgan was elected chairman in 1938, but proved more effective as gadfly than leader. Chee Dodge succeeded him in 1942. The fight against stock reduction required a united tribe, however, bringing the two men and their followers closer together than ever before.

Navajo herds grazed the land beyond redemption, and erosion washed silt downstream. The federal government feared for the future of newly built Hoover Dam on the Colorado River, its reservoir — Lake Mead — filling with sludge. The only solution — as far as Washington, D.C., was concerned — was to reduce the numbers of Navajo stock by 400,000 animals. The Bureau came to within 10 percent of meeting their goal by 1934.

Small herders lost their best animals to "voluntary" stock reduction in these early years of the thirties. The worst abusers were the *ricos*, who could afford to lose their unproductive ewes to the hated federal range riders culling herds. When forced reduction resumed in 1937, the large owners were cut back just as mercilessly over the next decade.

Sheep-dipping to control a scabies epidemic beginning in 1905 had already sensitized the People to federal interference with their most prized possessions. When dipping sheep in chemicals to kill mites became mandatory, however, the People turned the spring dip into something like a chapter picnic.

Eighty-five years later, Christine Benally earned her Ph.D. by studying the residues of the insecticides lindane and toxiphene left in soils around the old vats. The young Diné scientist told me: "There was no awareness of the chemicals being poison. Ladies and kids were out there practically bathing in it; intoxicated people would fall into the vats. No one paid any attention to the dosage: in some places, people were paying just to get their sheep wet!

"Once they were done, they would just let the water out; the vats were often located next to springs or windmills." Happily, Benally found that the toxic wastes remain concentrated around the vats and have not contaminated groundwater. The tribal council finally banned sheep-dipping in 1986, and by 1991, even the most stubborn dipper abided by the new law.

Ironically, the Depression probably would have thinned herds with much less trauma, as the bottom dropped out of markets and Navajos ate or sold most of their animals. The methods the BIA used in the 1930s, however, created an embittered and angry Navajo Nation.

In 1934, for instance, thirty-five hundred goats were shot and left to rot near Inscription House, because the railroad was too far away to bother with meat transport. Thousands of other animals were left to starve in holding pens. Piles of bones could be found in isolated canyons forty years later.

Navajo memories of stock reduction remain strong and sad.

Howard Gorman: "All of these incidents broke a lot of hearts of the Navajo people and left them mourning for years . . . The cruel way our stock was handled is something that should never have happened."

Buck Austin, Bitter Water Clan, Black Mesa: "Hundreds of men and women were arrested because they simply refused to limit their herds. We went through extreme hardship, hunger, thirst, being beaten by police, arrested, and being thrown in jail at places far away from our homes."

Martin Johnson, north of Teec Nos Pos: "There, inside the corral, the Navajo men who worked for the government slaughtered every one of our goats. There was blood running everywhere in the corral as we just stood there and watched. My wife was the one who had raised the sheep and goats in her younger years. She cried about her goats as they were killed. Then we just left to go back home."

Chahadineli Benally: "It was a tragic time that never will be forgotten . . . So now the Navajo wonders what will come next! What will the White Man want?"

Ernest Nelson, Red House Clan: "The reason why there is no grass is because of little rain. Before stock reduction, it rained all the time. There was a lot of livestock everywhere, and it rained and rained. Then, when John Collier put a blockade on livestock, the rain ceased altogether."

At the brink of the Depression, Navajos owned about 760,000 mature sheep and goats—about one hundred per family of five. This put them over the threshold for making a subsistence living from wool, lamb, and rug sales. By 1949, only 414,000 remained—about 44 per household, far less than the number necessary for a living. Per capita figures show the same decrease: from 21 in 1931 to 8 in 1940 to 3.6 in 1974 to 2.4 in 1988.

Chairman Sam Ahkeah called livestock reduction and the resulting impoverishment of his people, "the most devastating experience in [Navajo] history since the imprisonment at Fort Sumner." One route to solace found many followers: the Native American Church (NAC) grew strong on the Navajo reservation in the forties, to the distress of many traditionalist and Christian Navajos—Jacob Morgan, in particular.

The NAC began to spread south of the San Juan River—south from its stronghold at the Ute Mountain Reservation—in 1936. For most Navajo NAC members, peyote provides another way of access to power, of reaching communion with God, and of curing ills and restoring balance. Peyotists should avoid alcohol. The NAC incorporates some Christian elements but remains distinctly Indian. Harry Walters describes the faith as "Pan-Indian: NAC uses the basic core of all Indian religions." Anthropologist David Aberle describes NAC practitioners as "dignified and serious," "passionate and zealous." The NAC's ability to enhance self-esteem was critical for Diné devastated by stock reduction.

Another major event, of course, came for the Diné in those same years: World War II. The People would never be the same after the war.

The Code-Talkers Come Home

Just twenty-five Navajos served in World War I. As draftable U.S. citizens, however, as many as 3,600 Diné served in World War II, with another 10,000 to 14,000 leaving the reservation to work in defense and industry—all out of a Navajo popula-

Registering for the draft during World War II, Fort Defiance, Arizona, 1942. Draftable U.S. citizens since 1924, over 3,600 Diné served in World War II. The heroes of this era were the code-talkers, some 420 Navajo marines who used their native language as a code — never broken — to confound the Japanese. Photo by Milton Snow. (Courtesy National Archives, photo no. 75-N-NAV-370)

tion of 50,000. Over half of the population of Navajos nineteen and over had wartime jobs. In 1941, the Navajo earned $150,000 from industry; in 1943, wages brought in $5 million.

The heroes of this era were the "code-talkers." An Anglo dreamed up the idea: Philip Johnston knew the Diné language from his years with his missionary parents on the reservation. He suggested that the U.S. Marines use Diné as a code to confound the Japanese. Some 420 Navajo men subsequently served as code-talkers in the Pacific, and the Japanese never did crack their secret. Diné words acquired new meanings in the code: "sparrow hawk" became "dive bomber," "egg" became "bomb."

These men remain among the most honored of Navajo elders. When I have met them by chance, they identify themselves as code-talkers soon after — and sometimes before — they identify themselves by name. As Cozy Stanley Brown, a Deer Spring Clan member from Chinle, remembers of his time as a code-talker: "It was like the old saying of our elderly Navajo people, 'Only the Navajos had the whole world in their hands . . .' "

The forties opened up Navajo society to the wider world in countless ways. Elders watched as the educated youth won promotions and higher-paying jobs. The war itself brought prosperity after the dismal decade of stock reduction. As of 1948, Indian people in Arizona and New Mexico finally could vote in state and national elections.

The soldiers returned home to few jobs, however. Annual family income for the 65,000 Navajos averaged $400 in the late forties, one-third of minimal subsistence. Stock raising no longer offered a feasible life of self-sufficiency. Almost without exception, the veterans arranged Squaw Dances (Enemyway ceremonies) to cleanse themselves of the contaminating effects of the war. But the singers could not create jobs. Another time of transition descended on the People.

The death of Chee Dodge in 1947 symbolically marked this fulcrum. Historian Robert Young put it this way: Dodge "became the ladder along which the Navajo people tortuously made their way out of the early post-treaty period into the modern age." Indeed, Chee Dodge's son, Thomas, became a symbol of the change: the first Navajo attorney and an early tribal chairman.

The old chief died at the age of eighty-seven, just after election as vice-chairman — losing the chairmanship to Sam Ahkeah. Ahkeah was the first chairman to see his job as full-time; he moved to Window Rock in 1947 and served until 1954, overseeing enormous changes in the life of the People.

The crisis of unemployment and imminent starvation after the war led to the 1950 Hopi-Navajo Rehabilitation Act. This legislation opened the Colorado River Reservation to Navajo and Hopi colonists, gave the Navajo Council authority to allocate its own revenues, and authorized more than $100 million to build schools, public works, and roads across Diné Bikeyah. (In 1950, pavement ended at Shiprock, Cameron, and Window Rock on the outer fringes of the reservation. Pickups were beginning to replace wagons — the latter widely used only since the early thirties. By 1974, nearly two-thirds of all Navajo households owned a car or pickup.)

Intermountain Indian School in Brigham City, Utah, opened in 1950, originally intended exclusively for older Navajo students. As the fifties progressed, Navajos began to pour into boarding schools; Peterson Zah explains how Diné students coped with sudden uprooting: "We lived the life we were taught back home within ourselves." In 1954, for the first time, the Bureau could find seats in classrooms for every school-age Navajo, and within four years, the percentage of Navajo children in school jumped from 62 to 93 percent.

Stock reduction had eliminated the distinct levels of wealth generated by the livestock economy. After the war, the old high-status families maintained their status by urging their children to become educated. Many old *ricos* today live alone, taking care of the small family stock holdings, while their educated children live in Tuba City or Salt Lake City. They managed to pass on their values of achieving; the results are bittersweet.

Ahkeah reacted to the new Claims Commission by hiring a tribal attorney, Norman Littell, who became the "sparkplug of tribal political development" in the fifties, according to Robert Young, longtime observer of the tribe. Eventually, Littell acquired so much power that Raymond Nakai based his successful campaign for chairman on the pledge to fire Littell.

In one of Littell's first great successes, legislation passed that formally ended stock reduction. It took the Council until 1956 to institute grazing policies of its own, however, and these have not prevented further degradation of the range. In 1978, Navajo agricultural scientist Dr. Bahe Billy documented the devastation wrought by more than two million Diné sheep; he also noted overcutting not just of trees but of shrubs, especially four-wing saltbush, for firewood. Billy warned that "soon this overutilized land will blow or wash away."

The tribal council became the permanent institutional vehicle for the Navajo Nation's striving toward self-sufficiency. Nationalism was a fine ideal, but how could impoverished Indian people aspire to anything approaching real self-rule?

Energy development gave the Navajo Council income to fight for sovereignty and against the federal trend toward termination. With the discovery of the Aneth Oil Field on Utah Navajo land in 1955 came the first great flood of money to the tribal treasury, $34.5 million in royalties in 1956 alone. Tribal programs expanded drastically—building new chapter houses, establishing a tribal scholarship fund, bringing electricity to new areas, and creating a system of tribal courts.

With freedom came responsibility, of course. One Navajo tribal employee described to anthropologist Mary Shepardson the increasing power of the council over decisions formerly made exclusively by the BIA: "They have given us a knife and said, 'Now go and cut your own throats.'"

In Fruitland, New Mexico, construction jobs with a gas line gave the local Diné their first surplus income. Sudden affluence had its challenges. According to anthropologist Tom Sasaki: "Drinking became rampant at sings and squaw dances; young people married clan-mates; co-operative work on farms lost its place; transmission of Navajo culture from old to young and relationships among members of the kinship groups deteriorated."

Annie Wauneka, daughter of Chee Dodge and for years the only female council member (serving from 1951 to 1978), adopted as her personal mission the fight against

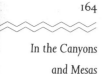
tuberculosis. With funding support and the aid of new antituberculosis sulfa drugs, her crusade reduced the number of Diné with the disease by nearly half between 1953 and 1960. In 1963, she received the Presidential Medal of Freedom. Today's Diné revere Wauneka, eighty-two years old in 1992, as the "legendary mother of the People," who speaks out against alcohol with undiminished passion.

Paul Jones, with more experience "on the outside" than Sam Ahkeah, held the chairmanship from 1955 to 1963; his vice-chairman, Scott Preston — an elder and medicine man — balanced Jones's modernity. Jones's administration reaped the rewards of the blossoming Navajo energy industry — from bonus payments due upon lease signings, royalties, and rents. Uranium mills opening in the mid-fifties, the Aneth oil field boom, and the beginnings of strip mining and coal-fired power plants all contributed to an annual average energy income for the tribe of $14,250,000 in the sixties. Wise council members consistently avoided per capita payments and invested much of this income in a tribal scholarship fund and other restricted accounts.

Tribal programs mushroomed. Jones hired a young Navajo administrator named J. Maurice McCabe who created the entire administrative structure of the tribe virtually singlehandedly. The tribe took over from the Bureau all responsibility for law enforcement, irrigation, and drilling and maintaining wells. The council created the Navajo Tribal Utility Authority in 1959; the *Navajo Times* and Navajo Forest Products Industries (which continues to support the sawmill community of Navajo, New Mexico) in 1960; the Navajo Housing Authority in 1964. Federal money augmented the budgets of each agency, climaxing with the creation of the Office of Navajo Economic Opportunity.

The Navajo Nation

Chairman Raymond Nakai's approach suited the stridency of the sixties. Elected in 1963, he had lived in Flagstaff since World War II and had long hosted a radio program broadcast in Navajo across the reservation. Zealous as only an outsider can be, Nakai pledged to curtail the power of Norman Littell and Maurice McCabe and to return power to the People.

Nakai hinted that he might go easy on grazing regulations, and he spoke out against Paul Jones's enforcement of the prohibition of Native American Church peyote use. The People wanted individual rights restored; they voted for Nakai in droves. During his first administration, the council fought him at every turn. His reelection, however, swept into office a more sympathetic council.

The new council finally approved the religious use of peyote, after twenty-seven

Coal slurry line plunging off Black Mesa, 1991. Each year, 4½ million tons of coal travel by pipeline from the nearby Black Mesa Mine almost 300 miles to the Mohave power plant on the Colorado River. The slurry water represents a major commitment of Navajo water resources.

years of persecution. Ending years of battling for his job, Norman Littell resigned in 1967. The Claims Commission made their award to the Navajo soon after, in 1970.

To take advantage of federal money — and jobs — pouring into the reservation during the sixties, the tribe created the Office of Navajo Economic Opportunity. A young Navajo engineer named Peter MacDonald returned home from California to serve as director of ONEO for five years — until he moved his files into the office of tribal chairman, which he won for the first time in 1970.

During fiscal years 1965 to 1968 alone, ONEO funneled over $20 million into such programs as Home Improvement Training, Local Community Development, and Neighborhood Youth Corps. As Peter Iverson puts it: "ONEO worked because it had money, because it involved bread-and-butter issues, because it encouraged local involvement, and because it had Navajo administrators."

One of the critical programs under ONEO was the grass-roots legal aid organization Dinébeiina Nahiilna Be Agaditahe (DNA): "Lawyers Who Contribute to the Economic Revitalization of the People." The DNA almost drowned in politics in its early years. By the mid-1970s, however, a thriving DNA provided the only source of legal help to poor Navajos throughout the reservation; DNA lay counselors constituted a third of the staff. The vitality of the DNA inspired many of the Navajos who have since become attorneys.

Chairman Nakai meanwhile initiated many of the economic ventures that came to fruition (and controversy) in later years. With the promise of free land and cheap labor, Fairchild Semiconductor opened a plant in Shiprock and General Dynamics came to Fort Defiance. Today, only General Dynamics remains. Fairchild laid off most of its workers in 1975, Navajo protestors occupied the plant, and the corporation closed its operations, leaving the tribe with a huge investment in buildings and equipment. Navajo labor may be cheap, but Taiwanese and Korean laborers are twenty times cheaper; the People have suffered the old Western cycle of "boom and bust."

The Diné signed coal leases to supply the Four Corners Power Plant at Fruitland, New Mexico, in 1961; in 1970 this was the largest coal mine in the world. The Black Mesa leases with Peabody Coal Company followed in 1964 and 1966. The tribe felt an imperative to develop these resources quickly before nuclear power made coal obsolete. One BIA administrator remembered attorney Norman Littell "walking up the Council aisle, waving papers for the Council to approve, like the Saviour had returned."

By the late 1970s, every Navajo chapter involved in mineral development had passed resolutions opposing any further development. Clean air advocates continue to protest pollution from the power plants, while the traditional elders of Black Mesa protest the destruction of their lands.

Black Mesa was reservation backcountry. A Black Mesa Diné told James Downs: "It's hard to make a living out here with our sheeps and cattles, but we love them and will keep on trying no matter how hard it is." The mine, however, made it harder than the People could have imagined. Many Mules' Granddaughter said: "Where they are mining now is my land. My father is buried there. His grave was torn up in the strip mining. I never approved of anything in the agreement to mine this area. I don't know of anybody who agreed to the contract."

Tully Frank, a Native American Church leader from Kayenta, says: "We've been up to the mesa in NAC meetings. The elders cry and shed tears. They say, 'They shouldn't have destroyed our sacred mountain.' One lady says she doesn't know where she's at; she can't find the hills. That's the way it goes: the young people want the jobs, the elderly people disagree all the way."

Councilmen at the time admitted in later years that they did not fully discuss the Peabody Coal leases on Black Mesa. The council also sold Navajo water rights to provide sufficient water for the power plant at Page and the pipeline that carries Black Mesa coal slurried with water almost three hundred miles to the Mohave power plant. In 1987, the tribe renegotiated the slurry water contract with Peabody, with terms that discourage waste of what Danny Blackgoat, from Big Mountain, describes as "wonderful sweet-tasting water." By then, the Navajo Division of Water Resources employed two hundred people, a formidable information-gathering arm for Diné executive and legislative negotiators. The coal company nonetheless remains the largest single employer of Navajos, and the royalties from these projects fuel one-fifth of the Navajo tribal budget (with the better royalty rates renegotiated in 1987).

Another dream for economic development initiated in the sixties has proved frustratingly slow to realize. The Navajo Indian Irrigation Project passed Congress in 1962, with the approval of Navajo Dam on the San Juan River and the guarantee of a half-million acre feet of water annually to irrigate some 110,000 acres of Diné fields south of Farmington. It would be the largest such Indian enterprise ever attempted. The original scheme envisioned family farms for nine thousand Navajos. In the late sixties, without much public discussion, the goal became a huge corporate tribal farm: Navajo Agricultural Products Industries (NAPI).

In 1991, irrigation water from the maze of canals that begin at Navajo Reservoir thirty miles away had reached only a little more than half of the farmlands. NAPI showed its first profit in 1986, and now produces high-value harvests of potatoes, onions, and pinto beans (and shiitake mushrooms, as well!). At full operation — if funding ever matches the legislative commitment — NAPI should generate at least three thousand jobs.

In 1969, the Navajo Tribal Council passed a resolution christening their land "the Navajo Nation." They spoke for more than ninety thousand Navajos.

The Two Petes

Peter MacDonald dominated Navajo politics for two decades. In the beginning, the newly elected reformer looked like the ideal leader for the People — the first college-educated chairman. Raised traditionally in Teec Nos Pos, MacDonald joined the marines as a code-talker in World War II and subsequently earned a B.S.

in engineering. He worked for the defense contracting industry in California before returning to Navajo Country in 1963. He knew how the non-Indian corporate world worked; some would say he knew too well.

MacDonald beat Raymond Nakai for the chairmanship three times, in 1970, 1974, and 1978. He made his mark as an articulate and aggressive Navajo nationalist. Mac-Donald even forced the BIA to appoint its first Navajo superintendent. These words come from his first inaugural address: "What is rightfully ours we must protect; what is rightfully due us we must claim . . . What we depend on from others, we must re-place with the labor of our own hands and the skills of our own people . . . What we do not have, we must bring into being. We must create for ourselves."

MacDonald became chairman of the Council of Energy Resource Tribes in 1976. With his characteristic flair for oratory, in a 1977 speech he christened CERT "a domes-tic OPEC." But MacDonald did not always deliver what he promised with his con-summate political rhetoric. In 1975, at the height of the Navajo energy boom, less than 5 percent of Navajo workers had found jobs in mineral development; another 67 percent stagnated — unemployed or underemployed. The median Navajo household income declined in the 1970s, to $2,520 in 1978.

Energy extraction has its risks even for those who can find lucrative work at the mines and mills. Health problems associated with coal and uranium mining plague the Diné; cancer rates are far higher than those of other populations, and far too many Navajo families tell horror stories of the sufferings of dying miners. The 1990 "downwinders" bill will provide compensation for families of the men and women "sacrificed to serve the national security interests of the United States," as Congress belatedly admitted.

Diné troubles with uranium climaxed at Church Rock, New Mexico, in 1979. When the tailings dam at United Nuclear Corporation's uranium mill northeast of Gallup failed one summer day, one hundred million gallons of radioactive water spilled into the Puerco River, the largest release of radioactivity in United States his-tory. According to Rose Hulligan, the government posted the river, "Unsafe waters: do not drink," in perfect academic orthographic Navajo — which few local Diné could read. A decade later, local Navajos still cannot drink their water, because of both the spill and long-term pollution.

The first charges of corruption against MacDonald (submitting false invoices to a utility company) whittled at his standing in 1976. The charges were pursued enthusias-tically by Republicans upset with MacDonald's support of Democratic gubernatorial candidates in the 1974 election. He survived a deadlocked jury trial, however, and

went on to win reelection as the Navajo Nation's first three-term chairman in 1978.
Only in 1982 did he find himself challenged by an opponent who gave him pause.

Peterson Zah came from the same grass-roots political background as had Mac-Donald fifteen years before. He grew up at Low Mountain in what would become the disputed Hopi-Navajo joint use area. His mother spoke no English, though her son says: "I had the best teacher in the world, my mother." His father had a third-grade education but served on the tribal council.

When Peterson Zah graduated from high school, he wanted to go to college. Every teacher but one said: "We don't want you to embarrass Phoenix Indian School." Only his basketball coach supported him. When he graduated from Arizona State University four years later (after attending on a basketball scholarship), he invited all his high school teachers to attend. None came. Zah says today: "That's when I decided to always *not* follow what the BIA tells me."

Zah came home to the reservation, "without knowing what my role was. The university didn't teach that." He found his role quickly, however. In 1972, he was elected to the first all-Navajo Window Rock school board. In telling the story of that time, Zah says: "This was the time of Alcatraz, Wounded Knee. The students at Window Rock High School really wanted to be Navajo. They said, 'We want Navajo language to be taught, Navajo culture to be taught, more Navajo teachers.' They wanted to practice all of those things that make them a unique people."

In 1974, though not a lawyer himself, he assumed the difficult role of DNA administrator. Two years later, in a case that went to the U.S. Supreme Court, Zah forced Apache County, Arizona (with its 70 percent Navajo population), to allow Navajos to serve on its board of supervisors. In the 1976 elections, Navajos for the first time endorsed a slate of candidates in a local election (and for the first time endorsed Democrats).

In the 1982 race for chairman, Peterson Zah beat Peter MacDonald. Zah's quiet style created considerably fewer waves than MacDonald's, but he ran into several problems during his four years as chairman that no style of leadership could have made to go away quickly. One was a national recession. The other was Big Mountain and the relocation tragedy.

"To Relocate Is to Disappear"

Sources for Navajo history often include a map of additions to the reservation over time. They show a huge rectangle added in 1882, surrounding the Hopi mesas. This executive-order withdrawal from the public domain was intended as a

Peterson Zah, Navajo tribal president, 1991. Elected in 1990 to a second term as leader of the Diné, Zah says: "Someday the coal, oil, and gas are going to be gone. What's going to happen to the Navajo children then? You have to think about the future."

Hopi Reservation by Congress, though the document's language acknowledged protection for "any other Indians" settled there by the Secretary of Interior. In 1882, these arbitrary boundaries took in some eighteen hundred Hopi and four hundred Navajo.

Over the years, Navajos continued to increase within the "Hopi Reservation." These Navajos, of course, saw this land as home. As one Diné elder from the area puts it today: "We know the land, we know the sacred places, we know where all the waters are and the land knows us."

The Hopi acknowledged no boundaries other than their ancestral boundaries. When their elders gave permission to the original Navajo families (refugees from Kit Carson) to live on Black Mesa, both peoples agreed that the land was Hopi land. The Diné lived there because the Hopi had granted permission to live there.

By the 1950s, however, the nine thousand Navajos on the 1882 reservation outnumbered the Hopis. Hopi people were concerned for their future. The development-oriented Hopi Tribal Council wanted to clarify its rights in order to proceed with the BIA's plan for energy development. In the subsequent drama that led to relocation, a case could be made that *everyone* lost — except the lawyers and the energy companies.

The BIA wanted to lease Indian minerals; in 1950, the BIA superintendent kept at least twenty oil companies up-to-date on efforts to reorganize a Hopi Tribal Council that could sign off on mineral leases. Attorney John Boyden arrived in Hopiland soon after, and succeeded in seating a council in 1955. Mineral leases, however, had to wait for resolution of the conflicting claims to the 1882 reservation by both Navajo and Hopi. Court cases followed; the *Healing v. Jones* decision awarding joint ownership of mineral rights to both tribes came in 1962, and four years later, the two tribal councils signed leases with Peabody Coal for the Black Mesa mines.

The Hopi council wanted further clarification of its rights, and Boyden's bill partitioning the Joint Use Area passed Congress in 1974. The Hopis lost half the 1882 reservation to the Navajo — land all Hopis believe to be Hopi land. One hundred Hopi would leave this half of the old Joint Use Area. Between eight thousand and ten thousand Navajo, on the other hand, would have to vacate the Hopi half of the partitioned land.

But where would they go?

Relocation began in earnest in the following years — the largest relocation in the United States since the Japanese-American concentration camps of World War II. Thousands of Navajos signed up for the voluntary program, accepting a $5,000 cash payment and a new house in Flagstaff or Gallup or Winslow. About nine hundred relocated into reservation communities. The Relocation Commission generally moved households individually, ignoring the interdependent relationships of Diné families in outfits. Isolated from the seasonal rhythms of their lives, older people whose existence circled around sheep and corn felt disoriented in their suburban homes. Inexperienced in the finances of ownership and without wage work, a third of them subsequently lost their houses. Heartbreaking interviews with relocated Diné aired on national television.

The Navajo were promised up to 400,000 acres of land in exchange for the land they had lost. The Hopi received no new lands. In the 1980s, the Navajo acquired a coal-rich ranch in New Mexico and several ranches southeast of Winslow, many of which were allotted lands the Navajo had lost to non-Indians in the past. A sufficient number of Diné have moved to these new lands to warrant the formation of new chapters.

Other Diné resisted, and continue to resist, at Big Mountain, Coal Mine Mesa, Teesto, and Cow Springs. When the mostly Navajo fencing crew came past Katherine Smith's hogan on Big Mountain in 1979, she took out her shotgun and fired over their heads. In interviews, she has said: "It's our land and I fired over their heads to keep that fencing crew away . . . This is our land, I know it . . . The federal government took me to prison because I would not relocate. My crops need my care, but I will go to prison again if they try to take me from my land."

Traditional elders from the Diné resistance meet in kivas with traditional Hopi leaders. They agree with the Hopi spokesman Thomas Banyacya: "Together we will realize the danger of losing our land and our culture. We must come together with all people to protect this land and repeal this law." Lakota people have brought the Sun Dance to Big Mountain to support the resisters. Some Diné feel this is inappropriate. However, Rose Hulligan, a Diné woman working on Big Mountain issues, points out: "People are offering you their prayers; you aren't going to say no."

The controversial documentary film on the Hopi-Navajo land dispute, *Broken Rainbow*, quotes one Big Mountain Diné elder: "There is no word for relocation in the Navajo language. To relocate is to disappear and never be seen again."

Roberta Blackgoat, another Big Mountain elder, says: "I call the law a monster. It's true. We need to repeal this law because it is harming my people. They're suffering, hungry, dying. The monster is licking our table clean."

The situation remains intractable. Peter MacDonald pushed in vain for repeal of the partitioning law in the late 1970s. Peterson Zah beat MacDonald in 1982 in part because he promised to work out an agreement with his counterpart at the time, Hopi Chairman Ivan Sidney, a classmate of Zah's from Phoenix Indian School. But the two old friends failed to reach any new solutions. MacDonald won back the chairmanship in 1986 (by just 750 of the 61,000 votes cast), in part because of Diné frustration with Zah's inability to solve the partition dispute.

Zah says today: "Prior to my coming into office in 1983, the Hopis and Navajos were fighting. Ivan Sidney and I used to meet, but the Hopi people didn't want us to do that. The Navajo people didn't want us to do that. This situation was created for us by the federal government. It has a life of its own. I don't know when it's going to end. Only through friendship can you end it.

"The Navajos who were convincible have moved. The two hundred families who are staying will stay no matter what happens." The conflict emerged from federal mediation in late 1992, with a new proposal involving seventy-five-year tenure for the remaining Navajos and a grant of almost 500,000 acres of forest land on the flanks of the San Francisco Peaks for the Hopi.

Many Navajo and Hopi people believe that the ultimate reasons for this entire fiasco lie in secret understandings between the government and the energy companies. Rose Hulligan says: "It is not a Navajo-Hopi land dispute; we are more interdependent than enemies. It's multinationals pushing native people off to make a profit. Why do they have to relocate?"

She answers her own question with firmness and frustration: "The coal."

No one has proof. Historian Peter Iverson believes that relocation would have taken place even with no mineral resources involved. Alice Luna, active in helping her Big Mountain elders to speak out, says: "No one ever said to me, 'We want to split the land to open it up for mines,' but don't tell me the fence and the mine came together by chance. When I looked behind the scenes of both issues I found the same people and heard the same names." Even Peterson Zah has said: "I can't really say, without any concrete documents or concrete evidence, that the energy resources have a lot to do with the push for relocation, but my intuition tells me that they have a lot to do with it."

Zah goes on: "The main obstacle to progress being made is the lawyers. The lawyers have made a career out of the Navajo-Hopi land dispute. We cannot continue to have non-Indian lawyers run our lives."

One crucial and irrefutable fact: the Hopi Tribal Council has printed maps showing potential sites for new strip mines on Big Mountain. Another fact: the people of St. Louis (Peabody's corporate headquarters) derive more economic benefits from the Black Mesa mines than do the Navajo or Hopi people.

The Peabody Coal literature I was given at the Black Mesa Mines (before being asked to vacate the premises when I identified myself as a writer and photographer) states that the Kayenta Mine "is Peabody's largest mine nation-wide, producing over seven million tons of coal annually. Eighty-seven percent of Kayenta Mine's 525 employees are Native American." The nearby Black Mesa Mine processes 4.5 million tons annually. Kayenta Mine coal fires the Navajo Generating Station at Page. Black Mesa Mine coal is slurried off to the Colorado River to fuel the Mohave Station.

Subsequent pages describe reclamation efforts aimed at "protecting the land we cherish . . . to restore the land to its original beauty and productivity." But the resulting graded and seeded hills look disturbingly out of place, however healthy their stands of introduced wheatgrass. I stood at the end of the pavement, with these reclaimed hills rolling northward behind me toward the devastation of the mines. The big Bucyrus dragline—capable of scooping ninety cubic yards in each bucketful—raised its neck from beneath the horizon like some mechanized dinosaur. I looked south down the dirt road toward Big Mountain, over the black stands of piñon and juniper that give the mesa its name.

I can only begin to imagine how the contrasts of this view make the Diné of Black Mesa feel. Many Mules' Granddaughter says: "We wanted them to make the land beautiful again. We wanted them to plant trees and saltbush and greasewood and cliffrose." Her son, Ned Yazzie, works at the mine. As Sam and Janet Bingham write in *Between Sacred Mountains*: "He cannot stay on Black Mesa and live any other way." Christine Benally, who has worked in environmental quality for the mining companies on the reservation, says that Diné miners must simply, "close their eyes, bite their teeth, and dig."

Steve Darden, educator and orator, has a suggestion for them: "When we went to take the corn, we made a corn pollen offering. When we went to make the cradle-board and we went to the juniper tree, we did not just cut, we made an offering. And yet we are not doing that today. We are not taking our medicine bundles . . .

"Those people that work at Peabody Coal, it would be beautiful for us to sit and talk to our Mother Earth every day before we went to work. Get to work early and talk to her. And say to her, 'I have to do this. I have to take this out of you to feed my family.' What mother who loves us wouldn't cut her own arm off if it was to save us? She would give us her heart. If it meant our life."

Ned Yazzie says: "In the beginning we agreed to everything without knowing what a mine is like. In the future, if it happens in another place, the people should say, 'No.'"

Peter MacDonald's predilection for development and deal making led to his downfall. In 1989, MacDonald was accused of secretly accepting kickbacks and conspiring to defraud the Navajo Nation of more than $7 million in arranging the purchase of the nearly half-million-acre Big Boquillas Ranch. In 1990, MacDonald was found guilty and sentenced to seven years in tribal jail and fined $30 million dollars. In 1992, federal courts convicted MacDonald of racketeering, conspiracy, burglary, extortion, and fraud in related cases. As Navajo Community College student Mike Yazzie put it: "We had one sharp leader, and he became a crook." (Navajos, with sly irony, have coined a Diné word for "politics:" *na'adlo*, which translates literally as "deception by trickery.")

The Diné entered a very hard time. Two men were killed in protests in Window Rock. Pro- and anti-MacDonald forces struggled for control of the tribe. Leonard Haskie, a little-known council delegate from Sanostee Chapter in New Mexico, became interim chairman. In an effort to curb the power of the chairman, the Navajo Council reorganized tribal government into executive, judicial, and legislative branches. In the election of 1990, Leonard Haskie ran against Peterson Zah for "tribal president" rather than chairman.

Haskie and his running-mate Steve Darden ran on a platform of traditional values. They said in their speeches: "We are the ones with the hair buns. We are the Warrior Twins" (Monster Slayer and Born for Water of legend).

Their pose was easy to ridicule, but Darden (who has served as a city councilman and director of the Native Americans For Community Action in Flagstaff) sees his political role as the modern expression of his clan role, the "Clan Who Walks Around You." He says: "In the traditional role, I would be living outside the camp, watching for the Ute, watching for the Apache. Today, I work in the enemy environment with non-Navajos. I'm still a warrior — a social warrior: I speak on behalf of my people."

Zah ran on his record of experience and honesty, wearing a tweed jacket over his velvet shirt and turquoise necklace — the quintessential moderate. Zah won, and politics in Diné Bikeyah have settled down.

In the spring of 1991, Zah said: "The only people who can resolve these problems are the Navajo people themselves. There are positive things that came from this turmoil. We reformed our government. Now, two years later, we have a new government, a three-branch government that we take very seriously. It is quiet on the Navajo Reservation now. People are tired of what they went through. Sometimes the quietness bothers me. But maybe, in this quiet, people can talk, and people can listen."

Education: Finding the Right Path for Moccasins

Dr. Jennie Joe, Diné educator and medical anthropologist, says of the history of Navajo education: "We have spent so long trying to fit into this shoe that doesn't fit; there are also these moccasins that take you down the same road, to the same end."

Ernesteen Lynch, a Navajo teacher in the Bloomfield, New Mexico, schools, says: "Give us a little time to undo those 130 years. Right now, Navajo parents are just beginning to learn how to be involved with our children's education."

Diné parents began their involvement in the sixties, with the first community school programs. Wilson Aronilth, Navajo culture teacher at Navajo Community College (NCC), calculated the magnitude of the challenge for me in 1991: "They started bilingual/bicultural education in 1964 — almost one hundred years since the reservation started. It will take another hundred years to put us back. It's been twenty-seven. We've still got seventy-three years to go yet, to re-understand what we're about. That's how much damage was done.

"The only answer is our little grandchildren."

In those first twenty-seven years, Diné educators have created impressive programs to fight what Navajo educator Gloria Emerson calls the trend toward educating Diné "to become 'biological Navajos' without knowing their tribal history, culture, language, or land." By the end of the fifties, local public schools had taken over half of the education of the People. As longtime tribal leader Howard Gorman put it, the Diné "began to realize that Navajo education belonged to the Navajo and not to people in Washington or Phoenix or Santa Fe."

Innovation blossomed first in Rock Point, an already existing BIA school where the community gradually took over control of the "contract school," largely funded by the BIA but under local Diné direction. At Rough Rock Demonstration School, starting from scratch in 1966 with financing from the OEO, Navajo parents formed a school board, and a curriculum center began developing texts written in Navajo. Two Anglo men married to Navajos led these schools at their beginnings: Robert Roessel and Wayne Holm. Soon, Navajos like Dillon Platero took over.

Community schools first flowered in the isolated heart of the reservation, where traditional values hold their own more than in border or agency towns like Shiprock, Chinle, or Window Rock. In 1960, one anthropologist described Shiprock as "active, articulate, politically sophisticated, and bellicose." In 1992, the Shiprock council delegate is Genevieve Jackson, who speaks strongly for the rights of Navajo women in council deliberations.

In the seventies, Rough Rock and Rock Point added high schools to their programs. Ramah Navajo High School began classes in 1970; Borrego Pass (just east of Crownpoint, New Mexico) opened in 1972. Abe Plummer, Diné official at Ramah School, described its goals — goals that spilled over into the reservation's public schools by the late seventies: "The school intends to help the students to be articulate in Navajo and English. The school intends to help students attain strong egos so they can compete in anyone's society without fear of stigmas, condescension and prejudices. The school intends to help the students to be analytical and critical without fear of reprisals."

In 1991, seventy percent of Navajo students attended public schools. Rough Rock's

Shirlene Begay, second grader, with her self-portrait, Rock Point Community School, 1991. Each nine-week quarter, elementary-age children write and illustrate a book in Navajo and in English. Rock Point has become a model for integrating Navajo culture into the school curriculum.

underfunded program had dwindled to a few classroom visits by Diné resource specialists. Borrego Pass and Ramah (later moved and renamed Pine Hill) continue to have active community schools. Curriculum materials come from Blanding, Utah (published for the San Juan School District), Navajo Community College Press, and the Native American Materials Development Center in Albuquerque.

Rock Point has become the bastion for weaving Navajo culture into its curriculum. Director at Rock Point, Jimmie C. Begay, says: "I've been in Indian education for twenty years and there isn't another program as thoroughly bilingual as this one." With that reputation, visitors come to observe in sufficient numbers to prompt Priscilla Chee, English language evaluator for the elementary school, to admit, "sometimes we feel like a zoo!"

Stella Tsinajinnie, Navajo language principal at Rock Point Elementary, outlined the program to me. Of fifty-four teachers in the primary grades, only one is non-Navajo. Classes in both Navajo (reading and writing, social studies) and English are required from kindergarten through grade twelve. Math classes begin in Navajo; after grade three, they are taught in English. English reading does not begin until grade two, "after they get Navajo reading pretty much in place."

Every nine-week quarter, elementary-age kids write and illustrate a book in Navajo and in English. High school students publish an award-winning newspaper in Navajo and English and run the local television station: Purple Cow TV.

Says Tsinajinnie, "At Navajo Community College, in Navajo Language 1 they are teaching what we're teaching here in the second grade!" And yet, "even my generation has lost a lot of words; we're at the fourth grade level. We're giving that fourth grade level to the kids. The rest of it is gone."

Everyone I spoke with at Rock Point preached the philosophy behind their program. Jimmie C. Begay held his hands about six inches apart: "If you're monolingual, you have this much. In terms of concepts, thinking . . . with Navajo and English, you have twice that." Johnson Dennison, principal of the high school, said, with vehemence: "All the times I have spent in high school and universities, I have discovered as long as I know my language, as long as I know who I am, I can learn better, faster. I feel better about myself."

Rex Lee Jim represents the ideal. He told me, "I was raised by a traditional family. Parents, uncles, aunts, grandparents, always informed me that this was where my roots are — whatever I planned to do, this is where I plant the seed." He graduated from Rock Point Elementary School when there was no local high school. He finished his secondary education on scholarships in North Carolina and Colorado. He then attended Princeton University.

Jim says: "It was easy to attend these institutions because I firmly believe in my culture. People who are not strongly rooted are the ones who question everything."

Navajo poet Rex Lee Jim, 1991. Jim came home to teach at Rock Point Community School after completing his degree at Princeton: "I want to make younger people realize that you can come from a traditional family and be successful in both worlds."

Rex Lee Jim has published a book of poetry in Navajo; he is working on a libretto for the first Navajo-language opera. He dreams of founding a Navajo School for the Performing Arts: "It has to be on the reservation." He came home to teach English at Rock Point High School, "mostly to be with family. To participate in ceremonies. I try to encourage my students to maximize their potential. Not many people say, go out and be a poet, writer, dancer, photographer. We deprive ourselves of nourishing the human spirit. Do something that you want to do. I want to make younger people realize that you can come from a traditional family and be successful in both worlds."

I asked to photograph a charming book created by a Rock Point second grader, Pedro Lee. He turned out to be a "problem" student, from a very poor family, living with his grandmother and two brothers in a tiny shed in the orange dunes below the buttes scattered around Rock Point. When I complimented his art, his aunt said, "That's the only good thing anyone has said about Pedro." But what did he title his book? "I'll Be A Singer."

Pedro wrote in Navajo: "I want my grandfather to help me. He'll help me learn to sing. We'll be singing while we're herding sheep. When I learn one song pretty well, I'll teach my brother to sing. When we learn how to sing very good, we will sing over our own brothers and sisters."

Other Diné educators dreamed of a Navajo college — the first community college on any U.S. reservation. First discussed in 1952 by Chairman Nakai, the idea of a bilingual college on the reservation, sensitive to Diné values, took hold in the sixties and led to the founding of Navajo Community College in 1968. Robert Roessel left Rough Rock to serve as the first NCC president; the next year, Ned Hatathli took over. In 1973, the college moved from temporary classrooms at Many Farms to the permanent campus at Tsaile; a branch campus offers classes in Shiprock.

Since then, tribal politics have digested several NCC presidents, but the school remains central to the study of Navajo culture. As a truly Navajo institution, it also offers advantages like a rodeo coach in the athletics program; winning top honors at the National Intercollegiate Rodeo Association Finals guarantees hero status for NCC students.

Lawrence Gishey, president of NCC in 1991, reminded his students: "Once you build up your self-esteem inside, there's no limit to what you can do. If there is anything you can get from this institution, it's that culture and language; that's what fills up your soul, that's what you survive on." Harry Walters, curator of the NCC museum, points out that the college also provides "foundation studies" to bring people up to college level in English and math, in preparation for moving on from their associate's degrees.

Though a pawn in the broader political wrangles of the Navajo Nation, NCC has continued to employ teachers like Wilson Aronilth, whose Foundations of Navajo Culture class gives students the background knowledge they might have received from their family's elders in previous generations. The morning I sat in on his class, he spoke of clan origins, of "cosmic laws": "Life is very short; every day is important. You should be up with the morning star. If you sleep late you will be lazy and ruin your life."

He spoke of Bluebird and Fox and Deer and Blue Jay. He spoke of Changing Woman and "the sacred sites we keep to ourselves. Near Spider Rock there is a sacred footprint of Changing Woman and her sons. There is one in New Mexico, one near Page, one near the Grand Canyon. We don't tell where these are; a museum might even go there and cut it out."

Aronilth spoke of the meaning of religion: "The word is used by people in the way they feel comfortable. The meaning of hózhǫ́? You can have all the medicine man's interpretations, but, really, it's *you!*"

Danny Blackgoat, NCC Navajo language instructor, says: "I'm working to get myself out of a job — deprogramming students from English to Navajo, educating all Navajos, as many as I can. The language comes to us from the land, the stars, the sky.

Sound from the natural world is incorporated in our vocabulary. For this reason, we live and speak the language of the earth."

Harry Walters describes his museum as "an Indian museum, run by Indians, for Indians." The collection protects medicine bundles, *jish*, many recently repatriated to NCC by the *other* kinds of museums — the ones run for non-Indians. Walters consults with the Navajo Medicine Man's Association about the proper way to care for them. He says: "These were never meant to be showpieces or aesthetic art pieces, but living beings that possess power for healing. We have a program for local medicine men to borrow these and use them in ceremonies." In turn, "medicine bundles are restored during the ceremonies."

Courses at NCC incorporate a Navajo Native Healing program — training young people in Navajo healing arts. Says Walters: "Traditionally, the teaching of ceremonialism belongs in the family, in the clan. It was not done in the classroom. But very few teachings are done now in the home. Most homes around here have serious problems with alcoholism. We shouldn't completely abandon these kids."

And so, "we need a medicine man entrance exam, like college boards." He looked at me across his desk: "You might be at the third grade level in your knowledge of Navajo culture. Navajo students working here at the museum are higher. High school level people like myself know what's what, but couldn't perform a ceremony. College-level people know some songs, can follow along with stories. Our program is aimed at this level.

"Only the medicine men are at the doctoral level."

The NCC staff works with a wide variety of students. One of them, outspoken twenty-eight-year-old Mike Yazzie says: "A lot of students here are really intelligent, but it's a really young population of students; a lot of them are just playing with education. You have good-thinking Navajos who can't speak English. And you've got kids taking calculus and they can't speak Navajo. If they could do both, then you'd really have something."

Yazzie grew up in Los Angeles, returning to the reservation each summer. He says: "I came here with the intention of becoming a councilman, a chairman. But Navajos need lawyers. Navajos need *good* lawyers, lawyers that can wheel and deal with these big slugs and not be intimidated by their stares and their language. I'm going to study Indian law."

Yazzie says: "I know I belong here. I'll take my stand for my beliefs. Even if it takes a *revolution*."

Navajo Borderlands: Struggle and Success

Though just six thousand Diné live in Utah — only 3 percent of the Navajo population — they live on one of the ten richest oil reserves in the United States. In 1978, over 90 percent of the workers in these rich oil fields were non-Navajo; in protest of their exploitation by the energy companies, the Utah Navajo shut down the entire operation for seventeen days.

Utah was the last state in the Union to allow Indians living on reservations to vote, in 1957. In 1989, 75 percent of Utah Navajos still lived without electricity or running water.

It is time for Mike Yazzie's revolution. And Mark Maryboy is leading it.

In 1984, the U.S. Department of Justice ordered San Juan County, Utah, to re-district to guarantee fair representation for the Navajo, who total 50 percent of the population. Maryboy won election as a county commissioner the next year — the first Native American ever elected in the state. In 1990, he won elections for both com-missioner and for Navajo Nation council delegate from Montezuma Creek.

In these same 1990 elections, a slate of Indian Democrats ran for San Juan County office. A registration and get-out-the-vote campaign added 20 percent to the numbers of Navajo voters, though only Maryboy won. "This is the beginning," he said.

The beginning continued in 1991 when Maryboy and his Indian and Anglo allies pushed a bill through the Utah legislature giving control over interest from the oil royalties from the Aneth fields to a committee of Utah Indian people. The state has held this money in trust for the Utah Navajos since the 1933 legislation that added the Aneth Extension and Paiute Strip (the latter once reserved for the San Juan Paiute) to the reservation. The 1933 bill guaranteed to the state of Utah 37.5 percent of royal-ties from any oilfields developed, with remaining royalties paid directly to the tribal government in Window Rock.

More than 80 percent of the $60 million that passed through this fund over the last thirty years is gone, much of it wasted through mismanagement and corruption on the part of both Navajo development officials and Utah state trust administrators. Utah Navajos have sued the state of Utah, seeking repayment. The state, tired of com-plications, has tried to transfer royalty payments to the Navajo tribe. The Utah Navajos remain steadfast in their fight to administer the funds, and they have threatened to secede from the Navajo Nation before seeing all royalties paid directly to Window Rock. The People are taking control of their own destiny, and they are doing so by using Anglo institutions.

The Diné have lived in Utah for centuries, with some hogan sites dating to the 1600s.
The Bears Ears region on the flanks of the Abajo Mountains east of Blanding has long
been home to Navajos. Many Utah Diné, in fact, call themselves Kaiyellis, after the
nineteenth-century Bears Ears headman, K'aayeli (Kigalia), whose territory reached
north to the La Sal and Henry mountains. A few Navajos have continued to raise their
families in these high mesas beyond the reservation, eating wild foods, singing songs
to the Earth, clashing with southeastern Utah Anglos over schools and culture.

Mark Maryboy grew up on the reservation, in isolated country across the San Juan
River from Bluff. He returned home from the University of Utah with a history degree
and two years of experience working for K-Mart as a manager of training programs.
Maryboy smiles when he thinks back to that time: "People thought I was Japanese in
my three-piece suit, all clean-cut."

At home, he was shocked by his mother's poverty: "It just broke my heart." He
wrote a grant for water, power, and HUD housing for twenty-nine homes belonging
to his relations, and the money came through. Says Maryboy: "People just couldn't
believe it, way out in the desert, twenty-nine homes!"

He expanded this program to all seven chapters represented in Utah. Soon,
at thirty ("young and foolish," in Maryboy's words), the charismatic and ambitious
Navajo found himself running for the county commission and winning the right
to sit across the conference table from the late, legendary Calvin Black, feisty sagebrush rebel and model for outrageous Bishop Love in Edward Abbey's *The Monkey
Wrench Gang*.

"There is a lot of anger at Native Americans in San Juan County," says Maryboy.
"San Juan County has been spending only 5 percent of its total budget on 50 percent
of its people — the Utah Navajos. But I have to think about all the people I represent;
anybody in my situation cannot afford to be limited in terms of understanding.

"Utah Navajos live in no-man's land. The Navajo tribe ignores them; the state of
Utah ignores them. Each thinks the other is taking care of them." With his ability
to attract media attention and his dual elected positions, Mark Maryboy plans to
change that.

Ramah, Cañoncito, and Alamo, the three isolated New Mexico satellite reservations,
face similar complexities. Each looks to Window Rock with ambivalence: desiring independence but needing support. The old Navajo concept of band survives here most
strongly. The "tribal band" owns more of each of these reservations than do allottees
or the Navajo Nation.

Closest satellite to the big reservation, Ramah remains a bastion of old ways because of its rural nature. When Mormons founded the village of Ramah in the 1880s,

they drove the Diné south. Today, the state highway rolling through meadows, fragrant pines, and sandstone buttes of the Zuni Mountains carries tourist minivans — and even greater numbers of Acoma, Zuni, and Navajo pickups — between El Malpais and El Morro national monuments and on toward Gallup. All but one Ramah Diné community lies well off this road.

Clyde Kluckhohn, talking with Ramah people in the 1940s, could find no adult over the age of thirty who had not been the patient in at least one ceremonial. Twenty percent of family income went to singers in those days. An ethnobotanist working at Ramah at the time identified five hundred native plants; Ramah Diné could name all but three in Navajo.

In the 1990s, livestock and weaving remain important here. The Ramah Weavers Association does well in marketing its rugs. A Ramah man, Benny Coho, served on the Cibola County commission in the 1980s and accomplished much for the community. Ramah people have seen increasing numbers of paved roads and HUD housing developments.

The fifteen hundred Ramah people are closely related, mostly descended from seven families who returned here after the Long Walk, primarily members of the Green Meadow and Bitter Water clans. Indeed, the community of Mountain View is still one large extended family. After about 1890, no new families joined the "founding fathers." New blood came from individuals marrying into Ramah.

In 1963, the BIA transferred Ramah from the Pueblo Agency to the Navajo Agency, opening up many tribal programs to Ramah people for the first time. In 1986, Ramah took over managing its own government, working directly with the BIA. Martha Pino, from Ramah, says: "Being isolated from the main reservation is a good thing for us. We can do our own thing."

I spoke with Pino, one of four producers, in the broadcast room of Ramah's FM radio station, KTDB, "Navajo Radio," housed in the Pine Hill School. KTDB began broadcasting in 1972, mostly in Navajo — providing not only entertainment but a key communications link for isolated communities. Bertha Dutton quotes a characteristic message overheard on KTDB: "Leonard Jose will be at the bus station at Gallup between 7:30 and 8:30 P.M. Someone please pick him up and give him a ride to Fence Lake, Bread Springs, or Ramah."

Ramah offers limited jobs: the community school, tribal government, woodcutting, firefighting. Some tensions remain with the small Mormon settlement. Electricity and water have yet to reach everybody. But Pino says: "I've lived in cities and I come back. It's peaceful out here. I can't live in the fast lane. Here you can spend time with your kids and still work 40 hours in the evenings. I like living here."

Martha Pino, producer at KTDB, "Navajo Radio," on the Ramah Navajo Reservation, 1991. KTDB provides entertainment and a key communications link for isolated communities. Says Pino: "Being isolated from the main reservation is a good thing for us. We can do our own thing."

The seventeen-hundred-strong Cañoncito Diné feel much the same way. Nora Morris, chapter secretary, says: "We have privacy from the big Navajo. We don't have so many people coming in and out of our reservation. A lot of people on the big Navajo Reservation didn't know where we were until this big turmoil of 1989 and 1990."

The turmoil she speaks of had to do with a tribal council delegate from Cañoncito who wanted to secede from the Navajo Nation. His notion was "unilateral," according to current delegate Lawrence Platero. "The old guard overspent in their roles of Business Committee. It was a big mess for a while."

Platero tells his people: "You want a change, you need to communicate. You have to tell me what you want in order to progress." I spoke with him one afternoon when a chapter meeting was scheduled. He needed twenty-five people for a quorum, and was patiently waiting for members to drift in over several hours. Only half a dozen had arrived when I left, but Platero was cheerful. He is used to the Diné way of decision making. Even in council, the votes are rarely close; people have already talked the issues through. Says Platero of Window Rock politics: "The lobbying happens over at the Navajo Nation Inn!"

Navajos deliberate slowly, think about things, and strive for consensus votes. As Kathryn Polacca, Navajo teacher, told Stan Steiner: "We communicate by listening and being quiet." Jennie Joe says: "A traditional speaker talks like a weaver, pausing to think about a line after it's woven, to think about whether it was woven well."

Once the home of the Enemy Navajo, the most acculturated and Christian of Diné, Cañoncito today no longer carries that negative tag. Dillon Platero, pioneer Navajo educator in the sixties, came from Cañoncito. Lawrence Platero discovered "a lot of people in the council in my clan."

Less than forty miles from Albuquerque, Cañoncito has rampant unemployment. There is a local BIA school, though many students bus into westside Albuquerque each day. Says Morris: "Younger people have to go elsewhere to get further education; few come back." Lawrence Platero believes: "What this place needs is economic development, housing, communication. People have been asking for help for years and have never received assistance. We're trying to work with Alamo on roads, water, a new BIA liaison."

Nora Morris points out that "the reservation stops at Stuckeys," at the Rio Puerco crossing — the first truck stop west of Albuquerque on Interstate 40. "Albuquerque's ten-year plan goes that far. If Albuquerque expands, that would bring access."

"The 'Big Tribe' teases us about getting tired on the Long Walk and not getting all the way back home!" Michael Secatero, Community Service Coordinator for the Alamo Navajos, laughs. "We tell them we didn't need to go so far; we chased away the Army and moved back into our own hills. We have a place we can call home. We've been fortunate."

Even so, the modern Alamo Band of Diné faces its own problems, compounded by isolation and boundary and land issues. In 1959, the average adult Alamo Navajo had only one and one-half years of education. After years of boarding away, the community opened its first successful community school in 1979. Today, this contract school provides the primary source of employment and pride for the Alamo Diné.

Alamo families cluster in nine villages serviced by power and water. Though the first powerline reached the reservation in 1967, more rural people still need services. Water and mineral rights remain clouded.

Only recently connected to Magdalena, New Mexico, by pavement, the 64,000-acre Alamo reservation lies some seventy miles west of Socorro — the nearest city with abundant wage work. The two-thousand-member band hopes to find funding for completing the pavement north for forty-five miles to connect with Interstate 40 near Mesita. This will ease access to Albuquerque, Cañoncito, and Window Rock. And then, says Michael Secatero, "our isolation will end."

Meanwhile, the Henderson Ranch lease offers new opportunities for stock raising, woodcutting, and blue corn production. And negotiations continue toward purchase of additional ranchland north and west of Alamo. Secatero dreams of passing on his government post to someone else and going into ranching: "I want to be my own boss." Like his People, to succeed he will need to balance that urge for independence with the need for help from the band, the BIA, and the Navajo Nation.

One last borderland holds nearly thirty-thousand Diné — 15 percent of the Navajos — living beyond the reservation boundary in the New Mexico "Checkerboard." Here, interspersed among Anglo and Hispanic ranches and federal land over an area of seven thousand square miles, Navajos live on allotted lands (and some simply on traditionally used and uncontested BLM lands). The Checkerboard grew from awarding alternate sections of land to western railroad companies and from the withdrawal of much of this land in 1907, partial allotment to Diné, and then hasty restoration to the public domain in 1908 and 1911. Efforts in the thirties to exchange lands and create blocks of Diné land resulted mostly in the Navajos losing access to almost half the public land they had been using beyond their 160-acre allotments.

Today, the Navajo chapter system continues eastward far past the reservation boundary; the Eastern Navajo Agency lies in Crownpoint, within the Checkerboard. Jurisdictional questions (at least fourteen different kinds of land ownership exist) and struggles over water, mineral, and grazing rights create constant troubles. Even when the Navajo Nation buys out a retiring Anglo rancher, Window Rock may lease the grazing rights on the new Diné land to nonlocal families — to the distress of Checkerboard people. In 1991, the Navajos negotiated a major agreement with federal land management agencies, exchanging 20,000 acres for 80,000 acres of consolidated Checkerboard lands.

The Checkerboard contains rich deposits of uranium, coal, oil, and natural gas, but rights to the minerals are a nightmare. The first big strike of uranium in the Southwest came within the Checkerboard in 1950; it was made by Navajo Paddy Martinez, who soon lost his claim to whites. In the 1970s, Checkerboard Navajos sued to slow uranium development in the San Juan Basin. In the 1980s, fourteen thousand Navajo allottees learned that the federal government, not the Diné, had the sole right to determine if allotted lands would be strip-mined for coal — and that Washington, D.C., not the Diné, would receive the proceeds. The Diné sued once again; the case remains in the courts.

Meanwhile, energy corporations contact individual allottees, arm-twisting rural Diné with misrepresentations about rights-of-way and payments, and the Navajos suffer the disadvantages of being single landowners bargaining with corporate lawyers.

One such Navajo landowner, Mary Largo, told journalist John Aloysius Farrell, after signing away her mineral rights to a Navajo representative of Mobil Oil: "The land is like a piece of material. If you put too many holes in it, it becomes a rag. They made a rag of my land. It is like a desert now, and the topsoil blows everywhere."

Claudeen Bates-Arthur, the first female Navajo attorney, worked as a lawyer for the Interior Department in the early 1980s. She was fired for protesting the Bureau's lack of action concerning energy corporations taking advantage of Navajo allottees. (She later won a court case and was granted back pay.) She came home to the Navajo Nation to work as tribal attorney general and, in 1991, legislative counsel. Says Bates-Arthur: "We must develop our own experts if we want 'self-determination' instead of 'self-extermination!' "

Today, the allottees have formed an association and have hired their own attorney.

The New Navajo

The Diné continue to define and redefine their identity — in the face of never-ending challenges. Today, many educated Navajos live far from the reservation and no longer participate in their family's pastoral life. Homesick Navajos say, "I haven't seen the sheep in a long time," or "I want some fresh mutton." Artist Shonto Begay, living in Santa Fe, calls his reservation home, "the sanctuary of my childhood."

Urban Navajos send money to their families on the reservation, however. Diné who live in agency or border towns, close enough to visit home most weekends, help with woodcutting, water-hauling, and with the stock. The older people herd sheep, and the homestead depends on the one younger wage-earner who commutes to the nearest power plant, mine, mini-mall, tribal office, or boarding school. The rest of the older and less educated people suffer chronic under- and unemployment.

One's local chapter has begun to take over from clan and kin as the primary source of identity. The traditional headman or naat'aani has evolved into an elected representative or tribal judge. Jennie Joe says: "Younger people raised on the reservation now define land (where they were raised) in terms of freedom: 'When I'm home I can do whatever I want.' Older generations define land in a more sacred way." And yet, she adds: "I know many Navajos who don't speak the language who are as Navajo as they come."

Diné parents continue to teach Diné values, no matter what scenarios their children subsequently live through. For years, many Navajo children lived with Mormon families during their school years on placement programs, but they usually came home — and in more than just a physical sense. As Frank Talker, today a Mormon Navajo business consultant living in Orem, Utah, says: "I was always told on placement that honesty, loving my parents, working hard — that these were Mormon values. But I finally realized that I learned these things from my parents."

Kalley Musial remembers what her grandmother taught her when she was growing up: "Without your family, you were nothing. She taught me to be there for all my family. When I am there for them, I expect them to be there for me when I need them. It's not very easy these days to teach that to people who are younger than you, who have grown up in San Diego and Salt Lake City. I do not know how it will be for my kids.

"Families are very important. There would not be so many people lost and wandering if families were all there for one another."

Being Navajo has much to do with what Anglos — *bilagaanas* — call religion. Even this powerful measure of ethnicity gets complicated.

Martha Jackson, a strong-willed middle-aged woman who teaches Navajo language at NCC, says with pride: "My grandfather was a medicine man; my father sang the Blessingway. I'm a Christian. It's not bilagaana. It's *mine.*"

Believing in Christianity certainly does not preclude being Diné. In one 1976 survey of Navajos, 25 to 50 percent of Diné (varying with region and gender) called themselves Christians. In a 1989 tribal sourcebook on Navajo chapters, the list of "Civic" facts included a listing of churches, each chapter supporting zero to several, depending on location. Every write-up also contained the line, "traditional Navajo religion and Native American Church are active in the Chapter." Twenty-five thousand Navajos belong to the NAC; thousands more attend peyote ceremonies but do not belong to the church.

Susie Yellowman says this about her belief in the power of the peyote religion: "The more peyote you eat, it's very spiritual. The NAC and Bible study are the same — both put God first. Nature is God, too. Every prayer counts. There's only one God."

Many Christian and NAC members also attend sings and use medicine men. Even Jacob Morgan, the most famous of Navajo Christians, secretly arranged a sing, according to some elders, to treat himself for an illness in his old age!

Sharing and reciprocity form a central tenet of Diné identity. Anthropologist David Aberle puts it this way: "If a favor is done, a favor can be expected in return; if an injury has been done, an injury can be expected in return, unless compensation is provided." Aberle notes that "Navajos call it 'helping out' when they speak of it in English — and the ethic that accompanies it is generosity."

Former NCC President Lawrence Gishey says: "When you see a white family picnicking in a park, you see a young couple, an infant, and a dog. When you see Native Americans or Hispanics, you see all the aunts and uncles and relations. It's the same when you give a paycheck to a Native American: it's supporting a lot of people."

Money coming into the family comes from diverse sources. William Kien, World War II code-talker and retired marine, lives out past Crownpoint; I spoke with him at the Gallup Flea Market where he sells his silverwork and his wife's beadwork. Kien called the marines his "second home—you got paid every two weeks. You couldn't beat that, not over here." Now he makes sure to swing by the Gallup post office every two weeks so he can pick up his retirement check—what he calls, with a smile, his "buffalo hunter's check."

At Cañoncito, I gave a ride to Thomas Platero—officially unemployed, but making a little riding bulls (with purses from $300 to $1,500), leatherworking, jewelrymaking. Platero usually rides his horse over to Mesita to visit his Laguna girlfriend. He unfolded himself from my truck with difficulty: the bulls left him with a gimpy leg.

Unemployment remains chronic, at about 34 percent in 1991. The tribal budget exceeded $100 million in 1991, but Peterson Zah says: "We have a fifty percent dropout rate. We don't have good houses, roads, phone lines. We need infrastructure."

Plans for developing new employment opportunities range from a marina at Antelope Point on Lake Powell to an electronics assembly plant being built by General Dynamics near Farmington to an array of shopping centers (at Pinehill and Navajo, New Mexico, and at Piñon, Arizona) and motels (in Chinle and Crownpoint). The Holiday Inn in Chinle exemplifies the never-ending tension between old and new among the Diné. Local people submitted a proposal to restore the ruins of Garcia's Trading Post as an old-time post to attract tourists; Holiday Inn also wanted the site. The tribe chose the new, and the Chinle Holiday Inn opened in 1992.

Local communities have rejected other ideas for development. Navajos in Dilkon, in the southwest part of the reservation, successfully defeated a hazardous waste incinerator proposed by their chapter officials in 1988. The People also must remain vigilant to prevent development of sacred sites that lie beyond the reservation, such as the San Francisco Peaks.

The tribe has resolved to pursue tourism as a number-one priority. Navajo tribal parks draw hundreds of thousands of people yearly. When I photographed sunrise at Monument Valley Tribal Park, I set up my tripod in line with ten other photographers—all speaking German and Japanese. Developing tourist attractions is a means, not an end. As Navajo journalist Marshall Tome puts it, "scenery won't help children get to school in bad weather or make it possible for sick people to be taken quickly to a hospital. And scenery won't help you get to Gallup for what happens on Saturday night or for what follows on Sunday morning."

The Navajo health care system has worked out an exemplary compromise between old and new. Rose Hulligan describes the common modern Navajo belief: "Some illnesses doctors can cure; some illnesses traditional medicine can cure; some

Navajo Tribal Council in session following the Persian Gulf War, 1991. In this grand rock hogan built by WPA workers in the 1930s, with murals by Gerald Nailor, the 88 members of the Navajo legislative branch administer a budget of more than $100 million.

can be helped by both; some can be helped by neither." New Indian Health Service hospitals incorporate a room in which Navajo medicine men conduct cures. Numbers of Navajo doctors and nurses steadily increase; the plan for an American Indian School of Medicine at Shiprock lies dormant.

Jennie Joe emphasizes that "physicians do not need to fear competition from native healers. They don't put up their shingles outside their hogans, saying 'Medicine Man: Open for Business 9–5.' They see themselves as catalysts, not gods." She goes on: "A Navajo chanter takes his patient on a healing journey. Purification and preparation call into this healing circle family members as well as the patient. Everybody contributes to that journey.

"Native ceremonies have an *end*, they have closure. The ceremony returns patients to harmony, gives them the strength and right frame of mind to heal themselves, reaffirms the person's value, and reinstates them in the community. In western medicine, closure comes when the bill arrives!"

Hospitals also serve the Diné well as a neutral place for death; in the old days, when a Navajo died in a hogan, that hogan had to be abandoned or burned — often along with the dead person's belongings and favorite horse. Now, when a person dies in a hospital, his or her home remains uncontaminated by death. The family can continue to live there — and so, homes safely can become more elaborate.

Navajo homesteads look more modern by the year, with gabled multiroom houses common — most often with a basketball hoop, too — and access to radio phone service promised by 1995 to the 88 percent of the reservation without phones in 1992. Still, the hogan remains as the spiritual core of the home place, the only space appropriate for ceremonies.

Navajo identity can be simple and elemental. It is, as Scott Momaday once wrote of Indian identity, "an idea which a given man has of himself." Listen to Diné weaver Kalley Musial explain her values to writer Tryntje Seymour: "I can look at my people and say, 'These are my people.' And I can actually sit down with an old lady on the side of a trading post and just say Ya'ateeh [hello], and just sit there quietly with her — and actually come away feeling like I communicated, because she didn't expect anything of me."

Diné emerging from boarding school, relocation, or employment in distant cities can remain proudly and tenaciously Navajo, even with the outer trappings of Anglo culture. Today's Diné range from those oriented toward traditional values, who speak Navajo only, to thoroughly acculturated Diné who have adopted Anglo values wholesale. In the middle are the marginal people, who do not feel they belong to either, and the masters of adaptation, who feel comfortable with both cultures. One can't make snap judgments about who falls in which category. Rex Lee Jim points out that in the classroom: "The more sociable kids speak English only. You tend to believe that's the trend. You have to go beyond them to the shy ones; you need to speak to *them* in Navajo."

Frank Goldtooth, a prominent elder and medicine man from Tuba City, said: "Our strength in the future must come from our faith in the past." Elaine Walstedter, a young Diné graduate of the University of New Mexico, found that her history classes "put me in touch with what my elders talked about around the campfire, put my father's oral history in context. I could see my father's whole life running parallel to federal Indian policy."

Poet Luci Tapahonso traveled to Europe and prayed from the top of the Eiffel

In the Canyons and Mesas

Rainbow over Acoma Pueblo, New Mexico, 1985.

Hosteen Mud Kid, Navajo
elder, at his hogan in
Monument Valley. Navajo
Reservation, Utah, 1990.

Our Lady of Guadalupe
Mission Church and hornos,
traditional bread ovens. Zuni
Pueblo, New Mexico, 1984.

A young boy rests between
rounds of the Comanche Dance
at San Juan Pueblo's annual
feast day. New Mexico, 1984.

Dancers returning to the kiva during

San Ildefonso Pueblo's feast day

Comanche Dance. New Mexico, 1984.

Christmas Eve luminarias light up five-storied

Taos Pueblo and the chill night sky below Pueblo

Peak. New Mexico, 1986.

Lois Sandy and Rachel Weahkee, Zuni Pueblo
olla maidens, await their turn to dance at the
O'odham Tash celebration. Casa Grande,
Arizona, 1992.

Tony Naki's mother takes her sheep out to graze on Red Mesa. Navajo Reservation, Utah, 1984.

Supai Village in winter. Havasupai Reservation, Grand Canyon, Arizona, 1980.

The track and athletic fields at Monument Valley High School. Navajo Reservation, Arizona, 1991.

The late Bertha Russell,

Hualapai elder and storyteller.

Peach Springs, Arizona, 1984.

Tower, watching the yellow corn pollen float away below her. She "understood that what I am is my mother, her mother, and my great-grandmother, Kinlichii'nii Bitsi, whom I never met but always knew."

Tapahonso teaches at the University of New Mexico. She says: "I live in Albuquerque because that's where the job is. Intellectually, I need the stimulus of my colleagues. And I have the professional support of access to books and poetry readings. It's also nice to call out for a pizza.

"But I miss my support system at home in Shiprock. I have seven sisters who can help with the kids when they're sick, with cooking. My brothers can fix my car. Just being around my relatives — I miss that connection. We can't get good mutton or Bluebird flour for fry bread in Albuquerque.

"People make compromises. It makes you appreciate your beliefs more."

Every Diné must perform a delicate balancing act in trying to live true to these wise words about past and present and future. Some, caught up in the frustration of meeting this challenge, start drinking. Child abuse is rampant; Frank Talker believes that the reasons lie in "punishment suffered by Navajos in BIA boarding schools." Johnson Dennison, Rock Point High School principal, says: "The 'New Navajo' means having economic, social, and health problems. We are killing each other."

Steve Darden lives in Flagstaff. He says: "I don't feel like I'm in an urban environment. I'm in my environment, culturally, traditionally — I'm in Flagstaff, at the base of my sacred mountain. I personally garner strength from this mountain. This is my place, a Navajo place, a holy place.

"I survive because I know who I am culturally."

None have a more difficult job balancing past and future than the councilmen and elected leaders of the Navajo Nation. Marshall Tome imagines what goes on in the mind of a thoughtful councilman pondering his or her job:

"Sometimes we accomplish a lot and other times we get in each other's way and once in a while we try to work against each other because we are afraid that we might lose our jobs or make someone who has more influence than we do mad at us. Sometimes we think that the best thing to do is nothing because then no one can say that we made a mistake. We want to hold on to our jobs for as long as we can. There aren't many jobs here that pay money and we all need money if we are going to live."

The Navajo leader with sufficient vision, charisma, and irreproachable ethics to unify such people must be an exceptional person indeed. He or she must understand another of Tome's maxims: "Now we must decide exactly how we will live as Navajos in this radically changing world."

"Where is our educated few?" worries Clyde Benally. "They are in Los Angeles. A lot of the educated people don't see anything out there, so they stay away." Later in life, many will come home to help. More than four thousand Diné were college students in 1987.

Johnson Dennison says: "We're not going to be stuck on that bottom line forever. I hope our kids are not going to remain imprisoned by American society. Using our language, our culture, to wake up — to be self-reliant again, like our forefathers — this time using our *own* government, to solve our problems. I'd like to see all of that for the Navajos."

Anthropologists Klara Kelley and Peter Whiteley sum up the challenges facing any Diné leader: "The Navajo Tribe is forced to beat the clock of dwindling natural resources by cranking up a self-sustaining economy with one hand, while the other is tied behind its back, dispensing welfare and jobs." Peter MacDonald summed up these dual goals as "building the Nation as well as defending the Nation."

Peterson Zah says: "Someday the coal, oil, and gas are going to be gone. What's going to happen to the Navajo children then? Pete Zah won't be around then. I'll be over at Chinle Extended Care; you have to think about the future.

"Navajo people have survived for thousands of years. Why? It's the culture, it's the language, it's the heart. These things will bring us through these times."

The Pai

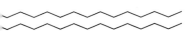

Mooney Falls and travertine, Cataract Canyon, Arizona, 1988. The boom of visitors venturing down the trails to Supai and its exotic waterfalls — the "Shangri-La of the Grand Canyon" — began in the 1960s. Tourism remains the foundation of the Havasupai economy.

The land we were given   Down at the source

The land we were given   A spring will always be there

It is right here   It is ours

It is right here   It is ours

Red rock   Since a long time ago

Red rock   Since a long time ago

Streaked with brown   In the land that is ours

Streaked with brown   Moving down the center

Shooting up high   Bright blue-green

Shooting up high   There moves a line

All around our home   This is what I'm thinking

All around our home   This is what I'm thinking

Red rock   At the edge of the water . . .

Red rock

Shooting up high

It is right here   Dan Hanna, Havasupai Medicine Song, 1965

"Anthropologists have an explanation for everything, but for us, it's simple." The young Havasupai James Uqualla, Jr., former tribal chairman and manager of the tribe's lodge, fixed me with a steady gaze.

"We are the People. We've been here forever. Any group of Indians will say that; it's a strengthening thing."

Wilfred Whatoname, former chairman of the Hualapai people, says: "To us, the land is somewhere where we can live and be in peace. The land means something to us. You go in to big cities: skyscrapers everywhere, you can't see anything. Then you come home, and there's just one street going this way, another street going this way. You can see a lot more. You look out here — it's so dry, no water. But I belong to this place."

Hualapai camp, Grand Canyon, 1883. In this year, President Chester Arthur designated nearly a million acres of rough canyons and rolling plateau on the south rim of the Grand Canyon as the Hualapai Reservation. Two years earlier, the railroad had reached Peach Springs. Photo by Ben Wittick. (Courtesy Museum of New Mexico, neg. no. 16257)

Once, Uqualla's people and Whatoname's people were one people. The Huala-pai and Havasupai were the Pai, the Pa'a, the People. Thirteen bands of Pai ranged across the northwestern corner of Arizona south of the Colorado River, hunting, farming, and living off the land. They spoke a Yuman language. They came from Spirit Mountain.

After Mađwiđa

Mađvil created humans by praying life into canes cut from along the Colo-rado River below Spirit Mountain (Wikahme'). In *Spirit Mountain: An Anthology of Yuman Story and Song*, Hualapai elder Elnora Mapatis tells what happened next:

> The Mojaves remained at Wikahme'
> They lived there
> "I shall remain a Mojave," they said.

The other peoples traveled eastward. First, the Southern Paiute left and moved north of the river. The remaining humans descended to live together in a side canyon of the western Grand Canyon called Meriwhitica on Anglo maps — a rough translit-eration of the Hualapai, Mađwiđa. Here all lived in peace. "They survived in this way."

But then a fight erupted between the people. The leaders said,

> "This battle is not good
> From now on our language will not be one
> From now on we all will leave and scatter one by one
> When we come out at the rim."

So the peoples emerged from the canyon. The Pai settled at nearby springs and at Supai. Though they spoke the same language, the Yavapai quarreled with the People and left, going south to become "The Enemy," the "Almost-People to the East." Other families moved east to Indian Gardens below modern Grand Canyon Village, to Moen-kopi Wash at Tuba City, "moving on and on." But, from Tuba City on, "their languages were different." Beyond, the Hopis, Navajos, Apaches, and Pueblos all settled.

> "Mah, I will remain Hualapai."
> "I will be Havasupai"
> "I will be Yavapai"
> "I will be Hopi," they said
> "I will be Navajo," they said
> This is what they said as they went.

The Pai remained. They remained for over twelve centuries, for archaeologists have found the same simple brown pottery in excavations at Willow Beach below Lake Mead, pots made in A.D. 750 by prehistoric Patayans, and on the knickknack shelves of modern Hualapai family homes, pots made by the Pai in the nineteenth century and now tenderly displayed by their great-grandchildren.

By historic times, according to anthropologists Henry Dobyns and Robert Euler (who worked with the Pai on their land claims case), three Pai subtribes held Arizona between the Grand Canyon and the Bill Williams Fork, east as far as Hopi country. The Middle Mountain people lived closest to Spirit Mountain, in two bands. Seven bands made up the Plateau People, including the large Ha vasuwa 'baaje band, the Blue Water People who farmed in Cataract Canyon with the spring-fed turquoise waters of Havasu Creek and who came to be called Havasupai. On the southern rim of Pai country lived the largest subtribe, the four bands of Yavapai Fighters, who faced the enemy across the Bill Williams Fork.

Several family camps made up each band, a camp averaging twenty people and moving through its home range in seasonal visits to resource-gathering sites. Band size ranged from 85 to 250; band territory ranged from 350 square miles to almost 1,500 square miles. The Blue Water People of Havasu (the largest band) may have ranged through a wider elevation span than any Southwestern Indians, gathering desert plants from along the Colorado River at eighteen hundred feet and hunting at twelve thousand feet on the upper slopes of the San Francisco Peaks, their "Center of the World."

Philbert Watahomigie thinks about the huge expanse of Hualapai land when he drives the sixty miles from Peach Springs to Kingman: "I look at these places and I wonder, did Hualapais really live around here? How were they able to walk these many miles, from, say, Chloride down into Mađwiđa, down into Peach Springs or over to Mohawk Canyon? It's amazing."

Camp headmen shaped group decisions and gave advice. Band headmen wielded still more influence, and subtribe chiefs led the People in war with the Mojave and Yavapai and served as spokesmen with outsiders. Their highest honorific meant "superlatively good." As with all Yumans, shamans dreamed their power and their songs; they wielded their power for curing, controlling the weather, or fixing fractures or snake bites by calling on the spirits of Wikahme', of Spirit Mountain. "This mountain is so powerful," said Hualapai elders George Walker and Old Mike in 1929, "that a doctor does not dare approach it directly. He must get his spirit to do it for him."

Weldon Mahone, son of a Hualapai tribal leader and now a parole officer for the tribe, remembers: "In the time of the medicine man, I was told that the hills and the mountain has a life in it. The ground which we stand on has a life in it, that we must

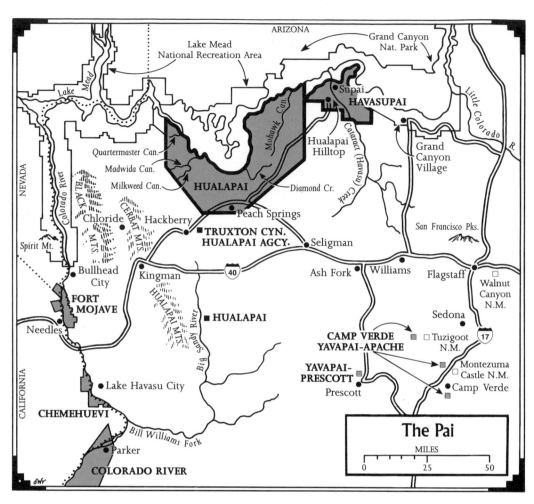

The Pai

MILES

0   25   50

try and worship the land and the ground and the stars and the skies, for they are the mighty spirits, which guides and direct us, which help us to survive.

"Now we have Indian Health Service here, and all these modern drugs. And all the people are banking on that!"

Cremation was a time of wailing and sorrow. In the old days, funerals included the burning of the deceased's house and belongings. Today, the Hualapai at Peach Springs hold their centuries-old memorial powwow in summer to honor the dead buried during the previous year. The People sing, dance, and cry under a ritual *ramada* for a day and a night. At dawn, they heap onto the *ramada* roof their mourning costumes, along with such offerings as bolts of cloth, and set fire to the structure as the sun rises.

Hualapai councilwoman Sylvia Querta lived at Milkweed Spring with her grand-

parents when she was small: "We were taught to pray to the land and talk to the water.
We ask it to forgive us for walking on it, if we make any marks, or if we drink of it we
ask it to be blessed so that we can get strength from the Mother Earth. We really meant
it from our hearts when we prayed. Now, my kids, I take them to the same place and I
teach them. They kind of laugh, but I know that down inside they're serious about it.

"Right now Milkweed is deserted. But my children, they want to go back and live
there because they have the same feelings that I have about that place."

The People built simple thatched brush and bark dome houses at each camp —
shades in summer and sturdier mud-plastered huts in winter. Men used sweat lodges
both for curing and as clubhouses; women entered them less frequently, primarily
for healing. The Pai practiced a wide variety of irrigation techniques at canyon springs
and along the Big Sandy River and Havasu and Diamond creeks, living near fields during the spring planting, summer irrigating, and fall harvest seasons. Havasupai leader
Sinyella told anthropologist Leslie Spier in about 1920: "We have a creek to irrigate
with; the Hopi plant prayer plumes in their fields because they have none and have to
pray for rain all the time."

The rest of the year the Pai cycled through a round of harvests elsewhere in
their territory. The Cataract Canyon band was typical, equally dependent on wild and
domestic foods, gardening between thirty and forty acres at Supai each season, staying
together as a band for the piñon harvest in fall, and hunting and gathering from eight
or nine family camps on the plateau through the winter. The Havasupai told anthropologist Al Whiting in 1941: "We used to live on top all the time. We just had gardens
in the canyon." The People set fires to stampede game, and in the wake of the blaze,
gathered the seeds of sle', the bushy annual, blazing star, that grew up in the burns. The
Pai litany of wild foods resembles those eaten by the other Southwesterners: cactus
and yucca fruits, piñon nuts, agave hearts, mesquite beans, small mammals, pronghorn (the number-one game animal), deer and mountain sheep, chuckwalla lizards
(not eaten by the Havasupai, who jeered at the western Pai for doing so).

Bighorn became more important to the Havasupai after they were restricted to
their inner-canyon reservation. Several families tell of shooting sheep from their front
doors. Lee Marshall watches the canyon from his house and sometimes sees sheep
on the ledges and on top of the cliffs looking down over the rims at the village. He
says: "The boys don't like the meat; if they did, there wouldn't be any more sheep!"

Hualapai elder Annie Querta likens ground mesquite to popcorn balls, ground
piñon nuts to peanut butter, pounded squawbush berries mixed with water to Kool-
Aid. She says: "I miss that food. I always tell this young grandchildren that we do that.
But when they don't see it, they don't believe it!" Philbert Watahomigie is impressed

by records of hundreds of pounds of piñon nuts in Hualapai camp larders (noted by the U.S. Army as they destroyed them): "It takes all day just to go out and fill up a two-pound coffee can. You can just imagine how many days and hours they spent out there gathering that stuff."

The People wove yucca-fiber nets, wore rabbit-skin robes in winter (over fifty rabbits per robe), made lovely baskets (women's work), and tanned buckskins (men's work). The richest men owned quivers made from mountain lion skin; lesser men used fawn or bighorn lambskin. The Pai also gathered rich red ochre pigment from a cave in Diamond Creek Canyon, a prized item that made them a vital link in the Southwest trade network.

When drought struck the Hopi mesas, the Hopi took refuge in Havasu Canyon with the Cataract Canyon band (whom the Hopi called Cosnino). Some Havasupai families, in turn, visited Oraibi in the fall and spring, watching the dances and trading, and bringing home the first peach trees to Supai. Thus, when non-Indians approached Pai country from the east, from Hopi country, they called the Pai "Cosnino." When Anglos approached from the west, from Mojave country, as they did increasingly after the Mexican War, the first band encountered was the Hualapai Mountain band, the Pine-Clad Mountain People, the Whala Pa'a. All the western Pai eventually came to be called the Hualapai (or Walapai).

The Hualapai Wars

The northwest frontier for Spanish missionaries in the Southwest stopped at Hopi. European diseases, however, reached far beyond the paths of explorers. And trade routes brought the Pai wheat, fig, peach, and melon seeds, along with manufactured leather items and wool blankets traded for Diamond Creek red ochre — for the women of Santa Fe wanted the red pigment to mask smallpox scars.

Non-Indians took a long time to penetrate Pai country in person. In 1776, Fray Francisco Garcés visited Supai, where he saw both horses and cattle. No missions followed him, only the beaver hunters (of the 1820s) and the surveying parties (of the 1850s) during the early American period, whose mules and horses made welcome additions to the Pai diet. Lieutenant J. C. Ives came exploring in 1858, writing for the first time of "Hualpai" (as he spelled it), who guided him down Diamond Creek to the bottom of the Grand Canyon.

Pai interaction with outsiders accelerated after 1857, when Edward Fitzgerald Beale pioneered a wagon road from the Rio Grande to California along what Congress called the "35th Parallel route." The Pai lay squarely on this path that would eventually see the Santa Fe Railway, U.S. Highway 66, and Interstate 40. Trouble between Indian and Anglo was inevitable.

Mojave raids grew fierce enough to force the army to build Fort Mojave in 1859 on the western edge of Pai country. The early years of the Civil War brought the Pai a brief respite, but in 1863, prospectors struck rich ore in the western Pai mountains, the Black, Cerbat, and Hualapai ranges. The Prescott mines opened in 1863, Arizona Territory was created the next year, and the Pai found themselves on the major supply line between Hardyville, where Colorado River steamboats unloaded, and Fort Whipple at Prescott. The principal leader (the Tokumhet) of the Middle Mountain people, Cherum, knew what was coming. He and his half-brother Susquatama (later called Hualapai Charley) traded Pai buckskins for blankets, and blankets for guns and ammunition (obtained from Utah via Moapa Paiutes). They also traded for horses — to be used as mounts, not food.

The Hualapai War lasted from 1865 to 1869, the longest period of armed resistance to Anglo settlement by any Yuman tribe. In between, the leaders of the three Pai subtribes became the legendary heroes of their people. A group of Anglo prospectors and freighters murdered Wauba Yuma, leader of the Yavapai Fighters, in a despicable way that sparked the angriest fighting of the war. Hitchi-Hitchi, chief of the Plateau People, died in battle. The remaining subtribal chief, Cherum, gained in influence because he survived to dominate the new young leaders of the two other subtribes.

Cherum's brilliant battle tactics made him the only Hualapai war leader to force the U.S. Army to retreat. Not even Cherum could beat back the cavalry consistently, though the People sent more than 250 men into battle (up to one-fourth of their total population). Cherum remained suspicious of Anglos throughout his life. Hualapai Charley and Leve Leve (band leader of the Whala Pa'a), were more inclined to make deals with the invaders, and whites thus chose to see them as principal chiefs. Leve Leve sued for peace first, and he and his band were interned. Cherum and Charley were sent off to prison in California, but Cherum repeatedly escaped.

During the year and a half after the U.S. Army joined the initial Anglo force of territorial rangers, government troops lost only seven men (four of them "civilian tenderfeet," according to Dobyns and Euler) to 175 Hualapai dead. The northeastern Pai bands, the Grass Spring, Pine Spring, and Blue Water People, all mostly escaped the disasters brought by war.

By the spring of 1869, the army considered the Hualapai sufficiently conquered to enlist Pai warriors as scouts. Even Cherum was persuaded to serve, blackmailed with the threat of further action against his own people. Pai scouts played crucial roles in the defeat of the Yavapai and Tonto Apache, especially in General Crook's 1872–73

campaign. Though the rest of the tribe tried to withdraw to their old haunts, the army had destroyed fields and food, and prospectors were pushing hard at the Pai frontier. The military created a small reservation at Beale's Springs in 1871, issued rations, and made the scouts the arbitrary authorities in the camp. The Pai were being coopted into government dependency, like so many other tribes.

Leader of the Cataract Canyon band, Chief Navajo, went home after the Yavapai War. The Army thought of Havasu as an isolated place far from the main group of "Hualapai" and treated Navajo as an independent leader. Differentiation of the Pai into two "tribes" intensified.

Inventing Tribes

In January 1874, Captain Thomas Byrne, commander of Hualapai scouts and administrator of the Beale's Springs reservation, opened orders from the Office of Indian Affairs he did not much like. Intent on its concentration policy, the government had decided to move the Pai to La Paz, on the Colorado River Indian Reservation. Byrne stalled, two-thirds of the People bolted, but the scouts who remained convinced all western bands but the Peach Springs band to surrender. The army made no effort to round up Cataract Canyon people.

During two weeks in April, the captive Pai were forced to march south to the desert. The late Bertha Russell, a Hualapai elder in her eighties in 1984, told me the stories told to her by her grandmother, Haika, who had been a teenager when she walked with her family on the march. As Bertha Russell spoke, she *became* her grandmother.

"When grandmother would tell that story, tears would spill down her face. She says, 'I don't know how I stood this march to La Paz. My feet were sore and torn, my toes were broken. We were so thirsty.

'I see what was done on this march.

'My grandfather was whipped to death.

'I cry in my heart.'

"La Paz is way down below Parker. They throw them in no-man's land, just sand, just stickers. It was so hot, many of them died — two, three people die in a day; babies die.

"One day, they said, 'Why should we just stay and die all of us? We should go back to our country, to our land, to our water where we were raised.' They had a big cry, shake hands, tell them, 'If we ever live we would see you again, if not, you know that we tried.' So, they travel by night, they rested by day."

"In later years, we hear her crying in her sleep. She says, 'I see these things still in my own eyes yet. When, when will I ever forget?'"

The internment at La Paz lasted exactly one year. Heat, epidemic disease, spoiled rations, and starvation killed many people. On the anniversary of their arrival at La Paz, the six hundred Pai left for home, as Russell described. They filtered back into a land now largely held by Anglo settlers and miners. Cherum paid a visit to the territorial governor in Prescott and promised that the Pai would stay at peace and find work. With the support of the army and governor, the People were able to remain in their homeland.

The pioneer local newspaper clearly stated Anglo perceptions when, in 1882, it stated that Hualapais had "taken the place of Chinamen." The People formed the underclass, the pool of cheap laborers for mines and ranches. Leaders like Cherum and Charley became hay cutters, and Cherum maintained his authority over his people by contracting for their labor with mine operators.

As much as they wished peace, the Hualapai found themselves in opposition to virtually every act of the settlers. Cattle companies took over the springs that gave Pai bands their names and identities as well as their water. Both Pai and Anglo hunters using rifles drastically reduced game populations; fire-drives no longer made sense. Lack of rejuvenating fires along with catastrophic overgrazing diminished the seed-producing plants favored by the People.

The railroad (called first the Atlantic and Pacific, and later the Santa Fe) came to northern Arizona at the very beginning of settlement. And so northern Arizona's towns are railroad towns: Holbrook, Winslow, Flagstaff, Williams, Ash Fork, Seligman, Peach Springs, Hackberry, Kingman. When the railway crews reached the territory of the Peach Springs band in 1881, they diverted the spring water, forcing the Pai to abandon the canyon fields below. The new Peach Springs depot site grew into the primary Hualapai village.

The railroad brought jobs; many Hualapais moved into the new towns. Only the Big Sandy people remained at their old field camps. The railroad brought disease to the Indians concentrated at the townsites, as well, and smallpox, "lung fever," and measles took their toll in the 1880s. Hualapai men re-enlisted as army scouts to track Chiricahua Apaches. Women found wage work as washerwomen or by going into white homes to work as servants and nannies. But the poverty of the People finally brought the army, concerned for the welfare of its scouts, to recommend a Hualapai reservation. In 1883, President Chester Arthur designated nearly a million acres of rough canyon country and rolling plateau on the south rim of the Grand Canyon as the Hualapai Indian Reservation — land formerly held by the Plateau People. Middle Mountain and Yavapai Fighter territory remained unprotected and eventually was lost to Anglos.

Meanwhile, settlers finally pushed into the Cataract Canyon people's territory. An 1880 executive order set aside sixty square miles along Havasu Creek to protect the People from lead mining developments. But as finally designated in 1882, the Havasupai Reservation included just 518 acres within the canyon, immediately surrounding the gardens at Supai.

The Havasupai leader, Navajo, evidently agreed to the smaller, easier-to-survey boundaries because he feared removal or extermination, but he did not intend to thereby forfeit rights to land outside the reserve. As the unprotected parts of their old territory became more and more heavily used by non-Indians, however, the Havasupai realized that they had lost virtually all of their land — and the resources responsible for some seventy percent of their ancestral economic base.

Hualapai and Havasupai to this day intermarry and speak dialects of the same language. But the diverging histories and administrative distinctions of the reservation communities indeed make them separate Indian nations. Two tribes exist where, before, all were Pai.

The Hualapai Nation

The Hualapai Nation had a slow start. The Santa Fe Railroad settled the town of Peach Springs and discouraged the People from living on their reservation. The BIA leased the eastern reservation lands to white ranchers.

Wovoka's Ghost Dance vision sidetracked the People in 1889, when Hualapai shaman Indian Jeff organized five hundred Hualapai to dance at Grass Springs. Several more large Ghost Dances followed, involving even Leve Leve's assimilationist group. But the vision promised by the shamans — of disappearing whites and Indian dead restored to life — failed to occur. Hualapais went back to work, though forty years later some remained convinced that the only reason the dead had not risen and the whites not gone away was that the Pai neither performed correctly nor danced long enough.

The year 1890 saw the conversion of Fort Mojave from military post to Indian boarding school. By 1894, the Hualapai had their own school at Hackberry, and in 1896, a day school for Kingman Hualapais (both Leve Leve's and Hualapai Charley's bands camped there most of the time). Hualapai educator Malinda Powskey heard her father and grandfather complain of "being told they couldn't eat in the same place as white people in Kingman." She says of such prejudice: "It didn't ever quite go away."

In 1902, the Hualapai collected their first grazing fees. The BIA superintendent

Havasupai students, Supai, 1900–1901. The BIA was slow to establish services in Cataract Canyon —
Supai was just too isolated. The first government farmer arrived in 1892, the first teacher in 1895, and
the first medical care provider in 1906. The government purchased the first cattle for the tribe in 1912.
Photo by J. H. Bratley. (Smithsonian Institution photo no. 53413-C)

said in 1905 that "scarcely a dozen families" lived on the reservation (out of about
six hundred Hualapai). The rest were scrabbling for a living in the railroad towns.
In 1914, the BIA started Hualapai cattle herds, but Anglo cattle on the reserve still
outnumbered Indian stock by a thousand to one.

World War I brought the first local acceptance for the Hualapai, when Mohave
County became proud of its Pai war heroes. The county (along with national Indian
rights groups) even helped the Hualapai fight off Santa Fe Railroad claims to up to
half the reservation. A fledgling tribal council worked to wrest control over Hualapai grazing from the BIA and put to use the experience they had gained working on
outlying ranches. Hualapai leaders Fred Mahone and Jim Fielding started the Peach
Springs rodeo in the twenties, leading to the first Hualapai-run roundup of tribal herds
in 1930.

In those early days, Hualapai traditions remained strong. Cattleman Hardy Smith
remembers: "When I was young, just playing anywhere, you could hear those gourds
in the houses — old-timers singing. My grandmother's brother sang the bird dance,
my father sang the salt songs. Now, when I'm out there driving, I sing a little bit."

Making a living still proved difficult. Nearly all of the Hualapai cattle-owners ran just a few head. The railroad shut down its Peach Springs operations as long-haul trains needed less frequent servicing. And in the thirties, few of the BIA jobs at the Truxton Canyon agency were held by Hualapais — and most of those were lower level.

Under John Collier's reforms, the tribe's relations with the Bureau slowly began to change. Purebred Hereford cattle were added to Hualapai herds, Hualapai CCC crews worked on range improvement projects, and in 1938, an IRA constitution passed. The first elected tribal council president was Phillip Quasula, grandson of Wauba Yuma himself.

Through the forties and fifties, council leaders Leo Bill Andrews and Grant Tapija, Sr., negotiated further settlements of land claims with the Santa Fe Railroad and worked to make the tribal herds support more than a few families. Dominating tribal leadership over the next twenty years, Sterling Mahone and Rupert Parker struggled with a major drought that made both Hualapai cattle and cattlemen suffer.

In the sixties, the council began to oversee the array of federal programs initiated by the OEO and saw real gains in housing, schools, and health facilities. Malinda Powskey's family was the last to leave the small allotted area on the Big Sandy and move up to the reservation. But, as Philbert Watahomigie notes: "One of the sad things is, when they built all these homes, Hualapais left jobs in Kingman to come here to live, and now they have no jobs. Or they have to commute, which is a hundred miles a day; it takes most of their paycheck to pay for their gas."

In 1968, the Claims Commission awarded the Hualapais almost $3 million, parceled out to investment trusts, resource development, and individual shares. The same year saw the passage of the Central Arizona Project, ending the Hualapai dream of a Bridge Canyon Dam on the reservation's stretch of the Colorado River, for which the tribe had given permission years before, pinning their hopes for economic development on the project.

Hualapai chairman in the mid-1980s, Edgar Walema, an army sergeant who returned to Peach Springs after retirement, still had to fight to take his people beyond the bitterness of the Bridge Canyon Dam defeat. In campaigning, he said: "To continue to plan and dream a useless cause is not worthwhile. Today the Hualapai Nation faces Economic Crisis . . . If no economic developments are created on the Hualapai Reservation soon . . . what will become of our People?"

Sustained-yield timber harvests and cattle provide little more than supplemental income; a doll factory opened in 1973 and closed in 1980. Interstate 40 bypasses Peach Springs now, limiting the possibilities for developing tourist facilities. Most Hualapais depend on jobs with government programs. "We have a false economy," says Wilfred Whatoname. "We live from month to month, from one program year to another." Hualapai unemployment remains sky high: 70 percent by some estimates.

Elnora Mapatis, Hualapai elder, 1984. For a series of booklets in Pai, the Peach Springs Elementary School Bilingual/Bicultural Program relied heavily on Mapatis's knowledge of food preparation, ethnobotany, cattle ranching, cradleboards, and baskets.

One hope for jobs is to develop the spectacular Grand Canyon viewpoints on the western part of the reservation. Vice-Chairman Dallas Quasula told me of plans in 1988 to promote "Grand Canyon West," bringing in tourists by plane, busing them to viewpoints. The tribe hopes eventually to build a "big resort." Meanwhile, they earn income from permits sold to hunters (guide, food, and fees for bighorn sheep permits run as high as $20,000), campers, and Colorado River runners who take out at Diamond Creek.

Peach Springs Elementary School has become the number-one employer in town and the most conspicuous Hualapai success story. The school owes its prominence to Lucille (Cindy) Watahomigie, now its principal. Watahomigie was working in teacher training at the University of Arizona when she agreed to come home and direct the Bilingual/Bicultural Program for her tribe in 1976. With her cohorts Malinda Powskey and Philbert Watahomigie, she has created a nationally known model program. Over half the staff is from Peach Springs, including the teachers; in earlier years, according to Philbert Watahomigie, the only Hualapais were "the janitors and the kids." Parent involvement is crucial; the goal: "a culturally and linguistically integrated curriculum."

The school relies heavily on the knowledge of elders like Elnora Mapatis. Malinda Powskey says: "She gives us the language, she gives us the culture." Powskey adds: "When I was growing up, my Mom and Dad used to fix a lot of traditional foods, and I hated it. Now, I make corn mush. I grind fresh corn on the metate, because it gives it the right consistency, and, at the same time, you've got to have bits and pieces of dirt in it. That's what flavors it!"

The success of the program in building self-esteem has increased the numbers of Hualapais graduating from high school at boarding schools and in Seligman and Kingman, and of those going on to college. Grant money funds a computer room, a video studio, and a bookshelf of bilingual instructional materials. A video newsletter running continuously on the school's VCR system announces everything from school lunch menus to cub scout meetings to student-of-the-week awards. Dance groups practice traditional steps; students harvest and roast agave hearts, visit the old sites important in Hualapai religion, learn to make baskets, and run the Colorado River. The curriculum places "a high value on the children's experiences, their culture, their community, and the natural environment familiar to them." Students see their teachers going to in-service trainings and attending classes themselves; they have role models.

The program is doing what former tribal chairman George Rocha described to me as the prescription to "correct the negative things about the younger generation. We have to take our young people and show them what belongs to them. Teach them the Indian names — here's your history, here's your land — teach what belongs to us, what was Hualapai, what is Hualapai, what is going to be Hualapai." The fifteen hundred Hualapais remain pragmatic and hopeful. "Improvising — we're good at that. It's our way of life," says Malinda Powskey. "Indian people are tough."

Every day starts fresh. Sylvia Querta rises at 4:00 each morning and watches the sun appear over the plateau to the east. She says: "It makes me feel good. To me, every new morning is history. Whatever happened yesterday is gone with the wind." She prays and give thanks to the Great Spirit "for us being here together where there is no rat race."

Querta's grandmother taught her to "run to the sun" every morning. She said: "Get up before the sun and run toward it. You'll be stronger than the sun. You're going to be a hard worker. You will be faster than the sun." Bertha Russell's grandfather summed up these attitudes in his advice to her: "You don't look back. You go forward."

The Havasupai Nation

As I walk the eight miles down Hualapai Canyon to Supai, I think about living with this eroding and cross-bedded red rock. Such a world must make the mineral-laden turquoise waters of Havasu Creek plunging over great waterfalls and the ribbon of woodland that lines the stream seem miraculous. Indeed, the Havasupai see their home canyon as sufficiently miraculous to take the place for their name: "People of the Blue Water," or, in an alternate translation, "The People Who Live at the Place Which Is Green."

After the 1880s, the Cataract Canyon band of Pai came to grips with newfound isolation. They lost their fields at Moenkopi (near Tuba City), first to Mormons, then to Navajos. They lost their upland hunting and gathering grounds. Forced to produce more than ever before from the only fields remaining to them, they planted up to one hundred acres at Supai and intensified their cultivation of peaches, as well.

The BIA was slow to move into Cataract Canyon. Supai Village (the name shortened from Havasupai in an invention of the U.S. Postal Service, today used by the People alternately with Havasupai) was just too isolated. The first government farmer came in 1892, the first teacher in 1895, the first medical care in 1906, the first government purchase of cattle for the tribe in 1912 (grazed on 100,000 acres of Forest Service land to which the Havasupais were granted exclusive grazing rights). By 1912, wages earned in the canyon ($4,144) already exceeded the value of crops grown ($3,983). After 1930, acreage in crops steadily declined to the five acres or so today gardened by elders and plowed by Rod Putesoy on the tribal tractor. Putesoy says: "The elderly farmers are passing away; the young people aren't interested."

And yet, when Leslie Spier interviewed the Havasupai between 1918 and 1921, he still could describe them as "obscure," living in "isolation quite complete." He believed that the "social life, religion, and to only a lesser extent, the material culture, of these people is practically intact." They still used precarious direct routes into the canyon, which included ladders, along with the more gradual horse trails.

The traditional harvest festival survived. Hualapais, Hopis, and Navajos came to Supai in the fall for this "Peach Festival." They gambled, ate, danced, sang, raced horses, traded, and had a wonderful time, before the Havasupai left the canyon for winter plateau camps. With the demand for American and woven Hopi clothing, metal tools, and rifles, cash took over from dried agave or buckskins as the medium of exchange. In 1941, the standard price for Pai red ochre paint at Hopi and Rio Grande pueblos was 25 cents for a heaping teaspoon, $10 for a full baking powder can. Today, the People still celebrate the harvest, but over the years have moved the date up to August, to remind children of the old ways before they head off to boarding schools

for the winter. As time passed, horsemanship replaced war skills as a measure of male achievement.

The primary Havasupai ceremony, cremation and mourning of the dead, gave way in the early twentieth century to Mojave-style ritual mourning after burial. Acceptance of the Ghost Dance came in 1891, and remnants of the ritual survived into the twentieth century. The Havasupai also tried out their own version of Hopi katsina dances. Their prayers for rain worked too well, however: a flood roared through Supai on 1 January 1910, destroying every building and causing tremendous damage to the fields. The People gave up masked dances. One Havasupai raised by Navajos brought home songs from the Blessingway that Havasupais still sing as "Horse Songs" a century and a half later.

One trade item remained crucial: the Havasupai basket. During the last decade of the 1800s, the Hopi passed through a Havasupai coiled basket craze. When that fad waned, the tourists at Grand Canyon took over as primary consumers. The 1930s saw the greatest achievements of some thirty Havasupai women weavers, giving them extra status in a culture where women traditionally owned no property and in general were submissive to men.

Grand Canyon Village also became the primary source of short-term wage work for Havasupais. The preservation of the Grand Canyon first as forest preserve, then as national monument, and finally, as national park, protected the land but blocked the Havasupai from traditional use of their territory, impoverishing them. With epidemic disease introduced by close contact with whites, Havasupai numbers hit bottom in 1906, at one hundred and sixty-six. Influenza after World War I wiped out almost an entire generation of children.

Chiefs gained in influence after the People were concentrated in one village year-round. Boarding schools and the day school created English-speaking Havasupai young people. World War II brought the young men out of the canyon to fight, and when they returned (as did ten of the eleven vets), Havasupai life began to change more rapidly.

Electric generators powered Supai's radios and refrigerators after 1948. But the dismal 1950s saw the generators broken, the day school closed, and one-fourth of the Havasupai in poor health. Wage labor receipts dropped to less than the 1930 total. For the nine years after 1955, children left the canyon for boarding school at age six, just as they had in assimilationist times at the turn of the century. The National Park Service secretly bought out the mining claims between Havasu and Mooney falls, building on the old cremation and burial site a developed campground for Havasu Canyon visitors. Before 1960, tourism remained minimal, only a few dozen Anglos each year venturing down the trails to Supai and its exotic waterfalls: "Shangri-La of the Grand

Minnie Marshall, *Havasupai basket maker, 1974. The twentieth-century tourist market for Havasupai baskets raised their makers' status. In Pai culture, women traditionally owned no property and generally were submissive to men. Photo by Laurance Herold. (All rights reserved, Photo Archives, Denver Museum of Natural History)*

Canyon." As late as 1963, resolutions were drafted at the BIA agency 100 miles away at Truxton Canyon and brought to Supai for ratification by a powerless council.

The fight for land rights began in the late 1880s, when army reports acknowledged the People's need for plateau lands. In the 1890s, BIA field agents understood that Havasupai uplands were "necessary for their support, as they can not keep stock in the canyon," but for decades such requests were rejected by the higher levels of the bureaucracy.

The Grand Canyon Forest Reserve allowed grazing, and the Havasupais developed stock ponds and continued to live in their old plateau homes in winters through 1919. But that year saw the establishment of Grand Canyon National Park. Pressure mounted over subsequent years to contain the Havasupais in their canyon. During the twenties, park rangers began to break up winter camps on the plateau, and even the few stubborn families who used isolated plateau areas for a few years afterward (one holding out until 1950) eventually gave up, feeling the pressure of "too many white people up there, too close by," as Mack Putesoy remembered it.

Swedva, called Big Jim by the whites, continued to plant at Indian Gardens on what became the Bright Angel Trail in Grand Canyon National Park until he was over eighty. But he was a "progressive," and the traditionalists, led by such men as Manakaja, the head chief until 1942, and Captain Burro, who also planted at Indian Gardens, did not fare so well. When Burro was forced from his home in 1928, he looked back from the rim and wept. He died the next year, his wife the year after.

After 1926, Havasupai ties to the national park became stronger. A telephone line and the Supai mail packtrain both came down the Topocoba Trail, which began at the end of the road arriving from the park village. A Havasupai colony of some ten families lived on land set aside for them at the South Rim, working summers for the Park Service and its concessioners. In 1934, afraid of the Havasupai establishing squatter's rights, the Park Service destroyed their traditional homes during the winter, built cabins for the People, and began charging rent.

The People continued to feel severely confined in their canyon. As Stephen Hirst puts it in his tribal history: "The canyon that summer visitors view as a landlocked Polynesia the Havasupai viewed in winter as a prison." Only five hours of direct sun penetrate the canyon at winter solstice. Snowstorms can isolate Supai from the outside world for as long as a week (an isolation pierced today by emergency helicopter flights).

With their acceptance of the IRA, the Havasupai elected a tribal council in 1939. The second tribal chairman, Dean Sinyella, stepped up pressure to obtain permanent rights to grazing lands on the plateau. Through the early 1940s, Sinyella added

Captain Burro, Havasupai, 1900. Captain Burro planted his fields at Indian Gardens on what became the Bright Angel Trail in Grand Canyon National Park. When park authorities forced him from his home in 1928, he looked back from the rim and wept. He died the next year, his wife the year after. Photo by Frederick Maude. (Courtesy Museum of New Mexico, neg. no. 82454)

to the reservation only one small parcel surrounding a spring. Earl Paya, Reed Wata-homigie, and the council of the early 1960s renewed the fight for plateau lands and pushed for control of the Havasu Canyon campground as Havasupai morale reached its lowest point. Just prior to 1966, when OEO money began to flow into Cataract Canyon, only five salaried jobs existed in Supai: policeman, postmaster, managers for the tribal store and Tribal Tourist Enterprise, and mail carrier (serving the only U.S. post office still using packtrains, as it does today). The 1960 on-reservation population had declined to a number less than the 1940 figure.

The Havasupai could not be self-sufficient in the canyon alone, nor could they make a decent living from the menial jobs available at Grand Canyon Village. In 1963, according to anthropologist John Martin, about two hundred people made their livings full-time in the canyon; sixty lived off-reservation; and a hundred mostly young people floated between jobs in the two worlds. With each additional generation, the tribe has become more desperate in its need for land and employment. Inheritance in the rapidly increasing population after 1940 (from 207 in 1938 to 347 in 1960 to more than 500 today) split fields and family holdings into unmanageable patchworks.

The sixties brought increasing tourism that helped create public awareness of Havasupai poverty. Federal funding, with some private help, built new housing, a new store, a tribal cafe, and tribal offices. Powerlines reached Supai for the first time; a water system went in. In 1969, the Claims Commission awarded the tribe $1.25 million for more than two million acres of their land lost to non-Havasupais. The BIA administered three-quarters of that cash, releasing money to the tribe for resource development only after bureaucratic deliberation. In 1973, individual Havasupais divided the remainder in $651.37 per capita payments.

By 1974, only half the arable canyon floor remained open for planting; irrigation ditches could reach only half of that. Lack of firewood had always been a problem, and now cottonwoods had to be managed carefully for fuel, further usurping croplands. With the best income coming to families who worked at horse-packing tourists and their gear, more and more bottomland was diverted to pasture for pack stock (while the upland pasture was crucial for rejuvenating worn-out animals).

Grand Canyon National Park officials did not even map the Havasupai Reservation on their 1971 draft plan to expand the park. They did suggest managing the Hualapai Trail, which since the thirties had become the primary trail to Supai, for "high visitor use." The Havasupais finally had the chance to protest the plan in May 1971, when Chairman Lee Marshall, grandson of Manakaja, spoke for the tribe.

Marshall opened with: "I heard all you people talking about the Grand Canyon. Well, you're looking at it. I *am* the Grand Canyon!" His presentation converted an important Park Service official, who proposed returning more than sixty-thousand acres

Lee Marshall, Havasupai, on his front porch at Supai, Arizona, 1988. When Marshall testified as tribal chairman in 1971 congressional hearings, he opened with: "I heard all you people talking about the Grand Canyon. Well, you're looking at it. I am the Grand Canyon!"

of park land to the tribe — still nowhere near what the Havasupais needed to create a workable stock enterprise on ancestral lands.

When the land restoration proposal bogged down in the bureaucracy for a year, off went Lee Marshall to Washington, D.C., to testify before Congress. Marshall spoke strongly: "We have homes and burial grounds on our permit lands. We fear for them if we are not there to protect them. No other lands except our permit lands are available to us. Our permit lands are the heart of our homeland, and we are not leaving our home.

"So hear us now and remember. We will go on grazing our animals on all our permit lands forever. We will go on keeping our homes on them forever. We will not be pushed from the plateau for Sunday recreation ever.

"We have never stopped using these lands, and we will not go from them now. They belong to us."

With the assistance of Anglo attorney Joe Sparks and the leadership of Havasupai elder Ethel Jack, Havasupai people moved to Washington, D.C., to argue their cause. The Arizona congressional delegation united behind the tribe, for reasons summarized by Representative Morris Udall: "This is not a giveaway of national park land. It is simply a protection of this tribe in the legitimate, honorable uses they have had."

The Grand Canyon bill that became law on 3 January 1975 restored to the Havasupai the most land so far returned to any United States tribe: 185,000 acres (plus exclusive use of an additional 95,300 acres within the park). After the restoration, Ethel Jack said: "The land is our grandmother and our grandfather, for it feeds us and provides for us. Then the land was taken from us, and we were alone for many years. But now we have our grandmother and grandfather back."

The expansion bill passed with restrictive language that limits the use of the restored lands primarily to grazing, which can bring in no more than $100,000 a year; the bill specifically prohibits commercial tourist developments on the plateau. A master plan for the uplands was approved in 1982; however, the return of the plateau lands gave the People a symbolic refuge and outlet as much as a resource to develop.

Tourism remains the most stable foundation for the Havasupai economy. The boom began with an *Arizona Highways* story in 1963. By 1975, visitation had reached ten thousand annually, and restrictions hold the current total below twenty thousand. The tribe actually prohibits village people from going down to the campground during the summer months. (Other side effects for the People, according to Lee Marshall, include fewer rattlesnakes than in the old days: "I think they're afraid of the tourists!")

Most members of this parade of strangers understand the isolation of Supai by the time they arrive. Some fly in by helicopter from Grand Canyon Village. The rest drive from Kingman sixty miles to the Hualapai community of Peach Springs and

Main Street, Supai, 1988. Most visitors reach Supai on foot or with the help of Havasupai horse packers. Upon reaching the village, the eight-mile-long Hualapai Trail becomes "Main Street."

then another sixty miles through Hualapai and Havasupai plateau lands to where the road abruptly ends at the Hualapai Hilltop parking lot. Supai Village lies in the canyon below, eight miles on foot or with the help of Havasupai horse packers. The Hualapai Trail becomes "Main Street" once it reaches the village — a dusty lane penetrating the world of the People. On the elementary school's field day, Havasupai kids running races must dodge tourists, horses, and every motorized vehicle in town: the tribe's tractor, backhoe, fire truck, and the two or three three-wheelers used by the community health workers. The adjacent helipad is the "town square," the site of softball throws, balloon take-offs, cultural exchanges (Hawaiian dance performances), parades, round dances, and band concerts.

Tourists stay in the campground, hostel, and in the new lodge. They bring in hundreds of thousands of dollars in income, though as Stephen Hirst points out, a family involved in packing must also pack in feed, hay, and salt for their horses: they "make almost enough to feed their horses but not quite enough to feed their families." One family member receiving a salary from elsewhere makes a packing enterprise solvent.

James Uqualla, Jr., managed the lodge with enthusiasm and elan when I spoke with him in 1988. He said: "This job uses all my talents — creative talents,

James Uqualla, Jr., former Havasupai chairman, *was manager of the tribe's lodge in 1988 when he told me:* "*We assume the responsibility for the people who are coming into our living room. You have to make it clear that you are not an attraction but the caretakers of this gorgeous place in the canyon.*"

administrative talents, Indian talents." Uqualla loves to talk, and sees his volubility as a responsibility: "Anyone that has a horse can provide transportation; anyone willing to talk can work as a guide. We become hosts for the people who come to visit. They are coming into our living room. We assume the responsibility to orient them, which makes it easier for us in the long run. You have to make it clear that you are not an attraction but the caretakers of this gorgeous place in the canyon."

Tourism has helped to rejuvenate Havasupai pride in their traditions, in being Indians. Basketmaking nearly disappeared by the mid-1960s, but now has revived to meet the demands of the growing market. Barbara Sinyella sells baskets from the new Tribal Arts Center she manages along Main Street: "I have the traditional background, and through this job, I thought I could maybe somehow bring that back to the people."

Federal and tribal jobs (half office jobs, and half federally financed construction work) generate reasonable incomes for tribal members, but always they depend on the whims of funding. Nonetheless, the village offers real opportunities for making a living today, and many Havasupais have moved home after "graduating from the outside," as one older Havasupai man put it to me. He said: "There's nothing to do, but I'm never bored."

In 1975, the tribe took over administration of its school from the BIA; in 1982, it completed a new building to house classes through eighth grade (upper school students still go to boarding school in Riverside, California, or stay with relatives in Peach Springs for the long bus ride to nearby towns). A bilingual, bicultural program began in 1978. The tribe dreams of having its own high school.

Angie Watahomigie directs the bilingual program for the tribal school. Her goal is the reverse of most such programs: "to get kids more and more aware of the outside," for most Havasupai kids come to school speaking only Pai. If their house happens to be along the trail into town, they may have picked up some English, but Havasupai is still spoken in nearly all homes. Parents tell her: "Bring it back, keep it up," when talking of the old ways. Elders teach classes in crafts and farming. All the teacher's aides are Havasupai, and several are close to finishing teaching degrees. The "outside" teachers rarely stay longer than two or three years. Watahomigie "talks to the kids about how lucky they are, lucky to be here with Mom and Dad. They should be thankful for that."

Contrasts abound. Most Havasupais "go out" about every four months to shop, see doctors and dentists, or to visit friends and family. Others never leave the canyon, while younger people may go out every two weeks. Barbara Sinyella says: "Going up there really makes me tired — all those cars, the smell of the gas. Phoenix gives me a headache. It's nice to go out once in a while, but when I come back down the trail it just gets so peaceful." She adds: "The elderlies want to stay down here. When they go out, they get put in nursing homes and get homesick and lonesome."

Many Havasupais still spend a great deal of time on horseback, though today the younger people do so with a Walkman clipped to their belt and headphones in their ears. Barbara Sinyella says: "Long time ago, we did a lot of walking around, exploring, listen to our grandmother tell us stories, and have a big family gathering with a fire. Now the kids have the satellite dish bringing in who knows what!"

Indeed, four or five families have satellite dishes; one family runs a video shop for the people (a majority) with VCRs. Still, the phones "get funny," as Angie Watahomigie puts it, for as long as a month. Kids stay along the creek swimming until seven or eight o'clock on summer evenings. Barbara Sinyella says with pride: "Even the one- and two-year-olds splash around at the shore; pretty soon they are going in swimming."

Rod Putesoy, manager of the tribal store, says: "Families mail in their groceries; regular postage gets it delivered to Supai. Perishables they pack in themselves. A meat company in Kingman packages frozen meats for them. Packers are punished — ninety days without work — for getting drunk and losing stuff." The store itself must charge well over twice outside prices because of supply difficulties. Putesoy told me that "being store manager is difficult. People always are saying we charge too high. We never know when to order, how much to order."

Tricia Tapija, Hualapai fifth-grader dressed for traditional dance practice, Peach Springs School, 1988.
The elementary school has become the number-one employer in town and the most conspicuous
Hualapai success story — primarily because of its dynamic principal, Lucille (Cindy) Watahomigie.

Today, the Havasupai live as nuclear families in new (though still in short supply) housing. Younger people — and women — serve on the tribal council. Intermarriage beyond the Hualapai remains rare. Havasupai is spoken widely, and younger people like James Uqualla still can say that "it's breathtaking to listen to a traditional orator speak. You hear that oratory every occasion that there's a public meeting."

One such orator is Lee Marshall, seventy-six years old when I talked with him in 1988 and still fiery in Havasupai or English. We sat on his porch and looked out over the green fields of Supai below red canyon walls shimmering in early summer heat. "In the old days you just heard birds singing along the creek there where it's cool. Now you hear helicopters, planes, the tractor with that small motor. The changes are good for young people. Old people don't care about jobs."

He sees the problems: "All these young kids getting married, they need houses. Why don't they build houses up top for young kids? Let the old people stay down here.

"The bootlegger is the guy that's hurting the tribe. I tell my son, if you drink, you won't have nothing when you're old. No money, no food, no clothes. Nothing.

"And they've got this uranium mine up there. It's going to wipe us all out — that's what we're afraid of. There'll be no future for anybody if they keep mining this uranium."

The mine (under construction in 1991) Marshall fears lies some miles above Havasu Canyon on Forest Service land. The tribe fears contamination from a spill of radioactive waste and has banned uranium mining on Havasupai land. The mining company insists that such accidents are a remote possibility. But sudden flash floods of sufficient magnitude to move mountains are not so unlikely: a devastating flood swept through Supai on Labor Day in 1990, wreaking havoc on the village and requiring major rebuilding.

Barbara Sinyella can list the problems and advantages of living in Supai, but sums up life in the canyon straightforwardly: "We're down here, we like being down here. This is our home. That's just the way we are. People say, what a beautiful canyon we have — people are so friendly.

"We just want to stay that way."

In the Dry Mountains

UPLAND PEOPLES

Tipi, Stone Lake encampment, annual Go-Jii-Ya ceremonial relay races.
Jicarilla Apache Reservation, northernmost New Mexico, 1987.

The Southwest surprises. This desert harbors the world's largest continuous stand of ponderosa pines, windblown alpine tundra twelve thousand feet in elevation, and mountains too rugged for roads or towns. On the north rim of Grand Canyon, aspens turn autumn gold on plateaus with Paiute names. Mist rolls through the dark spruce-fir timber of the White Mountains on the Fort Apache Reservation. The Mescalero Apache operate a ski area on America's southernmost glaciated peak.

Faulted, folded, and pushed up from beneath the surface of the Earth, these mountains mark the landscape with sacred summits, give refuge to nearby desert dwellers, and increase the ways people can live in dry country. Harsh mountain winters dictate seasonal migrations, but increased water supplies make for a dependable round of food ripening throughout the year.

From the north come the Rockies — the shining mountains of the West, watershed to the great western rivers. These last ranges of the Rocky Mountains reach into the Southwest with the southern San Juan Mountains spilling across the Colorado–New Mexico border and the Jemez and Sangre de Cristo mountains flanking the Rio Grande at Santa Fe. To the south, the hot deserts flourish in country labeled Basin and Range by the physiographers, dry basin alternating with dry mountain range, some ranges rising high enough to stand as sky islands of coolness and coniferous forest. Similar island mountains stud the Colorado Plateau. All offered their harvests to the People.

Most transitions between the Southwest's geographic provinces happen unmistakably. One major exception exists: the Colorado Plateau appears to end abruptly across much of north-central Arizona at the Mogollon Rim, an escarpment that can stand two thousand feet high. From the Rim, however, transition ranges tumble southward to the Basin and Range deserts. For Yavapai and Apache, these transitional mountains provided a rich larder of plants and animals — a mixture of the best of desert, mountain, and plateau. The People found similar resources on the southern fringes of the Rockies and in the isolated mountains of the deserts and the Colorado Plateau — a seasonal cycle of foods that carried them through the year from low to high elevations and back again.

Each increase in elevation brings an increase in available moisture. Throughout the Southwest, at about five thousand feet desert shrublands give way in rocky soil to piñon-juniper or oak woodland, to oaks and chaparral, or to desert grassland in deeper soil. Woodland gives way to ponderosa pine forest at seven thousand feet. The dry foothills where the Ute hunted mule deer at the base of the Rockies around Durango, Colorado, typify this mosaic in their juxtaposition of a scrubby fur of Gambel oak with an occasional flare into the hot green and autumn gold of small patches of aspen.

Even the higher and wetter places risk the unpredictability of dry country. Though Santa Fe lies at seven thousand feet and averages fourteen inches of precipitation each year, since 1950 annual averages have ranged from less than seven inches (Phoenix's average) to twenty inches (San Francisco's average).

In the dry mountains of the Southwest, Indian peoples responded to such variation by moving through the landscape in tune with the seasonal gathering cycle of food plants and game. The Yavapai held the northern Sonoran Desert mountains and the western transition from plateau to desert. At the northern edge of the Southwest, the Southern Paiute claimed the mountains and plateaus between the Grand Canyon and the Mojave and Great Basin deserts; the Southern Ute, who spoke the same language as their Paiute relations, lived on the southern flanks of the Rockies. The Apache swept into this land by the 1500s, filling the wilder spaces in a huge semicircle from the White Mountains and Mogollon Rim country of central Arizona, eastward to Texas, and northward to where the New Mexico mountains end at the tawny sweep of the Great Plains.

Sandstone canyons carry red rivers beyond the horizon; the desert falls away below. Here, these dry mountains bestow the gifts of forest, meadow, and alpine lake. Light, mountain light, drenches the landscape—tinted with the lush colors of exposed rock and a sky filled by sun and storm. High elevation and dry air intensify clarity and hue. Winter sunsets over the Sangre de Cristos in the Jicarilla Apache homeland or summer clouds gathering over the Bradshaw Mountains in Yavapai country near Prescott leave you stunned and exhilarated. Diverse and productive, these dry mountains make a fine place to gather one's living from the land.

John Smith, Yavapai, 1988. First chairman of the Fort McDowell council when it formed in 1934, Smith has seen his people fight for their land and water all his life. For decades the People lived with the threat of Orme Dam flooding their homes. In 1990, they finally obtained secure water rights.

The Yavapai

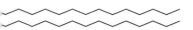

I don't know about the white people. I don't know who they are, where they come from. But we people don't come from nowhere across the ocean. We were raised right here in this country. We come out at Sedona, the middle of the world. This is our home.

My people used to teach the kids every day about these things. Teach them about everything. Tell them how to live, how to do everything. My grandmother used to tell me these things every day, every night. She told me how we got raised in Sedona.

We call Sedona Wipuk. We call it after the rocks in the mountains there. Some of my people, they call themselves Wipukpa. That's the ones who live up there around Sedona. All Yavapai come from Sedona. But in time they spread out.

North of Camp Verde there is Montezuma Well. We call it Ahagaskiaywa. This lake has no bottom and underneath the water spreads out wide. That's where the people come out first.

Mike Harrison and John Williams, *The Yavapai of Fort McDowell,* 1979

"When the white people come, lots of Yavapai get killed."

With these words, Yavapai elder John Williams summed up the basics of Yavapai history. His people, like every tribe that depended on far-flung resources, faced terrible odds of holding any territory sought early on by whites. Pursued to starvation and surrender by the U.S. Army, these central Arizona mountain people abandoned their vast homeland to undergo forced relocation. The Yavapai also have endured. They trickled back to remnants of these original lands and fought successfully to keep them.

The Yavapai themselves are beginning to forget this story as they "melt into American society," as Camp Verde Yavapai David Sine puts it. John Smith, first chairman of the Fort McDowell council when it formed in 1934, says to young people today: "Where is your culture? What do you know about it?"

Smith said to me, sadly: "Nobody even sings the Indian songs anymore; 1924 was the last big Yavapai dance up here." He regrets not asking more questions of his elders and sums up his regrets with: "We don't have a written history." The reason? "Indian

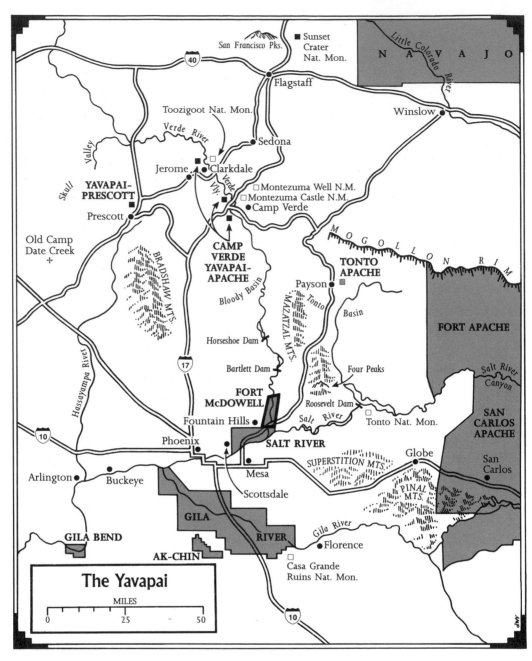

The Yavapai

MILES

0   25   50

people don't like to talk about their dead. The first time my mother mentioned her parents' names in my hearing was when I took her in for her Social Security registration. I can't tell you what our culture is. I guess our culture is what we *used* to do."

Mountaineers

The Yavapai ranged across more territory than any other Yuman people — almost ten million acres of Arizona. The four Yavapai subtribes compared themselves to mountain sheep in their ability to traverse their rugged home. Historically, the Tolkapaya (Western Yavapai) lived in the northern mountains of the Sonoran Desert from the Colorado River almost to Prescott. The Yavepe (Central Yavapai) held the Prescott-Jerome area. The Kewevkapaya (Southeastern Yavapai) controlled the Bradshaw Mountains, the lower Verde Valley, the Tonto Basin, and the Superstition and Pinal mountains; anthropologist E. W. Gifford called them "mountaineers."

Wipukpaya people (Northeastern Yavapai) lived in the middle Verde Valley, the Bradshaws, and the red rock country around Sedona. Their land included Montezuma Well, the limestone sink where Yavapai people entered this world, climbing up on a cornstalk (some say wild grapevine) that grew from the previous world up through the pool. The Sedona country also protects the sacred caves where Old Lady White Stone, Kamalapukwia, the first woman, survived the flood that destroyed the third world of existence, and the cave where her grandson, Skark'a mca, Lofty Wanderer, taught all beings the right way to live before he left this world.

Elders still identify themselves as descendants of these subtribes. Younger people link themselves to one of the three Yavapai reservation communities: Fort McDowell, Camp Verde, or Prescott.

The Yavapai speak a Yuman language, closer in dialect to the other upland Yumans, the Pai (Hualapai and Havasupai), than to the river Yumans. Some anthropologists lump the Yavapai culturally with the Pai for this linguistic similarity, but the Yavapai and Pai were traditional enemies and saw themselves as different people. A strip of neutral territory separated their lands; on the south, a similar buffer divided the Yavapai from the enemy Pima and Maricopa. Yavapai allies included the Quechan and Mojave on the Colorado River and the Apache to the east.

Apache people began moving into Yavapai country after 1700, intermarrying and trading bits of culture. Though outsiders thoroughly confused the Eastern Yavapai with the Western and Tonto Apache, Yavapai and Apache always remained separate in language and identity. Nevertheless, Anglos consistently called the Yavapai "Apaches," "Yuma-Apaches," or "Mohave-Apaches." Fort McDowell people — who are Yavapai — still must tolerate this confusion in the official name of their "Mohave-Apache" Reservation. The modern Camp Verde community includes both Yavapais and Tonto Apaches.

Yavapai bands moved through the landscape in rhythm with the sequence of ripening plants: spring greens for boiling, summer cactus fruits and mesquite beans, the

Yavapai camp, Date Creek, 1905. Marched from their homes to the distant San Carlos Reservation in 1875, the Yavapai lived in exile for a generation. By 1901, most Yavapai had left San Carlos singly or in small groups and returned to their former homes, where small reservations eventually were established. (Smithsonian Institution photo no. 53591)

abundant resources of autumn — acorns, piñons, walnuts, and seeds and berries. Fall also saw the harvest of corn planted months before (with beans and squash) and left to ripen on its own. Agave (mescal) was crucial year-round, its central heart barbecued in pits and dried and cached strategically. Yavapai elder Mike Burns called it "the essential food." Hunters brought home everything from deer, quail, rabbit, and fox to lizards, caterpillars, and yellow-jacket nests. John Smith remembers an old blind man barbecuing a mountain turtle: "It was just delicious."

Bands usually camped in groups of up to ten families; winter gatherings could number one hundred households. Many bands set up winter camps in caves, often the caves that sheltered the ruined cliff dwellings of prehistoric Salado and Sinagua people. Yavapai belongings had to be simple enough to take along on these cyclic travels on foot: skins for pole-supported huts, baskets (the primary currency when Yavapais traded with the Navajo for blankets), bows and arrows, clubs, buckskin ponchos, a few pots and pitched baskets. Not much else.

Each camp awoke to an elder orating from the roof of a hut, instructing the People on the right way to live. They listened, and then ran to the east for a half mile or so, often to a spring, to clear their minds for the day. Yavapai people listened to the land, as well, and it was good to them. As Fort McDowell Yavapai David King says today: "Being poor is only a state of mind."

This lifestyle continued with little disruption right up to the 1850s: Yavapai country was too rough to attract much attention from the first Spanish, Mexican, or American settlers. As Ted Smith, at Camp Verde says, "From 1500 to 1800, this was a silent place." In 1863, however, gold was discovered on the Hassayampa River and on Lynx Creek near Prescott; in 1865, the frontier reached the Verde Valley when the first farmers arrived. The Yavapais' food-collecting rounds were disrupted forever. Starving Yavapai raided the settlers. The U.S. Army was not far behind, and with it came what Camp Verde chairman Ted Smith calls "a ten-year Vietnam War."

The Yavapai Wars

Skull Valley. Bloody Basin. Skeleton Cave. These central Arizona place names come from the Yavapai wars. The casualties at these places were Indian families, not soldiers, for the Yavapais, unlike Apaches, had few guns and even less ammunition. Their weapons for hunting became weapons of war.

Two thousand Yavapai, probably Tolkapayas, tried farming on the new Colorado River Reservation in 1866, but competition for land with whites and Mojaves forced a return to the mountains. Other bands came in to the army posts — Camp Date Creek, Fort McDowell, Camp Verde — and asked for peace. The army had few rations to give them, and each time, hungry Yavapai returned to the hills to forage.

General George Crook came to Arizona in 1871 to bring Apache and Yavapai raiding to an end. As a man sympathetic to Indian welfare — as his era defined it — he wanted to see the tribes confined to reservations, where newly "civilized" individuals could learn that "every drop of honest sweat meant a penny in his pocket." As an effective military man, he wanted to bring this about as quickly as possible.

Though a reservation was established in the Verde Valley in 1871, Yavapais accustomed to their wide range of foods could not subsist on its limited resources. Raiding continued, and Crook took to the field the next winter. Campaign records kept by the Camp Verde post surgeon William Corbusier and by Captain John Bourke muddled the Yavapais and Apaches, but the Yavapai clearly took the brunt of Crook's force.

Calling Yavapais "Apaches" served as a good excuse to kill them, for the word meant marauding renegade to white pioneers; it meant enemy.

In April of 1873, Yavapai headman Chalipun surrendered to Crook and to the Apache and Yavapai scouts who made Crook's campaign possible. Chalipun told Crook that he and his people

> could not go to sleep at night because they feared to be surrounded before day-break; they could not hunt — the noise of their guns would attract the troops; they could not cook mescal or anything else, because the flame and smoke would draw down the soldiers; they could not live in the valleys — there were too many soldiers; they had retreated to the mountain tops, thinking to hide in the snow until the soldiers went home, but the scouts found them out.

By summer, the Rio Verde Reservation held more than two thousand Yavapais. Disease reduced them by a third; healthy people could not keep up with the crema-tions necessary to honor their dead. On 23 December 1873, Yavapai resistance ended with the massacre of a Yavapai band, babies and all, at what came to be called Skele-ton Cave, high above Salt River Canyon. Yavapai elder John Williams helped to bring down the bones from the cave for burial at Fort McDowell in 1923; he summed up the massacre: "It is here that all our people died. For nothing."

In 1874, the Verde reservation Yavapai and Tonto Apache dug an irrigation ditch five miles long using discarded army tools "from rusty and broken shovels to spoons." Corbusier called it an accomplishment "worthy of a place in the greatest annals of the West." The tribes then succeeded in bringing in such an impressive harvest from fifty acres that government contractors in Tucson, intent on selling low-quality rations to dependent tribes for huge profits, were roused to action.

Self-sufficient Indians? The contractors were horrified. Within a year — contrary to the recommendations of the army and General Crook — they succeeded in push-ing the government to abolish the Rio Verde Reservation and remove the Yavapai and Tonto Apaches to San Carlos, where they could be "herded with the other tribes," in the words of an outraged but powerless Bourke.

Not all officers were as enlightened as Crook and Bourke. The two-week forced march across 150 roadless miles took place in February 1875 under the direction of Edwin Dudley, who listened to a request to allow children and older men and women to take a longer route by wagon and responded with: "They are Indians; let the beggars walk." Many Yavapai died or were killed or mutilated by the soldiers on the march; others escaped to hide in the mountains and eke out a traditional subsistence or work for Verde Valley farmers.

At San Carlos, the Yavapai found themselves beyond their homeland, a minority among Apaches. Rations were meager. They began irrigating once again; they acquired cattle. They worked for wages as army scouts, detailed to help recapture Geronimo and his feisty band of Chiricahua Apaches. They did their best to farm well and to help the whites in their war, trusting General Crook to live up to his promise to allow them to return to their homes.

In the 1880s, floods washed out their ditch system; in the 1890s, both coal miners and dam builders wanted the Yavapai-held land at San Carlos. With their foothold so tenuous, even after a generation in this new location, and their desire to return to their homeland still strong, the government relented. John Smith says: "They finally decided we weren't Apaches." By 1901, most Yavapai had left San Carlos.

Some returned to the Verde Valley, where the army post at Camp Verde had been abandoned. A few Central Yavapai returned to the Prescott area; Western Yavapai settled in several places, including Arlington, in the desert west of Buckeye. Other Yavapai went to Fort McDowell — also abandoned by the army — on the lower Verde River outside Phoenix. Returning families found the best agricultural land in all these places taken by non-Indians.

Against the prevailing run of history of the times, the BIA recommended reservations for the Yavapai. Fort McDowell was established in 1903, Camp Verde and Middle Verde (small fragments of the original Rio Verde Reservation) from 1910 to 1916. The Prescott people were granted a piece of old Fort Whipple in 1935. Of the four historic subtribes, only the Western Yavapai obtained no reservation, and today they are nearly gone — with just one Tolkapaya family at Arlington, and the rest absorbed into other reservation communities.

The Fight for Fort McDowell

On the new Fort McDowell reserve, the Yavapai chose Yuma Frank as their headman. By 1905, the government had bought out the non-Indians farming the bottomlands. The Yavapai moved from their camps on the ridges (where, says John Smith, they "were living on wild rats [pack rats], on ladies selling their baskets") down to the floodplain. They began irrigating once again, farming with "ponies and walking plows." One Indian agent said of the McDowell Yavapai: "Their desire to be self-sustaining amounts to a mania." But their fight for their land seemed never to end.

Though the Yavapais had lost most of their land, what was left to them at Fort McDowell, ironically, included that rarity in the desert, a flowing river — the Verde. After the Salt River Project completed Roosevelt Dam in 1906, the Yavapais became entangled in water rights struggles, battling the powerful, monied, and growing metropolis of Phoenix for their right to live at Fort McDowell and use the Verde River.

By 1911, the Yavapai had constructed fifteen miles of main ditches and thirty miles of laterals, but the Verde kept flooding them out. Yavapai farmers asked for funds to build permanent irrigation works. Instead, the federal government planned to move the Fort McDowell people to the Salt River Pima Reservation, where the Yavapai supposedly would use Salt River Project irrigation water.

The Yavapai had had enough of forced relocation. They weren't about to live again as a minority with questionable promises of land and water rights. The Fort McDowell people protested formally in a petition offered by Yuma Frank to the Interior Department. The last line was crucial: "We hereby appoint Carlos Montezuma as our representative in these matters."

Carlos Montezuma remains a hero to the Yavapai. In their current promotional sheet aimed at attracting business to the reservation, the Fort McDowell people devote half the limited space allotted for tribal history to his story. Anthropologist Patricia Mariella described him as a "unique insider who had the skills of an outsider." Montezuma, like the Yavapai themselves, deserves to be better known than he is.

Born Wassaja to a Kewevkapaya family in about 1865, the little boy was captured in an 1871 raid and adopted by a Pima man. Pimas tell varying stories of succeeding events: that he was sold to a white man named Carlos Gentile because his adopted father simply could not afford to keep him, or that Gentile initiated the transaction, wanting to take Wassaja and educate him. Either way, in Florence, Arizona, in late 1871, before moving to a new life in Illinois and New York, Gentile baptized the Yavapai boy with a new name, Carlos Montezuma.

Gentile, too, came on hard times, and young Montezuma acquired other guardians. All encouraged him to pursue his studies, and he graduated from Chicago Medical College in 1889. Montezuma worked as an Indian Service doctor on reservations and at Carlisle Indian School, as a surgeon in Chicago, and, increasingly, as a national spokesman for Indian rights. With the eternally vague public perception of Yavapai identity, Montezuma became known as "the fiery Apache," an important voice among the first educated Indians crusading for their people.

In 1901, Montezuma visited Arizona and met the Pimas who had captured him; he then tracked down the remnants of his family at Fort McDowell. He found two cousins, George and Charles Dickens, active in tribal leadership at Fort McDowell. He returned to his people at a crucial time in their history, and they welcomed him.

Montezuma saw reservations as prisons and advocated abolishing the Indian Bureau. To promote his opinions, he started his own newspaper, *Wassaja*, in 1916; he gave speeches and made passionate friends and bitter enemies. Montezuma lost a good number of his political battles and has been dismissed by many historians as a

Carlos Montezuma, about 16 years old, 1881. Born Yavapai, captured by Pimas, and sold to a white man, Montezuma grew up in Chicago. He became a doctor and returned to Arizona to help his people fight for their land. A pivotal figure in the national struggle for Indian rights, Montezuma remains a hero at Fort McDowell. (Smithsonian Institution photo no. 53532.)

stubborn factionalist. But he waged his most successful fight for the people of Fort McDowell, against what he called the "persistent and wicked duplicity of management" intent on robbing them of their land.

Reservations might be "prisons," but the Yavapai had won their right to this home, and Montezuma would fight for their right to remain. He earned the reputation of troublemaker and agitator with the Indian Bureau. He gave articulate, conspicuous voice in Congress and in the national press to the positions of the Yavapai. He found them a sympathetic attorney. And his efforts extended to other southern Arizona tribes. Anna Moore Shaw wrote, in *A Pima Past*: "His fighting words changed our lives. In those times of prejudice, he made us realize that the Indian is not inferior, but a person of great dignity and worth. We set out to prove this to the world."

Montezuma kept up his barrage of activities until 1922, when he sickened with tuberculosis. At the end of that year, he returned to Arizona to die. In the words of his biographer, Peter Iverson: "His life was a circle."

John Smith remembers Montezuma's last days at Fort McDowell, before the doctor's death in early 1923. Smith used to go walking with Montezuma before the dying man became bedridden in his wickiup. "He was always full of jokes — almost like Wallace Beery in his humor." But when Montezuma "used to go deer hunting with his cousins, the Dickens, up there by Skeleton Cave, he would sit there sad all day long by the cave.

"When we walked way up on the hill, he would say, 'Boy, get out of this place; tear down this fence; go out into the world.' But he fought with all his might to save this place, to keep these people from being moved."

Montezuma helped stave off the move to Salt River, but for years afterward, no significant funds were budgeted for McDowell because the Yavapais' residence always was seen as temporary. As John Smith told me: "They've been fighting all their lives."

In 1921, Phoenix built a pipeline channeling Verde water from Fort McDowell to the city. In 1935, Bartlett Dam was built above the reservation; in the 1940s, Horseshoe Dam was completed just upstream from Bartlett. These projects offered short-term employment (and long-term jobs with the city water plant) to the Yavapais, and some control over flooding, but with the lack of funding for permanent irrigation systems, farming remained small scale. Through the 1960s, the Yavapai received just $360 annually from the City of Phoenix for the pipeline operation — the only tribal lease. Today, only seven hundred acres are farmed, though an irrigation system is finally in place to work more than four thousand acres.

For decades the Yavapai lived under the threat of yet another dam, to be built below the reservation at the confluence of the Verde and Salt rivers, potentially flooding 17,000 acres of their 24,680-acre reservation — destroying essentially all of the tribe's usable resources, along with their homes and cemetery. With this Orme Dam threatened as early as the 1950s (and authorized by Congress as part of the Central Arizona Project in 1968), the tribe could obtain no federal housing money for use in its residential areas on the floodplain; irrigation repair money was held up once again.

Not until 1973 did anyone ask for the reactions of the Fort McDowell community to the proposed flooding of their reservation. They held a tribal referendum and voted 144 to 57 against it; they refused $33 million offered in compensation. In statements to Congress, the Yavapai spoke their minds.

Councilman Hiawatha Hood spoke of the 1800s, when the Yavapai were "rounded up like cattle" and moved to San Carlos: "Today we are again faced with forced removal from our home. Again we will be moved at the command of the United States government.

"When will this stop?

"When will this stop?"

Ralph Bear wrote: "For those of you in government who are for the dam, how would you feel if your heart was taken out of you? That is what's going to happen to the Yavapai tribe if the dam is built."

Other Yavapai asked the same strong questions: "Why here?" "Where are we going to go?" "Where will I be buried?" "Why should we trade the land which supports us for money which won't support us?" "Why are we supposed to be better off if we are moved to a crowded place where we will be slum people?"

Outsiders saw the dam and its reservoir *increasing* the value of tribal land, for the shoreline surely would be valuable recreational real estate. The Yavapai saw their hearts ripped out. One elderly Yavapai summed up this difference in values: "The land is like diamonds; money is like ice."

After years of effort and marches on the state capitol in an historic alliance with environmental and taxpayer groups and articulate and outraged individuals (Anglo activist Carolina Butler pivotal among them), the tribe won its battle. In 1983 the Bureau of Reclamation withdrew the Orme Dam proposal.

The fight had permanent repercussions, however. A 1973 HUD housing area could be built only above the floodplain (the Yavapai call the new ridgetop community "Beverly Hills"), cleaving the community, scattering families. Tribal headquarters moved "up above" as well, isolating social services and political meetings from the community's old center below. A land claims settlement of $5 million was entangled in legal complications from Orme Dam.

The Yavapai beat back the dam — for now, at least; dam proposals in the West have a pattern of resurfacing. Meanwhile, the 450 Fort McDowell Yavapai are working to develop their resources — on a reservation never allotted and thus easier to manage. A historic water settlement signed into law in 1990 finally grants the tribe sufficient water rights from the Verde (36,350 acre-feet guaranteed annually) to develop their reservation — with $25 million in federal and state funding to accomplish that development.

The Fort McDowell bingo hall (under non-Indian management) grossed a million dollars a month in 1988 — the largest bingo operation in Arizona. The gaming business employs one hundred tribal members, and the tribe's profits support the preschool and senior citizens center. A sand and gravel operation soon may exceed bingo as the main tribal moneymaker. Nearby, at the reservation boundary, the smooth contours of the desert hills give way abruptly to the sharp angles of houses, subdivisions, and roads — the dream of Phoenix's real estate magnates come true in the Valley of the Sun.

On the reservation, the *whit-whit-whit* of a cactus wren breaks the hot but cooling air of a spring evening. The breeze carries a sweetness from creosote bush and ironwood in bloom. Just to the east is Fountain Hills, with its eerie 560-foot fountain vaporizing in the dry desert air, catching sunset light above the silhouette of a cactus-studded ridge.

The retirement community responsible for the fountain offers little to Fort

McDowell residents; for jobs and schools, Mesa is still "town." Fountain Hills does have a mall, and as tribal chairman Clinton Pattea said to me with a pleased grin: "Bashas Supermarket is now so close!"

The Beeline Highway cuts across the southern Fort McDowell reservation. Pattea described to me the leasing of land for highway widening as a rich source of potential income. Plans include a tribally run hotel and resort, and a commercial strip of businesses: "We want tribal members to have the first options on those."

Years of fighting for their land give the tribe a special cohesion, but as Fort McDowell social services director Joan Enos says: "The quiet, leisurely life is gone." John Smith remembers when "you could be gone for a week along the river, not worried about anything in the world, kill a quail or rabbit and cook it on coals in a driftwood fire." Or "take five dollars and go to Scottsdale in a wagon and bring a box of groceries home. Forty or fifty dollars from a wheat sale would go pretty far."

Today, unemployment hovers above 50 percent. Underemployment is chronic. What outsiders see as "terminal lethargy," Yavapais see as being close to their land, going down to the river and sitting on a mesquite log, watching the birds come in to roost in the cottonwoods. Fort McDowell residents still cut mesquite for firewood and run a few head of cattle. They garden. They hunt. And two or three basket makers gather materials along the river.

John Smith says his granddaughter gets acorns from Apaches to make acorn stew; she loves cooking in the old way. "My wife likes to make you think she still believes in the old ways, but you put her by the fire and she hardly knows what to do."

David King is a good example of these mixed feelings. He lived and worked in Phoenix for twenty-nine years; now he lives again at Fort McDowell. In 1988, we sat on his porch and watched the saguaros cast longer and longer shadows and the setting sun turn Four Peaks a deeper and richer mauve. King said: "After years of sitting at a desk, supervising, now I work as a pick and shovel man. It's cured me of high blood pressure, diabetes, back trouble." King went on to serve as Fort McDowell chairman during 1991–92.

"I never *really* left," says King. During all those years away, "I came back here every weekend. There's no place like it: out here the air is pure and clean and fresh. We produce water for the whole valley."

King sees both sides in his small tribe's predicament: "We Yavapai assimilate; we have a great learning ability. [John Smith calls that skill "Indian ears."] But 99.99 percent of the kids don't know Yavapai; the language is lost. The kids are not taught values: respect, honor, integrity. But I think a person knows within himself where he's going, where he's coming from."

David King, Yavapai, 1988. King's life mirrors that of many Indian people. Raised at Fort McDowell, he left to live and work in Phoenix for almost 30 years, visiting the reservation on weekends. After retiring, he moved back to Fort McDowell, where he served as chairman in 1991–92.

David King's confidence in the resolute identity of the Yavapai proved well founded. In the spring of 1992, the Fort McDowell Yavapai once more marched on the Arizona capitol, after blockading FBI agents on their reservation. At issue were three hundred video gambling machines from the tribal bingo hall, which federal law had declared illegal. The FBI moved in to confiscate the machines and the Yavapai resisted, angry at yet another denial of their chance for self-sufficiency. Six months later, a compromise agreement allowed the tribe to operate up to 250 machines under state oversight — estimated to yield $25 to $30 million a year.

Camp Verde and Prescott: Living on History

At Camp Verde, Yavapais share several small reservation fragments with equal numbers of Tonto Apaches. The Apaches tend to dominate, and so the Yavapai find it hard to keep their heritage alive. Ted Smith, an Apache who is Camp Verde Yavapai-Apache chairman, does his best. He told me: "Everybody lives on history. If you have a history, that gives kids something to shoot for." Smith claims that his tribe has the highest percentage of students going to college of any reservation in Arizona.

The modern Verde reservations began with a forty-acre reserve at Camp Verde in 1910. More than 400 acres of land (280 of it farmable) were added at Middle Verde by 1916. A permanent Yavapai-Apache community grew up at Clarkdale to take advantage of work in the smelter and copper mines, and in 1969, when Phelps-Dodge closed the Clarkdale mining operation, the company gave sixty acres to the Interior Department as a permanent land base for the Clarkdale Indian community. An additional seventy-five acres of tribal land surrounds the Montezuma Castle National Monument tourist complex off Interstate 17 — a focus for employment and revenue.

The three communities elect a council headquartered at Middle Verde; enrollment numbers some 1,200, half of whom live on the reservation. The Verde people place their economic hopes on tourism. Retired tribal coordinator David Sine says: "Here we are in a gold mine; we need economic development people, resource people — high-caliber people." An architect's sketch of a motel proposed for the Montezuma Castle tourist center graces Ted Smith's office; the tribe has asked for a 6,500-acre addition to their lands in the White Hills just to the north, land they already use for religious purposes. Meanwhile, unemployment reaches 65 percent, and, says Ted Smith: "Since we're almost landless, we're in town most of the time scratching for a living."

David Sine points out: "We're dragging people that are old, dragging the illiterate, dragging the non-high school kids. We can pull our community with us, but it's a hard pull up front." Ted Smith is proud of his tribe's progress. "Before, we were just a whipped people. Now you can walk down the street and look people in the eye. This year [1988] an Indian boy is salutatorian at the local high school."

Education clearly is the key to the future for Camp Verde Yavapai-Apaches; their land base is too small for self-sufficiency from farming or any other natural resource. They, like Southern Paiutes or barrio Yaquis, must rely on people — educated people. Says David Sine: "If they don't give us the land we have asked for, we'll work with what we've got."

The Yavapai-Prescott people began to recreate their community in much the same way as other Yavapai returnees — scraping by, hunting and gathering, working in the mines or as maids for Prescott families. A Presbyterian mission gave a focus to the community beginning in 1922 and helped push through a seventy-five-acre reservation in 1935. The reservation was expanded in 1956 by 1,300 additional acres. A little more than one hundred Yavapais live there today, and they have done well at "working with what they've got."

The matriarchy of Yavapai-Prescott in action: *Viola Jimulla (front right), tribal chief from 1940 until her death in 1967, teaches basket making to Ruth Mitchell Welch (front) and (rear, left to right) Grace Jimulla Mitchell (who served as tribal leader after her mother's death), Julia Moore, and Edna Moore. (Courtesy Sharlot Hall Museum)*

Rejecting the Indian Reorganization Act, the Prescott people continued to rely on a hereditary chief. Sam Jimulla led the tribe in the early 1900s, and his family leads the community still. Jimulla's widow, Viola, served as chief from 1940 to her death in 1967 and remains the best known Prescott Yavapai. Her daughters Grace Mitchell and Lucy Miller served after her, and her granddaughter Patricia McGee after them (from 1972–88). Mitchell was particularly influential, working with linguists to preserve the Yavapai language.

The 1988 election brought a major change to Yavapai-Prescott politics, with the Jimulla family losing power to someone from the "other side" of the tribe, Stan Rice, Jr. Rice hoped to "heal the hurt," both within and without the tribe. He believed his biggest obstacles on both fronts to be "stupidity, bigotry, and greed."

Pat McGee returned to the office of tribal president in 1990, ready to put to use the traits noted by her grandmother when Viola Jimulla asked McGee to return to her people in 1966: "You're as crazy as your grandfather — you're so impartial, you'll help everybody, even your enemies."

The Yavapai-Prescott community has transformed its economic status in recent years. Taking advantage of the growth of the city, which they surround on three sides, they have built an industrial park, a commercial park, and a hotel complex, and have initiated planning for a state-of-the-art tribal museum. Pat McGee hopes the museum/cultural center will recapture language and culture for young Yavapai-Prescott people, "a place to go to know where we came from." The hotel, a Sheraton, looms over Prescott from a bluff above U.S. Highway 89; the commercial park includes a Wal-Mart, initially protested by some Prescott residents but now patronized by nearly everybody. The Yavapai-Prescott, for so long barely visible in the community, are invisible no longer.

John Williams, the late Fort McDowell elder, wrote: "Before the white people live here, we have no trouble at all. At that time we all stay together, not like now, all separate. Now there are few of us left and that is why we are scattered out."

Today, the scattered Yavapai are pulling together. Joan Enos, at Fort McDowell, told me: "We found that the only time we were getting together with Camp Verde and Prescott was when there was a death. Now we have one get-together a year that rotates, and not at a funeral."

The Apache

White Mountain Apache Gaan dancers, 1906. These impersonators of the mountain spirits are also called crown dancers. They come to girls' puberty ceremonies, often at night, to dance with the girl, casting startling shadows beyond the circle of the bonfires. Photo by Edward Curtis. (Smithsonian Institution photo no. 76-6283)

Ojo Caliente is my home. All of my people so far as I can remember have lived there . . . It is my country. I have not forgotten it . . . I was taken away from there for no reason whatever. Loco, who was my grandfather and a chief, was moved from there for no cause. From that time until the time of his death here at Fort Sill he always asked to be sent back to Ojo Caliente. Now I am asking for that country myself . . .

From San Carlos they took me to Fort Apache. We had trouble at San Carlos and Fort Apache both. Both of those times we were on land belonging to other Indians. From Fort Apache I was sent to St. Augustine, Florida. At St. Augustine I was told that my way was a bad one, that my thoughts and life had been bad, to put it away from me, get away from it and go to school and learn the ways of the white people. They sent me to Carlisle, Pennsylvania . . . When I got back to Alabama I found lots of my People from Ojo Caliente there. In Alabama lots of them died. They brought us from Alabama to Fort Sill and there was lots of them died here. But they gave us strong words, strong thoughts . . . And they stayed in our hearts and are there today.

Talbot Goody, Chiricahua Apache, Fort Sill, Oklahoma, 22 August 1909

Smoke drifts along the northern shore of Stone Lake, wafting from tipis sculpted from white canvas. Red or white pennants flutter high from ridgepoles, the streamers crackling in the breeze in colors that signify the Jicarilla Apache Ollero and Llanero bands. Each family camp has an additional square canvas tent, a pickup truck or two, maybe a tent-trailer, a shade of oak boughs. Against the hillside of grass golden in early morning light and the gray-green sagebrush wet and aromatic from a dawn rain, turquoise portable toilets gleam like gemstones.

At my own camp across this lake in northernmost New Mexico, I catch snatches of singing — the higher pitch of the lead answered by the voices of the chorus. Songs to the sun and the moon, to the rain, to the clouds trailing black tendrils over the bluffs and through the Jicarilla encampment. I hear meadowlarks, ravens, ducks, an occasional exalted whoop from a singer, cars and chain saws revved. A great blue heron hunts in the shallows.

This annual three-day Jicarilla encampment brings long life and health to all participants. Tom Vigil, a Jicarilla singer, calls it "the Jicarilla New Year's, Mardi Gras, and state fair, combined." The high point is the 15 September relay race between Ollero and Llanero teams that ensures a beneficent harvest — and a food supply balanced

Derwin McIntosh helps prepare a young San Carlos Apache Gaan dancer, O'odham Tash parade, Casa Grande, Arizona, 1992.

between the animals (and sun) of the white Olleros and the plants (and moon) of the red Llaneros.

So much of these three days feels like an Apache camp must have felt in the old days. People walk from tent to tent, visiting, courting, sharing food. Horse-mounted, cowboy-hatted Apaches ride through camp exultant, following a man carrying a staff flagged with the white Ollero banner decorated with four red suns. Men lead pairs of ponies down to the water. One girl practices barrel racing in a corral. Teenagers ride to a ridgetop to watch the finish of a five-mile horse race, sitting astride their animals in dusty gold light, a tipi to the left, layers of junipers behind them leading to higher ridges dense with ponderosa pines and Gambel oaks, crested by creamy cliffs.

The women preside over the cooking fires, the men parade and boast and cheer the young boys running heats to determine the lead racers. I talk with a man who doesn't want to return to his tent for fear his wife will "capture" him and he won't have any more fun. Leaders bless the stones marking the racecourse — stones brought from the ancestral Jicarilla homeland around Cimarron, New Mexico — and offer them to the four directions.

This scene of vitality seems far removed from any common image of Apaches, who remain romanticized and misunderstood. Apaches still find photos of their sacred Mountain Spirit dancers captioned "Apache devil dancers." Bookshelves of Apache literature focus mostly on the Apache Wars with the U.S. Army in the late 1800s. The names of Cochise, Geronimo, Naiche, Juh, and Victorio strike chills in people who know little more of these men than that they were reputed to be fierce and bloodthirsty. Narcissus Gayton, a Chiricahua Apache at Mescalero, says: "When you go off the reservation, you say you're an Apache, and people say it couldn't be true!"

The late San Carlos medicine man Philip Cassadore spoke to me of "urban Indians who only know they look like an Indian." He said: "The movie industry has really destroyed our image. Even the word 'Apache' means 'enemies' and 'warlike Indian.' So everybody's scared of us.

"White people call us Apache, but we call ourselves Ndee, the People. Apaches were happy when they were by themselves, way up in the mountains. Now, when they see all these push-button things, Apaches get confused. Should I be an Apache or should I join those people? Because they think that white people have more to offer. They think the Apache has nothing.

"I grew up with nothing. But there was love. There might be no food but there was love."

Apaches have long been seen through the narrow lens of their success in war. In 1630, Fray Alonso de Benavides called them "a people very fiery and bellicose, and

very crafty in war." But he praised their upright morals, their value of chastity, and
added that "they pride themselves much in speaking the truth."

I have found that truthfulness in abundance in today's Apaches. They have a forthright bluntness that is impressive, attractive — and challenging. Ned Anderson, former chairman at San Carlos, says: "To this day, if an Apache says something, that's the way it will be." (His opponents in tribal politics, of course, might not agree!)

These Apaches, not the ones in the movies, held an enormous territory against all comers for centuries. Though vanquished, they have not vanished. Twenty thousand Apaches remain in the Southwest. Fort Apache is the nation's third most populous reservation (as of 1990), San Carlos the seventh. They have their struggles, but they continue to strive, in the words of San Carlos artist Delmar Boni, to "stand for life, family, goodness, and understanding."

The People from the North

No one knows just when the Apaches arrived in the Southwest. The Apaches, of course, don't worry about such technicalities. They know they climbed into this land from the underworld, clambering up a cane stalk behind the Red Ants, the first people. They know that Yusn, the Life-Giver, created the Universe and that Changing Woman and her sons, Child Born of Water and Killer of Enemies, then prepared the earth for Ndee, the People. The two brothers later killed the Monsters. The Apaches know, too, that Coyote stole fire, loosed darkness, and made death inevitable. Anthropologist Morris Opler said in his study of the Chiricahuas: "All that man does 'Coyote did first.'"

Any stories about the failings shared by humans and Coyote (gluttony, lying, theft, lust, adultery, incest, and the rest) insult Coyote, a risky thing to do. Apaches end such stories with diversionary tactics, a pledge to Coyote that they really have been talking about something good.

I have told stories here about Coyote. I am talking about fruit.

When the world was simpler, power was everywhere. Any Apache could possess power and become a medicine person. Some had power from the Mountain People, involving them with the Mountain Spirit dancers, the Gaan. Others had curing powers (they knew how to give "good hope," in the words of one Apache) or knew the long song cycles of the creation story, to be sung for the girl's puberty ceremony.

These beliefs underlie the Apache lifeway. The people called Apache lived in extended families organized into local groups, which, in turn, were loosely tied together in bands. Neighboring bands with shared cultural traits came to be seen as tribes, but to the Apache, the local group was always the most important unit. "Chiefs" were

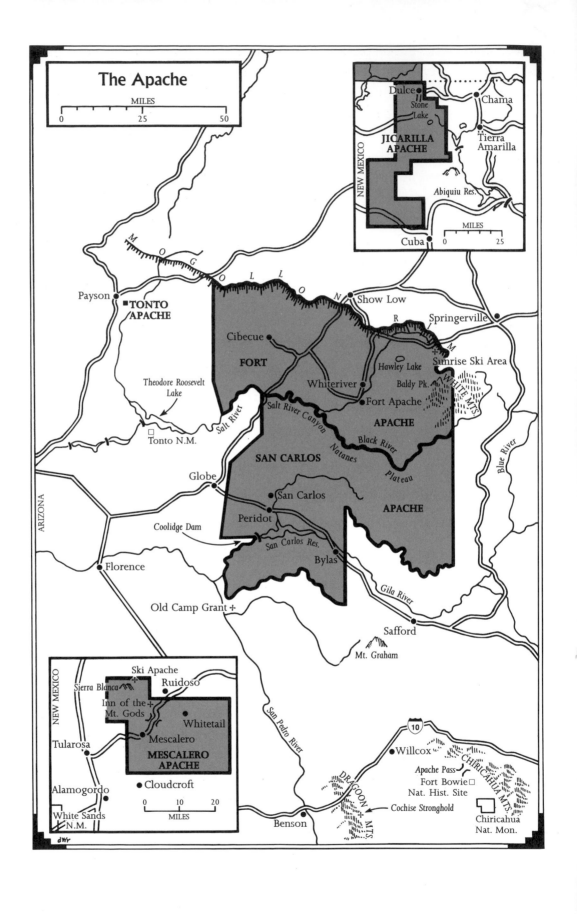

The Apache

MILES

0   25   50

JICARILLA APACHE

NEW MEXICO

Dulce
Stone Lake
Chama
Tierra Amarilla
Abiquiu Res.
Cuba

MILES

0   25

Payson
TONTO APACHE

MOGOLLON RIM

Show Low

Springerville

Cibecue

FORT

Hawley Lake

Whiteriver

Baldy Pk.

Sunrise Ski Area

WHITE MTS.

Fort Apache

APACHE

Theodore Roosevelt Lake

Salt River Canyon

Salt River

Natanes Plateau

Black River

Blue River

Tonto N.M.

SAN CARLOS

Globe

San Carlos

APACHE

Peridot

Coolidge Dam

San Carlos Res.

ARIZONA

Florence

Bylas

Gila River

Old Camp Grant +

Safford

Mt. Graham

Ski Apache

Sierra Blanca

Ruidoso

Inn of the Mt. Gods

Whitetail

Tularosa

Mescalero

MESCALERO APACHE

NEW MEXICO

San Pedro River

10

Alamogordo

Cloudcroft

0   10   20

MILES

Willcox

CHIRICAHUA MTS.

Apache Pass

Fort Bowie Nat. Hist. Site

White Sands N.M.

DRAGOON MTS.

Cochise Stronghold

Chiricahua Nat. Mon.

Benson

dWr

elected to lead these small groups (numbering about 35 to 200 people). They maintained their influence only as long as their counsel brought success to their followers in hunting, raiding, and warfare. Philip Cassadore said: "The person that give the most, that provide food for the most, was the one they call the leader. It's not a warrior that's called a leader, it's not a warrior that's called a chief—it's the one that really care for people, not kill people."

Chiefs wielded influence in long discussions that led to group decisions; their styles varied. Chiricahua historian Donald Cole writes of the leaders of his people: "Cochise led by sheer integrity and moral example. Geronimo held his followers by enigmatic behavior and examples of raw power. Victorio was successful as long as his sister Lozen's war power sustained him [and the remarkable warrior Lozen herself rode with Geronimo until the final surrender]. Juh, inhibited by a speech impediment, let others speak for him. Ulzana led by dash and Nana by stealth."

Delmar Boni says: "Leadership that we had a long time ago took spirituality, it took understanding for the mountain, it took those real simple things, getting up in the morning and the addressing of the Sun, towards family, towards sacred places where the clans came from. It took all these things. If you remove yourself from these basic elements, Indian leadership suffers."

From the shreds of evidence remaining on the land, in dialectical differences in Apache language, and from their best hunches, anthropologists have structured a timeline for the differentiation of the Apaches after their arrival in the Southwest. By 1300, the group called Kiowa-Apache broke off to become Plains people, in historic times living in Oklahoma as allies of the Kiowa. The remaining migrating Apacheans moved into the Southwest, probably about A.D. 1400.

At first, they hunted buffalo at the margins of the mountains. The Western Apache (the San Carlos, White Mountain, Cibecue, and Tonto people of central Arizona) and the Navajo seem to have moved westward early. The Lipan and Jicarilla Apache were not in contact with them after 1600, themselves dividing to set up territories in the west Texas plains and northern New Mexico mountains, respectively.

Mescalero and Chiricahua Apache people moved into southern New Mexico by the early seventeenth century. By the time Spaniards wrote of them, the prosperous Mescalero held the land east of the Rio Grande to the Pecos River and beyond, venturing out onto the plains for an annual buffalo hunt. The Chiricahua roamed west of the great river into southeastern Arizona and northern Mexico.

The Navajo became a tribe distinct from all other Apaches, picking up strong doses of Pueblo culture—though only a century has passed since outsiders called them "Navajo Apaches." All the rest of these peoples remain Apaches: Ndee.

Apacheans moved into Pueblo country late, after the Anasazi had abandoned their great cliff dwellings and moved to the Rio Grande, to Hopi, Zuni, and Acoma. Initially, Pueblo and Apache seem to have adapted to one another peacefully. When the Spaniards arrived, Apaches lived in the mountains surrounding the Pueblo villages; Apache warriors immediately began raiding the newcomers for food and horses.

The Knowledgeable People

"Nomads — always going and going. They're a very knowledgeable people; they don't get lost."

This is how White Mountain Apache museum director Edgar Perry describes his people — living in their chosen homelands, moving with the seasons. About 25 percent of the Western Apache diet came from their fields. Women did most of the gathering and the limited work in farm plots, generating the basics of life; men did most of the hunting, providing meat for the women to cook. Men led raids for food and stock and conducted war for revenge. Women set up camp, in the mountains building wickiups (*gowa* — also the word for family) and on the plains erecting tipis. Either sex could conduct ceremonies and curing rites, obtaining power from the earth, from dreams — though most specialists in ritual were men. Both men and women carried on the oral narrative traditions.

Apache families were structured around women; sisters and daughters lived together throughout their lives. Men entered the group by marriage. For Western Apaches, membership in one of the sixty clans further tied families together; Philip Cassadore said: "Clan is Apache way. Band is white man's description." Wesley Bonito, from Fort Apache, says: "Cousins go on and on and on — the extended family goes on forever!" These relationships formed the basis of Apache life; an Apache living alone was inconceivable.

Each year the plants gave their gifts to the people, who moved camp with the seasons and harvests. The Chiricahua named the year's divisions in accordance with these cycles of growth, from the "Many Leaves" time of late spring to "Thick with Fruit" in late summer to the "Ghost Face" of winter.

One year was "one harvest": yucca shoots, tule roots, yucca flowers, roasted mescal, locust flowers, wild onion, ponderosa pine bark, sumac berries, juniper berries, strawberries, chokecherries, wild potatoes, mulberries, pitahaya cactus, screwbean mesquite, saguaro fruit, datil yucca fruit, prickly pear, mesquite, walnuts, piñon nuts, greens, acorns, grasses, amaranth, sunflower seeds, tule pollen, honey.

Jeannette Larzelere's puberty ceremony, Whiteriver, Arizona, 1984. An older woman sponsors and instructs the White Mountain Apache girl as she dances through four days of ritual. Anyone attending the ceremony may bless the girl with sacred cattail pollen, and, in turn, ask her to share her power and blessing.

One conspicuous affirmation of power in the Apache universe came when a young woman reached puberty, when the entire community danced her into adulthood. During this time, the girl became Changing Woman, White Painted Woman, the progenitor of all humans; with her power the girl could cure those blessing her. As a raiding initiate, a young man became Child Born of Water — just as a pubescent girl became Changing Woman.

Today, not every Apache girl has a nai'es, a "getting her ready" ceremony. Not every modern Apache girl wants one; not every family can afford the costs (as much as several thousand dollars); not every family believes it appropriate. But for the Apache girls who go through the ceremony, it is an unforgettable experience. In Philip Cassadore's words: "During this four days is the most important part of her life." Elbys Hugar, at Mescalero, recalled that importance when she spoke to writer Henrietta Stockel, looking back from the age of fifty-nine: "It's still part of me and it's going to be that way for the rest of my life. I'll never forget the good it did for me and how it helped me over the hardships."

"Traveling on the medicine man's chants," the girl becomes Changing Woman and acquires the longevity and desirable qualities of this powerful being. The girl dances with a feather-decorated cane which absorbs the power of the ceremony; when she is an old woman she may use this same cane as a walking stick, to give her strength. An abalone shell hangs from her forehead, representing the shell in which Changing Woman survived a great flood to become the first Apache.

First, she dances alone, then she kneels, dancing as Changing Woman danced when the Sun impregnated her before the birth of Monster Slayer. An older woman, unrelated and with unquestionable reputation, sponsors and instructs the girl as she dances through the four days. The sponsor massages the girl, who is malleable like wet clay, to mold her into a strong woman. The girl runs to the four directions, and the gathered community runs behind her, running through the four stages of life, to ensure she will live through each of them.

Persons attending the Sunrise Dance may bless the girl with sacred cattail pollen, and, in turn, may ask the girl to share her power and bless them. According to anthropologist Keith Basso, the Apaches ask for everything from rain and good harvests to help for keeping out of trouble "my son in Dallas, learning to be a barber."

The Gaan, the Mountain Spirit dancers, come to dance with the girl at night, casting huge shadows beyond the bonfires. Finally, on the last morning, the girl is painted with earth to give her the power of the earth, and the assembled people dance behind her through the ceremonial tipi, made from the four kinds of wood lightning cannot strike.

"In the Apache, there is no adolescence. They just become a woman." This is the way Philip Cassadore summed up the significance of the ceremony he sang. In watching a puberty ceremony at Whiteriver with him, I was moved by the power and good will of the group assembled to dance the girl into womanhood. Cassadore said: "Everyone is in one accord, for the girl." And it remains so, despite whatever other reasons people might have for attending: free food, alcohol, courting, partying.

The Apaches still have power, and each girl undergoing her *nai'es* still acquires the mythic power of Changing Woman. A few weeks after her ceremony, I saw Jeannette Larzelere, the girl I had photographed during those four days, in jeans and t-shirt instead of ceremonial buckskins, at the Apache Tribal Fair. Walking with her friends, she still looked transfigured.

Philip Cassadore's power as a medicine man, a *diiyin*, came from his knowledge of the song cycle for the girl's puberty ceremony. He said: "My stories are Apache, from older Apaches. What they know is hundreds of years old. I ask older people if I'm doing it right. That's how you learn. That's how you keep it the way it was a thousand years ago. It will be taken away if it's not done right."

A singer like Cassadore first gained power by a sign ("power finds you"), not from a teacher ("you find power"). He told me: "You hear voices from another world if you become a medicine man. I am here, but when I look at the cloud, that's where I'm at. I'm up there with those medicine people. When the thunder and lightning come close, they're talking to me. When the thunder roll, it goes inside me. The closer it comes, the better I feel. I have a lightning shield — all around me."

The greatest source of power is the Sun. Edgar Perry says: "East is very important because it's a direction that represents the Sun, the moon, the stars, the darkness, the day. The first thing that hits the Apaches in the face in the morning is the Sun. It's like getting up with God."

Delmar Boni adds: "When the Sun sets in the evening, we can put all the things aside — obstacles, misunderstandings — put it behind. The Sun will bless us before we take our rest for the evening. And then the Sun greets us again in the morning. And the songs come out with a lot of strength and understanding."

A Cibecue Apache told Keith Basso: "You can't talk about power like other things. You can't hold it with words." The Apache maintain an intense intimacy with the powers of their world. Tom Vigil, at Jicarilla, says: "No one can see the world the way I see it, unless he's experienced the world the way I have."

Edgar Perry, at Fort Apache, says: "The core of being Apache is the language. If you can't speak Apache, you can't think Indian." Ned Anderson explains this: "For everything you say in Apache, there is something it means absolutely — but you have to know the context to really know what it means."

At Mescalero, Evelyn Breuninger has been working on a dictionary for her people. She sat with me in front of her house and looked away at the forested horizon: "In the puberty ceremony, how do the sponsors tell the young maidens all the things you should know? In English you just can't say some of these things." Lucille Shorten, San Carlos elder and councilwoman, says: "You need to know big words in Apache to understand big words in English. Learn English in school, put them together, and you'll be smarter than anybody who just speaks English."

Sometimes silence matters most. Wesley Bonito, education director for Fort Apache, talked with me about how he "may speak at a meeting and no one says anything. That means approval. If they have an objection, they speak out. It could be a silent meeting, but yet it gets done. They observed." Lucille Shorten agrees: "I speak up in council only when I don't approve."

Apaches "observing" can be unnerving to non-Apaches. The silent Apaches are neither uninterested, aloof, nor playing at being the stereotypical dignified and impassive Indian. They are simply refraining from speaking because at times this is appropriate for an Apache. They are listening.

Delmar Boni's advice for *anyone* going to a Sunrise Dance also has to do with silence and listening: "Be yourself; open up from your heart and your mind. Watch, be a part, see. Through that you can come to an understanding." That understanding goes beyond the ritual itself to the core of what it means to be Apache.

Apachería

The Apaches set the northern limits to New Spain. Confrontation began early; when Apaches raided Spanish expeditions for horses, the soldiers retaliated, and by doing so brought down the brunt of Apache revenge in full-scale war expeditions.

The Spaniards, in turn, gave a name to the greater Apache homeland — Apachería — and to each Apache band they encountered. The Spaniards traded with the Apache but sold them into slavery, as well. Apaches felt they had to avenge such wrongs. Relationships among Pueblos, Apaches, and Spaniards deteriorated through the 1600s. Indeed, "Apache" may derive from a Zuni word for "enemy."

Conflict came first in the south, in Sonora and Chihuahua. Apaches (and other lesser-known peoples evidently later absorbed by the Ndee) began raiding Spanish and Piman agricultural settlements for food and stock. By the early 1700s, the Apaches reigned north as far as Zuni. In this swath of land, the Spanish — and later the Mexicans — may have claimed sovereignty, but they had precious little to prove it. Apachería completely isolated the New Mexican settlements around Santa Fe from the Sonora-Chihuahua frontier.

Within this huge territory, the Apaches developed their culture through the eighteenth century; the roughest mountains in the Southwest became their strongholds. The Ndee treated the sedentary peoples as a crop, raiding whenever opportunity or need arose but never wiping them out — and refusing to fight in formal battles. As Edward Spicer put it, the line of Spanish presidios intended to protect the villagers "was a sieve through which the Apaches penetrated at will."

Warfare and raiding distanced Apaches from the surrounding tribes. Each Apache group raided the larder nearest at hand. The Chiricahuas raided south into Mexico; Western Apaches raided the Maricopa, O'odham, and Navajo; the Tonto Apache raided the Pai. Jicarilla and Mescalero raided Rio Grande Spanish and Pueblo settlements between more peaceful trading times. The Lipan plundered Texas.

Pressure from the Apaches weakened the Spaniards, contributing to the successful Pueblo Revolt of 1680. After the Spaniards reconquered New Mexico, the Camino

Real north from El Paso to Santa Fe came to be called the Jornada del Muerto, the "Journey of Death," for its risk of Mescalero Apache attack. In the early 1700s, however, the Comanches pushed south, inexorably reducing the lands of Lipan, Mescalero, and Jicarilla. These full-time raiders and hunters gained ground consistently from the Apache, who stubbornly continued to farm part of each year, making easy-to-locate targets.

After 1725, the Mescalero were forced into the mountains—and into relative poverty after their easy life as plains buffalo-hunters. Jicarilla were caught between expanding Comanche, Ute, and Navajo, and in a critical choice allied themselves with the Spaniards to stand some chance of survival. They lived close to Pueblo and Spanish villages from the 1720s on. Raids still occurred, alliances shifted, but the Spaniards were kept busy elsewhere—Christianizing the Pueblos and fighting the Chiricahua and Mescalero.

In 1786, after three generations of war, the Spanish Governor Bernardo de Galvez tried a new tack. His directions were cynical but effective (at least for some southern bands): make peace with the Apaches, persuade them to settle near presidios, feed them well, keep them drunk, give them rifles good enough for hunting but too rickety for war, stir up fighting between bands, and by any means necessary, keep them dependent.

After 1821, the struggling revolutionary government of Mexico could not afford to buy dependency as had Galvez. By 1835, the Apaches had demonstrated that the intervening years had not erased their raiding skills. Sonora and Chihuahua placed a bounty of one hundred dollars on every male Apache scalp. This desperate attempt to respond to the Apache warriors made for ineffective genocide, but it effectively aroused Apache hatred of Mexicans.

Chiricahuas called those Ndee who trusted whites "the foolish people." Bloody encounters with scalp hunters ended the Apache custom of gathering in large winter encampments: such concentrations just weren't safe. Chiricahuas ceased taking adult males as prisoners; instead, they generally began to turn them over to female relatives of slain Apache men for torture. War still raged when the United States took over Apachería in mid-century.

Tom Vigil, Jicarilla entrepreneur (owner/operator of the Jicarilla Inn in Dulce) spends considerable time thinking about who he is, about the history of his people. He says: "Too much of history is as we would like to remember it. We play right into the hands of the John Wayne movie. I refuse to accept the general notion that we have to be heroes.

"There is a story about some hungry Jicarillas killing some cows; all of a sudden they were 'Jicarilla warriors.' The army ends up chasing a Jicarilla family that is just try-ing to avoid extermination: these were the wars. You chase me and my family around the hillside with the army, and I'll become a pretty good tactician real fast. You come into my house, and I'll become brave real fast.

"Those were the wars. That's our history."

Much of Apache life has been obscured behind the ruckus of such battles. The Apache Wars with the United States were a short, though pivotal, period in the People's long history — the only time well known, but a time as full of exaggeration and myth as any time. Apache identity actually has more to do with language and reli-gion than warfare. As Daklugie, son of Juh and nephew of Geronimo, put it: "Religion is the one thing of which we cannot be deprived" — except perhaps by time, lost with the passing of the elders.

"A Good Day to Die"

When the United States assigned the first Indian agent to New Mexico Terri-tory (which included modern Arizona) in 1847, there were about six to eight thousand Apaches ready to trade with the newcomers. The Americans had beaten the Apaches' perpetual enemies, the Mexicans, so the People assumed that the Americans would be pleased to see the Apaches continue raiding their mutual enemy south of the border.

The Apaches reacted to the Americans' vow to pacify them with surprise and disgust. Apaches could not survive without raiding, an uncomfortable fact even be-fore Anglo settlers began to filter into the Southwest. Now that white appropriation of Indian lands began to disrupt traditional food-gathering rounds, raiding became even more crucial. As a group of Mescalero chiefs put the dilemma to an army quarter-master in 1850: "We must steal from somebody; and if you will not permit us to rob the Mexicans, we must steal from you or fight you."

The choices left to the Americans were three: exterminate the Apaches, feed them, or give them reservations and teach them to become self-sufficient. Historian C. L. Sonnichsen summed up these options from the perspective of the Apache: "Was he supposed to be a pensioner, a farmer, or a corpse?"

In the 1850s in New Mexico, the Jicarillas, the Sierra Blanca Mescaleros, and the eastern Chiricahuas (the latter known as Mimbreños, Warm Springs Apaches, and to the Ndee, as Chihene, Red Paint People) did their best to stay out of trouble. They signed treaties and were promised reservations and rations. They planted fields under the supervision of agents. But when the treaties went unratified and the government delivered neither protection nor adequate food, the Ndee were forced to raid.

Battles followed: Apaches would kill a settler's family in a raid, soldiers would

massacre entire camps of (often innocent) Apaches in return, and Apaches would
slaughter whites in retaliation. In the midst of this downward spiral, group after
Apache group kept trying to pledge peace in return for food rations and payment for
their lands.

In the 1860s, the turmoil of the Civil War reached the Southwest. Supply lines
passed through the country of the southern Mescalero (in the Davis and Guadalupe
mountains of west Texas), the eastern Chiricahua (the Mimbreños, led by Mangas
Coloradas), and the central Chiricahuas (the Chokonen, led by Cochise). When General
James Carleton occupied New Mexico with Union forces in 1862, his aim was to
keep the supply lines open; his method was to exterminate the Apaches.

By the spring of 1863, Carleton had forced the starving Mescaleros to leave their
informal reservation in the Sierra Blanca and move to newly built Fort Sumner, at
Bosque Redondo on the Pecos River. More than eight thousand Navajos joined the
four hundred Mescaleros, and with each new wave of prisoners, the situation at
Bosque Redondo grew worse.

The little grove of cottonwoods made a decent camp for a family but was no place
for ten thousand people. Alkaline water, disease, crop failure, and inedible rations
made Bosque Redondo a place of heartbreak and death.

On the night of 3 November 1865, the Mescaleros decided that they had had
enough. All but nine ill or crippled Apaches escaped from Fort Sumner, scattered,
and vanished into the mountains — for seven years. Big Mouth, who was at Bosque
Redondo when he was a child, spoke to historian Eve Ball of returning to "our country
and our freedom," where "there was pure, cold water and plenty of wood and no
worms, no bad smells, no Navajos, and no soldiers."

On the western edge of Apachería, the Prescott gold strike of 1863 led the Tonto
Apaches into the same tragic cycle of raid, murder, and massacre. By 1865, the army
had built a string of forts across Apache country. They were no more effective than
the Spanish presidios at preventing raids — and little better at protecting settlers. The
forts did house plenty of troops ready for battle, however.

Tragic stupidities by individuals contributed immensely to the sad story. Miners
at what became Silver City, New Mexico, bullwhipped Mangas Coloradas in 1860,
turning him to war; Mangas was tricked into capture and murdered in 1862. An inexperienced
Lieutenant George Bascom alienated Cochise, an immensely respected
leader who otherwise might have kept the peace. Chiricahua Donald Cole calls the
Bascom attack on Cochise and the murder of Mangas his people's "Pearl Harbor."

Through the 1860s, the Apaches held the field — particularly the Chiricahuas. By
one estimate, the U.S. Army spent $38 million from 1862 to 1871 to kill one hundred

Apache Camp Arizona

Chiricahua Apache camp, San Carlos River, circa 1885. After disastrous government efforts to concentrate all 5,000 Western and Chiricahua Apaches at San Carlos, many White Mountain people moved to Fort Apache. All Chiricahua bands, both peaceful and rebellious, were sent into exile. Photo by Ben Wittick. (Courtesy Museum of New Mexico, neg. no. 15873)

Apaches (including old men, women, and children). The Apaches themselves killed over one thousand American troops and civilians during the same period.

One particularly brutal massacre of San Carlos Apache women and children near Camp Grant in Arizona's Arivaipa Valley in 1871 finally pushed President Grant to formulate the Peace Policy. The administration planned to concentrate tribes on reservations and "promote peace and civilization among them." Success would require stellar leadership on both sides.

In New Mexico, the Mescaleros living on Sierra Blanca under their peace-making leaders Santana and Cadete were acknowledged with a reservation in 1873 — though with little support for their efforts to maintain themselves. The Jicarillas continued to promise to stay at peace, but the government provided insufficient rations, allowed their lands to be usurped, and made no move to establish a reservation. The Jicarillas remained in limbo throughout the 1870s, raiding for stock in desperation at times, but not really at war.

The Peace Policy had better luck in Arizona, at least for a few years. Vincent Colyer, Peace Commissioner, proclaimed reservations; General George Crook set out to confine the Indians on them. Crook's campaign against the Tonto in 1873 brought them permanently under military control. The Camp Verde, San Carlos, and Fort Apache reservations — together home for the modern Western Apache — all date from this time.

Guided by the trader Thomas Jeffords, a longtime friend of Cochise, another peace emissary sent by President Grant met with the Chiricahua leader deep in the Dragoon Mountains. Years of war and disease had whittled away at the Chiricahua: women and children outnumbered men by two to three times. Cochise promised peace; the Great Father in Washington promised a reservation in the Chokonen homeland surrounding Apache Pass; Jeffords reluctantly agreed to sign on as agent. Within two months, six hundred southern Chiricahua (Nednai) led by Juh and others joined Cochise's 450-member band, and a presidential order sanctioned the new reservation.

Jeffords strove to deliver rations in the face of an uncooperative bureaucracy. Cochise strove to limit raids but could not control the Nednai (whose numbers included a *diiyin* for war named Geronimo). By the time Cochise died in 1874, he could no longer control even his own Chokonen. A frustrated Jeffords had already submitted his resignation once, and the Indian Bureau was trying to move the Chiricahuas eastward to New Mexico. The Apaches said, simply, that "they would rather die here than live there."

Cochise created a new definition of Apache leadership. He started as war chief and the favored son-in-law of Mangas Coloradas. By force of personality, integrity, and his unusual friendship with Jeffords, he claimed leadership over other Chiricahua bands as well as his own. When he died, he ordered the same allegiance to his son Taza. The subchiefs agreed and elected the young man chief, but Taza lacked his father's wisdom and experience and never wielded the same authority.

Young Apache men had only one route to manhood and leadership: raiding (literally, in Western Apache, "to search out enemy property" — in contrast to warfare, "to take death from an enemy"). Their initiatory raids were the equivalent of the girl's puberty ceremony, the "equivalent of a Bar Mitzvah," as Donald Cole puts it.

Generally, only an accomplished warrior won the favor of his chosen woman. Only a successful raider could provide for his wife's family — indeed, a major goal of Apache life was "having a lot of relatives." Only a raider's surplus could accommodate the huge feasts and gifts necessary for his daughters during their puberty ceremonies. Only by demonstrating power and wisdom in war could a man earn the votes required for leadership.

Chiricahua men continued to slip away to Mexico to earn their successes, growing bolder as Jeffords' ability to deliver supplies decreased. Their reservation fell apart in 1876, with skirmishes between Apache factions, raids on settlers, and army reprisals.

Chaos filled the next ten years. Bands moved on and off reservations, fleeing to Mexico, returning peacefully, drifting away into the mountains once more. Warriors shifted allegiance between the primary dissident leaders: Taza, Geronimo, Juh, and Victorio. At one point, Agent John Clum succeeded in concentrating at San Carlos all five thousand Western and Chiricahua Apaches, most of whom had never associated with each other on such intimate terms. Juh's son, Daklugie, described San Carlos as "a terrible place, the worst in all our vast territory."

Concentration and forced marches continued. Geronimo and a few others were held in chains, awaiting civil trial. Clum took Taza to Washington, D.C., to show him off, and Taza died of pneumonia on the trip. Cochise's youngest son, Naiche, succeeded him as chief. While thousands of Apaches lived in peace on reservations, Victorio, Geronimo, Juh, and their few dozen followers made their last stand for the warrior's path. Daklugie put it this way: "All of us knew that we were doomed, but some preferred death to slavery and imprisonment." The warrior Chihuahua's son, Eugene, said they "were fighting for their freedom, their families, and their homeland. And their self-respect."

While the dissidents fought for their last, short interval of freedom, the concentration of the other Apaches began to ease. The first five hundred White Mountain people left for Fort Apache in 1879. Corrupt agents and voracious settlers continued to whittle away at reservation boundaries at both San Carlos and Fort Apache, lopping off the more desirable areas for mines and farms, appropriating upstream water, and in New Mexico stealing horses from the impoverished Mescaleros.

After years of being shuffled between his home at Ojo Caliente, the hated San Carlos, and Mescalero, Victorio took his final stand. He and his Mimbres people had lost their holy lands; what was there now to live for?

The leader fled with his warriors; their women and children were taken to San Carlos. Victorio's attitude must have been much the same as Philip Cassadore's: "I'm a human being, not a 'peaceful tribe.'" For a year, Victorio and his men (as many as 300) battled thousands of American and Mexican troops — usually winning and sometimes losing to the most canny of the army officers — who had the skilled help of Apache scouts recruited from bands at peace, including some Chiricahuas.

The army eliminated Victorio's sanctuary in the Sierra Blanca by disarming (and humiliating) the reservation Mescaleros in April 1880. Victorio, chased hard, retreated to Mexico, where he was surrounded and his band annihilated by Mexican troops in October 1880. Apache tradition says that Victorio took his own life with his knife when he realized that without ammunition his people were doomed to death or capture.

The surviving Mimbreño leader, Nana, escaped into the Sonoran mountains. In

July 1881, Nana led a raid across southern New Mexico with about forty Chiricahua and Mescalero warriors unencumbered by their families. Lieutenant Gatewood described old, lame Nana, seventy-three, as "palsied, aged and decrepit." Nana, however, could call on the power of Goose — for speed and endurance. He covered more than a thousand miles in six weeks, some days riding seventy miles, and won more battles than he lost, leaving the countryside in an uproar. If Apache warriors had always traveled without their families, the long wars would have been even longer.

During Victorio's campaign, Geronimo and Juh stayed at peace. But in 1881, Juh, Geronimo, Naiche, Nana, Loco (tricked into joining the fighters by Geronimo), Chatto, and Chihuahua led some seven hundred of their people into a Sierra Madre stronghold. The army took them seriously: in September 1882, General George Crook returned to Arizona.

Crook clearly stated his intentions toward the Apaches: "First, to make them no promises that could not be fulfilled. Second, to tell them the exact truth at all times. Third, to keep them at labor and to find remuneration for that labor. Fourth, to be patient, to be just, and to fear not." The general reorganized San Carlos, brought the Apache scouts to full strength, put his pack trains in order, and headed for Mexico.

In May 1883, the Apaches surrendered — now led in battle for the first time by Geronimo, after the death of Juh in an accident. It took until the following spring to force all of the bands to return, and the last was Geronimo's. Once again, all the Apaches tried living together on the reservations. Crook allowed nine hundred more White Mountain people to move back to Fort Apache country.

Too many competing factions existed — both Apache and white — for San Carlos and Fort Apache to settle down. One hundred and thirty-four Chiricahuas bolted a last time. More pursuit, more raids. More death. Ten months later, in March 1886, deep in the Mexican Sierra Madre, Chihuahua, Naiche, Nana, and Geronimo surrendered to Crook. On the ride north, bootleg mescal liquor roused the leaders again; Geronimo and Naiche escaped with thirty-five others. Of the seventeen warriors among them, all but Naiche were related to Geronimo by blood or marriage.

Jasper Kanseah reminded Eve Ball of Geronimo's burdens — so different from the needs of the professional army soldiers who traveled without their families: "Geronimo had to obtain food for his men, and for their women and children. When they were hungry, Geronimo got food. When they were cold, he provided blankets and clothing. When they were afoot, he stole horses. When they had no bullets, he got ammunition. He was a good man."

The last chase was a sad one. General Nelson Miles replaced Crook; he commanded five thousand troops — one-fourth of the U.S. Army. To intimidate the thirty-seven free Apaches, Miles deported to Florida not only the surrendered group led by

In 1885, 134 Chiricahuas fled one last time. In March 1886, deep in the Mexican Sierra Madre, the leaders Chihuahua, Naiche, Nana, and Geronimo surrendered to General George Crook, as recorded in this famous photograph. Geronimo sits third from left, Crook second from right. Photo by C. S. Fly. (Courtesy Museum of New Mexico, neg. no. 2116)

Chihuahua and Nana but all 382 Chiricahuas living peacefully at San Carlos — including the scouts who had served loyally under Crook. Within a few days, Geronimo and Naiche each surrendered to Lieutenant Gatewood and his two Apache scouts, Kayi-tah and Martine. This time they did not bolt when Miles showed up with his troops. On 8 September 1886, the last Chiricahuas (including Kayitah and Martine) left Fort Bowie, Apache Pass, and their homeland as prisoners of war headed for Florida by train. Eugene Chihuahua summed up the sorrow of his people: "It would have been a good day to die."

The Strong, Sad Odyssey of the Chiricahua

"I'm history myself, just sitting here!" That's how Elbys Hugar introduced herself when I walked into the Mescalero Cultural Center she curates. Hugar is granddaughter to Naiche and the great-granddaughter of Cochise. Her father knew

Geronimo's medicine songs — handed down from Naiche — and she says, "When I
need strength every now and then, I take out a tape of my father singing and play it."
As White Mountain Apache historian Edgar Perry says, songs (which are also prayers)
are "the Apache heartbeat."

Hugar remembers lying awake as a child listening to her parents and grandparents and their peers reminisce: "At night, they would keep the fire going after dinner, burned down to embers. They would tell stories way into the night. Those things you never forget."

Across the parking lot at Mescalero, Narcissus Gayton works in the tribal office building; her great-grandmother was Victorio's daughter. Gayton listened to my request for an interview and said: "Don't you think you're a generation too late?" Perhaps so. Chiricahuas who had been the youngest members of those last defiant bands lived into the 1950s and 1960s. They told their stories to historian Eve Ball and to anthropologist Morris Opler. Even so, we live close to the days when Apaches freely roamed their sacred lands. We cannot talk with anyone who lived that life. But we can talk with those who knew them. In another generation, that link, too, will be gone.

In 1983, thirty-eight Apaches toured the Chiricahua Trail of Tears by bus. They visited the forts in Florida and Alabama where their grandparents had been imprisoned. Says Narcissus Gayton: "You just don't know how it makes you feel when you visit those places. It does something to you." Gayton had heard her grandmother talk about the cells in which they lived, and at Castillo de San Marcos in St. Augustine, she saw the rooms.

In 1886, General Miles promised the Chiricahuas that they would be held in Florida for just two years and then returned to their homeland. Instead, they remained prisoners of war for twenty-seven years and never returned home.

When Eugene Chihuahua saw the main contingent arrive in Florida from San Carlos, stacked like cordwood in locked freight cars, he said: "I don't know how those poor people could have lived through that horrible trip." For the first two years, the men of Geronimo's band were separated from their families, imprisoned at the opposite end of the state.

By 1888, all had been transferred to Mount Vernon Barracks in Alabama, a place even worse, in the Apaches' judgment. Eugene Chihuahua said: "We didn't know what misery was till they dumped us in those swamps. Everything moulded — food, clothes, moccasins, everything. There was no place to climb to pray. If we wanted to see the sky we had to climb a tall pine."

The crowded prisons, humid climate, tuberculosis, and malaria devastated the people of the desert mountains. By the end of 1889, one fourth of the captive Chiricahuas had died. Many of the younger Apaches were shipped to Pennsylvania, where the staff of Carlisle Indian School did its best to destroy their identity as Indians.

Finally, eight years after surrender, with the help of political pressure from generals Oliver Otis Howard and Crook, and Crook's trusty Captain Bourke, in 1894 the 407 remaining Chiricahuas were moved to Fort Sill, Oklahoma. They built villages based on old family groups, and they were delighted to be free to support themselves by gathering, farming, and cattle raising. The time they called "The Lonesome Years" had ended.

Eugene Chihuahua spoke fondly of Oklahoma: "We could see the mountains. They weren't tall like ours but they were mountains. There were trees, and we didn't have to climb one to see the Sun. The best of all was to hear the coyotes sing, and the cry of the quail too."

Daklugie, with eight years of training at Carlisle and the support of every influential Apache, took over the tribe's cattle-raising operation. He married Chihuahua's daughter Ramona, interpreted for Geronimo, and declined election as "working chief" in deference to Naiche. Factions remained, of course.

The military threat posed by the Chiricahuas gradually lessened — even in the minds of the Arizona settlers still frenzied with fear at the thought of the legendary raiders' return. Nana died in 1896, Chihuahua in 1901, and Geronimo in 1909. Even so, a handful of Juh's group had never surrendered, escaping the roundup of the 1880s and continuing to live free in Mexico's Sierra Madre. Battles with miners, ranchers, and loggers occurred as late as the 1930s; today, Chihuahuans still will admit to being terrified of Chiricahua Apaches. No more than a dozen Mexican Chiricahua descendants can exist, mostly men cowboying discreetly on isolated ranches.

In 1913, the federal government granted the Chiricahuas in Oklahoma full freedom, though no reservation. One hundred and eighty-seven chose to move to the Mescalero Reservation, while eighty-four of the more acculturated stayed in Oklahoma on land purchased from Comanches and Kiowas.

Allan Houser, sculptor and painter, is perhaps the best known Chiricahua to have grown up in Oklahoma (spending his youth "sketching chickens and motorcycles" and sculpting bars of soap). Sitting among monumental stone and bronze Apaches at his studio in Santa Fe, he told me: "My dad [Sam Haozous — a grandson of Mangas Coloradas] moved out onto an allotment. The nearest Apache family was on a farm five miles away. Chief Naiche's daughter was another neighbor, but I was raised pretty much like an Anglo.

"I tried to learn as much as I could growing up. At my first unveiling [of a sculpture], I wanted to speak about my dad, tell him how he was responsible for everything. But I froze up.

After Juh's death in 1883, Geronimo led the dissident Chiricahuas in battle. By 1886, he and his last 17 warriors surrendered, an act he regretted until his death in 1909. Today, young Apaches must make sense out of Geronimo's violence, while honoring his skills. Photo by DeLancey Gill, circa 1900. (Courtesy National Archives, photo no. 75-N-MISC-47)

"My father was thirteen in the big battles; he knew many songs. He was more familiar with Geronimo's war songs than anyone. It's how I learned to respect our people. And it was a hard time to be proud of who you were."

Geronimo himself regretted surrendering to the last. He was not loved by all Apaches, but to Daklugie, he "was the embodiment of the Apache spirit, of the fighting Chiricahua." Today, young Apaches still must make sense of his violence while honoring his skills as a leader. Delmar Boni, San Carlos artist and teacher, went to Fort Sill to visit Geronimo's grave.

"The words came. I spoke to him in our language. I said, 'I'm here. We still hear your words quite strongly. Young and old alike, they still talk about you: your leadership, the things you stood for — our standards and values. We realize that your intentions were good. Your intentions were all for the betterment of the People.'

"I talked and talked and told him how glad I was to talk to him. And he listened. He listened. I just gave real freely of my words. And yet I could feel on the other end, that spirit listening. I said, 'As a young Apache, my love goes out to you. I will cherish this meeting and always uphold those things that you have put out before us.'"

The Fort Sill Apache community has continued to exist, though intermarriage and the lack of a tribal land base has tended to disperse the Apaches throughout the local community. Alan Houser says: "When I go back to Oklahoma, I have no one to speak Apache with."

When Mildred Cleghorn, Houser's cousin and chair of the Fort Sill Apache, attended the 1986 centennial of Geronimo's surrender at Fort Bowie, she was seventy-six: "We . . . stood where the old ones stood, camped where they camped, prayed where they prayed, and we completed the circle. That was something that I always dreamed of doing. And I can understand now more why they yearned so much for the country. And how they fought almost to the last person in order to keep it."

In 1988 there were more than three hundred enrolled tribal members but only four full-blooded Chiricahuas left in Oklahoma. For the rest of the tribe, their continuing history is the history of the Mescalero reservation, where Chiricahua, Lipan, and Mescalero together have created a new Apache community.

The Mescal Makers

The Mescalero Reservation had its drawbacks. Surrounding Sierra Blanca, summer range for the largest Mescalero band, it made a harsh home in winter and was too small to support traditional food gathering and hunting (and too high for many staple foods, including the mescal that gave the tribe its name). The Apaches did not gain clear title to the land until 1922, and the Mescalero Apaches of today include more peoples than a century ago. Still, they live on a portion of their sacred lands. They have a home.

The Mescalero future looked bleak in 1880. In the panic over Victorio's raids, the army had disarmed the People and penned them in a manure-filled corral. Disease forced their release, but they remained under martial law until January 1881.

By the mid-1880s, the Mescaleros had resigned themselves to the inevitability of reservation life. Gambling replaced raiding as an outlet for frustrated Apaches. A day school and the first missionary (by chance, a Catholic) arrived. From a population of about three thousand in 1850, the Mescaleros hit bottom in 1888 at 431 tribal members. Gradually, they came back from the nadir, surviving tuberculosis epidemics and further attempts to steal their lands — including a proposal to add the reservation to a national forest and a promotion scheme disguised as a bill to transform Sierra Blanca into a national park.

Through the next generation, the Mescaleros dealt with a series of dictatorial Indian agents — some honest and some not. Historian C. L. Sonnichsen summed up the problem: "Apparently, the way to make fourth-rate citizens out of the Indians was to send fourth-class white men to manage them." One agent misinterpreted the girl's puberty ceremony so completely that he justified his attempt to suppress it with: "These dances had been used principally to advertise the grown girls for sale to the highest bidder."

Mescalero lands became a haven for displaced Apaches, the Mescaleros absorbing immigrants in the hope that increased numbers would help them in retaining title to their land. In 1903, thirty-seven Lipan Apaches who had been living in Mexico were accepted into Mescalero. In 1913, the Chiricahuas came from Fort Sill by train — wagons, dogs, and all. They had sold their cattle herds in Oklahoma, so they had to rebuild them at Mescalero. Nearly all the Chiricahuas moved to Whitetail, an isolated part of the reservation, living in tents for four long, cold winters before houses could be financed.

Gradually, these disparate groups began to evolve into the modern Mescalero community. A Tribal Business Committee formed in 1918. Logging operations began in 1923, though federal control of tribal income did little to nurture self-determination. After the Indian Reorganization Act passed in 1934, the business committee functioned as a tribal council, and its president became the functional Mescalero chief.

Cattle raising and timber sales became more and more lucrative. In the three years following the organization of a Cattle Growers Association and the abolition of leases to non-Indians, the income from stock rose from $18,000 to $100,000. The Indian New Deal of the 1930s really seemed to work for the Mescalero, and the reservation became a prime example of advances resulting from government programs.

Daklugie, 80 years old, 1950. Late in life, Daklugie had his doubts about "progress." The son of Juh and nephew of Geronimo, Daklugie had been free — he had lived the life of a roaming, raiding Apache, under great leaders. His death in 1955 marked the end of an era. (Smithsonian Institution photo no. 44767)

Day schools replaced the hated boarding schools. Health programs, tribal courts, new homes, stock improvements — all began in the thirties. By 1942, every family had a house, though many were scattered across the reservation in places unlikely to yield a living.

Daklugie had his doubts about this "progress." In his later years (he died in 1955), he viewed the Chiricahuas' move from Oklahoma as "a terrible mistake." He told Eve Ball: "Those at Fort Sill became dependent on themselves by the farming experience, and they seem to have been strengthened . . . Here at Mescalero . . . they have been deprived of all initiative . . . All decisions are made for them. There is nothing ahead for themselves or their children. They have never been free." Daklugie, of course, had been free. He saw what no one now living has seen. He had lived the life of a roaming, raiding Apache, under great leaders. He also had seen his mother and youngest sister killed and his eldest sister wounded in a single battle with Mexican attackers.

Intermarriage began to fuse Mescalero, Lipan, and Chiricahua into a new people. Cooperative management of the reservation and universal dependence on agency services increased this trend. World War II opened up the reservation to a vastly wider world. The Mescaleros began to take advantage of the rich resources of their half-million-acre homeland and of newly experienced leaders.

When the Indian Claims Commission turned to the Apaches, the three peoples living at Mescalero agreed to share equally in judgments that eventually reached $25 million. A new tribal constitution, adopted in 1964, defined the Mescalero Apache Tribe without regard to original bands (though in the 1980s, when community members suggested I speak to a neighbor they usually identified each individual as Chiricahua, Lipan, or Mescalero). All children with one "Mescalero" parent are enrolled members.

For almost forty years, one man has led this newly defined community. "We owe everything to Wendell Chino," proclaims Mescalero entrepreneur Frederick Peso, former assistant to the BIA superintendent. Narcissus Gayton says: "We have to give a lot of credit to Mr. Chino for putting up with us. He's spoiled us — he's spent most of his life trying to make things better for us." Other tribal members form an opposition, concerned that Chino has too much power.

Chino, half Mescalero and half Chiricahua, has made an enormous difference for his people. Seminary educated, he has provided strong, honest, consistent leadership since the 1950s, both for the Mescaleros and as a national Indian leader, gaining the reputation of being "the conscience of tribal leaders." John Gonzales, the San Ildefonso president of the National Congress of American Indians in 1989, calls Chino "the E. F. Hutton of Indian country — when he talks, people listen."

During Chino's tenure as president at Mescalero (all but four years since 1953), the

*Reverend Wendell Chino, circa
1951, two years before his first
election as tribal chairman. Chino
has dominated life at Mescalero ever
since, revolutionizing the tribal
economy and ruling with savvy and
strength — too much strength, some
would say. Photo by Keller.
(Courtesy Museum of New Mexico,
neg. no. 111755)*

tribe has diversified economically in creative ways — partly in response to bad years
for cattle and timber in the late fifties. In 1962, the Apaches borrowed $1.5 million
from the government to purchase a ski area on the slopes of Sierra Blanca. A decade
later, below the reassuring silhouette of their sacred mountain, the Mescaleros created
a reservoir as a scenic backdrop — and fishing hole — for a resort hotel complex called
the Inn of the Mountain Gods, complete with golf course and dude ranch. (Chino
found a contractor to build the small earth dam for one-sixth the cost estimated by
the BIA; to serve alcohol at the Inn, he took his case to the U.S. Supreme Court.)

In a recent interview with Judy Gaines, Chino said: "Too many tribal leaders want
consensus because they're afraid to exercise real leadership." He told journalist Stan
Steiner: "Some tribal chairmen are not dedicated to their people. They are dedicated
to their job. Instead of serving their people, they serve themselves. They are interested
in power." A panel in the Apache Cultural Center proclaims Wendell Chino's own
goals: "As the Apache people continue to adjust to a new culture, we hope that we
can hold on to the best of the old — the wisdom and beauty of ancestral traditions."

President Chino recently may have gone too far for the taste of his people in his willingness to "adjust to a new culture." In 1991, he agreed to accept Department of Energy money to study storing high-level nuclear waste adjacent to the reservation. The DOE has promised enormous amounts of money to the tribe for its acceptance of the deadly spent fuel. Many of Chino's constituents are not willing to take the risk, and they are upset with the man they now call "Chernobyl Chino" for considering it. Harlyn and Joseph Geronimo, leaders of the opposition, repeatedly lose to Chino in tribal elections. Says Joseph Geronimo of the potential difficulty in maintaining tribal control over nuclear waste: "Every single treaty we've ever made with the U.S. government has been broken. What recourse do we have if the government breaks this?"

Today, three thousand Mescaleros live along the highway between Tularosa and Ruidoso, most of them close to tribal headquarters at Mescalero itself. Only a few families live off-reservation. Many still speak Apache, though intermarriage and the loss of extended families are making inroads on fluency; the modern dialect is more Mescalero than Chiricahua.

Only two elders in their eighties survived to work with Evelyn Breuninger on her Mescalero dictionary — one, "an old Lipan man whose memory is shaky." Breuninger says: "If we had done it earlier, we could have gotten all the names for different birds, rocks, bugs, flowers, foods." Just two families (both descendants of Chatto) make baskets, twining burden baskets rather than weaving the more spectacular coiled pieces with yucca patterns.

Narcissus Gayton, a nurse and community health representative, believes: "If you compare Mescalero to other communities, alcoholism here is nothing." Evelyn Breuninger worked for many years as a social worker: "Compared to New York City, our problems are mild. With child welfare cases, there is always an aunt or cousin to take kids when they need to be taken from parents. We're all kind of a big family here."

Many Mescalero girls still pass through the ritual of becoming Changing Woman. Though most participate in a joint ceremony held each year at the Mescalero Fairgrounds on July Fourth, more and more families arrange their daughters' ceremonies themselves, "out and about on the reservation" — part of a "cultural renewal" that Evelyn Breuninger sees.

Elbys Hugar laments the loss of the old days, when "people lived long. Now there are hardly any elderlies — too many kinds of food introduced, air that is not clean. Nothing but machines now — it makes time for people to get in trouble."

And yet, "the tribe is a multimillion dollar corporation. We have a good portfolio," according to Frederick Peso. Unemployment (running about 35 percent) and underemployment are problems, but more than one-half the three-hundred-person staff of the Inn is Apache. Mescalero lift operators help Texas tourists (among the

Fred Peso, 1988. Peso keeps these photographs of his grandfather, the Mescalero chief Peso, on the walls of his café on the road from Mescalero to Ruidoso. Says Peso: "We know who we are, we know where we came from."

300,000 annual users) onto the chairlifts at Ski Apache, where the tribe recently invested $35 million. The tribal cattle herd has been a one-brand corporation with shareholders since 1962, and now numbers some seven thousand head. Income from the Inn, Ski Apache, and a new sawmill supports the tribal government, and some money reaches tribal members as dividends.

Frederick Peso says: "We don't feel we're part of a minority, we think of ourselves as the chosen few. We know who we are, we know where we came from. We're fortunate that the elders looked out for us, and now we are constantly looking forward to the unborn. We still work as a tribe — the tribe comes first, the individual second.

"The day we forget that, we'll be like everybody else."

The Western Apache Melting Pot

"They keep asking us, 'Why don't you live in the beautiful pine country? San Carlos is so dry.' The traditional people know why we were there. Because they are in the middle of that four sacred mountain." Philip Cassadore explained his unlikely

Sierra Blanca and the Inn of the Mountain Gods, 1988. Built in 1972, the inn — with its reservoir, golf course, and dude ranch — constitutes a major achievement by Mescalero tribal president Wendell Chino. Apaches total more than half of the inn's 300-person staff.

home this way, but his heritage shaped his attitude: his great-great-grandfather Casidor was chief of the San Carlos "subtribal group" of the Western Apache. San Carlos was home to Casidor, and it became home to other Apaches (some more willingly than others) — the "Western Apache melting-pot," in the words of ethnographer Grenville Goodwin.

The five groups or subtribes of Arizona Apaches now called, together, the Western Apache, varied in their isolation before "melting-pot" times. The White Mountain people, then as now largest in territory and numbers, lived in close contact with the San Carlos and Cibecue groups, who, in turn, were friendly with each other. The Northern and Southern Tonto groups lived on the northwestern Apache frontier, interacting with each other but rarely in contact with other Apaches.

The Tontos became the most distinct of Western Apaches. Cibecue Apaches farmed more intensively. Cibecue and, especially, White Mountain and San Carlos Apaches owned more horses and spent more time raiding.

Only the Northern Tontos had a territory that did not include agaves to harvest. They traveled south below the Mogollon Rim once each year to make mescal in the country of their neighbors, the Southern Tonto. Agave expert Howard Scott Gentry has noted that the ranges of *Agave parryi* and its allied species and the territory of "the wide-ranging Apaches" coincide nearly perfectly. Apacheria could just as easily be called Agaveria.

All these Apache groups were on the move for most of the year, cycling through the rough mountains and deserts from pines to saguaros in rhythm with ripening plant foods. Western Apache groups ranged through nearly ninety-thousand square miles of territory — three-fourths of the state of Arizona. Raiders struck north to the Navajo and south to the O'odham and to Mexico. In peaceful times, traders took the place of raiders. One White Mountain Apache horse purchased six or seven Navajo blankets; one bundle of mescal, one medium-sized blanket; one good tray basket, one blanket. At Zuni, an Apache buckskin was worth one sack of corn in trade; a fringed burden basket bought one big blanket.

Group distinctions began to break down when the United States army began its concentration policy, bringing the Apaches together at San Carlos. No Western Apache group, however, has been so dislocated as the Chiricahuas. Cibecue people and western White Mountain people can be found today in their ancestral homes; so can San Carlos people. Many eastern White Mountain people live in the San Carlos Reservation community of Bylas — part of their original band territory. (Demands that children attend school full-time ended the seasonal migrations to winter camps at lower elevations.)

The Tontos, more dispersed, today live in Camp Verde, Middle Verde, and Clark-dale, where they have intermarried with Yavapai, and in a tiny reservation community of their own in Payson. Agnes Curtis, for instance, told me that she is the only Tonto Apache weaving baskets at the Middle Verde Reservation, where her grandmother made big storage baskets that "she used to trade to the man at the Wingfield Store for two to three months groceries." But Curtis has no grandchildren who are full-blooded Apaches.

After the San Carlos and Fort Apache reservations were administratively divided in 1897, the San Carlos people continued to see gradual encroachment on their lands by whites. By 1925, nearly the entire reservation was leased to non-Indian cattlemen, who devastatingly overgrazed the land. In 1930, Coolidge Dam was completed, flooding Old San Carlos, whose residents moved to Peridot or to the little community of Rice, now known simply as (New) San Carlos. As Edward Spicer put it: "The Apaches had become doubtful, so completely had they been left out of the planning and preparation, whether the land was really theirs any longer." During the building of the dam,

San Carlos men had jobs; when it was completed and the Depression hit, wage work evaporated.

Ironically, the reservoir—intended for irrigation use—effectively ended San Carlos farming. In response, the BIA ceased renewing Anglo grazing leases and provided cattle for the Apaches. By the end of the 1930s, the San Carlos Apaches had been transformed into stockmen.

This was the time, too, that anthropologist Grenville Goodwin lived at San Carlos, sitting with elders, encouraging them to tell their stories. He came to San Carlos in time to listen to Anna Price, eldest daughter of the powerful White Mountain chief Diablo, tell of her father's exploits from nearly a century before. Goodwin listened to John Rope recount his experiences as one of Crook's scouts and to Palmer Valor tell the story of a raiding party that reached the Gulf of California. Goodwin's work forms our bedrock source for understanding traditional Western Apache kinship and social organization.

A business committee dominated by the BIA superintendent in the 1920s evolved into a tribal council that today runs the tribe as a corporation. Through the mid-twentieth century, cattle, farming, and mining leases became the primary management concerns, but no San Carlos leader has galvanized the People or transformed their relatively dismal economy.

Councilwoman Lucille Shorten spoke to me in 1988 in her office, below a bumper sticker that proclaimed, "I'm Apache Indian and Proud of It." She comes there each week to wait for anyone who wishes to speak with her: "We're here for the people, not just our friends and relatives." She told me: "I was raised the hard way, when this place was Rice, Arizona, when San Carlos was where the lake is. Only a few of us have lived here all our lives. Now lots of people have moved here and they're fighting over land and leases."

San Carlos has plenty of undeveloped land but few resources to match. Grazing and timber cutting produce short-term profits but must be curtailed periodically to let the range and forest rejuvenate. Only a few individuals mine the semiprecious peridot gemstones. Recreational concessions on San Carlos Reservoir, according to Shorten, "help the white people, not the Indians."

Edward Parmee studied San Carlos education programs from 1959 to 1961 and came to depressing conclusions that in large part still apply. San Carlos, he wrote, shows what can happen when "a community . . . is manipulated by outside sources and its people are neither trained nor given an increasing share of the responsibility for their own affairs, when they are deprived of their traditional heritage while pressured to accept change, and when their social, political, and economic institutions

Lucille Shorten, San Carlos Apache councilwoman, 1988. Shorten comes to her office each week to meet with anyone who wishes to speak with her: *"We're here for the people, not just our friends and relatives."*

are disrupted without provision for immediate or adequate replacement."

As Lucille Shorten puts it: "Apache people are a proud people — too much pride. Even though there is something that could be done for them, they won't ask. An Indian has a feeling to make his or her own choice, and not to let someone tell them."

Parmee found that the goals of assimilation built into the program were diametrically opposed to the goals of most Apaches. The system is certainly better today than it was thirty years ago, but the battle for effective education remains the key to the San Carlos Apache future, as it is for all Indian communities.

Katie Stevens Begaye, director of Indian Education for Arizona, is Seneca/San Carlos Apache and married to a Navajo. She says, bluntly: "Language, history, and culture are one and the same." And yet: "The elders' position that 'without the language you aren't Apache' is worth striving for, but it's not realistic. Meanings are transmitted from one generation to the next; they will be carried on, but the medium won't be a tribal language."

Begaye fiercely remains an optimist. She told me: "You *have* to be an optimist! I am amazed at the incredible continuity of values across urban and traditional upbringings."

Though more and more young San Carlos Apaches move from the reservation to look for work, most Apaches still have little interest in accumulating capital. They would prefer to remain at home even if that means sacrificing financially. Their primary desire is to remain Apache.

San Carlos has struggled with its economic and educational troubles. Lucille Shorten says there are only a few jobs: "The BIA jobs are for people with degrees, with qualifications. San Carlos people are afraid to apply, so many have been turned down. There are low-paying jobs in Globe, but you use up all the money just getting back and forth [the twenty miles each way]. People are cutting wood, digging their own peridots. Married couples with children get general assistance. Poor people who want to get their kids educated don't get help; scholarship money goes to the people who are well off."

Exceptional people still break through these barriers. Ned Anderson, for instance, was the middle child of a family of twelve. He did not speak English until seventh grade, but, highly motivated, he "ended up valedictorian without even knowing he was competing for it." In junior college, an aptitude test told him he should be an artist. Anderson said to his advisor: "I'm an Apache, I'm already an artist. I want to be an attorney."

Anderson earned his law degree, clerked for large law firms, worked in legal aid, and then served as San Carlos chairman for almost ten years. He is proud of his record, though the succeeding administration would disagree. Anderson told me sadly in

1988: "Here I am, a person with all the credentials, but around here no one has any use for me."

Anderson's goal is to become a college professor. But he "would like to live here and be with the People." He cannot do both.

Anderson is concerned about San Carlos: "People worry about Panama, Nicaragua, or South Africa; here on our reservation is a microcosm of that. Alcoholism and drugs are real problems. So many of our people are moving off the reservation for greater opportunities. The problem: management is in non-Indian, BIA hands. There is no real incentive."

Unemployment runs over 50 percent among the more than six thousand San Carlos Apaches. Nonetheless, the tribal cattle operation generates a million dollars annually in sales. San Carlos women are among the most prolific of all Apache basket makers, crafting twined burden baskets from miniature to full-sized, plus a few finely coiled pieces with intricate designs in black devil's claw.

Both San Carlos and Fort Apache have kept many such traditions alive — the Apache language, the girl's sunrise ceremony, curing rituals. I spoke with Ned Anderson while he took a break from preparing for his daughter's puberty ceremony, scheduled the following week. He said: "I may sound ethnocentric when I say this, but I've always felt that without the American Indian the country as a whole would be in turmoil.

"No real war has come to our country from foreign places. I attribute this to the faith of the American Indian. The Great Spirit has protected us. No matter what we do or say, the foremost thing in our minds is the Great Spirit, the Giver of Life. We always pray before we do anything. We always believe, always try to keep ourselves in harmony with nature."

Philip Cassadore would have agreed with Anderson's belief in Apache spiritual power, if not with his politics. Cassadore said: "When I look at the problem of the Apache here, I look at the whole universe. Not just the narrow problem, the drinking problem. You communicate with everything. When we communicate, we meditate, we stand on the ground, on the dirt ground. That's why when I build my own house I want to have a dirt floor. I don't want cement.

"You're standing on the earth with no shoes on and pray. And your prayer is very effective that way. Being modern, our prayers are not effective. The ground, the Earth itself, give you a lot of energy. It's very important we take care of this Earth."

Craig Goseyun, who grew up in Bylas and now is a promising young sculptor, has his own concerns about how well we are taking care of this Earth. He told me: "When I was young, there was an abundance of game, and now it's sparse. Elk used to be abundant. The Gila used to go over my head; now it reaches just to my knee, and it's polluted."

Philip Cassadore orating at a puberty ceremony, Whiteriver, 1984. The San Carlos medicine man, who died in 1985, knew the complete song cycle for the girl's puberty ceremony. "I ask older people if I'm doing it right," he said. "That's how you learn."

Mount Graham, long sacred to the People, stands on the southern horizon of San Carlos territory. Today, the San Carlos traditionalists (led by Philip Cassadore's sister Ola) are fighting a proposal to place a massive complex of telescopes atop the 10,720-foot peak. The mountain is a sacred source of medicinal herbs — as well as home to the *Gaan*, an endangered squirrel, and a unique forest. Construction continues on the mountaintop while the Apaches sue.

Delmar Boni is one San Carlos Apache who has forged a way for himself between these conflicting demands. An artist living in Phoenix, he travels widely, conducting sweat-lodge ceremonies and talking with young Indian people. Boni says: "There is hope for Apache youth. You can be a part of both ways. When you take on another, you don't have to defy the other. There is a place there — right down the middle. Not too far to this side, not too far to this side, but down the middle, between pairs of opposites.

"Our people define that as the Life Way. The Apache Way.

"Fifty years from now — although one may have to commute from Albuquerque or Phoenix to go back down to the Sunrise Dance — the dances will still be going on, the songs will be just as strong. The language will be strong.

"We will survive in this Way."

"Our Mountain Is the White Mountain"

"The Indians always look to the mountains; our mountain is the White Mountain. Our people in the valley here in Whiteriver are praying to that mountain in the east." Fort Apache Museum director Edgar Perry loves to talk about his people. He goes on, looking out the window at the sun:

"In the old days, we just ran by that big yellow thing that's always going up and down. There weren't many people, water was clean. As long as they were traveling they were very healthy. There were plenty of edible foods along the way. No horses, no cattle — they were on foot.

"Imagine them going cross-country, crossing rivers after rains. As they move on, they've been where no one has ever been before. They use only what they need to survive. If they see an herb, they just take what they need for curing the person that needs it."

The White Mountain people still have what they need. Perry says: "Apaches here have water, they have land, cattle, cornfield, lot of materials — timber, rock. They could be self-sufficient if they could use the best of two worlds." There's the challenge again — to use the best of both cultures. And Perry is right: the White Mountain Apache Reservation has as good a chance as any of meeting this challenge.

Most of all, they have stability. The Fort Apache Reservation, ranging from 2,700 feet to almost 11,500 feet, includes the traditional territories of the Cibecue and White Mountain Western Apache groups (collectively, the Coyoteros) north of the Salt and Black rivers. Many sacred sites still lie within sight of Apache homes. Freshly constructed HUD suburbs spread across lands enshrined in myth. Curing ceremonies remain strong, particularly in Cibecue, the most conservative Fort Apache community.

Anthropologist Keith Basso has been listening to his Western Apache friends at Cibecue for many years, and they have told him what this living with the land means. Annie Peaches: "The land is always stalking people. The land makes people live right. The land looks after us." Stories are tied to the names of places; stories teach you how to live right; the place-name and the place itself keep you on the right road, the Apache Way. Benson Lewis: "Stories go to work on you like arrows."

White Mountain and Cibecue people never made full-scale war with the Americans. Happenstance helped: their territory lay beyond Anglo pioneering and mineral strikes, and the White Mountain and Cibecue continued their life of hunting, farming, and "living right" longer than other Apaches, who early on were forced to defend their lands.

As the reservation system took over their lives, the Western Apache adapted to that, too, mostly peacefully. In 1863, they did not resist the founding of the military post that became Fort Apache. The Army restricted hunting, and with the resulting decrease in available buckskins, tipi use ended; women began making flounced "camp dresses" from bolts of cloth, emulating the peasant-style Mexican dresses they knew from their travels or the gowns of army officers' wives and daughters.

Many men joined Crook's scouts, encouraged by the White Mountain chief Alchesay to sign on for wages even though it meant campaigning with the army against their cousins, the Tontos and Chiricahuas. Alchesay himself won the Congressional Medal of Honor for his bravery as a scout in the Tonto campaign of 1872–73. He lived until 1928, continuing to urge his people toward peace and education in the face of BIA authoritarianism.

A century has passed since the battles ended. Whiteriver became the dominant settlement on the reservation after Fort Apache was decommissioned in 1922 (a small Apache scout unit remained on duty until 1943). The United States government has done its best to force assimilation; Keith Basso summarizes the current results: "Contemporary Western Apaches remain marginal to national American society and retain a cultural system that is distinctly Apachean and entirely their own."

Though new communities have split bands and disrupted the rules against intermarriage, newly united clans (once dispersed among isolated groups) now are primary definers of identity. Apaches still work fiercely to promote the welfare of their kin. "Our tribe is still overprotective of our family," says Edgar Perry. "Politics and jealousy come from our loving our relatives. During the political time, everybody is like a mean dog ready to bite each other." Wesley Bonito told me how he must approach these factions, these "new combinations" of people that in the old days may not have spoken to each other: "Gently." Nonetheless, for most of the 1980s and early 1990s, chairman Ronnie Lupe has presided over a relatively stable tribal government.

Women still form the strongest thread in the fabric of Fort Apache society. They are the trunk of the family tree, their children its branches, their husbands sometimes described as leaves. The Apaches say: "The leaves may drop off, but the trunk and the branches never break." Nuclear families have replaced the family cluster and local group in primary allegiance, but clan relatives are still crucial, particularly when girls reach the time to become Changing Woman for the four days of their nai'es.

Apaches say that women are the trunk of the family tree, their children its branches, and their husbands its leaves. Sisters and daughters lived together throughout their lives; men entered the group by marriage: "The leaves may drop off, but the trunk and the branches never break."
(Courtesy of the Arizona Historical Society/Tucson)

Fort Apache has achieved enviable economic progress since the Depression of the 1930s, when the People survived by eating as many wild foods as any Indians in the lower forty-eight states. The last Anglo grazing lease expired in 1932; cattle and timber have both become integral to the community economy.

Misty spruce and fir forest and fragrant ponderosa pines cover half of the Fort Apache Reservation's 1.6 million acres, and the tribe owns a sawmill that generates 100 million board feet of lumber and $30 million annually, and keeps 450 people employed year-round — 90 percent of them Apache. The tribal Recreation Enterprise, begun in 1954, has blossomed into Sunrise Ski Area and summer resort, with seven lifts and $9 million in revenues per year. Unemployment among the 8,500 resident Fort Apache tribal members hovers at about 20 percent; less than a third of families received public assistance in 1989.

Additional money comes from summer cabin leases and from camping, fishing, and hunting permits. This did not happen easily. To build Hawley Lake in the late 1950s, the tribe blockaded the construction site with armed guards and completed the dam in ten round-the-clock days — to circumvent the threat of legal action intended to stop them.

Wesley Bonito, tribal education director, says: "Timber, wildlife, mining, agriculture, tourists, cattle — we have a gold mine in resources in each one, but we have to develop the resources that go with it — the people, the human resources." Those human resources remain undeveloped. Alcoholism follows, to "downgrade our people real bad, downgrade the culture, downgrade the health, as well," as Edgar Perry laments.

In the old days, sharing fermented *tulapai* made "people feel good about each other and what they were doing together," as an older Apache told Keith Basso. Today, alcohol provides an anesthetic against demoralization. In one recent analysis, over 85 percent of the major crimes at both Fort Apache and San Carlos involved drinking.

The key to progress against these obstacles, say the Apaches, is education. In the 1890s, assimilationist government and mission schools came to Apachería; by 1952, 80 percent of Arizona Apaches spoke English. Today, public schools at both Fort Apache and San Carlos have bilingual/bicultural programs, most extensive in the elementary grades.

I hear the same refrain from everyone I speak with: "We've got to teach our people to be a manager of a shopping center, forestry (all the way from choker to trucker to sawmill), geology, game and fish, cattle, ski industry, restaurant, motel — computers, too." So Edgar Perry lists the needs at Fort Apache. Wesley Bonito says: "We have a dream that each one of these will some day be managed by our own tribal professional experts."

Tribal leaders want Apache culture remembered, as well. Says educator Bonito:

"We really want Apaches to share their culture and teach the children. If a medicine man dies without passing on what he knows, it's gone forever. If what he knew was made from metal, he could pass it on. But it's up here in his head, and if he doesn't share it, it's gone.

"If Apaches are going to be here in two hundred years — and be Apache — they're going to need to maintain both worlds, cross the bridge by day and come back safe by night. Go out in the dominant society and work 8 to 5 and wear a necktie — what's wrong with that? — but then come home and spend their evenings in their own culture, speaking Apache, going to Indian dances.

"If they don't, the world will just absorb us."

The Jicarilla

Hascin, the Creator, gave to the Jicarilla sacred lands between four rivers: the Arkansas, Canadian, Rio Grande, and Pecos. The People camped between modern Albuquerque and Colorado Springs, from Chama, New Mexico, in the west, to Oklahoma on the east. Unfortunately for the Jicarilla, this was coveted country, and they had a difficult time holding their homeland. Today, they live outside this sanctified ground.

Of the two modern Jicarilla bands, the Ollero are the Jicarilla proper, longtime residents in the eastern Sangre de Cristo Range, where they lived almost like Pueblo people — in adobe houses with fields nearby. (Indeed, Navajos and Mescaleros still call the Jicarilla the *kinya-inde*, "the people who reside in houses.") Proximity to Picuris, Pecos, and, particularly, Taos pueblos exposed the Jicarilla to many useful things, from pottery making (*ollero* means pot maker in Spanish) and the Pueblo scheme of social relations to ritual and song, all incorporated into Jicarilla culture with typical Apache creativity.

The Llanero once were Plains buffalo hunters (*llanero* means plainsman in Spanish) who farmed only seasonally. The Llanero today include the Apaches who once held the southern Colorado mountains and the plains of Colorado, Kansas, and Nebraska, as well as eastern New Mexico. During their years in buffalo country, this Jicarilla band picked up traits from the Plains tribes: tipis, travois, parfleches. These blended with the Pueblo influences of the Ollero to evolve into the distinctive Apache complex called Jicarilla.

The Spaniards applied a bewildering variety of names to these Apaches. Even "Jicarilla," often translated as "little basket," is tricky. The first thing Tom Vigil said to me about his people was that he found that translation "almost nauseating."

Jicarilla Apache camp, circa 1935. The modern Jicarilla formed from two bands: the Ollero ("pot makers") brought Pueblo traits from their neighbors at Picuris, Pecos, and Taos; the Llanero ("plainsmen") brought traits from the Plains tribes — tipis, travois, parfleches. Photo by T. Harmon Parkhurst. (Courtesy Museum of New Mexico, neg. no. 2089)

Vigil went on: "The person that originated that probably got it from some lady that didn't speak Spanish. 'Xicarilla' had something to do with chocolate [in fact, in Mexico, *jicara* is a calabash-tree gourd with chocolate or other liquids in it]; our pitched baskets and micaceous pots looked sort of like chocolate. And so I think Jicarilla means something like 'chocolate pot, chocolate basket.' But that doesn't stop us from making 'little baskets' to sell to the tourists who ask for them!"

A pivotal event for the Jicarilla came in 1841. Pushed into the mountains by the formidable Comanche, the Jicarilla were left virtually landless when, without consultation with the Apaches, the government of Mexico granted 1.7 million acres of Jicarilla land to two citizens of its northern frontier, Carlos Beaubien and Guadalupe Miranda. By the time the United States took over in New Mexico — and, in Tom Vigil's words, "all of a sudden things went chaotic" — Lucien Maxwell had inherited the grant from Beaubien, his father-in-law.

An 1851 peace treaty with the Jicarilla stipulated that they remain fifty miles from all settlements. For a people dependent on trade with Pueblo and Hispanic villages, this was impossible. Misunderstanding, raiding, and retaliation characterized the next few years of Jicarilla-Anglo relations. The Ollero attempted to settle beyond the conflict-ridden frontier. The Llanero resisted, for their stronghold was Cimarron, the center of the Jicarilla world — unfortunately, well within the enormous Maxwell Land Grant.

Drought hit, and starving Jicarilla farmers began raiding for meat. A full-scale campaign in 1854–55 (which consisted of little more than the army pursuing the beleaguered Jicarilla through their rough mountain home without decisive action) led to another treaty, and the U.S. government set up agencies at Abiquiu, Taos, and, later, at Cimarron — each "a feeding station just like you would for animals," in Vigil's words. To reach the agencies for ration day, Jicarilla families were forced to raid along the way to survive. Vigil shakes his head: "It's hard to accept the fact that your ancestors just sat around the agency begging for food." But in reality the homeless Jicarilla had little choice.

The tribe avoided internment at Bosque Redondo during the 1860s only because the concentration camp failed before the army could gather the Jicarilla along with the Navajo and Mescalero. By 1873, the Jicarilla were the only New Mexico tribe without a reservation or land grant. Gold strikes in the Cimarron country compounded their problems.

During the 1870s, Ollero and Llanero band leaders began consulting with each other before negotiations, for the first time creating a tribal consciousness. A joint delegation of chiefs traveled to Washington, D.C., to plead the Jicarilla case, though some factionalism remained. The whites wanted to move the Jicarilla south to the Mescalero Reservation; the People resisted. Two executive-order Jicarilla reservations in northwestern New Mexico came and went on paper, stymied by cries of whites intent on settling and mining any proposed Apache reserves and by the fears of the Jicarilla themselves of moving into new country. In 1883, the 721 Jicarillas finally were marched south to Mescalero.

Once again, concentration simply did not work. The Mescaleros had already

In the Dry Mountains

David Sine, Yavapai, stands before his mural of Changing Woman,
titled "The Pollination of a Nation." Camp Verde Yavapai-Apache
tribal headquarters, Arizona, 1988.

White Mountain Apache women dancing
at Jeannette Larzelere's puberty ceremony.
Whiteriver, Fort Apache Reservation,
Arizona, 1984.

San Carlos Apache Mountain
Spirit (Gaan) dancer. Casa Grande,
Arizona, 1992.

McKay Pikyavit, chair of the Kanosh band of the Paiute Tribe of Utah. Kanosh, Utah, 1992.

Looking south from Natanes Plateau

on the San Carlos Apache Reservation.

Arizona, 1984.

The White Clan procession at the Stone Lake Go-Jii-Ya
ceremonial relay races. Jicarilla Apache Reservation, New Mexico,
1987.

Opposite:
The Ute Mountain Bear Dance. Towaoc, Colorado, 1992.

Top: *An old Southern Ute beaded belt worn by Chief Antonio Buck in a Sun Dance (belt courtesy of Mike Santistevan). 1990.*

Bottom: *Mabel Lehi, from Navajo Mountain, finished this San Juan Paiute coiled basket decorated with horses in one month in 1983 (basket courtesy Indian Arts Research Center, School of American Research). 1992.*

Tyler Charles, Paiute Tribe of Utah. Cedar City, Utah, 1990.

taken the best lands, and the Jicarillas had little chance of supporting themselves.

Jicarilla leaders, especially the Ollero chiefs, continually pushed the authorities for a solution, even suggesting that they take up homesteads and give up their rights to federal benefits (benefits that looked pretty meager just then). Jicarillas began to escape northward in groups, reclaiming their children from Mescalero boarding school dormitories under cover of nighttime snowstorms, seeking refuge with their friends at San Juan and San Ildefonso pueblos.

Finally, with the help of honest army and agency officials, including General Miles (fresh from the Geronimo campaign), the withdrawn 1880 executive-order reservation, with new boundaries gerrymandered to meet the demands of mining interests, was restored in 1887. Homesteaders and squatters had taken the best land and springs, and their abundant herds had nearly stripped the land of vegetation; land claims would be a continuing problem. Nevertheless, Jicarilla historian Veronica Tiller calls the land restoration won by the leaders of her people "the most important act of self-determination" in the tribe's history.

This Jicarilla Reservation along the continental divide turned out to be high, dry, rugged, and with a painfully short growing season — a poor place for Apaches to resume farming. The government refused to buy out resident Hispanic ranchers. Allotment confusions complicated efforts to begin tribal livestock and timber enterprises, and financial control by the BIA and Congress further slowed economic progress.

Initially, each Jicarilla leader set up a separate group camp on the reservation. Those families with livestock (who tended to be Ollero) quickly became the wealthier class; those without struggled to farm, dependent on government rations. Employment opportunities were few. Ollero headmen tended to be more "progressive," pushing for education; Llaneros developed a reputation as conservatives, the guardians of tradition.

Strong Jicarilla leaders continued to speak clearly on behalf of their people: Augustine Vigil and Garfield Velarde for the 350 Olleros, Santiago Largo and Juan Julian for the five hundred Llaneros. Their situation nonetheless deteriorated; Veronica Tiller calls the first two decades of the twentieth century "the twilight years." Poor and malnourished, 90 percent of the Jicarillas had tuberculosis by 1914. Their numbers dropped from over eight hundred in 1900 to less than six hundred in 1920. They did not again reach eight hundred until after World War II. Tom Vigil says, "Almost everybody remembers people with TB."

No schools operated on Jicarilla land until 1903. Once established, the boarding school, and later, several day schools, unfortunately served as distribution centers for tuberculosis bacteria. In Tiller's words, "school became an accessory to misery." Eventually, the Dulce Boarding School was converted to a sanatorium and the Dutch

Little sister Julia tags along as Dan and Alice Vigil pick up their son, Wallace, from the Dutch Reformed Mission School in Dulce, Jicarilla Reservation, 1939. The Vigils left their older child at the mission for the full school year while they tended sheep elsewhere on the reservation. Photo by Hendrina Hospers. (All rights reserved, Photo Archives, Denver Museum of Natural History)

Reformed Mission School took over education (most Jicarilla Christians still belong to this denomination).

Gradually, the Jicarilla began to forge a new life. A major 1907 reservation addition to the south gave them acreage with a milder climate — winter range for sheep herds started in the 1920s. This brought the reservation to almost three-quarters of a million acres, stretching along the eastern rim of the Colorado Plateau south almost to Cuba, New Mexico.

In the twenties, sheep made a profit for their owners; in 1932, 70 percent of the herds died in a bad winter. By 1940, the Jicarilla had rebuilt their herds; in the same year, the Apaches were sufficiently healthy to warrant closing the sanatorium. With increased income, families could once again afford ceremonial feasts like the girl's puberty ceremony and the Jicarilla Bear Dance (a healing ceremony). The 1937 Indian Reorganization Act (IRA) constitution chartered a tribal government whose initial act

After the devastating winter of 1929–30, the federal government purchased 12,000 sheep to compensate for Jicarilla losses. Here, Apache ranchers sign up for small replacement herds. By 1940, the Jicarilla had rebuilt their economy. Photo by E. K. Edwards and Son. (Courtesy Colorado Historical Society)

was to buy out the agency trader, who had wielded absolute economic power over the People for fifty years and dictated agency decisions as well.

That first elected council revealed the tenacity of Jicarilla culture in the face of long struggle. Five of the eighteen men were traditional leaders from chiefs' families; ten were medicine men or spiritual leaders; the five wealthiest men on the reservation served on the council — resonant with the old Apache value of success in raiding bestowing importance.

The council moved quickly to buy out most non-Indian holdings within the reservation and to return allotted land to the tribe (valuing allottees' share in tribal assets according to the size of their former allotments). Tribal income went up; after World War II, it skyrocketed with oil and gas development in the southern reservation. Individual income paradoxically did not keep pace.

Drought hit the stockmen hard. By the end of the 1950s, with little reason to live on isolated ranches, 90 percent of Jicarillas lived in the vicinity of the agency town of Dulce. Per capita payments began in 1952, with the hope that funneling tribal income back to the People would revitalize the economy.

The per capita payments and tribal funds for scholarships and assistance to minors kept families going until jobs in Dulce became more abundant. Federal programs exploded in the sixties, and twenty-five years of testimony on Jicarilla land claims came to fruition in 1970 with a judgment of close to $10 million.

Today, the tribe's oil and gas, livestock range, timber, and big game for recreational hunting have the potential to support the People. The wildlife management program has become a model for New Mexico, complete with aerial surveys and radio telemetry. Steve Martinez, law enforcement director for the Department of Natural Resources, says that the reservation has the best deer hunting of any comparable-sized area — anywhere. A trophy elk license costs $3,500 (Fort Apache collects up to $10,000 for similar permits); regular customers come every year from as far away as Germany and Mexico.

The Jicarillas received about $25 million in oil and gas revenues in 1986 — some 85 percent of the tribal budget, which supported a wide range of social programs. To avoid having constantly to audit the energy companies, the Jicarillas take much of their royalty payments as a share of oil and gas, which they then market themselves. They also have moved toward ownership of as many wells as possible. In 1987, the tribe made one-fourth of its energy-related income from the 2 percent of the wells in which it shared ownership.

The Jicarilla decision to impose a severance tax on energy extractors led to a crucial United States Supreme Court decision in 1982, affirming the right to tax as "an essential attribute of Indian sovereignty." Unfortunately, taxation by both state and tribe has scared some energy companies away. That fact, combined with the early-1990s recession, sent Jicarilla royalties down to a projected $11 million in 1992.

Jicarilla economic planner Richard TeCube says: "We should be able to leverage our natural resource money. We should, we shall, we must. But do we have the will?"

As the economy has become a tribal affair, so has the allegiance of individual Jicarilla families shifted from extended family group and band to the tribe. Only during the annual relay race do Olleros and Llaneros once again separate into rival groups. This two-day holiday, when virtually the entire tribe moves out to Stone Lake, is more than simple recreation; some 70 percent of Jicarillas still practice their Apache religion.

The race also marks the time to pick band chiefs for the coming year; now, in Tom Vigil's words, little more than "chief for a day." The runners sprint in sneakers, ribbons trailing from their headdresses, their bodies painted with clay and blessed

Jicarilla runner refreshed by a wet cottonwood branch, Stone Lake, 1987. Only during this annual relay race do the two Jicarilla clans, the Olleros and Llaneros, separate into rival groups, each team trying to lap the other twice for victory — and resulting prosperity for the year.

with eagle-down feathers, each team trying to lap the other twice for victory — and resulting prosperity for the year. Cheered on by their families and friends, they run into the Jicarilla future, carrying with them their past.

What survives from that past grows more and more fragile. In 1978, half the reservation residents spoke Jicarilla, and one-third of the households used the language regularly. Few younger people today learn to speak Jicarilla, however, according to Wilma Phone, language and culture director for the Jicarilla Education Department. "I feel bad about it, but if young people aren't interested, you can't force them." The elders who can teach them are hard to understand, according to Phone: "You have to have good ears." She believes that there are few elders — no more than ten people in their eighties — because "we lost a lot of people when they were young. Only about six or seven sit at the Senior Citizens Center. I wonder how they feel about the TV."

Phone knows how *she* feels about television. "When TV came, we started losing communication with our family life. You can all sit in the room together, but you don't talk to each other, you don't tell stories. That's family life now. You lose contact and then you wonder why you have problems at home."

Wilma Phone's sister, Lydia Pesata, also has chosen to fight "a one-person campaign against the odds." She taught herself basketry and pottery making beginning in 1971 and now teaches others the old skills. She talked with me in the Cultural Resources Center, the simply furnished frame building she uses for her classes: "The language dying out isn't my problem; the crafts are my problem. Pottery completely died out in the fifties, and now we have pottery. Dye plants completely died out, and I brought that back."

Pesata and her students make coiled willow and sumac baskets like the "professional ladies" down the street at the tribal arts and crafts museum, but Pesata's group uses natural plant dyes instead of brilliant chemical dyes. She says: "Some say the colors are too dull, but to me, they're beautiful." Her soft reddish browns, tans, yellows, mauves, and blacks come from mahogany root, alder bark, squaw apple, chokecherries, and sumac — using recipes concocted through trial and error. Pesata says: "It's not my art only, it's to share with other people. It's my lifework, to continue for the future."

Several Jicarillas spoke with me about the loss of medicine men, how "white people think you can learn from recordings" of their songs, but that the Jicarillas know better. You have to be there in person, whenever the medicine man wants to teach. "When he feels you have it, he gives it to you, and you accept it." Such a commitment must be the focus of your life, and Jicarilla people who want to learn but could not make that commitment speak sadly of their decision.

"Dulce is an Indian community, but it's not that different from any other rural community," says Richard TeCube, whose perspective reflects a decade living off-reservation, including time with the Peace Corps in India. He goes on: "You don't have to be poor to be Indian. The state will take us to court on taxation issues and then issue a brochure showing us in feathers, saying, 'Come visit Indian Country.' It causes people wonderment to find us not living in shacks."

The Best Western Jicarilla Inn is cause for some wonderment, too. This motel is Tom Vigil's creation. After a twenty-year "whirlwind tour" on the outside, with jobs as diverse as advisor to southern California city governments and working in Washington, D.C., on the Indian Self-Determination Act, Vigil came home in 1982. He had been saying to himself, "How long am I going to go around the world trying to prove myself? I want to be home in my peak professional years."

When he returned, the tribe was considering building a high-quality motel for the oil and gas executives who were parking their planes in Dulce and "walking around in the mud in suits." Vigil said to the tribe: "Lease me the land. I'll build it, you guarantee the loan. And I'll build it for a third the cost per square foot projected by the

BIA." Vigil's entrepreneurial drive made good his pledge, and (with 80 percent of his capital from the tribe, the rest from the BIA) his top-of-the-line family operation now is making a profit — a national model for Indian-owned business.

Vigil believes his motel can trigger "a multiplier effect" in the community's economy. His goal: to make the motel an "information center." Tourists, he told me, "come in with interests and guilt. They are puzzled, and want conversations like this one I'm having with you more than dances. I just want to be honest with them."

More and more, the Jicarillas have become part of the regional economy The school district, incorporated in 1959 with the surrounding Hispanic towns, had a 1989 board that included four Jicarilla members, including TeCube and tribal newspaper editor Mary Polanco, board president. In 1988, it was chosen New Mexico School District of the Year. Some college classes are taught in Dulce through Northern New Mexico Community College.

Polanco, editor of the *Jicarilla Chieftain* for twenty years, says: "When I was young, you needed to know how to brand cattle, how to mend fence, how to milk a cow. If someone had told me that I would have learned how to run a computer, I would have laughed my head off."

She goes on: "People my age went to boarding school because we had to. We were not close to our homeland, culture, parents. There is a new emphasis on education, but at the same time there has been a rebirth of the quest for personal knowledge. Children now are beginning to say, 'Hey, I'm Jicarilla, it's important.' We are so few, we have to protect ourselves. I hope we never can cope with the outside world, for if we do, we will have lost our identity."

Few outsiders hear much about the Jicarillas. TeCube shakes his head about this: "It's a dichotomy. We're not well known, yet we're known as progressive, too." Mary Polanco dismisses outsiders' ignorance of her people. "Being invisible is their problem, not ours. We've been here forever and ever."

The Jicarilla, and all Apache people, see themselves still moving in the flow of their history and culture, but they do not depend for their identity on any one facet of that culture — not the techniques for roasting mescal, not the language, not the success of a young man on a raid. Tom Vigil says: "Our attachment to the land is more than just being Indian. At one time we lost our land; down deep inside our animalness, we still care." Steve Martinez explains his desire to stay in Dulce: "There's not much money here, but there is seclusion and serenity."

Dulce seems particularly serene in fall, when each family collects its winter supply of firewood, the ready-to-split rounds of ponderosa and piñon stacked in yards.

Magpies flap across deep blue skies, yellow rabbitbrush blossoms along the roads, scrub oak deepens to burnt gold in late afternoon light.

Richard TeCube speaks of the predicaments of his people: "We are a people. We want to keep the link; it's oral — there is a core. I think there will always be traditional culture with tribes. But our repository of tradition and culture is dying out with the elders. No tribe is as traditional as they were twenty-five years ago. It's a sobering thought to think about those lost opportunities. And yet, who am I to judge what should or shouldn't be? It's so difficult to do things right."

Indeed it is.

The Ute

Weeminuche camp below Ute Mountain, 1915. The Weeminuche occupied this dry westernmost end of the reservation and refused to budge, forcing the BIA to leave their land unallotted and eventually to create the Ute Mountain agency. Photo by William J. Carpenter. (Courtesy Library of Congress)

One thing . . . every Indian student has to face is, are you willing to go back and work with your

own people? Dress like your own people? Think like the white man, but still be able to work right

alongside your own tribal organization and your own people?

. . . I've learned that the only way to be able to work with an individual is to try to live like him,

think like him, sing with him, dance with him . . . try to participate with 'em, dress just

like them . . .

At White Rock Sun Dance, I came in on a plane; I had a tie, dress clothes, everything, and you

know, . . . I felt out of place . . . I decided to go back over to the camp, where my Dad's camp was,

and I took all my dress clothes off, changed into Levi's, and put on my hat, and got my Levi jacket

on and went back over there and I was just like the rest of them . . .

This is the only way you're going to work with people — especially when you're working with

older members of your tribe . . . And then when they talk to you, they talk to you in the Ute

language.

Guy Pinnecoose, Southern Ute college student and counselor, 1970

"This is our homeland. This is our one last acreage; it sounds big, but it's small compared to what we once owned: the whole western slope of Colorado." Ute Mountain Ute Arthur Cuthair sums up the history of his people with these words and a sweep of his arm up and around, through a blue sky stirring with thunderheads — taking in the green tableland of Mesa Verde, the stub of Chimney Rock, and the sleeping curves of Ute Mountain.

Once, his people lived unchallenged throughout western Colorado and eastern Utah, in the Rocky Mountains and the drier plateaus and valleys sloping southward to merge with the Southwest. The Utes held this homeland in the face of all immigrant invasions, perhaps for as long as ten thousand years — right up until a century ago. And then they lost nearly all of it to the last invasion, to the Anglos who came to settle and mine and own land the Utes felt could not be owned.

But they did not disappear. Vivian Frost, a young Southern Ute woman, says: "In Colorado they think we don't exist, but we do." The southern bands of Utes continue to exist today at two reservations in the southwest corner of the state. All other Colorado Indian tribes were removed. Northern Colorado and Utah Utes live at the Uintah-Ouray Reservation in northern Utah — beyond the Southwest.

Singers (left to right) *Bob Jenkins, Charlie Knight, Homer Tom, and Scott Jacket, Ute Mountain Bear Dance, 1992. Rasps made from notched axe handles make the sound of Bear growling when rubbed against the corrugated-metal-topped wooden box.*

Norman Lopez, editor of the Ute Mountain tribal newspaper, the *Echo,* says: "We need to understand that there *are* Indians in Colorado. These dances, the Sun Dance and the Bear Dance, still exist today."

The Utes endure.

From the Wasatch Range above the Salt Lake Valley east to the Great Plains, and from the Uinta Mountains at the rim of the Wyoming Basin south to the San Juan River and Santa Fe, eleven historic Ute bands divided this huge expanse of the West. Several bands had access to abundant mountain game and garnered half of their food from hunting. Others lived on lakeshores, and a third of their diet came from fish. The driest territories dictated more plant gathering.

At their frontiers, the Utes came in contact with a wide variety of other Indian cultures. Western Utes, in modern Utah, were most like their Great Basin linguistic cousins, the Paiute and Shoshone. Eastern Utes, in modern Colorado, adopted more Plains traits. The southernmost Eastern Utes had the closest contacts with Pueblo and Apachean peoples — trading at Taos and Pecos, allying with the Jicarilla, a few bold Ute farmers even planting cornfields long before Indian agents came along and insisted they do so.

Reservations isolated these three southernmost Ute bands from northern bands, and today there are Southern Utes and Northern Utes. The Mouache and Capote bands merged to become the Southern Ute Tribe. The Weeminuche band became today's Ute Mountain Ute. All other Utes came to be called Northern Utes.

The Mouache lived along the eastern edge of the Rocky Mountains from Denver to Santa Fe, and westward to the San Luis Valley. Capote Utes spanned the Colorado–New Mexico border south of the summits of the San Juan Mountains and west from the San Luis Valley as far as Durango. Still further westward, the Weeminuche held the San Juan River drainage, from the snowy San Juan and Abajo mountains to the arid mesas and plateaus surrounding the confluence of the San Juan and Colorado rivers in Glen Canyon, where they overlapped the San Juan band of Southern Paiute.

These Utes were the northernmost of Southwestern Indians. Beyond them to the north, beyond the spine of the San Juans and the high desert of the San Luis Valley, land, plants and animals, and culture changed. The Southwest ended.

Grizzly Bear's People Acquire the Horse

After making the world and all the animals, the He-She — Sinawaf, the One-Above, the Creator — realized the animals would always be quarreling, particularly with Coyote around to cause trouble. So Sinawaf made the Grizzly Bear to rule over the others with wisdom and strength. Coyote still makes mischief. But Bear is there for the Utes to learn from.

Eddie Box, the Southern Ute Sun Dance chief, told writer Nancy Wood some of what the Utes have learned. "The bear . . . was able to bring people together, to teach them to live in harmony all year long, not just at Bear Dance time. The Creator used the bear to teach the Ute strength and wisdom and survival."

The Utes have needed every bit of that learning to survive. They began long ago. Archaeologists suspect that Ute culture grew right out of the Archaic–Desert culture tradition, which would place them in their homeland thousands of years ago. Scientists cannot prove this with data; Utes prove it by faith. Either way, the Spaniards found the Utes in the mountains. The People hunted deer, pronghorn, elk, buffalo — indeed, they had more access to big game animals than virtually any other western North American tribe.

Ute families foraged alone from spring to fall, moving through the mountains with the game and the ripening harvests of fruits and seeds. They trained their dogs to help carry their gear on canine-sized travois. Southern Ute elder Edna Baker says:

Ute Mountain Bear Dance, 1992. With their age-old Bear Dance, the Utes awaken Bear from his winter sleep; in turn, Bear leads them to food. After women flick their shawls at their chosen partners, men and women start the dance in facing lines, then break into pairs.

"In those days, we walk up the hill, down the hill—no one was fat." Even in those pre-equestrian days, the Ute's mobility through enormous mountainlands distinguished them.

In winter, families came together in warmer parts of the band territory—river bottoms in northern Arizona or New Mexico for the three southern bands. They

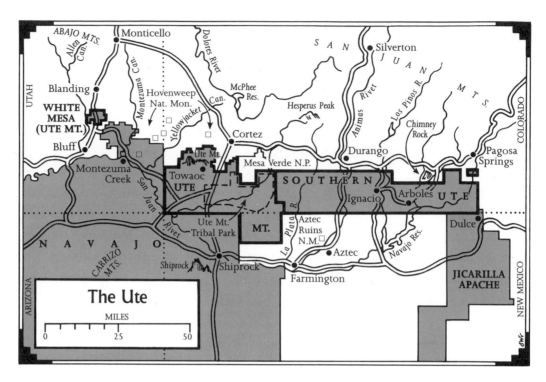

The Ute

MILES

0   25   50

told stories, lived on nuts and dried meat in good years and on boiled skin bags and peeled ponderosa bark in bad, and waited for spring. The month of March for the Weeminuche was "Melting Side, Snow on One Side of the Trail, Bear Rolls Over in This Time," followed by April, "Spring Moon, Bear Goes Out." The spring Bear Dance began a new year.

The Bear Dance is the oldest of Ute ceremonies, still performed today at both Southern Ute and Ute Mountain. By dancing, the Utes awaken Bear from winter sleep. In turn, Bear leads the People to roots, berries, and nuts throughout the summer. Women choose their partners (who should not be relatives), and the courting that follows has always led to many marriages. On the sidelines, feasting, horse racing, gambling, and stick-and-hand games make these four days the most important coming together of the Ute year.

In the 1600s, the horse revolutionized the Ute way of life. Before 1640, Utes held captive by the Spaniards in New Mexico escaped with horses, making their tribe one of the first to be mounted. Within ten years, the Utes were following buffalo herds on the plains, horse-packing their belongings on full-sized travois made from tipi poles and loaded with possessions and skins (a single tipi required six to ten elk or buffalo hides). One Ute Mountain tribal history summed up the intensity of the People's feeling for their herds: "Much as later Americans would love their cars, the Weeminuche loved their horses."

Horses gave the mountain people freedom to remain in bands through summer. Their herds gave them mobility, their mounted warriors gave them protection. Larger camps required more powerful leaders, more food, more horses: resource consumption accelerated with the rise in the standard of living. Stealing was the easiest way to expand the resource base, and the Utes became raiders, buffalo hunters, and enemies to their neighbors.

The Utes raided the Pueblos and kept peace with the Spaniards well into the 1700s. Only after the Ute joined forces with their linguistic cousins, the Comanche, to raid northern New Mexico, did the Spaniards campaign extensively against them. In 1750, the Utes reestablished peace with Spain, and trade picked up once more. Relations with the Navajos alternated between alliance to fight outside forces (while trading fine Ute buckskins for Navajo blankets) and raiding each other when not threatened by other tribes. The Jicarillas remained Ute allies after the mid-1800s.

The Utes continued to hunt and raid from their mountain stronghold while political authority shifted from Spain to Mexico to the United States. In 1851, however, the first settlement in Colorado was established just past the New Mexico line, at San Luis. Ute life would never again be the same.

Peace and Defeat

In 1852, the U.S. Army built Fort Massachusetts at the foot of the Sangre de Cristos' Blanca Peak to protect San Luis. Ute raids flared to small-scale war, however, in 1854–55, ending with unratified treaties negotiated by the governor of New Mexico.

The "Rush to the Rockies" triggered by gold strikes near Denver in 1858 signaled doom for the People. Every prospector believed his fortune lay waiting in some private ore vein in the Ute mountains, back up that draw where no one had yet wielded a pickaxe. The flood of miners overwhelmed Ute resistance. The bands of the People kept the peace and began a dreary saga of submitting to treaty councils that whittled away at their lands.

1863: A treaty signed at Conejos ended Ute claims to "all mineral rights, all mountain areas settled by whites and the San Luis Valley." The Weeminuche refused to attend the council. The Capote and one Mouache leader attended but refused to sign. Several chiefs from northern bands signed, ceding lands they did not use and preserving their own territories.

1868: Most Colorado Ute bands signed a treaty reducing their lands to about 15 million acres, the western third of the state. The government continued to try to keep the Utes away from settlers and miners, off the plains, out of the San Luis Valley and New Mexico, and near the agencies. In short, out of trouble. The Utes continued to roam their lands as always — indeed, using the plains more than ever after the defeat of old enemy tribes by Anglos. To collect their annuities, most southern Utes used New Mexico agencies.

1874: The Gold Rush to the San Juan Mountains began almost immediately after the 1868 treaty, and miners wanted the Utes out of their way. One of President Grant's peace commissioners, Felix Brunot, persuaded the Utes to cede the San Juans — one-fourth of their reservation — in the devastating Brunot Agreement. Brunot told them that this would be the "last request the government would ever make of the Ute." The loss of the mountains meant the loss of the Utes' summer home — and the loss of most of their deer harvest.

The strongest voice in the southern Ute bands was Chief Ignacio, of the Weeminuche. But the government had fixed on Ouray, a northern Ute of the Taviwach band, as "Head Chief of the Utes" (granting him a $1,000-per-year salary and a house complete with fine china for his wife, Chipeta, a writing desk, and a stack of calling cards for visits to Washington).

Ouray, a strong leader, was convinced the Utes would disappear entirely unless they peacefully accommodated the Anglo invasion. His position did not please more militant leaders, and in Ute political structure, Ouray could only speak for the Taviwach. But he did his best to fight for what he believed right for the People, and Ouray and Chipeta remain the Utes best known to outsiders.

Ouray's limited influence could have had no more upsetting demonstration than the events at the White River agency at the end of the 1870s. A new agent arrived in 1878, to take over this agency for all northern Colorado Ute bands. Nathan Meeker, a self-righteous and rigid man, pushed the White River Utes down a narrow path he believed was the only true path to God (who was Christian, of course). A list of values alien to the Utes charted Meeker's way: farming, arbitrary discipline, and a stern view of such "immoral" Ute pastimes as horse racing and gambling.

When Meeker's agency men plowed up bottomland that Chief Douglas used as pasture and cut an irrigation channel through his racecourse, the White River Utes fired a few warning shots over the heads of the diggers. Meeker called in the army. In the ensuing tragedy, the Utes killed Meeker and eight agency employees, and thirty-seven Utes and twelve soldiers died in battle. Ute oral history states that it was "the old ladies" who killed Meeker himself, and that the troops called in were marching under orders to annihilate the Utes. Three weeks later, the southern Ute chief

CHIEF IG-NA-CI-O
OF THE WEEMINUGHS

COPYRIGHT. 189
ROSE AND HOPKINS

The strongest leader in the Southern Ute bands was Ignacio, chief of the Weeminuche, photographed here in 1898. Ignacio detested the idea of allotment, and his defiance created a new entity, the Ute Mountain Ute Tribe. Today, the Ute Mountain Reservation covers more than half a million acres. Photo by Rose and Hopkins. (Courtesy Denver Public Library, Western History Department)

Buckskin Charlie rode in to White River country cautiously, alone in a buggy, to re-trieve the five Anglo women and children held captive by the White River people.

Ouray could not prevent the Meeker outbreak, though his sister, Susan, was mar-ried to a prominent White River shaman. But he did prevent war spreading across the rest of Ute territory. He had achieved more unity among the bands than they would ever know again.

In April 1990, I stood at the roadside monument commemorating the "Meeker Massacre" with a delegation of Southern Ute elders, educators, and children—the first official tribal visit by Utes to the site since the 1879 battles. Edna Baker, whose grandfather, Weaselskin, had been with the group that took the Meeker women hos-tage, listened to the description of historic events matter-of-factly. She turned to me and said, simply: "I often wondered where the place was. Now I know."

Governor Pitkin of Colorado proposed a handy solution to the Meeker fiasco: all Colorado Indians "must necessarily be exterminated . . . The advantages that would accrue from the throwing open of 12,000,000 acres of land to miners and settlers would more than compensate all the expenses incurred."

1880–1881: All White River and Taviwach Utes (the latter also known as Uncom-pahgre) were removed from Colorado by the army to join the Utah Utes, long since subjugated by Mormon settlement, near the Uintah Reservation (the whole complex now to be called the Uintah and Ouray Reservation). "Brothers and sisters got mixed up in that move," says Neil Buck Cloud, Buckskin Charlie's grandson.

The southern Utes remaining (including the Mouache removed from New Mexico in 1878) were assigned to the agency at what came to be called Ignacio, on Los Pinos River, but it took fifteen years to finalize their reservation. Ouray died as these negotiations proceeded, saddened by and disgusted with his white friends.

By 1880, tribal numbers dropped to half the early-nineteenth-century total of perhaps eight thousand Utes. The Mouache-Capote and Weeminuche dwindled to about 500 and 650, respectively. Their numbers would continue to decline for another forty years.

Pressure continued to concentrate all the Utes on the Uintah Reservation, or even to banish the Colorado Utes to Oklahoma Indian Territory. Meanwhile, the southern Utes continued to live in the country around the Los Pinos agency on the remains of their 1868 reservation, resisting removal.

This remnant of their lands grew ever more crowded—especially after the Den-ver and Rio Grande Railroad reached Durango in 1881. Random violence occurred, usually triggered by confrontations with white ranchers using Ute land. Any mur-der of Ute families or hunters went unpunished; any retaliation by the Utes brought out the U.S. Cavalry from Fort Lewis, near Durango, in an overreaction inflated into

Southern Ute horsemen crossing the Los Pinos River, near Ignacio, Colorado, 1899. Horses gave the mountain people freedom and mobility. As camps grew larger, they required more powerful leaders, more food, and more horses: the Utes became raiders, buffalo hunters, and enemies to their neighbors. Photo by Horace S. Poley. (Courtesy Denver Public Library, Western History Department)

"America's Last Indian Wars" by the press. That the Utes remained mostly peaceful through these frustrating years testifies to the wisdom and patience of their leaders.

Meanwhile, the government blackmailed the Utes into sending their children to boarding school by withholding rations until they capitulated. In the 1883 to 1885 school sessions, twelve of twenty-seven Ute children sent to school in Albuquerque died. Ignacio lost his last child; he said: "When they go away, they die, we cannot account for it."

The Utes were pleased by an 1888 treaty granting them a huge reservation in southeastern Utah. They knew the land, which included both mild wintering areas and the high La Sal and Abajo mountains, but they were wrong in their belief that white people would not like that country. Mormon settlements at Moab, Bluff, and Blanding, plus a few large ranches, already existed. The Utes were too weak to force these settlers off the land. And they were too late.

Small numbers of Weeminuche continued to live in southern Utah canyons. The Mormons called them Cowboy Indians. They remain today — at White Mesa, south of Blanding, since 1935 officially part of the Ute Mountain Tribe.

In 1895, Congress passed a plan to allot a strip of land measuring 15 miles by 110 miles along the Colorado border — the land left the southern Utes after the Brunot Agreement, land that had always been transitional between summer and winter territories, the wrong elevation for either season's traditional rounds of activity. Any land not taken by Ute families would be thrown open to non-Indian homesteaders at $1.25 an acre. By April 1896, 72,811 acres had been allotted to 371 Utes. Only the Capote and Mouache bands agreed to the new scheme, led by Severo and Buckskin Charlie (Ouray picked Buckskin Charlie to assume his leadership role when he died).

Ignacio, however, detested the idea of allotment. Some time before, the Weeminuche had occupied the westernmost end of the reservation strip — the area around Mesa Verde and Ute Mountain — and they now refused to budge. The BIA was forced to leave the western reservation unallotted and to set up an agency for the Weeminuche at Navajo Springs in 1897 (moved to Towaoc in 1914).

The Ute Mountain Tribe

Ignacio's defiance created a new entity. No one fought the Weeminuche, those stubborn Utes, for the eroded dome of Ute Mountain, the curtained slopes of Mancos Shale skirting the dry canyons at the south edge of Mesa Verde, the sudden sweep of Chimney Rock's cliffs. No one wanted the land because it offered so little.

It yielded a safe haven, however, to the conservative Weeminuches, who, today, are the Ute Mountain Ute. Their reservation covers more than a half-million acres, with one block extending into New Mexico. They have carried their conservatism right on through to the present, remaining always the most isolated from Anglo influence of Ute bands. "We're just now coming out of our shell," says Art Cuthair.

BIA policy allowed for nothing but turning Indians into farmers, but the nearly waterless Ute Mountain Reservation made extensive farming impossible. The People survived on government rations (issued until 1931) and what traditional foods they could gather. By 1905, only 454 Weeminuche remained; in 1925, they had declined to 437.

In 1911, the Weeminuche provided the acreage for Mesa Verde National Park — the high tableland dissected by canyons whose alcoves harbor the greatest of Anasazi cliff dwellings. This was an ironic twist, since it was the Ute man Acowitz who told the Wetherill brothers about the Mesa Verde cliff dwellings in the first place, guiding

them to their "discoveries." For the land they lost to the national park, the government granted to the Utes twice as much in trade, including most of northern Ute Mountain.

Ignacio died in 1913. The People turned to the leaders Mariano and Red Rock; when they, too, died, Mariano's son-in-law, John Miller, became the Ute Mountain leader. He was succeeded in 1936 by Jack House, last of the Weeminuche traditional chiefs.

Not all Weeminuche stayed on the reservation in its early days. Mancos Jim led a group that lived in Yellowjacket Canyon on the Colorado-Utah line. John Benow (also known as Green Ute) and his followers made their home in Montezuma Canyon. In 1907, hoping to force the Utes' retreat to the reservation, Anglo cattlemen burned a cedar fence Benow and his people had constructed to try to protect their land from trespass.

The Utes near Blanding, Utah, had an even more difficult time. Forced by Navajos to concentrate near Allen Canyon in about 1900, they were determined to maintain these homes — just as determined as the Anglo ranchers were to displace them. Led by Mancos Jim, Old Polk (a Weeminuche), and Posey (a Southern Paiute married to Polk's daughter), leadership shifted to Posey and the Paiute faction as Mancos Jim grew older. In 1914, tensions flared when Polk's son, Tsenegat (Everett Hatch), was accused of killing a sheepherder. Though he claimed innocence, he was afraid to turn himself in — fearing lynching.

The local marshall led a posse of half-drunk cowboys after Tsenegat, murdering several Utes in a surprise attack on a camp where Tsenegat was staying. Old Polk and Posey took their hundred terrified "renegades" to hide near Navajo Mountain while *The New York Times* editorialized about the "Ute Wars." The U.S. Army finally intervened, and charges were dropped against all but Tsenegat, who was tried and acquitted.

Another mini-war erupted in 1923, when two Allen Canyon Utes were found guilty of stealing sheep. One escaped with Posey, the sheriff and posse gave chase — this time in cars — and everyone but Posey surrendered after two days. Posey died of a wound in the hip (or, as the Utes believe, from poisoned food given him by whites). The remainder of the group agreed to keep the peace and filtered back to their homesteads, which were allotted that year.

In the 1920s, in order to force Allen Canyon and White Mesa children to attend the Ignacio boarding school, Ute Indian police corralled the People behind barbed wire in Blanding and denied them food and water until they gave up their children. Even then, some children had to be taken by force.

The White Mesa community officially became part of the Ute Mountain tribe in

1935, and its representative holds one of the six tribal council seats. Mary Jane Yazzie, White Mesa delegate to Towaoc in 1989, also heads the local council; she says, with a laugh: "I'm the mayor!"

In contrast to Utes living in Towaoc, White Mesa people still garden in Allen Canyon during the summer; Yazzie suggests that this is because at Towaoc, "those guys are closer to the big grocery stores." In addition, White Mesa runs a community cattle herd of about seven hundred head. Other traditions continue at White Mesa: women basket makers (says Yazzie: "that's how they make their living") and one flute maker — Yazzie's eighty-nine-year-old grandfather. Her great-grandfather was Jim Mike, the Southern Paiute who led the first Anglo expedition to Rainbow Bridge. Mike lived to be 115, dying in 1976, and remains White Mesa's most illustrious son.

White Mesa people consider themselves Ute, but they have become mixed with Navajo and Paiute over the years. White Mesa elder Meyers Cantsee says: "The Utes was clear down to Tuba City and Flagstaff; now, nothing but Navajos — the Navajos are taking over." Cantsee is blunt about the absolute lack of work at White Mesa: "The uranium boom changed things for whites, not Indians. Nobody found uranium or oil around here." Another White Mesa elder, Stella Eyetoo, thinks the old days were easier: "Families got along better back then. They planted their cornfields together. Food was plentiful."

Mary Jane Yazzie speaks more positively — about her hopes for a pipeline from Blanding to bring in drinking water (the wells currently used tap water contaminated by uranium mills). She told me that most White Mesa people are Mormon, and the connection with the church makes job-hunting easier.

Meyers Cantsee isn't so sure about the Mormons, suspicious of what he sees as their intolerance of other religions (Cantsee was baptized a Catholic in boarding school). But he says: "If I understand more white man's words, maybe the Book of Mormon would be good." He adds, with a twinkle in his eye: "If I had finished school, I'd probably have been the president of the United States — or the governor of Utah. I might be well-off!"

Not many Ute Mountain Utes have become "well-off," education or not. The BIA formed a Ute Mountain business committee in 1920; its five members included John Miller, John Benow, and Jack House. They had little power, for though the Utes had won the first of their land claims in 1910, they could not spend the money without allocation from Congress and transfer of funds through the BIA. Clubs formed to promote adult education in the 1920s and 1930s provided other settings for adding Anglo leadership skills, particularly for women; there were garden clubs, rock clubs, goat clubs, pig clubs, and sewing clubs.

The tribe formed its first council in 1940. Jack House remained the most powerful

leader until his death at eighty-six in 1971 — able to pull together families and factions
in a way no one has achieved since.

In 1940, when anthropologist Marvin Opler wrote of Ute Mountain, he described the tribe as still living "a nomadic existence," wandering seasonally "with movable tents and flocks of sheep." Syphilis claimed a quarter of the population; gonorrheal arthritis, tuberculosis, and trachoma were epidemic. Only half a dozen of the 450 Towaoc Utes spoke English; gambling consumed most of the People's time and money. One educated young Weeminuche told Opler: "The old people had better brains. We youngsters have nothing and we do nothing." Opler summed up his observations: "The gap between Ignacio and Towaoc is deep and wide."

World War II ended tribal isolation for Ute Mountain, most dramatically for the young men. An additional land claims check arrived in 1950, and the tribal council had enough power to control the fate of this $6 million. Coal leases and oil and natural gas discoveries in the fifties brought the tribe its first real income — and per capita payments to tribal members of up to $1,500 every sixty days. Seasonal work in the pinto bean fields north of Cortez gave decent wages to some. The reservation population began to concentrate in Towaoc. Though some of the most prudent tribal members used the per capita money for houses and cattle, many Utes, unfortunately, were easy marks for unscrupulous businessmen in Cortez, who fleeced them of most of their windfall.

The Utes took to cattle raising better than they had to sheepherding. Ute cattlemen gradually took over from non-Indian lessees. In 1957, the tribe bought twenty-thousand-acre Pinecrest Ranch, between Gunnison and Lake City, for additional summer range. But today, "nobody lives exclusively on cattle," according to tribal librarian Janice Colorow. Twenty families run fifty to one hundred head; there are just three or four big owners.

More land claims money arrived in the 1960s. The decade brought federal housing programs, as well. Changes began to accelerate. But the tribal government descended into a morass of factionalism, embezzlement, and bankruptcy, sadly detailed in Nancy Wood's controversial book, *When Buffalo Free the Mountains.*

Since then, the lot of the tribal elite, at least, has improved. Ernest House, grandson of Jack House, took over as chairman. The Ute Mountain bingo operation and pottery cooperative (the latter begun in 1970) generate income for a few families and for the tribe. A high-stakes gambling casino opened in 1992 will expand that financial base. A challenging court battle led to a 1978 restoration of year-round hunting rights in the land ceded in the Brunot Agreement. The tribe negotiated a model mineral lease with the Wintershall Corporation in the 1980s; in addition to excellent financial terms, the company agreed to train Ute workers and to restrict activity in the tribal

Ute Mountain Casino, 1992. The 1,700 Ute Mountain Utes are working to counter unemployment that exceeds 50 percent. Tribal efforts include a model mineral lease, a park that protects Anasazi ruins, and this high-stakes gambling casino, which opened in 1992.

park. Unfortunately, the known oil and gas reserves will be pumped out by the end of the century.

Half of the forty-eight program heads who work in the new tribal headquarters building (opened in 1988) are Indian; all but two of those are tribal members, most of them in their thirties. But, as Janice Colorow points out: "There's only so many positions available with the tribe. A lot of the children feel they'll be lucky to work on a construction job." And yet, "the reservation is like a beacon, always calling home. Almost inevitably, everyone comes back." The economic and social dilemma is, as journalist Jim Carrier puts it, that of "a community of people struggling to be individuals."

The seventeen hundred Ute Mountain Utes (325 of whom live at White Mesa) come home to face unemployment that runs over 50 percent. Life expectancy averages thirty-eight years; alcoholism rates, by some estimates, surpass 80 percent. A staggering 98 percent of all cases in the tribal court are alcohol or drug related. Ute Mountain has one of the highest fetal alcohol syndrome levels in the world. A sky-high birth rate is nearly offset by a high death rate.

Defying these grim statistics, one of the most hopeful of Ute Mountain people is Arthur Cuthair, longtime Ute Mountain Tribal Park director. Wrapped around Mesa Verde National Park, the 125,000-acre tribal park constitutes almost a fourth of the reservation area, and, according to Cuthair, protects "some of the most pristine Anasazi sites left."

The tribal park was one of the last enterprises initiated (in 1967) by Jack House, who lived in these canyons as a young man, painting pictographs that are now an attraction on park tours. During the seventies, the ruins were stabilized (with Arthur Cuthair on the crew), and tours began in 1981. Cuthair says: "We want to complement the National Park Service at Mesa Verde, with a primitive, private park experience and native Ute tour guides. We're not just taking care of the park, we're *caretakers* of the park. It's not just another job. Somewhere deep down inside, the Anasazi is happy we're taking care of the ruins."

Ute Mountain people remain proud of their culture. As tribal journalist Norman Lopez said to me of his grandparents: "They didn't believe in Christ; they believed in the sun, night, day, light, and the spirit. They believed in human life being a gift from someone. They tell me that I have to go through these certain stages of life, but I'll always be Ute — these things I will always go back to."

The People conduct their Sun Dance in seclusion several miles up Ute Mountain from Towaoc. In 1989, they celebrated the one-hundredth recorded Bear Dance. Janice Colorow says: "Our Bear Dance ground is dirt; at Southern Ute, they have black-topped it. The old people say the dust that the wind kicks up, that's what makes it what it is."

Ute Mountain potter Norman Lansing believes the symbolism of this cultural "tradition should only be used for ritual, ceremonial purpose." To decorate his pottery — cast, kiln-fired, and sgrafitto-etched — he dreams his designs, "contemporary ones." He told me that he had to go out and "try to explain this new concept in art to museums and galleries: they always want to know what the tradition is. Tradition shouldn't be exploited."

Lansing lives on the Southern Ute Reservation (in Arboles, at the corner of Wandering Hills and Hoot'N Holler). I asked him why he didn't live in Towaoc. He explained: "I guess I was just meant to be here; the mountains — it's where I find the energies I need."

The Ute Mountain community has always spoken Ute; indeed, as late as 1953, few Weeminuche could converse in English. Fewer and fewer children learn Ute today. Norman Lopez says: "My wife is a Head Start teacher; Head Start is where we try to teach who is a Ute. Some white kids who went there thought they were Ute — they learned Ute language better than the Utes!"

For the rest of their schooling, Ute Mountain children bus to Cortez, as they have since 1961. Says Lopez: "Our goal is to elect a tribal member to the school board. The Cortez teachers from big universities ask our kids, 'What's your telephone number? What's your street number?' The teacher gets angry with the child when they don't know. They say, 'We live in Towaoc, that's all.'

"But they know what a horse is; they know what a sheep is — the kids in town only see those on TV."

The shale and sandstone cliffs of the Weeminuche turn gold in the sunset, their mountain turns purple, a full moon rises over Mesa Verde. The storm clouds that roll in from Navajo country, over the Carrizo and Lukachukai mountains, over the mighty landmark of Shiprock, bring little water. But soon water may reach the Ute Mountain nation in a new way.

In 1986, the Animas–La Plata water settlement was signed; ratified two years later, the settlement promises sixty-thousand acre feet annually to Ute Mountain (with forty thousand more for Southern Ute, if the project goes through). In 1990, threats to endangered Colorado River basin fish from these new dams brought the entire project to a halt, but a compromise reached in 1991 may allow the project to proceed. Lawsuits continue from opponents who question the validity of yet another massively expensive reclamation project in the West; their success could stop the project permanently.

Meanwhile, a twelve-inch pipeline to Towaoc from the Cortez water treatment plant has been built, ending a century of hauling drinking water for the People. Irrigation water will arrive via gravity flow from McPhee Reservoir on the Dolores River in the mid-1990s, given sufficient funding. Tribal members credit ex-chairman House, current chair Judy Knight (elected in 1990), and Anglo natural resources director Joe Keck with this triumph for Indian water rights.

What does Animas–La Plata mean for the tribes? Will the Utes become corporate farmers? Janice Colorow thinks that "we're not ready to deal with the water coming — not psychologically ready. We never have been farmers. If we can't use it ourselves, the tribe may lease to people. It would be good for our economy, but our isolation and privacy will deteriorate. The more people we get coming in, the more we'll change."

But the water could give the Ute Mountain people their first real shot at self-sufficiency. "We've got to do what we've got to do with what little we've got," says Arthur Cuthair. "We're still one nation."

As Norman Lansing says: "You can't give up. It's worth the struggle. You've got to know that what you believe is right."

The Southern Utes

In the early days of the reservation, Chief Buckskin Charlie described the plight of the Southern Ute warrior:

> He had been a brave man — he had fought the enemies of his tribe by day and by night; he had something to think about all the time, and got the full enjoyment out of the busy and active days as they passed. But now he had nothing to do but eat and sleep and be lazy like a child. The dullness of his life took away all the pleasure of living, he would not be sorry when his time came to die. He believed that the only alternative left for his people is to strive to learn to read and write and farm, and do the other things that are done by the white people, but he has grave doubts as to whether his people will ever be able to succeed in the new life that is being forced upon them.

Allotment forced that new life on the Mouache and Capote with a vengeance. In 1899, with the allotment of seventy-two thousand acres completed, the remaining half-million acres of the Southern Ute Reservation were thrown open to settlement. Ignacio, the agency town, evolved as a Southwestern tricultural village, and the Southern Utes learned to cope with Anglo and Hispanic cultures — something unnecessary at isolated Ute Mountain.

Coping became a crucial skill for the Southern Ute. In the first fifty years of the Ignacio agency, twenty-two different agents and BIA superintendents determined the tribe's destiny. Even the honest government men weren't around long enough to come to any real understanding of Ute culture.

Until his death in 1936, Buckskin Charlie continued to urge education and farming on his people. By 1912, almost all Southern Ute children attended school, and by 1920, they attended the Ignacio public school.

As for many tribes, the twenties were the nadir at Southern Ute. By 1921, when allotments were supposed to pass into full Indian ownership, one-third of the acreage had already been sold to non-Indians, mostly by agents who controlled the fate of land in "heirship" status and could judge Ute owners "competent" or "incompetent" in sales decisions. Less than half of the allotted Utes lived on their land, and few of those actually farmed. The government supplied only meager help. Maintaining rights to irrigation water was a chronic problem, and as generations passed on, inheritance of allotted lands became a legal nightmare. The People meanwhile lived on rations, annuities, lease income, some hunting, and still less farming and stock raising.

Only 334 members of the tribe survived in 1920. John Collier sparked the subsequent national concern for the plight of Indian people, and from those concerns grew the IRA. In 1936, the year that Buckskin Charlie died and was succeeded as

Southern Ute leader Buckskin Charlie and his wife To-wee, 1899. Charlie led his people from Ouray's death in 1880 to his own in 1936. Photo by Rose and Hopkins. (Courtesy Denver Public Library, Western History Department)

hereditary chief by his son, Antonio Buck, the Southern Ute tribe adopted a constitution. Antonio Buck became the first elected tribal chairman.

The next year, 1937, saw 222,000 acres of reservation land never homesteaded restored to the tribe. The Southern Utes regained control of about half of their original reservation, though the resulting checkerboarded ownership has been difficult to manage (with non-Indians outnumbering Utes within the reservation). Ironically, these restored lands turned out to be energy rich, providing the Southern Utes with windfall income decades later. As Neil Buck Cloud says: "The prospectors made the Utes settle on bare ground, and today we're sitting on oil fields." Southern Ute Byron Red puts it succinctly: "Without the land, the People wouldn't be here."

By the time Marvin Opler wrote of the Southern Utes in 1940, he could describe "money-minded" people (in contrast to Towaoc), "vigorous farmers over sixty insisting upon the virtues of White medicine, White morality, and even White law." He saw "complete assimilation" looming just ahead.

Total assimilation has not happened, though as Byron Red says: "We have a lot more than many other tribes, but we've given up our culture for it." Everett Burch, Ute language and culture specialist for the tribal education department in the late 1980s, says simply, "We're too much modern." Of the Ute reservation communities, Southern Utes have the lowest level of surviving cultural traditions but the greatest economic success. As Southern Ute Linda Baker Rohde says: "It comes down to 'What do you sacrifice?'"

Eddie Box knows that "We're not living in the times of the elders. I live in the days when my child and grandchild don't speak Ute anymore." Shirley Frost, a middle-aged Ute woman who works as medical records technician, puts the challenge simply: "We can't go out and hunt buffalo."

The land claims settlement awarded in 1950 required the Southern Utes to write a "Rehabilitation Plan" detailing their budget and vision for health, education, and resource development. The plan, written under the leadership of tribal chairmen Sam Burch, John E. Baker, Sr., and Julius Cloud, has given order to Ute tribal government ever since. Leonard Burch has been chairman for most of that time, from 1966 until the 1990s.

Oil, and, especially, natural gas royalties, additional land claims money, and quarterly per capita payments have brought superficial affluence to tribal members at times. In 1972, the tribal motel complex opened. Unfortunately, it has been a money-losing operation: on one of my visits to Ignacio, the "Sky Ute Convention Center" was booked with a "holistic metaphysical fair" sponsored by the Center for Alternative Realities in Durango. No Ute customers were visible.

By one 1968 estimate, splurging with land claims money left the average Southern Ute family owing $17,000 against an average annual income of less than $2,000. Today, insufficient housing exists for young and single people. Unemployment remains above 50 percent. Only about eight hundred of the twelve hundred enrolled Southern Utes live on the reservation. Ute families earn about half the annual income of other American families, and female-headed Southern Ute families earn only half that. "The world is passing us by," according to council member Orian Box. "We need people with business sense; the council needs to be more aggressive in economic development."

Box was repairing an eagle feather dance headdress while he talked to me in his studio. He fumbled for thread in a briefcase, pushing aside sunglasses and eagle plumes in his search. A bold mural he had painted filled the wall behind him. "I've dreamed about going to New York City, talking to Donald Trump, finding out how they made their millions. The Animas–La Plata water will allow our development — all these things can be in place, but you have to teach people how to use them."

And yet: "People here, they have it easy: a beautiful place to live, jobs with the tribe." Box's uncle David agrees. David Box lives in Denver now. But he comes back to Ignacio frequently, staying up half the night talking Ute with his brother Eddie. "There are certain advantages the Indians have. We have a place, a sense of belonging. Here you live a life that's less demanding." Melvin Peabody, a young Ute working as a carpenter, says: "It's easier to live here; you know everybody. In the city, everybody is a stranger."

When Shirley Frost went away to business school in Denver years ago: "I didn't know how to use a telephone. It was my first bus ride — I almost got off in Pagosa! In Denver, the sirens scared me. I got up and dressed when I heard them. But my parents would say, 'We could never go back to the way we lived.' They told me I would learn the different ways of living."

Shirley Frost speaks fluent Ute. Her children understand "but won't talk it — I don't know why." Linda Baker Rohde may have the answer. She says she feels "like the lost generation," a product of parents taught to "not learn your own culture." She grew up in Durango, one of only two Indian families in town. Her mother is Navajo, her father Southern Ute. "They didn't teach me, but now they are teaching these kids. My four-year-old son Daniel can speak more Navajo and Ute than I can. The hope lies in the little people now. I can't teach them the songs, but my Dad can."

Rohde and her husband manage the tribal recreational area at Lake Capote; she gives tours of the Anasazi ruin at Chimney Rock, on U.S. Forest Service land. She says: "Our ultimate dream is to run the lake as a camp for tribal members. Tom [her Anglo husband] could teach environmental things; I could teach beadwork, sign language, stories."

The tribe requires one-fourth Southern Ute blood for enrollment. Shirley Frost says: "The council makes these rules about who is going to be enrolled without thinking about the future; Ute blood will go within twenty years." Linda Baker Rohde says: "For my sons' kids to be enrolled, it would almost have to be an arranged marriage!"

David Box asks: "Twenty years from today, where are we going to be? Our chance of making it looks good, because of the younger people." Everett Burch says: "About 50 percent of the kids go on to start college now. They have to bump heads and rub elbows out there. But they tend to quit after a couple of years."

The competitiveness they learn doesn't always transfer home with ease. Says Burch: "When a tribal member gets going on individualism, the tribe pulls you down." Shirley Frost says: "It's hard for an Indian to become a leader in a community where there is so much criticism. You have to go on no matter what people say; I've gotten to be tough. Jealousy breaks down the oneness that tribes should have."

Religion still can create oneness for the Southern Utes. Everett Burch said to me: "You've taken away our language, our land, our water. You're not going to take the dances away. This is our way of life."

The Southern Utes still hold sacred the Bear Dance and Sun Dance. Everett Burch says: "There's one big church — there's no getting away from it. The whole universe is one big tipi." There is an active Native American Church, as there is at White Mesa and Towaoc (where, in 1950, 90 percent of the community practiced peyotism).

Youngsters are joining powwow dance groups, learning what David Box learned: "The older people say a powwow is to establish yourself among other people in good spirits — teach your children what it means to be an Indian." Linda Baker Rohde remembers: "In Durango, the school never understood how important it was to get away for powwows. If they want to keep what's left of the real Native American, they will have to learn how to work with them."

The most powerful part of "what's left" of the Ute spirit comes out each year in the Sun Dance. And to talk about the Southern Ute Sun Dance means talking about Eddie Box.

Consistently described as "the self-proclaimed spiritual leader of the Southern Utes," Eddie Box is a controversial character. Nancy Wood tells the story of Box's return to the reservation in 1954 after some years away, of his restoring the Sun Dance that had disappeared with the death in 1941 of the last Sun Dance chief (the grandfather of Eddie Box's wife). She tells of the risks he has taken — and the criticism his actions have brought.

Eddie Box, Southern Ute Sun Dance leader, Ignacio, 1989. Box speaks of the Sun Dance with passion: *"We've got so much power within ourselves to help ourselves, but we don't use it. The Sun is an energy, it is created by the Creator. Accept it. It fills you up, then you let it flow out."*

Eddie Box stepped in to fill a vacuum. The grumblings from the rest of the community about his conspicuousness and his celebrity seem to come not so much from people who wish to displace him as from the jealousy extended toward anyone who has the confidence to stand alone.

I spoke with Eddie Box in his living room under the gaze of a great shaggy mounted buffalo head; on the walls, bold paintings by his son faced a reproduction of a classic Remingtonesque cavalry-and-Indian skirmish. On the mantel were black-and-white photos. a mysterious vision of Jesus appearing in the Canadian clouds taken by a Cree friend of Box's, and a portrait of the Comanche leader, Quanah Parker — a Box ancestor. Eddie says that he has a little Cheyenne and white in him also, from his grandmother, daughter of trader George Bent and his Cheyenne wife. Many Box family members, including Eddie, have Bent as a middle name.

Box served sixteen years on the tribal council; retired now, he makes Ute "love flutes," signing them with the name he prefers, Red Ute. He says, "Back in the fifties, they call me agitator, they call me activist. They call me many names. All I was telling the people was 'wake up — we cannot let somebody else think for us all the time.' "

He speaks most passionately about ceremony: "When I talk about these things, it kind of sends chills down my back. We've got so much power within ourselves to help ourselves, but we don't use it. That's what the Indian ceremonies are all about. The Sun is an energy, it is created by the Creator. Accept it, it fills you up, then you let it flow out."

Eddie Box says: "I didn't become the Sun Dance chief overnight." Like any Sun Dance chief, he received a vision directing him to sponsor the dance. He speaks thoughtfully, sincerely, and movingly; he seems the real thing. Who are we — Ute or non-Ute — to question the validity of personal visions?

The Sun Dance came to the Ute from the Shoshone, who learned it from the Comanche, who learned it from the Kiowa. Ute Mountain Utes performed their first Sun Dance in 1900, their shaman Tonapach learning the ritual from the Northern Utes; he, in turn taught the ceremony to Southern Ute shaman Edwin Cloud in 1904.

In his fine book on the Sun Dance religion, Joseph Jorgensen suggests that the Utes adopted the Sun Dance after the Ghost Dance failed to rid their world of whites, after they had resigned themselves to reservation life. The Sun Dance "promised only that men could cope with life as it was, promised only that it could make men well and make communities happy to the exclusion of whites, yet in a white-dominated world." And it delivers on these promises to its participants still. As Eddie Box says: "Some of the things Indian people feel are not written in books, they are written in their hearts. The teachings of the Sun Dance are about peace and harmony."

Sun Dancers pledge to dance in twelve dances. In each, they dance for three days and three nights (at Southern Ute, four), seeking to acquire power, *puwa*. They dance and sleep in a corral, the "thirst house," without drinking or eating, with the hope that power will come to them — for themselves, the community, relatives in mourning, or to make themselves shamans. Singers and drummers accompany them, spectators watch and bring them armfuls of cattails, cottonwood branches, and other water-loving herbs to cover themselves with. The women who sit by the singers brandish these same sprays of green plants, keeping time to the music with them. The women sing for a line or two alone when the drum stops — a benediction.

The dancers move back and forth toward a central cottonwood pole, in the crook of which rests a bison head. They charge and retreat, blowing eagle-bone whistles, meditating, pondering their dreams, giving themselves to the power of this religious experience. The symbolism of the corral and the dance is complex, mixing Ute ritual with Christianity: indeed, Utes told Jorgensen, "No one knows the complete meaning of the dance."

I watch Eddie Box direct the third day of a summer Sun Dance. He announces that the afternoon is for blessing and healing anyone who wants to come into the lodge. An old man is pushed beneath the center pole in a wheelchair; next come mothers with babies and little children — the kids solemn, uncrying.

Eddie Box wears a crown of greenery and uses a swatch of it as a wand, along with an eagle wing, working over the bodies of the patients. The eagle wing makes a dry tapping sound, light, soft, with a vibration — of power. Other dancers do some curing and "shamanizing" for their own patients.

The Southern Ute Sun Dance lodge stands a couple of miles north of Ignacio. Beyond its circle is a circle of brush shades and the tipis and pickups of spectators' camps. Beyond camp is a circle of sheltering reddish hills; on ridgetops and along the base of the rise stand ranch houses, the more affluent with satellite dishes. The cattail sprays brought to the dancers come from the marshy edges of fields, some with cattle grazing, a few marked by the rhythmic clanking of oil-well pumps. Further still is the circle of mountains, big ones, including Hesperus Peak in the La Platas. Los Pinos River flows between cottonwood trees, a little to the east.

This truly is a dance to the Sun. Sunlight blasts the spectators, too, but we have it easy, retiring to shade and food and cold drinks whenever we feel the need. All that greenery warming in the sun makes the lodge smell sweet and moist — and I smell sage, too.

The drum and the singing and the sharp thin chorus of eagle-bone whistles mesmerizes. The drum goes on and on; it rests on the earth; its vibrations come through earth and air to each listener's breastbone. Breastbone, eagle bone.

The dancers hold eagle wings or a single wing feather, to amplify their prayers and to bless the pole, each other, themselves, and family members who approach. Eddie Box says: "When you come out of the Sun Dance, you have to do it in steps, like a decompression chamber. We hope they won't go down *all* the steps, back to where they started."

A last dance, last song, and last blessing end the ritual. Gift giving and a feast end the gathering. The Southern Ute dance begins the annual cycle of Shoshone and Ute Sun Dances, and people from all the reservations attend and dance at others.

Linda Baker Rohde said something to me that explains how the Utes have maintained their spirit in the face of change. "You are everything that is in your family line. No matter who you are, you are an old person with someone new inside of you. You reflect who you once were, yet you have new experiences that your great-grandmother couldn't have."

Eddie Box says, with hope: "One hundred years from now, our kids probably will be more understanding than us. I understand my elders; these people in the future will understand me *and* my elders.

"One hundred years from now, Utes will still be Sun Dancing."

The Southern Paiute

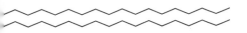

Paiute summer homes, San Juan County, Utah, 1870s. The Paiutes' creative energy went into the weaving of burden baskets, winnowing trays, water jugs, boiling baskets, mush bowls, cradles — some of the most remarkable baskets made in North America. Photo by John K. Hillers. (Courtesy Utah State Historical Society)

The hungry Indians gathered on top of the mountain . . . Shinob came to them and . . . said, "The deer, the antelope and all the big animals went away to find food when there was none here. They were smart. The ducks and sage hens and all the birds went away to find food when they had none here. They were smart. The squirrels and rabbits and all the little animals went away to hunt for food when they were hungry. They were smart. You should have as much sense as the animals and the birds. The country is large and somewhere there is always food. If you follow the animals and the birds they will lead you to it. Go out now and follow their tracks." So saying, the god went away.

From that day to this the Pahutes have been a nomadic people. Leaving their homes in the caves, they have followed the game from high land to low and gathered in gratitude the foods which the gods distribute every year over the face of tu-weap, the earth.

William R. Palmer, *Why the North Star Stands Still*, 1946

"We're nomadic people; we went where the food was." The late Beverly Snow, former chair of the Shivwits Paiute band, spoke with pride. She went on in exasperation. "When the Mormons came in and fenced everything — built their homes at our water sources — we became beggars. What else could we do?"

Outsiders have had difficulty understanding the Southern Paiute from the time they first met. Kaibab elder Dan Bulletts fixed me with a steely eye: "White people killed lots of helpless Paiute people. Books leave all this out, leave out how they paid for Indian scalps in Salt Lake." Gary Tom, a Kaibab Paiute who directs education programs for the Paiute Tribe of Utah goes on: "In reality, *we* wore the white hats. Without our knowledge and skills, when the non-Indians came here, they would not have survived."

The Paiutes chose a life of peace, agriculture, and harvests of game and wild crops. Skilled botanists, they were prepared to eat anything of nutritional value, from seeds and roots to deer and antelope to ant larvae and lizards. In turn, Anglos dismissed them as "Diggers." Neighboring raiders — the Navajos and Utes — took advantage of their pacific ways and kidnapped Paiutes for the slave trade. Mormons and Navajos usurped Paiute lands, and the federal government long ignored the tribe.

Anthropologists Richard Stoffle and Michael Evans believe that "the pre-contact Kaibab Paiutes were as different technologically, socially, and culturally from Euroamericans as any Native American group ever contacted."

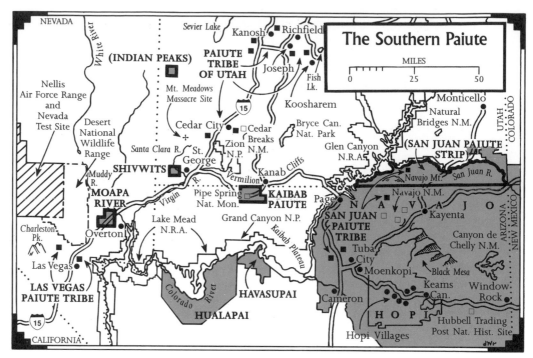

Knowledge from the Past

"I'm glad I'm born in the time I am, but I wish I had that knowledge from the past." Geneal Anderson, chair of the Paiute Tribe of Utah, knows enough of traditional Paiute ways to know what she has missed.

Once, the Southern Paiute, the Nuwuvi, the People, lived from Death Valley to Monument Valley, from Utah's West Desert south to Arizona's Painted Desert. It was "the Paiute Nation all the way — every spring, every mountain," in the words of Clifford Jake, an Indian Peaks elder.

Fifteen bands, or groups, subdivided this huge arc of land in the northwestern corner of the Southwest. All spoke dialects of Numic, a language similar to that spoken by their closest relatives, the Chemehuevi to the south and the Shoshone and Ute to the north. McKay Pikyavit, from the northernmost Paiute band at Kanosh, Utah, says: "Paiute is like English, but reversed; we have a drawl. The farther south you get, the faster the Paiute gets. Down in Las Vegas it goes so fast you can't tell how the words fit together." Indeed, northeastern groups are called Paiute by some and Ute by others. The Chemehuevi, today a Colorado River tribe, form a particularly distinct Southern Paiute group.

These peoples evidently expanded from the Death Valley area into their historic territories not long after A.D. 1100. The Southern Paiute moved through the land with the seasons and harvests, using every available resource within about ten miles of camp, at a sequence of sites visited each year. Stoffle and Evans judged this lifeway more protected from climatic disasters and capable of supporting a larger population of Kaibab Paiutes than Anglos can support now in the same country with their "mixed ranching-farming strategy."

The annual cycle of hunting and gathering varied with the ecological zones available to each band. And with personal taste. Clifford Jake told me: "Some people that like rabbits stayed low; some that like bigger game stayed high, using rabbit-fur blankets to keep warm. Indians followed deer up in spring, just like white men with sheep and cows." Many Utah bands spent spring and summer fishing at Fish Lake.

The western Nuwuvi hunted and gathered piñon nuts on the small ranges rising from the Great Basin and Mojave deserts. Eastern bands used the high terraces stair-stepping away from the Grand Canyon toward Zion and Bryce canyons in the same way, and mapmakers have applied Paiute band names to many of these plateaus: Uinkaret. Shivwits. Kaiparowits. Kaibab — "mountain lying down."

Paiutes managed wild foods, burning grasslands to increase new growth and seed production, transplanting wild grapes and mesquite, cultivating "weeds" like amaranth that provided nutritious seeds. Most bands farmed a bit at springs and in the lower river valleys. Gary Tom thinks the Cedar City people may have had the best territory of all: "They could winter in St. George and move up with the summers."

The "old people" used to tell Elva Drye, at Kaibab, "that they used to have *so* much — deer meat and all of that good food. My grandmother would still collect the seeds. She would grind them on a grinding stone and make soups and things." She laughs: "I don't remember which ones she collected. I'd get poisoned if I tried it!" Other elders miss the traditional foods, as well. The late Marie Lehi, a San Juan Paiute, said: "Sometimes I miss cornmeal and getting up and grinding the corn. It was a lot of work, but I liked the food. I don't like to eat potatoes all the time. When I can, I still gather and eat the old foods."

Clifford Jake says: "They didn't call a bow and arrow a weapon. It was to provide food." Men hunted; some bands honored "dreamers" who hunted large game. Women collected plant foods — the staples. Clothing and shelter were simple, designed for comfort and, in the case of brush huts and shades, for use during a single season. Topsy Swain, a Moapa Paiute elder who died in 1989, laughed when she said: "When I pass by Overton [Nevada] now, I see places where we used to camp and I point and say, 'I had a bed there in that bush!' We had no tent — just sticks and a piece of canvas. But the rain never got in and we never got cold." Swain's granddaughter Vickie Wyatt says: "We're different because of the land that we live in. We should be proud that we could survive here. The people who did survive had to be tough."

Kaibab elder Dan Bulletts, 1988. Bulletts fixed me with a steely eye: "White people killed lots of helpless Paiute people. Books leave all this out, leave out how they paid for Indian scalps in Salt Lake."

Men wore skin caps, women favored conical basketry hats. Creative energy went into burden baskets, winnowing trays, water jugs, boiling baskets, mush bowls, cradles — some of the most remarkable baskets made on the continent. (Today's basket weavers have to compete for materials with farmers and cattlemen trying to eradicate willow and squawbush. Gary Tom says that "older people talk of getting sick from splitting herbicide-sprayed willows in their mouths.")

Nuwuvi lived and foraged as families, claiming ownership of a particular spring. Extended families joined together in economic groups, with headmen. Leaders were advisors more than chiefs, to the distress of pioneer Anglos trying to negotiate with the Southern Paiute. The San Juan Paiutes call their leaders "chief elders."

Bands became much stronger after the arrival of whites, who recognized men of prestige as "chiefs." Such leaders, in turn, found new roles in this time of stress, combining the dwindling remnants of camp groups. They acted as orators and advisors with limited power but with great moral authority, working toward consensus.

Shamans dreamed their songs. Storytellers kept alive the old stories and dreamed new stories. Elders instructed the young in the virtues of a mature person: self-restraint, self-discipline, hard work done willingly. Paiutes conducted a lively trade with the Hopi, Havasupai, and Mojave to the south, crossing the Grand Canyon easily enough when motivated by such an enterprise.

The Nuwuvi gathered together in large groups for the "Big Times": piñon harvests, round dances, or funeral ceremonies. The eastern bands adopted Yuman-style "cries" for mourning only recently — the San Juan conducting the ritual only once, in 1983. In later years (and still, today), the Ute bear dance became a Paiute dance.

Most bands lived in peace, for no other people coveted their land. When the Spanish explorer-priests Dominguez and Escalante came south along the western edge of the Colorado Plateau in southern Utah in 1776, they became the first non-Indians to write of meeting the Nuwuvi. Escalante summed up his impression of them: "a large number of people, all of pleasing appearance, very friendly, and extremely timid."

The Nuwuvi first felt the presence of these European newcomers through a more mysterious vector than the few trappers and traders who appeared in person: smallpox and measles reached far beyond the frontier of settlement. The Kaibab population alone fell from an estimated 5,500 to around 1,175 by the mid-1800s.

And those good-looking, friendly, and timid people noted by Escalante made favored prey for Navajo, Ute, and New Mexican slave traders. By 1830, an annual wagon train passed westward from Santa Fe to California, trading goods first for horses and then for Nuwuvi children. The traders sold Paiute slaves for more horses or trade goods in California, and on the return trip, stocked up again on Paiutes to sell in New Mexico — where, in 1851, a boy brought $100 and "a likely girl" up to twice that.

Losing their young ones, watching herds of up to four thousand horses trample and graze the grasses, shrubs, and crops they depended on for food, the Paiute fought back occasionally. Mostly, however, as Clifford Jake puts it: "When the white men comes, they shot a few little ones and the rest of them went off to hide." The Paiute began to starve; when they stole horses from a caravan, the People ate them.

Today's Paiutes have called the Santa Clara River the central core of Nuwuvi territory, and the best wagon route to California went down this small southwestern Utah river from the resting place of Mountain Meadows high in the Pine Valley Mountains. The Southern Paiute rivers, "you can jump across in summer," according to Gary Tom: "Up north, rivers are rivers." Still, wagon trains needed Nuwuvi water. The springs at Las Vegas, the Moapa Valley of the Muddy River in southern Nevada, and Mountain Meadows all were favored Paiute oases, and all, unfortunately, lay on or near the Old Spanish Trail.

The Nuwuvi needed uplands, canyons, valleys, and rivers to survive through the demands of the year's cycle of seasons. Driven away from one habitat, they suffered. Driven away from all, they starved.

The Coming of the Mormons

In 1847, Brigham Young looked into the Great Basin for the first time and proclaimed this the place to establish a permanent home for his fugitive band of Mormons, members of the Church of Jesus Christ of Latter-Day Saints. When the Mormons began to colonize southward from Salt Lake City a couple of years later, the Paiutes at first welcomed them, seeing them as a new market for trade.

Looking back on this time, however, a Kaibab Paiute with the perspective of age told anthropologist Isabel Kelly in 1932: "After the Mormons come, all the Indians died." A Kaiparowits woman visited her old haunts with Kelly for the first time in forty years and dismissed what she saw with: "This country is no good any more; everything is dry; the creeks are cut deep; the food plants are all gone."

The Utah Territorial Legislature outlawed the Spanish Trail slave trade in 1852, but did so in a roundabout way, setting the stage for the Mormons themselves to take over the "adoption" of young Nuwuvi. The Book of Mormon declares that American Indians are Lamanites, descendants of one of the lost tribes of Israel, and this gives Indian people a privileged position and a special importance as converts.

Brigham Young visited southwestern Utah settlers in 1851 and advised them to use indentured servitude (not to exceed twenty years for each servant) as an effective means of missionary work among the Paiute. He called the practice "purchasing them into freedom instead of slavery," and hoped Mormons would "buy up the Lamanite

Mormon baptism of 200 Shivwits Paiutes, 1875. The Mormons took over Paiute land, but also gave the People what little employment and support they received during the decades before the federal government began to honor trust obligations. Photo by Charles R. Savage. (Courtesy Church Archives, The Church of Jesus Christ of Latter-day Saints)

children as fast as they could, and educate them and teach them the gospel, so that many generations would not pass ere they should become a white and delightsome people."

Within ten years of their arrival in Utah, the Mormons had established several towns in the territory of the Cedar City band, had replaced Paiute irrigation dams on the Santa Clara River with Mormon dams, and had sent missions to Moapa and Las Vegas country. Within another five years, the industrious Anglo villagers were moving into the rest of the Southern Paiute lands.

Wherever Paiutes and Mormons competed for resources, the Paiutes lost. In the early 1860s, Mormon ranchers moved to Kanab and onto the Arizona Strip (the remote country north of the Grand Canyon but within Arizona); in a single year they appropriated all Kaibab water sources. Paiute farmers became dependent on the settlers for food.

The 1860s brought the Paiutes a brief respite. Navajos were pushing hard at the Mormon frontier, forced to raid northward when the U.S. Army prevented Navajo raids into New Mexico. Mormons encouraged Paiutes to farm near Kanab if they would help defend the community when Navajos threatened. Even this proved a risky bargain for the Nuwuvi: after a raid, Mormon militia did not always distinguish between Navajo and Paiute when taking their revenge. And there remained the unsettling legacy of the infamous Mountain Meadows Massacre, when Mormon men murdered the members of an emigrant train in 1857, with Nuwuvi assistance.

By 1870, of the nearly three million acres in Utah's Kane County — Southern Paiute land, all of it — Mormon farmers had "improved" 1,244 acres; county officials guessed that only twenty acres of potential agricultural land remained undeveloped and thus open to Indian use. By 1873, only 207 Kaibab Paiutes remained; the 80 percent reduction in their numbers in a generation came as much through starvation as disease.

Two white men figure prominently in the beginnings of modern Paiute reservation communities. Jacob Hamblin, the head of the Southern Indian Mission, spearheaded Mormon exploration in the 1850s and earned the trust of the Indians through his fairness and honesty. One of his six wives was Paiute. Legend has dubbed him "the Buckskin Apostle."

Hamblin was a natural advisor to Major John Wesley Powell when the geologist-explorer began his work along the Colorado River in 1869. Hamblin knew the country better than any other non-Indian. When three men who left Powell's Grand Canyon river expedition disappeared, Hamblin helped the major make contact with the Shivwits Paiutes in 1870. The Nuwuvi admitted killing Powell's men, whom the Paiutes believed to be miners who had recently murdered a Hualapai woman across the river.

Powell's visits with the Nuwuvi over the next several years gave him an opportunity to study Indians, as he put it, "more nearly in their primitive condition than any others on the continent." His photographers brought back images that have become the iconic photos of the Nuwuvi, though some have a staged romanticism, silly captions, and pose the People in atypical Ute-style buckskin clothing. Powell was doing pioneer ethnography; he also earned $4,100 from the sale of Paiute photos in the first six months of 1874 alone.

In 1858, Hamblin shifted his missionary attention from the Nuwuvi to the Navajo and Hopi, and the Paiutes began to sink into official invisibility. Mormon colonization and mining strikes had impoverished them, and the fact that they were ignored (unless they were raiding) made things worse. Hamblin sympathetically noted "a considerable change . . . in the spirit and feelings of the Indians."

In 1865, six Nuwuvi headmen (those whose names are known today were all Mormon converts) agreed to a treaty removing all Southern Paiutes to the Uintah

Ute Reservation (where, in Gary Tom's words, they would live with "the ones who came down here and killed and raped and kidnapped and sold us"). Unratified, the treaty was meaningless. In 1869, the first Indian agent came to Moapa, but few annuities followed. The withdrawal of the Mormons from Moapa in 1871 did not help: with traditional food rounds made impossible, the Nuwuvi needed the support of the settlers.

Suggestions from agents (G. W. Ingalls, especially) and from Powell led to the establishment of the first Southern Paiute Reservation: 3,900 square miles set aside for all Nuwuvi at Moapa in 1872. In 1874, Congress enlarged the reserve, but in the next year, bowing to political pressure from a local settler, reduced it to just a thousand acres.

Powell and Ingalls had recommended federal jurisdiction for the Kaibab Paiute, as well. Hamblin wrote to Powell in 1880, detailing the "very destitute circumstances" of the ninety-nine remaining Kaibab people — destitution brought on by food resources "all et out" by the settlers' stock.

In the same year, the Moapa Paiutes deserted the reservation because they could not protect their fields from trespass. They had "scattered over the surrounding country for 200 miles around," according to their agent, "eking out a precarious existence by working, begging, root-digging, and insect-eating — a life not of their choice." Corruption and neglect at Moapa continued past 1900.

Salvaging Homes

Dispossessed of their homes and resources, the Utah Paiute lived on the fringes of Mormon villages. The villagers, in turn, gave them work. When Bishop Robert Gardner lectured the Nuwuvi headman Moqueak in 1879 southwest of St. George, on the occasion of giving the Paiute ten acres to farm, Gardner made clear the relationship: "You need not trouble me anymore, for more land. I know better what is good for you than you do for yourself."

Some Koosharem Paiutes sold fishing rights at Fish Lake in 1889 to the Fremont Irrigation Company. The price: nine horses, five hundred pounds of flour, one beef steer, and one suit of clothes. Koosharem irrigation water rights were controlled by the Mormon church until 1958, when the band sued and their rights were restored.

By 1890, just one group of Shivwits people lived in the most isolated part of their territory. The frontier finally reached them that year, when the ranching operations of St. George mayor Anthony Ivins expanded into Shivwits land deep in the Arizona Strip. Cattle made tempting food for foraging Paiutes, and Ivins began pressuring Congress to remove the Shivwits to the Santa Clara River west of St. George — where, in

Nellie Snow (the older girl) and Lucis John, Shivwits Paiute Reservation, Utah, 1930s. Only 85 of the reservation's 28,000 acres could be used for homesites or agriculture, and water rights were a source of constant conflict. Photo by D. E. Beck. (Courtesy Utah State Historical Society)

his words, "they would be among civilized people, and subject to proper government supervision." When Congress did so a year later, they appointed Ivins to spend the appropriated money on land and supplies and move the Shivwits.

A few remaining members of other nearby groups also gathered on the new Shivwits Reservation. The Santa Clara River — once the Nuwuvi heartland — again had a Paiute community. Official recognition came in 1903. Additions in 1916 and 1937 increased the reservation area, but only eighty-five of its eventual twenty-eight thousand acres could be used for homesites or agriculture, and water rights were a source of constant conflict.

This exchange of traditional homeland for reservation symbolized the irony of the Mormon-Paiute relationship. The Mormons took over Paiute land, but the church also gave the Indian people what employment and support they received during the decades that passed before the federal government began to honor its trust obligations.

At Cedar City, the Paiutes concentrated in a small colony living in town on church land. Parowan LDS leader William Palmer was the force behind moving the Cedar colony to a larger tract of land in 1926. Paiutes became dependent on Palmer and other church leaders for their dealings with the non-Indian world; in turn, Palmer published collections of Paiute legends, working diligently as a self-taught historian. A contemporary Paiute talking to anthropologist Ronald Holt complained about "Mormon paternalists" treating the Nuwuvi as "their Indians . . . always taking care of them — looking after them like some livestock." The Cedar people (without federal recognition until 1980) nonetheless have lived for a century on church land, thirty-five acres of which recently has been donated to them "in perpetuity."

In Arizona, by 1907 the church had convinced the residents of Moccasin Ranch to grant one-third of the flow of Moccasin Spring — usurped almost fifty years before — to the original Kaibab Paiute owners. In 1909, a twelve-by-eighteen-mile Kaibab Reservation was designated surrounding the spring (again, with the local Mormons supporting the wish of the Kaibab Paiutes to stay in their territory rather than be moved to the San Juan Paiute reservation). Additions during the next decade enlarged Paiute holdings to more than 120,000 acres straddling the Vermilion Cliffs. Cattle herding supported a few families, but wage work lay in Fredonia and Kanab, and many Kaibab Paiutes lived off-reservation.

Elva Drye spoke to me of these years. She married in 1934 and spent the next twenty years in Delta, Utah, where her husband worked in a hay mill. "We didn't get lonesome: it was kind of far but we still came back home to visit."

Other Nuwuvi communities have similar histories, with small reservations providing some security, but with many people working in nearby towns. For example, Moapa people looking for work lived in a colony at the edge of Las Vegas, forming a pool of cheap labor for the local farmers and miners. In 1911, Helen Stewart, an Anglo who had employed many Paiutes to work on her Las Vegas Ranch, sold the federal government ten acres (for $500) for the Las Vegas colony to use for homes and a day school. Alfreda Mitre, Las Vegas Paiute educator, says: "She needed stability in her work force so she gave us a place to live." The agency at Moapa left the Las Vegas people on their own for years. By 1913, discouraged by disease and economic pressures, Las Vegas Paiutes believed "they would soon pass away and leave their homes to the whites."

The railroad reached Las Vegas in 1904, bringing tourists; by the 1920s, Helen Stewart was encouraging Paiute basket makers to make pieces for sale. To weave large baskets, however, could require months of part-time work yet bring in only a few dollars or some groceries and cheap clothing in trade.

In the desert out at Moapa, the community survived influenza and tuberculosis epidemics, allotment (1914), alcoholism, and in the 1920s, repression of traditional religion by the BIA. The thirties began a mild turnaround, and in 1941, allotments reverted to tribal ownership. A business council and constitution passed in 1942.

The Indian Peaks Reservation was established in 1915 west of Cedar City in isolated country near the Nevada line. A few independent families farmed and ran cattle there, but by 1935, even with additions to the reserve, most had abandoned the small reservation and moved to Cedar City. Band members told anthropologist Martha Knack of the last family to leave: skidding down forty miles of dirt road through an autumn blizzard in a Model-T piled high with belongings and two wide-eyed children.

Other small Utah reservations at Koosharem (1928, with later additions) and Kanosh (established in 1929, and still being enlarged in 1937) suffered similar fates. Many Koosharem people migrated to yet another small-town ghetto, a tract of land at the edge of Richfield, where the Mormon church constructed some homes and community buildings for winter quarters: summers saw the families migrating from farm to farm, living in tents in their employers' fields. Piñon nuts continued to be crucial to twentieth-century Utah Paiutes — as a cash crop, gathered and sold to Anglos.

The concepts of band and local community began to blur through intermarriage, movement between Paiute enclaves, and through helping a complicated network of kin. Such interactions nonetheless reduce the isolation scattered pockets of Paiute families otherwise might feel. Family is the "focal concept of Paiute social organization," as Martha Knack put it.

Into the 1950s, the Paiute communities received minimal federal assistance while struggling to live from the limited resources of their reservations or from wage work in local towns. The seasonal cycle of wage work prevented their own farming operations from becoming self-sufficient, though by the late 1940s, the Kanosh band was close.

Survival and Self-Sufficiency at Kaibab, Moapa, and Las Vegas

Lucille Jake had taken a break from weaving baskets to answer phones in the Kaibab Tribal Offices one winter afternoon when I stopped by. She told me: "Young people work here in the office, and then when they get a better job, they move on, and we get new people here."

"Moving on" is an old pattern. At the beginning of settlement, once the number of Mormons grew sufficiently, the Paiutes weren't even needed for cheap labor. One-fourth of the Kaibabs left their community during the droughts in the early 1900s. Not

until the sixties, when federal programs began to create more on-reservation jobs, did
this drain of people reverse direction.

The 1970s brought HUD housing and land claims money; the Kaibabs invested 70
percent of their share of the latter to support tribal programs. Particularly for women,
soft money remains the main income source, from jobs created by federal grants funneled through tribal administration. Working men, whose skills often involve heavy
outdoor labor, are the most mobile people in the community.

Families must be creative to support themselves. One Kaibab extended family
living in a single household (interviewed by anthropologist Allen Turner in 1976)
earned its $16,000 annual income from wages, cattle sales, land claims funds, and
social security benefits; this worked out to $1,396 per person. The expertise repre-
sented in the household included basket weaving, buckskin tanning, weather prediction, ethnomedicine, ethnobotany, ceremonial procedures, singing, childrearing,
food preparation, gardening, livestock management, carpentry, welding, heavy equipment operation, automobile repair, and secretarial skills.

For the three hundred Kaibabs a stream of tourists is one promising resource:
their reservation surrounds the Mormon pioneer fort at Pipe Spring National Monument, and the visitor center itself is leased to the National Park Service by the tribe.
Community projects have included a campground, trailer park, traditional crafts festival, and cafe, but the long, quiet winters and relatively low visitation rates have hin-
dered these developments. The Bear Dance was revived in 1977, the first in twenty
years, but it remains a mostly Indian affair.

The Kaibabs number too few to live in self-sufficient isolation — either socially or
economically. Half the community consists of non-Kaibab spouses. Kaibab people go
to Keams Canyon, at Hopi, for health services (and to Hopi shamans for native cures,
since no traditional Paiute doctor survives). Shopping takes Kaibabs to St. George,
Cedar City, and Las Vegas — all places with Paiute relations. Children attend a one-
room school in Moccasin through grade three, along with local Anglos. After that, all
bus to Fredonia.

As Gary Tom puts it, for both Kaibab and Utah Paiutes: "Size is the main difference between us and other reservations. A Navajo can get lost out there and never
have to deal with the white man at all. A Papago might deal with whites once or twice
a week." A Paiute does not have that choice.

In 1980, Kaibab leaders summarized their hopes for the future: "Survival is
our problem." The best possible future? Self-sufficiency in agriculture, with land and
water rights guaranteed and adequate for building "the new ways on the old." New
wells and freshly cleared springs just may provide the water needed for such food

production. The search for profitable "new ways" leads in unlikely directions: in 1990, the Kaibab Paiutes first approved and then rejected a hazardous waste incinerator on their reservation.

Elva Drye says: "There was more cattle when I was young; we don't spend as much time outside now. Paiute people live here just like white people — only it's harder to find jobs." She laughs affectionately about confused visitors to Pipe Spring: "The tourists are surprised by no tipis. They tell the park rangers that they couldn't find the Paiute homes; they 'just saw houses!'" The Kaibab insisted on redesigning one recent HUD housing complex, placing houses on alternate lots to allow for the Paiute need for privacy.

And yet, the past remains so close. One Paiute elder said to Turner, while pointing to a woman gazing out from a print in a stack of photos from Powell's 1869 visit to Chuarumpi-ak's band of Kaibabs: "This one is my grandmother; I learned from her." Lucille Jake says: "We have never given up our crafts." Drye adds, "Sometimes when there's a bunch of us together we tell each other what we can remember of the legends. We're the last."

Moapa people invested 60 percent of the land claims money that arrived in 1971. In 1968, they took over all non-Indian leases and established a cooperative farm that today employs two men and provides hay for many Las Vegas area horses. The tribe also ran a beaded leather company and a tomato greenhouse operation in the 1970s.

Unemployment remains near 90 percent, with the guarantee of 10 percent Paiute employment at a nearby Nevada Power plant unenforced. Randall Simmons, tribal employment officer, says: "The experts brought in as consultants on different business ventures didn't train our people before they left." Vickie Wyatt says: "There is a big difference between the haves and have-nots here."

The late elder Herbert Myers responded to my questions about Paiute culture: "The language? That's all gone." Says Vickie Wyatt: "Our tribe wasn't studied. Our old people are dead. We're scrambling to save something, but it's almost too late." Everline Begay, who clerks in the Moapa Tribal Store, told me that her mother quit making baskets when she lost her teeth: "You had to use your teeth a lot" to split the basket materials. She says: "Indian things fascinate me. Why? I'm Indian!" The kids are not learning the language: "They go so far, and that's it." And yet, when the community gathered for a memorial sing for Topsy Swain in 1990, Begay (Swain's daughter) told me that all of her mother's things would be burned in a hole, plus the clothes worn by the mourners. As recently as twenty years ago, when Begay's brother died, his horse was shot, in the old way.

In the early 1980s, the Moapas were granted an additional seventy thousand acres

Dean Brown, Moapa Paiute, working at the tribal fireworks stand, 1990. This tribally owned business on Interstate 15 in Nevada provides Moapa with nearly all of its income.

of land, though the three hundred Paiutes continue to live mostly in HUD homes built in 1970 on the old reservation. The new land may be "all hills and deserts," in the words of Moapa security guard Nathan Lee, but it has attracted many developers looking for leases and created plenty of "political upheaval," in Vickie Wyatt's words.

The new lands include ten miles of frontage along Interstate 15, and it is here that the tribe has built the fireworks stand and smoke shop that employs Lee and some twenty others. Herbert Myers said that the stand "is the only thing keeping this reservation going." Annual profits run to six figures. Vickie Wyatt, the young tribal finance clerk, talked to me in her office in the Moapa community center: "This is our first successful business. We're barely getting our feet on the ground. We used to not even be able to keep the lights on in this building at night; now we're newly computerized."

Wyatt went on: "We're just a small place. Everybody takes their turn in politics." Nathan Lee told me: "We live in a white civilization now, even if we do live on a reservation." As I rose to leave, he jabbed a sturdy finger toward my notebook. "We still live in poverty. You got that down there?"

The Moapas speak with ambivalence about fifty-mile-distant Las Vegas. Herbert Myers said: "I don't like Vegas, there's too much of this and that." When he talked about water rights problems, he understood that casinos hold the power in Nevada: "All that big club down there, that's who controls the water." Of the Las Vegas Paiutes, Everline Begay says that they are "kind of particular." Vickie Wyatt says: "They are city Indians, into gangs and girls!" Nathan Lee says simply: "They are a lot richer."

As Las Vegas kept growing, engulfing the Paiute colony, road access became a problem (unresolved until 1975). A well drilled in the 1930s provided irrigation water until it gave out in 1945. Kenneth Anderson, chair of the Las Vegas Paiutes in the 1970s, remembers that "people went to work and provided for themselves."

The community spent much of the 1950s and 1960s campaigning for decent water and sewer facilities (achieved in 1962) and fighting the BIA plan to sell their land and relocate them. Electricity and telephone service did not arrive until 1965. The tribe adopted a constitution in 1970, largely to cope with issues surrounding land claims money. "We were at poverty level until 1977," says Alfreda Mitre, Las Vegas chair from 1990 to 1992.

Today, the Las Vegas Paiute tribe has virtually no unemployment, due to its urban locale and an immensely successful smoke shop operation. By 1979, the smoke shop grossed an estimated $1 million to support community social programs. Indian smoke shops based their discount cigarette prices on the non-taxable status of reservations, but a 1980 Supreme Court decision changed the rules. Now tribes must collect tobacco and sales tax from non-Indian customers. Alfreda Mitre says, "We've agreed to tax ourselves at a rate equal to or greater than the state. Our prices can be beaten, but promotions and large quantities bring the people in. Only 19 percent of our tribal funding comes from federal funds.

"But we don't want cigarettes to be the sole source of our economic self-sufficiency. We believe in diversification, and we have purchased contiguous acreage. We want to stay in retail businesses, serving the current bargain-hunter consumers."

In 1983, the seventy-person colony was granted thirty-seven hundred acres thirteen miles northwest of Las Vegas. They needed the land, as Chairman Billy Frye testified before Congress in 1982, to create "the opportunity to become families again and to reverse the deterioration of our spiritual and cultural values," a trend initiated by the dispersal of tribal members from the overcrowded ten-acre colony and into the city's suburbs.

An imaginative "land graphic sculpture" designed by Arapaho architect Dennis Sun Rhodes forms the heart of a 1986 master plan for the new land (called Nuvakai, Snow Mountain, for its views of Charleston Peak). Rhodes created a yin-yang symbol in streets and buildings. As seen from the air, one half of the development will form the shape of a Wolf, a sacred Paiute symbol, including housing (the Wolf's head), schools, the cemetery, and recreational and open space. Commercial and industrial buildings and a golf course development together outline the other half, the profane Coyote. By 1992, some Paiutes had moved to the new land, but a long fight for funding a highway interchange for Snow Mountain delayed development.

Thoughtful chair Alfreda Mitre told me: "A lot of credit needs to be given to the strength and spirituality of our people. A small group here is struggling to hang on to the remnants of our culture. We're acculturated but not assimilated. We're noted for your basic necessity — survival. That's the essence of mankind, but it's not glamorous or tangible. We don't have elaborate dances and artifacts, not even the ticky-tacky things that tourists want." The key: "Education, both formal and informal, will allow the tribe to exist."

The Termination and Rebirth of the Utah Paiutes

In 1953, Utah Paiutes learned a new word: termination. A wild swing of the federal policy pendulum took it out to one of its extremes, the one that said, "cut-the-Indians-loose-on-their-own-so-they-can-be-independent-and-integrated-Americans."

Senator Arthur Watkins of Utah happened to be chairman of the Senate Subcommittee on Indian Affairs in the early 1950s. When Congress passed a resolution supporting the Bureau's intention of terminating federal responsibility for administering Indian affairs (and dismantling the BIA itself), Watkins opened his hearings with an investigation of the Utah Paiutes — who had not been included on prior lists of tribes ready for termination.

Perhaps Watkins wished to use a tribe in his home state as the first example of this new policy, one he strongly supported. Perhaps he believed that since the federal government had done little for the Paiutes, they might as well cut them off entirely. He stated his belief in the Southern Paiute as "ambitious, deserving people who should and will prosper once the yoke of federal supervision is removed."

Whatever the motivation, Congress removed "the yoke," voting in 1954 to terminate the Indian Peaks, Kanosh, Koosharem, and Shivwits reservations. Though they had no reservation to terminate, the Cedar City band received no further federal assistance, and termination affected them just as abruptly.

The Nuwuvi did not protest termination effectively because they did not fully understand its implications. Gary Tom points out that "Paiutes didn't have a word for 'termination'; they couldn't explain it to the elders." When Clifford Jake attended the only hearing held on the matter in southern Utah, he testified that his Indian

Peaks band had no livestock, no income, and made their homes from "what the white people throw away." He remembers being "the one that spoke up, but the rest didn't."

Jake asked Senator Watkins: "Do you ever check on Indian people down toward the reservation? Do you know how they live? Did you ever visit them?" The senator told him: "You'd better sit down and mind your own business and shut up."

Termination took effect in 1957. Prior to that, federal aid may have been minimal ($284 per Paiute family in 1953), but with an average family income of just $375, it had made a difference in Nuwuvi lives. They were now at the mercy of the local economy and population, where they suffered job and social discrimination — more severe in larger towns like Cedar City and St. George. One Shivwits woman who could see what was coming for her people threatened the BIA "withdrawal director" with a broom.

The Paiute were left without health care, with their lands subject to taxation. The Kanosh band soon lost nearly all its 4,280 acres — by selling individual allotments and losing tribal land for nonpayment of taxes. McKay Pikyavit, band chair, told me: "We had some friends in downtown Kanosh who bought our land during termination under the tax sale. They kept it and we lived on it. After restoration, they gave eighty acres back."

Seizure for taxes took all of the Koosharem's four hundred acres. The Indian Peaks band sold their 8,900 acres before it could be taken (for $1,374.10, to the Utah Division of Wildlife to be used as a pronghorn reserve). At Shivwits, the band preserved their holdings by using lease money: "The gravel pit paid taxes all those years while we tried to hold on to our land," said Beverly Snow. The after-tax surplus from leases paid each community member $5 per year. At one point, the band read in the local newspaper of plans by the bank trustee to sell their land without their knowledge and had to move quickly to stop him.

Only four years after termination, a report concluded that the policy had failed. The Utah Paiutes were almost invisible for the next decade. Travis Parashonts, from Cedar City, says "termination for our people was a nightmare" marked by welfare, heavy drinking, child neglect, theft, alcohol-related auto accidents, substandard housing, nonexistent medical services, diabetes, malnutrition, and suicide. The only meat they could afford was rabbit and venison they hunted themselves. And the rabbits at Shivwits, according to Beverly Snow, "are not healthy to eat anymore. They have growths and things because of fallout" from nuclear explosions at the Nevada Test Site.

The Southern Paiute agreed to a controversial settlement of their land claims case in 1965, arranged by the tribe's lawyers without the usual careful documentation of historic territorial rights and land values. Payment arrived in 1971; the terminated Utah Paiutes, without a tribal government, took their share in per capita checks of $7,522 —

quickly used up for housing and vehicles. (As Gary Tom says: "If you've got money, you spend it.")

In 1970, the BIA officially notified the Cedar band that they had not been terminated. This opened the possibility of Cedar people having access to federal programs denied their neighbors from the terminated Indian Peaks band. Worried about such injustice, Clifford Jake began investigating restoration for all Utah Paiute bands.

The late Woodrow Pete spoke for the Cedar City band in Salt Lake City's *Deseret News* in 1968:

> We have received no money from the government or anyone else for the loss of our land. A lot of our children have been taken away by welfare and we see them no more. Our mothers have cried many tears for their children are gone. Even if we received money from the government, maybe we couldn't get our children back . . .
>
> We are grateful for what help we have been given, but soon we will all be gone unless something different happens to us. We want to live like everyone else and see our children healthy and happy. In the name of SHINAALV, the name we use when we pray to our God, please help us. Please give us some of our land back, enough to dignify our lives.

In 1971, the Utah Paiute Tribal Corporation incorporated as a de facto tribal government—an innovation combining all Utah Paiute bands under one leadership for the first time. A housing authority formed in 1974, and the first HUD houses were built in 1976. While termination dragged on, a whole generation of Paiutes matured. Travis Parashonts, Cedar band chair at the time, says: "We lost a lot of our traditions; young people have to learn from ground level now, we have so few older people."

All band leaders in the restoration fight were under thirty at the time. Beverly Snow "wore out two cars driving back and forth to Salt Lake City during all the meetings to restore our reservation." With the help of attorneys Larry Echohawk and Mary Ellen Sloan and the leadership of interim tribal chair Travis Parashonts, the Paiute restoration bill passed on 3 April 1980.

Travis Parashonts oversaw the struggle for land by the newly restored tribe, then resigned to become Director of Indian Affairs for Utah; Geneal Anderson took his place in 1984 as tribal chair of the six hundred Utah Paiutes. She says: "Growing up, I didn't really understand what this word 'termination' meant." She does now.

She bragged to me of the advances since restoration: "Our resources are people. That's why education is so crucial. Our dropout rate has dropped from 40 percent to 3 percent. Tribal sewing plants in Kanosh and Cedar City have even sewn jackets for

Ashley Cuch (left) and Lindsey Wall attending a summer school/daycare program, Paiute Tribe of Utah, Cedar City, 1990. Termination of federal recognition in 1957 led to dismal times for the Utah Paiutes. Since restoration in 1980, the tribe has cut the school dropout rate from 40 percent to 3 percent.

NASA." Yet, as Gary Tom points out: "It will be a generation before we see a strong educational background as a given."

Travis Parashonts says: "You had to be an optimist during the restoration era. Prior to 1980, we had three deaths to every birth. We were a vanishing tribe, slowly going into extinction. Restoration gave us access to health service, and we reversed those figures in two to three years."

In 1984, Utah Paiutes were granted 4,770 acres of land (in addition to the Shivwits Reservation, which remained in Paiute ownership all along). The tribe lobbied hard for National Forest land with mineral resources. At the time, Travis Parashonts said: "Our purpose is to develop ourselves and become self-sufficient — and we need good lands in order to accomplish this."

"We asked for 15 thousand acres; it should have been 15 million!" says Gary Tom. The meeting called in Parowan to discuss this proposal, according to Tom, was the biggest gathering the town has ever seen: "People went bananas." The tribe was refused the forest land. The Paiutes asked for ancestral land on the shores of Fish Lake and again were refused. (Clifford Jake remains philosophical about such holy sites: "Power booster stations may get put on a sacred place; below it still is a sacred place.")

Most of the BLM land granted the Utah Paiutes consists of grazing land or small parcels surrounding exits from Interstate highways 15 and 70 — reasonable places for developing tourist facilities near Cove Fort, Joseph, and Cedar City. Koosharem people have built houses on the Joseph tract. In addition, a $2.5 million trust fund passed; the fund's interest helps support tribal administration and economic development. A BIA field agency opened in Cedar City in 1982 specifically to administer to Southern Paiute tribes.

The politics of reunification challenge the bands to work together. Geneal Anderson, chair, working out of the Cedar City tribal headquarters, comes from the smallest band — Indian Peaks, with less than thirty people. Shivwits, the most rural site left, is home to one-third of the tribe — about twenty families, mostly female single parents and their children. Dolly Big Soldier looks out from her home at Shivwits: "In the fifties, that whole valley down there was filled with homes. A lot of people moved away during the termination years. Some died off; we're the ones who stuck it out here."

Kanosh and Koosharem people think of themselves as more Ute than Paiute. When once-transitional Ute-Paiute Kanosh was left out of the Ute land claims case, according to McKay Pikyavit, the attorneys said: "The Paiute case is still open; why don't you join that?" They did, and today administrative designation and intermarriage combine to make the Kanosh members of the Paiute Tribe.

Restoration created a tribal entity, but the outlying bands, says McKay Pikyavit, "are so far from the tribal office that we lost authority with reinstatement. We can't get enough tribal money to plow up the fields for hay. Grants require matching funds; loans require income. We're just sitting here going to waste.

"There are thirteen homes today, with seventy-five people (though we might have to count the dogs!) As far as the future goes, we don't have any. The tribe has all the money."

Even with money, the tribe's depressing social statistics change slowly. From 1981 to 1984, 95 percent of Paiute deaths were alcohol related; in 1984, 68 percent of health needs still went unmet, and the life expectancy for a Utah Paiute was just forty-two years. Paiutes without health records may be ineligible for restitution money promised to families of "downwinders," who died from cancer caused by open-air nuclear testing in Nevada.

Dolly Big Soldier attributes the many medical problems of her family to radiation.

She says: "We can't even plant a garden here anymore. I don't want to be called activist; I'm just trying to fight for my kids' future — all the other kids, too, white or any kind. The whole planet is radiated; *everybody* is a downwinder."

Big Soldier's late sister Beverly Snow hoped that the Shivwits would eventually encounter "somebody smart enough to come in and start some money-making project and not cheat us. The schemes people have proposed to us — pistachio farms, golf courses, condos — are always to benefit outsiders." Says Geneal Anderson: "I don't know if we're ready for economic development. We need more tribal involvement; how can we go out and make a difference in the world if we can't make a difference at home?"

During termination, says Travis Parashonts: "Our people lost something that you can't feel or touch or see. Once we went through restoration, we got that spirit back. Now that we own something again, a spirit of change has come over our people." The "resiliency" of his people amazes Gary Tom: "The Paiutes just have such a strong tie to the land."

The Paiute Tribe of Utah shares its problems with all small Indian tribes; as put succinctly by Martha Knack, they live in "a never-ending flux of attraction through need and repulsion through overfamiliarity." Geneal Anderson says: "We call them problems, but we should call them opportunities to make us a better people." Travis Parashonts has one dream ("We're supposed to dream; visions are part of our culture!") that might help: "I can see a unification of the Paiutes. They are all small bands, but the more they stick together, the stronger they will be. It's hard to be Indian in a white world."

The Struggle Continues: The San Juan Paiute

Sometimes it's hard to be Indian in a red world, too. The San Juan Paiutes live as a tiny minority surrounded by the Navajo. Their struggle for survival and recognition has lasted for more than a century so far.

San Juan people always have been the only Paiutes east of the Colorado River. They scattered in summer to farm along the San Juan River, in Paiute and Navajo canyons on the flanks of Navajo Mountain, in marshes near Kayenta, and at springs along the Echo Cliffs between Tuba City and Page. In winter, families camped together.

Northernmost Arizona was Paiute land all the way to Marsh Pass, above Monument Valley — with the exception of the Hopi village at Moenkopi. By 1776, San Juan Paiutes forced Hopis and Havasupais to retreat from the Moenkopi area, but the Hopi reestablished their farming outpost in the early 1870s, with the protection of Mormon colonists.

The oldest San Juan lands surrounded Navajo Mountain, whose isolated turtle-back rising above the horizon spreads a motherly presence over all of northern Navajoland. The Diné hold sacred its summit, though not as one of the four mountains defining their home. Once, however, "Navajo Mountain" was "Paiute Mountain."

Few Navajos lived in this land until after the Long Walk, when Paiutes helped those Navajos who escaped the net of Kit Carson's troops in 1864. By the 1880s, Navajo stock were beginning to trespass on Paiute Canyon farms. By 1884, this northern section of Paiute territory had been added to the Navajo Reservation, to cope with the Navajo tribe's extraordinary population growth. Nevertheless, the Paiutes claim that no Navajos settled permanently in the Navajo Mountain area until the 1920s.

In 1900, the San Juan Paiute winter home at Tuba City–Willow Springs became Navajo Reservation land, though the local Navajo population was still small. The Mormon ranches at Tuba were bought out in 1902–03 to make room for the Western Navajo Agency and school. Moenkopi Wash was parceled out to Hopi and Navajo.

While the western Navajo Reservation still had its own agency (through 1935), the BIA provided some services to the San Juan Paiutes. Once the entire Navajo Reservation was administered from distant Window Rock, however, the BIA became confused about Paiute identity, and administrators forgot the San Juan people.

By the turn of the century, the Paiutes had added sheepherding to their repertoire of skills, trading baskets to the Navajo for their first flocks. They moved back and forth from the southern lands to Navajo Mountain, and this migration further confused the BIA whenever they tried to pin down who and where the San Juan Paiutes were.

In 1907, government inspections led to the establishment of both the Kaibab Reservation in Arizona and the "Paiute Strip" San Juan Reservation in Utah, south of the San Juan and Colorado rivers and east to Monument Valley, which protected grazing lands around Navajo Mountain but not the Paiute farms at either Paiute Canyon or Willow Springs. In 1909, a BIA agent described the San Juan Paiutes' land, the slick-rock maze surrounding Navajo Mountain and Glen Canyon: "the roughest, driest, and most inaccessible country I ever saw."

The 1918 influenza epidemic devastated Monument Valley Paiutes, young people especially. San Juan Paiute numbers dropped from three hundred to less than eighty between 1900 and 1940. When mining interests in Monticello, Utah, pushed for access to the Paiute Reservation, a poorly informed BIA inspector made a quick trip to Monument Valley in 1922 and saw no Paiutes. Within weeks, Secretary of Interior Albert Fall, an exploiter soon to be disgraced by scandal, had thrown open the land.

Almost immediately, the one Navajo family living in Monument Valley began campaigning to regain the old Paiute Strip (it had been Navajo Reservation land in the 1800s). The miners found no major strikes, and Navajo politicking overwhelmed the silent Paiutes. The Strip again became Navajo land in 1933.

For the next fifty years, the San Juan Paiutes were largely forgotten. The Navajo Tribal Council claimed that the Paiutes intermarried and "became Navajo." In reality, the minority Paiutes have been the butt of ethnic jokes, harassment, and job discrimination — especially at Navajo Mountain, where Navajo and Paiute still compete for limited resources. The BIA sometimes included Paiutes in the Navajo census, and in the 1980s a random 55 percent of the San Juans were "officially" enrolled as Navajo.

From the 1930s until his death in 1969, the chief tribal elder of the San Juan Paiutes was Alfred Lehi. Though a strong leader within his community, particularly in sacred matters, Lehi did not like working with non-Indians, and he did not fight federal neglect, seeking instead assistance from Kaibab and Kanosh kin (such as finding agricultural jobs in Utah for his band members).

In the thirties and forties, the San Juans began settling into their winter camps as year-round home bases, pulling back to the remaining farm areas at Willow Springs and Paiute Canyon in summer. Pickups and cars made visiting possible and kept the tribe (the southern "Sand People" and the northern "Mountain People") tied together. Annual harvests of piñon nuts — still an important cash crop — brought the tribe to one joint camp each fall.

After Lehi's death, San Juan leaders grew more forceful. They started from scratch: at the time, the band received no government aid at all. In 1969, Kaibab, Cedar, Kanosh, and Shivwits people went to San Juan and compared ancestries; they agreed to take almost a hundred San Juans into the Paiute Land Claims judgment, though each added person diminished the per capita payment to all. The Kaibab leader, Ralph Castro, helped the San Juans begin their fight for federal recognition, admonishing both the Navajo and United States governments in 1970: "Keep it up — you are doing a good job — there is now less than 100 Paiutes left in the area. In a few years, there won't be any left and the Navajo Nation and the U.S. Government can say well done."

The quagmire of the 1974 Navajo-Hopi Relocation Act opened the way for the Paiutes to sue for their land. With the help of Native American Rights Fund attorneys — and under the leadership first of Alfred Lehi's daughter, Anna Whiskers, and now, his granddaughter, Evelyn James — the Paiutes became full participants in the legal battles to clarify jurisdiction over the three tribal homelands. The San Juans began writing a constitution in 1986, a historic chance to incorporate the traditions of their people in the Anglo-inspired document.

While Navajos persist in dismissing the Paiutes as disgruntled Navajo "converts," the Hopis support the Paiute drive for recognition. The formal petition from the San Juan Paiutes finally brought federal recognition in 1989. The fight for a designated reservation continues.

Anthropologists Pamela Bunte and Robert Franklin have documented in detail the cultural integrity and vitality of the modern San Juan Paiutes. They note that Anna Whiskers is considered by elders from other Paiute bands to be "one of the foremost living orators in the Southern Paiute language" (she passed on the leader's role to her daughter in 1980 because of James's greater mobility and her skills in English).

San Juan is the only remaining Southern Paiute community where Paiute is a child's first language and the language of all everyday transactions. Kaibab elders leave their children with San Juan families to give them a dose of "traditional" Paiute culture. Coyote tales ("winter stories") are still told in their full repertoire. Menstruation and childbirth rituals are still the norm. In meetings, if dissent remains after discussion by elders, the San Juans simply put the matter aside. Consensus remains the only way to action.

These are the ironic results of federal neglect and of isolation from the non-Indian world: poverty maintains tradition.

San Juan Paiute women have adopted the Navajo women's velveteen blouses and gathered skirts. They herd sheep, and some weave. But as tribal leader Evelyn James (a widow) has said: "My husband was a Navajo . . . He used to say that after a visit with his family, when he came back to me, it was like coming into a different world. When I would go to visit his family, it was like another world for me. We would go in between, and we would both get confused and go through a culture shock . . .

"My people want to be recognized for what we are. We are not Navajos. We are Paiutes."

Only recently have the San Juans received credit for another of their skills — their basketry. For more than a century, they have made baskets to trade and sell to the Navajos, and this has been a major source of cash. San Juan Paiutes make nearly all "Navajo" wedding baskets required in so many Diné ceremonies — the coiled plates with their distinctive not-quite-closed circle of red outlined with zigzag terraces of black. Many Diné believe that Paiute-made baskets have special healing properties.

In the 1970s, trader Bill Beaver, an Anglo, and his Navajo wife, Dollie Begay, at Sacred Mountain Trading Post north of Flagstaff, began encouraging the San Juan weavers to experiment. The Beavers bought Paiute baskets and saw to it that they were exhibited in museums. Basket making has since flowered into a full-blown industry for the band, which formed a cooperative in 1985 to market baskets directly.

The Lehi-Whiskers family has been central to this basketry revival, just as they dominate tribal leadership. Alfred's widow, Marie Lehi, was the family matriarch until her death in 1992. She said: "I never forced my girls to make baskets, but they just started doing it as play when they were in a good mood. Even the bread making was like that. When they were willing to do it, they started to."

San Juan weavers today make "old-timer baskets," the utilitarian pieces that keep tradition alive. They make "wedding baskets," the mainstay of their economy. And they make "fancy baskets," or "design baskets," to nurture both their market and their artistic needs. Over 10 percent of all band members are weavers, many of them younger women — and even a few men.

Evelyn James has visionary dreams about her two hundred San Juan Paiute people. She told Robert Franklin in 1984 of her worries and fears in dealing with the large and powerful Hopi and Navajo tribes, of her search for strength: "I was on top of Willow Springs . . . I went to let the sheep out . . . And I cried, I never felt like this before. I never felt so brave before, never felt so, so strong before . . . I looked around me. And the Great Spirit said, you're a human, you have a strong bones, strong back-bone. And that's when I found out that somebody that is greater than anybody else is on my side, that I . . . wasn't alone after all."

As you drive along the base of the Echo Cliffs from Cameron north toward Page, remember that the hogans and the bead-sellers along the road, the sheep flocks crossing between small stands of juniper and creamy sandstone cliffs, are a thin Navajo veneer over another, older place. The Paiutes, too, live here, raising their children in some of those homesteads you pass. They, too, call this land their sacred home.

The Paiutes' Great Spirit, Shu-nangwav, may well talk to non-Paiutes. But to Evelyn James, he said, "not to be afraid. He told me to do this in happiness, because he knows, he told me, that I am a winner."

THREE

In the House of the Sun

DESERT PEOPLES

The emergence place of Yuman peoples: Spirit Mountain,
Newberry Mountains, Nevada, 1992.

The O'odham say that saguaros are people, too. Branching, tree-like cacti give the Southwest desert a human scale, making this intense land surprisingly reassuring when compared to the stormy bulk of mountains or the long bare cliffs and moonscape badlands of plateau country. Saguaros stand upright like men and women; chollas surround them, with the presence of animals.

Where this southwestern land lies lowest, in the lower reaches of the Colorado, Gila, and Rio Grande basins, the air shimmers with summer heat: these are the North American desertlands. Across them, faulted mountain and down-dropped basin create a landscape in two:four time, an endless alternation that gives this huge sweep of the continent its physiographic name: Basin and Range.

Only the great Colorado and Gila river systems flowing through these arid lands bring abundant water to Indian farmers. South of the Rocky Mountains (which are too cold to farm extensively) and the canyons of the plateau (too tortuous to irrigate large areas), oasis peoples live and farm where the sere land bakes under the desert sun — alongside lazy red rivers. The Mojave, Chemehuevi, Quechan, and Cocopah of the Colorado River. Pima and Maricopa people of the Gila and Salt rivers. Yaqui who migrated north from Mexico's Río Yaqui. The true desert people, the Tohono O'odham and Sand Papago, live away from the rivers, dependent on springs and thunderstorms for their water. They dance to bring clouds; they sing for rain.

When humans moved down through North America during the Ice Age twelve thousand years ago, they found the Southwest cool and wet, with woodland and forest plants growing much lower than they do today. About ten thousand years ago, the climate began to warm. Woodland and forest species retreated to the cooler mountaintops; desert shrubs and cacti moved north from Mexico as the glacial climate withdrew. Little more than five thousand years ago, the Southwest became the land of hot deserts, the land of creosote bush.

Today, ecologists recognize four North American deserts, each of them distinct. One lies on the Southwest's northern borders: the Great Basin Desert, with cold winters and vast stands of sagebrush stretching between lightly forested mountain ranges. Within the Southwest, the Sonoran Desert surrounds the head of the Gulf of California in Arizona, California, and Mexico. Its lower reaches are its most arid, too dry even for most cacti; to the east and north lies its higher, well-watered border: saguaro country.

The smaller, transitional Mojave Desert, symbolized by the Joshua tree, separates the Sonoran and Great Basin deserts; some see it as a distinctive part of the Sonoran Desert rather than a full-fledged bioregion in its own right. The Chihuahuan Desert — reaching up the Rio Grande and Pecos valleys through Texas and New Mexico and westward to the upper Gila River in Arizona — covers the largest area of the four deserts, with over 80 percent of its expanse within Mexico.

Winter rains come from the west, from the Pacific. Summer rains — crucial for agriculture — come from the southeast, in thundershowers fueled by Gulf moisture that create high drama in the southwestern skies. At the western and eastern extremes, the Mojave has extremely arid summers, the Chihuahuan, arid winters. In between,

the Sonoran Desert, Southern Rockies, and Colorado Plateau receive both winter and
summer moisture.

Undependability compounds problems posed for people and wildlife by these meager amounts of water. Yuma, Arizona, received more than eleven inches of precipitation in 1905, only a third of an inch in 1953; four inches fell during a single day in August 1909.

The Yuman-speaking Mojave, Quechan, and Cocopah lived along the Colorado River from the beginning — dreaming, fishing, and farming. Piman-speakers held southern Arizona — the Pima in their villages along the Gila River, the Tohono O'odham (once called Papago) with their quiet culture carefully tuned to the Sonoran Desert uplands, the Sand Papago in the most arid reaches of what the Spaniards called Papaguería. The other desert peoples came to their homes later: the Chemehuevi breaking away from other Paiutes in the Great Basin; the Maricopa (Yumans like the other Colorado River tribes) driven to the Gila by tumultuous competition for limited space on the Colorado; and the Yaqui fleeing from Mexico as political refugees only a century ago.

All live in dry country, yet all speak of their land not as desert. They speak of it as home.

The O'odham

Pimas crossing the Gila River, Sacaton, 1907. By 1867, Anglo settlers had begun the long series of tragic diversions from the Gila. Within 20 years, Pima fields no longer had a dependable water supply, and O'odham farmers were forced into a wage economy. (Courtesy Museum of the American Indian, Heye Foundation)

The green of those Pima fields spread along the river for many miles in the old days when there was plenty of water.

Now the river is an empty bed full of sand.

Now you can stand in that same place and see the wind tearing pieces of bark off the cottonwood trees along the dry ditches.

The dead trees stand there like white bones. The red-wing blackbirds have gone somewhere else. Mesquite and brush and tumbleweeds have begun to turn those Pima fields back into desert.

Now you can look out across the valley and see the green alfalfa and cotton spreading for miles on the farms of white people who irrigate their land with hundreds of pumps running night and day. Some of those farms take their water from big ditches dug hundreds of years ago by Pimas, or the ancestors of Pimas. Over there across the valley is where the red-wing blackbirds are singing today.

George Webb, *A Pima Remembers*, 1959

From a hill above San Xavier Mission, I watch rush hour on the reservation. It is 5:30 P.M., and Tohono O'odham people are coming home from work. In the foreground, stucco HUD houses scatter around the old Franciscan church. Kids on bicycles wheel in figure eights around junked cars and burning trash, ducking under fresh laundry line-drying in the sun. Beyond, golden fields lead off toward Tucson and the Catalina Mountains — the O'odham's Frog Mountain.

The last red rays of light glint off picture windows in foothill homes far away on the lower flanks of the Catalinas, twinkling in distant starbursts behind the creamy white church now flushing with gold. On my hill are petroglyphs and pictographs — old spirals carved in the black volcanic rock and new designs spray-painted in blues and greens.

Newcomers in Phoenix and Tucson appear to have learned little from the O'odham about how to live with the desert. The cities seem dumped on the ancestral Indian homeland — subdivisions pushing against reservation boundaries, pools, lawns, irrigated fields, and fountains using up fossil groundwater at a shortsighted pace. San Xavier vice-chairman Daniel Preston says: "Developers are looking over our fences."

When Gila River Pima medicine man Emmett White took his Basket Dance group to Ahwatukee, a Phoenix development, he found that his audience was expecting stereotypical beads and feathers. Says White: "We're not entertainers. We're Pimas."

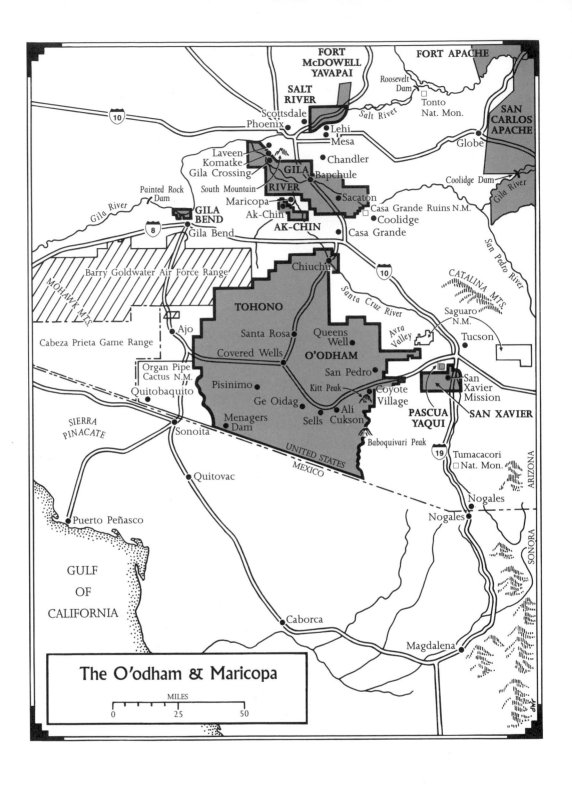

The O'odham & Maricopa

MILES

0   25   50

Though the reservation boundary was less than a mile away, the people were surprised to learn that Indians lived right next door.

White told me: "These are our songs and dances. We want you to see this and know who we are. Our songs and dances are our symphony music; powwow beads and feathers are the 'hard rock.'" The late Dorothy Lewis, leader of a Basket Dance group at Salt River, discovered "that some of these songs and dances and legends are really history."

Diane Enos, a Pima from Salt River, says: "We're running back and forth to jobs and classes in Scottsdale, but not all of us want to integrate. There has to be a revival of what we hold dear—what we eat, what we do with our families, how we feel for this land that we came from. All this is different from outside people."

Just what are these differences? Tohono O'odham, Sand Papago, Ak-Chin, Pima—all are O'odham people. But each group has made its own bargains with its desert homeland.

Reconciled with the Earth

No one knows whether the O'odham carry the heritage of the Hohokam within them—not even the People themselves agree. When the first non-Indians arrived in the Sonoran Desert, the O'odham lived in the same country as had the prehistoric Hohokam. Some O'odham told the early explorers that, though they held the ruined villages sacred, they knew of no connection between their people and the Hohokam (from Huhugam O'odham, "the people who have vanished"). Some Pimas tell a legend of their ancestors driving wicked chiefs from the Hohokam cities and taking the Phoenix Basin for themselves. Many modern O'odham believe, however, that they are the descendants of the Hohokam.

Tohono O'odham Joseph Enos says: "I know that the Hohokam were a very spiritual people, and they understood the Earth and prayed with the Earth and understood the desert." Pima storyteller Archie Russell says: "The older people talked about the Hohokam as if they were the older generation. They had a connection." In 1959, Gila River elder George Webb described his father and his grandfather. From them, he said, "I think I know what those old Huhugam were like." Daniel Preston says simply: "Everything is connected to the past."

In the 1600s, the Spaniards penetrated what they came to call the Papaguería and Pimería Alta (two hundred miles to the south in Mexico there was a Pimería Baja, a lower Pima country where Indian people also spoke O'odham). They called the

Emmett White, Bapchule, Arizona, 1988. The Gila River Pima medicine man and Basket Dance group leader sits with his youngest son in front of their "sandwich house," built from layered adobe and planks.

speakers of the O'odham language by a variety of names. Sobaipuris lived along the Santa Cruz and San Pedro rivers; Pimas lived along the Gila River (allied with the Yuman-speaking Maricopa); Papagos lived in the desert away from the rivers; and Sand Papagos lived in the western and most arid parts of the Sonoran Desert. Pima and Papago were Spanish-applied names that had no meaning to the People, the O'odham.

Nonetheless, life-style and dialect did vary across the basins and ranges marching across southern Arizona. The O'odham themselves speak of Akimel O'odham (River People), whom outsiders call Pimas; Tohono O'odham (Desert, Country, or Thirsty People), the Papago; and Hia C-ed O'odham (Sand People), or Sand Papago. All shared a world view — what the O'odham call the Himdag: the "way of life," embracing Anglo concepts of culture, heritage, history, religion, values, tradition, custom, belief, and language.

Another analysis of the O'odham neatly divides them into One Villagers, the Pima, farmers who lived in permanent villages along rivers with permanent water; Two Villagers, the Tohono O'odham, who divided their time between a summer village where they irrigated fields with seasonal floodwaters and a winter home higher in the mountains near a permanent spring; and No Villagers, the Sand Papago, many of whom moved through the year, through the most extreme desert, farming a little, but gathering and hunting for most of their food.

By 1751, Spanish colonization had become sufficiently onerous to motivate one band of O'odham, led by Luis Oacpicagigua, to attack missions and ranches and push the Spaniards back into Sonora. Spain reconquered Papaguería by 1754, but never re-established missions within the interior of Tohono O'odham territory or in the Gila River Pima villages.

At the same time, Apaches were expanding westward and pushing the eastern O'odham frontier with them. O'odham people fought as allies with the Spaniards against the Apache, and in the process, many of the Desert People clustered around the new Spanish presidios and missions, such as Tumacacori and San Xavier — transforming Two Villagers into One Villagers. Apache raids and, especially, epidemic European diseases periodically wiped out these settlements, until the Sobaipuris ceased to exist, their survivors being absorbed into the Tohono O'odham and Gila River Pimas.

The O'odham nevertheless became Catholicized. Tohono O'odham linguist Ofelia Zepeda speaks of how her people "have taken the religion and mixed it with their culture. There are little churches in tiny villages — and no priests. Maybe just a saint's table and a candle. The villagers go in and say rosary together, and that's it. And yet even very traditional Papagos have thought about these things a lot and come to their own views of heaven and hell."

Joseph Enos says: "We were Christians before we even knew what Christianity was all about. We don't need to be saved, we need to be reconciled — reconciled with the Earth."

Enos told me this as we sat and talked in a desert arroyo, in the soft blackness of a summer night. In such a place, well-spoken words carry more meaning than their simplest content suggests. Enos works with young O'odham people, conducting workshops on self-esteem. This O'odham man, himself both a Catholic and a believer in traditional O'odham ways, speaks of carrying saints' medals: "They are medicine people, too." He speaks of what he learns from the desert tortoise, who says to him: "Come to the desert and I will tell you about creation."

He speaks of his people's values — the Himdag — paralleling Judeo-Christian values: family first, reliance on community, generosity, modesty. He speaks of what the Tohono O'odham need now: a turning away from the competition for power and property taught by Anglo society and a return to the bedrock source for O'odham people — a return to acknowledging the Earth as their teacher.

Once, life was a seamless whole. Food came from the land, brought forth by the rain; rain came from prayer and ceremony; ceremony from the past and from God.

Saguaros topped with iron crosses at the San Jose Mission, Pisinimo, Tohono O'odham Reservation, 1988. The village's resident artist, Frank Mariano, painted the church interior with basket designs. To worship here is to pray inside an O'odham basket.

The land, the desert — put simply, *home* — tied the world together. This was the place from which all grace and wisdom came. These age-old rhythms endured.

People of the Desert

In living with the desert, the Tohono O'odham adapted to its seasons, its aridity, and its heat. The attentive pioneer anthropologist Ruth Underhill, who lived with the People, said that three things distinguished the Tohono O'odham: they never raise their voices; their movements are deliberate; and they are always laughing. It is that patient movement that makes them Desert People — in Underhill's words, "the rhythm slowed down by desert heat to the slow swing of a wave under a ship's bow in a dead calm."

Jim Mattia, Tohono O'odham artist, lives in the pine woods of northern Arizona, near Flagstaff. He told me how he feels living so far from home: "When I go down home to Menagers Dam and speak Papago again to my parents and be part of those people down there, my people, I feel good for a long time after that. In Flagstaff, I try to find my own tranquility in just thinking about the mountains, going through my photo album, speaking to myself in Papago a lot, speaking to the dogs and the cat in Papago." He laughs.

"I miss the animals, the quail — you always hear the quail — the mourning doves, out there. And the heat itself, it's so soothing to the body. I like pines, but they're not mine."

"No matter where we go throughout this world, we will come home to our Tohono O'odham land," says Tohono·O'odham educator Bernard Siquieros. "Once you pass those cattle guards that are the reservation boundary, you feel so much at home. Who would want to live in the desert other than us?"

Ofelia Zepeda says: "The place makes you who you are — the village where you were raised. Other Papagos know your complete life history, your family's history, if they know your place."

I understood just how one can be misled by the huge size of the Tohono O'odham Reservation one day when I drove one hundred and fifty miles across it. After visiting a swap meet in San Pedro, I drove on, asking after several people I hoped to meet; all were guessed to be at the swap meet. In fact, it seemed that the entire population of the northeastern reservation was at the swap meet. These villages and homesteads may look isolated, but they are tied together by an invisible but sturdy network of relationships built on kin and clan, friend and church.

I headed west to Pisinimo and watched Baboquivari Peak framed through a notch as I drove into the village. The great buttressed mountain — sacred home of I'itoi, the Papagos' Elder Brother, who gave this land to the People — looks out over many such far-flung points across the reservation.

I wanted to photograph the saguaros crowned with iron crosses in front of the Pisinimo mission, as well as the church interior painted with basket designs by the village's resident artist, Frank Mariano; to worship here is to pray inside an O'odham basket. But the nuns were rushing off to a festival in a Pisinimo home a few doors away where many cars were gathering. I had time only for a quick look before they locked up.

Later that day, I stopped to visit Joseph Enos in Chiuchu. And where was his mother? At the festival in Pisinimo, seventy miles away.

Tohono O'odham people have long been accustomed to moving through this desert of theirs. In winter, they moved up to the mountains to their "well home" next to a permanent water source — in the old days, a spring, more recently, a deep, drilled well. They moved down to arroyo mouths in summer, building brush dams to spread flash flood runoff over their fields in ak-chin agriculture, planting desert-adapted varieties of corn, cowpeas, melons, tepary beans, devil's claw, and squash in

A mesquite tree and corral frame Baboquivari Peak, sacred mountain of the Tohono O'odham, seen from Ali Cukson, Arizona, 1988.

July and August, hoping for a harvest in October or November that would provide a fifth of their yearly food supply.

Joseph Enos says: "I love corn; it has a nice ancientness about it." Tohono O'odham elder Maria Chona told Ruth Underhill in the 1930s: "Wheat flour makes me sick! I think it has no strength. But when I am weak, when I am tired, my grandchildren make me gruel out of the wild seeds. That is food."

The People of the Desert farmed; they also gathered the wild foods — saguaro fruit, cholla buds, prickly pear fruits and pads, mesquite, agave, amaranth greens and other kinds of "wild spinach," and in the nearby mountains, wild chiles and acorns.

But for the cushion that ensured survival the Desert People relied on the River People, the One Villagers, and their more dependable agricultural resources.

Tohono O'odham traded their labor and their goods — wild foods, baskets and pottery, salt and shells gathered by pilgrims at the Gulf of California, mineral pigments mined from pits at Ajo, and macaws from the Mexican Sierra. In return, they obtained corn, and later, wheat, from the Pima. This yearly visit to the Gila (or south to the Sonoran river valleys) has always been a crucial part of the Two Villagers' economy, and has bound together the bands of O'odham.

Houses came from the desert: saguaro ribs and mesquite for the superstructure, ocotillo ribs for the walls, brush and dirt over it all. Outdoor *ramadas* without walls sheltered most of the daily activity in good weather: sleeping, cooking, eating, visiting, sitting quietly and listening for the breath of the desert.

The Tohono O'odham year began when the saguaro fruit ripened. Women and children gathered the sweet crimson cactus fruits by knocking them from the cacti with long poles made from the woody ribs of the dead cacti themselves. Setting aside pulp and seeds (manufacturing eleven other foods from the fruit besides ceremonial wine), they boiled the fruit down to juice, each family saving a little to donate to the village ceremony. The medicine men fermented this syrup in the "rainhouse" for two days. Then all the men of the band gathered to "drink down the clouds," to "sing down the rain," drinking and drinking until they were as saturated as rain-soaked earth, until the saguaro wine was gone and clouds came to their fields as the summer monsoons began.

This *nawait* is the most sacred ceremony of the Tohono O'odham year. Many families still collect saguaro fruit, even if only during a Saturday afternoon picnic outing. Jim Mattia believes the teachings are still there: when he goes back to Menagers Dam for a ceremony he sees a lot of teenagers involved. But some O'odham complain that the wine feast has become a party, that as much beer as saguaro wine is drunk, that some villages no longer have an elder who knows the proper songs.

Danny Lopez is one who laments these changes. The Tohono O'odham educator dreams that one day he will be able to put on a ceremony in his own village. As he drives back and forth between his family in Tucson and his job in Sells, he sings the old songs. He says, "I need to *remember*."

Traditionally, Two Villagers lived on the narrow edge of self-sufficiency. There were few resources untouched, few new places for villages. Even today, only a sprinkling of the fifty or so Tohono O'odham villages have more than the traditional handful of related families; scarcely a dozen number more than one hundred people. Danny Lopez says that kids take this open space for granted: "They don't realize how

Coyote Village, Tohono O'odham Reservation, 1894. The Tohono O'odham, "two villagers," divided their time between a summer village where they irrigated fields with seasonal floodwaters and a winter home higher in the mountains near a permanent spring. Photo by William Dinwiddie. (Smithsonian Institution photo no. 2789F)

lucky they are." He came with his family one night to sleep in their village — a weekend respite from Tucson. But even in isolated Ge Oidag, "some boys were playing music as loud as their amplifiers would go."

Not until the twentieth century made drilled wells feasible did Tohono O'odham people stay all year in field villages — permanently changing their relationship with water, the land, and their world. For the first time, they built adobe homes with the newly abundant water. For the first time, they could relax in their adherence to the ancient dictum of the People: "Drink only a little water!"

The Sand People lived close enough to the Gulf of California and the Colorado Delta to depend on these resource-rich places during hard times. They harvested shellfish on the Gulf and traded with Yuman peoples on the river. But their *home* was a vast, dry curve of the planet out among the sands of El Gran Desierto, the lava flows of Sierra Pinacate, the spring-fed pools at Quitobaquito and Quitovac, and the rugged mountains along the present international border.

The O'odham word to describe the direction that led southwestward into the lands of the Sand Papago meant "the direction of suffering." Padre Garcés passed through Sand Papago country in 1774, and thought that the People here must be more "ingenious . . . industrious, and have a more alert intelligence than those of the rivers," where living was easier.

Here the No Villagers, the Hia C-ed O'odham, knew where every rock tank might hold a few gallons of moisture after a rare thunderstorm. They knew exactly where to dig in the dunes for sandfood, a delicately delicious parasitic plant that was a staple, along with many other easily overlooked resources. Ethnobotanist Gary Nabhan tallies at least forty animal species and more than sixty plant species that Sand Papagos have spoken of using as food and drink. These Hia C-ed O'odham hunted mountain sheep for food only when all other resources failed, asking I'itoi to send them an old ram that he no longer needed. The hunters left the great curling horns of their prey in piles scattered as shrines across the desert and cremated the bighorn bones to pacify their spirits.

"The books said we were buried under the sandstorms somewhere," Lorraine Eiler told me with an ironic smile. She grew up at Darby Well, an O'odham community off-reservation, near Ajo. Today, she lives and works in Phoenix. In the mid-1980s, she and some twelve hundred other Sand Papagos won their fight for recognition from the tribe.

Until then, Eiler says, "I considered myself an Indian but I couldn't prove it." The Sand Papagos still have no land of their own, but tribal enrollment provides them with access to the same social services, education, and health benefits as all Tohono O'odham. More recognition will come; while Virgil Lewis served as Tohono O'odham vice-chairman, he said: "They have a distinct heritage, a distinct culture, a distinct dialect, and we should not be hampering that. They should be allowed separate representation."

The late Miguel Velasco said: "We are from the sand, and known as Sand Indians, to find our way of life on the sand of the Earth. That is why we go all over to seek our food to live well." Today, however, Velasco's idea of living well is no longer possible.

The Changing World of the Tohono O'odham

The changes began early. When Padre Kino pushed the Spanish mission frontier into O'odham country in 1687, the native farmers already were raising European wheat and watermelons from seeds obtained in trade. Winter wheat gave them a second harvest and a crucial hedge against starvation. The Tohono O'odham quickly adopted such labor-saving miracles as horse- and oxen-drawn plows and wagons, picks, and shovels.

New Spain became Mexico in 1821. By coincidence, modern O'odham "written" history began not long after — when the keepers of calendar sticks began marking a saguaro rib with cuts and slashes to help them remember important happenings since "the night the stars fell," a great meteor shower on 13 November 1833. By the 1840s, immigration brought some bands of O'odham in Mexico to war. They surrendered in 1843; the loss of their land to non-O'odham continued. (The calendar sticks made little mention of these events. More important were snowstorms and earthquakes, Apache raids, births and marriages, lynchings of evil shamans, and the intervillage tally of races, skipping dances, and kickball scores.)

Later that decade, Mexico lost a war — and much of the American West — to the United States. When the victors needed to secure a railroad route along their new southern border, they persuaded a needy Mexico to sell them Arizona south of the Gila River (the 1853 Gadsden Purchase), splitting the Tohono O'odham in two. The United States relied for years on the Pima-Maricopa Confederation and Tohono O'odham warriors to protect the supply routes in these new lands from the Apache.

For decades, this newly invented border made little practical difference to the O'odham people. But in the late twentieth century, the lives of Mexican and American Papagos have diverged so drastically that Mexican Papagos today number only a few hundred, living between the border and Caborca, Sonora. Within southern Arizona, many Sonoran Papagos now live scattered in small ranching and mining towns.

Tohono O'odham tribal chairman Josiah Moore says: "I've always grown up with the idea that the Rocky Point people [at Puerto Peñasco, Sonora] are O'odham — just speaking Spanish. They don't acknowledge this; they call themselves Indians from Mexico. And at the same time, other Tohono O'odham see the people not even ten miles away across the border as being Mexican."

The most powerful connection to Mexico for many O'odham — no matter their origin or current home — occurs each fall during the Fiesta de Magdalena. For more than a century, in one grand October celebration O'odham pilgrims have combined an old-time trading fair, an ancient harvest ceremony, and payment of their respects to the statue of Saint Francis in the cathedral in Magdalena, Sonora. The statue combines the qualities of the Jesuit Saint Francis Xavier, the Franciscan Saint Francis of Assisi, and of Padre Eusebio Kino — first Jesuit to work in Papaguería in the 1600s — whose bones lie with honor in Magdalena's plaza.

The O'odham celebrate in Magdalena with that distinctive mix so characteristic of their approach to life: they wish glory to the saint and then visit the local herbalist. They stock up on Mexican goods and foods (they say that they prefer the texture of Mexican flour, that the coffee is richer and the chiles better). Then pilgrims dance all night — in between rounds of beer and tequila. They twirl and shuffle to

Joseph Head, Pima, holding a calendar stick, Gila Crossing, 1921. Beginning with "the night the stars fell," a great meteor shower on 13 November 1833, O'odham calendar-stick keepers began marking their saguaro ribs with cuts and slashes to help them remember important events. Photo by Edward H. Davis. (Courtesy Museum of the American Indian, Heye Foundation)

chicken scratch, *waila* music in O'odham, a sort of mariachi polka. Ofelia Zepeda says of chicken scratch music that even though it sounds Latin, "it's Papago, not Mexican. It's very much a part of the people's culture; they made it fit what they like."

Until recently, bilingual O'odham spoke Spanish as their second language, not English. Likewise, O'odham names became hispanicized, then anglicized. In the old way, O'odham people had names dreamed by the medicine man, the *makai*, magic names normally replaced in conversation by an often outrageous nickname or a simple kinship term. Missionaries bestowed saints' names in Spanish; later surnames were added by turning a father's name into a surname: thus all the Joseph Franciscos, Mary Juans, and Pablo Joses. When English-speaking Anglos came along, their interpretations of Papago-pronounced Hispanic names changed once more: Xavier became Harvey; Antonio shortened to Antone; Candelaria became Condolorey. Pedro Maria turned into Puella; and Miguel, McGill.

Alliance with the outsiders to fight Apaches encouraged O'odham acculturation. The San Xavier calendar stick keeper felt the mark for 1857–58 and said, simply: "The Whites and the People together started taming the Enemy." By 1872, most Apache bands were officially defeated and confined to reservations. The federal government unfortunately paid less heed to their O'odham allies' need for protected lands. Without hostilities, there were no peace treaties to negotiate with the O'odham. The first Papago Reservation consisted only of the small San Xavier reserve, established in 1874, which did not include the most fertile lands along the Santa Cruz River farmed by the O'odham for generations.

An even smaller reservation was established to protect O'odham living at Gila Bend in 1882 (though most of this reservation was lost in the twentieth century, to executive withdrawal and flooding by Painted Rock Dam). The 1880s also brought the completion of the railroad to Tucson; non-O'odham cattlemen and miners began expanding into Papaguería. Cattle lost by Spanish, Mexican, and Anglo owners formed the initial Papago herds — by the 1870s, the most important resource in the economy of the People.

Not until 1916 did the large Tohono O'odham Reservation surrounding Sells begin to take shape. Sells itself had been a minor O'odham village; with a new Anglo name and the agency established there in 1917, offices and stores expanded until Sells became the reservation's major town and capital. As people from traditional villages began to move there, says Ofelia Zepeda, "for the first time, they lived next door to strangers, not relatives. That was odd for Papago. Enough people live there now so that people can move to Sells and have an aunt or sister already there. But they always say, 'I live in Sells but I'm from someplace else.' "

By the time the San Xavier calendar stick record ended in the 1930s, the decrease in community vitality showed in its entries, a transition from gossipy commentary on village life to a litany of deaths of elders. Instead of noting a champion runner who could shoot off a piece of rainbow with his arrow and wear it on his shoulder in a race — always keeping ahead like a rainbow is always ahead — the last entries tell of skipping dances transformed into commercial events for whites.

When complete, in 1940, the Tohono O'odham Reservation protected only a portion of the traditional lands of the Desert People, although it ranked as the second-largest reservation in the United States (when combined with the areas of San Xavier and Gila Bend). The Sand People lost all rights to their domain, most of which now lies within Organ Pipe Cactus National Monument, Cabeza Prieta Game Range, and Barry Goldwater Air Force Range. In 1976, the Tohono O'odham accepted $26 million in payment for their claims against United States appropriation of their lands.

This judgment validated the long-ignored words spoken by a Papago elder to the whites in 1856, passed down by the keepers of the San Xavier calendar stick:

> Every stick and stone on this land belongs to us. Everything that grows on it is our food — cholla, prickly pear, giant cactus, Spanish bayonet, mesquite beans, amaranth, all the roots and greens. The water is ours, the mountains. There is gold in the mountains. Everywhere I go I walk on gold; I lie down at night as though on a bed of gold, my head rests on gold and silver. These mountains, I say, are mine and the Whites shall not disturb them.

Pulling Together: The Modern Tohono O'odham Community

Over the centuries, outsiders have insisted on viewing the so-called Papago and Pima as "tribes." These foreign ideas have never made much sense to the scattered bands of O'odham, all of whom were most loyal to their families and clans. In the old days, village councils of elders chose headmen. The headman, the Keeper of the Smoke, influenced decisions only a little more than war leaders, hunting leaders, singers, and criers. The entire council talked through any decision until they reached unanimous agreement.

Spaniards introduced "governors." Americans insisted that a chief governor be chosen to speak for all O'odham. During the early twentieth century, a variety of Papago leadership groups formed to fight for land and water rights. The Good Government League formed among boarding-school-educated Presbyterian-converted O'odham. The conservative League of Papago Chiefs, mostly headmen and mostly Catholic, opposed them.

Tohono O'odham women playing an exhibition game of tóka, a double-ball game, at the Tucson Rodeo, 1941. (Courtesy of the Arizona Historical Society/Tucson)

The 1930s brought men from all over Papaguería together to work in the Civilian Conservation Corps (CCC) camps, breaking down some of the isolation between villages and bands, drawing them into a wage-based economy. World War II did the same thing on a grander scale. A tribal constitution was created in 1934, and the tribal council — based on nine political districts on the main reservation, plus one each for San Xavier and Gila Bend — has run tribal political affairs ever since. The late Thomas Segundo remains the best-known tribal chairman, serving during two pivotal times in recent decades. When he first took office in 1947, Segundo was a young veteran of World War II who went to Washington, D.C., the next year to lobby directly for his people's needs in Congress and with the BIA — a crucial innovation in tribal leadership.

Carol Antone, a Tohono O'odham who lives at Ak-Chin, says: "The closer you get to a bigger city, the faster the pace. At home, there is more family time. We eat our meals together — there is the longest dinner time down there!" Tohono O'odham still live in extended families and try hard to carefully talk through each issue in all its nuances. This makes for slow decision making, but it makes for unanimity, too. Take education.

Bernard Siquieros and Rosilda Lopez-Manuel supervised the Tohono O'odham education plan approved in 1987. They are proud of including the viewpoints of "elders, young people, professionals — *everybody*." Siquieros says: "Our original form of government called for complete consensus; we strive for that still." Lopez-Manuel adds: "As a people, we've known we had to pull together to be strong; you can't be successful unless you do."

Each school uses local resource people to teach language and culture. Lopez-Manuel calls it "parent power. Grandparents cry because they can't communicate with their little ones. They *ask* for bilingual education. It made me want to go ninety miles per hour on my programs."

The modern educators do their best to carry on the old ways of teaching. Chona told Ruth Underhill how she learned: "My father went on talking to me in a low voice. That is how our people always talk to their children, so low and quiet the child thinks he is dreaming it. But he never forgets." Danny Lopez hopes that parents will still "teach the kids about listening." Everyone wants to avoid what Tohono O'odham cattleman Joe Enriquez admits: "I wished I'd asked more of the old folks — when there still were old folks."

Siquieros points out that "elders want their children to know how to build fences, to learn the basic skills necessary to manage a herd of cattle. We can use these traditional things to teach math and science." The educational plan lists additional examples: teaching the concepts of probability with Tohono O'odham stick games; asking a high school student to write a computer program to produce the "man in the maze" tribal symbol; and dramatizing O'odham legends in puppetry when storytelling season comes round (Lopez-Manuel says, "Students love it!").

She goes on to describe the program as "a double-shot of education. The two languages reinforce each other." And the program itself reinforces the changing concept of community. "It all comes back to that concept of community," says Juana Jose, another Tohono O'odham educator: "Indian peoples have historically banded together because they needed each other's support. Cooperation, not competition, is crucial in classes."

Ofelia Zepeda says: "Papagos are not in a hurry. Apaches have the right kind of land to make money. Papagos do not. What can you do?" Joe Enriquez, from Queens Well, agrees: "There's no place to spend money anyway, even if we have good jobs." He puts his faith in the Central Arizona Project eventually bringing water to the reservation — legislation passed but not yet funded: "We've got a lot of land that's just wasting."

Enriquez looks through the open door of his house and points to Santa Rosa Peak. "From here to there it's all wasteland; from there on to Santa Rosa, the same, for the same distance. A person with knowledge about agriculture could develop land, scatter fields around *charcos* [stock ponds], grow hay — all they need is water."

Enriquez notes that "there's always someone who jumps up and says 'that's not the O'odham way.' But there's got to be something done. Even if our development is a failure, we will have tried." Danny Lopez, however, points out that "it's hard for people to change. Your *life* is what you're talking about."

The early years of an O'odham cash economy saw Papago potters selling and trading their huge water-cooling *ollas* all over southern Arizona — until electric refrigerators came along. Men cut firewood to sell; basket makers sold tightly-coiled baskets for use as milk pails.

When irrigated cotton took over along the Gila, cotton picking regulated the O'odham work year, until machine pickers displaced people in the 1950s. Most Tohono O'odham today work for wages at least part of the year in Sells, Tucson, Phoenix, Casa Grande, Ajo, and other towns adjacent to the reservations — an extension of the age-old migration to the Gila to work for the Pimas during harvest season.

Basket makers still work with yucca, beargrass, and O'odham-domesticated white-seeded devil's claw — creating art and making a living for their families. Tohono O'odham run cattle, but their grazing land, unfortunately, has been devastated by running too many animals over the years, both by sharing families running too-big herds and greedy families running too-big herds.

Beyond such traditional subsistence, copper mine lease money and a very few jobs with traders and with Kitt Peak Observatory just about sum up reservation-based income for the eighteen thousand enrolled Tohono O'odham, except for the shifting bureaucratic maze of civil service jobs with tribal programs and federal agencies. Unemployment on the Sells reservation claimed one-third of the labor force in 1986.

More than half the tribe now lives full-time off-reservation; Bernard Siquieros says: "We're pushing entrepreneurship. We have to teach our kids that they can create a business, not just be a civil servant." Danny Lopez wants kids to "dream to be the best runner, not just on the reservation, but in the world, period. Whatever they dream, they should work for it. Even those girls, I tell them to dream of being chairperson. Dependency on the government? We can break out of that. Education is the way." Siquieros says: "Today, Indians *can* live in both worlds. It amazes me how some people can feel very comfortable in a college setting and then drive fifty miles to a village and feel comfortable with that."

Sometimes living in both worlds can lead to simple but clever additions to the

Papago Himdag, their way of life. One young Tohono O'odham 4-H member won an award for feeding saguaro seeds to chickens as a high-protein supplement.

The San Xavier reserve must deal with the most relentless confrontation between two worlds because of its huge neighbor, Tucson. Daniel Preston, vice-chairman at San Xavier when I spoke with him, fears that when an O'odham "goes out there, you forget who you are and where you're from. You're competing. You can't say, 'This is my land, this is my people, this is who I'm doing it for.' For us, it's all connected, all simple: home, land, family. We need to move on and understand modern civilization but remember our own culture, too."

San Xavier suffers from the difficulties of an 1890 allotment that parceled out more than half of the tribal reserve to individuals. Luckily, little land was lost to non-Indians, but today, with division by inheritance, four hundred to five hundred people may jointly own an acre, complicating farming, mining leases, and resource management by the tribe. Daniel Preston says: "Allotment didn't work because O'odham people don't understand ownership of something God gave them — especially water. How can anybody own something that God made and gave to his people?"

Tohono O'odham may live in cities, but they say their home lies out on the reservation, and they name their village. They speak in soft voices, at a slow pace, with lilting accents, breathing between the syllables as only an O'odham can. City or reservation, the Tohono O'odham keep an eye out for clouds. Whether they plant petunias and ornamental cacti in their suburban yards or tepary beans, cushaw squash, and dipper gourds in their *ak-chin* fields, they watch the sky; they sing and hum songs to themselves, songs of power.

They wait for rain.

Two Thousand Years of Ak-Chin Farms

For more than two thousand years, O'odham people have farmed the floodplain of Vekol Wash with the runoff waters from summer thunderstorms. In prehistoric times, they grew cotton, squash, and corn. As the first Spanish crops were traded northward, they added Sonoran winter wheat. Later came melons and fruit trees. Today, says Ak-Chin leader Leona Kakar, "we are farming ourselves right out of the residence area" of Ak-Chin Village.

With the end of Apache hostilities and the building of the Southern Pacific Railroad in the 1870s, Tohono O'odham made the Ak-Chin summer field camp site into a permanent village. Nearby, they could work in Pima fields and find jobs with the railroad (Maricopa Station, in 1879, numbered 1,500 people — making it bigger than Phoenix). When Maricopa Station was moved to Maricopa, two miles from Ak-Chin, in 1887, the jobs moved still closer. As agriculture declined along the Gila and the 1918 influenza epidemic hit some Pima villages hard, some Pima families migrated to Ak-Chin.

Today, Ak-Chin people speak a unique O'odham dialect and tend to think of themselves as neither Papago nor Pima but as the Ak-Chin O'odham. They number not much more than five hundred people, but they have taken their reservation from poverty to a model of self-sufficiency.

In 1911, the seventy-one people living at Ak-Chin filed for sixty-three homesteads — a rare tactic for Indians seeking title to their own land. All were eventually voided, but in 1912, the Maricopa–Ak-Chin Reservation was established to protect the village's farmland.

In the old days, Ak-Chin O'odham people could reach the water table — and drinking water — with ten-foot hand-dug wells. Groundwater pumping began about the same year the reservation was established, and by 1914, the water table had dropped thirty feet. By 1970, it had dropped below three hundred feet.

By the 1930s, subsistence farming at Ak-Chin had disappeared. At the end of World War II, only 600 acres of the 21,000 acres of reservation land had been developed. The BIA began leasing the community's farmlands to non-Indian farmers, though the Ak-Chin people profited little. At the same time, chances for work on the big farms of the Casa Grande Valley disappeared in the late 1950s. In 1953, nearly fifty thousand cotton pickers worked for wages from September to December. In 1963, there were little more than five thousand such jobs. The pickers had been replaced by mechanized technology.

At Ak-Chin, under the leadership of Richard Carlyle and with a $12,000 budget, the community created Ak-Chin Farms in 1962. The O'odham started canceling leases and farming the reservation themselves with the help of a non-Indian farm manager. Leona Kakar admitted to me: "We worried and worried and worried. What if we fail?" But by 1964, the 4,900 acres of the new cooperative farm yielded a $21,000 profit. Cotton gin owners financed the crop; the community borrowed and begged for equipment money. By 1977, the tribal farm netted more than $1 million.

After Richard Carlyle's death in 1965, his brother Wilbert and sister Leona Kakar served as chairs, in turn. Kakar began working for the farm in 1963 and remains a moving force behind Ak-Chin Farms today, though she is no longer chairperson. She says of the Carlyle family leadership: "Nepotism doesn't apply here because we're too

Leona Kakar, Ak-Chin O'odham leader, 1988. With hard work and persistence, Kakar won a 28-year fight for water rights for her people. Central Arizona Project water reached Ak-Chin in 1987, making the farming community truly self-sufficient.

small a community. I have made a deal with the good Lord to not let me die until somebody else is trained."

Kakar loves to tell the Ak-Chin success story. She says, simply: "To make the farm succeed, I was willing to do whatever was required of me." What was required of her was "hard work and persistence," a twenty-year fight for water rights for her people.

By 1967, the water table was dropping twenty feet a year and Ak-Chin farmers were getting desperate. After sinking a $100,000 dry hole, they even tried water witching for new well sites. Despite assurances of water rights in the reservation charter, not until 1984 did a negotiated water settlement guarantee 75,000 acre feet annually from Central Arizona Project canals. Delivery began in 1987. With a certainty of irrigation water (as long as the Colorado River can keep the CAP canals full) — and additional funding — Ak-Chin Farms tripled in size, until fully 16,500 acres of the reservation's 21,000 acres has been turned over to cotton and wheat fields, with some recent experiments with potatoes for the potato chip market.

As Leona Kakar watched the last bit of desert by the residence area disappear under the plows, she said to herself, "Oh my god, what have I done!" But she adds: "The only thing we have is agricultural land; we don't even have a mountain on our reservation." Having developed that single resource completely, the community has become truly self-sufficient. Unemployment runs just 10 percent. After expenses, farm profits are split evenly between farm operations and community programs.

Such success brings compromise, as well. Ak-Chin council member Martin Antone points out that the community is so close to Anglos — unlike the isolated Tohono O'odham — that the O'odham language has mostly disappeared. He points to a Hohokam metate freshly dug from the fields sitting on the table before us and says: "I don't think we even knew we had a culture here until we started finding things like this under our land. Kids would just say 'it's a piece of rock.' We have to teach them. Maybe the elders have stories to tell, but somebody's not listening."

His wife, Carol Antone, directed planning for the community museum project — a model " 'eco-museum' reintroducing the culture to the younger generation. It's for the community first; the public comes second." Opened in 1991, the museum describes itself as "a place of memory and a catalyst for dialogue between generations," with programs in oral history, language classes, and archiving of tribal records. Seven community members work full-time — and in the course of their work, earn associate of arts degrees in museum and archive management. The staff knows it will take years of effort to incorporate the institution fully in community life.

Carol Antone speaks of the Hohokam people who lived at Ak-Chin before her: "They were here when times were hard, and they survived. We are a continuance of that. Today we have hard days — but it was nothing like they had it. If you think about that, you get a lot of power. There's no problem too big that you can't handle. Because they did."

Though the Ak-Chin O'odham have chosen to develop their reservation, Carol Antone says: "At Ak-Chin, we can go either way. The culture, it's in there — it's just bringing it out. When someone grows the old crops, everyone wants them. We even used three bags of wild spinach as a prize in bingo. The people who took it said they didn't want to go get it, though they knew the plant — they might miss that soap opera while they were out!"

Martin Antone says: "With the building of the museum, we're giving our kids back their past." With the self-sufficiency of Ak-Chin Farms, today's leaders have given to their children a future, as well.

People of the River

The Pima, the Akimel O'odham, were the People of the River — the Gila River. They figured strongly in the historic Southwest; the Spanish captain Juan Mateo Manje, who accompanied Padre Kino, described them as "haughty and proud." The Pima tried to live by the words of one of their elders: "not to steal, not to go out nights, get up early and go to work, always kill Apaches, and help everyone who needs anything." The resources of the Gila Pimas made their lives less a gamble than those of most desert Indians. They obtained about 60 percent of their food from their fields; their "country cousins," the Tohono O'odham, came each year to help with the harvest.

Archie Russell, raised on the Gila River Reservation, remembers that "as long as we had water here, we had plenty of things to eat. Instead of having telephones, the chief of the village would get up on his house and holler early in the morning, 'We're going to build dams and get ready for the water!' " The bottomlands offered mesquite and other wild plants. Fish came from the river; deer from the mesquite bosques; rabbits from the brushlands. Pima baskets with abstract designs in black devil's claw were prized only a little less than Pima cotton blankets — the paragon of Southwestern weaving before Navajo weavers began making blankets for trade.

During the Hispanic years, Pimas lived beyond the frontier, and both Spanish and Mexican authorities valued them as a strong buffer against raiding Apaches. The addition of winter wheat made their farms super-productive year-round; their population grew, their military defenses against the Apache strengthened and included the new-found ability to muster a cavalry of horse-mounted warriors. Wheat, in fact, became so important that some Pimas began calling May the "wheat-harvest moon," and considered it the beginning of the O'odham year (rather than the traditional new year, "saguaro-harvest moon" in June).

Pima farmers harvested as much corn, cotton, squash, tobacco, gourds, and beans as they could conveniently give away. Two thousand O'odham lived along the Gila when the Spanish first arrived, and One Villager population density along the Santa Cruz and San Pedro rivers may have been even higher.

The first decade of American rule brought boom times: with an enormous new market for their crops, the Pimas did well even though prices were low. The Akimel O'odham grew sufficient food to feed the twenty thousand overlanders migrating through Pima country in the 1850s, as well as all the Civil War troops west of the Mississippi. The U.S. Army purchased two million pounds of surplus Pima wheat in 1862.

The Pima-Maricopa military confederation protected Anglo from Apache at the request of the army and rescued wagon trains from starvation and thirst as they approached the Gila. In the Civil War years, Pima and Maricopa companies served in the Arizona Volunteers. From the 1850s well into the twentieth century, three generations of Azuls — the Pima generals Culo Azul, Antonio Azul, and Antonito Azul — led the confederation. Gila River medicine man Emmett White says of the westward-bound immigrants: "Without the Pimas being here with their wheat and horses and water, they would never have made it to California."

In 1870, the Pima-Maricopa confederation constituted the largest ethnic group in Arizona Territory (even though that year was the low point for their population); by 1880, whites outnumbered them. When Anglos came to the Gila to stay, they accelerated the overgrazing initiated by the Spaniards in the river's headwaters, triggering erosion that led to devastating downstream floods. They diverted the Pima's water.

Despite the eloquence and forceful leadership of Antonio Azul, the Pimas, successful farmers and generous people, were impoverished. Earl Ray, a Salt River Pima, puts it this way: "We're on a tin-can diet because the water was cut off. Our men, instead of tending the fields, went out to the edge of the dry river and drank. The Pimas used to be paternal, with strong men; now the women lead the home. The Pima man is stuck with alcoholism, diabetes, and death."

Gila River elder George Webb sounded only a little gentler in ending his 1959 memoir, *A Pima Remembers*: "The Pimas are a very humble people who like to farm. Perhaps they have been too humble . . . the pace of progress is a little hard on them. I have heard several white men say that the pace of what is called progress today is almost too much for them.

"Think how it must seem to a simple Pima who remembers the Gila River when it was a running stream."

In 1859, the first reservation in Arizona was established for the Gila River Pimas and Maricopas. The end of the Civil War brought Americans west in unimagined numbers. Phoenix was founded, and by 1867, the new settlers were beginning the long tragedy of water diversions from the Gila. Their actions coincided with the worst drought in six centuries.

In the mid-1870s, when even the mesquite crop failed, a group of Pimas and Maricopas moved to the Salt River above Phoenix, hoping for better luck. The Salt River Reservation was created in 1879 to guarantee land for these new villages. Executive orders added acreage to the Gila River Reservation. Water rights remained unprotected, however, and by 1887, no water reached Pima fields along the Gila.

Pimas were forced to shift to a wage economy. They could not weave their clothes, for without summer irrigation water, they could not grow cotton. They had to buy food, since they couldn't grow it. They had to cut down their mesquite forests to sell for firewood in Anglo towns.

Pima calendar-stick keepers called these years "the years of famine" and the first ten years of the twentieth century, "the black decade." By 1904, there had been no crops for six years and most cattle herds had been sold. In 1911, Gila River Pimas created a business committee to lobby for their interests. Even a moderate upswing in Pima fortunes beginning afterwards did not change the fact that Pima culture had been as devastated as the river the People had watched die. Ethnobotanist Gary Nabhan points out that some foods mentioned in the Pima creation legend were never again grown, eaten, or prepared after 1900.

But the Pima remember. Gila River farmer Albert Cooley remembers jumping off the wagon that was to take him to St. Johns School and swimming in the Gila all day. He would jump back on the wagon on its return trip and tell his mother, "school was good."

Sally Pablo lives in Komatke on the Gila River Reservation. She says of her youth: "I look back now and see that the old people were clever in their teaching by example; we learned a lot through trial and error. We didn't have books, but we had the earth, the trees — we had the river to fish and swim in. We drank the water. We stayed out there all day; we never got into trouble. We were rich because we grew up the way we did."

The land speculators continued to defeat Pima interests in water rights battles. Allotment of reservation land between 1911 and 1923 further decreased the clout of the People. Coolidge Dam at San Carlos, intended to save Pima farms, could not even fill its reservoir until 1941, a wet year; non-Indians appropriated its water for their own use once again. An intended rehabilitation of Pima-Maricopa irrigation systems in the thirties destroyed centuries-old ditches and fields and negated age-old Pima soil-conservation techniques. A 1936 Indian Reorganization Act (IRA) constitution at Gila River began the long road toward political power for Pimas to counter such disasters.

World War II did not affect the acculturated Pimas as much as it did more isolated tribes. The war, however, produced an American hero in Pima marine Ira Hayes, one of the men photographed raising the American flag on Iwo Jima. Hayes came home to fame, but no emotional support for his bewilderment. Tragically, he died of alcoholism in 1955 at the age of thirty-three. Other Pima war heros fared better: army captain Sam Thomas managed the tribal farm in the fifties, making it profitable for the first time; J. R. Morago, Jr., served as tribal governor from 1954 to 1960, overseeing revision of the tribal constitution.

By the 1950s, 94 percent of Pimas were literate and 98 percent spoke English. Most were Presbyterian. Anthropologist Edward Spicer spoke of them in 1962 as probably the "most nearly culturally assimilated" of all Southwest Indians. Today, one thousand students a day bus from Salt River to the Mesa public schools. Gila River students bus into Chandler, Casa Grande, and Coolidge. And yet the old days are still close.

Archie Russell remembers his wife Adeline's grandmother: "She had tattoos — the Pima way of being beautiful." Adeline's grandfather wore his hair in the traditional "long hair in curls — like French curls, but thinner." Her father lived in a brush round-house (an *olas-ki*) when young — and in 1988 was still alive at ninety-six. Her mother put mud on Russell's hair to turn it black and glistening, leaving it on for two to three days. She laughs when she remembers: "I couldn't stand it. It was too heavy; I looked like a Hindu!" Russell used her grandmother's basket to winnow wheat in her suburban Phoenix backyard until her boys said: "Don't do that, Mom; people are looking at you."

Winning, Losing, and Living Fully

Weldon Johnson has seen the latest generation of changes come to Pima country. He says: "In our progress, we've lost a lot." Johnson grew up at Gila River in the 1960s, living with his grandparents in a "sandwich house," the layered adobe and plank home that took the place of traditional brush roundhouses.

"If you wanted warm water in the morning, you had to go out in the wagon, gather mesquite, chop wood. You gathered wild spinach, killed rabbits. People call it poverty but it was the happiest time of my life. When I smell mesquite wood burning, it takes me back, it has a story. Today, that mesquite wood is just smoke; it has no story. A lot of youth just don't know what it's like to live without air conditioning, VCRs, telephones."

Johnson told me in 1988: "I'm only twenty-nine and I can remember when Phoenix had clear blue sky. Reservations aren't mobile populations. They can't up and move if the air gets bad, the water gets bad, or the hazardous waste truck flips. They're not snowbirds." Emmett White adds: "We were put out here for a reason: we can stick it out in 100-degree heat without cooling systems!"

The twelve thousand Pimas (and the several hundred Maricopas who live with them on the Gila River and Salt River reservations) must cope with forces seemingly intent on pulling them apart. Water rights remain their primary issue. Phoenix creeps ever closer.

As quiet as St. Johns can feel — just minutes from the city, beyond South Mountain — "Indian culture is being inundated by development," as Weldon Johnson says. George Webb summed up their recent history: "Sometimes I think what is happening to the Pima Indians today is a legend, only it is harder to believe."

Interstate 10 bisects the Gila River Reservation. More and more land at both Gila River and Salt River is leased to industrial parks and to agribusiness using San Carlos Project irrigation technology, creating both jobs and complications. Diane Enos, working with native crops in her garden at Salt River, was sprayed with pesticides by crop-dusters aiming at a nearby leased field.

One result of early acculturation: the Pima have no shortage of educated leaders to deal with these challenges. Alexander Lewis served as tribal chair for twelve years, beginning in 1971. The tribal counsel, Rodney Lewis, was the first Arizona Indian to pass the state bar. His brother, John Lewis, directs the Arizona Intertribal Council. Many Pimas commute from Phoenix suburbs to tribal jobs on the reservations, or from reservation villages to work in the cities.

Farmland, almost all of it leased, covers thirteen thousand acres at Salt River, with cotton the number-one crop, along with watermelons, cantaloupes, onions, carrots, lettuce, grains, and alfalfa. Agriculture employed only 6 percent of Salt River people in 1992, but the water rights settlement that became effective in 1991 could create more jobs by boosting yearly supplies from 15,000 to 85,000 acre-feet. The tribal budget increases by $1 million each year, and as Gerald Anton, chair in 1988, says: "It is not going to go down."

Salt River is caught in a battle over additional freeway development that will pay allottees along the highway route millions, their neighbors nothing; Diane Enos says: "It's tearing the community apart." At Gila River, Sally Pablo has heard "even my little grandson say, 'they're spoiling the desert.' I don't want to ever see the day when this whole area gets turned into big business farming."

Another difficult problem for the O'odham is that "tin-can diet" Earl Ray spoke about. As late as 1919, Tohono O'odham farmers tended 16,000 acres in *ak-chin* fields.

Today, the People plant less than one hundred acres of native crops; few gather the wild foods. Sand Papago elder Miguel Velasco believed that "the reason so many Indians die young is because they don't eat their desert food." He was right.

Diabetes and other nutrition-related diseases virtually unknown among the O'odham in the 1940s now affect up to 35 percent of all Pima adults (and more than half of those over 35) — the highest documented diabetes rate of any ethnic group in the world. The Tohono O'odham suffer sky-high diabetes rates, as well, and chairman Josiah Moore worries that: "If we don't turn this around, as a nation we're down the tubes." Researchers have confirmed that the O'odham evolved a metabolism attuned to the high soluble fiber content of traditional foods such as cactus, mesquite, chia, beans, and tansy mustard. These harvests came each year in half a dozen pulses of bounty, separated by lean times when stored staples like corn and mesquite pod flour fed the people.

O'odham people survived best by storing up calories during the good times, and thus avoiding starvation during the hard times. Mesquite, cactus, and beans constituted half their diet — all are notably slow to release carbohydrates while undergoing digestion. Turn this efficient metabolism loose on a steady diet of highly processed surplus-commodity white flour, lard, sugar, coffee, canned fruits and vegetables, and junk food snacks bought with food stamps at the Mini-Mart, and obesity and diabetes are sure to follow — as O'odham bodies prepare for the famine that never comes.

The traditional diet looks better and better as research results accumulate. Tepary beans and the gums in mesquite flour slow digestion and reduce blood sucrose levels, a possible aid to today's diabetics. Mineral salt from the Gulf of California contains crucial trace minerals. Cholla buds and the O'odham's favorite wild greens are loaded with calcium; saguaro, gourd, and devil's claw seeds with B vitamins; saguaro fruit, wolfberries, and wild chiles with vitamin C. The mucilage coating many of these seeds (to protect them from drought) also slows their digestion and eases glucose tolerance. Reservation education programs aimed at changing diets and encouraging exercise give the O'odham hope. Many young people, however, no longer know the old foods.

Bert Cooley worked most of his adult life for the painter's union in Phoenix; now at home and on pension, he grows the old Pima crops, "just for myself and to keep the hungry Indians supplied. Kids? Heck, you can't get them out there in the fields." (Sally Pablo is more optimistic: "Lots of people grow the old plants. I grow my grandfather's seeds in my garden, I take them into the schools.")

Pablo says: "People may live in a big home in Scottsdale and still have the Pima way. But they've given something up, too." She motioned toward the Komatke senior center's hallways where we talked: "Look at these apartments for the elderlies; we've separated the families — grandparents from grandkids. Grandchildren have to come

The late Dorothy Lewis, Salt River Pima, and the drum for her Basket Dance group, 1988. "I'm an Indian," she told me, "but I'm a modern person, too. My past is behind me, but I'm looking to the future."

visit. The way we grew up, we always had grandparents living with us. We've lost that support system."

The late Dorothy Lewis worked to rebuild a little of that Pima pride. As I left her house at Salt River on a soft spring day in 1988, she walked over to a frame crowded with portraits. She was looking for the photos of her four girls who participated in her Pima dance group. Looking out from the frame were her thirteen children, with birth dates ranging from 1945 to 1968. She began ticking off names and pointing to faces. Her family became a microcosm of the challenges and opportunities facing the People: "I've lost four. This one died when he was a baby; this daughter burned up with her husband and baby when their house burned; these two boys died of alcoholism."

She told me which children had kids, which did not, which boys were singers, which girls spoke Pima. Some always wore their hair long. Some had short hair in Indian School class photos. One daughter studied anthropology at Arizona State University. One grandchild was murdered. One was retarded.

Her husband was resting in the back room of her house, recovering from surgery — a leg amputated after complications from diabetes. Dorothy Lewis remained matter-of-fact, cheery, telling stories, at ease. She walked back to her couch, the drum for her dancers resting on the floor at her feet.

She counseled her children and the young people who joined her Basket Dancers: "Who are you? You're a Pima Indian. You live on the Indian reservation, you make your tortillas on the wood stove, you have your heritage. You know your history. Your ancestors were the first ones to make canals and watered plants and made them to grow. Learn these things and be proud, but be plain, for it's not the Indian way to brag."

Dorothy Lewis told me: "I'm an Indian but I'm a modern person, too. My past is behind me, but I'm looking to the future." Alfretta Antone, vice-chair at Salt River, says: "We choose not only to survive, but to live fully." And as Archie and Adeline Russell say in the Pima benediction that ends their storytelling sessions for kids in schools and museums: "There's no end to learning."

The Maricopa

For most of the twentieth century, Maricopas have been nearly invisible in Phoenix, the metropolis that surrounds them. A few Maricopa women still make pottery — the aspect of the People's culture that surfaces most frequently in non-Indian awareness. Photo by Edward H. Davis, Laveen, Arizona, 1921. (Courtesy Museum of the American Indian, Heye Foundation)

There is still another generation of children coming, one after the other.

When you get older there will be things you know, good things will be coming to you.

You must listen to people; think; listen; you will be happy; you will be strong. All of these things have been going on since the beginning. When you see an old lady or old man you love them, you help them. From the very beginning, you know your relations, you see your relations, you listen to them, you help them. This will go on and on and on.

We are still together, we are still all around here; we're still all here together. Things will be good again. Learn from your elders. Go in a good direction. This knowledge will go on from generation to generation. It will help you go in your life's direction. I have heard this from the beginning many times. We are like one.

It's still the same. It will always go on and on.

Ralph Cameron, Spirit Mountain, 1984

A thicket of mostly unfamiliar names turns up on maps of tribal territories and in the technical literature about the Gila River tribes: Maricopa, Halchidhoma, Kavelchadom, Kahwan, Halyikwamai, Opa, Cocomaricopa.

Only one sounds familiar: Maricopa. *Piipaash.* The People.

"Maricopa" is a common place name around Phoenix, including the name of the county that encompasses the sprawling urban center, but Phoenicians who can say anything about the cultural heritage embodied in the word number few indeed. One memory surfaces most frequently: mention of the great Maricopa potter, Ida Redbird, who died in 1971. As Maricopa elder Ralph Cameron says: "We're still unknown."

The Migration Home to the Gila

Some seven hundred of the people we call Maricopa live today among twelve thousand Pimas on the Gila River and Salt River reservations. (Maricopas do not live on the Maricopa Reservation surrounding the O'odham community of Ak-Chin.) Long ago, the Maricopa lived along the Colorado River among their linguistic relations, the River Yumans — Quechan (Yuma) and Mojave. In those days, four other tribal groups lived nearby on the river: Halchidhoma, Kavelchadom, Kahwan, and Halyikwamai.

These people began moving from the Colorado to the Gila in the time of legends — first the Maricopa proper left, then the Kavelchadom. The Maricopa say that no Pimas lived in their new country when they first arrived. From the 1600s through the 1800s, Yuman migrations continued, mostly in response to the pressures of formal warfare between rival groups—the Quechan and Mojave allied against the smaller tribes. Ralph Cameron says: "We had some kind of misunderstanding at Yuma—fishing rights—and we came here." Another Maricopa elder, Nick Sunn, puts it this way: "The Yumas and Mojave would sneak up there and steal and kill. Our chief said, 'This is no good.'"

When the Spaniards traveled down the Gila River, they found Yuman villages from its confluence with the Salt, at the edge of O'odham country, west to the Mohawk Mountains sixty miles beyond Gila Bend. The Spanish explorer-priests called these warriors the Opa and Cocomaricopa. The Gila villagers farmed a little, but depended largely on mesquite beans, jackrabbits, and fishing. They made pottery in preference to baskets—as they still do, shaping the wet clay between a curved paddle and a stone anvil or pottery mold.

Oral traditions of the Maricopa suggest they were first of the Yumans to come to the Gila; they were the people the Spaniards called Opa. Likewise, the Kavelchadom were called Cocomaricopa but were one people—next to move up from the Colorado River to a section of the Gila downstream from Maricopa villages. In the beginning, they came tentatively, leaving goods and seeds cached in a cave back home in the Colorado River Valley. Mojaves and Chemehuevis quickly took over their old territory; Kavelchadom never again lived along the Colorado.

Migrations of the other three peoples that would become Maricopa happened recently enough for their story to remain vivid for twentieth-century Maricopas. On the basis of interviews with elders in 1930, anthropologist Leslie Spier could state matter-of-factly: "The Halchidhoma fled the Colorado about 1825–1830, going to Sonora, and shortly after joining the Maricopa near the Pima. Ten years later the linked Kahwan and Halyikwamai followed them eastward. The Kavelchadom joined the Maricopa community at about the same time."

In 1846, Anglos settled on the word Maricopa to describe this brand-new community of about one thousand Yuman people. By then the immigrants had moved still farther eastward, to live near their Pima allies in villages on the western flank of Pimería Alta, in the shadow of the sharp spine of the Sierra Estrella. Sometime in the mid-1700s, these Maricopa had joined the Pima in a confederation to fight the Apache. The confederation became the major military force in the Southwest in the mid-1800s and made Anglo settlement possible—a tragic irony, given the later treatment of the People by the Anglos they had protected.

Today the Maricopa live primarily in two communities on the Salt River and Gila River reservations—near Lehi, in the former reservation, on the Mesa (southern) side of the Salt River; and west of Laveen, in the latter, where the Gila and Salt rivers meet. The Laveen Yumans (originally the Maricopa proper) absorbed all the migrant peoples except the Halchidhoma, who today live mostly at Lehi and identify themselves still as a unique people. They speak a different dialect than the Laveen people, who call themselves Maricopa. Persons marrying from one community into the other retain their ethnic identity.

Elders distinguish lineages by tribal names, remembering grandparents who were Kahwan, speaking about women of Kavelchadom affiliations and of Maricopa-Halchidhoma men. In Laveen today, neighborhoods (not unlike the *rancherías* of old) and church congregations are tied to these specific heritages.

Maricopa think of themselves as a united nation in spite of their diverse origins. Says Ralph Cameron: "We call Lehi people 'upriver people.' We're related, we always keep in touch." Nick Sunn says that "there are hardly any Maricopas left at Lehi; they intermarried with Pimas and the grown men have died off." Not quite all of them, however. Hollis Chough, Lehi counterpart to the Laveen elders, does his best to "keep the old ways going."

For years, writers dismissed the Maricopa as a mostly dead culture. They assumed they had lost their ties to their history and become a minor subvariety of Pima. Not until the 1970s, when anthropologists Henry Harwell and Marsha Kelly took the trouble to ask the Maricopa what they believed about themselves, did more outsiders realize that the peoples once known as Halchidhoma and Maricopa had not disappeared. As Ralph Cameron makes clear, his people may be "a tree half fallen down with its roots showing," but he believes, too, that "We will stand again . . . The people will walk again, I say."

Living in a Pima World

Maricopa history since Anglo settlement resembles that of the Pima: ravaged by disease, forced to give up farming when the rivers died and to look for wage work in the nearby cities of the Phoenix Basin, disrupted by allotment, subjected to the whims of reservation and BIA politics. According to Ralph Cameron: "White men came in and allotted land to us — only ten acres, not enough to farm. The whole community was allotted in 1915. I've got about nine acres to divide up among my children, and then it just goes on and on and on. It comes out infractionated." Says Nick Sunn: "Pretty soon you'll have nothing big enough to bury yourself on."

Cameron also told me of his childhood, when the nearby Salt and Gila rivers still ran: "We swim there, we hunted there, we fished there. It breaks my heart to see those rivers dry. That's where I started out my life. That's where I learned to build my con-

Ralph Cameron, Maricopa elder, at the Laveen Community Center, 1992. Some 700 Maricopas live today among 12,000 Pimas, west of Laveen on the Gila River Reservation and at Lehi on the Salt River Reservation.

fidence, my patience. Sometimes I sit there all day long and I don't catch a fish, but I learned something valuable. I learned how to be calm and collected here; when I was in the South Pacific in World War II, I already knew."

Ralph Cameron spent his working years in a Los Angeles steel mill via the BIA relocation plan of the fifties, but he returned to Laveen when he retired. He told me that as retirement approached, he counted the days: "I had the pickup all ready. I got in and came back the next day."

I spoke with Cameron in the Laveen community service center in 1992 as several Maricopa men unloaded a truckload of commodity foods passed on to the tribe — surplus from the Persian Gulf War: "In my day we had nothing. Now people have the opportunity to work in the city, but nobody takes it." He waved toward the cans and boxes. "It's all on account of that. Younger people here don't even know food comes from the ground."

Across a patchwork of fields I sat with Nick Sunn, who at seventy-nine had just lost both feet and one eye to diabetes: "Our old folks ate fried foods but they could work it out. We used walking plows; there was lots of physical activity. When I was young, we used to sleep all in a bunch. My grandmother was in the middle and she would tell us stories till we go to sleep. Then the machine came in."

Laveen residents believe that urban sprawl may yet push them from the land they hold dear. Their once-isolated community butts up against a persistently growing metropolis. Irrigation water from their wells is insufficient for their farmable acreage and has become too alkaline to use on gardens — good only for cotton and alfalfa.

These Yuman peoples have long lived near the Pimas. They shared the old earth-covered brush roundhouse architecture; Western Apache called the O'odham and Maricopa together the "sand-house people." Today, they share tribal government — with the Maricopa colony at Laveen and Lehi's Halchidhomas represented as distinct districts in tribal councils. On the Gila River Reservation, as Maricopa/Pima educator Lucinda Williamson points out, "they have only one vote out of seven, so the projects tend to go elsewhere." Nick Sunn is more blunt: "The Pimas outnumber us considerably. Anything they get from Washington, they use; we hear about it afterwards. We've been neglected here for such a long time." Ralph Cameron believes that "we need leaders. When you lead, you have to work, give a little out of your own pocket — and stand to have a few rocks thrown at you."

Day to day, Pima and Maricopa communities remain remarkably distinct. Nick Sunn says: "Even though we've been living together for many years, there has been intermarriage only with the closest Pimas." Ralph Cameron told me: "We try to keep away from politics as much as we can; we follow our own way." Says Lucinda Williamson: "There isn't anybody down there in District 7 [the Laveen Maricopa community] that *doesn't* speak Maricopa. It's always amazed me." Her observation may be dated. Ralph Cameron says: "The young people can't speak it; Papago and Navajo are easy compared to Maricopa."

The Maricopa sometimes contemplate a separate existence. Lucinda Williamson said to me: "Nobody can really tell me why the two tribes are on the same reservation. I wonder what it would take for the Maricopa to petition Congress to be an independent tribe. They could get their own services, schools."

Both Maricopa communities strive to pass along something of the old ways. They tell stories of their warriors in the great Pima-Maricopa Confederation, including the massacre of Quechan and Mojave at Maricopa Wells in 1857, the last major formal battle between Indian nations in the Southwest. They tell of their leader Juan Chevería, who led the Maricopa company of Arizona Volunteers protecting the southwestern flank of the Union during the Civil War.

They tell of the power of dreams: the oldest way of learning, and one that helps define the Yuman world view. Last Star, a Maricopa elder, told Leslie Spier: "Everyone who is prosperous or successful must have dreamed of something. It is not because he is a good worker that he is prosperous, but because he dreamed."

Lucinda Williamson says: "Maricopas have a better sense of their religion than Pimas. You don't hear them talk about it, but you sense it." They mourn their dead in solemn cremation rituals; until this century, Maricopa villages constantly shifted location, moving when someone died and his or her residence and possessions were burned, forcing survivors to build a new home elsewhere.

The mourning ceremony is the most visible part of Maricopa-Halchidhoma culture today — though Ralph Cameron worries that the cremation ceremony is dying out. It is this tradition that keeps the people in touch with other Colorado River tribes, participating in a network of church events, funerals, singing, and visits to friends and relatives.

Ralph Cameron speaks of Maricopa children needing to be taught the traditions, helping "fill in those empty spaces" left by public schools, "to know who they are, where they came from, where they are going. The desert speaks, if you want to listen to it. That's what every kid is looking for — a part of that emptiness being filled in with what he is supposed to be fully."

What will fill this emptiness? Cameron, and his son Leroy, say that it is the right to live on the land, to eat native foods, to have their Maricopa religion, to maintain family and community relationships. To be "culturally aware of who we are, where we came from, and where we are going." In this way, Ralph Cameron reconciles his worries with his faith in the strength of his people.

The Colorado River Tribes

Irrigating fields, Colorado River Reservation, Arizona, 1988. At CRIT, cotton, alfalfa, melons, and lettuce are the big crops, and the tribal cooperative farm is the largest on the reservation.

Then Mastamho . . . put the stick into the ground again and, as he drew it out . . . stepped aside and

watched the water run. This time it ran to the south. It made the [Colorado] river.

. . . Then a boat came out and floated on the river . . . He put the Mohave into it, and the

Yavapai, the Yuma, the Maricopa . . . Then he entered himself and let the boat float. It went south

with the river . . . He said: . . . "I make the boat lean to one side because I want the country to be

wide there. I make it lean to the other side because I want the land to be flat there too." When they

came to the Needles Peaks, the boat went straight along and the river became narrow. Wherever the

boat went straight, the river went straight; where the boat turned, the river now bends. When they

came farther down, where the Parker reservation is now, Mastamho wanted to make more valley, so

he again tipped the boat to each side and made flat land on both sides of the river. So they arrived at

Yuma. Here he tipped the boat first to the right and then to the left; so that there the flat land is very

wide and there are no mountains except in the distance. Then they came to the sea. Then Mastamho

took the people out of the boat and let it float away.

Nyavarup, Mojave creation narrative, 1902

The People emerged at Spirit Mountain.

In southernmost Nevada just west of the Colorado River, this peak that Anglos call Newberry Mountain tumbles down from its great cream-colored double crest, its sharp ridges contrasting with rounded outcrops of granite boulders. At its base, Grapevine Canyon leads east, toward the river. On the canyon walls, petroglyphs tell the sacred stories. On the canyon floor, the rusty olive-green of creosote bush hazes the dry air with color just above the desert pavement. Chollas and Mojave yuccas grow scattered among the shrubs.

Here, all peoples spilled into this world — created by Mastamho, according to the Yumans. Here, each people began their journey home. The Yumans stayed closest to Spirit Mountain. They live there today.

I stand here where the People emerged from the underworld to live on the Earth. I imagine this time — small bands of people lost in the rugged ranges, their campfires mirroring the fire of the stars; shamans singing at the edge of the red river, asking for guidance, for a dream, for a sign. They moved out from this canyon and fanned into the desert. Most turned to the right down the broad alluvial plain of the Colorado to

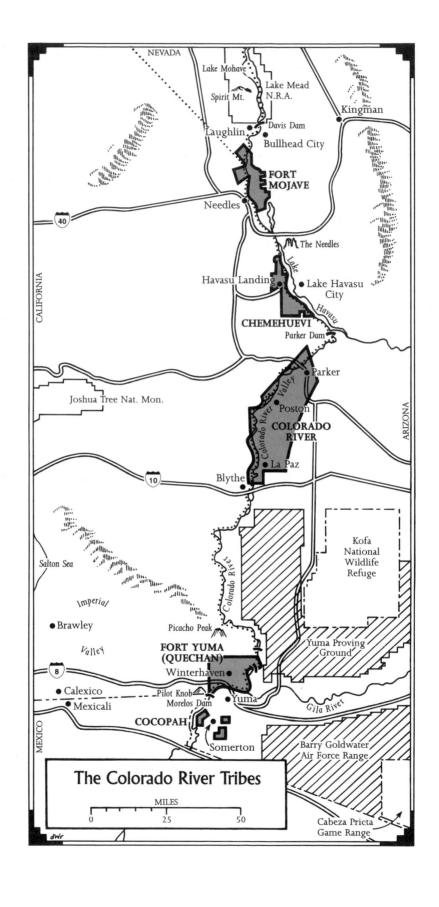

The Colorado River Tribes

NEVADA

Lake Mohave

Lake Mead N.R.A.

Spirit Mt.

Kingman

Davis Dam

Laughlin

Bullhead City

FORT MOJAVE

Needles

40

The Needles

Havasu Landing

Lake Havasu City

Lake Havasu

CHEMEHUEVI

Parker Dam

CALIFORNIA

Parker

Colorado River Valley

Poston

Joshua Tree Nat. Mon.

COLORADO RIVER

La Paz

10

Blythe

ARIZONA

Kofa National Wildlife Refuge

Salton Sea

Colorado River

Imperial

Brawley

Picacho Peak

Yuma Proving Ground

Valley

FORT YUMA (QUECHAN)

8

Winterhaven

Calexico

Pilot Knob

Yuma

Mexicali

Morelos Dam

Gila River

COCOPAH

MEXICO

Somerton

Barry Goldwater Air Force Range

MILES

0   25   50

Cabeza Pricta Game Range

dwr

become river people; others bore straight ahead, up and over buttresses of the first range to the east, drawn by distant summits.

The word that embraces the People from Spirit Mountain, "Yuman," describes a linguistic and cultural group and includes many tribes. On the Colorado live the River Yumans: the Mojave people, under the shadow of Spirit Mountain itself; the Quechan (or "Yuma") downstream, where the Gila and Colorado join; and the Cocopah, all the way down the river at the delta. (Later, a band of [non-Yuman] Southern Paiute, the Chemehuevi, came to live on the river, as well in Mojave country.)

Other Yumans live beyond the world of the Colorado River. The Maricopa emigrated from the Colorado to the Gila. Upland Yuman people moved beyond the river, to live in the mountains and plateaus of northwest and central Arizona as the Hualapai, Havasupai, and Yavapai. Still other Yuman tribes live in the deserts of southern and Baja California, beyond the American Southwest.

River people were people of plenty, living in an oasis valley in a nearly rainless desert. Before the river was dammed, spring floods brought rejuvenating silt to the fields each year; the river carried a heavier silt load than either the Mississippi or the Nile. Farming produced rich harvests; the river provided fish; bottomlands nourished mesquite trees heavy with bean pods; and hunters came home with small game and an occasional deer or desert bighorn sheep. Trips for wild plant roots and berries could take the People sixty miles from home.

Yuman river people shared a belief in the power of dreaming that formed the "basis for everyday life," in the words of Mojave storyteller Herman Grey. He goes on: "Knowledge is not a thing to be learned . . . but something to be acquired by each person through his dreaming . . . Conscious learning seems to him nearly impossible, and he is convinced he has dreamed for the first time, or has dreamed repetitiously, the things which all Mohaves know in common."

Patrick Miguel, a fiery Quechan leader who died in 1959, said: "You know how some men are quick and strong and know the things to do, how people like to do things for them, and how they have a gift for getting everybody cheerful. Well, those men were leaders (*kwaxót*). When a man knew he had the power to be a good leader, he told his dreams. If his dreams were good, his plans would be followed, but if they were poor and stupid others would tell him so and he could do nothing."

Today the river tribes remain in the haven of the fertile Colorado River Valley, with the stunning desert on either side. As Curtiss Martin, a young Mojave man, says, "You're not really in the desert when you're on the river."

THE MOJAVE

The Mojave people were warriors, farmers, and fishermen who dreamed their way to positions of authority and cried for their dead in moving cremation ceremonies. "Mojave" (and the alternate "Mohave" preferred by some anthropologists and tribal members) comes from the hispanicization of the word these people use for themselves, *hamakhav*, which may have no literal translation or may mean "people who live along the water."

In prereservation days, the Mojave tribe — and it truly was a tribe, with the ability to come together as one people for warfare — lived along the Colorado River from about fifteen miles north of present Davis Dam south for 170 river miles almost to modern Blythe, California. Throughout this region, bands and family groups lived in scattered settlements — *rancherías*, more like farms than villages. Total Mojave population may have reached twenty thousand. On rises above their crops and the fickle river, the People built their summer *ramadas* and their winter houses of thatch insulated with mud and sand. Mojaves wandered far, mostly for the wonder of the journey itself rather than for trade, reaching even to the Pacific Coast and covering much of the distance in long, loping runs of up to one hundred miles in a day.

Mojave elders speak of mesquite as their "tree of life." Fresh mesquite beans yielded juice to drink. Powdered pith from bean pods could be eaten as mush or baked into cakes. The People used the bark to make shoes and clothing; they dyed their hair with mesquite. Roots could be carved into cradles, instruments, and tools. Sap made glue. Pottery was fired with mesquite wood. Mojave people used mesquite in every phase of their lives from birth until death, when the tree fueled the fires for their cremation ceremonies. Today, the Colorado River Reservation has discussed preserving part of their mesquite *bosque* — the largest stand remaining in the state — as a permanent wood supply for cremations.

Mojave leaders were skillful orators who earned their position by dreaming "great dreams." More mundane dreams were important as omens. Some great dreams conferred power in battle against the Mojave's old enemies, the Maricopa and Cocopah. Other dreams gave a person the power to cure or taught a new song or a special funeral oration. Young people hoped to have great dreams, but no one could fake power; unless successful deeds followed a dream, the dream could not be authentic.

The elderly Mojave shaman Nyavarup spoke to anthropologist A. L. Kroeber at Needles in 1902 about some of the implications of dreaming: "I saw all that I am telling about Mastamho . . . I shall see it all again tonight when I dream . . . Doctors do not learn from older doctors: they are born to be doctors; they learn only from Mastamho."

Mojave camp, circa 1885. Mojaves lived in scattered rancherías, more like farms than villages. On rises above their crops and the fickle river, the People built their summer ramadas and their winter houses of thatch. Photo by Ben Wittick. (Courtesy Museum of New Mexico, neg. no. 15965)

The most powerful of Mojave rituals was the cremation ceremony. Mourners sang their song cycles (of which there were thirty, with two hundred songs in each); orators spoke of the good deeds of the mourned. And the departed person's possessions went up in flames with the body — originally including his or her house and offerings from the mourners. Still more elaborate ceremonies were performed for dead warriors or leaders.

Traditionally, Mojave people depended more on agriculture than did any other Colorado River tribe, growing about 50 percent of their food. Men planted panicgrass, tepary beans, corn, pumpkins, and melons in the flooded bottomlands along the river in spring, and women did much of the fall harvesting. Only in drought did famine threaten, and the People then would spend more time hunting, fishing, and gathering wild food plants.

The river flowed through their lives, their seasons, and their dreams. The People swam across the Colorado, sometimes with a log for extra flotation, and pushed food or small children ahead of them in large "ferrying pots." They used rafts only on long trips.

The Division, Recombination, and Evolution of a People

The river brought the Mojave their first experiences with non-Indians, though few exploring soldiers and priests penetrated to this far corner of Spanish and Mexican territory. In the 1800s, visitors began to come more frequently.

American fur trappers en route to California forded the river in Mojave country, and the People did not always welcome their presence. The Mojaves helped Jedediah Smith in 1826, but when the intense young leader of the mountain men returned to the Mojave villages in 1827, the People had recently tangled with a party of New Mexico trappers. The Indians took their revenge on Smith's group, killing ten men while Smith escaped with eight others to cross the desert to the Spanish missions on the coast.

Mojave warriors stayed busy with their own wars, ousting the Halchidhoma tribe (whose descendants migrated to the Phoenix Basin to join the Maricopa) from the Colorado River Valley between 1827 and 1829, and raiding and battling against other tribal alliances. Not until the California gold rush did many Anglos venture into Mojave country, but when they did come, they came for good. Mining and railroad towns were their beachheads.

Introduced disease devastated the Mojaves long before they began to fight Anglo encroachment face-to-face. Already weakened by a great loss to the Pima and Maricopa in 1857, they chose few battles with whites. When the U.S. Army built Fort Mojave in 1859, the Mojave settled for permanent peace.

With the building of the fort, the Mojave leader Irrateba (also spelled Yara Tav) convinced a large group of followers to move to the Colorado River Valley area. The territorial Indian agent sent Irrateba to Washington, D.C., in 1865, to prove to him that Mojaves could never defeat the army and to have him speak with Congress in favor of a reservation. The same year, pressured by an 1862 gold strike at La Paz, at the south end of the Colorado River Valley (and the south end of Mojave country), Congress created the Colorado River Reservation for "all the tribes of the Colorado River drainage." As in many stories from tribal histories, this was a complicated time.

Irrateba was a progressive, making his move with encouragement from whites, believing it best for his people. Conservative Mojaves (about 70 percent of the People's total numbers) stayed behind in Mohave Valley, their land protected by a reservation

Mojave leader Irrateba permanently divided his people when he and his followers moved to the Colorado River Valley when Fort Mohave was built in 1858. In 1865, Congress created the Colorado River Reservation for "all the tribes of the Colorado River drainage." (Smithsonian Institution photo no. 53567)

in 1880; for years they called the Colorado River Valley Mojaves "the weak ones." In turn, the Colorado River Reservation Mojaves accused the Fort Mojave people of not being able to take care of themselves, and therefore tied to living near the fort.

Today these old animosities have dimmed. Fort Mojave chair Nora Garcia says of the Colorado River Reservation Mojaves: "They are us. They are our people. They are our bloodline." Still, the Mojave now live in two groups, with separate tribal councils, separate problems, and separate futures. The Fort Mojave Reservation covers parts of Nevada, California, and Arizona along the Colorado River near Needles, California. It includes the Mohave Valley, the ancient traditional homeland of the People, within sight of Spirit Mountain. Fort Mojave enrollment numbers more than eight hundred. Most Mojaves, however, today live sixty miles to the south, on the Colorado River Indian Reservation between Parker, Arizona, and Blythe, California, a community unique in combining Mojaves, Chemehuevis, Hopis, and Navajos on a single reserve.

Both reservations include some of the most fertile irrigable land retained by Southwestern tribes, and farming remains important. Both groups of Mojave still cremate and mourn their dead with the old ceremonies that give them an unqualified reason to maintain their language and their songs. Fort Mojave councilman Lew Barrackman knows this is Mojave land: "We're placed here by the Almighty — from the beginning. 'People along the river' is what the Almighty calls us. All our land around here is named in Mojave."

The late Herman Laffoon, a Mojave elder from the Colorado River Reservation, laughed when he told me: "I want to start a World War III to get back Spirit Mountain for our reservation. They should have included it in!" Lew Barrackman, at Fort Mojave, is proud of his roots below Spirit Mountain: "We didn't move; we didn't budge. Why should we go down to Parker and be placed in a place we didn't know? If necessary, we'll die along with the land."

The amalgamation of tribes on the Colorado River Reservation began immediately after its establishment in 1865. About eight hundred Mojaves settled close to the Indian Agency, near Parker, Arizona, at the north end of the new reservation. On their south, some two hundred Chemehuevis joined them — Paiute speakers who had moved to the river from the deserts during the half century before, with the intermittent approval of the Mojave.

Influenza swept through the reservation after World War I, and whites encroached on Indian land. During the 1930s, dams on the Colorado made traditional floodplain agriculture impossible. In the Bureau of Reclamation's own words, the lower Colorado River — between reservoirs — changed "from a natural-looking stream to something resembling a canal."

The tribes understood that if they did not develop their land, non-Indians would. They also knew that Mojaves and Chemehuevis simply did not exist in numbers sufficient to fill the reservation. Mojave elder Joe Sharp looked at my fair skin and put it this way: "We were fought into a corner. It was dry in there; so you can dry up in there. Later it started to get green in there, so you came back with your claws and tried to get some of it back."

During World War II, the federal government interned thousands of Japanese-

In the House of the Sun

Saguaros at sunset below the Sierra Estrella.

Gila River Reservation, Arizona, 1988.

Bert Cooley, Pima farmer,
still grows the old crops — including
two annual harvests of tepary beans.
Gila River Reservation, Arizona, 1988.

Danny Soliz, five-year-old
Ak-Chin O'odham boy, on
a float in the O'odham Tash
parade. Casa Grande, Arizona,
1992.

Juanita Ahil, Tohono O'odham,
gathers saguaro fruit. Avra Valley,
Arizona, 1984.

Spirit Mountain, Nevada, as seen from Spirit Mountain Drive in the new HUD housing project.

Fort Mojave Reservation, Arizona, 1988.

Contemporary Maricopa effigy pot by Therena Bread.

Gila River Reservation, Arizona, 1992.

A chicken scratch band plays at the Tohono O'odham Nation Spring Arts Festival. Sells, Arizona, 1988.

Jose Guichapa, Yaqui,

stands in front of Joe Acuña's

mural of his people's history.

Guadalupe, Arizona, 1992.

San Xavier mission and cemetery. Tohono O'odham Reservation, Arizona, 1984.

Fields stretch southward on the resource-rich reservation of the Colorado River Indian Tribes (CRIT). Poston, Arizona, 1988.

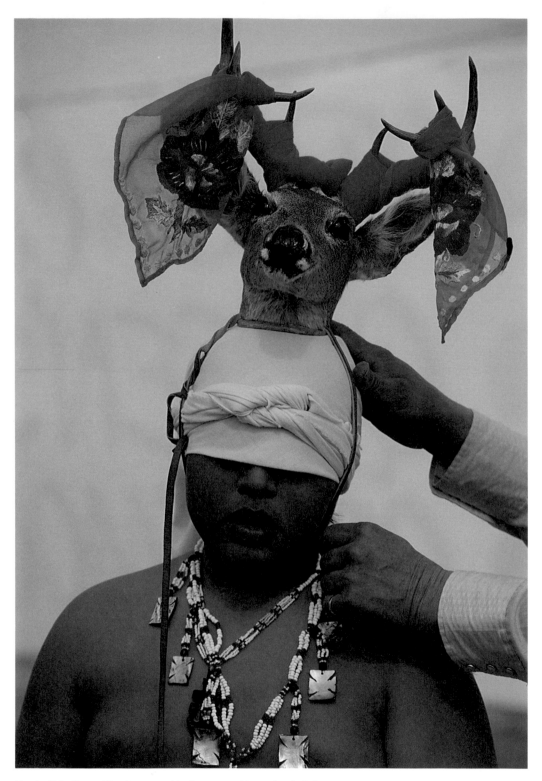

Narciso Bule, Pascua Yaqui, prepares his eleven-year-old son, Angelo Bule,

to perform as a deer dancer. Casa Grande, Arizona, 1992.

Mr. and Mrs. Lubbock (*Arenaya* and *Oacha*), Mojave, listen to a Bureau of Reclamation official describe the wonders of the new Parker Dam, circa 1939. Parker Dam flooded the Chemehuevi Reservation, driving most of its residents to the Colorado River Reservation. Photo by William Fox. (*Courtesy National Archives, photo no. 75-N-CO-45*)

Americans on the Colorado River Reservation, creating the town of Poston. To do so, it appropriated twenty-five thousand acres of reservation land without the approval of the tribe. After the war, the BIA acted on that almost-forgotten clause in the reservation's charter calling for a reserve for "all the tribes of the Colorado River drainage." They opened the land to Hopi and Navajo immigrants, families on hard times from the Depression days of drought and stock reduction in their own reservations — families in need of land and water.

These plateau peoples moved into the empty barracks left from the Japanese-American concentration camps, then onto the reservation itself, colonizing land south of the farms already developed. The same ruling that allowed immigration guaranteed — for the first time — title over their northern reservation lands for the Mojaves and Chemehuevis.

When the Mojaves and Chemehuevis became concerned that they would be overwhelmed by these "outsiders," they stopped immigration in 1952. By then, 148

Navajo and Hopi families had become part of the unified Colorado River Indian Tribes (CRIT).

Today all four peoples call this place home, and with intermarriage, a new tribe is evolving, the "CRIT Indians." The few remaining Mojave elders resent these facts. Amelia Flores, a younger Mojave woman, says: "My children can't know the hurt the elders felt when they went through that. They lived it and fought it; my generation just accepts it." Tribal education director Dennis Patch, a Mojave, notes: "A lot of tribes in the past have disappeared. The four tribes here were tough; we have to adjust even more than most. Though over half the Mojave families still speak their language in their homes, eventually all four tribes may lose their languages. But we gain something, too: we adapt easier."

Patch says: "The outside world is at our doorstep: HUD housing, satellite dishes, paved roads, newspapers delivered to our doors." He cannot know the future, but he believes that "an Indian can never stop being an Indian." The values — "respect your elders, cherish your children, respect Mother Earth, treat each other right — that alone gives you a sense of tribalism."

Mona Fernandez, whose parents were immigrant Hopi and Havasupai, feels that the Colorado River Reservation is home, a place filled with a "simple richness." "This place, it's my heart and soul. I feel like I have a real close relationship with this land here. My kids are part Mojave, so that helps."

The Mojaves still dominate in numbers and political power, and the three other tribes respect that position: it is indeed the Mojaves who have the ancient ties to this land. Navajos and Chemehuevis have taken their turns as CRIT chairmen. Nonetheless, the Navajo and Hopi have been known to say: "You guys would still be living in mesquite brush if we hadn't come down here. We wouldn't have all this area farmed and producing."

"Now, We're All Mojaves."

Immigration to CRIT has affected Fort Mojave people as well. Their chairperson, Nora Garcia, told me: "I am a creation of that governmental setup. My father, a Mojave, met my mother, a Hopi-Tewa, down there when her family immigrated to CRIT."

Garcia has struggled with her identity. She told me: "I was only twenty-eight when I became chairman. I knew there was a reason for me sitting at this desk. But I didn't have any answers. I had a lot of problems dealing with the responsibility; I felt a sense of loss about our beliefs. But I grew up in a hurry.

"All we can do is instill the pride that was lost with the language and the culture.

We can't bring the past back. But we can give people pride for the future. We're here. Maybe we are a bit more modern than some reservations, but we will remain here."

Weldon Johnson, a Pima/Maricopa who has directed the CRIT tribal museum, knows why the museum exists: "Twenty years from now, when the CRIT Indian decides he wants to be Mojave, he can come back here and find out what that means." Allie Welch has already found the museum the place to go when he "feels a little bit lost." The young man, of Navajo/Mojave/Chemehuevi/Anglo heritage, told me: "When I want to find my identity, I have to go to that little museum. I'll look back and I'll see that this is the way it was when my parents were younger. They lived here and it was 'pure.' Everything they were taught was from their parents, and their parents, and nothing had changed in all those years.

"I look at the old pictures. I look at the old artifacts. And I see the way it used to be. You see pictures of the old people — who now live like Anglos — when they were children and they were living in these native homes. Mud walls, thatched roofs: it looked like a wind could come along and blow it away. They were content and didn't know anything better than that."

Welch says, wistfully: "These things are not clear anymore."

Conner Byestewa came to CRIT from Hopi when he was seven years old. He says: "Ceremonial things are taken care of at Hopi; we left all that behind. Since I was born at Hopi, I've got to understand what Hopi is, just like I have to understand Mojaves since I live here. I have no regrets. Now, we're all 'Mojaves.'"

As "Mojaves," what the CRIT Indians have that other reservations do not is the river and the iridescent oasis green of the fields its waters irrigate. Curtiss Martin, a young council member, emphasizes that "we have to rely on the river, and we have the resources to go where we want to go."

The riches of the Colorado River Reservation's resources mean jobs. Unemployment at CRIT (with a population of about three thousand) dropped from 33 percent in 1980 to 10 percent in 1985. Fort Mojave, checkerboarded with private land and therefore hard to irrigate successfully, cut unemployment in the 1980s, but the actual numbers remained distressing, with 46 percent of the tribe's labor force still unemployed. Lew Barrackman says: "We've got some good farmland, but water has been the issue." Some fifteen thousand acres of Fort Mojave Reservation land is leased.

At CRIT, cotton, alfalfa, melons, and lettuce are the big crops, and the tribal cooperative farm is the largest on the reservation. Agricultural development approaches the maximum area possible with available water rights — more than 130,000 acres of irrigated land. In spring, neatly furrowed fields line the highway south from Parker, the rhythmic lines of the plow leading away to the ragged horizon studded with the sacred mountains of the Mojave. Ducks fly through the sky; kingfishers perch on the power lines. Egrets and herons fly up from irrigation ditches and canals into crimson sunsets.

Leased land brings pesticide spraying into backyards, but it brings income, as well, particularly from farming operations and from tourist development along the "Parker Strip." This stretch of the river, mostly within the reservation, can see 125,000 southern California tourists on a single weekend. Lease money from tribal land is reinvested in tribal programs; privately owned lease land helps some individual families.

The northern Mojaves did not form a tribal council until 1956, twenty years after the Colorado River Reservation. Only then did they push agricultural leases from five-year to long-term ninety-nine-year leases, attracting investors capable of staying in business. Their first improved housing in thirty years was built on the outskirts of Needles in 1976; housing on the Arizona side of the reservation has been added since.

Plans for a one-thousand-acre casino development on the Nevada portion of the reservation are close to completion, after "years of hurdles," in Nora Garcia's words. Fort Mojave people also plan to lease land for homes on the northern reservation border, near the booming communities of Laughlin, Nevada, and Bullhead City, Arizona.

I asked Lew Barrackman, at Fort Mojave, how a reservation ensures that it is paid fairly for its leases. His answer: "A good attorney."

Both the Fort Mojave Reservation and the Colorado River Reservation have valuable resources: good farmland and booming tourism nearby. In addition to managerial skills and fair leases with non-Indians, both resources require considerable capital to be successfully cropped. "Creating jobs," says Nora Garcia, "is a business. You must separate it from politics and government. And it will happen only in short spurts; you can't put everybody to work at once, without having management in place."

Mojave elder Thomas Stevens says: "Young people talk about money, they talk about gambling and bingo. We older people, we learned from the old people. They don't talk about money; they talk about *land*, about the future, about what's going to happen to our people."

Development plans cause a certain amount of tension with the Anglo enclave communities of Parker and Needles. Balances of power must be worked out. Hiawatha Polacca, a Hopi/Havasupai freshman at Parker High School, told me: "It means something to be Indian. Some people give us more respect. Some people give us dirty looks."

The late Elmer Gates was the only active Mojave potter when I spoke with him in 1988, when he was still "playing with the clay, picking his designs from petroglyphs on old mountainsides." Young Mojaves did not learn what he knew; his people have

The late Elmer Gates, 1988. Gates was the only active Mojave potter at the time, still "playing with the clay, picking his designs from petroglyphs on old mountainsides."

little connection with their traditions beyond the surviving cremation ceremony. Allie Welch calls the new way of life they are forging "an experiment — pushing a reservation as far into Anglo society as possible. I think it succeeds, but of course we lose our traditional ways."

Mona Fernandez says: "My hope is that CRIT can maintain its existence as an Indian community. For that to happen will take teaching the young people something of their relationship with the land, teaching them about their forefathers." Amelia Flores says, with hope, that even now, "it all ties in. I was raised in a Christian way, but dreaming directs your way."

The dangers are clear; Dwight Lomayesva, a Hopi member of the Colorado River Tribes, states them bluntly: "Without a unique religion, language, or culture, these Indians become just another pocket of poverty without a clear understanding of their heritage."

Herman Grey wrote: "It is impossible to tell through the words of another culture and another language the meaning of a Mohave dream." As long as there is a single person who understands Mojave, who dreams the age-old Mojave dreams, there will be someone who can say, as does Grey when he begins a tale: "I am a Mohave."

THE CHEMEHUEVI

Long ago, the Chemehuevi broke away from the Las Vegas band of Southern Paiute. Tribal legend suggests that they wiped out a group of "Desert Mojave" as they moved southeastward, perhaps before they split from the Las Vegas band. In the 1700s, they ranged across the eastern Mojave Desert, hunting and gathering in a land of naked mountains and shimmering desert valleys. They wandered through the seasons, camped at the springs, and numbered no more than a few hundred people.

To the east beckoned the fertile bottomlands of the Colorado River, held by Yuman peoples. Warfare stepped up between the river tribes in the 1800s, culminating in the expulsion of the Halchidhoma. With the invitation, permission, or at very least, tolerance, of the victorious Mojave, the Chemehuevi moved into the rich Chemehuevi and Colorado River valleys by the early 1850s. They also came to live with the Mojave on Cottonwood Island — now submerged under Lake Mohave.

The desert nomads became floodplain farmers. This southernmost band of Southern Paiute became distinct from their kin; they developed a much stronger tribal consciousness, based, in part, on their interest in warfare. They adopted enough of the Mojave religion that they even acquired some of the powers of dreaming.

Beginning in 1865, the Chemehuevi and Mojave made war on each other; the

Chemehuevi, hugely outnumbered, lost but made a good showing. They retreated from the river and resumed their desert life. In 1867, however, the fighting ended and most Chemehuevi returned to the California side of the Colorado River Valley. The two-year-old reservation was extended to include them. By 1904, one agricultural scientist judged the Colorado River Valley Chemehuevi the most successful Indian farmers on the river.

In 1885, the river failed to flood the Colorado River Valley bottomlands adequately, and some Chemehuevis returned to the Chemehuevi Valley to farm. They stayed, a reservation was established in 1907 to protect their land, and the Chemehuevis were split into two groups. Gertrude Leivas was born just fifteen years later, in the early 1920s. I sat with her on the porch of her HUD home at Chemehuevi Valley and looked out over the waters of Lake Havasu sparkling in the clear winter sunshine. "I made a vow to myself," she said. "My mother always talked about the Chemehuevi Valley, and I made a vow to myself that I would come up here for her. I lived in Parker for over fifty years. But I loved the desert, and I came up here. So here I am."

Leivas heard stories about one of her great-grandfathers, who was with the first Chemehuevis to come into the valley. They found a whole forest of mesquite heavy with beans that nobody was harvesting. She says: "When they saw that land full of mesquite beans, they rushed down into the valley like a roadrunner, and that is what Chemehuevi means: 'nose in the air like a roadrunner.'" The Chemehuevi call themselves The People, Nuwu, as do all Southern Paiutes.

As a child, Leivas watched the red river rise in flood in the spring, when Chemehuevi Valley people would put in their garden plots using rough barricades of mesquite to divert the water. She and her friends would swim in the lakes formed as the waters subsided. They made dolls and toys from the dried mud curls at the edge of the shrinking lakes.

"Times were rough, then," Leivas says, "but I think it was the best time in the world. There were no bills, we didn't have to worry about running out of gas. We used kerosene lamps, fireplaces. That land along the river was filled with cottonwoods, mesquite trees, arrowweeds — it was *pretty*."

Disaster awaited, however. Hoover Dam was completed in 1935, and the rejuvenating floods came no more. In 1939, Parker Dam closed its head gates and Lake Havasu flooded most of the Chemehuevi Valley. Chemehuevi livestock drowned in the rising waters. The lake covered the homes of the People and the bones of their ancestors. Mary Lou Brown, a Chemehuevi basket maker who lives in Parker but was raised in the Chemehuevi Valley, says: "I have to throw flowers on the water here if I want to honor my people, because that's where they are — underneath."

Most of the Chemehuevi Valley people joined their kin at the Colorado River

Reservation reluctantly, feeling the pressure of being a minority among the Mojave. In the 1960s, Chemehuevis both on and off the Colorado River Reservation began to work toward a return to the Chemehuevi Valley; the late Georgia Culp was a pivotal leader.

In 1970, the tribe adopted a new constitution and members began trickling back to their old reservation. They remodeled a resort catering to boaters on Lake Havasu, and business at Havasu Landing now is booming for the one hundred and fifty resident Chemehuevis. The resort has a paradoxical feeling, isolated at the end of a fifteen-mile dead-end road that winds down bajadas past sere desert mountains to the lake, facing across to the burgeoning subdivisions of Lake Havasu City.

Gertrude Leivas made good her promise and returned home — with four of her seven children. She remains concerned about their future, however: "You need money to make money, and we don't have much." One of her daughters, Mary Drum, had been working as a nurse in East Los Angeles. She heard stories about the Chemehuevi Valley all her life, but did not see it until after she graduated from high school. "The stories made it sound enchanted and green. When I first came up, I was disappointed; it was nothing but desert. Now I feel different. I'm safe and I'm home. I don't need anyplace else."

The Chemehuevis hoped to keep the tribal rolls limited to people with one-fourth Chemehuevi blood. But there simply were not enough Chemehuevis to hold to that. They have extended their tribal rolls to include about five hundred people with one-sixteenth Chemehuevi blood.

Some outsiders joke about this rule, saying it makes for a lot of "Chicano-huevis." But Gertrude Leivas, a full-blooded Chemehuevi and (in 1988) one of only two adult tribal members born in the valley, has a different attitude. She has grandchildren from Chemehuevi, Sioux, Navajo, Winnebago, Omaha, Mojave, and Mexican parents. When her family gets together, she says: "I've got the whole United Nations under my roof."

The majority of Chemehuevi people remained at the Colorado River Reservation, but they understand these issues. Intermarriage with Mojaves, Hopis, and Navajos forces them to remain tolerant. When Abby Stevens, a Chemehuevi woman, married a Mojave man, she had to learn "to be comfortable. If I didn't, I would be in limbo. I wasn't used to the Mojave sense of humor, to their hard teasing. My mother was worried about the conflict between cremation and burying. It took five or six years to get comfortable."

In 1970, when she was twenty, Stevens chose not to join the move to the Chemehuevi Valley. She says: "I was born and raised here. What does that tribe have to offer me? How long will it take them to be as developed as CRIT?"

Some Chemehuevi traditions still can be maintained at CRIT, even in the face of

Leroy Fisher watches his aunt, Mary Lou Brown, dean of Chemehuevi basket weavers, at the CRIT Tribal Museum, 1988. Fisher has learned the craft well, and these two individuals hold the tradition of Chemehuevi basket making in their hands and hearts.

intermarriage and land development. When Mary Lou Brown, dean of Chemehuevi basket weavers, taught the craft to her nephew, Leroy Fisher, "I start him underneath a willow tree when it's ready to harvest. That's the way to teach."

Today, Leroy Fisher has learned that "money really does grow on trees." He makes his living from baskets. He explained to me: "The coils in the center of the basket are like the rings of life in the tree. Mary Lou told me, 'Once you start, there's no end. You'll dream about designs, you'll always be picking up blades of grass and wanting to weave; you won't be able to quit. Like any artist, your work is never ended.' "

In practicing their art, Brown and Fisher stay connected to their land. They know where the willow and the sumac and the juncus grow; they know the seasons to gather them. They experiment with "little whiskers of palm trees" for basket starters, with growing their own devil's claw for black fiber, with new drying schemes for willow — just as their ancestors experimented with materials and techniques. Today, however, Fisher and his "auntie" must go sixty miles round trip for some of their materials because so much of the land nearby is farmed.

These two people clearly value each other. They hold the tradition of Chemehuevi basket making in their hands and hearts.

"I really miss that big old river," said Harold Chaipos. "Those were good old times." When he talked about how rich the bottomland soil was after flooding ("when the river was loose"), the late Quechan elder rubbed his hands together — remembering the feel of it. "The Colorado River was a lifeline, a wonderful thing. Today it's a small brook. And something's got to happen to keep the river from getting too salty to use."

Before the Quechan god Kumastamxo (the Mojave call him Mastamho) transformed himself into four different kinds of eagles and flew away, before he took the People to Spirit Mountain and instructed them in the right way to live, he made the Colorado River flow by thrusting a spear into the Earth. Kumastamxo then cut a channel for the river with his spear.

The Quechan people lived along Kumastamxo's river at its junction with the Gila. In the late nineteenth century their six most important settlements dotted adjacent Arizona, California, and Mexico. The largest of these *rancherías*, Xuksil ("Sandstone"), lay below the small mountain now called Pilot Knob, California, and it housed more than eight hundred people when the Spaniards wrote of it.

Like their Mojave allies to the north, the Quechan were warriors and farmers who dreamed great dreams and who traced their origin to Spirit Mountain. (Indeed, their tribal name comes from a word that means "another going down," a reference to their migration from the holy mountain far to the north. The Spanish called the Quechan by the O'odham name for the People: Yuma.) Pioneer anthropologist A. L. Kroeber said that the Quechan and Mojave were "virtually identical" in their agriculture, manufacture, clothing, hairstyles, houses, warfare, and definition of tribal sense. Warfare, in anthropologist Robert Bee's words, was "a tribal passion." Today, Quechan Barbara Antone notes: "We still have a close relationship to the Mojave, and the Cocopah still remain enemies in some ways. But intermarriage has put us closer together."

Unlike the Mojaves, the Quechan lived close to exploration routes, astride the important river crossing at what is now Yuma, Arizona; the Spaniards came early to Quechan country, and as Barbara Antone says: "We do play a big part in history." Unfortunately, disease reduced the more than ten thousand Quechan to four thousand, and then by another 25 percent. Said Harold Chaipos: "If the Spanish hadn't come, I imagine today we'd be a big tribe."

In an effort to secure the Colorado River crossing, Spain entertained four Quechans in Mexico City in 1776; their leader, Olleyquotequiebe, called Salvador Palma by the Spaniards, agreed to welcome missionaries for his people in return for a supply

When the late Harold Chaipos talked in 1988 about how rich the bottomland soil used to be after flooding, "when the river was loose," the Quechan elder rubbed his hands together, remembering the feel of it: "The Colorado River was a lifeline, a wonderful thing. Today it's a small brook."

of European firearms. Fray Francisco Garcés established a mission on the hill by the river crossing in 1780. But the settlers that came with the padres arrived without food or supplies, assuming the Quechan would support them. The Spaniards became more arrogant and destructive with each reinforcing expedition; finally, the Quechan wiped out the mission in 1781.

Not until 1852, after both Spaniards and Mexicans had passed through their eras of influence in the Southwest, did another permanent non-Quechan settlement appear at the crossing. When the California gold rush began, the Quechan ferried California-bound forty-niners until American competitors arrived. Tensions rose along with the numbers of Anglos. Baited into war, the Quechan soon saw the U.S. Army's Fort Yuma rising on the ruins of the Garcés mission on "Indian Hill" overlooking the river.

The soldiers left in 1884, and the BIA took over the site to administer the new Fort Yuma Indian Reservation; Fort Yuma grew into the town of Yuma, Arizona. The Quechans worked for the river steamships as pilots and woodcutters until the railroad brought an end to the industry. They also worked as laborers, but the town gradually became glutted with unskilled workers. Subsequent Quechan history is the familiar one of disenfranchisement of the native people and devastation of their original numbers by disease. This cultural eclipse took only thirty years.

The People had always reached consensus after orations by their leaders — "real men" — who established their authority through dreaming, prowess in war, and care for their people. As Robert Bee puts it: "Dreams only signaled the potential for greatness"; action had to follow. The most powerful dreamer of the tribe was the primary religious leader, the kwaxót.

Pressures from the nearby town made it difficult to balance factions and fiercely loyal family groups and to present a united front opposing outside influences. Anglos unilaterally appointed Quechan leaders. Clan and village affiliations broke down when young Quechans were taken from their families and sent to school.

Meanwhile, the 1884 reservation boundaries shrank as Anglo farmers protected by federal policy took over more and more land traditionally farmed by the Quechan. Chief Miguel lost both his fight against allotment and his office in an 1893 power struggle, suffering public whipping and imprisonment with seven followers. His nemesis was Sister Mary O'Neil, superintendent of the Fort Yuma Boarding School and de facto agent until the end of the century.

By 1910, the best reservation land had been sold; only 834 Quechan people survived. Quechan farmers had to pay for their irrigation water. Much of the Indian land was either too far from the river to irrigate or in bottomlands no longer flooded be-

Quechan women picking cotton, California, 1940. By 1910, the best land on the Fort Yuma
Reservation had been sold, and only 834 Quechan people survived. The tribe descended into poverty
for decades, with most of its farmland leased to non-Indians and few jobs available. (Courtesy
National Archives, photo no. 75-N-CO-Yuma-3)

cause of upstream dams. As Harold Chaipos said: "Man's quest for development has
destroyed everything."

The tribe descended into poverty for decades. Allotments were subdivided beyond practical use through inheritance; most of the farmland was leased to non-
Indians; and few jobs were available. Harold Chaipos told me: "In 1925, some well
drillers thought they found some oil on our reservation. Older people said: 'Leave it
alone until we can get along with our neighbors.' We haven't touched it yet."

Passage of an Indian Reorganization Act (IRA) constitution in 1934 gave political factions platforms during election time but no real power. In 1935 the boarding
school became a public day school. Not until the 1960s, however, did the drive toward
economic and cultural assimilation lessen, when the federal War on Poverty poured
money into the Quechan community for new housing and economic development.

One land claim was settled in 1965, providing funds for the first full-time salaries for the council; twenty-five thousand acres were returned to the tribe in 1978. The second land claims settlement brought $15 million in 1983, 80 percent of it distributed in $6,000 per capita payments. A major piece of fertile land exposed by the eastward wandering of the Colorado River in 1920 remains mostly in Anglo hands — and in dispute, even after dramatic road blockades set up by the Quechan in 1960 and 1973 focused attention on their case.

Federal development made the reservation *look* different: new homes, new water systems, new schools and clinics. The daily lives of the People changed less; local employment depends on Congressional funding of tribal programs, and whenever that funding lapses, so do the jobs. The tribe raised sufficient capital in the 1970s to start a hydroponic tomato and cucumber farm and a cooperative farm in the river bottomlands. By 1987, both had failed, destroyed by bad luck with crop disease, a hurricane, and competition from low-priced Mexican-imported produce, as well as management problems and lack of capital. Tribal businesses in the 1990s center on three recreational-vehicle parks, a sand-and-gravel operation, and an irrigation project. The twenty-five hundred Quechan hope to establish a closed economy, with no reliance on the job markets of Yuma — now flooded by unskilled workers from Mexico.

Farming remains problematic: flooding by the Colorado River in 1983 left one-third of Quechan allotments too alkaline for crops. Any future plans for the Quechan agricultural economy depend on establishing water rights and obtaining irrigation water; the fight continues in the courts.

"Being out in the desert, it makes you feel good, a part of it all," said Harold Chaipos. "You can just *feel* the creation out there." Quechan painter Victor Curran feels much the same way. When he attended Arizona Western College in Yuma, Curran's art history teacher insisted he read all the ethnographic material on the Quechans. Curran made his way through the scholarly literature grudgingly, but in the end, he found it important. He realized that "there was no Southwestern Indian artist inspired by this area."

And so he has made Quechan country his artistic as well as his ancestral home. Though he sees himself as an "artist, not just a Quechan artist," he learned about the sacred mountains that rise at the horizons — Picacho Peak to the north and Pilot Knob to the southwest. When he camps north of Picacho Peak he is "amazed by the colors." Curran is certain the colors reemerge in his art.

Pauline Jose, manager of the Quechan Tribal Museum, says "home is home." Many people in their forties still speak Quechan fluently, but few people learn the language today. Jose believes that without the language, "they're just Indians, not Quechan." Harold Chaipos maintained that unless a child can fully understand Quechan, "it's just words." Yet he said, too, that although the older people "are all gone, the traditions are still with us. That's one thing that will never change."

Chaipos spoke to me in 1988 of Quechans who grew up in Los Angeles and who "were stunned to come home and see our rituals going on. They have to learn these things, for they will be coming home one day. Most of them do, even if in a box." The bastion of traditional Quechan culture is the tribal mourning ceremony and the kar?úk, the latter both a commemoration of any deceased person important enough to warrant the expensive ceremony and a reenactment of the original kar?úk, celebrated at the death of Kukumat, the creator, father of Kumastamxo.

"We have songs for everything," said Chaipos. "Songs for the departed ones. Songs for the lonely. Songs for the sick. Songs for the future." He understood about that future, about the dilemma of trying to live in both the traditional desert world of the Quechan and in the modern non-Indian world: "We have some old-timers that have some experience — but that's not good enough. You have to know today's world, the computer world. The Quechan never wanted anyone to know about them in the early days. Then there comes a time when we *need* people to know us."

Barbara Antone, a Quechan woman who has worked for many years in Phoenix, believes that "We made ourselves invisible because we kept so many things to ourselves. What we have, we want to keep. We have a lot of pride." She notes the difficulties that outsiders have in "saying to my people, 'Tell me your stories.' We're not monkeys in a cage that sing and dance and get fed peanuts. But when another Quechan comes up and says, 'I'm having trouble raising my daughter,' an elderly woman would tell us anything they know that could help — traditions that we might not be aware of."

Harold Chaipos said: "Today, there's no line, everything is open, though growing up sometimes takes a long time." But the key for the Quechan, he believed, is to teach "some kind of responsibility," so educated Quechans like Antone will not all remain off the reservation for good: "It takes a lot of guts to leave the opportunities in the outside world and come back and say, 'I've got to help my people.'" But if enough Quechans do just that, "our younger people will survive."

Returning is just what Barbara Antone hopes to do as soon as her son graduates from high school. She too believes in a viable future for her people: "We need to stand up and put our thoughts together, our feet together, our future together. We survived yesterday; we're going to survive tomorrow."

Downstream, the Cocopah held the delta. They were living there in 1540, when a sea party under the Spaniard Hernando de Alarcón attempted to resupply the faraway Coronado expedition. And they remained there beyond the next three centuries, until Americans began their dam building and irrigation schemes and the Colorado River ceased to flood.

Like their upstream enemies the Mojave and Quechan, Cocopah people farmed in the rich silt as the springtime floods receded from the fifty thousand acres of potentially usable delta land. They gathered the nutritious seeds of a wild saltgrass on thousands of acres. They fished, both in the river and in the Gulf of California. Their dreams gave them songs and success in war and curing. And they burned their dead along with their possessions — with ceremony and oratory.

As one Cocopah orator described his people for an early visitor to his homeland: "There is among us no quarreling or fighting for another man's property. We live happy and contented among ourselves, and respected by our neighbors, who know that in war we are invincible, as in peace we are courteous."

This world began to change in the mid-1800s. Cocopah leadership circled around warfare, and when the ancient wars with the Quechans ceased, there was nothing to replace warfare as the uniting force in the tribe. The American riverboat trade gave the Cocopah employment for a generation, but when the railroad reached Yuma in 1877 and the steamships no longer sailed, the wage economy evaporated overnight.

The most permanent blow to these river people, however, was the disappearance of their river. First came the debacle of the Salton Sea in 1905. In an effort to irrigate the Imperial Valley, Anglo land boosters diverted the whole Colorado River by mistake, creating the Salton Sea. The fifteen hundred delta Cocopahs had no choice but to disperse.

Though the Salton Sea overflow was stopped in 1907, Colorado River engineers were not finished with their work. Dams, channelization, canal building, and increasing salinity of what river water was left put a permanent end to traditional Cocopah life. Mexico built Morelos Dam in 1950 to divert the leavings of the great river one last time, and today only a sad, small flow of overused irrigation water trickles toward the Gulf.

For sixty years the Cocopah were simply forgotten in this scurry to make the desert blossom. As the river dried up, the traditional home of the tribe could not support them. Two bands remained in Mexico, in Sonora and Baja California. The other two moved north, settling around Somerton, Arizona.

In 1917, the far-sighted Cocopah leader Frank Tehanna persuaded the federal gov-

*Cocopah men on board Admiral George Dewey's survey ship, the Narraganset, at the mouth of the
Colorado River, 1874. When the railroad reached Yuma in 1877, the riverboat trade died out and the
Cocopah wage economy evaporated overnight. Photo by Henry von Bayer. (Smithsonian Institution
photo no. 2819)*

ernment to set aside a small Cocopah reservation near Somerton. In the late 1930s, the
U.S. Immigration Service cracked down on Cocopah movement back and forth across
the border, splitting the tribe into American and Mexican groups; today, the American Cocopahs are working toward restoring dual citizenship for Mexican Cocopahs.
Fred Miller, tribal chairman for most of the 1980s, says: "That was all the attention
the government paid us. There was nothing else, no administration, no help, until
the 1960s."

When Miller returned home after World War II, only fifty-eight Cocopahs were
enrolled members of the tribe. Most of the rest lived off-reservation in the surrounding area in extreme poverty. A 1970 issue of *Look* magazine exposed the plight of the
Cocopahs in an article titled: "Sometimes We Feel We're Already Dead."

Cocopah people have moved steadily upward since their nadir in the 1950s. A
tribal council formed in 1964. Adequate housing, with modern plumbing and electricity, has been built. Paved roads reach the reservation now, and each morning,
school buses take Cocopah children to Somerton schools. Today, tribal enrollment
nears one thousand. A land claims settlement returned to the tribe four thousand
acres of leasable land in 1985. And in winter, an excursion train brings tourists down
the banks of the Colorado River from the north, giving the Cocopah a market for
selling beadwork and fry bread with beans under traditional *ramadas*.

Frank Tehanna, Cocopah leader, 1920.
In 1917, this far-sighted man persuaded the
federal government to set aside a small Cocopah
reservation near Somerton, Arizona.
Photo by Densmore. (Smithsonian Institution
photo no. 2809)

Isolation has one positive side effect: it has preserved the Cocopah language. Ninety percent or more of Cocopah speak their language. "Our songs are not dying," says Frances Evanston, who manages the tribe's hot lunch program for senior citizens. "Younger people are taking up singing. It's not something you learn, it's something that's gifted. It comes to you in very mysterious ways."

Ruth Miller, a young Cocopah woman who served as Tribal Queen in 1986–87 understands what Evanston means: "Some Indian people think you should go away for an education and work off the reservation. Some think you should come back. I grew up during the American Indian Movement years, and they encouraged people to go out and then come back and help their people." Miller now works for the Tribal Housing Authority. "I used to have this hang-up about being from a tribe no one knew. Now I know that's what I am, and I'm proud."

Peter Soto, a Cocopah raised in Blythe, with a master's degree from Harvard, now lives in Phoenix. But after college he too returned to the reservation to work with the tribe in education: "When I left the East Coast and went back to the tribe, I felt I really had an impact. I've been gone a great number of years, but I still feel I'm from there." He adds, with a smile: "If you can work for your own tribe, you can work for anybody."

Still, Ruth Miller says: "There are a lot of people who won't work off the reservation. They are afraid." Frances Evanston describes the "seniors" who live in the tribal elderly home: "Every one of them is lonely. We bring in people from out on the reservation for hot lunches, and that seems to help a lot."

Optimism is built into their language. Hope Miller, wife of tribal chairman Fred Miller, comes to the lunch program and talks with her friends in Cocopah throughout the meal. One way she refers to the Cocopah homeland translates as "this land which goes on." When she says in Cocopah where she lives, it means far more than just a street address: "I am here and own this land with my heart." With the strength that comes from such emotional certainties and the "common sense" that Fred Miller says is the main reason for their recent political success, the Cocopah hope for a vital future.

The Yaqui

The pascolas . . . pray to the little animals of the desert because they have to dance all those songs on the desert. They say to help because they learned the songs from the desert. They do not do this for fun, they are serious about it. They say . . .

Saint Bullfrog, I pray to thee. Thou art amphibious, who can stay under water and out of the water as well. Help me.

Saint Horned Toad, thou who has the crown like the Virgin of Guadalupe, help me.

Saint Turtle, thou who are known never to be afraid, even if you see your enemy coming to kill you, you always walk slow and never run away, help me.

Oh, Saint Lizard, thou who can resist the heat of the summer and bury thyself in the soft dust of the desert, help me.

Thou Holy Cricket, thou who is able to stay awake all night and sing for me to sleep. Let me not feel very hard about staying up all night tonight.

Muriel Thayer Painter, *With Good Heart*, 1986

"We're the new ones," says Pascua Yaqui council member Yvonne Acuña.

"New," as Acuña uses the word, means both new to Arizona and new to the list of "official" American Indian tribes. The Yaquis have been in Arizona barely a century; they have begun to think of themselves as American Indians only since 1978.

In the time beyond history, Yaquis lived along the Rio Yaqui, deep within the modern Mexican state of Sonora. They and the Mayo Indians are the only tribes left today from more than eighteen neighboring peoples who spoke related dialects — a language called Cahita by linguists. The Spaniards named the Yaquis after a word that probably referred to their river; they call themselves Yoemem: the People. A unique religion has given the Yaquis stability through tumultuous events; in turn, their history has affected their religion.

A deer dancer, pascolas, and matachinis at Old Pascua, 1955. Ceremonies at the Yaqui village church always draw the congregation together, no matter how dispersed its members. Yaqui scholar Felipe Molina believes that Yaqui dances "remind us of what it is to be a Yoeme," a Yaqui. (Courtesy of the Arizona Historical Society/Tucson)

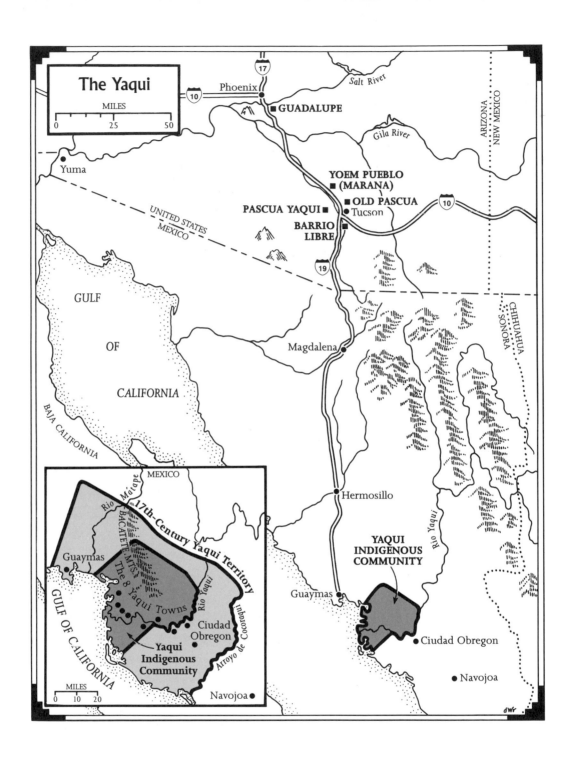

The Yaqui

MILES
0   25   50

Salt River

17

Phoenix
10
GUADALUPE

Gila River

Yuma

YOEM PUEBLO
(MARANA)
OLD PASCUA
PASCUA YAQUI
Tucson
BARRIO
LIBRE

10

UNITED STATES
MEXICO

19

ARIZONA
NEW MEXICO

GULF

OF

CALIFORNIA

Magdalena

CHIHUAHUA
SONORA

BAJA CALIFORNIA

Hermosillo

Rio Yaqui

YAQUI
INDIGENOUS
COMMUNITY

MEXICO

Rio Mátape

17th-Century Yaqui Territory

BACATETE MTS.

Guaymas

The 8 Yaqui Towns

Rio Yaqui

GULF OF CALIFORNIA

Ciudad
Obregon

Yaqui
Indigenous
Community

Arroyo de Cocori

Inhbioooii

Guaymas

Ciudad Obregon

Navojoa

Navojoa

MILES
0   10   20

dwr

People of the Flower World

The Yaqui River watered rich soil in the midst of desert and gave the tribe's ancestral home an oasis feeling similar to the homelands of the Colorado River tribes and Gila Pimas. And like these other streams, the Yaqui River today has been dammed, its valley made first into a Green Revolution breadbasket for wheat, then into the winter vegetable warehouse for the western United States. Modern Yaquis in Mexico farm in rhythm with the rise and fall of water in irrigation canals. Banks own most of the land and hire the Yaquis at low wages to work in their own fields.

In the almost-forgotten time before European contact, Yaqui *rancherías* and fields checkered the river bottoms. Into this world came the Jesuits, sent in 1617 to civilize the "savages" of this far northwestern corner of New Spain.

The Yaquis first demonstrated their backbone to the Spanish troops, then negotiated a peace unprecedented in Spanish-Indian relations, which lasted for 125 years. They asked for and welcomed the Jesuit missionaries, but maintained political control over their villages.

The Jesuits and their Christian-European culture did not destroy the Yaquis. Instead, for 150 years, the Yaquis and the Jesuits "collaborated," to use the word chosen by the foremost Anglo student of Yaqui culture, the late Edward Spicer. Though no more than six friars lived with the Yaqui at any one time, they reported baptizing all thirty thousand Yaquis by 1623. The Spanish priests also convinced the Yaquis to gather along the river in eight towns surrounding new churches.

In the years that followed, the Yaquis accepted some concepts offered by the Jesuits, rejected others, and evolved a new culture — a new way of being Yaqui. The Indian people managed to keep control of their lands — too densely populated to be easily taken over by Spanish settlers. No mines attracted boom-town rushes to Yaqui country. The Yoemem maintained their power and their numbers in relative isolation. Ironically, this peaceful small-scale penetration by the Spaniards led to greater acculturation than the more thorough conquests of most tribes; even the Yaqui language became an amalgam, with some 65 percent of modern Yaqui words borrowed from Spanish.

The strength of the Yaquis, nurtured in that first peaceful century of adaptation to the new ways, sustained them in difficult times. Yaqui educator Octaviana Valenzuela Trujillo says: "We are still known for our bullheadedness and our stubbornness. Maybe that's one reason for our survival." The Yaquis knew who they were; they still do. They became more and more urban, and the eight Yaqui towns, like the land itself, came to be seen as sacred gifts.

Yaqui religion, of course, was sacred as well. With no Catholic hierarchy, Yaqui church leaders from each village (the *maestros*) took their place. Men and boys under vows to the Virgin Mary make up the Matachin society, active all year except at Easter. The Matachin dance — the violin and guitar music, the intricate patterns of the dancers crowned with their colored ribbons of "flowers," and the infectious rhythm of the rattles and the joy of the participants — is irresistible.

The flower world symbolizes the most sacred Yaqui realm — an enchanted wilderness of nature, represented by the deer dancer. This ancient pre-Christian world threads through Yaqui Catholicism, especially at Easter, when the Yaquis reenact the Passion of Jesus in ceremonies rooted both in Jesuit liturgical dramas and in the flower world. "The Easter Ceremony," says Yvonne Acuña, "is the clincher to our culture."

In Easter season, as one Yaqui *maestro* put it: "The blood of Christ is the flower. All the flowers. That is why we use flowers so much. That is why the pascolas [the *pahkolam*: the "old men of the fiesta" — dancers, ritual hosts, orators, and clowns] and deer wear them on their heads, and the musicians and singers and everyone."

During Lent and Holy Week, the *kohtumbre* (the "keepers of our most sacred traditions") take over the village, conducting both normal village business and the re-enactment of the Easter Passion. Two groups make up the kohtumbre, the *caballeros* (Horsemen) and the *fariseos* (Pharisees — whose masked members are also called *chapayekas*). Members of both societies are under vow to Jesus to behave "with good heart." They, in Yvonne Acuña's words, are "the core of Yaqui culture."

Revolution and Dispersal

Gradually, the Jesuit bureaucracy and Yaqui leadership grew apart. The first Yaqui rebellion came in 1740. The Jesuits turned over New Spain to the Franciscans and secular authorities in 1767. For the next two centuries, Yaquis came under increasing pressure to open their lands to non-Indian settlement. The more desirable the Yaqui land became to outsiders, the more passionately the Yaquis believed that their land was a sacred gift, never to be lost.

War did not erupt again until the 1830s, after Mexico had won independence from Spain and had begun pressuring Yaquis to integrate and to pay taxes like good Mexican citizens. Yaquis fought for their land and their rights throughout the next century. Tribal pride coalesced around the victories of their slain guerilla generals: Juan Banderas, Cajeme, Tetabiate. Treaties were signed and broken. Through most of these decades, Yaquis fought the dynastic armies of the great landowners of Sonora eager to extend their holdings and force the Yaquis into a state of serfdom. In the end, it took the full force of Mexican federal troops to disperse the Yaquis.

Beginning in the 1880s, many Yaquis scattered across Sonora and into what became Arizona, seeking jobs (with railroads and farms — in part to earn money for arms and ammunition to aid the guerrilla war back home) and peaceful escape from war, massacre, and harassment. Small numbers of Yaquis remained in the eight sacred towns; others retreated into the Bacatete Mountains east of Guaymas, to continue the campaign against the hacienda families and Mexican army. The Mexican government began deportation of thousands of Yaquis to Yucatan plantations, where they were sold into peonage. The Yaquis became the most widely dispersed Indians in North America, scattered across thirty-five hundred miles. But they remained Yaquis.

A thousand or more Yaquis may have entered the United States by 1910. Another wave of immigrants came in 1916–17, when Mexican troops struck in another campaign of repression; a last exodus occurred in 1926. These refugees settled in southern Arizona on unwanted land at the edge of the then-small cities of Phoenix and Tucson.

By 1909, Arizona Yaquis had reestablished ceremonial activities in their new home villages, organizing their lives around the church. In the early years, especially, each Arizona Yaqui family continued to identify as well with its ancestral village on the Rio Yaqui. Octaviana Trujillo says: "We were in limbo — not Mexican, not white, not Indian, but Yaqui." Even now, says Old Pascua resident Dolores Bravo, "our identity sometimes is confusing even to us."

In 1921, the U.S. government tried to concentrate the Yaquis living near Tucson in one spot north of the city center. This cluster of households came to be called Pascua Village. Other Yaquis lived in south Tucson (though their village, Barrio Libre, was disrupted after 1958, when a freeway cut through their neighborhood, right past their church). Some Yaqui families gained ownership of their land, at times charitable foundations subsidized them, but most remained squatters without secure title. The Yaqui community of Guadalupe in the Phoenix Valley (probably the oldest of Arizona Yaqui villages) and the smaller colony of Yoem Pueblo at Marana have similar histories. Lack of land became a growing problem for young families, even when urban renewal came to the Yaqui barrios.

For work, Yaquis adapted first to the cotton harvest, moving out to cotton farms to work at chopping (weeding and thinning) the growing plants and harvesting the ripe crop, returning to their villages for ceremonial seasons. Mechanized pickers replaced human cotton choppers in the fifties, and the Yaqui were forced to live full-time in their villages and seek new work.

Once rural, Yaqui barrios became urban. Once quiet, the Yaqui villages watched

Yaqui family making tortillas, Tucson, 1942.
From the forties to the sixties, quiet, rural Yaqui
barrios became urban as the booming cities of
Tucson and Phoenix surrounded them. (Courtesy
of the *Arizona Historical Society/Tucson*)

as the cities of Tucson and Phoenix surrounded them with what Octaviana Trujillo, from Guadalupe, calls "a community completely in conflict with their values." "Being in an urban area," says Dolores Bravo, "made us more political."

In spite of drugs disabling their young people, in spite of chronic poverty and unemployment that turns some Yaquis to *viciados* (people ruled by vices), Yaqui ceremonies (run by men) and Yaqui families (held together by women) have stayed remarkably strong. Dolores Bravo says: "What makes us Yaquis is the caring for one person to the next — the closeness. My mother lives four blocks down, my old aunts and uncles a block away — and cousins, godmother, godfather, nephews, nieces . . . We'll keep our kin until they die." Those kin include a vast network of ceremonial godparents, *comadres* and *compadres*, as well as blood relations — a skein of obligations and dependencies always important to Yaquis but particularly crucial in the Arizona villages where fragmented families and solitary refugees assembled after their escape from persecution in Mexico.

The Pascua Yaqui Tribe

In 1964, Yaqui leaders persuaded Congress (through Representative Morris Udall) to grant 202 acres of federal land southwest of Tucson to the Yaqui for new housing. About one-third of the Yaquis at "Old" Pascua moved to this "New" Pascua, as well as many Yaquis displaced from Barrio Libre by the freeway.

In 1978, the federal government granted the Pascua Yaqui Tribe of Arizona access to the same health and social service programs as all Indian tribes, and placed their land in the familiar "trust" administered by the Secretary of the Interior. With these amendments to their status, the Yaquis could obtain funding to continue their housing improvement programs. In 1982, the Pascua Yaqui Reservation, just west of San Xavier, was increased to 892 acres.

By 1979, New Pascua had displaced Guadalupe as the largest Yaqui community in Arizona. Though no other Arizona Yaqui community has reservation status, from 1978 to 1980 all of the more than five thousand Yaquis (those with at least one-half Yaqui heritage) could enroll as members of the tribe with access to federal benefits. The rolls reopened ten years later with certain limitations; many full-blooded Yaquis remain unable to enroll.

"This whole notion of a reservation," says Octaviana Trujillo, is new. "It's what 'contemporary Yaqui' is all about." Still, neither place of residence nor purity of blood means as much to Yaquis in defining an individual's identity as does ceremonial association.

Anselmo Valencia can be given primary credit for the success of the Pascua Yaquis in obtaining land and federal recognition. Some Yaquis praise him for this; others bemoan his consolidation of power, leading to what one Yaqui described to me as ten years of a "dictator" situation. Many Yaquis were proud of the People's independence and saw no need to tie themselves to the government. But Valencia's eloquence in speaking for the Yaquis before Congress during the 1977 hearings cannot be argued with:

The Yaquis are Indians in every sense of the word. We have our own language, our own culture . . . In the deer dance, we sing to honor the great mountains, the springs, the lakes. We sing of our father the Sun, and of creatures living and dead. We sing of trees and leaves and twigs. We sing of the birds in the sky and of the fish in the ocean . . . We could have been Mormons, Baptist, or any other denomination, and we would still have retained our Indian culture. It just so happened that the so-called conquerors were of the Catholic faith. The Catholic faith and the various governments under which the Yaquis have had to suffer have tried for centuries to undermine our "Yaquiness," but after 400 years they have not succeeded. We have retained our language, our culture, and our Indianness.

Raul Silvas, Pascua Yaqui chairman in 1988, says that the Easter ceremony remains the symbol of the new unity of his people: "All year long we've been preparing ourselves. It's a new beginning for us. Everybody takes time off. There's no stopping us — even if we have to lose our jobs." The Yaqui village church always draws together its congregation, no matter how dispersed its members may be.

New Pascua continues to grow, drawing Yaquis with its availability of good housing; in fact, HUD housing projects have begun to push at the limits of New Pascua's limited acreage. Younger Yaquis have been amazed at the willingness of their elders to leave strong roots in Old Pascua or Guadalupe and move to the new village. Octaviana Trujillo says: "Some have chosen to return to their own villages. In New Pascua, it will take them a while to bond. It's like building a community from scratch."

In contrast, Yoem Pueblo, at Marana, remains isolated and rural. Guadalupe voted to become a municipality in 1977, after the threat of annexation by Phoenix; alone among Phoenix Valley communities, it has retained its Indian-Mexican character.

Luis Lopez Gonzales, from Guadalupe, told me: "The Yaquis and Mexicans in the community keep separate in culture, though the community as a whole shares a lot." Like all Indian groups living far from tribal headquarters, Guadalupeños feel they could use more direct help. Says Gonzales, who works with the 175 Guadalupe Yaqui high school age kids: "The tribe counts on us, but only one of eleven members on the last council was from Guadalupe. The tribe has no satellite administration now; we finally received tribal money to build twenty houses here. We need an activity and cultural center; we need Yaqui programs for Yaqui kids."

The first truly open elections for Yaqui tribal offices took place in 1988. Tribal consciousness is growing, knitting together the far-flung villages — though each still has its distinctive reputation. Says Octaviana Trujillo: "Guadalupe Yaquis are always seen as the radical ones, the politicians. Marana — isolated and surrounded by Anglo ranchers — is seen as the center for traditionalists. They have retained the language most strongly, speaking Yaqui at home, English in school. Guadalupe has the most traditional dances, with Barrio Libre second. And during Easter Week, of course, *everybody* comes home." And everybody, Anglos included, is welcome to watch the Easter ceremonies; to watch is to participate — to share "with good heart."

Raul Silvas said to me, with a smile: "If we start talking in Yaqui, I speak Yaqui. If we start in Spanish, I speak Spanish. And if we start in English, I speak English till I run out of words." Each village emphasizes one or two languages, but many Yaquis remain trilingual. Yaqui is the crucial language for ceremonies and is much spoken at home

Freddy Valenzuela (right) and Vincent Chiago, Yaqui, in front of a mural by Joe Acuña, Guadalupe, Arizona, 1992. With a reputation for being both traditional and political, Guadalupe became a municipality in 1977 to avoid the threat of annexation by Phoenix.

by older people; Spanish dominates in the Catholic church and in many social situations; English is most formal, associated with school and with legal and economic interactions with Anglos. Yaquis themselves sometimes feel they cannot speak any of the three languages well.

After decades of increasing the number of Yaqui speakers, today the urban Yaqui communities are losing their native language; Marana is losing its Spanish. New Pascua, thoroughly Yaqui and proud of it, is becoming "Mexican-Americanized" less rapidly than the barrios, and seems to be holding on to the Yaqui language more strongly. Other Indian tribes tend to dismiss the Yaquis as Mexican, not Native American, because they speak Spanish. "It's like we're the invisible culture," says Octaviana Trujillo.

Silvas notes, in contrast, that "it's a matter of pride for the Yaquis in Mexico," who live on a federal reserve where they have rebuilt the life of the eight sacred towns, "that we're recognized, too. The United States really is a land of opportunity."

American Yaquis maintain ties to their relatives in Hermosillo barrios and on the Rio Yaqui Reserve. Some Arizona villages must import a Sonoran Yaqui to conduct certain ceremonies; Luis Gonzales told me of driving all the way down to Mexico to pick up *maestros* and *cantoras* (singers) needed in Guadalupe. Many Arizona Yaquis go to Mexico for visits and for the Magdalena Fiesta and pilgrimage in the fall. Dolores Bravo of Old Pascua says: "I would never think of living there." Octaviana Trujillo agrees — with regard to a permanent move — but can see herself "going down to the Rio Yaqui for a year or two and just living. They may dress, eat, and live a little differently, but the core of the tradition and culture is the same." For their part, Sonoran Yaquis allow Arizona Yaquis to return to live and even cultivate land if they can marshall local relations to attest to their family background — if they can prove themselves genealogically Yaqui.

The most famous Sonoran Yaqui — apart from the romanticized deer dancer of the Ballet Folklorico — is, of course, don Juan Matus, the sorcerer Carlos Castañeda has written about for more than twenty years. Considerable controversy swirls around Castañeda's books — and the very existence of don Juan. Though many of the details in the books clearly come from other Mexican tribes, witchcraft and sorcery do thread through Yaqui culture, and elders can remember burnings of evil witches on the Rio Yaqui. No Arizona Yaquis, however, claim don Juan as a compadre.

In the 1970s, broken-down Volkswagen buses with California plates began to show up at New Pascua, driven by "long-haired hippies" full of questions about don Juan. One New Pascua leader was in the habit of being persuaded, after much smoke-screening hesitation, to tell the visitors where don Juan lived in the village. There was

Octaviana Valenzuela Trujillo, Yaqui educator, 1992. Trujillo believes that "the future of Guadalupe and other Yaqui settlements may be questionable, but not Yaqui culture or people."

indeed a don Juan in New Pascua, an old man full of stories, who obliged the would-be apprentice sorcerers for a little money, cigarettes, and beer — until they realized they had been had.

Entertaining such visitors is not a full-time profession. In the Arizona barrios, Pascua Yaqui unemployment remains at 50 percent. The tribe hopes to attract industry — "any kind of enterprise that brings jobs," in Silvas's words. Octaviana Trujillo points out that "We don't have the land, the mining — we need to depend on human resources." Luis Gonzales notes: "Several families in New Pascua live entirely on money from selling pascola masks. Here in Guadalupe, people have never sold their arts. The Guadalupe Mercado is all Mexican, no Yaqui."

Developing those Yaqui human resources can take a person far from home: Dr. Eddie Brown, a Pascua Yaqui, has been Assistant Secretary for Indian Affairs in President Bush's Interior Department since 1989. Indeed, every Yaqui I spoke with emphasized the importance of education for their young people. Octaviana Trujillo says: "We need to look at education from the Native American perspective. We don't learn in a linear, abstract fashion. We are cyclical thinkers. We have to determine our own destiny."

The Yaqui always emphasize ceremonial participation when speaking of the future. Octaviana Trujillo believes that "the future of Guadalupe and other Yaqui settlements may be questionable, but not Yaqui culture or people." Luis Gonzales says: "Within myself, I will always be a Yaqui. A lot of people say the Easter dances are fading away, but I don't see it." Yoem Pueblo scholar Felipe Molina believes: "We Yaquis are a spiritual people." Our dances "remind us of what it is to be a Yoeme."

My favorite image from Yaqui ceremony is the deer dancer. Molina says, "good deer dancers can actually dance the meaning of the song, and these dancers are greatly respected because they help the Yaqui people to see the close connection all living things have in common on earth." Molina and his Anglo collaborator Larry Evers write of the deer singers that accompany the dancer, that their "water drum is said to represent his heartbeat, their raspers his breathing, their words, his voice."

The deer dancer *becomes* a deer. He stands in the swirl of the pascolas, detached, graceful, at rest but still taut, smelling the wind, ready to run. He looks to the left, he looks to the right. He looks out into the present with the wisdom of the past. In his power and understanding lie the future. The deer singers sing. The deer dancer stamps his foot, and his cocoon rattles shush. The deer song ends:

> Growing flower, growing flower . . .
> beautifully, endlessly, sparkling, you go.
> With the enchanted dawn wind, you went.

Conclusion

WE ARE THE LAND

In popular and persistent folk belief, The Indian is, among other things, male, red-skinned, stoic, taciturn, ecologically aware, and a great user of metaphor. Or, he is cunning, mercurial, wild, lusty, and a collector of blond scalps. At nightfall he silhouettes himself in the sunset, or dances, shrieking, around his campfire. Before vanishing, he was prone to skulking, sneaking, and sundry other double-dealings. Rather than defend himself, he "uprose"; rather than resist the occupation of his land, he "outbroke"; rather than defeat a foe, he "massacred" . . . The Indian, by and large, is a motif embedded in Americana, not perceived as a part of the American present. The confusion comes when we realize that Indian people, too often mistaken for The Indian, are still very much around . . .

Never has there been a greater misnomer than to call Indians the "vanishing Americans"; against the greatest of odds over the past five centuries they have proved their staying power . . . Tribal allegiance and identity have weathered disease and removal, allotment and termination, war and indifference. Of all the myriad rich and diverse customs that are identified with one tribe or another, a single tradition — survival — unites them all.

Michael Dorris, *Daedalus*, 1981

Land and family make Indian people who they are; they give them an absolute sense of home. Millie Touchin, from Laguna Pueblo, puts this simply and strongly: "Some people don't have a place, a beginning. We're lucky. We have something and somebody." Paula Gunn Allen, also from Laguna, sums up this fundamental value: "We are the land."

"The American public have no idea of the affection the Indian people have for the land," says Navajo historian Harry Walters. "The Navajo say your home is where your umbilical cord is buried, in a hogan or sheep corral. Where you grew up, you herded sheep, where your mother and grandmother are buried, it means a lot. Relocation — to leave the place and turn it over to other people, it's unthinkable."

Hazel Merritt painted her satellite dish with the traditional design of a Navajo wedding basket, Aneth, Utah, 1991.

Taos Pueblo filmmaker Diane Reyna says: "For Pueblo people, there's more to come home to. There's a cattle guard right past the Allsup's station on the north edge of town — there's a sigh of relief when you pass it."

Rival tribal councils may dispute land and water rights, but the elders take a more philosophical view of land tenure. Hopi Fermina Banyacya says: "All native peoples' lands overlap each other's boundaries. That's how we hold it, overlapping, like a chain."

Indians are not the universally wise and spiritual tenders of the Earth that New Age simplifiers would imagine them to be. The People understand consequences, however. They live as if their land is their home, permanently. They do not plan to move on to the next boomtown. That attitude alone explains much of their religion; that attitude can teach non-Indians a great deal about paying attention — to the land, to the stars, to the most humble plants and animals.

Tohono O'odham cattleman Joe Enriquez describes the extended family, a bedrock Indian value: "The father and wife could get jobs. So older folks cared for the youngsters. Lot of youngsters grew up with their grandparents. It's been that way as far back as anyone can remember, even in the old days when they were just farming."

Indians who still have ties to the reservation always have a home to return to. Says Millie Touchin at Laguna: "We don't have any homeless; even an alcoholic, there's always an old aunt or a grandmother that will take them in." Ute Mountain Ute Janice Colorow says: "We touch each other's lives." Colorow has turned down a higher-paying job off-reservation, because it would do nothing to "help people." Such work would "feel like you haven't done anything worthwhile."

Millie Touchin explained to me another aspect of extended families that has become critical in modern Indian communities: "My brother has three families: his, mine, and my sister's." Touchin and her sister, both single parents, relied on their brother for a male role model for their children. Says Touchin, "He's only 5′2″, but to us he is seven feet tall."

Housing projects and nine-to-five jobs gradually shift the definition of family from extended to nuclear. Laura Graham, from Laguna, works for the National Indian Council on Aging. She told me: "In my mother's time, and before that, the extended family just took care of each other. You hardly ever heard of anyone in nursing homes. My grandmother died at home, in her own bed.

"Now you can't really do that. I couldn't quit my job and take care of my mother. I don't even expect my kids to take care of me. The elderly need to know that our whole Indian society has changed. They need to keep their relationship with their family, but they need to talk to each other."

Still, those nuclear Indian families come back together whenever necessary.

Acoma potter Juana Leno spent the winter of 1985–86 living in the old family house on top of the mesa at Acoma Pueblo; her husband was the field chief that year, and their presence was required. Few other Acomas live full-time at Sky City; most live below, in more modern and accessible HUD homes.

Statistics show that the lower and less stable the family income, the larger the household size. The collective Indian ethic allows survival when kin lose jobs and need help. Newly married young people move in with parents; grandparents take over childrearing when parents drink; ailing grandparents move in with their children. Each of these extended families shares its resources.

Cocopah Frances Evanston tells her own children: "You're like a chameleon. When you are out in the white society, you have to change color. When I grow old, you'll have to change to my color to take care of me."

Life on a Roller Coaster

Steve Darden, Navajo, former director of Native Americans for Community Action in Flagstaff, points out that "over 50 percent of the Native American population now lives in urban areas — because of the economic depressions on reservations, because of the cultural genocide that has occurred on the reservation, because of the pursuit of the American Dream." In 1990, only 35 percent of American Indians lived on tribal lands.

When Sylvia Querta first married, she moved from the Hualapai Reservation to spend two years in the Bay Area in California. "I was young and I thought I wanted to live in the city — get caught up in the excitement of shopping, of having a car, going to the movies and concerts and games. We lived in an apartment. We didn't even know who lived next door or under us or on top of us. We were used to being in a community where we all know each other, where if anything happens we are all close.

"I missed home. I missed the not-so-busy everyday life. I missed my family, being around Peach Springs, out to Milkweed; I missed Quartermaster and Madwida canyons."

Gail Russell, Chemehuevi/Apache director of the Indian Walk-In Center in Salt Lake City, says: "By living in urban areas, Indian people have seen that what they have is meaningful and precious. If there was an economy on the reservation, they would choose to live there. They would not *choose* to live in cities." They would not choose to live as Fort McDowell Yavapai David King laments too many of us live: "We drive, we go — 'I gotta get here, I gotta get there.' And when we get there, we don't know why we came."

Those 1.3 million off-reservation Indians (in 1990) have their problems. In 1989, for instance, thirty thousand Indian people lived in Bernalillo County, New Mexico, surrounding and including Albuquerque. Sixty percent were under 25 years old. Nearly 60 percent earned less than $15,000 a year, and more than 20 percent less than $5,000. About 23 percent were homeless.

As Steve Darden points out: "If a man cannot continue his planting, if he cannot continue his livestock, how then can he survive? We have had to move because you have taken the lifeway from us in your relocation efforts. A government-to-government relationship excludes urban Indians, who are not tribes, not governments, from any appropriations." Providing deserved social services equally to Indians living in cities and on reservations remains a critical need.

Many people may grow up in a reservation community, leave for the military, college, or a career, and retire (at a relatively young forty-five or fifty) and come home to work in tribal government, start a small business or herd, or take up an old love for pottery making or silversmithing. The classic tour of duty "on the outside" is the twenty to thirty years it takes to reach retirement.

During the years they live in cities, most Indian people stay in close touch with their families and with reservation life. "Navajos in cities live in an invisible bubble with an umbilical cord that goes back to the reservation," says Jennie Joe. Martin Antone, an O'odham from Ak-Chin, says: "You always come back home — it's just like migrating animals, like salmon that always swim upstream to spawn."

Ada Melton says: "It's damned hard to be a good Indian these days. It's labor intensive, it's expensive. You have to make choices, compromises. And no one else is required to understand the compromises."

She had been talking to me about driving up to Jemez Pueblo from her job at the University of New Mexico in Albuquerque every night that week to practice in the kiva for the coming feast day. "I'm here in the office during the day, to make money, for my profession. And my father is a *fiscale*: we're *obligated* to show our support by dancing. By night I'm up at Jemez practicing in the kiva.

"It's really comforting, that kiva. It's the same as it always has been. It smells the same, it feels the same. There are new songs, but the motion is the same, the rhythm is the same. It is a very familiar place, a place where all of us belong.

"Off come my professional credentials as an American career woman when I go to Jemez. I'm Ada, daughter of so-and-so. When I'm in the kiva, I'm in the ranks. The doctors and lawyers don't dance in the front row. The officials' families dance toward the front. What's important up there isn't important here in Albuquerque."

Sally Pablo, Pima educator, understands this. We spoke in Komatke, on the Gila River Reservation: "If we're going to survive on the outside, in the dominant society, we have to learn to live there, too. When you go out in the work world, you have to sell yourself to get a job. But don't do that here: it sounds like bragging. Besides, in the Indian world, everybody knows us anyway!

"In our Indian lives we're taught that we're all equal. There's a certain code of ethics. I know what's expected of me here, what I can and can't do. As a woman, different things are expected of me at whatever age I am." As another Pima, Earl Ray, says: "I know when I have to change my mask."

This wrenching between worlds has become almost second nature for Indian people. Their lives both as individuals and as peoples have been filled with such swings for decades. Their ability to move back and forth can disrupt and confuse or create a distillation of "urban and rural life in a nationalistic continuum," in the words of Vine Deloria, Jr. Santa Clara educator Dave Warren is continually astonished by the "amazing resilience and viability" of his people — who have been subjected to a "whiplashing almost unimaginable for anyone who hasn't lived with that circumstance."

Peterson Zah, president of the Navajo Nation, says that "Indian life is a roller coaster. When we are at the very top of the roller coaster, we have to do things to allow the survival of the Indian people. That's the only time you can accomplish things, when people are willing to listen."

Vine Deloria, Jr., notes that America comes around to being interested in Indians about every twenty years. After a brief flurry of press attention, Indian issues disappear again from the national agenda. Stan Steiner's *The New Indians* appeared in 1968, Deloria's *Custer Died for Your Sins* in 1969, and Dee Brown's *Bury My Heart at Wounded Knee* in 1971. (As Deloria bitterly points out in *God Is Red*, however, the public still feels more comfortable reading about the noble natives of one hundred years ago than about the struggles of today's Indians.)

Indian activists riveted the nation's attention through 1972. Navajo Community College and the revolution in community-based bilingual education developed in these years. A surge in the Indian population resulted not only from high birth rates but from the increasing numbers of mixed-blood people who were willing to identify themselves as Indian. And then, for nearly, twenty years, silence.

In 1990 came the film *Dances With Wolves*. At the 1991 Academy Awards, Doris Leader Charge translated acceptance speeches into the Lakota language. In the weeks that followed, Senator Daniel Inouye, longtime chair of the Senate Select Committee on Indian Affairs, found prominent senators knocking on his door daily, requesting a seat on his usually neglected committee. For the first time ever, he had a designated committee room and a full slate of members. Inouye joked with Peterson Zah that the new converts were the "*Dances With Wolves* senators."

The balance between tribal governments, Congress, the courts, the BIA, corporate America, and the electorate in reservations, counties, and states remains as delicate as ever. Redistricting after the 1990 census will restructure that political balance once again, with enormous consequences for Indian nations. The endless roller coaster of cycling budgets, policies, and laws — reflecting the changing public image of Indians — testifies to how easily the balance can be upset. This endless journey carries the People round and round, always returning to their beginnings on the land. Roller coasters stand rooted in place; they are not trains bound for the far horizon and exotic new possibilities.

Within the Rainbow of Sovereignty

Tribes hoping to move beyond the self-government granted by the Indian Reorganization Act (IRA) to a true tribal government must in the end control their own destinies — must accomplish what Vine Deloria, Jr., calls "retribalization." Public support for Indian self-determination and sovereignty, however, is heartfelt only as long as Indians are weak and poor.

Non-Indians still do not quite believe that Indians do not wish to assimilate. As tribes become more competitive and powerful, the "special relationship" that boils down to their right to a separate and distinct existence — while still receiving the support obligated by treaty — comes under increasing fire from assimilationists. Most non-Indians do not know how to cope with Indians who do not fit into romanticized roles.

Edgar Walema, chairman of the Hualapai tribal council for most of the 1980s, talked with me about his economic worries and his dreams in 1984. At first he read stiffly from his campaign literature, but as he relaxed, he leaned back in his chair and looked thoughtfully out his window over the rooftops of the neat HUD houses that make up Peach Springs, Arizona: "We can no longer wait and let the federal government keep us going. We need something to show our sincerity and self-determination in achieving self-sufficiency.

"All the income made here on the reservation goes to supporting other communities. We have 95 percent of our income going into Mojave County. We have to do all our shopping in Kingman, in Flagstaff, in Phoenix. Every cent that we make goes out.

"When we talk about unemployment at the state level, at the national level, I wonder if they ever include reservations. Here alone we have 70 percent unemployment. We have to provide something for the people. We're a sovereign nation. We live in our world. But we're in a situation where there's just no justification for our existence."

Peterson Zah says: "Sovereignty means everything. We are very jealous, very sensitive about our sovereignty. It's a way of life, of keeping your land intact. Navajos like to call it 'rainbow.' Indian people have to develop everything you have at the state level inside the rainbow. That's the whole reason to go out and get educated."

John Lewis, Pima director of the Arizona Inter-Tribal Council, says: "We have to struggle to maintain understanding that tribal governments are not just another minority group, but equal to the state governments. It should be a given. To take all those government functions — like court systems and law enforcement — and do them well and appropriately is a tremendous feat. The next step for Indian people is to take over their hospitals and clinics."

Politicking their way through a myriad of government programs (what Navajo Danny Blackgoat calls "white tape") leads to what Dennis Patch, Mojave education administrator, notes as "a new word surfacing in Indian Country: 'burnout' — with deadlines, grant timelines, stress-related illness."

Alfreda Mitre, Las Vegas Paiute chair, says: "You can't hire Indian leaders; they have to be bred within. Tribes have to make a decision about the kinds of leaders they want and had better instill those qualities." Tribal governments seem to work best under a strong and visionary leader (like Wendell Chino at Mescalero) or where the community still maintains a solid identity allowing a citizens' government to twine through the lives of its people (as at several of the pueblos). Other tribes have been paralyzed by political infighting or the inaction of old guards fearful of losing power.

The Salt River Reservation is caught in a battle over additional freeway development that will pay allottees along the highway route millions of dollars, their neighbors nothing. In 1988, Pima activist Diane Enos erected this sign in her yard protesting the development. She says, sadly: "It's tearing the community apart."

Tribal governments face many of the same challenges as Third World nations: undeveloped resources, poor people, lack of capital. They must choose between corporate leasing and local entrepreneurism, as noted by Tom Vigil at Jicarilla: "Economic development can create income or develop jobs — completely different scenarios." In many ways, these choices in development are the same choices faced by the rural West in general. And as the West both desires and fears development, so do Indian people.

At Zuni, when a Zuni-Cibola National Historical Park was created in 1988, the press heralded this "prototype for an American Indian park system," largely managed by the People themselves. (A Hohokam-Pima National Monument, with similar aspirations, has existed on paper for years, with no public development or facilities.)

In 1989, Dave Warren, Pueblo museum administrator, could hardly contain his excitement when he described the project to me: "Zuni-Cibola is the future — a community-based institution with native people in it." In 1990, however, Zuni people voted eight to one against the park, galvanized by traditional religious leaders who fear torrents of tourists who will surely disrupt the spiritual life of the pueblo.

Judy Knight has served as both Ute Mountain and CERT (Council of Energy Resource Tribes) chair. She points out that no other governmental jurisdiction in the country grappling with the issue of economic development runs the same risks as tribal governments. None faces the same "enormous economic, environmental, and political consequences" or "a more hostile environment." None faces "political, economic, or social annihilation." She concludes: "Tribal government walks a high wire, most often without a safety net should we lose our balance."

Ted Jojola, Isleta, directs the Native American Studies program at the University of New Mexico. He says of his information specialist, a strong-minded young Navajo woman named Elaine Walstedter: "The agents of the revolution are going to have to be people like Elaine — people who can shake cages and say, 'Let's deal with problems.' The tribes are so damn rigid: they see Elaine as a fifty-pound hammer and they are a large crystal. They don't think of themselves as malleable, like a piece of clay."

Frances Evanston, a supervisor for the Cocopah Senior Citizens Center, says: "Making changes here is like going through a concrete wall." Everett Burch, Southern Ute educator: "Individuals are like a wheel, always getting a new tire. The tribal government is like the bearing: it just sits there, off to the side." Linda Baker Rohde, also a Southern Ute, believes that "the spiritual leaders should be the good heart in all this."

Every institution needs periodic renewal. The Institute of American Indian Arts stagnated in the 1970s and 1980s, but with a new charter from Congress, a new name (Institute of Native American and Alaskan Native Culture and Arts Development), a new site south of Santa Fe for the campus, a permanent museum just off the Santa Fe plaza, and a dynamic new director, Comanche Kathryn Harris Tijerina, the national Indian art school has once again moved into the news.

The BIA is more in need of such new blood than most institutions — though 88 percent of Bureau employees in 1992 are Indian and the BIA undersecretary in charge of Indian affairs is Eddie Brown, Pascua Yaqui, who is committed "to making the ideals of tribal self-government and self-determination a reality." Southern Paiute Gary Tom still finds the Bureau the "big bureaucratic bungle-jungle." Alfreda Mitre, chair of the Las Vegas Paiutes, deals with the jungle this way: "I'll learn the rules forwards and backwards and sideways, and I'll follow them. And I'll make sure they'll follow them, too. That way, you don't waste time bickering over semantics."

The debate over whether or not to abolish the Bureau goes on. As anthropologist Joseph Jorgensen points out, frictions constantly occur between Indians who need the BIA's services but hate its domination and incompetence and the BIA itself, which must maintain Indians in subservient roles in order to preserve jobs and the bureaucracy. Peterson Zah says: "The BIA has outlived its usefulness." However, many Indians feel as does Navajo Jennie Joe: "A great sense of threat that BIA elimination is termination in disguise, a convenient way to eliminate federal responsibilities entirely."

Though the BIA is prone to paternalism, overregulation, and bureaucratic paralysis, *somebody* has to deliver the services, preserve the rights, and protect the trust lands of American Indians — obligations guaranteed by centuries of treaties ratified and bills passed by Congress and repeatedly upheld by the courts. Such delivery of federal support could come from a variety of bureaus. A cabinet-level Indian affairs post could end the conflicts of interest between such agencies as BIA and Reclamation within the Department of Interior, but might promote its own new bureaucracy. The issue, like all Indian issues, is not simple.

Educating "the Devil's Children"

Gary Tom says: "In the old days, the classroom was not square. It was air-conditioned, but not with electricity. It was lit, but not by a coal-fired power plant somewhere else." Learning took place through living, through trial and error. Elders acted as guides in this "cooperative learning," a modern educational technique that corresponds, as Rose Hulligan notes, with the Diné style of education. Her father explains learning with a Navajo phrase that translates, "everything is transformed."

With fewer and fewer elders, proportionally, more and more young Indian people will have to learn in new ways. Lydia Pesata recreated traditional Jicarilla Apache baskets on her own. She says: "Teaching yourself is like walking around in the dark." Richard TeCube, Jicarilla planner, admits that "the demographic analysis of our tribe scares the hell out of me. There is a tiny number sixty-five and over and an enormous number eighteen and younger. What can we do?"

Education is the answer to his question. Education close to home, education that involves the whole culture and community — education that is the antithesis of the boarding schools. Vine Deloria, Jr., has pointed out that for Indians, "the universe is personal." He speaks of the Indian emphasis on the particular, of one's personal experience of life and energy and the relationships between things forming the bedrock of knowledge. Such particularities happen closest to home.

Specifically, Deloria suggests that local communities take over primary and part of secondary education — even if it means recreating one-room school houses — beginning their restructuring of the curriculum by teaching family genealogies and tribal traditions: "These two subjects provide a solid foundation for children's personal identity as well as serving as a context for teaching all manner of social skills and development of memory and recollection." He is working toward solving the same problems seen by Las Vegas Paiute educator Alfreda Mitre: "It's like we walked into the

White Mountain Apache Head Start pupils dressed for the annual Easter egg hunt, Fort Apache Reservation, Whiteriver, Arizona, 1988.

pages of history and disappeared. My son came home from grade school exposure and said, 'I don't know how to be Indian.'"

Bernard Siquieros, Tohono O'odham educator, worries about what happens after graduation. He says: "When we talk about preparing kids for jobs, kids look at us and say, 'Where are we going to work?' We have to start working with our kids to teach them that they can create a business, not just be a civil servant. We could use a model like Junior Achievement, use our successes now as models." Deloria sees educated Indian professionals in the same role as scouts in the old hunting culture, who "provided information on which the community could act."

The boarding school policy of forced assimilation moderated only recently. Indian people now in their forties can remember classmates who were struck with brooms for speaking their Indian languages, forced to wear a sign around their necks: "I spoke Indian in school."

When Joe Dishta, a Zuni man in his thirties, was initiated into his kiva as a boy, he wore an eagle-down feather to St. Anthony's Catholic School. He was reprimanded for being a pagan. Lea Pinto, also a Zuni in her mid-thirties, suffered the same accusations in parochial school when she would counter the prescribed stories with, "but my grandmother says . . ." The teachers called her "the Devil's child."

Today, the Zuni School District makes a special lunch for kids undergoing initiation and on dietary restrictions. Schools close for Shalako. Joe Dishta told me that though Zuni held night dances on weekends for a time, they recently have returned to following the Zuni calendar.

In college, Indian students often drop out after one or two years; some wait a while, gather their energies, and try again. Others never return. Stella Clah, Navajo, with an M.S. in sociology, works as ethnic student advisor at the University of Utah. She told me: "The students who come to this center are the ones who excel and finish school. They can come here and get more energy and go back out and do it again. We don't see them much in junior and senior years. The ones we don't see at all are the ones who don't make it." Nonetheless, the number of Indians enrolled in higher education rose from 2,000 to 70,000 between 1960 and 1990.

Dennis Patch, education director for the Colorado River Tribes, says: "Indian people make it hard for Indians to be Indians. They don't allow an educated Indian to be Indian. I bring education, not traditional bird singing to the tribe. Maybe that's what I was chosen to be. We have enough trouble with other people stereotyping us that we don't need to stereotype ourselves as mechanics, heavy equipment operators, or secretaries. Why don't we have more priests, more oceanographers?" As Quechan Barbara Antone says: "I've *been* a stereotype. I was walking backward, not forward. There is no 'white man' to blame in my world; it's an excuse. We need to get out there with our fighting tools and defeat the stereotypes, the discrimination, the barriers."

Tony Dorame, from Tesuque Pueblo, believes that resolution is possible, that the old excuses are "hogwash." He goes on: "Indian people who are firmly fixed in their values can operate in any setting because they derive strength from their world. In fact, there is no other 'dominant' world in existence. The so-called other world is in fact an amalgamation of many ethnic groups whose values overlap Indian values."

Rina Swentzell, Santa Clara architectural historian, says: "Change is good, but it has to happen with continuity. When that continuity gets broken, you lose your sense of connectedness to the world around you, you lose a sense of balance. It's good to change, it's good not to change — they always have to be brought together in some balance, so that they create a whole."

Creating a Whole, Living in Balance

So many issues reduce to this balance between Indian and Anglo values, the unresolved struggles, as Joseph Jorgensen puts it, between "individualism and collectivism, between capitalism and communitarianism, between white actions and Indian responses, and between a non-Indian ideology that promotes fair play and

Painted woodbox, Towaoc, Ute Mountain Reservation, 1989. Most native languages have no word for "art"; the concept is integrated with everything in the lives of the People.

compassion." The two sides can be brought together, but that takes creativity and thoughtfulness. Tony Ringlero, Pima/Apache, says: "There's a lot of power with Indian people — the power of the elements, the power of the medicine man. The power of white people is money. Sometimes you need both — the finances and the spiritual power." Weldon Johnson, Pima, laments what he sees happening with development on Indian lands: "Sooner or later, these things end up in lawsuits, where some judge is trying to decide whether your religion is valid or not. And that's wrong."

The crux of that religion remains straightforward. Tom Vigil, at Jicarilla, sums up the Apache — and Indian — view of the world this way: "It's simple, the world is God; all the forces in the world and in nature are important. We pray to the symbols of these forces. What it means to be Indian is to live in prayer and hope. The ultimate end is peace, peace of mind, being happy. It's not incompatible with anything in the twentieth century. I've tried being something I wasn't, and I came back to being what I am."

Rosanda Suetopka-Thayer, from Hopi, says: "Indians are real practical. That's why Indian religion lasts. You don't have to go anywhere; you don't need special equipment." Alfreda Mitre, Paiute, says: "This abstract thinking — believing that the wind is alive, that you can talk to the rain—is still with us. You learn this as a child. It makes us a little different from the average American." Chemehuevi/Apache Gail Russell: "Indian people don't need to go to church to read meaningless prayers." Indian prayers "combine everything, things that are here, now. Our people are still poor, so we have a lot to pray for."

More than anything, those prayers need to bring back Southwest Indian people from the devastation of alcoholism. One-third of all Indian people die before the age of forty-five from alcohol-related disease. One in four Indian twelfth-grade boys is a problem drinker; in turn, one in six Native American adolescents has attempted suicide—four times the rate for the general American population. One-fourth of the Indian students at one boarding school admit to a suicide attempt. Harold Chaipos, Quechan elder, sadly concluded that "Indians are usually the last ones to pick up good things, the first to pick up bad."

Gail Russell says: "The number one problem for young Indian people is alcoholism. *Every* Indian person has been touched directly or indirectly by this. We have lost a generation or two of people to diabetes and alcohol. But now there is more of an awareness, and I think the next ten years will be positive."

Mona Fernandez, Hopi/Havasupai, works as behavioral health services coordinator for the Colorado River Tribes. She says: "It is hard to be optimistic when you are working with eleven-year-old alcoholics. The system that exists can't help him because of understaffing, limited resources. It seems hopeless and overwhelming.

"But on the very day I was ready to give up, some kids came in and asked me to help. They said to me. 'We want to become Indian leaders, meet Indian professionals, learn about how the government works with Indians. We want a better future.'

"That gives me the hope that I didn't think I had. I know there are young people out there who have the motivation to do this."

Tom Vigil, Jicarilla, believes: "The biggest problem with alcoholism is that the drunk is usually our cousin or somebody we're willing to tolerate. We love them to death; we support their habit by not saying anything." Dave Warren agrees: "When you try to tell your mother or sister not to drink—talk about infighting! We have to do this with our peers; tribal chairmen have to intervene boldly. Otherwise there will be no us."

At the Hualapai Reservation, parole officer Weldon Mahone says: "My people are hurting. Drugs and liquor are tearing them up, tearing their minds, tearing their insides, tearing them all to pieces. There's no ending to it." But he also believes in the future: "We cannot turn time back. We must struggle. We must go forward toward the bright horizon."

Delmar Boni, San Carlos Apache artist and teacher, sees these challenges with both sadness and hope. He says: "I see a lot of creative people who are quite in tune with who they are on the reservation. But somehow they find it hard to find themselves a niche in what the Western man's concept of man defines them to be. Most of the time we see these people at bars, at reservation border towns. They are caught in a paradoxical situation.

"They adhere to the values of what the grandmothers and grandfathers talked about, to be in tune with themselves, to be in tune with their environment. But when it comes to applying for a job, they don't have the degrees.

"The most creative people that we have, that know about all these stories, that have something to say, are in fact people we know to be reservation winos, reservation dropouts."

And yet, there is always the ideal of the People — individuals who bridge the paradox. Boni goes on: "More and more I see young Indian people making it. Lawyers, doctors, degreed people with Ph.D.s, master's, that in the same breath know something about these things we are talking about."

Indian art creates another bridge across the gap. And yet, as Norman Lansing, Ute Mountain potter, says: "It's pretty hard to be an artist and a businessman at the same time." Success complicates the lives of native artists. In her poem, "Two Worlds," potter Nora Naranjo-Morse finds herself stricken by guilt on a vacation:

> Damn, Indian women,
> especially Pueblo women,
> don't drink Piña Coladas
>   on Kauai beaches
>   in December and enjoy it!

Finding balance in her identity as one of her People, the Towa of Santa Clara Pueblo, she resolves her feelings:

> I am a brown woman
>   who will always be a Towa
>   even under a hot Pacific sun.

Naranjo-Morse began her career selling pottery on the portal in front of the Palace of the Governors on the Santa Fe plaza. This often may be the only place where tourists on Southwestern vacations talk with a group of Indian people. Says Rodey Guerro, a Navajo silversmith who sells his work there: "We are living museum pieces." A Santo Domingo woman next to him adds: "People say 'Why don't you get a job?' They don't understand that this is our job. I've been doing this for nine years." Guerro agrees:

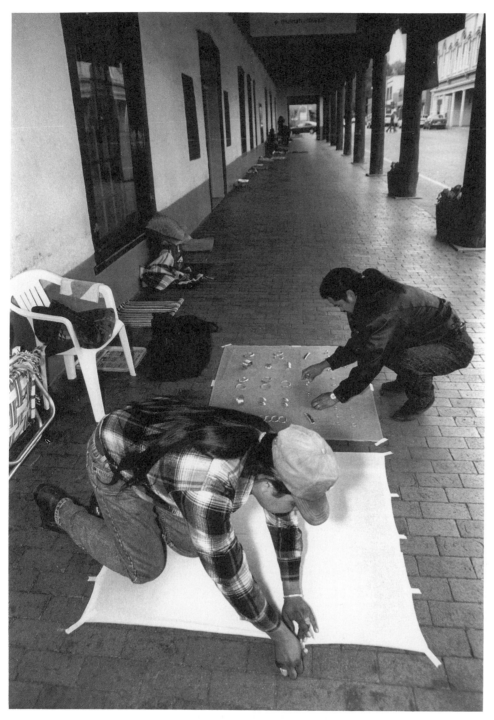

The portal in front of the Palace of the Governors on the Santa Fe plaza, 1992. Tourists visiting the Southwest may well talk with Indian people in no other place, and the portal vendors pride themselves on their ability to educate. Here, Neal Paquin (left), Laguna, and Allen Paquin, Jemez/Zuni — brothers who acknowledge different parts of their ancestry — arrange their silver for the day's business.

"Sometimes the wind-chill factor is below zero and we're still sitting here. The one that toughs it out gets the sale."

In trying to combine two worlds — to "tough it out" — the People have a fine line to walk. Salt River Pima Earl Ray says: "Our Indian kids today are going to find life twice as challenging as the non-Indian. They have to learn to take both ways and inter-weave them — taking things where they apply — take mythology and use it as political strategy."

Travis Parashonts, a Utah Paiute, warns of becoming "too Indian and too proud. I look for things that have value and truth in them, both in your society and mine. When I find them, I try to incorporate them in my life. We need to teach and preach balance."

Mentors from Inside

Darwin Roanhorse is looking for that balance. He is thirty years old, Navajo, and a candidate for a Master of Fine Arts degree at Goddard College in Vermont. Raised on the reservation, in 1991 he came back from Vermont for a term at Navajo Community College with a hunger for "Navajo history and spiritual knowledge." He feels it may be too late: "I am looking for the missing pieces in a flickering old eight-millimeter movie — trying to fill them in. It's almost like it's something I can hold in my hands and look at as I turn it — but I can't understand it.

"I've fallen from so far and splintered all over the floor. When I try to speak Navajo, it all goes upstairs to my analytical brain and comes back out in packages like laundered shirts."

He says: "I'm so discouraged. What is it that I want to learn? There are so many things that I want to do. What am I in this life for?"

Roanhorse wants to write about these things. He wants to "band together" with Navajos who have been to the city and Navajos "who are living *out there*, who are thinking, who are getting up with the sunrise. Then we can meet and decide how to maintain our sense of tradition and how we can still compete with the outside world."

Young Indian people like Darwin Roanhorse need role models (though of course people like Roanhorse are role models themselves). When Barney Mitchell, Navajo culture teacher at Rock Point, instituted Navajo song and dance contests in the seven-ties, he reasoned: "The younger generation copies what it sees, and when it sees the joy of acting like a traditional, respectful, thoughtful Navajo, it will start copying that."

Young Indian people need men like Larry and John Echohawk, Pawnee brothers who grew up in Farmington, New Mexico. Larry became Attorney General of Idaho in 1990, after working on legal issues for several tribes. As the first-ever Indian member of the Conference of Western Attorneys General, he brings a native perspective to a group that, he notes, has traditionally been filled with "opponents of tribal rights."

His older brother, John Echohawk, has directed the Native American Rights Fund (NARF) since the 1970s. Recently judged "one of the nation's one hundred most powerful attorneys" by the *National Law Journal*, Echohawk arguably is the most important champion of Indian legal rights today. A third brother, Walter Echo-Hawk, works as an attorney for NARF, and has been a leader in trying to strengthen the well-meaning but weak 1978 American Indian Religious Freedom Resolution.

In the twenty years since John Echohawk graduated from the University of New Mexico law school, he has seen the number of Native American lawyers in the United States rise from twenty to seven hundred. He and his staff have been involved in countless court cases that have helped tribes to become "legally defined, once and for all, in American society." Echohawk thinks the People have finally gone beyond the wild swings of the federal policy pendulum — "we've come too far for that."

Successful Indian women are even easier to find. They have continued their strong matriarchal roles, holding families together. And the traditional roles of women in camp — tasks like food gathering and basket weaving — involved the kinds of organizational and fine motor skills that translate well to success in office work and Anglo education. Men — warriors and hunters — don't have as many options that fit naturally into Anglo cultural norms. Some families work this out better than others. Janice Colorow works as the Ute Mountain tribal librarian; her husband stays home and works on livestock and raises their children.

Lucinda Williamson, Pima/Maricopa educator, has her own theories: "We women have been brought up handling babies, careers, money; men go out of the cave and bring home the meat! Men have a hard time handling multiple tasks, and men in any culture have that macho-ism to deal with. Indian men are trying to balance those two worlds, plus this macho-ism. They can't do all three, so they pick two." Vickie Wyatt, a young Moapa Paiute, says: "We don't have any strong men; they are all dead from drinking."

Christine Benally is another young Navajo who still is seeking to learn — at the same time that she has become a role model herself. Trained at Navajo Community College as a lab technician, she went on to work in industry and then returned to school. After finishing her B.S., she looked at graduate students and said: "If they can do it, I can do it." She obtained a Ph.D. in environmental health in 1990. She then turned down many higher-paying jobs to return to teach at NCC. She says: "Money can always come; family members can't."

She told me: "I just stayed at college — right through ceremonies, funerals, marriages at home. I had a hard time getting back into education, and once I was back into

Three generations of Navajo women, and — so far — two generations of weavers: Pauline Allen, her daughter-in-law Beverly Allen, and granddaughters Rebecca and Raberta Allen. Tsaile, Arizona, 1991.

the flow, I stuck with it. I had to give up a lot. Your family doesn't always understand."

Benally feels strongly about her return to NCC. "It was time to come home and spend time with my family. The culture is thinning. I want to get as much as I can."

Motivations for such success are just as hard to analyze for Indian people as for anyone else. How did Jennie Joe become a Ph.D. anthropologist? "I was a failure as a weaver and a sheepherder. My mother said, 'I guess we better explore other alternatives!' My grandmother gave me the gift of curiosity; that was why I failed at herding. I spent so much time being curious about so many things that I forgot about the sheep.

"Now, I tell my own kids when they go to school: 'Be like a detective; here's this culture, figure it out!' "

Nora Garcia became chair of the Fort Mojave Tribe when she was twenty-eight. She says: "The women I meet are so proud, it makes me feel good. There is the 'fishbowl syndrome,' too: everybody is watching. It's a lot of responsibility."

Yaqui educator Octaviana Trujillo talks about the "fishbowl," too, about the expectation that she be a "super Indian woman." She has directed Indian education programs for the Tempe and Tucson school districts and the University of Arizona. She adds, however, that "not all Yaquis should even graduate from high school. We need to provide all Indian children with the *chance* for education. We have to empower people to make the best decision for themselves."

This is a radical position for someone with Trujillo's experience. But she is well aware of what she calls her "balancing act — culturally, linguistically, emotionally, spiritually. It's very draining. You have to walk a fine line and you can't stray or you'll be in trouble with your own people, and worst of all, you'll be in trouble with yourself."

Reinventing an Indian Identity

Octaviana Trujillo says: "Being Yaqui and being able to place myself outside that culture and look inside from outside — I can do both. Before I was so immersed, I couldn't see the subtleties of who we are." Staying in touch with that sense of identity remains eternally challenging. As Southern Ute Linda Baker Rohde says: "People need to understand that not all Indians are the same." Just as "you can't say all Americans enjoy apple pie and eat spaghetti."

Richard TeCube, Jicarilla, admits: "I'm not sure what the Indian story is anymore. We're not feathers and buckskins. People live in houses with running water, pitched roofs. It's done, you can't take it back now. How does the influence countrywide finally filter down to an isolated reservation community? TV, books, movies. We have powwows and ceremonies all across New Mexico — packed with people from all over. That mobility is a profound influence." But as Tom Vigil says: "The worst place to learn culture is at a powwow; it just depends on the announcer, who makes it up as he goes along."

Powwows nonetheless serve powerful roles for maintaining Indian identity. The dances came from Plains tribes, while the powwow grew from a desire to honor twentieth century war veterans, creating a blended celebration of both patriotism and Indianness. In the sixties, intertribal powwows became crucial for growing communities of urban Indians, far from their own tribal traditions but in need of some way to nourish ethnicity.

Indian people living in Salt Lake City tell Gail Russell when they come to her Indian Walk-In Center's powwows in the winter months: "I don't know what I'd do if we didn't have powwows!" Russell believes: "Unless you come to a powwow when you're so far from any reservation, you have no contact with your culture."

Such non-tribal ways of being Indian can be crucial. Several people in their thirties and forties talked to me about taking over their high school Indian clubs in the 1960s from white "Wannabes." For many, this was the first time they felt proud of being Indian while in the heart of the dominant society. Nora Naranjo-Morse, Santa Clara potter, remembers the thrill of hearing drums in assemblies. Verna Williamson, former governor of Isleta Pueblo, says: "The sixties gave me the courage to do what I do."

Tony Ringlero, raised at Salt River, says: "Most of the Salt River people I grew up with, we didn't have an identity other than fry bread and speaking with a broken English accent — even though we couldn't speak our own language."

Anthropologist Edward Spicer noted that the best-known tribes "become a part of Anglo society." Minorities, yes. Victims of neglect and prejudice, yes. But Pueblo, Navajo, Apache — even the Havasupais in their "Shangri-La of the Grand Canyon" — have their niches in Anglo awareness. Whatever misinterpretations and stereotypes remain, these tribes have an edge on establishing self-esteem in the non-Indian world that mostly invisible but largely unacculturated tribes like the Cocopah, Hualapai, or Ute Mountain Utes do not. The latter tribes start in isolation; they start from poverty and anonymity. Paradoxically, they may be able to evolve a modern identity more easily, since no tribal stereotype exists that must be superseded. In isolation, they also can maintain old ways more easily.

The mass media, Christianity, education, disruption of the old housing patterns, and the need to compete for jobs in the dominant society all contribute to changes in culture. Intermarriage contributes to these challenges, as well; in 1980, 53 percent of married American Indians were married to non-Indians. Many others marry Indians outside their own tribes. Doreena White, a young Pima basket weaver, describes herself as "mostly Pima — but my mother is a Laguna." Gail Russell told me that when she introduces herself as Chemehuevi/Apache, "people only remember the Apache part." Chemehuevi? What's that?

Paula Gunn Allen calls her upbringing a "multicultural event"; the "confluence of cultures" in her bloodline include Laguna, English, Arabic, Spanish, Lakota, and German. Grandchildren in such families may not be able to communicate with their Indian elders who speak a native language. As Diné elder John Burnside says: "Today everyone speaks the English language. I do not speak English. I live in silence."

English has endangered the very existence of native languages. Hopi scholar Emory Sekaquaptewa predicts that half of Indian languages will become extinct within a generation. Perhaps 10 percent of Arizona Indians under thirty speak their native language fluently. Ninety-five percent of the 1991 incoming freshmen at the prestigious Navajo Preparatory School in Farmington could not speak Navajo. In 1990,

Toneya (left) and Camille Shanta, Hopi/Mescalero Apache, wait for the Grand Entry at the Gathering of Nations Powwow, Albuquerque, 1991. At major powwows such as this, the palpable sense of Indianness and the deep beat of the drums help sustain Indian identity far from the reservations.

Fort Apache museum curator Edgar Perry watched students at Alchesay High School in Whiteriver vote on the second language they would like taught in school: French came in first, Spanish second, and Apache third.

Sylvia Querta notes the inevitability of intermarriage and its consequences for young people in her little Hualapai community at Peach Springs: "We are at that point where they can't marry anymore within the tribe; it's too close. There will be very few full-blooded Hualapais left. I married a Hualapai from a family from the other side; my daughter is related to *everybody*. She can't marry anyone here."

There are many ways to nourish the feeling of identity, of strength, that comes from being Indian, and few depend on whether or not a person is "full-blood." Most involve family — the bastion of old ways even in the most acculturated Indian community. Many are nonverbal; as Nora Naranjo-Morse says: "I rarely talk to my mother about pottery. That connection is instinctively there. It's just part of you." Millie Touchin, at Laguna, talks about the importance of small things: "I have a daughter in Albuquerque, a son in Michigan, and a daughter in the navy who's been all over the world. They call me every two weeks. I have to send them chile — all the things they miss."

Pima medicine man Emmett White says: "Because of our 'Indian time,' we can take time to look at these things. Others are caught up in a world that's spinning out of control. The old people say in Pima, 'The Earth is round.' What you do comes around to you; that's what life is about."

That same Piman homily could be applied to most issues in Indian Country; the challenges rarely go away. Those who seek to extinguish Indian rights remain powerful: big business, fish and game lobbies, local and state governments, and pork-barrel Western congressmen. Members of the Native American Church, long subject to persecution, must now deal with a 1990 U.S. Supreme Court ruling that seriously weakens their First Amendment rights to practice their religion and to transport peyote off-reservation; Indian rights groups consider the current judicial climate to have created a crisis in religious liberty. "English-only laws" have "mobilized tribes . . . to plan for their own linguistic survival," in the words of Tohono O'odham linguist Ofelia Zepeda. Challenges to Indian water rights never slacken. And a new movement to abrogate treaty rights has touched off the most widespread demonstrations by Indian activists in years. The newer problems will not go away, either. Dave Warren, from Santa Clara, worries about the "plague-like" dangers of AIDS "in such tight situations."

As Felix Cohen, the codifier of federal Indian law in the thirties, said: "Like the miner's canary, the Indian marks the shift from fresh air to poison gas in our political atmosphere; and our treatment of Indians, even more than our treatment of other minorities, marks the rise and fall of our democratic faith."

Perhaps the most emotional of recent issues has been the realization on the part of Indian people that museums are warehouses for their ancestors' bones. In 1989, the Smithsonian Institution agreed to return its more than eighteen thousand Native American skeletons if any could be identified by tribe. Daniel Preston, a Tohono O'odham from San Xavier, is more than ready to see that happen: "I've been to the museum and seen what they do to the bones, spray them with chemicals so they'll last forever. Those bones are supposed to go back to Mother Earth. It's like me going into Tucson and digging up somebody's relative and putting them here in a museum and letting non-Indians come look at their grandmother. This is the most disrespectful thing anyone could do to a person's spirit, well being. If these people would give the bones back to the O'odham people, we can take care of them in our hearts. All the trees, all the foods that come from the ground are coming from the place where our ancestors are buried." Pima museum administrator Weldon Johnson agrees: "We want digs, nondestructive analysis, time-frames established, and after this, reburial. Archaeology helps culture — it's a wheel that brings you back. But there has to be respect, as Indians and archaeologists, and vice versa."

Daniel Preston says that a white man can understand Indians only if he, too, "knew where he was from, he knew where his ancestors were buried, what they had to sacrifice to keep their land, had a reservation somewhere he had to fight for. Whites have lost that. They are jealous of Indian people." Dennis Patch, Mojave, wants "the dominant society to become more aware of who we are — not a bunch of lazy, dumb, savage, bloodthirsty Indians but humble, reverent, beautiful people." To do this, both sides need to communicate. As Las Vegas Paiute Alfreda Mitre says: "Once you stop the dialogue, we really don't exist."

The media continues to do its best to make all Indians the same and to then freeze them in the "traditional times" of 1880; the same forces in corporate and political America insist that all Americans in the 1990s share identical goals, desires, and dreams — that they aspire to be rich, white, blonde — and frenetic consumers. Americans in general do not mold to these insults; American Indians do not, either. Both, as Americans are prone to do, constantly reinvent themselves.

Hope remains for understanding — and for the People to maintain their freedoms and vitality. At issue for each native group are reform of tribal government, cultural renewal, economic stability, and a stable relationship with federal and state governments. The futures of Southwest Indian nations have as many possible courses as their diverse origins and histories. But at the heart of both their past and their future lies a simple belief in the goodness of the Earth — a continuity, a certainty, a reverence, and a connection.

The People have been living with this land for at least thirty times as long as any non-Indians. They have lived with the land, not apart from it. They live here permanently. While permanence does not guarantee wisdom, it encourages thoughtfulness. As non-Indian Southwesterners sink their own roots, they can begin to look beyond quick extraction of resources and unlimited growth to nourish their communities. The People offer an ethic to all Southwesterners: that this is the land to fight for, to learn from, and to cherish. We all can take root; we all can learn who we are: natives, finally.

The unbroken continuity that the People feel stretches from the past right through the present and into the future. The past still exists in story and memory, and the future can be foretold by prophecy. Everything that exists matters; everything is related. Laguna writer Leslie Marmon Silko tells of her elders who refused to record "the stories and songs that would be lost when they passed away." These old people told the anthropologists: "What is important to our children and our grandchildren will be remembered; what is forgotten is what is no longer meaningful. What is true will persist."

Rooted in their families, the People find strength for the fight to survive. Rooted in their land, they move outward from home to meet their challenges. Rooted, they know who they are: "We are the People. We are the land. We will persist."

Faren Burch, Southern Ute dancer, 1990.

Notes

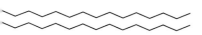

Quotations from Indian people in the text come primarily from interviews I conducted between 1984 and 1992. During the first four years, I was working under the auspices of The Heard Museum, Phoenix, and the School of American Research, Santa Fe; tape recordings of those interviews can be found in the archives of the two institutions. All other interviews are documented in my own notebooks. Quotes from published sources can be found in the books I mention in the following notes. To comment or inquire about sources for anything in my text, please write to me care of the publisher.

Preface and Introduction

The definition of the Southwest quoted in the preface comes from John H. Parry's article in *Plural Society in the Southwest*, edited by Edward H. Spicer and Raymond H. Thompson (University of New Mexico Press, 1972). The Taos Indian man's words in the epigraph come from Alfonso Ortiz's comments in *Indian Voices: The First Convocation of American Indian Scholars* (The Indian Historian Press, 1970), a book that strongly conveys the major issues confronting anyone trying to understand contemporary Indian people.

The Smithsonian Institution's *Handbook of North American Indians* is the primary source for Southwestern Indians. This enormously ambitious project will eventually result in twenty volumes — an entire bookshelf — summarizing what we know of all North American native peoples. Luckily, the volumes so far published include the three that cover the tribes included in this book: Volume 9: *Southwest* (Pueblo peoples; prehistory, history, and languages of the entire Southwest; Alfonso Ortiz, ed., 1979); Volume 10: *Southwest* (non-Pueblo peoples; Alfonso Ortiz, ed., 1983); and Volume 11: *Great Basin* (including Ute, Southern Paiute, and Chemehuevi; Warren L. D'Azevedo, ed., 1986). Volume 4: *History of Indian-White Relations*, edited by Wilcomb E. Washburn (1988), was also useful, especially for this introductory chapter. These authoritative books are packed with information and illustrations — and they are remarkable bargains, available from the U.S. Government Printing Office.

See also Bertha P. Dutton's *American Indians of the Southwest* (University of New Mexico Press, 1983) and the sweeping *Cycles of Conquest: The Impact of Spain, Mexico, and the United States on the Indians of the Southwest, 1533–1960* by Edward H. Spicer (University of Arizona Press, 1962). The Jack D. Forbes quote comes from his fine *Native Americans of California and Nevada* (Naturegraph, 1989).

For an introduction to the Southwestern landscape, see *Natural Regions of the United States and Canada* by Charles B. Hunt (W. H. Freeman, 1974); *The Mysterious Lands: A Naturalist Explores the Four Deserts of the Southwest* by Ann Zwinger (E. P. Dutton, 1989); *Biotic Communities of the American Southwest — United States and Mexico*, edited by David E. Brown (*Desert Plants*, vol. 4, 1982); and *The Audubon Society Nature Guide to Deserts* by James A. MacMahon (Alfred A. Knopf, 1985).

Narrower in focus are Tom Miller, editor, *Arizona: The Land and the People* (University of Arizona Press, 1986) and Stephen Trimble, *The Bright Edge: A Guide to the National Parks of the Colorado Plateau* (Museum of Northern Arizona Press, 1979).

For prehistory and archaeology, go first to Linda S. Cordell's *Prehistory of the Southwest* (Academic Press, 1984) and Robert H. Lister and Florence C. Lister's *Those Who Came Before: Southwestern Archeology in the National Park System* (Southwest Parks and Monuments Association, 1983). "Gardeners in Eden," by Kat Anderson and Gary Paul Nabhan, *Wilderness* (Fall 1991):27–30, clearly states the new understanding of native peoples as managers of the "pristine" continent's resources.

The best quick overview and introduction to the Southwest's peoples, both prehistoric and contemporary, is the exhibit "Native Peoples of the Southwest" at The Heard Museum in Phoenix. This permanent exhibit fills an entire wing of the museum. See also the book version of the audio-visual program from the exhibit, *Our Voices, Our Land*, edited by Stephen Trimble (Northland Press, 1986), which focuses on the vitality of contemporary Southwest Indian people.

The most comprehensive history of Indian relations with the United States is Francis Paul Prucha's monumental two-volume *The Great Father: The United States Government and the American Indians* (University of Nebraska Press, 1984). Prucha elegantly distills the ideas in this material in *The Indians in American Society* (University of California Press, 1985). Michael Dorris, "The Grass Still Grows, the Rivers Still Flow: Contemporary Native Americans," *Daedalus*, vol. 110, no. 2 (1981):43–69, and Joseph G. Jorgensen, "A Century of Political Economic Effects on American Indian

Society, 1880–1980," *The Journal of Ethnic Studies*, vol. 6, no. 3 (1978):1–82, also provide fine historic outlines of the legal and political status of Indian tribes.

For specific eras, see Frederick E. Hoxie, *A Final Promise: The Campaign to Assimilate the Indians, 1880–1920* (University of Nebraska Press, 1984); Kenneth R. Philp, *John Collier's Crusade for Indian Reform* (University of Arizona Press, 1977); Alison R. Bernstein, *American Indians and World War II* (University of Oklahoma Press, 1991); and a fine book edited by Philp, *Indian Self-Rule: First-Hand Accounts of Indian-White Relations from Roosevelt to Reagan* (Howe Brothers, 1986), from which the quotes from Alfonso Ortiz and Sam Deloria come. *One House, One Voice, One Heart: Native American Education at the Santa Fe Indian School*, by Sally Hyer (Museum of New Mexico Press, 1990), contains a wealth of quotes from Indian students commenting on a full century of the boarding school experience.

Vine Deloria, Jr., and Clifford M. Lytle collaborated on the superb *The Nations Within: The Past and Future of American Indian Sovereignty* (Pantheon, 1984). The quote from Mary Young appears in Calvin Martin, editor, *The American Indian and the Problem of History* (Oxford University Press, 1987); Gary Witherspoon's words come from his *Language and Art in the Navajo Universe* (University of Michigan Press, 1977). See my Southern Paiute chapter note for the Turner source. *Indians in American History: An Introduction*, Frederick E. Hoxie, editor (Harlan Davidson, 1988), also helped shape my thinking.

The best books on Indian activism in the recent past are by the idiosyncratic but eloquent Stan Steiner: for the sixties, *The New Indians* (Harper and Row, 1968), and for the seventies, *The Vanishing White Man* (Harper and Row, 1976). To understand modern Indian America, read anything and everything by Vine Deloria, Jr., especially the biting *Custer*

Died for Your Sins (Macmillan, 1969; University of Oklahoma reprint, with a new introduction, 1988), *God Is Red* (Grosset & Dunlap, 1973), and *Indian Education in America* (American Indian Science & Engineering Society, 1991). Michael Dorris's *The Broken Cord* (Harper & Row, 1989) devastatingly documents some of the horrors alcoholism has wrought on Indian families. C. Matthew Snipp analyzes 1980 census data for the Indian population in detail in *American Indians: The First of This Land* (Russell Sage Foundation, 1989). Joan Weibel-Orlando, *Indian Country: L.A.* (University of Illinois Press, 1991) analyzes how Indians maintain their ethnicity in cities.

A superb critical work on contemporary Native American literature, from which the epigraph for my book comes, is Kenneth Lincoln's *Native American Renaissance* (University of California Press, 1983). Simon Ortiz's eloquent words come from *Fight Back: For the Sake of the People, For the Sake of the Land* (Institute for Native American Development Literary Journal, vol. 1, no. 1, 1980). I recommend all of Simon Ortiz's work, much of which is gathered in *Woven Stone* (University of Arizona Press, 1992); his is a crucial voice.

The Pueblos

The literature on the Pueblos is rich, especially books on ceremony and religion. For basic Pueblo history and culture, in addition to the Smithsonian *Handbook* and Spicer (1962), the crucial works come from two Pueblo scholars: Joe S. Sando's *The Pueblo Indians* (The Indian Historian Press, 1976) and the updated *Pueblo Nations* (Clear Light, 1991), and Edward P. Dozier's *The Pueblo Indians of North America* (Holt, Rinehart, and Winston, 1970). See also Sando's fine *Nee Hemish: A History of Jemez Pueblo* (University of New Mexico Press, 1982); would that there were comparable

books for every pueblo by such eminent tribal historians.

Monographs on individual pueblos have been a staple of anthropology for over a century. A warning, however: regard all information regarding religion or spiritual matters in these books with suspicion. Pueblo people do not yield such information easily, and often modify the truth slightly to make it more appropriate for publication. The overall feeling is usually accurate; details may be vague or misrepresented.

The classic example is Frank Waters' *The Book of the Hopi* (Viking, 1963): his informant, Oswald White Bear Fredericks, was not initiated and therefore not privy to the core of Hopi culture. White Bear's material is further filtered through the Anglo sensibilities of Waters. Emory Sekaquaptewa calls the book "a fiasco," though other Hopis call it "credible." The book does communicate much of the mystery of Hopi, remaining a basic source for the tribe.

Monographs that helped me include the following: Elsie Clews Parsons, *Taos Pueblo* (Banta General Series in Anthropology 2, 1936); *The Pueblo of Santo Domingo, New Mexico* (American Anthropological Association Memoir 43, 1935) and *The Pueblo of Santa Ana, New Mexico* (American Anthropological Association Memoir 60, 1942), both by Leslie A. White; William Whitman, *The Pueblo Indians of San Ildefonso: A Changing Culture* (Columbia University Press, 1947); Charles Lange, *Cochiti: A New Mexico Pueblo, Past and Present* (Southern Illinois University Press, 1959); Shuichi Nagata, *Modern Transformations of Moenkopi Pueblo* (University of Illinois Press, 1970); Ward Alan Minge, *Acoma: Pueblo in the Sky* (University of New Mexico Press, 1976); *The Zunis: Experiences and Descriptions* (Pueblo of Zuni, 1973); and Henry Dobyns and Robert Euler, *The Hopi People* (Indian Tribal Series, 1971).

Alfonso Ortiz's work provides a window

into the Tewa world view. See *The Tewa World: Space, Time, Being, and Becoming in a Pueblo Society* (University of Chicago Press, 1969) and *New Perspectives on the Pueblos* (School of American Research Press, 1972). Rina Swentzell also writes eloquently of Tewa belief: "Bupingeh: The Pueblo Plaza," *El Palacio*, vol. 94, no. 2 (1988):14–19; "The Butterfly Effect: A Conversation with Rina Swentzell," *El Palacio*, vol. 95, no. 1 (1989):24–29; "Remembering Tewa Pueblo Houses and Spaces," *Native Peoples*, vol. 3, no. 2 (Winter 1990):6–12.

Tryntje Van Ness Seymour's *When the Rainbow Touches Down* (The Heard Museum, 1988) has a wealth of quotes from Pueblo artists about not only their paintings but also their lives. See also Fred Kabotie and Bill Belknap, *Fred Kabotie: Hopi Indian Artist* (Museum of Northern Arizona Press, 1977) and Victor Masayesva, Jr., and Erin Younger, compilers, *Hopi Photographers/Hopi Images* (University of Arizona Press, 1983).

The chapter epigraph comes from Simon J. Ortiz, *A Good Journey* (Turtle Island, 1988), a fine book of poems. The Pablo Abeita story about Teddy Roosevelt comes from *Ranchers, Ramblers, and Renegades* by Marc Simmons (Ancient City Press, 1984). The description of the 1980 Hopi Children's Art Show comes from Catherine Feher-Elston, *Children of Sacred Ground: America's Last Indian War* (Northland Publishing, 1988). I also quote from Sandra Lee Pinel, "Peter Pino: Zia Pueblo's Man of Many Hats," *New Mexico Magazine* (March 1990):56–65.

Quotes from Bacavi people and the story of Oraibi come from Peter Whiteley's *Deliberate Acts: Changing Hopi Culture Through the Oraibi Split* (University of Arizona Press, 1988). See Edward P. Dozier, *Hano: A Tewa Indian Community in Arizona* (Holt, Rinehart and Winston, 1966) for the inner workings of First Mesa cultures. Joanne Kealiinohomoku's piece, "The Hopi Katsina Dance Event 'Doings,'"

appears in *Seasons of the Kachina*, Lowell John Bean, editor (Ballena Press Anthropological Papers 34, 1989).

Pueblo literature lives both in old stories and recent fiction. See, in particular, Leslie Marmon Silko's *Ceremony* (Viking, 1977) and *Storyteller* (Seaver Books, 1981); *Finding the Center: Narrative Poetry of the Zuni Indians*, translated by Dennis Tedlock from performances by Andrew Peynetsa and Walter Sanchez (University of Nebraska Press, 1972); and the many books of Hopi tales collected and translated by Ekkehart Malotki (for example, *Hopitutuwutsi/Hopi Tales* by Herschel Talashoma [University of Arizona, Sun Tracks, 1978]).

For fascinating life histories of Hopi and Hopi-Tewa whose lives spanned the early years of Anglo acculturation, see *Truth of a Hopi* by Edmund Nequatewa (Museum of Northern Arizona, 1936); Leo W. Simmons, editor, *Sun Chief: The Autobiography of a Hopi Indian* (Yale University Press, 1942); Polingaysi Qoyawayma, *No Turning Back* (University of New Mexico Press, 1964); and Albert Yava, *Big Falling Snow: A Tewa-Hopi Indian's Life and Times and the History and Traditions of His People* (University of New Mexico Press, 1978). For the feel of modern life at Hopi, see the excellent *Hopi* by Suzanne and Jake Page (Abrams, 1982).

The story of the Tiguas comes from Bertha Dutton (1983), the "Tigua Pueblo" chapter by Nicholas Houser in the Smithsonian *Handbook*, and Stan Steiner's *The Tiguas: The Lost Tribe of City Indians* (Crowell-Collier Press, 1972). The history of Tortugas comes from "An Ethnological Study of Tortugas, New Mexico," by Alan James Oppenheimer in *Apache Indians II* (Garland Publishing, 1974), and from *Tortugas* by Patrick H. Beckett and Terry L. Corbett (COAS Publishing, Monograph 8, 1990). Both tribes provided photocopied, unpublished histories with additional information.

The Blue Lake story comes largely from Alvin M. Josephy, Jr.'s, *Now That the Buffalo's*

Gone: A Study of Today's American Indians (University of Oklahoma Press, 1984); Robert A. Hecht's "Taos Pueblo and the Struggle for Blue Lake," *American Indian Culture and Research Journal*, vol. 13, no. 1 (1989):53–77; and Nancy Wood's controversial, blunt, but honest (as always) book, *Taos Pueblo* (Knopf, 1989).

Most of the water rights stories (and many quotes) come from Sando (1972). Additional quotes from Frank Tenorio come from Steiner (1976), as does the Tesuque Pueblo subdivision story. For the latter issue, see also the Tesuque Pueblo chapter in the Smithsonian *Handbook*. Charles Wilkinson writes frequently of Indian law issues; see, for instance, *American Indians, Time, and the Law: Native Societies in a Modern Constitutional Democracy* (Yale University Press, 1987). Some of the Cochiti statistics come from the interesting "Pathways from Poverty: Economic Development and Institution-Building on American Indian Reservations," by Stephen Cornell and Joseph P. Kalt, *American Indian Culture and Research Journal*, vol. 14, no. 1 (1990):89–125. "The New Indian Wars," by John Aloysius Farrell, ran in *The Denver Post*, 20–27 November 1983, and includes a vivid retelling of the Laguna uranium mine story. Silko's "The Fourth World," *Artforum*, vol. 27, no. 10 (1989):124–27, offers a Laguna perspective and includes my quotes from her.

Isleta pollution problems are discussed in *Americans Before Columbus*, vol. 17, no. 2 (1989) and vol. 18, no. 2 (1990). Zuni land issues come from "The Impact of Federal Policy on Zuni Land Use," by T. J. Ferguson, in *Seasons of the Kachina* (cited above). Quotes from Governor Joseph Lujan on Sandia's land claims come from the *Albuquerque Journal*, 27 March 1988.

The Hopi-Navajo land and mining disputes have generated enormous numbers of words. Dutton (1983) provides details of the coal mine leases; see also Marjane Ambler, *Breaking the Iron Bonds: Indian Control of Energy Development* (University Press of Kansas, 1990). Richard O. Clemmer's excellent *Continuities of Hopi Culture Change* (Acoma Books, 1978) provides thoughtful insights into the last century of Hopi politics and history.

As Peter Matthiessen says at the end of *Indian Country* (Viking, 1984), relocation "remains the most painful and dangerous situation in Indian Country." For relocation, I have relied mostly on the book by Feher-Elston (cited above); Jerry Kammer's *The Second Long Walk: The Navajo-Hopi Land Dispute* (University of New Mexico Press, 1980) is more of a polemic — from a Navajo perspective — but it tells the story in dramatic detail.

For overviews of Pueblo attitudes toward art, see Seymour (1988) and Ralph T. Coe, *Lost and Found Traditions: Native American Art 1965–1985* (University of Washington Press, 1986). For specific art forms, see my own *Talking with the Clay: The Art of Pueblo Pottery* (School of American Research Press, 1987); the classic *The Navajo and Pueblo Silversmiths* by John Adair (University of Oklahoma Press, 1944); the fine *Southwestern Indian Jewelry* by Dexter Cirillo (Abbeville Press, 1992); and M. Jane Young's excellent and wide-ranging *Signs from the Ancestors: Zuni Cultural Symbolism and Perceptions of Rock Art* (University of New Mexico Press, 1988). Volume 2 of Thomas E. Mails' *The Pueblo Children of the Earth Mother* (Doubleday, 1983) is filled with illustrations of pueblo life.

My perspective on Pueblo health issues was shaped by the papers in "Contemporary Issues in Native American Health," a special issue of *American Indian Culture and Research Journal*, vol. 13, nos. 3–4 (1989).

The Navajo

The Smithsonian *Handbook* contains an abundance of Navajo material by the modern experts; see especially Marshall Tome's "The Navajo Nation Today." Most additional material on Navajo culture and philosophy comes from Witherspoon (1977; cited in full in the "Preface and Introduction" note); John R. Farella's *The Main Stalk: A Synthesis of Navajo Philosophy* (University of Arizona Press, 1984); *The Navajos* by Ruth Underhill (University of Oklahoma Press, 1956); and *The Navaho* by Clyde Kluckhohn and Dorothea Leighton (Harvard University Press, 1974). James Downs' *The Navajo* (Waveland Press, 1972) conveys a good feel for day-to-day life in back-country Navajoland about 1960.

I base the historical story on the *Handbook*; Spicer (1962); *The Navajo Indians* by Henry F. Dobyns and Robert C. Euler (Indian Tribal Series, 1972); *A History of the Navajos: The Reservation Years* by Garrick Bailey and Roberta Glenn Bailey (School of American Research Press, 1986); Bill P. Acrey's *Navajo History: The Land and the People* (Shiprock Consolidated School District No. 22, Dept. of Curriculum Materials Development, 1978); *The Navajos* (Chelsea House, 1990) and *The Navajo Nation* (University of New Mexico Press, 1983) by Peter Iverson, the pivotal scholar for the later twentieth century; and Clyde Benally's fine *Dinéjí Nákéé' Nááhane': A Utah Navajo History* (Monticello, Utah: San Juan School District, 1982), which serves as a much wider general introduction than the title indicates. This observation is also true for David Aberle's magisterial *The Peyote Religion Among the Navajo* (Aldine Publishing Company, 1966).

The Navajo perspective speaks loud and clear in *Navajo History*, *Volume 1*, Ethelou Yazzie, editor (Navajo Curriculum Center, 1971) and in Sam and Janet Bingham's *Between Sacred Mountains: Navajo Stories and Lessons from the Land* (University of Arizona Press, 1982), from which come the quotes from George Blueeyes, Alice Luna, Many Mules' Granddaughter, Ned Yazzie, Claudeen Arthur, Amos Coggeshall, and Charles Morgan. See *Navajo Blessingway Singer: The Autobiography of Frank Mitchell*, Charlotte J. Frisbie and David P. McAllester, editors (University of Arizona Press, 1978), for a fine sense of one prominent man's life. Navajo Community College Press has published a wonderful series of oral histories; see especially *Navajo Stories of the Long Walk Period*, Ruth Roessel, editor (1973); *Navajo Livestock Reduction: A National Disgrace*, Broderick Johnson and Ruth Roessel, editors (1974); *Navajos and World War II*, Broderick Johnson, editor (1977).

Sources for more specific aspects of Navajo history include Robert W. Young's "The Rise of the Navajo Tribe," in *Plural Society in the Southwest* (1972), and his *A Political History of the Navajo Tribe* (Navajo Community College Press, 1978); Lawrence C. Kelly, *The Navajo Indians and Federal Indian Policy, 1900–1935* (University of Arizona Press, 1968); Donald L. Parman's detailed *The Navajos and the New Deal* (Yale University Press, 1976); *A Navajo Confrontation and Crisis* by Floyd Pollock (Navajo Community College Press, 1984), focusing on the thirties; *Navajo Ways in Government: A Study in Political Process* by Mary Shepardson (American Anthropological Association Memoir 96, 1963); and Klara B. Kelley and Peter M. Whiteley, *Navajoland: Family Settlement and Land Use* (Navajo Community College Press, 1989). For energy-related stories, see Ambler (1990) and Farrell (1983).

Books on Navajo art fill several shelves. See, in particular, Adair (1944); Seymour (1988); Cirillo (1992); *Indian Silver: Navajo and Pueblo Jewelers* by Margery Bedinger (University of New Mexico Press, 1973); *Navajo Sandpainting: From Religious Act to Commercial Art* by Nancy Parezo (University of Arizona Press, 1983), which traces the motivations and demography of the makers of this new commercial art form in fascinating detail; and *Navajo Pottery: Traditions and Innovations* by Russell Hartman,

Jan Musial, and Stephen Trimble (North-land Press, 1987). For a good introduction to weaving, see Stephen Trimble, editor, "Tension and Harmony: The Navajo Rug," *Plateau Magazine*, vol. 52, no. 4 (1981).

The relocation story comes from Feher-Elston (1988), Kammer (1980), and an excellent summary of the land dispute that appeared in a special issue of *High Country News* (12 May 1986): "Navajos Resist Relocation," by Christopher McLeod. Additional quotes come from *Between Sacred Mountains* and from John Running's portfolio of Big Mountain people in "Visions from the Southwest," *Plateau Magazine*, vol. 52, no. 3 (1980).

Tom Sasaki paints a clear picture of the changes that hit the reservation in the fifties in *Fruitland, New Mexico: A Navajo Community in Transition* (Cornell University Press, 1960). See Kendall Blanchard for *The Ramah Navajos* (Navajo Historical Series No. 1, Navajo Tribal Parks and Recreation Research Section, 1971). Eric Henderson details striking continuity of social history in a huge section of the western reservation in "Wealth, Status, and Change Among the Kaibeto Plateau Navajo" (Ph.D. dissertation, University of Arizona, 1985).

The Scott Momaday quote comes from "The Man Made of Words," in *Literature of the American Indians: Views and Interpretations*, Abraham Chapman, editor (New American Library, 1975); the Shonto Begay and some of the Luci Tapahanso quotes come from two lovely essays in *Anii Anaadaalyaa'lgii: Continuity & Innovation in Recent Navajo Art* (Wheelwright Museum, 1988). For a powerful and poetic new translation of the Navajo Creation Story, read Paul Zolbrod's *Diné bahane* (University of New Mexico Press, 1984).

The Pai

Hualapai ethnography comes primarily from the work of Henry F. Dobyns and Robert C. Euler. See their *The Walapai People* (Indian Tribal Series, 1976) and *Wauba Yuma's People: The Comparative Socio-Political Structure of the Pai Indians of Arizona* (Prescott College Press, 1970). See also the pioneering "Walapai Ethnography" edited by A. L. Kroeber, *Memoirs of the American Anthropological Association* 42 (1935), and Thomas R. McGuire's "Walapai" chapter in the Smithsonian *Handbook*. The epigraph and the Elnora Mapatis Wikahme' narration come from *Spirit Mountain: An Anthology of Yuman Story and Song*, Leanne Hinton and Lucille J. Watahomigie, editors (Sun Tracks/University of Arizona Press, 1984), equally good for both modern groups of Pai. The Rupert Parker quote comes from "Support Asked for Hualapai Dam," *Indian Historian*, vol. 1, no. 2 (1968):15–16.

Havasupai sources start with *The Nation of the Willows* by Frank Hamilton Cushing (Northland Press, 1965 reprint of 1882 text) and Leslie Spier's "Havasupai Ethnography," *Anthropological Papers of the American Museum of Natural History*, vol. 29, no. 3 (1928), which contains a map of every household and a genealogy of most of the tribe; they continue with *Havasupai Habitat: A. F. Whiting's Ethnography of a Traditional Indian Culture*, Steven A. Weber and P. David Seaman, editors (University of Arizona Press, 1985). Dobyns and Euler's *The Havasupai People* (Phoenix: Indian Tribal Series, 1971) is a basic source, as is Douglas Schwartz's Smithsonian *Handbook* chapter on the Havasupai.

The two best references for recent Havasupai life are Stephen Hirst's lovingly written *Havsuw 'Baaja: People of the Blue Green Water* (Havasupai Tribe, 1985), which tells the moving story of the fight for the expansion of the reservation and includes rich reconstructions and reminiscences; and the more analytical work by John F. Martin: "The Havasupai," *Plateau Magazine*, vol. 56, no. 4 (1986) and "The Havasupai Land Claims Case" in *Irredeemable*

America: The Indians' Estate and Land Claims, Imre Sutton, editor (University of New Mexico Press, 1985).

See also Barbara and Edwin McKee's *Havasupai Baskets and Their Makers* (Northland Press, 1974), which emphasizes the 1930s; Carma Lee Smithson's excellent *The Havasupai Woman* (University of Utah Anthropological Papers 38, 1959); Smithson and Euler, *Havasupai Religion and Mythology* (University of Utah Anthropological Papers 68, 1964), which contains a unique detailed description of a funeral; and Leanne Hinton's *Havasupai Songs: A Linguistic Perspective* (Tübingen: Gunter Narr Verlag, 1984).

The Yavapai

The classic Yavapai ethnographies are Edward W. Gifford's "The Southeastern Yavapai" and "Northeastern and Western Yavapai," *University of California Publications in American Archaeology and Ethnology*, vol. 29, no. 3 (1932):177–252 and vol. 34, no. 4 (1936):247–354. Gifford based the Southeastern Yavapai ethnography entirely on sixteen days of conversation with Mike Burns, John Smith's father-in-law. The story of the Yavapai wars (and relevant quotes) comes from *On the Border with Crook*, by John G. Bourke (University of Nebraska Press, 1971 reprint of 1891 edition), and *Verde to San Carlos*, by William T. Corbusier (Dale Stuart King, 1969).

Anthropologist Sigrid Khera took on the telling of the Yavapai story almost as a sacred mission, and her publications, along with those of her student, Patricia Mariella, are the critical sources today. See their chapter in the Smithsonian *Handbook*, Khera's *The Yavapai of Fort McDowell* (Fort McDowell Indian Community, 1979), and Mariella's excellent "The Political Economy of Federal Resettlement Policies Affecting Native American Communities: The Fort McDowell Yava-

pai Case" (Ph.D. dissertation, Arizona State University, 1983).

Peter Iverson has contributed the important biography *Carlos Montezuma and the Changing World of American Indians* (University of New Mexico Press, 1982). Clyde P. Morris studied the Camp Verde community in 1968: "A Brief Economic History of the Camp and Middle Verde Reservations," *Plateau Magazine* 44 (Fall 1971):43–51. The Pat McGee quotes come from the *Prescott Sun*, 17 August 1990; the John Williams quotes from his Skeleton Cave story appear along with other Yavapai literature collected in *Spirit Mountain* (Hinton and Watahomigie, 1984).

The Apache

The six Apache chapters in the Smithsonian *Handbook* are the best introduction to the vast Apache literature. Thomas E. Mails's *The People Called Apache* (Prentice-Hall, 1974) also makes a good starting point, with excellent drawings of items of Apache material culture. James L. Haley's *Apaches: A History and Culture Portrait* (Doubleday, 1981) is another good general synthesis. See also Donald E. Worcester, *The Apaches: Eagles of the Southwest* (University of Oklahoma Press, 1979), which emphasizes the Apache Wars.

For the history of Apache relations with the Spaniards, see Spicer's *Cycles of Conquest* for western Apachería, and Dolores A. Gunnerson's *The Jicarilla Apaches: A Study in Survival* (Northern Illinois University Press, 1974).

The authoritative history of the Apache Wars is Dan L. Thrapp, *The Conquest of Apachería* (University of Oklahoma Press, 1967). See also John G. Bourke, *On the Border with Crook*, for an eyewitness account by Crook's perceptive captain, and *A Clash of Cultures: Fort Bowie and the Chiricahua Apaches*, by Robert M. Utley (U.S. National Park Service, 1977). C. L.

Sonnichsen, *The Mescalero Apaches* (University of Oklahoma Press, 1973) provides the New Mexico Apache perspective and is the crucial source for Mescalero history.

The bedrock of Apache ethnography was laid by Grenville Goodwin and Morris E. Opler. For Goodwin, see *The Social Organization of the Western Apache* (University of Chicago Press, 1942), *Myths and Tales of the White Mountain Apache* (American Folklore Society Memoirs 33, 1939), and *Western Apache Raiding and Warfare* (Keith Basso, ed., University of Arizona Press, 1971). Opler's more than three dozen major works include the basic Chiricahua ethnography, *An Apache Lifeway* (University of Chicago Press, 1941); *Apache Odyssey: A Journey Between Two Worlds* (Holt, Rinehart and Winston, 1969), an autobiography of a Chiricahua/Mescalero hunter, singer, herbalist, and incipient shaman; and three collections of Apache myths and tales published by the American Folklore Society, 1938–1942.

For specific historic periods, see D. C. Cole, *The Chiricahua Apache, 1846–1876: From War to Reservation* (University of New Mexico Press, 1988) and Veronica E. Velarde Tiller, *The Jicarilla Apache Tribe: A History 1846–1970* (University of Nebraska Press, 1983) — both written by members of the tribes chronicled. Eve Ball's remarkable *Indeh, An Apache Odyssey* (Brigham Young University Press, 1980) tells the story of the Chiricahua fighters from Cochise to the last old warriors at Mescalero, largely through the words of Daklugie and Eugene Chihuahua, whom I quote repeatedly (my chapter epigraph from Goody also comes from Ball's oral history). Edwin R. Sweeney, in *Cochise: A Chiricahua Apache Chief* (University of Oklahoma Press, 1991), covers much new ground in detail.

Keith Basso is this generation's Goodwin; his work is fascinating and shows great respect for his Western Apache friends. See especially *The Cibecue Apache* (Holt, Rinehart and Winston, 1970) and *Western Apache Language and Culture: Essays in Linguistic Anthropology* (University of Arizona Press, 1990).

For the biography of the Fort Sill sculptor, see *Allan Houser (Ha-O-Zous)*, Barbara H. Perlman (David R. Godine, 1987). For a detailed history of the Chiricahua prisoner-of-war years, see *The Apache Rock Crumbles: The Captivity of Geronimo's People* by Woodward B. Skinner (Skinner Publications, 1987). H. Henrietta Stockel's *Women of the Apache Nation: Voices of Truth* (University of Nevada Press, 1991) contains extensive quotations from contemporary Chiricahua women, including chapters on Elbys Hugar and Mildred Cleghorn.

Edward A. Parmee studied education at San Carlos; see his *Formal Education and Cultural Change: A Modern Apache Indian Community and Government Education Programs* (University of Arizona Press, 1968). *Apachean Culture History and Ethnology*, Keith Basso and Morris Opler, editors (University of Arizona Press, 1971), collects important papers about both Apaches and Navajos. Henry F. Dobyns wrote two volumes in the Indian Tribal Series, *The Mescalero Apache People* (1973) and *The Apache People* (1971; about Fort Apache). For baskets, see Clara Lee Tanner, *Apache Indian Baskets* (University of Arizona Press, 1982), and Barbara Mauldin, *Traditions in Transition: Contemporary Basket Weaving of the Southwestern Indians* (Museum of New Mexico Press, 1984).

The quotes from Wendell Chino come from Stan Steiner's *The Vanishing White Man* and from "Modern-Day Warrior Champions Dignity for Mescalero Apaches," by Judy Gaines, *New Mexico Magazine* (August 1989):67–76. Mildred Cleghorn spoke at the centennial of Geronimo's final surrender, as filmed by KUAT-TV, Tucson, in "Geronimo, the Final Campaign"; I also quote Cleghorn from Stockel's book. Howard Scott Gentry, *The Agaves of Continental North America* (University of Arizona Press, 1982) discusses "Agavería."

The Ute (and Southern Paiute) are classi-
fied as Great Basin Indians by ethnologists.
See volume 11 (*Great Basin*) of the Smithsonian *Handbook* for the primary source on
Ute people and history. Jan Pettit, in *Utes:
The Mountain People* (Century One Press, 1982),
provides a good summary of the historical
story; the Buckskin Charlie quote comes
from her book. See also *American Indians in
Colorado* by J. Donald Hughes (Pruett, 1987).
Joseph Jorgensen's excellent *The Sun Dance
Religion: Power for the Powerless* (University of
Chicago Press, 1972) provides not only a brilliant analysis of the Sun Dance but also a
detailed history of the loss of Ute land and
"the neocolonial reservation context."

Both reservation communities have published useful histories of their own. See *The
Southern Utes: A Tribal History* by James Jefferson,
Robert W. Delaney, and Gregory C. Thompson (Southern Ute Tribe, 1972); and a series
of booklets published by the Ute Mountain
Ute Tribe: *Early Days of the Ute Mountain Utes*
(1985), *Ute Mountain Utes: A History Text* (1985),
and *Ute Mountain Ute Government* (1986). See also
Ute Mountain Tribal Park: The Other Mesa Verde by
Jean Akens (Four Corners Publications, 1987)
and *The Ute Mountain Utes* by Robert Delaney
(University of New Mexico Press, 1989).

Marvin K. Opler studied the Utes in the late
1930s; see "The Southern Ute of Colorado," in
Acculturation in Seven American Indian Tribes, Ralph
Linton, editor (Appleton-Century-Crofts,
1940). C. Clark Johnson analyzed Southern Ute political and economic leadership
through the 1950s and early sixties: "A Study
of Modern Southwestern Indian Leadership"
(Ph.D. dissertation, University of Colorado,
1963). And Nancy Wood's *When Buffalo Free
the Mountains: The Survival of America's Ute Indians*
(Doubleday, 1980) provides a well-written
(and controversial) journalistic look at the

trials and tribulations of contemporary Ute
life, with fine black-and-white photographs.
Jim Carrier's *West of the Divide: Voices from a Ranch
and a Reservation* (Fulcrum, 1992) provides a
more balanced portrayal of three months
with Judy Knight's family at Ute Mountain;
it is a fine piece of work that addresses issues
shared by all contemporary Indian communities.

Wood's *War Cry on a Prayer Feather: Prose and
Poetry of the Ute Indians* (Doubleday, 1979) was
originally written as an opera libretto. Her
words are moving, and the book contains the
best available selection of historic photos of
the Utes.

See Ambler, *Breaking the Iron Bonds* (1990), for
energy-related history and for the source of
the quotes from Judy Knight in my conclud-
ing chapter. In "Canyons, Cows, and Conflict:
A Native American History of Montezuma
Canyon, 1874–1933" (*Utah Historical Quarterly*,
vol. 60, no. 3:238–58, 1992), Robert S. McPher-
son untangles the overlapping Ute-Paiute-
Navajo history of this area. The epigraph
comes from an interview with Guy Pinnecoose by Floyd O'Neil and Gregory Thompson in the Doris Duke Oral History Archives,
University of Utah. Thanks to Kathleen and
Reed Kelley of Meeker, Colorado, and to Neil
Buck Cloud of Ignacio, Colorado, for inviting
me to participate in the Southern Ute visit to
the Meeker Massacre sites in April 1990.

The Southern Paiute

Basic historical and ethnographic details
come from the Smithsonian *Handbook* "South-
ern Paiute" chapter by Isabel Kelly and
Catherine Fowler; Kelly's "Southern Paiute
Ethnography" in *Paiute Indians II* (Garland
Publishing, 1976); and, especially, *Nuwuvi: A
Southern Paiute History* (Inter-Tribal Council
of Nevada, 1976). The epigraph comes from
William Palmer, *Why the North Star Stands Still*

and Other Indian Legends (Zion National Park Natural History Association, 1978). The best single general source is Robert J. Franklin and Pamela A. Bunte, *The Paiute* (Chelsea House, 1990), with fine descriptions of contemporary Paiute life.

For additional details on each band, for the Kaibab, see *Kaibab Paiute History: The Early Years*, by Richard W. Stoffle and Michael J. Evans (Kaibab Paiute Tribe, 1978; also published in *Ethnohistory*, vol. 23, no. 2 [1976]) and Robert C. Euler, *The Paiute People* (Indian Tribal Series, 1972), which is especially strong on nineteenth-century contacts with Kaibab and other bands. Allen C. Turner's Ph.D. dissertation (University of Kentucky, 1980), "Housing, Water, and Health Care: The Anthropology of Planning in a Southern Paiute Community," contains a wealth of insights into the contemporary Kaibab community. For Las Vegas, see John Alley, *The Las Vegas Paiute: A Short History* (Las Vegas Tribe, 1977). I found more recent history in Las Vegas newspapers; see especially the *Las Vegas Sun*, "Searching for an Identity," 3–4 August 1986, and the *Las Vegas Review-Journal*, "Paiutes Struggle for Economic Development," 28 June 1987.

The termination story for the Utah Paiute has been carefully documented by Ronald L. Holt in "Beneath These Red Cliffs: The Utah Paiutes and Paternalistic Dependency" (Ph.D. dissertation, University of Utah, 1987). Martha Knack studied the terminated communities in the 1970s: *Life Is with People: Household Organization of the Contemporary Southern Paiute Indians* (Ballena Press, 1980). And the draft of the "Proposed Paiute Indian Tribe of Utah Reservation Plan" (USDI, BIA, 1982) was helpful.

For the San Juan, Pamela A. Bunte and Robert J. Franklin, *From the Sands to the Mountain: Change and Persistence in a Southern Paiute Community* (University of Nebraska Press, 1987), provides a remarkably detailed history. See also Lucille Jake, Evelyn James, and Pamela Bunte, "The Southern Paiute Woman in a Changing Society," *Frontiers* vol. 7, no. 1 (1983):44–49, from which my quotes from Marie Lehi come. Quotes from Evelyn James relating to the Hopi-Navajo land dispute come from *Children of Sacred Ground*, Feher-Elston (1988).

The San Juan Paiute basket-maker renaissance has been beautifully documented in Andrew Hunter Whiteford, *Southwestern Indian Baskets: Their History and Their Makers* (School of American Research Press, 1988) and Whiteford and Susan B. McGreevey, editors, *Translating Tradition, Basketry Arts of the San Juan Paiute* (Wheelwright Museum, 1985).

Catherine W. Viele kindly gave me a copy of her unpublished manuscript about the Southern Paiute written for the Zion National Park Natural History Association.

The O'odham

The key sources for Tohono O'odham people, in addition to the Smithsonian Handbook and Spicer (1962), are *The Papago People* by Henry F. Dobyns (Indian Tribal Series, 1972); *Of Earth and Little Rain: The Papago Indians* by Bernard L. Fontana with photographs by John P. Schaefer (Northland Press, 1981); and all of Ruth M. Underhill's work. Of the latter, see especially *Papago Woman* (Holt, Rinehart and Winston, 1979), from which my quotes from Maria Chona come; *Singing for Power: The Song Magic of the Papago Indians of Southern Arizona* (University of California Press, 1938); and "A Papago Calendar Record," *University of New Mexico Bulletin, Anthropology Series*, vol. 2, no. 5 (1938). The Tohono O'odham Tribe has published two very useful booklets: *Tohono O'odham: Lives of the Desert People* (1984) and *Tohono O'odham: History of the Desert People* (1985).

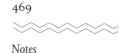

For insight into the lives of today's O'odham, especially traditional farmers, nutritional issues, and Sand Papagos, see Gary Paul Nabhan's elegantly written books, *The Desert Smells Like Rain: A Naturalist in Papago Indian Country* (North Point Press, 1982), *Gathering the Desert* (University of Arizona Press, 1985), and *Enduring Seeds* (North Point Press, 1989). Nabhan, Wendy Hodgson, and Frances Fellows summarize what we know about Sand Papagos in "A Meager Living on Lava and Sand? Hia Ced O'odham Food Resources and Habitat Diversity in Oral and Documentary Histories," *Journal of the Southwest*, vol. 31, no. 4 (Winter 1989):508–33.

Charles Bowden's *Killing the Hidden Waters* (University of Texas Press, 1977) chronicles the depressing history of groundwater misuse in the Papaguería. Marc Reisner's *Cadillac Desert* (Viking Penguin, 1986) gives the background for the Central Arizona Project. Additional insight into the relations of the O'odham with the desert appear in Frank S. Crosswhite and Carol D. Crosswhite's "The Sonoran Desert," in *Reference Handbook on the Deserts of North America*, Gordon L. Bender, editor (Greenwood Press, 1982).

For eloquent oratory and poetry, see *Rainhouse and Ocean: Speeches for the Papago Year* by Ruth M. Underhill, Donald M. Bahr, Baptisto Lopez, Jose Pancho, and David Lopez (Museum of Northern Arizona Press, 1979) and *When It Rains: Papago and Pima Poetry*, Ofelia Zepeda, editor (University of Arizona Press, 1982).

Historical background on Ak-Chin comes from a collection of papers (in press, 1988) prepared for the tribal museum project and edited by Richard Effland, Phoenix.

Pima sources overlap Papago sources. See Frank Russell, *The Pima Indians* (University of Arizona Press, 1975 reprint of 1908 edition); Paul H. Ezell, *The Hispanic Acculturation of the Gila River Pimas* (American Anthropological Association Memoir 90, 1961); and, especially, Henry F. Dobyns, *The Pima-Maricopa* (Chelsea House, 1989). Quotes from Gerald Anton come from *The Salt River Pima-Maricopa Indians*, John Myers and Robert Gryder, editors (Life's Reflections, 1988). Two eloquent Pima autobiographies are Anna Moore Shaw's *A Pima Past* (University of Arizona Press, 1974) and George Webb's *A Pima Remembers* (University of Arizona Press, 1959). (Anna Moore Shaw was Adeline Russell's mother.) Amadeo Rea's *Once a River* (University of Arizona Press, 1983) chronicles the destruction of the Gila River, primarily through looking at effects on bird life. *The Hohokam: Ancient People of the Desert*, David Grant Noble, editor (School of American Research Press, 1991) includes perspectives on the Hohokam-O'odham connection.

The Maricopa

Henry Harwell and Marsha Kelly's chapter on the Maricopa in the Smithsonian *Handbook* is the primary source, along with Leslie Spier's *Yuman Tribes of the Gila River* (University of Chicago Press, 1933). My spelling of the names of these Yuman tribes follows the *Handbook* — and I have standardized their use even in quotations. To unravel who is who, see Paul H. Ezell, *The Maricopas: An Identification from Documentary Sources* (University of Arizona Anthropological Papers 6, 1963).

The quotes from Ralph Cameron and Leroy Cameron come from *Spirit Mountain* (1984). *Massacre on the Gila* by Clifton B. Kroeber and Bernard L. Fontana (University of Arizona Press, 1986) examines the 1857 battle pitting the Maricopas and Pimas against the Quechans and Mojaves and is rich with details about all these cultures in war and peace.

Dobyns (1989), cited in the Pima note, makes clear the power of the Pima-Maricopa Confederation.

The Colorado River Tribes

Spirit Mountain, Hinton and Watahomigie, editors (1984), provides a rich introduction to both River and Upland Yuman oral literature. See Herman Grey's *Tales from the Mohaves* (University of Oklahoma Press, 1970) for additional Mojave material. *Crazy Weather* by Charles L. McNichols (Macmillan, 1944) is one of the few novels of river life and a fine evocation of Mojave culture at the beginning of the twentieth century.

A note about the spelling of Mojave. The fort and the desert both are spelled, by convention, Mojave; the valley, lake, and county are, conventionally, Mohave. The Fort Mohave tribe uses an "h," and CRIT a "j"; the BIA and many anthropologists use Mohave. I use Mojave throughout for the People.

A. L. Kroeber's beautifully written *Handbook of the Indians of California* (Bulletin 78, Bureau of American Ethnology, 1925) contains sections on Quechan, Chemehuevi, and, especially, Mojave. The epigraph comes from Kroeber's "More Mohave Myths" (*University of California Anthropological Records* 27, 1972). See also Bernard L. Fontana's "The Hopi-Navajo Colony on the Lower Colorado River: A Problem in Ethnohistorical Interpretation," *Ethnohistory*, vol. 10, no. 2 (1963):163–82, and Dwight Lomayesva's "The Adaptation of Hopi and Navajo Colonists on the Colorado River Indian Reservation" (M.S. thesis, California State University, Fullerton, 1980). Carobeth Laird's *The Chemehuevis* (Malki Museum Press, 1976) is the key ethnography for the tribe. The tribal museum in Parker offers exhibits on the Colorado River Indian Tribes,

a spectacular Chemehuevi basket collection, and crafts demonstrations.

For Quechans, the pivotal references are C. Daryll Forde, "Ethnography of the Yuma Indians," *University of California Publications in American Archaeology and Ethnology* vol. 28, no. 4 (1931):83–278, for traditional lifeways; and Robert L. Bee's *Crosscurrents Along the Colorado: The Impact of Government Policy on the Quechan Indians* (University of Arizona Press, 1981) for more recent tribal history. Bee also has written the single best general introduction to the Quechan for the Chelsea House "Indians of North America" series, *The Yuma* (1989).

For the Cocopah, see Anita Alvarez de Williams, *The Cocopah People* (Indian Tribal Series, 1974), and William H. Kelly, *Cocopa Ethnography* (University of Arizona Press, 1977). See also *A River No More: The Colorado River and the West*, by Philip Fradkin (Alfred A. Knopf, 1981), for the sad recounting of the exploitation of the Colorado River.

The Yaqui

Edward H. Spicer's work forms the keystone for Yaqui studies. See especially *The Yaquis: A Cultural History* (University of Arizona Press, 1980). The literature on Yaqui religion is extensive; start with Muriel Thayer Painter's *With Good Heart: Yaqui Beliefs and Ceremonies in Pascua Village* (University of Arizona Press, 1986). For Yaquis in Mexico, see *Politics and Ethnicity on the Rio Yaqui: Potam Revisited* by Thomas R. McGuire (University of Arizona Press, 1986). For discussions of trilingualism and education, see Sam A. Brewer, Jr., "The Yaqui Indians of Arizona: Trilingualism and Cultural Change" (Ph.D. dissertation, University of Texas, 1976) and Octaviana Valenzuela Trujillo, "Yaqui Views on Language and Literacy" (Ph.D. dissertation, Arizona State University, 1991).

The Yaquis themselves write eloquently about their culture and their lives. For life histories, see *The Autobiography of a Yaqui Poet* by Refugio Savala (Kathleen M. Sands, editor; University of Arizona Press, 1980), Rosalio Moises, Jane Holden Kelley, and William Curry Holden, *The Tall Candle: A Personal Chronicle of a Yaqui Indian* (University of Nebraska Press, 1971), and, especially, *Yaqui Women: Contemporary Life Histories* by Jane Holden Kelley (University of Nebraska Press, 1978) — from which the story about the New Pascua leader and don Juan comes.

Larry Evers and Felipe Molina, *Yaqui Deer Songs* (University of Arizona Press, 1987), and James S. Griffith and Felipe S. Molina, *Old Men of the Fiesta: An Introduction to the Pascola Arts* (The Heard Museum, 1980), give wonderful Yaqui perspectives on ceremonialism. See also *Yoeme: Lore of the Arizona Yaqui People* by Mini Valenzuela Kaczkurkin (Sun Tracks/ University of Arizona Press, 1977). The quote from the deer song comes from Evers and Molina (1987).

Conclusion

See the Introduction chapter note for the Dorris reference. The quote from Paula Gunn Allen comes from *The Remembered Earth: An Anthology of Contemporary Native American Literature*, Geary Hobson, editor (University of New Mexico Press, 1980). John Echohawk quotes appear in "John Echohawk is leading a (legal) revolution," *High Country News*, 2 July 1990. The Barney Mitchell quote comes from Iverson (1983), and the quote from Deloria is from *Indian Education in America* (1991). See Nora Naranjo-Morse, *Mud Woman: Poems from the Clay* (University of Arizona Press, 1992), for a wonderful revelation of the inner spirit of a funny and thoughtful twentieth-century Pueblo woman. My conclusion incorporates ideas from David H. Getches, "A Philosophy of Permanence: The Indians' Legacy for the West," *Journal of the West*, vol. 29, no. 3 (1990):54–68.

Calendar of Events

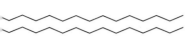

For additional information and phone numbers, see *Discover Indian Reservations USA: A Visitor's Welcome Guide*, Veronica E. Tiller, editor (Council Publications, 1992).

January

1   New Year's dances at most NM pueblos
6   King's Day dances at most NM pueblos
23 San Ildefonso Pueblo feast day, NM

February

2   Candlemas Day dances at San Felipe, Cochiti, and Santo Domingo pueblos, NM

Weekend before President's Day:
    O'odham Tash Celebration, Casa Grande, AZ

Saturday at end of February
    Exodus Days (commemoration of forced march to San Carlos, 1875), Camp Verde Yavapai Apache Reservation, AZ

Last Saturday in February
    Yuma Crossing Day, Fort Yuma Reservation, AZ

In February (date varies)
    Katsinas return to Hopi pueblos during Powamuy (Bean Dance), AZ

March

First Sunday in March
    St. John's Indian Fair, Gila River Reservation, AZ

19 St. Joseph's feast day, Laguna Pueblo, NM

Easter Week
    Yaqui dances, AZ
Easter Sunday
    Dances at most NM pueblos
First Friday after Easter
    San Xavier Fiesta, AZ

April

1   Spring Corn Dance, many NM pueblos
Early April
    Mul-Chu-Tha Tribal Fair, Gila River Reservation, AZ

May

1   San Felipe Pueblo feast day, NM
3   Santa Cruz feast day, Taos and Cochiti pueblos, NM
First Sunday in May
    Santa Maria feast day, McCartys (Acoma Pueblo), NM
14 Blessing of the fields, Taos Pueblo, NM
Memorial Day weekend
    Kaibab Paiute Cultural Fair, AZ; Southern Ute Bear Dance, CO

June

First week of June, Thursday to Monday
    Ute Mountain Bear Dance, CO
8   Buffalo Dance, Santa Clara Pueblo, NM
13 Sandia (NM) and Tigua (TX) pueblos feast days; San Antonio feast day, other NM pueblos

Second weekend in June
> Restoration Gathering and Powwow, Paiute Tribe of Utah, Cedar City, UT

20 Governor's Dance, Isleta Pueblo, NM

24 San Juan Pueblo feast day;
San Juan feast day, other NM pueblos

29 San Pedro feast day, many NM pueblos

Late June or July
> Katsinas return to San Francisco Peaks during Niman Dance, Hopi pueblos, AZ

July

4 Nambe Pueblo waterfall ceremony; Mescalero Apache girl's puberty ceremony, NM

14 Cochiti Pueblo feast day, NM

Second weekend in July
> Southern Ute Sun Dance, CO

Third weekend in July
> Eight Northern Pueblos Artist and Craftsman Show, NM; Little Beaver Round-Up, Jicarilla Apache Reservation, Dulce, NM

25 Acoma and Santo Domingo pueblos rooster pulls; Cochiti Pueblo Corn Dance, NM

26 Santa Ana Pueblo and Seama Village (Laguna Pueblo) feast days, NM

August

2 Pecos Bull Dance, Jemez Pueblo, NM

4 Santo Domingo Pueblo feast day, NM

10 Picuris, Laguna pueblos, and Acomita (Acoma Pueblo) feast days, NM

Mid-August
> Inter-Tribal Indian Ceremonial, Gallup, NM

12 Santa Clara Pueblo feast day, NM

15 Zia Pueblo and Mesita Village (Laguna Pueblo) feast days, NM

Weekend after third Thursday
> Santa Fe Indian Market, NM

28 Saint Augustine Day dances, Isleta Pueblo, NM

Late August
> Peach Festival, Supai, Havasupai Reservation; Snake Dance, Hopi Reservation, AZ

September

Labor Day weekend
> White Mountain Apache Tribal Fair and Rodeo, AZ; Zuni Tribal Fair, NM

After Labor Day, Wednesday to Sunday:
> Navajo Nation Fair, Window Rock, AZ

2 Acoma Pueblo feast day, NM

4 Isleta Pueblo feast day, NM

8 Encinal Village (Laguna Pueblo) feast day; San Ildefonso Pueblo Corn Dance, NM

Second weekend in September
> Southern Ute Tribal Fair, CO

15 Stone Lake Go-Jii-Ya races, Jicarilla Apache Reservation, NM

19 Laguna Pueblo feast day, NM

25 Paguate Village (Laguna Pueblo) feast day, NM

30 San Geronimo feast day, Taos Pueblo

Last week of September, Thursday to Sunday:
> National Indian Days celebration, Colorado River Reservation, Parker, AZ

October

First weekend in October
> Navajo Fair, Shiprock, NM

4 Nambe Pueblo feast day, NM; Magdalena Fiesta, Sonora, Mexico

17 Paraje Village (Laguna Pueblo) feast day, NM

Mid-October
> Fort Mojave Indian Days, Needles, CA

October
> Western Navajo Fair, Tuba City, AZ

November

12 Jemez and Tesuque pueblos feast days, NM

Veteran's Day Weekend
  San Carlos Apache Tribal Fair, AZ

Weekend in late November
  Tohono O'odham Tribal Fair and Rodeo, AZ

December

Early December
  Shalako ceremony, Zuni Pueblo, NM

First weekend in December
  Parker All-Indian Rodeo, Colorado River Reservation, AZ

10-12 Tortugas Fiesta in honor of Our Lady of Guadalupe, Las Cruces, NM

12 Pojoaque Pueblo feast day; matachines Dance at Jemez Pueblo, NM

24 Christmas Eve night procession and bonfires, Taos, Picuris, and San Juan pueblos, NM

25 Christmas dances at most NM pueblos

26 Turtle Dance, San Juan Pueblo, NM

Index

~~~~~~~~~~~~~~~~~~~~~~~~~~~~~~~~~~

References to photographs are indicated by **boldface**. *Photographs in the four color sections are indexed by section number in* **boldface Roman numerals**. *Color section I follows page 96; II follows page 192; III follows page 288; and IV follows page 400.*

STEPHEN TRIMBLE

Stephen Trimble has become a primary
narrator of the story of Southwest Indians
through his books *Our Voices, Our Land; Talking
with the Clay: The Art of Pueblo Pottery; The Village
of Blue Stone;* and an annual calendar based on
The People.

Trimble's books on western wildlands and
natural history include *Blessed By Light: Visions of
the Colorado Plateau; Words from the Land: Encounters
with Natural History Writing;* and *The Sagebrush
Ocean: A Natural History of the Great Basin,* for
which he received The High Desert Museum's
Chiles Award and The Sierra Club's Ansel
Adams Award.

Trimble has lived in the Four Corners states
all his life and makes his home in Salt Lake
City with his wife and two children.

Photograph by Ben Altman